ROUTLEDGE COMPANION TO MUSEUM ETHICS

The Routledge Companion to Museum Ethics is a the ... ...ed reconceptualization of museum ethics discourse as a dynamic soc... ... central to the project of creating change in the museum. Through twenty ...n chapters by an international and interdisciplinary group of academics and practitioners it explores contemporary museum ethics as an opportunity for growth, rather than a burden of compliance. The volume represents diverse strands in museum activity from exhibitions to marketing, as ethics is embedded in all areas of the museum sector. What the contributions share is an understanding of the contingent nature of museum ethics in the twenty-first century—its relations with complex economic, social, political and technological forces and its fluid ever-shifting sensibility.

The volume examines contemporary museum ethics through the prism of those disciplines and methods that have shaped it most. It argues for a museum ethics discourse defined by social responsibility, radical transparency and shared guardianship of heritage. And it demonstrates the moral agency of museums: the concept that museum ethics is more than the personal and professional ethics of individuals and concerns the capacity of institutions to generate self-reflective and activist practice.

Janet Marstine is Lecturer and Programme Director of Art Museum and Gallery Studies at the School of Museum Studies, University of Leicester. Her research focuses on museum ethics and institutional critique. Marstine is the founder and former director of the Institute of Museum Ethics at Seton Hall University. She is editor of *New Museum Theory and Practice: An Introduction* (Blackwell, 2005).

THE ROUTLEDGE COMPANION TO MUSEUM ETHICS

Redefining Ethics for the Twenty-First-Century Museum

Edited by
Janet Marstine

Routledge
Taylor & Francis Group

LONDON AND NEW YORK

Published 2011
by Routledge
2 Park Square, Milton Park, Abingdon, Oxon, OX14 4RN

Simultaneously published in the USA and Canada
by Routledge
711 Third Avenue, New York, NY 10017

Routledge is an imprint of the Taylor & Francis Group, an informa business

British Library Cataloguing in Publication Data
A catalogue record for this book is available from the British Library

Library of Congress Cataloging in Publication Data
A catalog record for this book has been requested

ISBN13: 978-0-415-56611-7 (hbk)
ISBN13: 978-0-415-56612-4 (pbk)
ISBN13: 978-0-203-81546-5 (ebk)

Typeset in Goudy Old Style
by Taylor & Francis Books

GIFT OF JESSICA JOHNSTON
2019

MIX
Paper from
responsible sources
FSC
www.fsc.org   FSC® C004839

Printed and bound in Great Britain by
CPI Antony Rowe, Chippenham, Wiltshire

To the memory of my beloved mother, Connie:
cheerleader, confidante,
queen of all things ethical

CONTENTS

List of Illustrations   x
List of Tables   xii
Notes on Contributors   xiii
Acknowledgments   xxi
Preface   xxiii

PART I
Theorizing Museum Ethics   1

1   The contingent nature of the new museum ethics   3
    JANET MARSTINE

2   The art of ethics: Theories and applications to museum practice   26
    JUDITH CHELIUS STARK

3   GoodWork in museums today ... and tomorrow   41
    CELKA STRAUGHN AND HOWARD GARDNER

4   Museums and the end of materialism   54
    ROBERT R. JANES

5   Changing the rules of the road: Post-colonialism and the new
    ethics of museum anthropology   70
    CHRISTINA KREPS

6   "Aroha mai: Whose museum?": The rise of indigenous ethics within
    museum contexts: A Maori-tribal perspective   85
    PAUL TAPSELL

7   The responsibility of representation: A feminist perspective   112
    HILDE HEIN

PART II
Ethics, Activism and Social Responsibility   127

8   On ethics, activism and human rights   129
    RICHARD SANDELL

9   Collaboration, contestation, and creative conflict: On the efficacy of
    museum/community partnerships   146
    BERNADETTE T. LYNCH

10 An experimental approach to strengthen the role of science centers in the governance of science 164
ANDREA BANDELLI AND ELLY KONIJN

11 Peering into the bedroom: Restorative justice at the Jane Addams Hull House Museum 174
LISA YUN LEE

12 Being responsive to be responsible: Museums and audience development 188
CLAUDIA B. OCELLO

13 Ethics and challenges of museum marketing 202
YUNG-NENG LIN

14 Memorial museums and the objectification of suffering 220
PAUL WILLIAMS

PART III
The Radical Potential of Museum Transparency 237

15 Cultural equity in the sustainable museum 239
TRISTRAM BESTERMAN

16 'Dance through the minefield': The development of practical ethics for repatriation 256
MICHAEL PICKERING

17 Visible listening: Discussion, debate and governance in the museum 275
JAMES M. BRADBURNE

18 Ethical, entrepreneurial or inappropriate? Business practices in museums 285
JAMES B. GARDNER

19 "Why is this here?": Art museum texts as ethical guides 298
PAMELA Z. McCLUSKY

20 Transfer protocols: Museum codes and ethics in the new digital environment 316
ROSS PARRY

21 Sharing conservation ethics, practice and decision-making with museum visitors 332
MARY M. BROOKS

CONTENTS

PART IV
Visual Culture and the Performance of Museum Ethics 351

22 The body in the (white) box: Corporeal ethics and museum
   representation 353
   MARA GLADSTONE AND JANET CATHERINE BERLO

23 Towards an ethics of museum architecture 379
   SUZANNE MACLEOD

24 Museum censorship 393
   CHRISTOPHER B. STEINER

25 Ethics of confrontational drama in museums 414
   BJARNE SODE FUNCH

26 Conservation practice as enacted ethics 426
   DINAH EASTOP

27 Bioart and nanoart in a museum context: Terms of engagement 445
   ELLEN K. LEVY

   Index 464

LIST OF ILLUSTRATIONS

1.1 Anthony Schrag, *Push*, 2008, Gallery of Modern Art, Glasgow   4

3.1 A Graphic Rendition of the Principal Elements of GoodWork, Courtesy of The GoodWork Project® Team, Harvard Graduate School of Education   43

6.1 *Te Kaoreore*, Auckland Museum   88

6.2 *Tama te Kapua*, Ohinemutu, Rotorua   89

6.3 Abbreviated *whakapapa* of creation according to Ngati Whakaue-Te Arawa traditions   90

6.4 Abbreviated *whakapapa* of some key events since light & enlightenment (consciousness) entered the world (Te Ao Marama)   91

6.5 *Pareraututu* and *Murirangaranga*, Te Papa-i-Ouru Marae, 29 April 2008, Ohinemutu, Rotorua   94

6.6 *Ko Tawa* exhibition, 2005–2008, Auckland Museum   100

9.1 Aurelie Lolingo, one of the 'Talking Objects' participants, debates the interpretation of museum collections at the British Museum, August 2008   158

11.1 Alice Kellogg Taylor, *Mary Rozet-Smith*, 1898, Jane Addams Hull House Museum, University of Illinois at Chicago   178

11.2 Mary Rozet-Smith with Jane Addams, circa 1898, Jane Addams Memorial Collection, Department of Special Collections, The University Library, The University of Illinois at Chicago   185

11.3 Mary Rozet-Smith with Jane Addams, circa 1930, Jane Addams Memorial Collection, Department of Special Collections, The University Library, The University of Illinois at Chicago   186

13.1 Importance–performance analysis   208

13.2 Visitors' importance–performance scoring of service attributes   210

14.1 Ingers being repatriated to Finland, Museum of Occupations, Tallin   224

19.1 *Gela Mask (The Ancient One)*, 20th century, African, Ivorian, Wee culture, Seattle Art Museum   300

19.2 Joseph Kosuth, *The Play of the Unmentionable*, 1992, Installation at the Brooklyn Museum of Art   303

19.3 Joseph Beuys, *Capri-Batterie*, 1985, Museum of Fine Arts, Boston   305

19.4 *Cow Figure*, 20th century, African, Burkina Faso, Mossi culture, Seattle Art Museum   307

19.5 Marita Dingus, *400 Men of African Descent*, 1997, Seattle Art Museum   311

21.1 Poster for the exhibition *Verschachtelt & Behütet* (Nested and Protected), Institute for Conservation and Restoration, University of Applied Arts, Vienna, 2008–9   340

21.2 Visitors at the 2006 exhibition *Mission Impossible? Ethics and Choices in Conservation*, Fitzwilliam Museum Exhibition, Cambridge, England   341

22.1 James Luna, *Artifact Piece*, in *The Decade Show*, 1990, New Museum/ Studio Museum of Harlem   355

22.2 Navajo Indians executing sand painting, March 26, 1941, during the exhibition *Indian Art of the United States*, The Museum of Modern Art, New York   357

22.3 Marina Abramović, *The Artist is Present*, 2010, The Museum of Modern Art, New York   368

22.4 Video still from Andrea Fraser, *Little Frank and His Carp*, 2001, Friedrich Petzel Gallery, New York   370

26.1 Armchair from a suite of furniture commissioned in 1765 for the Picture Gallery, Corsham Court, Wiltshire, UK. Composite image showing the chair before and after conservation intervention of 2009   429

26.2 Woman's Mantua, Stomacher, and Petticoat, circa 1700   432

26.3 Thomas Ridgeway Gould, *Kamehameha I*, 1878–1880, Kapa'au, North Kohala, Hawai'i. Composite image showing the sculpture before and after the conservation interventions of 1999–2002   434

26.4 William Turnbull, *Transparent Tubes*, 1968, Tate, London   437

27.1 Catts and Zurr, *Victimless Leather – A Prototype of Stitch-less Jacket* grown in a Technoscientific 'Body,' 2004   449

27.2 Paul Vanouse, *The Relative Velocity Inscription Device*, 2002   451

27.3 *GenTerra*, 2001, performance by the artists Critical Art Ensemble and Carnegie Mellon University robotic art researcher Beatriz da Costa   453

27.4 Victoria Vesna, *Zero@Wavefunction: nano Dreams & Nightmares*, 2002, Interactive Installation in collaboration with nanoscientist James Gimzewski   456

LIST OF TABLES

13.1 Participation in museums or galleries at least once in the
previous 12 months, EU–27, 2007   204
13.2 Participation in museums or galleries in Taipei City at least
once in the previous 12 months, Taiwan, 2004   205
13.3 Importance–performance rating of museum services   209

NOTES ON CONTRIBUTORS

Andrea Bandelli is an independent adviser on science communication initiatives and a consultant for various science centers and other institutions in Europe, the United States, Brazil and South Africa. He is the director of PlayDecide, a project to encourage deliberative democracy activities in science centers and museums. He is currently conducting Ph.D. research at VU University Amsterdam, the Netherlands, on the role of the public in the governance of science centers.

Janet Catherine Berlo, Professor of Art History and Visual and Cultural Studies at the University of Rochester, holds a Ph.D. from Yale University. She has written numerous books and articles on the arts of the indigenous Americas, has taught Native American art history as a visiting professor at Harvard, Yale and UCLA, and has received grants for her scholarly work from the Guggenheim Foundation, the Getty Foundation and the National Endowment for the Humanities.

Tristram Besterman is a freelance adviser, mediator and writer on museums, specialising in the ethics of cultural identity, representation, dispossession and restitution. He draws on thirty-five years' experience in museum education, curatorship and management, and the development of ethical standards nationally in the UK. After graduating in natural sciences at Cambridge, Besterman worked in London, Sydney, Sheffield, Warwick and Plymouth before his appointment as Director of the Manchester Museum (1994–2005). There, he led the redevelopment of one of the UK's leading multidisciplinary university museums, reorienting the museum to engage more effectively and imaginatively with the public, with higher education, with diaspora communities and with source nations. Among many national board appointments, Besterman served on the Museums Association Ethics Committee for nineteen years and as its Convener from 1994 to 2001. He was closely involved with the development of successive codes of ethics, and re-wrote the Association's definition of a museum in 1998.

James M. Bradburne is a British-Canadian architect, designer and museum specialist who has designed World's Fair pavilions, science centres and international art exhibitions. Educated in Canada and England he received a diploma in architecture from the Architectural Association and a Ph.D. in museum theory from the University of Amsterdam. He has developed numerous exhibitions, research projects and symposia for UNESCO, national governments, private foundations and museums worldwide during the course of the past twenty years. He has worked in senior management of cultural institutions in four European countries, and was Director General of the Museum für Angewandte Kunst in Frankfurt from 1999 to 2003. He currently is Director General of the Fondazione Palazzo Strozzi, which is responsible for transforming Florence's Palazzo Strozzi into a dynamic cultural centre.

Mary M. Brooks gained the post-graduate diploma in Textile Conservation at the Textile Conservation Centre after working in the book world and management consultancy. She has worked as a conservator and curator in Europe and America. Her research interests include seventeenth-century embroideries and modern materials. Her Ph.D. focused on the technical, social and cultural histories of regenerated protein fibres. She has a special interest in the contribution that object-based research and conservation approaches can make to the wider interpretation and presentation of cultural artefacts. She was Reader at the Textile Conservation Centre and Programme Leader for the MA Museums & Galleries and now works as a consultant specialising in museology and conservation.

Dinah Eastop studied the history of art and then trained as a textile conservator in the UK and Switzerland, before working at the Textile Conservation Centre, UK, most recently as Senior Lecturer at the University of Southampton. She is an accredited conservator restorer (ACR) and a Fellow of the International Institute of Conservation (FIIC). She was the Founding Director of the AHRC Research Centre for Textile Conservation and Textile Studies (2002–2007). MA studies in anthropology fostered her research interest in the dynamic interplay between the material properties and social attributes of museum objects and the effects of this interplay on conservation and curatorial decisions. Her Ph.D. dissertation focused on a material culture analysis of textile conservation. She is a consultant in conservation and heritage studies and Honorary Lecturer, Institute of Archaeology, University College London. She initiated and leads the Deliberately Concealed Garments Project: www.concealedgarments.org

Bjarne Sode Funch is Dr. Phil. and Associated Professor of Psychology in the Department of Psychology and Educational Studies at Roskilde University in Denmark. Professor Funch's research interests include personality psychology with a focus on phenomenological and existential theories and methods, the psychology of art and aesthetic education at art museums. He is the author of *The Psychology of Art Appreciation* (1997) and a number of publications that focus on the psychological theories of the aesthetic experience, strategies for museums education and art exhibition. Funch's teaching incorporates phenomenological studies in different areas of personality psychology as a point of departure for an existential understanding, particularly different types of art appreciation, including the aesthetic experience, the relationship between art and spirituality, artistic creativity and the influences of art in the individual and its importance in society.

Howard Gardner is the Hobbs Professor of Cognition and Education at the Harvard Graduate School of Education. For 28 years, he co-directed Harvard Project Zero, a basic research group that has focused on education in the arts. He is the author of many books, including *Artful Scribbles, Art, Mind, and Brain, Frames of Mind, Creating Minds*, and *Five Minds for the Future*. Since 1995, he has co-directed the GoodWork Project, an examination of ethics in the professions. Among his advisory positions, he is on the Board of the Museum of Modern Art in New York.

James B. Gardner is Senior Scholar, National Museum of American History, Smithsonian Institution. Prior to his appointment at NMAH, Dr. Gardner served as Deputy Executive Director of the American Historical Association and as Director of Education and Special Programs for the American Association for State and Local History. At NMAH, he previously served as Associate Director for Curatorial Affairs. His professional activities have included service on the AASLH Council, as President of the National Council on Public History, as chair of the Nominating Board of the Organization of American Historians, and on the Board of Editors of *The Public Historian*. He served as the first chair of the Smithsonian's Ethics Advisory Board. His publications include *The AAM Guide to Collections Planning*, *Public History: Essays from the Field*, *Ordinary People and Everyday Life: Perspectives on the New Social History* and contributions to *The Public Historian*, *Museum News* and other periodicals.

Mara Gladstone is a Ph.D. Candidate in Visual and Cultural Studies at the University of Rochester. She is a recipient of two grants from the Getty Foundation, and has organized several live art exhibitions, film programs and performances.

Hilde Hein is a resident scholar at the Brandeis Women's Studies Research Center and Lecturer in the Brandeis University Department of Philosophy. She is a professor of philosophy emerita at Holy Cross College, in Worcester, Massachusetts. Through her continuing research she strives to introduce feminist theory into the structure and practice of social institutions. Beginning with her 1990 book *The Exploratorium: The Museum as Laboratory*, she has studied the transformations of and within museums since the 1960's. Her subsequent books, *The Museum in Transition: A Philosophical Perspective* (2000) and *Public Art: Thinking Museums Differently* (2006), carry on that pursuit. Dr. Hein holds a Ph.D. in Philosophy from the University of Michigan. She has been an active member of the American Philosophical Association and the American Society for Aesthetics. Upon retirement, she served in the Peace Corps in Morocco, where she taught English and worked in the Jewish Museum in Casablanca.

Robert R. Janes is the Editor-in-Chief of *Museum Management and Curatorship*, Chair of the Board of Directors of the Biosphere Institute of the Bow Valley, a Fellow of the Canadian Museums Association and the former President and CEO of the Glenbow Museum in Calgary, Alberta, Canada. He is also a museum consultant and lives in Canmore, Alberta, Canada. His books include *Museums and the Paradox of Change* (1995; 1997), *Looking Reality in the Eye: Museums and Social Responsibility* (2005, with Gerald T. Conaty), *Museum Management and Marketing* (2007, with Richard Sandell) and *Museums in a Troubled World: Renewal, Irrelevance or Collapse?* (2009).

Elly Konijn is currently Professor in the Department of Communication Science, Faculty of Social Sciences at the VU University Amsterdam and was affiliated with Media Studies at Utrecht University until recently. She has conducted a number of research projects with theatre and film audiences, as well as studying the emotional processes of visitors and professional stage actors in Europe and the United States. Her recent research interests include the psychology of media, media entertainment, interpersonal communication and entertainment-education. She has published numerous journal articles and (co)authored various books.

Christina Kreps is Associate Professor of Anthropology and Director of Museum Studies at the University of Denver Museum of Anthropology. She specializes in the study of museums and heritage work from cross-cultural, comparative and international perspectives, and conducted research and participated in training programs in The Netherlands, Indonesia, Italy, Thailand, Viet Nam and the United States. Dr. Kreps serves on the board of the American Association of Museums Committee on Museum Professional Training and is former editor of *Museum Anthropology*, the journal of the Council on Museum Anthropology of the American Anthropological Association. Her publications include the book *Liberating Culture: Cross-Cultural Perspectives on Museums, Curation, and Heritage Preservation* (2003).

Lisa Yun Lee is Director of the Jane Addams Hull House Museum at the University of Illinois, Chicago, and a faculty member in the Departments of Art History and of Gender and Women's Studies, where she teaches courses on aesthetics and politics and on museum studies. She founded the Public Square at the Illinois Humanities Council, an organization in Chicago committed to creating radically democratic space and opportunities for civic dialogue and conversations about social justice. She holds a B.A. from Bryn Mawr College, and a Ph.D. from Duke University. She is the author of *Dialectics of the Body: Corporeality in the Philosophy of Theodor Adorno* (Routledge, 2006) and several articles about feminism and critical theory. She is the Chair of the Historic House Professional Interest Committee of the American Association of Museums and serves on the advisory boards of numerous cultural and political organizations, including *Ms. Magazine*, WBEZ Chicago Public Radio and the International Contemporary Ensemble.

Ellen K. Levy, a New York-based artist and educator, is Past President of the College Art Association (2004–2006) and specializes in art and complex systems. Levy has exhibited her work widely, both in the US and abroad. Awards include an arts commission from NASA (1985), an AICA award (1995–1996) and a Distinguished Visiting Fellowship of Arts and Sciences at Skidmore College in 1999, a position funded by the Luce Foundation. Her artwork was included in *Petroliana* at the 2nd Moscow Biennale, *Weather Report: Art & Climate Change* at the Boulder Museum of Contemporary Art and *Gregor Mendel: Planting the Seeds of Genetics* at the Field Museum, Chicago. She was guest editor of *Art Journal*'s special issue, "Contemporary Art and the Genetic Code" (1996) and has contributed to numerous publications involved with art and evolution. She is a Visiting Scholar at NYU while completing a doctorate at Z-Node (Zurich) on art and neuroscience.

Yung-Neng Lin is Associate Professor in the Department of Cultural and Creative Industries Management of the National Taipei University of Education, Taiwan. He holds a Ph.D. from the School of Museum Studies at the University of Leicester. His research focuses on museum management and audience development. One of his articles, entitled "Leisure – a function of museums? The Taiwan perspective", was awarded Best Paper for 2006 in the Management category by the international peer-reviewed *Journal of Museum Management and Curatorship*. He has been commissioned by the Council for Cultural Affairs, Taiwan, to establish key performance indicators for the museum sector. He is also the Joint Director of the Cultural Statistics project in Taiwan, 2009.

Bernadette T. Lynch is an academic and museum professional with twenty-five years experience at senior management level in UK and Canadian museums and has a reputation for reflective, ethical and innovative museum theory and practice. Dr. Lynch is particularly interested in conflict as central to democratic dialogue and debate in museums. Formerly Deputy Director of the Manchester Museum, she is now a freelance museum writer/researcher and consultant and Honorary Research Fellow at the University of Manchester, Centre for Museology. She was recently Visiting Fellow at the University of Sussex, Institute of International Development Studies, where she examined lessons on citizenship and participation from international development. She has just completed research into the impact of engagement and participation on twelve museums and galleries across the UK on behalf of the Paul Hamlyn Foundation, and is working on a book: *Practising Radical Trust: Museums and the Sharing of Authority*.

Suzanne MacLeod is a Senior Lecturer in the School of Museum Studies at the University of Leicester where she is also Deputy Head of School. Her research relates to architecture and exhibition design in museums and galleries with a particular focus on the architectural and spatial forms of museums and galleries and their histories of reshaping. She is editor of *Reshaping Museum Space: architecture, design, exhibitions* published by Routledge in 2005 and *Museum Revolutions* (with Knell and Watson) also published by Routledge in 2007. She is currently working on an edited volume entitled *Museum Makers: architecture, exhibition, narrative* (with Hale and Hanks) and a monograph which explores an architectural history of design and use at the Walker Art Gallery in Liverpool from 1877 to 2002.

Janet Marstine is Lecturer and Programme Director of Art Museum and Gallery Studies at the School of Museum Studies, University of Leicester. Her research focuses on museum ethics in theory and practice and on institutional critique and its impact on museum ethics. Marstine is the founder and former director of the Institute of Museum Ethics (IME) at Seton Hall University. At the IME she was project director for an Institute of Museum and Library Services Twenty-First Century Museum Professionals Grant. Marstine is editor of *New Museum Theory and Practice: An Introduction* (Blackwell, 2005). Her essay "Fred Wilson, Good Work, and the Phenomenon of Freud's Mystic Writing Pad" will be published in Richard Sandell and Eithne Nightingale's edited volume *Museums, Equality and Social Justice* (Routledge) in late 2011.

Pamela Z. McClusky is Curator of African and Oceanic Art at the Seattle Art Museum. With her primary focus on African art, and working across continents, she has organized national tours including *Long Steps Never Broke a Back*, and galleries devoted to: *A Bead Quiz, Intimate Information, The Ultimate Spectacle, Sorry Business, Painting Up Yams and Lizards, The War of Nerves, Elegant Plain Art from the Shaker World and Beyond, The Untold Story, Is Egyptian Art African? Passion for Possession, Two Visions of Slavery* and *Indigo Blues*. Her most recent article, "And to think that we saw it on East Marginal Way," is included in *Nick Cave:*

Meet Me at the Center of the Earth. In 2012, she will open an exhibition devoted to Australian Aboriginal Art.

Claudia B. Ocello, President & CEO, Museum Partners Consulting, LLC, has over 20 years' museum experience. She and her team of educators at The New Jersey Historical Society won the American Association of Museums (AAM) Excellence in Programming Award for *Partners in Learning: Teen Parents and their Children at Museums*. Joining the staff of Save Ellis Island enabled Claudia to continue developing education programs, training docents and advising on accessibility issues and exhibitions. In 2008, Claudia received the Award for Excellence in Practice from AAM. Currently Claudia serves as a consultant to US museums. She published articles in *Museum* Magazine and authored a chapter in *An Alliance of Spirit: Building Museum School Partnerships* (AAM, 2010). Claudia co-teaches in the M.A. in Museum Professions Program at Seton Hall University and is actively involved in mentoring young professionals. She earned an M.S. in Museum Education from Bank Street College of Education.

Ross Parry is Senior Lecturer and Academic Director in the School of Museum Studies at the University of Leicester. He is chair of the Museums Computer Group, since 2004 has co-convened the annual 'UK Museums on the Web' (UKMW) conference, and between 2007 and 2009 was chair of judges for the national Jodi Awards. In 2005 he was made a HIRF Innovations Fellow for his work on developing in-gallery digital media, and in 2007 was awarded a University Teaching Fellowship for his outstanding contribution to meeting the training needs of the cultural heritage sector. In 2009 he was made a Tate Research Fellow. He is the author of *Recoding the Museum: digital heritage and technologies of change* (2007), the first major history of museum computing, and is editor of *Museums in a Digital Age* (2010).

Michael Pickering is Head of the Aboriginal and Torres Strait Islander Program at the National Museum of Australia team and leads the Museum's repatriation program. He has previously worked as Head Curator with the Indigenous Cultures Program of Museum Victoria, Native Title Research Officer with Aboriginal Affairs Victoria, Regional Officer with the Northern Territory Aboriginal Areas Protection Authority, as an anthropologist with the Northern Land Council and as a consultant archaeologist and anthropologist. His research interests and publications include studies on material culture, cannibalism, Aboriginal archaeology and anthropology, Indigenous heritage management and repatriation. Dr Pickering is a member of the editorial boards of the journals *ReCollections* and *Museum Management and Curatorship*. He is also a member of the Collections Council of Australia's Experts panel in collection law. At time of writing he was a member of ICOM. Whether he still is awaits the reception of this paper.

Richard Sandell is Director and Head of the School of Museum Studies at the University of Leicester. He has been awarded research fellowships at the Smithsonian Institution (2004/5) and the Humanities Research Center of the Australian National University (2008) to pursue his research interests which focus on museums and human rights and the social agency and responsibility of museums. He is the editor of *Museums, Society, Inequality* (2002), author of *Museums, Prejudice* *and the Reframing of Difference* (2007); co-editor (with Robert R. Janes) of *Museum Management and Marketing* (2008) and co-editor (with Jocelyn Dodd and Rosemarie Garland-Thomson) of *Re-Presenting Disability: Activism and Agency in the Museum* (2010), all published by Routledge.

Judith Chelius Stark is a professor of philosophy and director of the Environmental Studies Program at Seton Hall University in South Orange, New Jersey, where she teaches seminars on Augustine, feminist theories and environmental and museum ethics. She also team-teaches in the interdisciplinary University Honors Program of which she is an associate director and former director. She publishes on Augustine, environmental issues and human rights and is the editor of *Re-Reading the Canon: Feminist Interpretations of Augustine* for which she wrote the introduction and one of the chapters (Penn State Press, 2006). Dr. Stark is the co-author (with Joanna Vechiarelli Scott) of *Hannah Arendt, Love and Saint Augustine* published by University of Chicago Press, 1995. In 2009 she was appointed to the Environmental Justice Advisory Council for the Department of Environmental Protection of the state of New Jersey. She is an avid (amateur) birder and sea kayaker.

Christopher B. Steiner is the Lucy C. McDannel '22 Professor of Art History and Director of Museum Studies at Connecticut College. He is the author of *African Art in Transit*, and co-editor (with Ruth B. Phillips) of *Unpacking Culture: Art and Commodity in Colonial and Postcolonial Worlds*. His current book project, *Performing the Nut Museum*, focuses on outsider art, visionary museums and the social construction of exhibitionary (dis)order.

Celka Straughn is currently the Andrew W. Mellon Director of Academic Programs at the Spencer Museum of Art, University of Kansas. Prior to this position she served as a research assistant at Harvard Project Zero on the "Developing Minds and Digital Media" study, as well as on the collaborative research project with the Harvard Art Museums, "Learning in and from Museum Study Centers." She has also held curatorial and museum education positions at the Harvard Art Museums/Busch-Reisinger Museum, the Smart Museum of Art and The Photographic Gallery (formerly The Sony Gallery for Photography) at the American University in Cairo. She received a doctorate in Art History from the University of Chicago.

Paul Tapsell belongs to the Maori tribes of Ngati Whakaue and Ngati Raukawa. He was formerly Curator of Rotorua Museum (1990–1994), Director Maori of Auckland Museum (2000–2008) and Co-convenor of the Museums and Cultural Heritage Programme at University of Auckland (2000–2008). He was also Co-Chair of Museums Aotearoa (2003–2004) and the Editorial Board Chair for *Te Ara — New Zealand Museums Journal* (2002–2007). After completing his M.A. in Anthropology at Auckland (1995), he graduated from Oxford with a D.Phil. in Museum Ethnology (1998). His Post Doctorate at Australian National University seeded his first book, *Pukaki* (2000), winning a national award. Paul later became an Eisenhower Fellow (2005) and, more recently, Professor of Maori Studies and Dean of Te Tumu: School of Maori, Pacific and Indigenous Studies at University of Otago (2009). A father of two, he continues to serve his family, his tribe and wider Maori communities on various boards, including Maori Maps, a not-for-profit service that assists re-linking dislocated descendants with home *marae*.

Paul Williams is a specialist in the interpretation and representation of social histories in museums. His most recent publication is *Memorial Museums: The Global Rush to Commemorate Atrocities* (Oxford: Berg, 2007). He has contributed many articles to history, heritage and museum journals, on topics such as postcolonial museology, genocide remembrance and memory and public history. After gaining his Ph.D. in Cultural Studies from the University of Melbourne, Australia, Dr. Williams spent several years as a professor in the M.A. Museum Studies program at New York University. Since 2008 he has worked for Ralph Appelbaum Associates, the New York-based museum planning and design firm, as a senior content developer.

ACKNOWLEDGMENTS

Funding for this publication was provided, in part, through a grant award to Seton Hall University through the 21st Century Museum Professionals Grants Program of the Institute of Museums and Library Services. I am grateful for the support of this remarkable federal agency which furthers change in the museum, in particular, Marsha Semmel, Christopher Reich and the anonymous reviewers who recognized the need for new conversations about ethics in our sector.

I thank my former colleagues at Seton Hall University for recognizing the promise of the IME and nurturing it through its initial three years of growth. The Office of the Provost; Office of the Dean, College of Arts and Sciences; M.A. Program in Museum Professions, Department of Communication and the Arts; and Seton Hall IME Advisory Committee all provided support for my work in museum ethics. Special thanks go to Petra Chu, Jürgen Heinrichs, Charlotte Nichols, Susan Leshnoff, Arline Lowe, William Haney, Michael Soupios, Judith Stark, Elaine Walker, Martin Finkelstein, Jeffrey Togman, Stephanie Hauge and to the IME Graduate Assistants Jennine Schweighardt, Lindsay LaPrad and Danielle Schallom.

Many friends and colleagues from museums and museum studies helped give me a sense of direction through the minefields of ethics discourse. They include Alexander Bauer, Pete Brown, Donna De Salvo, Margaretta Frederick, Elizabeth Greenspan, Alice Greenwald, Katherine Hart, John Haworth, Hilde Hein, Victoria Hollowes, Christina Kreps, Karol Lawson, Steven Lubar, John Mayer, Pamela McClusky, Steve Miller, Martha Morris, Michael Pickering, Jan Ramirez, Christine Reich, Anthony Shelton, Lois Silverman, Paige Simpson, Tom Sokolowski, Kevin Stayton, Christopher Steiner, Carole Wharton, Glenn Wharton and Paul Williams.

Richard Sandell and Robert R. Janes provided valuable insights into the project during its formative stages, as did proposal reviewers Marjorie Schwarzer, Haidy Geismar and Raymond Silverman. My editor Matthew Gibbons was a great advocate throughout the process, as were editorial assistants Lalle Pursglove and Amy Davis-Poynter.

Artists engaged with institutional critique have strongly impacted my understanding of museum ethics. I cherish my conversations with Fred Wilson, Ernesto Pujol, Robert Fontenot and Anthony Schrag.

My new colleagues at the School of Museum Studies, University of Leicester, have provided a supportive and inspiring environment for me to finish the project. It is a precious gift to be working among a community of people committed to the social responsibility of museums. I am especially grateful to my new Head of School, Richard Sandell, and to Deputy Head, Suzanne MacLeod, who have opened up for me a whole new world of possibilities.

I could not have done this project without the many kindnesses of Rosanne Harrison, Susan Nussbaum, Joyce Rosenbaum and Janet Strahosky. My husband Mark, father Sheldon, and children Jean and Jake have shown love, patience, humor and understanding through many challenging transitions during this project and I hope to make them proud.

Any views, findings, conclusions or recomendations expressed in this publication do not necessarily represent those of the Institute of Museum and Library Services.

PREFACE

At this moment of global economic recession, museum ethics is a timely topic. Museums and heritage sites around the world, from university art galleries to national parks, are facing some of the most serious challenges in their history. Most are under-resourced and scarce funding often means that innovative agendas to promote the common good are abandoned in favor of seemingly safe and conventional approaches. In addition, financial pressure is causing some museum directors and trustees to consider choices—from capitalizing their permanent collections to cutting educational programming—that may compromise their institutions' ethics long into the future. Ethics, as opposed to law, is ostensibly self-regulating but, amidst the tensions, an undercurrent is developing that calls for stronger enforcement of ethics. Museums and related committees and associations are writing, reviewing and tightening up their ethics codes and guidelines.[1] And legal intervention is being considered more closely.[2] The traditional museum ethics discourse, created to instill professional practice through a system of consensus and its correlative, coercion, is unable to meet the needs of museums and society in the twenty-first century.

This volume proposes a new museum ethics discourse as a way forward. It identifies both the critical ethical challenges to museums and the ethical opportunities that have arisen to reconfigure ethics. The 30 academics and practitioners who contributed to it come from diverse disciplines and international contexts to examine ethics in museum areas such as leadership, business practices, exhibitions, marketing, technology, conservation, collections management, visitor learning, community partnerships, repatriation and architecture. While the volume is by no means encyclopedic, it represents diverse strands in museum activity for, as Tristram Besterman notes, "there is no part of the museum that is free from ethical implications."[3] Essays convey a range of perspectives indicative of the rich texture of contemporary ethics discourse. What they share is an understanding of the contingent nature of museum ethics in the twenty-first century—its relations with complex economic, social, political and technological forces and its fluid ever-shifting sensibility. Together, they also assert the moral agency of museums: the concept that museum ethics is more than the personal and professional ethics of individuals and concerns the capacity of institutions to create social change. The volume is a theoretically informed reconceptualization of museum ethics discourse as a dynamic social practice central to the project of change, both inside and outside the museum.

Part I, *Theorizing Museum Ethics*, examines contemporary museum ethics through the prism of those disciplines and methods that have shaped it most. It situates museum ethics discourse within the larger discourses of philosophy and educational psychology. It considers the ethics of sustainability as it pertains to museum ethics. It identifies important theoretical and practical models from post-colonial and feminist theory. And it asserts the contingent nature of the new museum ethics; in so doing, it sets out three paradigms of ethical engagement for the twenty-first century: social responsibility, radical transparency and shared guardianship of heritage.

The multi-layered implications of social inclusion for the contemporary museum ethics discourse is the subject of Part II, *Ethics, Activism and Social Responsibility*. This section argues for ethics as an activist practice and articulates new models of participation from democratic pluralism to reciprocity. It examines the value of economic and programming initiatives to bring under-represented communities to the museum. And it anchors the new museum ethics in a social justice agenda.

The chapters in Part III, *The Radical Potential of Museum Transparency*, explore the liberatory aspects of museum communication that admits accountability—acknowledgement and assumption of responsibility for choices. This is not simply conveying knowledge but instead analyzing the power relations inherent in museological processes. This section demonstrates how the gesture of unpacking the political permutations embedded in concepts undergirding current practice can generate critical thinking among museum staff and diverse stakeholders which, in turn, leads to ethical change.

Part IV, *Visual Culture and the Performance of Museum Ethics*, considers a new paradigm of responsibility towards heritage. It asks what kind of ethics emerges from the ever-more-fluid dynamic between objects and experiences in museums. Several of the chapters engage the ethics of exhibiting the body in the museum—both the corporeal presence and the body represented by genetic material. Others look at the ways that museum ethics itself is enacted or performed in practices such as architectural design, conservation and educational programming. Part IV challenges traditional values of ownership, embracing instead for the museum a notion of "property" as a relationship that requires ongoing nurture and negotiation.

Together, the many strands of the volume chart a new museum ethics discourse with the potential to guide and drive change in the museum. It is my hope that recognizing the contingent nature of museum ethics today generates self-reflective and activist practice in support of a socially inclusive museum.

Janet Marstine

Notes

1 For example, much of the discussion of the Institute of Museum Ethics (IME) listserv from 2008–2009 focused on the writing and revision of ethics codes. This material is archived and available for listserv members to review on the IME website. Online. Available HTTP: http://www.museumethics.org/listserv (accessed 25 October 2010).

2 For instance, in the U.S. the Internal Revenue Service in 2009 introduced a revised Form 990 "Return of Organization Exempt from Income Tax" for non-profits which asks leading questions concerning potential conflicts of interest such as "Does your institution have a written whistle-blower policy?" In New York Assemblyman Richard Brodsky drafted a bill in 2009 with the New York State Board of Regents and the Museum Association of New York (it did not pass) legislating the circumstances under which museums, libraries and historic houses in the state could deaccession works from their permanent collections. See T. Chomicz and E. Waterhouse Wilson, "Get Ready for the New Form 990," *Philanthropy Journal*, 18 March, 2008. Online. Available HTTP: http://www.philanthropyjournal.org/

resources/managementleadership/get-ready-new-form-990 (accessed 26 October 2010); "Museums and Lawmakers Mull Sales of Art," *New York Times*, 14 January 2010. Online. Available HTTP: http://www.nytimes.com/2010/01/15/arts/design/15deaccession.html (accessed 25 October 2010). The bill died in part because New York museums with large holdings complained that the task of publishing an inventory of their collections was too costly and onerous.

3 T. Besterman, "Museum Ethics," in S. MacDonald (ed.) *A Companion to Museum Ethics*, Malden and Oxford: Blackwell Publishing, 2006, p. 432.

Part I

THEORIZING MUSEUM ETHICS

1

The contingent nature of the new museum ethics

Janet Marstine

Introduction

In 2008, Scottish performance artist Anthony Schrag scaled a column of the classical portico fronting the Gallery of Modern Art (GoMA) in Glasgow and, then, partway up, held on to the fluting while extending his legs until his feet reached the adjacent column (Figure 1.1). In this brief but expressive piece, entitled *Push*,[1] Schrag exerts both a physical and metaphorical pressure on the museum. Through bodily means *Push* calls for ethical change in the museum responsive to the needs of contemporary society. Schrag explains:

> It's an instinctual, responsive piece that came from my frustration at a museum's monolithic status within a cultural landscape. It was a symbolic gesture harking back to the myths of Samson, wherein he broke the pillars of the temple that held him. It was finding a way to both critique and belong within those systems, and attempt to add another, tangential pathway through and around the building. My desire is to disrupt expected modes to find new ways of speaking.[2]

In the Hebrew Bible Samson has so much rage towards the Philistines who blinded, seduced and imprisoned him that he draws strength from God to collapse the two temple pillars to which he is chained during a celebration; he thus destroys the temple and the Philistines who were inside it, sacrificing himself in the process.[3] Schrag mimics Samson's act to convey a similar alienation from an oppressive environment. Schrag's action compels the viewer to imagine dynamic and participatory new museum models defined by divergent voices. He asserts, "the impulse for this type of work comes from an interest in theories related to socially engaged practices and inviting a wide spectrum of the public into a shared cultural debate."[4] Schrag's *Push* adroitly encapsulates the thinking of the new museum ethics, an approach that, I shall argue, is a feminist-inspired mode of critical inquiry defined by its contingent nature.

Figure 1.1 Anthony Schrag, *Push*, 2008, Gallery of Modern Art, Glasgow. Copyright, Anthony Schrag.

It is common practice for ethics centers, institutes and think tanks to use symbols of measure, enlightenment and strength to represent the concept of ethics; images of scales, compasses, torches and pillars predominate.[5] But these icons connote moral certainty, a characteristic that does not define twenty-first-century museum ethics. I have found institutional critique—artists' systematic inquiry of the policies, practices and values of museums—a useful touchstone by which to grapple with the multi-faceted and contingent nature of museum ethics today. Schrag's performance functions as such. It refutes the rigidity of museum power with the realities of corporeal presence to model a process that admits complexity, contradiction and flux.[6]

Institutional critique such as Schrag's positions museum ethics as a discourse, a social practice which impacts the construction of knowledge and the way we behave. Foucault has established that discourse can function as a mode of asserting power but it may also serve to subvert social relations.[7] By examining museum ethics as social practice, I will illuminate the dynamics of authorized and alternative ethics discourse and offer a corrective to this under-theorized sphere of inquiry.

The authorized museum ethics discourse has both shaped and been shaped by the prioritization of skill development and standard setting that characterized the museum and museum studies sector for much of the last century. Gary Edson's 1997 seminal volume *Museum Ethics* advanced this notion of professionalization. "Museum ethics is not about the imposition of external values on museums, but about an understanding of the foundations of museum practices," he declared.[8] Ethics as professionalization has played a significant role in distinguishing public service from personal gain and political interests. But in this century the shifting terrain drives a critique of common practice to implement change that meets the current and future needs of society.

Social and cultural change lead to alternative discourses that undermine authorized discourse. Recent social, economic, political and technological trends have sparked in the museum sector a developing discourse about the moral agency of museums that contests the authorized view of ethics. Richard Sandell has argued persuasively that objectivity is an elusive stance and a default position that imparts value through the invoked authority of the institution. Sandell uses the term "moral activism" to suggest a direction for museums to realize their potential as change agents in promoting social inclusion and human rights both inside and outside the museum.[9] Hilde Hein identifies what she calls an "institutional morality," asserting that, while museums may not have conscience, they do have moral agency.[10] Hein's institutional morality moves beyond personal and professional ethics; it suggests that, while museum staff may come and go, their synergy across time and place, especially as built into the mechanisms of organizational change, creates an institutional ethics, as well as an ethics of the museum sector. In this chapter I will show how the discourse of contemporary museum ethics is founded on the concept that institutions have moral agency. And I will define three major strands of theory and practice through which museums can assert their moral agency: social inclusion, radical transparency and shared guardianship of heritage.

It is well documented that the museum sector has become increasingly more responsive to the shifting needs of society; museums have come to accept and even embrace change as a defining element of policy.[11] Nonetheless, institutional bureaucracies, the demands of funding sources and allegiances to common practice have typically prescribed incremental change in the museum, rather than the kind of holistic rethinking required to instill the values of shared authority and of social understanding among diverse communities.[12] In museums today creativity and risk-taking are often funneled through one-off projects.

In fact, a substantive policy and practice of change depend upon a museum ethics of change. The progressive museum is undergirded and invigorated by deep engagement with the key ethical issues of the day. Museums that are driven by a dynamic ethics discourse have a clear sense of the values that their decision-making conveys and continuously assess and reassess this alignment with the communities they serve. Evidence of this emerges from a range of institutional policy and planning statements, not only ethics codes. One result is that institutions invested in the new museum ethics discourse effectively communicate the public value of museums. The process empowers museums to change because it builds public trust through democracy, transparency and relevance.

In this chapter I posit that the new museum ethics is among the most pivotal concerns of museum professionals in the twenty-first century and central to good leadership. I examine the richness and fluidity of museum ethics today and explore how this shifting terrain can help the museum to acknowledge its moral agency. First, by considering what museum ethics is not, I will unpack the authorized discourse. I will then analyze the developing alternative discourse which I refer to as the new museum ethics, contemporary museum ethics and twenty-first-century museum ethics. I situate this alternative discourse within feminist theory and within the literature of ethics studies from a broad range of disciplines to advance the concept of the contingent nature of the new museum ethics. And I discuss the three key strands in museum ethics theory and practice today: social responsibility, radical transparency and guardianship of heritage. A central tenet of my argument is that museum ethics is an opportunity for growth, rather than a burden of compliance. I hold that change in the museum is anchored by change in museum ethics discourse.

What Museum Ethics is Not

What is contemporary museum ethics? We might begin by clarifying what it is not.

Museum ethics is not a duty to conceal unethical behavior within one's own institution and/or among a select group of colleagues. This assumption remains quite common, as is indicated by the many requests that I receive from well-intentioned and politically pressed parties to provide confidential advice concerning specific ethical quandaries at particular institutions. Museum ethics of the twenty-first century does offer insight to support museum staff in making appropriate choices that will help their institutions to flourish but it is a discourse that cannot and should not be contained within isolated pockets of the sector. Feminist experience suggests that shielding insiders can inflict significant damage. As Hein declares, "The appeal to privacy as an essential claim to immunity from public intervention can be divisive and dangerous."[13] Singularizing ethics dilemmas overly circumscribes the issues involved. Identifying and evaluating the options that arise from any one ethical dilemma require that those invested engage with the larger body of contemporary ethics debates. Clearly, ethics is not about airing the "dirty laundry" of individuals or institutions; such airings can betray trust and do not advance the discourse. But central to the project of museum ethics is the sharing of ethical challenges and opportunities with diverse stakeholders to understand and address larger patterns of behavior. This sharing is a mark of visionary, proactive and courageous leadership which encourages problem-solving and builds trust.

Museum ethics is not a universal set of values to be applied indiscriminately. In this light, it is important to differentiate between ethical principles—those ideals and values which a society holds dear–and applied ethics—the practice of employing those principles to specific arenas of activity, from medicine to business to museum work.[14] While ethical principles such as individualism have shaped applied ethics in western culture, other operative principles, for example, collectivism, have impacted applied ethics in many other parts of the world. It is critical to acknowledge the pertinence and the problematics of cultural relativism as applied to museum ethics.

Contemporary museum ethics is not a canon of ideas based on consensus. The principal ethical debates of the twenty-first century are marked by strong differences of opinion from diverse contributors, not neatly settled through negotiation, and this is a sign of health. Inspired by Socrates' ideal of examining ethics, through a dialectic process, consensus, as applied to museum ethics, has, until recently, been considered a professional, democratic and fair method of determining practice—relying on compromise among experts from the field and enforced through appealing to the desire for conformity.[15] I believe that, in a twenty-first-century multicultural context that respects difference, consensus has come to signal an exclusivity and like-mindedness among contributors, as well as fixity of thought. Museums seeking change foster collaborative relationships on equal footing with diverse stakeholders and willingly assume the risks entailed by entertaining novel positions.

Museum ethics is not a system of decrees and prohibitions instituted to control behavior, as does the law, but without the enforcement incentive. The technical, legalistic approach to museum ethics has functioned to oversimplify issues and scope and deaden the vitality of the discourse. This is not to suggest that legal studies itself is static or straightforward or to deny the vast overlap between law and ethics. Indeed, ethics and jurisprudence have had a long and contentious relationship that can be traced back to the writings of Plato.[16] Ethics provides purpose and rationale for law. Ethics also depends on the law to penalize certain behaviors that do harm. Ethics and jurisprudence often conflict. But the most significant difference between law and ethics is that the former is characterized by constraints—what one cannot do—while the latter concerns ever-shifting opportunities—what one can do—for the common good.[17] Understanding this difference is central to realizing the potential of the new museum ethics to effect change.

Museum ethics today is not defined by codes. Since the American Association of Museums (AAM) introduced the first such statement in 1925, ethics codes have been the mainstay of the museum ethics discourse.[18] Ethics codes and guidelines define appropriate behavior, establish responsibilities and offer means for self-assessment. Museum and professional associations, individual museums, non-governmental organizations (NGOs), institutes, congresses and other bodies depend on these instruments to establish professional practice. Ethics codes are not legally binding though they may influence the law. They function through group pressure; museum association censure, loss of accreditation and threats of professional isolation are the typical means of enforcement.[19]

Ethics codes are aimed at professionalizing individual practitioners and are culturally defined, based on western enlightenment ideals of virtue.[20] This focus on the individual practitioner inhibits museums from recognizing their moral agency. Hein asserts, "As institutional mediators, museums are positioned to shape as well as preserve values, but narrowly focused moral codes lack the creative idealism to bring this about."[21] Museum ethics codes are fraught with contradictions indicative of the diversity of voices that impact and are impacted by museums today.[22] These constraints do not suggest that ethics codes are no longer of use but that they need to be invigorated by contemporary ethics discourse so that a process of debate takes priority and the result is self-reflexive, acknowledges the complexities and contradictions of the contemporary museum context and has the ability to change as the needs of society change.

Museum ethics of the twenty-first century does not prioritize the institution's responsibility to objects above all else. Objects are the pretext for the founding of most collections-based institutions and museum rhetoric, grounded in the presumption of authentic experience, commonly attests that objects are what make the museum experience unique. But Hein reaches an alternative conclusion. "The containment of valuable things is not unique to museums, but is common to banks, private collections, and expensive stores. What distinguishes the museum is its agency, what it does with its resources, and for whom."[23] In my estimate the new museum ethics stresses the agency to do good with museum resources. This is not to say that objects lose out; when museums meet the needs of society, they meet the needs of objects in the process.

The Contingent Nature of the New Museum Ethics: A Feminist Approach

In addressing what museum ethics is not, what I am arguing for is its contingent nature. The term contingent emphasizes the conditional and relational qualities of the discourse. Contingency is commonly defined as a dependence on factors, circumstances and/or events in the future and thus suggests a lack of certainty. The Latin root of the word is *contingere*, to have contact with, from *tangere*, meaning to touch.[24] To reconceptualize museum ethics as a contingent discourse is to emphasize its dependence—the way it touches–upon social, political, technological and economic factors and to acknowledge its changeability. The contingent nature of contemporary museum ethics suggests that it is deeply engaged with the world around it and that it is adaptive and improvisational. Looking at the discourse through the lens of contingency helps us to understand the complexities of the relationship between museums and applied ethics.

Contemporary museum ethics is shaped by—and touches—a broad range of disciplines and methods. For example, philosophy helps us to understand the past and present of diverse theoretical and practical approaches to ethics and its study can help situate museum ethics. Educational psychology can offer insights into what might inspire ethical behavior in the museum context among staff and visitors. Environmental studies provides a model to assess the sustainability of museums. Acknowledging the contingent nature of museum ethics discourse entails rejecting the artificial divide between museum ethics and a broad range of other applied ethics studies, instead building upon issues of mutual concern. For example, how can medical ethics inform museums' treatment of human remains and vice-versa? How might the ethics of journalism converge with museums' perspectives on censorship? What kind of dialogue can be fostered between political ethicists and curators developing exhibitions about war? What values might computer ethics and digital heritage hold in common?

From my perspective gender studies and critical anthropology offer some of the most revolutionary implications for the new museum ethics. This is because methods that have recently emerged from feminism, queer theory and post-colonial theory have problematized the process of "othering" in such profound terms that they lead to the renegotiation of key museum relationships traditionally configured in binary positions. These include the binaries between museum director/curator and support staff; between museum staff and their publics; and between museums and source communities. In so doing, the methods of gender studies and post-colonialism call for a reconsideration of representation itself—the core function of museums.[25]

My focus on contingency in museum ethics is shaped by feminist theory. Hein asserts that theory in of itself is a means towards ethical behavior because it offers an overarching system by which to engage in self-reflexivity. Hein argues for the adoption of feminist theory to the museum context because of its focus on inclusion and process:

> I propose feminist theory as a point of departure for the reconstruction of museums, in part because of its open-endedness and inherent pluralism. There is no single feminist theory, nor even a projected design for one. There is no canon, although there are some pivotal declarations. Feminism makes no claims to ultimate doctrinal verities. I take this renunciation of universalism and concomitant lack of finality as an asset.[26]

The kind of feminism that Hein advocates for in the museum context is not an essentialized understanding of gender, nor is it an argument for equality. It is more deeply subversive for it challenges the "othering" that underpins museum policy and practice. She states:

> I do not minimize the achievements of gender equity that have been realized in modern society, inclusive of museums, but essentially these amount simply to the extension of rights and privileges traditionally confined to men, without alleviating the disequilibrium that underlies the very possibility of according such rights and privileges to anyone. That disequilibrium stems from a profound climate of ownership and entitlement implicit in the characterization of the human subjects, relative to an object observed, desired, cultivated, possessed, feared, tamed, conquered, or even revered. Feminist theory seeks radical revision of the very notions of subjectivity and otherness.[27]

Hein's feminist theory for museums converges with queer theory and post-colonial theory in its investment not in reversing the subject/object dichotomy but in the liberation from it, along with other patriarchal binary oppositions that impede processes of engagement, mutuality and fluidity.[28] She asserts feminism's potential for a museum ethics of sociality, "Feminist theory holds up an ideal of social life that promotes integrated relations between self and other, self and nature, in an environment that is non-repressive and caring."[29] Hein's feminism elucidates the contingent nature of contemporary museum ethics. She notes, "Feminist theory accommodates impermanence and does not assign priority to changeless immortality. It is responsive to the dynamic world that spawned it, in which alone its perceptions may be validated."[30]

The transformative potential of Hein's feminist perspective makes it a useful construct by which to reconceive museum ethics. Its focus on collaboration and inclusion leads to new understandings of the importance of social responsibility in the museum. Its emphasis on process over product points to the centrality of transparency in museum policy and practice. Its critique of canonicity opens up possibilities of non-hierarchic approaches to staff organization, museum-community engagement and the sharing of heritage. And its stress on care provides productive ways to imagine the "touch" of contingency as a bodily presence. Indeed, feminist theory, as Hein articulates it, is founded on contingencies that set a useful precedent for the new museum ethics. Hein declares, feminist theory "must be attuned to complexity, criticism, and change, and must admit its fallibility. I suggest that a similar pliability and readiness for redistribution and reintegration should model the use of things in museums and also the museum itself."[31] Contemporary museum ethics adapts the contingent nature of feminist theory to assert dynamism and self-reflexivity.

The contingency of contemporary museum ethics does not imply that the discourse is weak. The sensitivity of the new museum ethics to outside forces opens up possibilities for systemic transformation—towards social responsibility, radical transparency and shared guardianship of heritage. I put forth these aims not as circumscribed or universal principles but, from a feminist viewpoint, as constantly evolving ideals representative of human rights. And as Christina Kreps cautions, while culturally relative approaches are to be championed, respect for human rights is paramount; she declares, "The challenge is to reconcile our respect and need for cultural diversity with the need to acknowledge and respect the principles of human rights and cultural democracy."[32]

Social Responsibility

The feminist notion of contingency as a sense of touch or contact underscores the connectivity of the new museum ethics; museum ethics today is contingent upon the connectivity of museums with their diverse and ever-shifting communities. The relations between museums and communities rest upon the moral agency of the institution—its participation in creating a more just society. As Sandell asserts, the new museum ethics "positions contributions to social well-being, equity and fairness as an integral part of museum work."[33] Democratic pluralism, shared authority and social justice are distinct but convergent areas of policy and practice that together define the socially responsible museum.

Since the late twentieth century the sector and the associations and agencies that support it have been increasingly committed to creating a more socially inclusive museum.[34] But while many institutions have created exhibitions and programs to attract traditionally under-represented groups and have adopted learner-centered approaches to the interpretation of collections, patterns of participation continue to demonstrate inequalities of access. Sandell argues that equity and diversity depend on a revolutionary rethinking of the social responsibility of museums:

> Originally understood by many to be simply a synonym for access or audience development (concepts that most within the sector are at least familiar, if not entirely comfortable, with), there is now growing recognition that the challenges presented by the inclusion agenda are, in fact, much more significant and the implications more fundamental and far-reaching. A growing body of research into the social role and impact of museums suggests that engagement with the concepts of social inclusion and exclusion will require museums—and the profession and sector as a whole—to radically rethink their purposes and goals and to renegotiate their relationship to, and role within, society. In short, if museums are to become effective agents for

social inclusion, a paradigmatic shift in the purpose and role of museums in society, and concomitant changes in working practices, will be required.[35]

The ethical, socially responsible museum of the twenty-first century recognizes identities of its staff and its publics as hybrid and fluid, rather than simply boxes to be ticked. The ethical, socially responsible museum also problematizes concepts of the museum public. Museum professionals' continued reliance on the term "general public" attests to the monolithic status still assigned to visitors and non-visitors. The recent use of the plural "publics" accommodates diverse stakeholders and acknowledges the development of complex social spaces created by the internet. But, as Jennifer Barrett explains, no matter what the choice of term, there is no essentialized audience: "Merely substituting terms such as community, audience, and visitors conceals, but does not escape the central concern, that it is necessary to continually monitor and adapt the idea in response to a changing world."[36] Barrett advocates self-reflexive thinking about the use of the term public as a means to help museums become more socially engaged.

Social inclusivity is also dependent on new modes of democratic participation in the museum. Political philosopher Iris Marion Young described a sweeping kind of participatory process—soliciting, rather than shying away from, divergent or transgressive voices—as democratic pluralism, a socially just corrective to the sometimes exclusive properties of conventional democratic systems in which the majority can silence dissent.[37] In the museum context, this process, which results in civic discourse,[38] is often avoided because it presumes risk, the risk of unpredictability and of potential transformation of institution and self. The new museum ethics is conceived as a means to encourage democratic pluralism in the museum; the ethical museum today consciously chooses to assume risk to foster socially inclusive discourse. A truly engaged museum interaction "restores the intimacy of participation in the world,"[39] as Hein imagines it. Ultimately, democratic pluralism is a way of challenging the binary relationship between self and other which continues to shape museum policy and practice.

The contingent nature of the new museum ethics suggests not only that museums depend upon discursive practices with a diversity of stakeholders, but also upon innovative approaches to this engagement. These approaches encourage shared authority, defined by Robert R. Archibald as "relinquish[ing] traditional authoritarian roles in favor of new responsibilities as both resources and facilitators of dialogue about those things that matter most to people." Archibald asks, "How can we really allow communities to own museums?"[40]

Though not free of ideology,[41] the paradigm of social media has introduced new modes of non-hierarchal engagement to the museum. It has created a novel kind of public sphere—that realm between private and state in which opinion is formed and political action taken—though the ethical issues that emerge are not unfamiliar. Amanda Wong explains in the context of regulating social media at the US Memorial Holocaust Museum:

> Discerning ethical behavior in this emerging media landscape means navigating uncertain terrain, experimenting so as to understand its opportunities and limitations, and assessing its value based on its unique

conditions. Although no panacea, social media opens up new ways to be attentive to diverse audiences and draw them into discussion as ethical actors themselves.[42]

While power-sharing can be a difficult and complex process, social technologies provide a productive tool to embed shared authority.

Bernadette Lynch suggests reciprocity as an effective mode to nurture shared authority.[43] According to Lynch, reciprocity requires that each party recognizes, respects and draws from the expertise of the other; museum staff members acknowledge the social capital of collaborators and partners as no less significant than their own. Moreover, encounters expose and deconstruct inherent power relationships so that creative conflict can occur. Lynch argues that creative conflict is more successful in eliciting change than consensus which, she asserts, is ultimately coercive. Reciprocity fosters dialogue in which the values of the "margins"—those not at the centre of institutional power—transform those of the "core," destabilizing these categories in the process.[44] Reciprocity makes the ethics of the core contingent upon the ethics of the margins.

Reciprocity does not mean that staff members give up responsibility for their collections or areas of expertise. But it does mean that museum professionals share these resources and expertise equitably and usefully so that they empower communities to leverage their own experiences and knowledge in co-production. It also means that museum professionals develop a more diverse range of options by which stakeholders can participate and indicate when and how this participation has impacted the institution. And it means that staff show the vulnerability required to consider deliberately enough ideas and opinion from stakeholders so that these ideas and opinions lead to change. As Hein imagines a feminist notion of shared authority:

> The museum initiates, but should not dominate, conversation. It generates vocabulary to perpetuate communication. No single story is preeminent, but together they constitute reality. Museums and the public combine to articulate that reality, and no one is above it.[45]

Shared authority depends on museum staff members functioning as trustees, not in the traditional sense of the word, an institutional board of governors with all of the paternalistic baggage that is attached to that, but as Howard Gardner defines them, "individuals in one's community who are assumed to see the big picture clearly; who are concerned with the long-term welfare of the society; and who, most importantly, are expected to behave in a disinterested way—that is, to recommend and do what is right, rather than what improves their own lot or advances their own interests."[46] Gardner's societal trustee does not assume a position of disinterest to affect objectivity but to renegotiate power relations willingly in order to do what Gardner calls "good work," work that is "socially responsible, ethical and moral."[47] Trusteeship, in Gardner's sense of the word, is an indicator of ethical leadership. Only through this renegotiation of power and control can co-production and shared governance occur. And shared governance is the key to self-representation, a basic human right.

Social responsibility also extends to relationships among museum staff. Reciprocity and trusteeship are vehicles to reconfigure the power hierarchies within the museum as well as without, as, clearly, the institution mirrors the world. The new museum ethics imagines a collaborative organizational structure in which support staff–from preparators to visitor services employees to registrars—are equally respected for their expertise as are curators, educators and museum directors and engage in decision-making processes across the institution.[48]

While social responsibility is founded on new modes of inclusion and engagement, it is equally predicated on forwarding a social justice agenda. Sandell has shown that there is a growing acceptance—and evidence to substantiate the premise—that museums play a unique and significant role in contributing to social justice. Museums have the social agency to combat prejudice and foster social understanding.[49] This is not a new phenomenon. Lois Silverman traces a long history of social service in museums.[50] And as Sandell notes, this social justice agenda is integral to rethinking the terms of social inclusion:

> Museums can contribute towards social inclusion at *individual, community and societal* levels. At an individual or personal level, engagement with museums can deliver positive outcomes such as enhanced self-esteem, confidence and creativity. At a community level, museums can act as a catalyst for social regeneration, empowering communities to increase their self-determination and develop the confidence and skills to take greater control over their lives and the development of the neighbourhoods in which they live. Lastly, museums, through the representation of inclusive communities within collections and displays, have the potential to promote tolerance, inter-community respect and to challenge stereotypes.[51]

In fact, the museum can be an ideal laboratory for promoting social justice and human rights, as Jeanne Nakamura declares, "responsibility for others can be learned through practicing it in a small world designed with that purpose in mind."[52] Feminist theory claims a social justice role for museums; Hein asserts, "Museums could be tantalizing sites of reconciliation where contrast and discord join in a protected environment that cultivates sympathy and reflection."[53]

To be the compassionate and equitable institutions that the new museum ethics imagines, institutions must be willing to accept the responsibility of activism. The museum sector today conveys conflicting messages about this role. Professional codes of conduct typically portray museum work as a set of skills to be practiced in an objective manner and museum associations insist that their campaigns to change funding structures and public perception are advocacy—to support publicly a particular cause–in distinction to activism—to campaign to bring about political or social change. Nonetheless, the scope and ambition of these advocacy efforts convey an underlying recognition of the place and power of activism in museum dynamics.[54] Hein notes that in playing out their roles of instilling citizenship, museums have had an activist agenda since the enlightenment.[55]

Assuming an activist approach does not imply that the resulting interpretation is reductive. Instead, activism opens up debate in the museum around social justice issues, offering opportunities for museum staff and audiences to re-examine their own and societal assumptions as well as alternative views.[56] Moral activism presumes that such efforts will have an impact outside the museum—they will contribute to a more just society. In acknowledging the contingent relations between the museum and the world, activism also suggests that institutions assume ethical responsibilities outside the museum, some of which might conflict with the immediate interests of the museum. As Peter Welch notes in the context of tangible and intangible heritage:

> Should museums actively stand up for the rights of communities to sustain traditions *in situ* and exert pressure on states or other governmental entities where these rights are in jeopardy? Should museums devote resources to informing local communities of collections already in the institution that might enable them to preserve their heritage? Museums to some extent do all of these things. The extent to which an institution can implement the broadest spectrum of engagements with intangible heritage is, in my view, the most ethical position to take.[57]

For Welch, promoting intangible heritage as intellectual property and a human right is an activist agenda that may outweigh the short-term interests of the museum to collect objects but ultimately strengthens the museum by giving it ethical purpose.

Radical Transparency

Twenty-first-century museum ethics is also built upon a new theory and practice of transparency in museums. Social responsibility will not flourish in museum culture unless participants know the stakes: unless museums disclose what issues they are facing, the "hows" and "whys" of their decision-making processes and the larger impact of these choices. This is not transparency as Foucault critiqued it, the transmission of knowledge to assert or rationalize power.[58] This is neither the transparency of which feminists have been wary, a mode to justify convention and its unequal power relations.[59] Radical transparency is a liberatory antidote to the assumed alignments and readability of knowledge. Radical transparency not only describes but also analyzes behavior and considers its significance. It is a mode of communication that admits accountability—acknowledgement and assumption of responsibility for actions. A transparent wall text might tell us that an artifact is of unknown provenance; a radically transparent wall text would additionally engage the ethical issues of exhibiting works of unknown provenance. Radical transparency is necessary because museums continue to be perceived as a trusted source of knowledge.[60] For our publics radical transparency offers the freedom to make informed choices in order to experience what they wish and to participate as they'd like. For the museum sector it reveals choices and actions that can be assessed and amended. For all stakeholders it provides a means to think critically about museums and to engage in ethics discourse, thus leading to greater self-reflexivity.

As the economic downturn has caused some leaders of culture and industry to engage in questionable ethics practices, transparency has become a buzzword divorced from radical implications. Transparency is typically defined as being "evident" or "open to public scrutiny."[61] Given museums' increasingly diverse publics and complex responsibilities, contemporary museum ethics calls for a new, more assertive position of radical transparency contingent upon the changing needs of society. Radical transparency is declarative and self-reflexive, as opposed to a patriarchal authoritative voice. A feminist commitment to transparency, as Hein sees it, is a declaration of one's theoretical approach.[62] The Manchester Museum at the University of Manchester, for example, distributes a manifesto that declares its theoretical approach, informed by post-colonial theory, and that situates both its ethical past and future.[63]

Radical transparency does not require that an institution share all information equally. There will be concerns that remain private, such as some financial information concerning individual donors. Some issues may be time-sensitive and transparency might occur after a delicate negotiation, rather than during the process. Some indigenous cultures may restrict objects and knowledge because of the spiritual power and/or sacred knowledge associated with them.[64] What defines radical transparency is that the institution and its communities together establish clear guidelines for what can and cannot be shared, explain the choices behind these guidelines and review them routinely. The larger culture of openness that radical transparency creates within a museum instills awareness that all activities need to be carried out in such a way that they are consistent with institutional values.

Radical transparency hinges upon an array of broadly accessible communications tools from wall texts to web sites to operate effectively. Radical transparency also is a bridge to communication; it solicits data and commentary in diverse forms and employs these resources as a means to impact future decision-making. Museum blogs and web pages revelatory of the messiness of curatorial decisions;[65] live feeds that demonstrate and discuss conservation measures;[66] home pages that provide financial data, strategic plans, annual reports, collections policies, deaccession activity, staff and board directories and organizational charts;[67] wall texts that explain how some visitors might find it unethical to view certain materials on display, for example, human remains, and that provide alternative routes;[68] technologies that facilitate visitor-generated content;[69] exhibitions/artists' projects that critique the museum;[70] open storage and transparent glass-walled offices into which visitors can peer;[71] these are all indicators of museum transparency that offer pathways for stakeholders to engage in critical conversation. Some such efforts, however, fail to sustain a culture of transparency because they convey a sub-text that justifies behavior rather than analyzing decision-making.[72] For example, museum leaders planning controversial deaccessioning sometimes speak to the press before an impending sale so that they can claim they have been transparent while hoping to control the flow of information. Such efforts at transparency are often unsuccessful because their underlying motivations are externally elicited and reactive, rather than internally generated, analytical and responsive to social needs. Though these ventures speak the language of transparency, the institutions that develop them are pressed into action by law, the media, financial concerns or some other outside pressure.

Radical transparency embraces the uncertainties—the contingencies–of museum work and its ethics. The forthright, consultative and often personal voice of radical transparency can help communities to perceive a challenging exhibition, program or direction as difficult but appropriate, rather than merely controversial.[73] As Pete

Brown has demonstrated, unconventional approaches to exhibitions often require greater transparency than does common practice.[74]

Radical transparency is a strategy that can reinvigorate the ethics code. The concept of the "living" or "breathing" ethics code which prioritizes an ongoing and transparent process of debate among diverse stakeholders is developing from the new museum ethics discourse. This shift in emphasis from product to process underscores the contingencies of the ethics discourse today for it does not depend on consensus but instead welcomes conflicting views as a constructive contribution. The transparent, collaborative and self-reflexive characteristics of the "living" ethics code make it a mechanism appropriate to asserting moral agency.

The concept of the living ethics code has begun to take hold, for example at the Curators Committee (CurCom) of the AAM.[75] As John Mayer, a CurCom member who helped spearhead its new Code of Ethics for Curators, explains,[76] the initiative began with a creative process of rewriting, rather than a revising of an earlier document. Transforming static codes into living, breathing guidelines typically demands this kind of active rethinking. From 2006 to 2009, the CurCom Ethics Committee underwent a broadly inclusive and transparent interrogation of the ethics discourse for curators. By working together on a Yahoo group to which anyone could subscribe, the committee made all discussions and review available for comment and participation. The committee also created an electronic archive of the work for future review. It used listservs, mailings and conferences to enlist diverse constituents in dialogue. Nonetheless, it is indicative of the sway that traditional ethics codes have in the sector that, though over 5000 people were contacted for feedback, only 20 responded. The small number of responses reflects a lack of understanding of the transparent and consultative nature of the living ethics code.

Mayer asserts that transparency remains the defining feature of the initiative. The radicality of this transparency is that it is sustained into the future. He states:

> We listened to and considered the comments from all our reviewers, and perhaps most importantly, accepted the fact that developing a code of ethics is a process. To this end we have advocated for and created a standing committee on ethics for CurCom.[77]

But, as is sometimes the case, reality has checked idealism. A slow and politically sensitive approval process of the new CurCom code by the AAM Board of Trustees has hampered efforts for sustained ongoing review by the Standing Ethics Committee.[78]

More important, however, is that the ethics code, even the more contingent living, breathing ethics code, is just one tool in a larger museum ethics discourse informed by radical transparency. Ethics codes do not resolve ethics issues but can promote an ethics of social change when seen as part of a matrix of other mechanisms, from mission statements to vision statements to strategic plans, invested in the moral agency of museums and which are routinely interrogated and re-imagined.

Radical transparency has particular resonance for the current climate in which the museum sector is rapidly expanding in countries where government restricts freedom of speech. Accepting radical transparency as theory and practice sets a model for emerging museum professionals who are negotiating the complex dynamic of intellectual rigor and censorship in these countries.[79]

Radical transparency's most significant impact, however, may be its ability to offer up a process to enable negotiation among competing parties, each with claims to the museum. Meeting the needs of competing parties is one of the most difficult issues that museums of the twenty-first century encounter. Contested ownership of objects, performances and knowledge can become painful because of the intrinsic ties of heritage to concepts of identity, creativity and human rights.[80] Complicating the issue is that museums' various publics continuously reconstitute themselves and everyone, including museum staff, identifies with more than one group. How can museums be fair to all involved? How do they choose whose voices will be heard and unravel the politics of who speaks for whom? As Sheila Watson describes:

> Identity is about difference, and one community's difference will often foreground past or present disputes with others. For many museum workers such complex issues require not only good consultation skills but also, inevitably, some exercise of power over community representation. Such issues require visionary leadership and good management.[81]

Radical transparency is central to visionary leadership and good management. Radical transparency generates accountability in policies, processes and practices that diverse groups can trust and help shape. Though it's not an easy fix, radical transparency helps nurture understanding not only between the museum and communities but among communities themselves.

The Ethics of Guardianship

As it establishes new pathways to accountability, contemporary museum ethics reimagines the responsibilities to collections in the museum. Feminism, post-colonial theory and digital heritage studies have all contributed to the construction of a more fluid and contingent relationship between objects and experiences in the museum; this anticipates a corresponding transition from a stance of possession to one of guardianship. In contemporary museum ethics discourse the concept of guardianship is a means towards respecting the dynamic, experiential and contingent quality of heritage and towards sharing in new ways the rights and responsibilities to this heritage.

Today in the museum sector there is a focus on experience as the link between objects and people. This privileging of experience, the social engagement of objects, does not deny their materiality.[82] It does, however, "demote" the object, in the words of Hein, by problematizing singularity and emphasizing contingency.[83] Post-structuralist theory, as applied to museums, undergirds the emphasis on experience. Reception theory asserts that making meaning from objects is unstable and dependent upon the perspective of those engaging the object.[84] Heritage studies defines material culture as a social process, rather than a body of concrete things.[85] Performance theory holds that museums are a kind of theater in which culture is produced and enacted through institutional processes.[86] And post-colonial theory critiques the western reliance on vision as a definitive way of knowing, introducing indigenous paradigms for multisensory approaches to exhibitions.[87] In the museum itself the model of science centers and children's museums built on experiences, rather than collections, presents new pathways for learning in collections-based institutions. The paradigm of indigenous museums as cultural centers demonstrates the potential of the experiential to empower communities to thrive.[88] The example of feminist curation as a bodily act underscores the affective possibilities of museums.[89]

Privileging affect offers what Sandra Dudley describes as a subjective experience of objects, "physical, multisensory, aesthetic, emotional, immersive,"[90] and acknowledges the place in museums for intangible heritage. It is equally informed by new thinking in digital heritage, particularly Ross Parry's deconstruction of the binary relationship between virtuality and authenticity;[91] in a post-media world the virtual has authenticity and new understandings of the physical object can be produced through virtual means. As Lev Manovich suggests, user choice and organization of information now overshadow medium.[92] Privileging experience opens up new directions for ethical care and sharing of heritage.

The concept of guardianship effectively encapsulates these new directions. Guardianship is a term that Haidy Geismar has adopted from Maori culture to critique as consumerist the notion of cultural "property" and to promote instead a position of temporal caretaking, in partnership with source communities, which is appropriate to respecting the dynamic or experiential quality of heritage. She explains:

> The concept of guardianship, known in Maori as *kaitiakitanga*, acknowledges both the rights and responsibilities of the museum and other owners in the care of collections. Once it is understood that these are both acknowledged and respected, Maori groups are increasingly supportive of using the museum as a storehouse and exhibitionary context for their community treasures (provided there is an ongoing process of consultation). Rather than a condition of ownership, this notion of guardianship develops relationships of consultation and collaboration. The acknowledgment that property is a relationship rather than an object suggests an alternative view of cultural property, which acknowledges the political and social relations that objects are enmeshed within as vital to their identities.[93]

Sometimes equally referred to as stewardship, this idea of guardianship, as Geismar notes, is relevant not only to indigenous cultural heritage but to all cultural heritage, tangible and intangible.

Geismar's concept of guardianship as a strategy for care of objects makes sense from a feminist as well as post-colonial perspective. Hein declares that feminist theory "advocates diverting the focus on products and their consumption to the depiction of practices and processes that vitalize societies."[94] As a feminist practice guardianship enables collaborative relationships with multiple stakeholders including source communities. It eschews entitlement, instead proposing a model of nurture and sensitivity. And it enhances public engagement by emphasizing the dynamic, experiential quality of culture. As an ethical position, guardianship embraces the contingent nature of heritage.

Guardianship carries significant implications for understanding heritage as something animate, to be respected, and communal, to be shared. In acknowledging that property is a relationship, rather than an object, and thus experiential and contingent, guardianship is socially inclusive. It enables diverse pathways to engagement, encouraging a range of participatory encounters and visitor-centered learning around heritage in the museum, from community curation to performing rituals.

In recognizing the living quality of culture, guardianship leads to new thinking about collections management and access to this knowledge. It admits the fluidity and complexity of identity in the cataloguing of objects, rather than defining collections by the limits of software and taxonomic conventions. And it promotes technology as a means to challenge conventional distinctions between exhibitions and research.[95] Museums invigorated by notions of guardianship may pursue digital tools for visitors to extend their learning beyond what's on display to what Fiona Cameron and Helena Robinson refer to as "polysemic interpretive models," digital databases that invigorate the museum experience through visualization, sound, simulation and other means.[96] Parry predicts that the search process for digital interpretation will become increasingly more personalized with the development of the semantic web, given its sensitivities to context and profiling; he cautions, however, that such personalized research creates a host of new ethical quandaries to be considered.[97]

Guardianship prioritizes repatriation as a human right and emphasizes the strengthening relationships that the return of cultural "property" inspires. Guardianship also implies that repatriation alone is not enough; it suggests, as Nick Stanley argues, "a consideration of wider issues concerning ownership, rights and identity."[98] It involves agreements and partnerships with customary owners, including the owners of intangible heritage. Guardianship also instills dignified treatment of all human remains, regardless of their age; an ancient Egyptian mummy is equally as deserving of respect as are human remains from the Second World War.

Guardianship advances an ethics of sustainability, not accumulation. It encourages deliberate thoughtful acquisitions policies and deaccessioning practices.[99] Guardianship democratizes conservation as it acknowledges the organic, rather than eternal, nature of objects. It indicates the subjective character of conservation decision-making and supports community-based conservation as a participatory process.[100]

The concept of guardianship inspires consortiums, collaboratives, mergers and hubs to pool and distribute resources in ways that promote public access to collections, locally, regionally and globally. This pooling of resources is particularly critical at times of economic instability.[101] This can be painful in that loss of institutional identity may result but careful planning can mitigate the impact; moreover, guardianship as an ethical concept prioritizes shared access over institutional sanctity. Guardianship was the driving force behind the Brooklyn Museum of Art's transfer of its vast and historically significant costume collection to the Metropolitan Museum of Art when the Brooklyn came to terms with the fact that it could no longer adequately care for this material. Through a complex and thoughtful set of arrangements on issues from database cataloguing to future deaccession decisions, the Brooklyn Museum continues to maintain some association with and jurisdiction of the collection.[102] Nonetheless, it takes courage to make the ethical choice to pursue guardianship over ownership. Kevin Stayton, Chief Curator of the Brooklyn Museum, recounts the decision-making process:

> The mission of the Brooklyn Museum is to create a bridge between our great art collections and the public who ultimately own and use them. This could be accomplished, we imagined, without the literal and traditional ownership by the Brooklyn Museum. It is always difficult for a curator to give up a great collection, and I will not pretend that I don't have an occasional pang of regret that things could not have been different. But in the end I am extremely proud of the decision that was reached by the board and the staff of the Brooklyn Museum. The partnership we established allows Brooklyn to use its great collection, and in fact gives us greater access to it than before, when we did not know it completely and when we could not always afford to conserve it for exhibition. But more importantly, it creates a secure future for these great objects, and it allows them to be preserved and to be interpreted and exhibited to the public—who are, in fact, both the owners and the beneficiaries of the collection.[103]

Such difficult but visionary decisions, informed by the new museum ethics discourse, define good museum leadership of the twenty-first century.[104]

Conclusion: Thoughts on Using the New Museum Ethics

As a discourse, the new museum ethics is not merely an ideal; it is a social practice. Through debate among diverse stakeholders, ethical issues are identified, considered and acted upon. The contingent nature of the new museum ethics—its inherent changeability–suggests that the discourse be integrated across the museum sector and engaged on a consistent basis. Theoretically informed ethics discussions should not be reserved for crisis control or for a once-a-decade revision to ethics codes. Infusing the new museum ethics into the museum studies curriculum, museum professional development programming, museum strategic planning and museum/community collaboration is central to creating a changing and sustainable museum for the twenty-first century.

Some may counter that co-production and transparency confuse audiences, that living, breathing ethics codes are too porous and that guardianship betrays a trust to collections. Ethics is never easy. But policing is not an adequate response to the ethics quandaries of the twenty-first century. Training is. Critical consumption of museum rhetoric is a twenty-first century skill that the ethical museum leader must build among students, professionals and communities. To develop a level of comfort with the contingencies of museum ethics–its uncertainties and dependencies, its capacity to "touch" a range of other social concerns–is to accept the complexity and dynamism of the discourse that both reflects and shapes the real issues that museums encounter.

It is this contingent nature of museum ethics that performance artist Anthony Schrag expresses as his hands and feet "touch," on many levels, the columns of the

Gallery of Modern Art in Glasgow. And through bodily pressure Schrag asserts the moral agency of museums. By forcing us to imagine the consequences of his action—like those of Samson—a temple's ruins, he conveys the urgency for redistribution of power and authority in the museum. The agenda of social responsibility, radical transparency and guardianship towards heritage provides a way forward.

Notes

1 *Push* was part of a series of performances by Schrag, *The Legacy of City Arts Projects*, funded by the Gallery of Modern Art, Glasgow, through the Scottish Arts Council.
2 Anthony Schrag, email to author, 27 July 2010.
3 Judges 16:30.
4 Online. Available HTTP: http://www.anthonyschrag.com/Statement.html (accessed 6 September 2010).
5 See, for example, the websites of the Ethics Center for ASME, the American Society of Mechanical Engineers; the International Center for Ethics, Justice and Public Life at Brandeis University; the Applied Ethics Institute at St. Petersburg College; and the Rock Ethics Institute at Penn State University. Online. Available HTTP: http://www. asme.org/NewsPublicPolicy/Ethics/Ethics_Center.cfm; http://www.brandeis.edu/ethics/; http://appliedethicsinstitute.org/; http://rockethics.psu.edu/ (all accessed 30 August, 2010).
6 This piece is part of a larger body of Schrag's work, as catalogued on his website, that destabilizes the museum. Online. Available HTTP: http://www.anthonyschrag.com (accessed 6 September 2010).
7 M. Foucault, *The Archaeology of Knowledge*, trans. A.M. Sheridan Smith, 1969; London and New York, Routledge, 2002; L. Smith, *Uses of Heritage*, London and New York: Routledge, 2006, pp. 4–5, 11–17.
8 G. Edson, "Introduction" in G. Edson (ed.) *Museum Ethics*, London and New York: Routledge, 1997, p. xxi.
9 R. Sandell, *Museums, Prejudice and the Reframing of Difference*, London and New York: Routledge, 2007, p. x. See also R. Sandell, "On Ethics, Activism and Human Rights," this volume; R. Sandell and J. Dodd, "Activist Practice" in R. Sandell, J. Dodd and R. Garland-Thomson, *Re-presenting Disability: Activism and Agency in the Museum*, London and New York: Routledge 2010, pp. 3–22.
10 H. Hein, *The Museum in Transition: A Philosophical Perspective*, Washington, D.C.: Smithsonian Institution Press, 2000, pp. 91–93, 103.
11 See, for example, R. R. Janes and R. Sandell, "Introduction to Part One," in R. R. Janes and R. Sandell (eds.) *Museum Management and Marketing*, London and New York: Routledge, 2007, pp. 17–19.
12 On the need for such radical rethinking, see R. R. Janes, *Museums in a Troubled World: Renewal, Irrelevance or Collapse?* London and New York: Routledge, 2009.
13 H. Hein, *Public Art: Thinking Museums Differently*, Lanham: AltaMira Press, 2006, pp. 31–32.
14 On the difference between ethical principles and applied ethics, see Judith Stark's contribution to the concluding panel "A Discussion on Defining Museum Ethics," Institute of Museum Ethics Inaugural Conference "Defining Museum Ethics," 14 November 2008. Online. Available HTTP: http://www.youtube.com/watch?v=3pVKtoz_CY8 (accessed 9 September 2010).
15 See, for example, G. Edson, "Ethics and the Profession" in Edson, *Museum Ethics*, p. 21.
16 For Plato's ideas on the relationship between the law and ethics, see, for example, T. Pangle, *The Laws of Plato, Translated, with Notes and an Interpretive Essay*, New York: Basic Books, 1980.
17 For a helpful discussion on the relations between law and ethics in regards to bioethics, see C. D. Herrera, "How are Law and Ethics Related?" Online. Available HTTP: http://www-hsc.usc.edu/~mbernste/tae.ethics&law.herrera.html (accessed 17 September 2010).

18 On the history of ethics codes, see Hein, *The Museum in Transition*; T. Besterman, "Museum Ethics," in S. Macdonald (ed.) *A Companion to Museum Studies*, Malden and Oxford: Blackwell Publishing, 2006, pp. 433–35.

19 Even international treaties, declarations and charters are binding only in those countries where they have been ratified and national law overrides the international.

20 M. P. Alfonso and J. Powell, "Ethics of Flesh and Bone, or Ethics in the Practice of Paleopathology, Osteology, and Bioarchaeology," in V. Cassman, N. Odegaard and J. Powell (eds.) *Human Remains: Guide for Museums and Academic Institutions*, Lanham [MD]: AltaMira Press, 2007, pp. 5–6.

21 Hein, *Museum in Transition*, pp. 101–102.

22 See M. Pickering, "'Dance through the Minefield': The Development of Practical Ethics for Repatriation," this volume.

23 H. Hein, "Redressing the Museum in Feminist Theory," *Museum Management and Curatorship* 22: 1, 2007 (March), p. 38.

24 *The Concise Oxford English Dictionary*, Tenth Edition, Revised, J. Pearsall (ed.), Oxford: Oxford University Press, 1999.

25 On the transformational potential of anthropology for museum studies, see A. A. Shelton, "Museums and Anthropologies: Practices and Narratives," in Macdonald, *Companion to Museum Studies*, pp. 74-80. On feminism and reimagining representation, see H. Hein, "The Responsibility of Representation: A Feminist Perspective," this volume.

26 Hein, "Redressing the Museum," pp. 31–32.

27 Ibid., p. 32.

28 Ibid., pp. 33–34.

29 Ibid., p.33.

30 Ibid.

31 Ibid., p. 37.

32 C. Kreps, "Non-Western Models of Museums," in Macdonald, *A Companion to Museum Studies*, p. 470.

33 Sandell, "On Ethics, Activism and Human Rights."

34 See, for instance, American Association of Museums, *Excellence and Equity: Education and the Public Dimension of Museums*, Washington, D.C: American Association of Museums, 1992; Department for Culture, Media and Sport, *Centres for Social Change: Museums, Galleries and Archives for All*, London: Department of Culture, Media and Sport, 2000; "ICOM 2008-2010 Strategic Plan." Online. Available HTTP: http://archives.icom. museum/2strat_plan_eng/strat_plan_eng.pdf (accessed 5 October 2010).

35 R. Sandell, "Social Inclusion, the Museum and the Dynamics of Sectoral Change," *Museum and Society*, 1: 1, 2003, p. 46. Online. Available HTTP: http://www.le.ac.uk/ms/ museumsociety.html (accessed 2 October 2010).

36 J. Barrett, *Museums and the Public Sphere*, Malden and Oxford: Wiley-Blackwell, 2010, p. 164.

37 I. M. Young, *Justice and the Politics of Difference*, Princeton and Oxford: Princeton University Press, 1990; I. M. Young, *Inclusion and Democracy*, Oxford: Oxford University Press, 2002, Oxford Political Theory series. In a talk at the 2008 Inaugural Conference of the Institute of Museum Ethics, Lisa Yun Lee demonstrated the relevance of Young's ideas in the museum context. Online. Available HTTP: http://www.youtube.com/watch? v=k5kDGvtokMo (accessed 23 September 2010).

38 On civic discourse, see P. Korza and B. Schaffer Bacon (eds.) *Museums and Civic Dialogue: Case Studies for Animating Democracy*, Washington, D.C.: Americans for the Arts, 2005; S. Bodo, K. Gibbs and M. Sani (eds.) *Museums as Places for Intercultural Dialogue: Selected Practices from Europe*, London: MAP for ID Group, 2009; J. Koke and M. Schwarzer (guest eds.), "Civic Discourse: Let's Talk" [special issue] *Museums and Social Issues: A Journal of Reflective Discourse* 2, p. 2.

39 Hein, "Redressing the Museum," p. 35.

40 R. R. Archibald, "Introduction," in *Mastering Civic Engagement: A Challenge to Museums*, Washington, D.C.: American Association of Museums, 2002, p. 3.

41 On the biases of digital media, see L. Manovich, *The Language of New Media*. Online. Available HTTP: http://www.manovich.net/LNM/Manovich.pdf (accessed 7 October 2010).

42 A. Wong, "Ethical Issues of Social Media in Museums: A Case Study," in J. Marstine, A. Bauer and C. Haines (guest eds.) "New Directions in Museum Ethics" [special issue] *Museum Management and Curatorship*, 26: 2, 2011 (May), pp. 97–112.

43 B. Lynch, "Collaboration, Contestation, and Creative Conflict: On the Efficacy of Museum/Community Partnerships," this volume.

44 I cite these terms from the conference, "From the Margins to the Core? An International Conference Exploring the Shifting Roles and Increasing Significance of Diversity and Equality in Contemporary Museum and Heritage Policy and Practice," held at the Victoria and Albert Museum, 24–26 March 2010 and co-sponsored by the V&A and the School of Museum Studies at the University of Leicester. Online. Available HTTP: http://www.vam.ac.uk/res_cons/research/conferences/margins_to_core/index.html (accessed 24 October 2010).

45 Hein, "Redressing the Museum," p. 39.

46 H. Gardner, *Changing Minds: The Art and Science of Changing Our Own and Other People's Minds*, Boston: Harvard Business School Press, 2006, p. xiv.

47 H. Gardner, "Introduction" in H. Gardner (ed.) *Responsibility at Work: How Leading Professionals Act (Or Don't Act) Responsibly*, San Francisco: John Wiley and Sons, 2007, p. 5.

48 On the possibilities for ethical change when support staff have significant collaborative roles, see J. Marstine, "Fred Wilson, Good Work, and the Phenomenon of Freud's Mystic Writing Pad," in R. Sandell and E. Nightingale (eds.) *Museums, Equality and Social Justice*, London and New York: Routledge, forthcoming, expected publication date 2011, Museum Meanings Series.

49 Sandell, *Museums, Prejudice and the Reframing of Difference.*

50 L. H. Silverman, *The Social Work of Museums*, London and New York: Routledge, 2010, pp. 5–14.

51 Sandell, "Social inclusion, the museum and the dynamics of sectoral change," p. 45. See also Sandell, *Museums, Prejudice and the Reframing of Difference.*

52 J. Nakamura, "Practicing Responsibility" in Gardner, *Responsibility at Work*, p. 291.

53 Hein, "Redressing the Museum," p. 38.

54 On museum association advocacy programs, see the AAM web page "Speak Up for Museums." Online. Available HTTP: http://www.speakupformuseums.org/home.htm; and the MA web page http://www.museumsassociation.org/love-museums/advocacy-advice (both accessed 3 October 2010).

55 H. Hein, "What's Real in the Museum," lecture, School of Museum Studies, University of Leicester, 11 October 2010.

56 On the application of activist practice to a specific issue, see Sandell, Dodd and Garland-Thomson, *Representing Disability.*

57 P. Welch, "Q and A on Museum Ethics: Intangible Heritage," Institute of Museum Ethics. Online. Available HTTP: http://www.museumethics.org/qanda?page=4 (accessed 24 October 2010).

58 M. Foucault, *Discipline and Punishment*, London: Tavistock, 1977, p. 27.

59 See, for example, C. Belsey, "Writing as a Feminist," *Signs: Journal of Women in Culture and Society* 25: 4, 2000 (Summer), p. 1157.

60 S. Watson, "Museums and their Communities," in S. Watson (ed.) *Museums and their Communities*, London and New York: Routledge, 2007, Leicester Readers in Museum Studies, p. 10.

61 See, for instance, *The Concise Oxford English Dictionary.*

62 Hein, "Redressing the Museum," pp. 29–31.

63 *A Manifesto for The Manchester Museum* (brochure), Manchester: University of Manchester, Manchester Museum, c. 2009.

64 See, for example, Kreps, "Non-Western Models of Museums," pp. 459–69.

65 See, for example, an entry of the blog of the Los Angeles County Museum of Art, *Unframed*, in which a curator of contemporary art considers the implications of an artist's blog critiquing LACMA deaccessioning practices. Online. Available HTTP: http://lacma.wordpress.com/2009/07/23/raiding-and-recycling-the-collection/ (accessed 28 September 2010). On the range of museum activities that benefit from transparency on museum

websites, see S. Lubar and A. Bauer, "Q and A on Museum Ethics: Museum Ethics and the Web," Institute of Museum Ethics, 1 February 2010. Online. Available HTTP: http://www.museumethics.org/qanda?page=1 (accessed 16 October 2010).

66 See the Reveal Gallery at the National Conservation Centre, National Museums, Liverpool. Online. Available HTTP: http://www.liverpoolmuseums.org.uk/conservation/reveal/ (accessed 1 October 2010).

67 The web pages of the Indianapolis Museum of Art and the Glenbow Museum are representative of this trend. Online. Available HTTP: http://dashboard.imamuseum.org/ and http://www.glenbow.org/about/ (both accessed 28 September 2010).

68 See, for example, the warning labels concerning the exhibition of human remains at the Manchester Museum, University of Manchester.

69 See, for instance, the Communication Gallery and the Science Now, Science Everywhere program at the Liberty Science Center. Online. Available HTTP: http://www.lsc.org/lsc/ourexperiences (accessed 28 September 2010).

70 For a broad survey of such projects, see J. Putnam, *Art and Artifact: The Museum as Medium*, 2001; New York: Thames and Hudson, 2009.

71 For open storage that conveys the complexity of collections management, see the University of British Columbia Museum of Anthropology, as discussed by Anthony Shelton. A. Shelton, "Q and A on Museum Ethics: Open Storage," Institute of Museum Ethics. Online. Available HTTP: http://www.museumethics.org/qanda?page=9 (accessed 16 October 2010); for transparency in architectural design, see the Andy Warhol Museum with its glass-walled archives which enables visitors to watch staff examine Warhol's time capsules and other collections.

72 See, for example, Thomas Crow's review of the 1999 Museum of Modern Art exhibition *The Museum as Muse: Artists Reflect* which suggests that poor exhibition design and inadequate space robbed the project of its potential transformative power as institutional critique. T. Crow, "The Museum as Muse: Artists Reflect," *Artforum*, 1999 (summer). Online. Available HTTP: http://findarticles.com/p/articles/mi_m0268/is_10_37/ai_55015171/ (accessed 17 September 2010).

73 On transparency and self-reflexivity, see P. Chaat Smith, "Critical Reflections on the Our Peoples Exhibit: A Curator's Perspective," in A. Lonetree and A. J. Cobb (eds.) *The National Museum of the American Indian: Critical Conversations*, Lincoln and London: University of Nebraska Press, 2008, pp. 131–43.

74 P. Brown, "Us and Them: Who Benefits from Experimental Exhibition Making?" in J. Marstine, A. Bauer and C. Haines (guest eds.) "New Directions in Museum Ethics" [special issue] *Museum Management and Curatorship*, 26: 2, 2011 (May), pp. 129–48.

75 Online. Available HTTP: http://www.curcom.org/ethics.php (accessed 18 October 2010).

76 J. Mayer, "Developing an Ethics Code: Purpose, Process, Value," American Association of Museums Annual Conference, Philadelphia, 1 May 2009.

77 Ibid.

78 The author has served on this Standing Ethics Committee since 2009.

79 On the museum boom in China and in Abu Dhabi, see "A Museum Boom," *The Economist* 383: 8533, 2007 (16 June), p. 49; J. Seligson, "Can Museums Buy Happiness?" *Museum* 87: 6, 2008 (November–December), pp. 47–53.

80 N. Stanley, "Introduction: Indigeneity and Museum Practice in the Southwest Pacific," in N. Stanley (ed.) *The Future of Indigenous Museum: Perspectives from the Southwest Pacific*, New York and Oxford: Berghahn Books, 2007, pp. 10–11.

81 Watson, "Museums and their Communities," p. 18.

82 On objects and experience see S. Dudley, "Museum Materialities: Objects, Sense and Feeling," in S. Dudley (ed.) *Museum Materialities: Objects, Engagements, Interpretations*, London and New York: Routledge, 2010, pp. 1–17; A. Appadurai, *The Social Life of Things: Commodities in Perspective*, Cambridge: Cambridge University Press, 1986; Hein, *Museum in Transition*, pp. 51–87.

83 Hein, "What's Real in the Museum."

84 See E. Hooper-Greenhill, *Museums and the Interpretation of Visual Culture*, London and New York: Routledge, 2000, p. 103, Museum Meanings Series.

85 See, for instance, Smith, *Uses of Heritage*, p. 2.

86 B. Kirshenblatt-Gimblett, "Performance Studies," in H. Bial (ed.) *The Performance Studies Reader*, London and New York: Routledge, 2003, pp. 43–53.

87 See, for example, E. Edwards, C. Gosden and R. Phillips (eds.) *Sensible Objects: Colonialism, Museums and Material Culture*, Oxford and New York: Berg, 2006.

88 Stanley, "Introduction," pp. 1–20.

89 J. Fisher, "Exhibitionary Affect" in R. Baert (guest ed.) "Curatorial Strategies" [special issue] *n.paradoxa: international feminist art journal* 18, 2006, pp. 27–33.

90 Dudley, "Museum Materialities," p. 2.

91 R. Parry, *Recoding the Museum: Digital Heritage and the Technologies of Change*, London and New York: Routledge, 2007, pp. 58–81, Museum Meanings Series; see also F. Cameron, "Beyond the Cult of the Replicant: Museums and Historical Digital Objects—Traditional Concerns, New Discourses" in F. Cameron and K. Kenderline (eds.) *Theorizing Digital Cultural Heritage: A Critical Discourse*, Cambridge [MA] and London: MIT Press, 2007, pp. 49–75.

92 L. Manovich, *The Language of New Media*, Cambridge and London: MIT Press, 2001.

93 H. Geismar, "Cultural Property, Museums and the Pacific," *International Journal of Cultural Property* 15: 2, 2008 (June), pp. 114–15.

94 Hein, "Redressing the Museum," p. 39.

95 On how new media blurs these boundaries, see M. Henning, "New Media," in Macdonald, *Companion to Museum Studies*, p. 309.

96 F. Cameron and H. Robinson, "Digital Knowledgescapes: Cultural, Theoretical, Practical, and Useage Issues Facing Museum Collection Databases in a Digital Epoch," in Cameron and Kenderline," *Theorizing Digital Cultural Heritage*, pp. 165–191.

97 R. Parry, "Transfer Protocols: Museum Codes and Ethics in the New Digital Environment," this volume. See also R. Parry, N. Poole, and J. Pratty, "Semantic Dissonance: Do We Need (and do we Understand) the Semantic Web?", in R. Parry (ed.) *Museums in a Digital Age*, London and New York: Routledge, 2009, pp. 96–106, Leicester Readers in Museum Studies.

98 Stanley, "Introduction," p. 8.

99 On sustainability, acquisitions policies and the ethics of deaccession, see Janes, *Museums in a Troubled World*, pp. 84–93.

100 On participatory conservation, see D. Sully, *Decolonizing Conservation: Caring for Maori Meeting Houses Outside New Zealand*, Walnut Creek: Left Coast Press, 2007; G. Wharton, "Dynamics of Participatory Conservation: The Kamehameha I Sculpture Project." *Journal of the American Institute for Conservation* 47: 3, 2008, pp. 159–173.

101 On pooling resources when institutions are no longer viable, see A. Rogers Narzarov, "Ethical Considerations for Museum Closures," *Museum* 88: 4, 2009 (July–August), pp. 38–43.

102 K. Stayton, untitled lecture in the session "Deaccessioning in an Economic Crisis: Ethical Challenges and Solutions," Mid-Atlantic Association of Museums, 19 October 2009, Saratoga Springs, New York.

103 Ibid.

104 This is not to negate the separate ethical issues concerning funding of the Metropolitan Museum of Art's Costume Institute; the Costume Institute relies almost entirely on the fashion industry to support its work and has been criticized for conflict of interest. For such a critique, see A. Wallach, "The Unethical Art Museum," in E. A. King and G. Levin (eds.) *Ethics and the Visual Arts*, New York: Allworth Press, 2006, pp. 23–35.

2

The art of ethics

Theories and applications to museum practice

Judith Chelius Stark

Introduction

In this time of increasing specialization in the professions, the temptations to appeal to the "experts in the field" are great, but also need to be tempered by the ability to make good judgments about expert knowledge. Are there experts in ethics? Philosophers look to be in a good position to lay claim to this territory, yet where does that leave others in making good, ethical decisions? How does one distinguish between well-informed experts and those who are not? Must one appeal to the experts in ethics to understand the difference between right and wrong in human behavior? These questions involve cognitive and epistemological debates about expert knowledge that are difficult to sort out.[1]

These debates fill books and journals of philosophy, but such considerations are not the focus of this chapter. How then may the work of professional philosophers be brought to bear on this area of professional ethics? In what follows I set out some ways in which philosophers may contribute to the complex and fast-growing field of museum ethics.

The introduction sets out the broad framework within which the discussion of museum ethics may occur. In the second section, I describe the field of ethics (as a branch of philosophy) and the relatively new category of applied or practical ethics. In the third section, I explain an approach to ethics called discourse ethics and suggest how this might be used by museum professionals. In the final section, I look at professional codes of ethics and suggest ways in which the rational frameworks of discourse ethics may be understood as a kind of heuristic for interpreting and applying these codes. The chapter concludes with some comments on "know-how" in ethics.

In thinking about ethics and its connections to the museum professions, we do well to begin with a reminder from Aristotle about what to expect in ethical inquiry. In the first section of the *Nicomachean Ethics*, he writes:

> We must be content, then, in speaking of such subjects [ethics] and with such premises to indicate the truth roughly and in outline, and in speaking about such things that are for the most part true, and with premises of the same kind, to reach conclusions that are similar. In the same spirit should

each type of statement be received; for it is the mark of an educated person to look for precision in each class of things just so far as the nature of the subject admits. It is equally foolish to accept probable reasoning from a mathematician and to demand certain proofs from a rhetorician.[2]

As one of the major branches of philosophy, ethics is a very complex, rich and highly contentious area of study. It has a long history both in western philosophy and in the three religious traditions of the west—Judaism, Christianity and Islam. The approach to ethics in this chapter is philosophical and not theological or religious (even though the religious traditions have and continue to contribute a great deal to ethical inquiry and to moral practices). This chapter does not summarize the history of ethics nor does it refer to the many important debates that occupy philosophers who work in ethical theory. As important as these are, they are not a major focus here.

Here is what is presented in this chapter: an examination of what counts as an ethical dilemma; substantive discussion of ethical theories, their relevance and applications; and some guidance about how to frame and think through ethical dilemmas. In our moral lives we aim for the cultivation and expansion of moral imagination that enables us to appreciate and evaluate the experiences of others, thereby coming to insights that may help us make ethical decisions. In this chapter, one will not find a "one size fits all" mechanical process for simply inserting elements of a case into a formula and drawing out the answers. Nonetheless, even though formulaic answers are not the goal, we can still go a long way toward clarifying relevant issues and encouraging habits of mind and heart that help practitioners think through and make well-reasoned decisions about the ethical dilemmas they face in their professional lives.

Ethics and Applying Ethics

As a study, ethics is typically divided into three sections: descriptive ethics, normative ethics and metaethics. Briefly stated, descriptive ethics focuses on how people actually behave and what kinds of moral choices they make; normative ethics explores the theories that offer principles or norms for people and social institutions to guide their moral choices; and metaethics considers questions about the meanings and analysis of language that is used in moral discourse. Many disciplines contribute to descriptive ethics, for example, history, literature, law and the behavioral sciences, and, so, it is not the sole prerogative of philosophy or religion. The work of normative ethics and metaethics, however, tends to be the preoccupation mostly of philosophers and legal and religious scholars.[3]

Since the 1970s, there has been tremendous growth in what has come to be called applied or practical ethics. Spurred on by controversies and ethical dilemmas in an increasingly complex world, some areas of applied ethics are now well established: biomedical ethics, business ethics and environmental ethics. In addition, increasing attention has been devoted to clusters of concerns gathered together as professional ethics (e.g. in journalism, law, education and the arts). Applied ethics also deals with contemporary issues, such as war, global poverty, racism, distribution of resources, gender oppression and the death penalty (among many others). I place our current discussions of museum ethics at the intersection of professional ethics and contemporary issues. Their concerns overlap with many of the problems that other professionals face, such as the importance of truth-telling, fiduciary responsibilities, transparency and fulfilling contractual obligations. In the final sections of this chapter, I make some suggestions about approaches to ethical dilemmas specific to the museum profession.

At this point, however, more needs to be said about applied (and applying) ethics. What is actually going to be applied to the ethical dilemmas that museum professionals face? The short answer is–ethical theories and the principles derived from them. However, that short answer can also be the misleading one. Even though I am about to set out a brief description of the major ethical theories, the distinction between ethics and applied ethics is itself problematic, as has been discussed by the philosopher Mary Midgley. She states that the distinction between theories and applications contains within it an assumption of hierarchy and relative importance in which "pure" theory is considered more significant than applications.[4] It is as though, she writes, "the serious work—the hard and original thinking—would always be done by the pure theorists; the appliers would be the beta people who accepted their results, perhaps worked them out in minor details if that were necessary, and put them into effect."[5] She argues for an integration of theory and application as has been done by some of the best thinkers in the west, e.g. Plato, Kant, Mill and Nietzsche. These philosophers were not content simply to sort out and clarify ethical confusions, but were committed to "articulating their own positive counsel about better ways in which people ought not only to think, but also to live."[6] I agree with Midgley that what we are doing is "applying philosophy to the world" and "using conceptual skills, in which we can to some extent be trained, on problems which are not yet shaped and possessed to yield to them easily."[7] Part of that training involves a good grasp of the basic points of the major ethical theories, keeping in mind that we proceed not in order to master abstract theories, but for the sake of "applying philosophy to the world."[8]

A Foray into Ethical Theories

In western thought there are three widely recognized approaches to resolving ethical dilemmas and here we review the major elements of each.[9] The first theory is called consequentialism (or teleological ethics) and focuses its ethical evaluation on the probable consequences or probable results of a rule or action. The most prominent version of this approach is utilitarianism with its classical formulation of producing the greatest happiness (pleasure or benefit) for the greatest number of people. The basic principle seems at first glance to be accessible and straightforward, but this theory continues to generate great debate among philosophers on questions such as: the nature of happiness (is it pleasure?); gauging the probable consequences of actions (what about mistakes?); where does society as a whole fit into the picture?

The second approach is called deontological theory of ethics. In this theory one should do the actions that conform to one's duties without giving the decisive moral weight to the consequences of the actions. The moral agent evaluates the action by examining it according to ethical principles. Immanuel Kant is the most prominent philosopher who developed this ethical theory. He described the foundational ethical principle as the categorical imperative for which he gave a number of formulations: "Always treat a person as an end in himself, never as a means only; so act that the maxim of your action could become a universal law of nature; treat other people the way you want to be treated."[10] This theory is sometimes characterized as "respect for persons" and includes an emphasis on intentions of the moral agent and the intrinsic value of the morally good action. Of course, these points also raise many questions, e.g. how does one discover these principles (Kant would say that one needs to exercise practical reason); who counts as persons (for a very long time women, slaves and non-elite males were not considered persons); can species and ecosystems be accorded respect or do these entities have right (environmental ethics challenges these typically anthropocentric paradigms)? Can we, in any meaningful senses, have obligations to treat future generations of people (entities that do not yet exist with respect)? Questions and debates ensue on all these points.

The third theory, virtue ethics, takes a different approach from the other two theories. Philosophers working in this area examine principles related to the understanding of moral virtue and its cultivation for performing moral actions. Aristotle was the philosopher who fully developed this theory; he was indebted to his predecessors Socrates and Plato with their concern about cultivating moral virtue.[11] Contemporary philosophers who work in virtue ethics acknowledge the foundational work of these Greek philosophers, especially Aristotle, in their own work. In examining moral virtue (Aristotle discussed intellectual virtues as well), these philosophers cast ethical evaluations in terms of human good or fulfillment (flourishing) and also in the moral agent's cognitive and moral capacities to hit the mark in exercising moral virtue in particular circumstances. In this approach, developing moral virtues as habits is the best way for people both to understand and to choose the right thing to do. Of course, this theory, too, raises more questions than can be answered here: e.g. how does one develop moral virtue (as Aristotle well understood, family circumstances are crucial, but are not in the control of children in the family to evaluate or to ameliorate); does the possession of moral virtues alone (courage, generosity, truthfulness) give us sufficient wherewithal to make correct moral judgments in real life situations; are the understandings and practice of virtue so various across time, place and cultures that this approach gives scant ethical guidance for the exigencies of conflicts in a global context? As with the other theories, debates are ongoing.

Relativism and Subjectivism

This last point leads us to a brief consideration of two important positions in ethics—relativism and subjectivism—and each one has a long history in western philosophy. In essence, ethical relativism rejects the possibility of universal or universally applicable ethical principles and claims that principles are embedded in or relative to specific times, places and cultures. Subjectivism rejects the possibility of universal or objective ethical principles and claims that statements about ethics are actually statements about a particular person's beliefs, attitudes or preferences. Relativism does a good job of reminding us to pay attention to the particularities and pulls of specific times, places and cultures as we engage in ethical discourse, especially as we become more attuned to the varieties of cultural practices and norms. For example, is it a form of "cultural imperialism" for western feminists to reject female genital circumcision (as some cultural feminists in African countries that engage in the practice would argue) or is there an ethical ground upon which both western and cultural feminists could begin to analyze this practice (e.g. respect for persons)? A supporter of ethical relativism would have a difficult conceptual time establishing a standpoint outside the culture upon which to base an ethical evaluation. It is not enough to say, as would a subjectivist, that I disapprove of female genital circumcision, because that simply means I do not like it or I find it repulsive. On the other hand, subjectivism does provide a healthy reminder that an ethical analysis that gives no play to the feelings, beliefs and attitudes of the moral agent who is making the evaluation is lop-sided and incomplete. Ethical judgments should not be driven by feelings or emotions, but as many philosophers are beginning to appreciate, there is a role for the emotions to play in ethical evaluations.[12] As instructive as these two positions may be in some ways, the conceptual problems with relativism and subjectivism are legion. One need not defend a version of moral absolutism (and that has its own problems) to show some of the deficiencies in relativism and subjectivism.

The principle of relativism that states that one ought to abide by the norms and standards of one's time, place and culture presupposes that there is some common agreement within a culture about these standards. This is clearly not the case, especially in increasingly pluralistic and multicultural societies. In liberal democratic societies, gender equality is an important principle, but may not be in more traditional societies. What happens when one moves across cultures (gender equality is moral in one society, but not in another) or when members of a traditional culture move to a contemporary liberal society? In the latter case, one could argue that one should abide by the predominant cultural norms. However, if that were so, then there would have been very little progress, for example against slavery or gender inequality, since these were the norms of earlier times. Who would want to cast the abolitionists or the women's rights groups of nineteenth-century Britain or the United States as immoral for violating the standards of their times by working for racial and gender equality? One more point about relativism. This concerns the status of the foundational principle itself about abiding by the norms of one's culture. Is not this principle itself cast as a universal principle and, if so, how is that consistent with the principle of relativism? Is that principle alone above the standards and norms of one's time, place and culture and, if so, how is that principle justified?

Subjectivism, in fact, does away with ethical principles and norms and, in so doing, vitiates attempts to seek for a justification or grounding of ethical theories. It results in doing away with ethical theories entirely. Argument and debate about ethical matters would be pointless, or at least would devolve into trying to convince my opponent to feel the same way I do about a certain state of affairs, for example, I disapprove of or don't like stealing and you should feel the same way I do. This does not get us very far in resolving ethical differences. The best that one can hope for in subjectivism is ethical skepticism or agnosticism in which people attempt to convince others to feel the same way and to share individual preferences, instead of working out a shared understanding of the rightness or wrongness of actions.

Moral Pluralism

This review of ethical theories is not simply an exercise in getting to know them as part of the field of ethics, but is a prelude to a position in ethics called moral pluralism in which a range of theories is used in real-life situations. Moral pluralism challenges the attempt to find and articulate a unitary ethical theory that, through its principles and imperatives, would be suited to the entire range of ethical issues. The search for such a unitary theory presupposes that ethics functions more like the natural sciences or mathematics. Mary Midgley goes even further and calls the competition among philosophers to find "the perfect, final, all-purpose formula ... mistaken and trivial."[13] What she proposes is a kind of universality that offers:

> ... [A] wide appeal to thoughtful people, coherent with the other ideas they accept—an appeal strong enough to lead to action, and rational enough to fit in with important elements of existing morality.[14]

We can expect clarity and rigorous analysis in moral pluralism, but as Aristotle noted, we are seeking the truth roughly and in outline and consequently we should not expect mathematical certainty in what the Greeks called "the human things." Due to the incompleteness of every theory, I support moral pluralism in which principles are used from a variety of theories in order to discover the best fit given the contours of the situation as a whole. Moral pluralism seems well suited to the complex range of ethical issues that we face in the twenty-first century as well as to the increasing global settings in which these issues emerge and need to be addressed. Multiple approaches to museum ethics are brought to bear in thinking through and bringing together those particularities with the principles.

Ethical Dilemmas: What Makes Them Ethical?

Not all questions of value involve ethics. Although the domains overlap, aesthetics and matters of taste entail values and making judgments of value, e.g. "This is good art," "These strawberries taste delicious," but are not ethical judgments. What makes a dilemma ethical and how can it be identified as such? It is not enough to state that ethics involves making judgments of right and wrong in human behavior. That does not get us very far since it leads to discussion of what exactly is right or wrong in a particular situation.

Nevertheless, there are ways to scope out the terrain of ethical dilemmas with some markers for professionals to use. First, delineating the problem specifically as ethical or as involving ethical issues will help one decide if it needs ethical analysis. Second, to be ethical the issue entails dimensions of human choice and deliberation, e.g. it is not solely a technical problem—why doesn't the toaster work? Third, one should have knowledge of the relevant circumstances of the issue that is as much as is possible to glean. Fourth, one should consider whether or not the issue has some bearing on human life, well-being, liberty, rights or property of oneself or others, as individuals or groups.[15] Fifth, does the issue involve contingent actions, that is, actions that bring about a state of affairs that could have been otherwise, e.g. the person who intentionally and knowingly pads his expense account, but could have chosen not to do so? Often the issue engenders a conflict or confusion in which one is led to ask: what ought I to do in these circumstances or what is the right thing for me to do? For example, there is the case of family members who must decide about whether or not to initiate a feeding tube for a terminally ill elderly relative who is unable to make the decision for herself (and who does not have an advanced medical directive that covers this circumstance). Another way to identify the specifically ethical dimensions of an issue is to investigate the extent to which values are either explicitly or implicitly embedded in the issue, for example, values such as fairness, honesty, justice, integrity, responsibility, autonomy or care. Their presence in a dilemma at this point simply indicates that we are most likely dealing with a situation with ethical dimensions that needs further work. Finally, ethical dilemmas entailing principles and norms need to be distinguished from questions of etiquette and commonly-accepted behaviors in society. For example, the person who constantly checks his Blackberry while being interviewed for a position is being rude, but is not necessarily doing something unethical. Management issues in the workplace, e.g. establishing procedures for efficient handling of work-load, are not necessarily ethical issues, unless they entail matters of fairness of distribution to all members of the team. Without being exhaustive, readers may use the markers and distinctions offered here to begin to figure out if the dilemma they are facing is an ethical one and then begin to sort it out and come to some resolution.

Theories: Now What?

After having put down some markers for identifying an issue as an ethical one, what are the next steps? Briefly, they are: dilemma, deliberation and decision-making. After identifying the ethical dimensions of a dilemma, one moves to deliberation. The word *deliberation* comes from the Latin term for weighing on the scales. In the setting of museum ethics, deliberation entails giving ample thought and due weight to the principles and norms that are used to come to a decision. Deliberation is not an abstraction here, but is a process engaged in by professionals in facing challenges like de-accessioning, repatriation, conflicts of interest, increased accessibility for disadvantaged communities and curating difficult issues, for example, global climate change or contested access to natural resources.

What is at stake for museum professionals using the principles of ethical theories? As noted above, emphasis on the results of the actions entails theories whose main evaluative tool is analyzing the ethical weight of the consequences of actions. Do these figure more or less prominently than the concepts of duties, rights or responsibilities? If the latter are more prominent, then the analysis should focus on clarifying the claims of duties or rights. Moreover, does the dilemma entail or highlight acting according to a specific virtue, like fairness or courage, on the part of the professional, as in the case of whistle blowing? Is the dilemma covered by a principle or norm in one's professional code of ethics? One theory does not fit all situations and what a professional may do is use an appropriate repertoire of analysis, including knowledge of the relevant ethical theories, application to the specific dilemma and formulation of a reasoned decision.

Time pressures and the exigencies of real-life dilemmas require professionals to make decisions. In addition to the principles of ethical theories, what else could help them in this process? First of all, one should identify the relevant elements of the dilemma. This includes gathering all relevant information, marshalling evidence, bringing principles to bear that are pertinent to the issue at hand and aiming for consistency, coherence and validity of conclusions in the reasoning process. In form, these methods of critical thinking are used across disciplines, but differ insofar as the content is provided by the theories of ethics and by principles, norms and actual situations that museum professionals will encounter in the field.

How might professionals apply these suggestions in the dilemmas they face? The answer is similar to the question about getting to Carnegie Hall—"Practice, practice, practice." This is where the *art of ethics* comes into play. Teachers and other experts may provide knowledge and guidance, but these are complemented by actual practice in working through ethical dilemmas—real or hypothetical. This way the skills may already be in play when the crisis hits and discussions are not relegated solely to the committees charged with reviewing and updating the professional codes. In collaborative models of decision-making, all those with a stake in the outcome are involved in discussions about ethics and its applications. This would include managers and support staff; that is, members of the institution also participate in discourse about ethics beyond those ordinarily designated as the decision-makers in hierarchical models of governance. This model gives all stakeholders practice in ethical deliberations and decision-making.

Are There Experts in Ethics?

We return to the opening question of this chapter—are there experts in ethics? If one answers that such expertise entails knowing the major ethical theories, having the ability to explain and defend general ethical principles and applying them in analytical and critical ways, then this sort of expertise presumably lies with those who are trained to do these tasks. As such, philosophers and religious thinkers are good candidates to whom others may look for such knowledge. However, since many fields of knowledge are involved in applied ethics, a collaborative and multidisciplinary approach is more suitable than relying on a single profession to provide answers. With any claim to "expert knowledge," what are participants to do when the experts disagree? Call in more experts? Again the exigencies of real-life decisions press upon professionals as they seek to make decisions in a timely way. They proceed with the most complete analysis and with as much consultation as possible. And when not facing a pressing dilemma, they prepare themselves with the knowledge and practice they can bring to bear when they need to make the difficult decisions. In fact, this volume of essays is itself exactly the kind of intellectual training that museum professionals can use to prepare themselves to engage in deliberation and decision-making when the time comes. It would also be useful to include ethics education as part of graduate training in the museum professions. As an expression of the multidisciplinary approach that is being taken by the museum professions, this volume of essays advances the conversation in the field about current ethical challenges. In this process, the conversation is broadened and enriched and, no doubt, the interlocutors themselves will articulate new insights and employ greater expertise in dealing with the complex issues they face.

Discourse Ethics

As a multidisciplinary and collaborative method, the museum profession may find the approach to problem solving called discourse ethics particularly useful. Developed over the last few decades by Jürgen Habermas, Karl-Otto Apel and Albrecht Wellmer, it continues to generate interest and critiques from philosophers and social theorists. Taking its starting point from Kant, these philosophers develop an approach to ethics that emphasizes what they call the principle of universalizability (U). As with any new approach in ethics, many other philosophers dispute its claims and its findings, especially the justification of the foundational principle itself. The emphasis here, however, is on the ways that a version of discourse ethics may be of use to museum professionals and others working in the field of museum studies. Since so much current work in the professions is collaborative, any approach to solving dilemmas that puts communication at the center of the process could be very useful. Discourse ethics does precisely that and holds out the prospect that a decision for acting in a particular setting can be arrived at through a rational process. Habermas presents the principle of universalizability by focusing on the rational consensus that must be achieved in order to reach a proposed norm. Such a consensus is reached and the norm is thereby valid, if and only if:

> All affected can accept the consequences and the side effects its general observance can be anticipated to have for the satisfaction of *everyone's* interests (and these consequences are preferred to those of known alternative possibilities for regulation).[16]

Apart from the many questions raised by the theory as a whole, what is valuable for issues in the museum profession is the notion that the interests of those actually affected by the decision are morally relevant and that moral rightness depends on the real consensus of participants in the discussions. Habermas's emphasis on inter-subjectivity adds a very important dimension to this approach and has particular relevance for the kinds of disputes that arise in the public arena, in this case the ethical analysis of dilemmas facing museum professionals. In the domain of ethical theory, much has been made of Habermas's efforts to construct a clear way to come to rational consensus among people who do not share the same history, traditions or value systems. This effort, both fruitful and problematic, has yet to be fully explored in order to help professionals sort out the dilemmas that they face. As essential as the theoretical issues are, it is in the actual debates and discussions among participants that thorny conflicts arise. A kind of "application discourse" needs to be developed and drawing implications from Habermas's work would advance this project.

William Rehg has done much to draw out these implications in his work on Habermas in which Rehg argues that at the point of actual, real-life discussions, participants need to express a kind of "rational trust" that the legal and political procedures put in place in the spirit of the principle of universalizability (U) will be adhered to and fulfilled. This notion of rational trust seems to contain its own criteria of rationality and has its own moral weight apart from the U principle:

> On this view, the individual's confidence in the validity of a decision is based not so much on his or her overview of the relevant arguments as on the procedures for processing various arguments and how faithfully their administrators carry them out.[17]

Rehg imagines that on any particular issue many audiences may be involved, resulting, he claims, in dispersed consensus. Such a consensus, freely and fully arrived at by all participants, needs to be seen not merely as a compromise (i.e. the best one can hope for under the real circumstance of the debate), but as a genuine, moral decision that can be accepted by all as a morally, and not only legally or procedurally, binding. This is a tall order in the hurly-burly, real life conditions of such debates.

One way to address the overly rationalistic approach of Habermas's discourse ethics may be found in some feminist ethical and political theories. Seyla Benhabib has drawn on the work of Hannah Arendt to propose the construction of associational public spaces. Constructing these spaces requires that all participants cultivate an "enlarged mentality" in which all learn how to reason, understand and appreciate the standpoint of other participants.[18] For Arendt and then Benhabib, such understanding is the outcome of meeting and speaking in the public space that includes professional associations and meetings. The multiple perspectives that constitute the public space are only revealed in the speaking acts of those who are willing to engage in the public drama in the first place. Public space is thereby created by such collective and contested actions. Participants take the standpoint of others and exercise what Arendt called "transcending judgment" by which one accords each person the moral respect to consider seriously the other's point of view. This does not mean agreeing with or assuming the other standpoint by foregoing one's own; rather the challenge is to think from the other's standpoint and to listen in a genuinely open way to what the other's standpoint entails.[19] When this happens, the associational public space is enacted in which conflicts may occur but without win–lose struggles. And narratives of all sorts are included in creating these spaces. Discourse in this setting is not judged solely on principles of rationality or objectivity, but rather depends on the relational processes that are enacted within the associational public space. It is important to note that these relational processes do not presuppose the existence of a robust public space, but in fact lead to its creation through the enactment of the multiple discourses in the events themselves. In the new framework presented here, administrative, scientific, technological and creative discourses would be accorded parity within the context of the enlarged mentality of all participants who are committed to creating an associational public space. Negotiating discourses in this associational public space could be a more fruitful enterprise than the agonistic and competitive models currently in use. Conflicts and dilemmas emerging from the museum professions would constitute interesting cases in these associational public spaces that also use norms generated from discourse ethics and feminist ethical theories.

Actual discourses in museum settings would be created to include the following features:

- As many professionals already recognize, discussions need to be multidisciplinary in approach, including but not limited to museum professionals, board members, members' organizations, other non-profit groups, representatives of local populations, source communities, non-visitors, ethicists and policy makers.
- All stakeholders participate in debates, discussions and decision-making.
- All factors impinging upon a particular dilemma need to be considered: economic, social, political, ethical, environmental and aesthetic.
- Working groups accommodate "expert" and "non-expert" discourse and ways of thinking. Non-linear discourse is accorded due weight in discussion and decision-making, e.g. traditional myths, storytelling, rituals and religious beliefs are included in significant ways and not simply as tokenism.
- Advocacies are delineated, i.e. who speaks for non-rational, non-verbal and inanimate parts of the community. This is addressed and resolved before discussions take place.
- Indigenous peoples with claims to specific sites and artifacts have the right, if they wish, to participate or not in such discussions and decision-making.
- Models for conducting discussion and decision-making are decided upon before discussion of issues occurs. Facilitators, discussion leaders and group-process consultants who have no stake in the issues are given the task to implement and monitor the discussions and decision-making.

No doubt, elements of these frameworks are already being enacted. Museum professionals, members' organizations, community representatives, public officials and others are creating and participating in the process of dealing with ethical dilemmas facing museums and other public institutions. There is no doubt that working to create associational public spaces and operating within these frameworks is difficult and time-consuming. It also requires good will, openness and honesty on all sides. Vision and creativity are called for to help create such associational spaces. If participants do enact these spaces, fruitful and meaningful discourses may occur and ethical decision-making may have a greater chance of occurring.

Professional Codes

As fields of knowledge and the practices of professions become more complex and contentious, professional organizations have developed professional codes of ethics to inform and guide their members. While some codes have been adopted because of egregious ethical violations, e.g. the immoral practices of the Nazi doctors or the theft of art works during WW II, others have been enacted because professionals themselves realize the need for self-regulation and for a statement of best ethical practices within their professions. There has been an explosion of these professional codes of ethics in the last sixty years with many professions engaging in on-going review and revision of their codes on a regular basis.

At first glance, professional codes may appear to be fairly straightforward statements that express the values and norms of a particular profession. However, as in most areas of contemporary life and work, issues can quickly become complicated and contentious. Confusion may ensue for those professionals who have every intention of doing the right thing. Museum professionals have available to them the ICOM Code of Ethics and the American Association of Museum's Code of Ethics.[20] What more is required than these codes? In fact, interpreting and grounding these codes are themselves matters of debate among members of professional groups.[21] Here are some points to consider about codes of ethics: what they are and how they function; how they may be related to discourse ethics; and how they may be used and interpreted. In light of the recent serious ethical violations by business officials, clergy, and public officials, we should attempt to steer clear of the Scylla and Charybdis of skepticism or cynicism about the value or effectiveness of professional codes of ethics. Clearly, all the codes in the world will not prevent those few professionals from committing immoral actions, but this fact could also be used to argue for more effective codes than for rejecting them entirely.

First, the nature and functions of codes of ethics: these are sets of principles, standards, norms and practices that professional associations voluntarily adopt for the good working of their profession and its members. They are typically created and adopted by the profession itself and, as such, are expressions of the autonomy and self-regulating nature of the profession. Codes function as guidelines for members of the profession and in general are considered aspirational, regulatory and educational. Some codes include procedures for initiating complaints, adjudicating conflicts or dealing with violations of the code itself. Ordinarily, codes address multiple audiences with the first being the members of the profession itself. Other audiences include clients, customers and the community at large. For audiences outside the profession, codes function as a public statement of the roles and responsibilities that museum professionals take up in relation to those outside the profession, but who also have a stake in the good functioning of the museum and its personnel.

In format, codes of ethics often begin with general principles, a prologue, or mission statement of the profession. Then norms and standards that are specific to that profession are enunciated. For example, codes may enjoin honesty, integrity and public service on the part of its members and then in museum work relate these principles to the specific tasks of museum professionals. These might include connecting the values, for example of honesty and transparency, to the means by which museums acquire or de-accession objects; or relating the value of learning to the display of objects that it holds in trust for public benefit and not for private gain.

Codes of ethics should not be considered fixed or final in form or content, but as open to review and revision by their members on a periodic basis. The code itself may include provisions for review and revision, analogous to the amendment procedures for a constitution. As an example, ICOM's latest revision of its code was promulgated in 2004 after a series of consultations with its members. Prior versions of the code had been published in 1970 and in 1986 with an interim document issued in 2001 that formed the basis of the code of ethics accepted by its members in 2004.[22]

Codes of ethics are only effective when they are known, adhered to and put into practice by the members of the profession. To these ends, professionals have an obligation to be informed about the contents of their codes and to abide by them.

Periodic seminars and workshops are helpful to inform and encourage professionals to evidence a good working knowledge of and practice in using the codes. Since codes of ethics do not provide specific answers to particular and complex dilemmas, how do professionals use these codes effectively? Again, knowledge of the codes and practice in using them are essential aspects of a professional's training. However, when the actual ethical dilemmas emerge, how might professionals proceed? As presented in the section above, enacting the process from discourse ethics comes into its own. The features and stipulations given above are put into play so that all stakeholders take part in the process (pp. 34–36). The group comes to a resolution as a result of the process enacted, perhaps with assistance from facilitators who guide the process, but who are not stakeholders and whose only interest is that the outcome be arrived at reasonably and fairly. It may be necessary for stakeholders to meet to agree on the framework of the process before the process itself is enacted. This may seem time-consuming and burdensome, but agreement about the process itself is what leads to a real consensus about how to address the ethical dilemma. The group comes to a consensus as a result of this two-fold process and not by some mechanical application of a set of directives. Finally, the dispositions and attitudes of the participants themselves are important ingredients in enacting the consensus that may emerge. We now turn to these qualities for brief consideration.

"Phronesis" and Virtue Ethics

When Plato remarked in his *Seventh Letter* that, as valuable as rule by law is, it is only "rule by second best," he was pointing to the importance of the capacities and skills of the human beings who actually make ethical decisions.[23] Aristotle takes this examination further and develops his theory of ethics centered on the cultivation of virtues. One of the overarching dispositions or habits of mind that he enunciates is called *phronesis*. It is a difficult word to translate and translators have rendered it "practical wisdom" or "moral know-how." In essence, it means that the person with *phronesis* knows the morally right thing to do in a particular set of circumstances and is so habituated that she will choose to do it. In effect, such a person is able to understand and fit a general ethical principle to a particular case in life. As such, this disposition contains both cognitive and moral dimensions.

How does one acquire such a disposition? Aristotle takes a developmental view of the acquisition of both moral and intellectual virtues; they require understanding, skill, training and practice. The same could be said for *phronesis*—it takes practice to learn how to get it right and includes an understanding of what, for example, courage is, as well as the conviction (voluntary action) to act courageously when called upon to do so. We are not left entirely to our own devices, however, in trying to get the virtuous action right. In a passage in which Aristotle presents virtue as the mean between excess and defect, he makes two important points: first, the mean is determined by a "rational principle, and by that principle by which the man of practical wisdom [*phronesis*] would determine it."[24] Aristotle proposes that we exercise reason to figure out the mean that is "relative to us" in particular settings. He also presupposes the community as the context for making ethical evaluations since we also keep in mind the model of what the person of *phronesis* would do in these circumstances. Having that model in mind entails recognizing the person of practical wisdom in the community and exercising moral imagination to fit that model into one's own particular setting. And so, in addition to knowing how to put a version of discourse ethics into practice, we also need to pay attention to ourselves and to the cultivation of *phronesis*, as well as other moral and intellectual virtues. Then, we will be in the best possible shape to make morally correct judgments when ethical dilemmas come into our lives, as most surely they will. Codes of professional ethics are helpful guidelines for ethical best practices, but it also takes the skill of the professional who possesses *phronesis* to be in a good position to interpret and apply these guidelines.

Bringing these elements together—*phronesis*, knowledge of ethics and practice in ethical decision-making, understanding the nature and requirements of one's profession and enacting discourse ethics to address the challenges in one's field—may go far to help ethics become truly applied in the museum profession. After all, in the final analysis, this is where ethics and its practice as an art really matter.

Notes

1 A note on terms *ethics* and *morality* that are used in this paper: in their origins, ethics is from the Greek *ethos*, morality from the Latin *mores* and each term has a much broader meaning than we attach to them in English. In their original languages, they both mean human customs, norms or accepted ways of acting. In English, each term is used more narrowly to connote an investigation of the correct or principled standards of human behavior. For the purposes of this paper, I typically use *ethics* to apply to the theories and principles of correct action and *morality* to apply to the issues or actions themselves.

2 Aristotle, *Nicomachean Ethics*, trans. David Ross, Oxford: Oxford University Press, 1963, I, 3, p. 3.

3 We prescind here from questions about the relationship between ethics and law. The legal system certainly concerns itself with questions of right and wrong, but does so from its own prerequisites and presuppositions, i.e. from the various systems of law that govern societies. Both ethics and the law are concerned with matters of justice, but such matters take us far afield from the present discussion. This note simply serves as a reminder that unpacking the uses and meanings of terms that appear in both law and ethics is very important, but cannot be addressed here. Even though both law and ethics deal with questions of right and wrong, each does so according to the methods of its own discipline.

4 Mary Midgley, *Utopias, Dolphins and Computers*, New York: Routledge, 1996, pp. 33–4.

5 Ibid.

6 Ibid., p. 35.

7 Ibid.

8 Ibid.

9 Readers should note that there are many debates among philosophers about the principles and claims made in each of these, but such "in-house" debates need not concern us greatly. For a good introduction to the major ethical theories, readers may consult James Rachels, *The Elements of Moral Philosophy*, New York: McGraw Hill Publishers, 2002.

10 Immanuel Kant, *Foundations of the Metaphysics of Morals*, trans. Lewis White Beck, New York: Library of Liberal Arts, Bobbs-Merrill Co., 1959, p. 39.

11 The Greek term for virtue is *arête* and is usually understood as *excellence*. In Homeric Greek, the term can be used to describe the excellence of an inanimate object like a sword or sailing ship and later in Greek usage it comes to be associated with human excellences of all sorts, including what we would characterize as moral virtue, like honesty, generosity, and so forth. Obviously, in the ancient Greek usage, *arête* has a much more comprehensive denotation than the more limited use that we make of it as moral virtue alone.

12 Some researchers who are working on the value of the emotions in making ethical judgments include Carol Gilligan, Diane Ackerman, Sallie McFague, Daniel Goleman, Allison Jaggar, Charlene Spretnak and Linda Holler.

13 Midgely, *Utopias, Dolphins and Computers*, p. 132.

14 Ibid.

15 For the present discussion we bracket issues raised in environmental ethics about the moral status of non-human beings, species or ecosystems, as important as these issues are.

16 Jürgen Habermas, "Discourse Ethics: Notes on a Program of Philosophical Justification," in *Moral Consciousness and Communicative Action*, trans. Christian Lenhardt and Shierry Weber Nicholsen, Cambridge, Mass.: MIT Press, 1990, p. 65.

17 William Rehg, *Insight and Solidarity: The Discourse Ethics of Jürgen Habermas*, Berkeley: University of California Press, 1994, p. 237.

18 Seyla Benhabib, "From Identity Politics to Social Feminism," in *Radical Democracy: Identity, Citizenship and the State*, D. Trend (ed.), New York: Routledge, 1996, pp. 27–41.

19 Hannah Arendt, *On Revolution*, New York: Viking Press, 1963, p. 220.

20 ICOM Code of Ethics Online. Available HTTP: www.icom.museum/ethics.html (accessed February 22, 2010); American Association of Museum Code of Ethics Online. Available HTTP: www.aam-us.org/museumresources/ethics/coe.cfm (accessed February 22, 2010).

21 See Michael Pickering, "'Dance Through the Minefield': the Development of Practical Ethics for Repatriation," this volume.

22 ICOM Code of Ethics, Introduction, p. vi (www.icom.museum/ethics.html).

23 Plato, *Letter VII*, trans. L.A. Post, *Plato: the Collected Dialogues*, New York: Pantheon Books, Bollingen Series LXXI, 1966, pp. 1583–84; see also Plato, *Statesman*, trans. J. B. Skemp, *Plato: the Collected Dialogues*, pp. 1066–67.

24 Aristotle, *Nicomachean Ethics*, II, 6, pp. 38–9.

3

GoodWork in museums today ... and tomorrow

Celka Straughn and Howard Gardner

Published discussions of museum ethics in America first appear in connection with the 1917 *Proceedings of the American Association of Museums*. Referring to current museum policy discussions, L. Earle Rowe, then Director of the Rhode Island School of Design, finds that these emphasize "the need of proving the value of ... [museum] work."[1] Rowe characterizes such work primarily in terms of museum relationships with other institutions, dealers, members, scholars and staff, relationships that he places under the "head of museum ethics." Although Rowe does not explicitly link his articulation of museum ethics with establishing the value of museum work, his brief article suggests a connection between efforts to legitimize and professionalize museum work and efforts to develop a museum ethics.[2] As such, his article raises the question, how does thinking about ethics shape museum work and museum workers?

Although museum ethics had become a topic for discussion at least by 1917, the American Association of Museums (AAM) did not adopt its first code of ethics until its twentieth annual meeting in 1925. In this first *Code of Ethics for Museum Workers*, the main relationship stressed is one that Rowe does not particularly address – the relationship to the public. As the opening lines declare, the value of museums "is in direct portion to the service they render the emotional and intellectual life of the people." Therefore, "[th]e life of the museum worker, whether he be a humble laborer or a responsible trustee, is essentially one of service."[3] The *Code* continues that the museum worker's "conduct rests on a threefold ethical basis" consisting of devotion, faith and honor. Performing one's ethical duties of public service, the museum worker "approximates most fully the ideals and purposes for which the museum stands."[4] As Hilde Hein explains in her historical analysis of museum ethics in America, this first code belonged to a context of "community betterment" with its emphasis on public service and "the dissemination of knowledge."[5] Nearly a century later, museum work constitutes a well-established profession with a large number of professional categories that range from educators and conservation scientists to exhibition designers and collections managers.[6] How do we perceive the value of museum work in the 21st century? And, why museum ethics today?

The most recent AAM *Code of Ethics for Museums* (2000) reaffirms the first Code's commitment to public service as an enduring and widely shared value; it further posits public service as an ethic to frame the new code.[7] Yet what does public service mean today? According to the new code, public service appears intertwined with the notion of public trust, with museums in the role as stewards of their collections and information for the benefit of their publics. "Their collections and/or the objects they borrow or fabricate are the basis for research, exhibits, and programs that invite public participation."[8] While the current Code outlines major areas of museum work, such as governance, collections and programs, it makes no specific mention of the roles of museum workers and their relationship to the public.[9] Rather, in addition to AAM's general museum Code, there now also exist today multiple codes of ethics and practice developed by AAM Professional Committees and other professional organizations, such as the Registrars Committee (RC-AAM) or the Association of Art Museum Curators (AAMC).[10] Each of these codes attempts to respond to the changing professional landscape of museums and museums workers. The ways in which museums and museum workers perform their public service present one of the major changes and challenges to good work in museums today.

In this chapter we draw on the perspectives and findings of the GoodWork Project,® a large-scale social scientific research project investigating the ways leading professionals in a variety of domains perform good work. Ethics forms an integral component of good work. As the Project has come to view it, good work is comprised of three elements that begin with the letter E: It is technically Excellent, personally meaningful or Engaging, and conducted in an Ethical manner. In addition to examining questions of museum ethics through the lens of the GoodWork Project, we focus here on recent museum transformations and meanings of public service, directing particular attention to the changing roles, responsibilities and relationships of museum curators and educators.

The concept of GoodWork

The GoodWork Project® originated in 1995 under the direction of psychologists Mihaly Csikszentmihalyi, William Damon and Howard Gardner. As the Project evolved, it sought to identify, understand and educate about what constitutes good work and what characterizes those who seek to practice it at time of powerful market forces, globalization and technological change. Over the ensuing decade Project researchers conducted more than 1200 interviews with leading members of different professions in America that included, among others, journalism, genetics, higher education and theater. This research has produced a rich collection of data on professional values, goals, responsibilities, strategies and struggles. Publications derived from the study and its concepts continue, as do various associated projects and practical initiatives that seek to encourage good work.[11]

According to findings from the Project, good work is likely to occur when four key forces align:

1 The individual beliefs and values of the worker.
2 The domain of work (long-standing values of the profession).

3   The current professional field (comprised of organizations, gatekeepers, etc.).
4   The wider societal reward system.[12]

Reflecting these four forces are four principal elements, or controls on behavior, that the GoodWork Project identifies as impacting good work (Figure 3.1):[13]

1   Individual standards.
2   Cultural controls of a domain (including leadership, missions, professional codes, traditions, etc.).
3   Social controls (such as trust, community needs, ethics boards).
4   External or outcome controls (e.g. power, prestige, extrinsic benefits).

Each of these four components influences or controls behaviors that impact good work; individual standards are also often shaped by social and cultural controls as professionals often internalize the requirements and codes of their domain and field.

Rephrased with examples more specific to museums, the quartet of forces and their controls would include, respectively: (1) the value system held by an individual conservator, collections manager or educator; (2) longstanding values of collection, preservation, education, and public service; (3) the particular museum, professional associations like AAM and AAMC, along with donors and critics; (4) the current priorities of the nation and the world. Consensus of what constitutes good work needs to be negotiated, mediated and revisited frequently among these different forces.

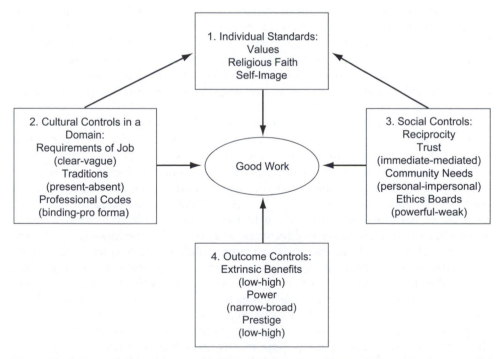

Figure 3.1 A Graphic Rendition of the Principal Elements of GoodWork, Courtesy of The GoodWork Project® Team, Harvard Graduate School of Education.

Creating conditions for good work among these different elements requires a strong support structure that makes clear professional needs and expectations, educates the public about the nature of the profession and allows for an open expression of individual values. Factors facilitating the emergence of good work include early training, mentors and colleagues, as well as an openness and flexibility of work and the domain to change.[14] Good work further entails a set of established core values with clear and strong standards that are constructed and enforced by the professional community and internalized by its individual members.[15] Drawing on its extensive research, the GoodWork Project locates characteristics of ethical work under two conditions:

1 Workers attempt to operate according to the longstanding values of their domain, even if these values clash with self-interest.
2 Workers recognize issues of moral complexity, take the time to think them through, seek advice and guidance and reflect on past actions and future consequences.[16]

One of the most important findings of the GoodWork Project is the concept of alignment as a major factor facilitating good work. "In alignment, all of the various interest groups basically call for the same kinds of performance; in contrast, when a profession is misaligned, the various interest groups emerge as being at cross-purposes with one another."[17] That is, to use an example of museum professionals, a curator is most likely to practice good work if the curator's own goals coincide with those of the professional role of the curator, with the expectations of colleagues, and with the attitude of the wider society toward work in general and museum work in particular. The relationship of alignment to good work is complex. While alignment helps to achieve good work, it may also complicate it by desensitizing workers to potential problems. Conversely, some workers are actually stimulated by the *lack* of alignment.[18] Moreover, both alignments and misalignments are temporary, necessitating continued reflection and adjustment.

Mission statements – and mutual adherence to missions by the relevant parties – can help promote alignment, but they may also come into conflict with competing purposes. In interviews with various professionals GoodWork Project researchers find that the highest form of responsibility to good work derives from a sense of duty "as defined by the traditions and current standards of the particular activity in which they [workers] are engaged."[19] This responsibility extends both to enhancing the status of the profession within the field and to society at large by enhancing the lives of those who are served, directly or indirectly, by the profession. In the museum field, these values, standards and responsibilities are frequently articulated in museum mission statements and further delineated in the various codes of ethics and practice, both for the museum field generally, as well as for different constituent professional groups. How the responsibilities to fulfill the mission are delegated and shared among museum workers impacts their abilities to uphold core values and standards. A fundamental GoodWork finding is that workers "feel comfortable with whom they are and have time and opportunity to reflect on their mission and to determine whether they are progressing toward its realization."[20] As noted, when the values, standards, and responsibilities as expressed by missions and professional codes misalign or come into conflict with each other and/or with the forces of the individual worker, institutions, professional societies or wider society, such conditions complicate the ability to practice good work and achieve ethical decisions.

Museum transformations and public service

Particularly with reference to the United States, numerous publications have characterized museums' relationship with the public dimension as their most significant transformation at the end of the twentieth century. This view is exemplified by AAM's report, *Excellence and Equity: Education and the Public Dimension of Museums* (1992), which takes as its premise that all activities contribute to a museum's public dimension and its provision of public service.[21] In his essay "The Museum and the Public" Stephen Weil proposes that "the relationship between the museum and the public must be understood as a revolution in process … The museum's role will have been transformed from one of mastery to one of service."[22] Museums, according to this proposed process, have shifted from inward, collection-oriented institutions that disseminate knowledge to outward, audience-oriented sites that offer educational resources, and, increasingly, experiences, which engage the public in their own knowledge making.[23] As Mary Ellen Munley and Randy Roberts recently state: "The once familiar 'collect, preserve, and interpret' mission that dominated twentieth-century museums shifted toward a new audience-centered focus. Across the field, museums have increasingly identified themselves as community-oriented, outwardly focused centers of education dedicated to reflecting and serving broad and diverse audiences."[24] Such transformations not only raise questions about the purposes and priorities of museums; they also throw into question the existing roles, responsibilities and relationships of museum workers, as well as established hierarchies, authorities and value systems. These questions may help generate change, but they may also generate points of conflict and/or confusion.

Many current museum mission statements reflect the recent turn to the public dimension, articulating a commitment to enhance public understanding and appreciation of the natural world and human creativity, or to serve and engage individuals and society through activities, exhibitions, programs, collections, research and publications. But museum missions are also shaped according to the particularities of their institutions' resources and values. Interpretations of a duty to public service, or to the notion of public trust, vary, depending on how museums respond to a myriad of different challenges. Glenn Lowry, Director of the Museum of Modern Art (MoMA), draws attention to "the challenges of increased competition, changing social values, and diminished financial resources." He argues that these forces "have compelled them [museums] to stretch the boundaries of acceptable museological practice."[25]

Lowry's statements come from a collection of essays by leading art museum directors, *Whose Muse? Art Museums and the Public Trust*, which attempts to retain the art object as the focus of art museums' public purpose. In contrast to Munley and Roberts's above-cited claim of a transformed mission, James Cuno, in his main essay for *Whose Muse?*, asserts: "Acquiring, preserving, and providing access to works of art is the basis for an art museum's contract with the public and the foundation of the trust that authorizes that contract."[26] Similarly Philippe de Montebello questions the shift in museums from "repositories, primarily, to being activity centers" that cede attention from the work of art to the public, and are driven more by market than by mission forces.[27] De Montebello precedes these comments with a critique of AAM's *Excellence and Equity* report as "fanciful" in its emphasis on educational experience and global citizenship.[28] Whether or not one chooses to critique the essays that comprise *Whose Muse?* as elite art museum voices steeped in the values of connoisseurship, they present an influential perspective of contemporary museum transformations. They further indicate a significant area of tension regarding museums and their service to the public, one that in many ways coalesces around the responsibilities of curators and educators within museum work.

Indeed, many conflicts experienced within the museum workplace concern the status of audiences and the role of education. Hein contends that "the concept of education" constitutes "the most significant change" in museums during the later decades of the twentieth century.[29] In her insightful volume, *The Museum in Transition*, she articulates contemporary museum conflicts:

> Today's museums perform their public service by offering themselves as resources and educational institutions, but it remains a matter of debate whether the goods they offer are to be valued as cultural treasures and means of education, or, especially in the case of artworks, whether these are sources of original experience. … Is the designated experience of the object exclusively for its own sake, or does the object serve as occasional stimulus for a broader, more encompassing experience? The answer to this question determines whether we think of museums as "object-centered" or "story-centered." … These concerns lie at the heart of the many 'culture wars' and political confrontations that currently rage inside the professional museum community and also subject it to attacks from outside.[30]

Challenging Hein's notion of "story-centered," we would claim that objects *always* evince stories, and that the argument concerns whose story, whether an historical or personal narrative or some other epistemological perspective, based on, for example, an object's materials, method of creation, or formal characteristics. Hein's distinction, then, might be recast as a conflict between object-centered and audience-centered. This conflict points to a common source of misalignment within museums, one frequently manifested in the relationship between curatorial and education departments.

Museums and the challenges of GoodWork today: the case of curators and educators

Tensions between curatorial and education work are well known, particularly within art museum settings. However, they do not appear to have been specifically examined within an ethical framework. As noted earlier in the introduction, the current AAM *Code of Ethics for Museums* does not directly address the roles and relationships of museum workers. Although AAM's *Museum Education Principles and Standards*, developed by the Committee on Education, emphasizes shared responsibility and "stresses the importance of interdepartmental teamwork in the achievement of the museum's education mission," neither it nor the recent *Code of Ethics for Curators*, developed by the Curators Committee, includes coworker relationships as noteworthy areas of ethical significance.[31] Yet when professional values and standards of practice come into conflict, compromising the ability to practice good work, workers are confronted with the dilemmas that merit the descriptor "ethical."

The Curator and Education Committee codes and standards, in addition to the AAMC *Professional Practices for Art Museum Curators*, outline the core values and responsibilities for the practice of each profession. These include, for curators, "the interpretation, study, care and development of the collection, and the materials, concepts, exhibitions and other programs central to the identity of their museum."[32] The recent ethics code for curators lists the interpretation of objects among their responsibilities, "with a respect for the needs of all potential patrons," as well as "to an object's creator(s) and culture of origin."[33] With a focus on objects and the collection, a primary duty of a curator remains scholarship, and, at least for art curators, their "responsibilities must be balanced with the ethics of their scholarly disciplines."[34] On the other hand, museum educators "serve as audience advocates and work to provide meaningful and lasting learning experiences for a diverse public."[35] Part of accomplishing these responsibilities entails that educators "develop interpretation with specific educational goals by integrating content and learning objectives for targeted audiences."[36] Broadly speaking, curators attend to the collections and educators to the public; with the reconceived public dimension of museums, both also attend to interpretation.

According to museum training manuals, curators are ascribed the intellectual and academic interpretation of the collection.[37] The AAMC guide to *Professional Practices* assigns curators the role of providing "information and expertise on the collections and exhibitions to educators," while "[e]ducators in turn provide curators with pedagogical strategies to fulfill public interests and needs."[38] Museum educators are, according to the *Museum Education Principles and Standards*, "specialists who help museums fulfill their educational mission." They "shape content and interpretation toward relevant issues and create a broad dialogue," as well as "develop interpretation with specific educational goals."[39] Acknowledging curators as "traditionally responsible" for interpretation based on their scholarly expertise, Lisa Roberts claims that it now is "the business of every member of the team," with educators presenting "views about the meanings of collections that will resonate with museum audiences."[40] This real, if subtle, shift brings into question the value and role of expertise, and as various scholars have noted, museum shifts toward audience views and voices have challenged curatorial voices and hierarchies of meaning.[41] Roberts argues that "[i]nterpretation is in part an act of negotiation – between the values and knowledge upheld by museums and those which are brought in by visitors."[42] How responsibility for interpretation is conceived and carried out matters significantly and may have ethical consequences.[43] For, as Lowry characterizes the art museum, it is a "mission-driven educational institution devoted to the display and interpretation of its collection."[44]

A recent job posting for the Director of Interpretation and Research at MoMA, a position within the Education Department, states: "MoMA's founding mission to 'help people to understand and enjoy modern art' is fulfilled through collaboration between curators and the interpretation and research staff. Curators bring deep knowledge and innovative perspectives on works of art and education and research staff bring knowledge of how visitors engage and learn within a museum context. The field of interpretation and research has been recognized as an essential priority for museums to achieve their public mission to engage audiences with art."[45] While MoMA's posting stresses collaboration – and curators and educators may work well together and with other museum workers on interdepartmental teams – as Roberts and others recount, questions of interpretive authority as well as of priority to collection or audience needs remain sources of potential conflict.[46] The roles and responsibilities assigned to museum curators and educators today, in particular with regard to interpretation, may in certain ways place them at cross purposes in carrying out the museum's mission and, accordingly, pose ethical dilemmas.

What are the ethical dimensions inherent in museum worker relationships, such as those that involve cooperation between curators and educators? Three scenarios highlight potential conflicts and how they may impact the conditions for good work, with attention to core values, professional standards and alignment across the four forces of workers, the domain, the field and society. In the first example, a classic about didactic interpretations, the professional values of the educator and curator clash, complicating effective collaboration. Conflicting values with regard to collections and audiences also challenge curators and educators in the second scenario. With the third example curators and educators contend with media (both old and new) and market forces, and they negotiate a means to remain true to both their core values.

1   An educator requests that a curator change a text label that the curator has written for an exhibition. The educator claims the text is "too academic" as it introduces and defines terms that the public might not know, limiting its accessibility. The curator argues that, at some level, interpretation involves learning new terms and concepts, and that not all academic language is inaccessible, especially when explained. The curator also maintains a sense of a duty to bring a certain amount of scholarly knowledge to the production of exhibition texts. For her part, the educator believes that expressing the text in technical terms compromises her responsibility to communicate to an audience that deserves the clearest and least obfuscatory information. Both find themselves challenged as to how to adhere to their personal and professional values and responsibilities as well as to support the museum's mission.

2   Staff at a museum have completed work on a small touring contemporary art exhibition – everything is ready to go. At the last minute, the first venue suffers a problem with the climate-control system; this abrupt turn of events means that staff conservators cannot approve the display of several works in the show. Essays and other materials have already been published that include these works. For multiple reasons, it is not possible to reschedule or cancel the show.

In order to maintain key aspects of the exhibition's concept, curatorial staff propose illustrated captions for each of the removed works, in addition to a clear explanation of why they are missing from this venue of the show. For curators, this seems the professional course of action and is sufficient for public interpretation purposes. Educators, on the other hand, disagree. The proposed solution conflicts with their professional responsibility to engage diverse audiences in dynamic learning experiences; they wish to have large-scale reproductions or facsimiles created in order to make an impact similar to that of the removed pieces. Curators agree that the texts with their small-scale illustrations do not approximate the power of the actual objects, and cite the importance of showing original works rather than reproductions. For them, as stewards of the collection and with their professional obligations as curators who value original objects, it is crucial to uphold the integrity of the works of art and the artists.

3   The producers of a popular television program offer a museum the opportunity to buy into its next season. In each show five aspiring artists create new works of art. A group of celebrities critiques each piece and the audience gets to vote for each episode's winner. Select winning works are acquired by the supporting museum, as stipulated by the contract. The museum would receive publicity in every episode and its pick of six of the program's winning works of art. The educators advocate for participation. They argue that it not only provides publicity outreach, but it also enables the museum to be directly involved with a widely shared public art experience, one that allows the audience the role to play an active role in the selection of works of art. The curators, however, take issue with the stipulation to acquire the works of art, particularly ones that they do not find of sufficient quality; to do so would violate their responsibility to professional collection practices.

After discussion, the curators and educators agree that the artworks do not fit the museum's standards for acquisition and decline the program's offer. Through their discussion they also develop the idea of presenting new acquisitions in a special interactive section of the museum website that shares elements of the museum's process and justification for the new works; it also encourages visitors to contribute their own evaluation of the works' qualities and benefits for the museum.

As these scenarios reveal, curators and educators may face ethical choices when their respective core values and professional standards do not align. Ethical minefields may erupt between collections' care and interpretation. Museum workers – be they curators, educators, collections managers or exhibition designers – need to assess the long-standing values of their domains and field, as well as the expectations and demands of society; to recognize and reflect upon areas of conflict; to seek ways to share the responsibility for both the collections and the public; and to stretch to achieve alignment. The scenarios described above portray three of the multiple kinds of dilemmas that arise, while offering a solution to one that appears to uphold the core values of all the participating professionals.

Values of GoodWork today and tomorrow

Returning to our earlier question of the value of museum work today, we may ask: what are the core values, standards, responsibilities and goals of museum work and museum workers? How do museum workers share the responsibility for the public trust? Where does the public dimension fit in? Whose values and voices take priority, and for what purpose?

The challenges posed by museum transformations impact the four forces identified by the GoodWork Project – the worker's individual beliefs and values, the long-standing values of the domain, the influences at work in the current professional field and the priorities of wider society – and, in particular, the roles, responsibilities and relationships of museum workers, as we have seen in the case of curators and educators. When the values, standards and purposes of these four forces align, it facilitates the ability to achieve meaningful, high-quality and ethical work. Good work is more likely to occur when workers have opportunities to participate in the "three Es": excellent, engaging and ethical work.

While the principles of good work are quite constant, they must continually be rethought as voices, values, authorities, responsibilities, standards and practices are challenged and transformed. The preservational priorities of elite institutions a century ago are now complemented, if not overwhelmed, by the public service priorities of a far more democratic era. The professionals working in today's museums cannot ignore this shift, but, by the same token, they need to be vigilantly reflective about how best to realize core values in a changed – and continually changing – environment – one that now prominently includes the Internet, among other new technologies. Making ethical conflicts public can be uncomfortable; engaging in serious discussion and debate about them is time consuming. But in a democratic society, these are the most promising, and quite possibly the only, means to bring about the best possible work.

Acknowledgments

The authors wish to acknowledge Madeleine Trudeau for her thoughtful suggestions and careful reading of this chapter, as well as Amanda Martin Hamon and Janet Marstine. We would also like to thank John Abele, Count Anton von Faber Castell and Susan Noyes.

Notes

1 L. E. Rowe, "Museum Ethics," *Proceedings of the American Association of Museums*, II, 1917, pp. 137–43. Reprinted in H. H. Genoways and M. A. Andrei (eds.) *Museum Origins: Readings in Early Museum History and Philosophy*, Walnut Creek, CA: Left Coast Press, 2008, p. 147.

2 Robert Macdonald, specifically referring to the first American museum code of ethics in 1925, claims: "The promulgation of ethical values by museum workers early in their organizational history makes clear that they viewed themselves as belonging to a profession willing to formalize principles that would inform individual and collective activities."

R. Macdonald, "Museum Ethics: The Essence of Professionalism," in J. R. Glaser with A. A. Zenetou, *Museums: A Place to Work: Planning Museum Careers*, London and New York: Routledge in association with the Smithsonian Institution, 1996, pp. 35–40, quote p. 35.

3 Committee of the American Association of Museums, *Code of Ethics for Museum Workers*, New York: American Association of Museums, 1925, p. 2.

4 Ibid., p. 3.

5 H. S. Hein, *The Museum in Transition: A Philosophical Perspective*, Washington, DC, and London: Smithsonian Institution Press, 2000, p. 93.

6 A response to the establishment of the museum profession is the growth of museum studies and various training programs, as well as more practically oriented publications on museum careers. For example, see G. Edson, *International Directory of Museum Training*, London and New York: Routledge, 1995; Glaser and Zenetou, *Museums: A Place to Work*.

7 American Association of Museums, *Code of Ethics for Museums*, 2000. Online. Available HTTP: http://www.aam-us.org/museumresources/ethics/coe.cfm (accessed 16 December 2009).

8 Ibid.

9 This shift in emphasis from museum workers to museum work is reflected in the change of titles from a code "for museum workers" to one simply "for museums," indicating a transformation from earlier attempts to establish a generalized museum profession to the particularization of today's more specialized professional roles.

10 See, for example, Registrars Committee of the American Association of Museums, *A Code of Ethics for Registrars*, 1984. Online. Available HTTP: http://www.rcaam.org/pdf/Part3-Appendix.pdf (accessed 13 November 2009); Association of Art Museum Curators, *Professional Practices for Art Museum Curators*, New York: Association of Art Museum Curators, 2007.

11 The first major publication appeared in 2001. H. Gardner, M. Csikszentmihalyi and W. Damon, *GoodWork: When Excellence and Ethics Meet*, New York: Basic Books, 2001. For the most recent publication, see H. Gardner, ed., "Good Work: Theory and Practice," unpublished manuscript, 2010. The GoodWork Project web site provides a detailed accounting of publications and related studies. Available HTTP: http://www.goodwork project.org (accessed 22 February 2010).

12 GoodWork Project® Team, *The GoodWork Project:® An Overview*, 2008, p. 19. Online. Available HTTP: http://www.goodworkproject.org/docs/papers/GW%20Overview%204_08.pdf (accessed 12 November 2008).

13 GoodWork Project® Team, *GoodWork Project Overview*, pp. 19–22, figure p. 20.

14 H. Gardner, "The Ethical Responsibilities of Professionals," GoodWork Project Report Series, No. 2, July 1998 (updated February 2001), p. 9. Online. Available HTTP: http://pzweb.harvard.edu/eBookstore/PDFs/GoodWork2.pdf (accessed 12 November 2008).

15 H. Gardner, "Introduction. Who is Responsible for Good Work?" in H. Gardner (ed.) *Responsibility at Work: How Leading Professionals Act (or Don't Act) Responsibly*, San Francisco: Jossey-Bass, 2007, pp. 1–18, quote p. 12; GoodWork Project® Team, *GoodWork Project Overview*, p. 23.

16 Gardner, "Introduction," in Gardner (ed.) *Responsibility at Work*, p. 13.

17 GoodWork Project® Team, *GoodWork Project Overview*, p. 28.

18 Ibid., p. 29.

19 M. Csikszentmihalyi and J. Nakamura, "Creativity and Responsibility," in Gardner (ed.) *Responsibility at Work*, pp. 64–80, quote p. 67.

20 GoodWork Project® Team, *GoodWork Project Overview*, p. 42.

21 American Association of Museums, *Excellence and Equity: Education and the Public Dimension of Museums*, Washington, DC: the Association, 1992. This report, prepared by the AAM Task Force on Education, is frequently cited as fundamental in numerous museum education publications.

22 S. E. Weil, "The Museum and the Public," *Museum Management and Curatorship* 16: 3, 1997, pp. 257–71, quote p. 257.

23 For example, Weil calls for museums to provide more "stimulating, interactive, visitor-centered, and cross-disciplinary experiences." S. E. Weil, "Foreword," in J. S. Hirsch and L. H. Silverman (eds.) *Transforming Practice: Selections from the "Journal of Museum Education," 1992–1999*, Washington, DC: Museum Education Roundtable, 2000, pp. 11–13, quote p. 11. More recently, educators at the Detroit Institute of Arts claim that the "new institutional priorities" for interpretation are to "facilitate dynamic, dialogic experiences that will ignite visitors' imaginations, ideas, and emotions and encourage self-reflection and social engagement." J. W. Czajkowski and S. H. Hill, "Transformation and Interpretation: What is the Museum Educator's Role?" *Journal of Museum Education* 33: 3, 2008, pp. 255–264, quote p. 256.

24 M. E. Munley and R. Roberts, "Are Museum Educators Still Necessary?" *Journal of Museum Education* 31: 1, 2006, pp. 29–39, quote p. 31.

25 G. Lowry, "A Deontological Approach to Art Museums and the Public Trust," in J. Cuno (ed.) *Whose Muse? Art Museums and the Public Trust*, Princeton, NJ, and Oxford: Princeton University Press and Harvard University Art Museums, 2004, pp. 129–49, quote p. 145.

26 Cuno continues: "The museum ... is also a center of a very special kind of research and education ... research and teaching are object-based: prompted by the object, engaged with the object, and offered up by the particular way objects are experienced as physical things ... " J. Cuno, "The Object of Art Museums," in Cuno (ed.) *Whose Muse?* pp. 49–75, quote p. 52. Similarly advancing these familiar goals, AAMC's guide opens: "Members of the Association of Art Museum Curators (AAMC) believe that the core mission of art museums is to collect, preserve, study, interpret, and display works of art for the benefit of the public." Association of Art Museum Curators, *Professional Practices*, p. 6.

27 P. de Montebello, "Art Museums, Inspiring Public Trust," in Cuno (ed.) *Whose Muse?* pp. 151–69, quote p. 157.

28 Ibid., p. 156.

29 Hein, *The Museum in Transition*, p. 116.

30 Ibid., p. 7. Hein herself questions whether the "displacement of objects by experiences ... risks compromising the uniqueness of the museum's educational agency," p. 109.

31 Committee on Education, *Excellence in Practice: Museum Education Principles and Standards*, American Association of Museums, 2002, p. 2. Online. Available HTTP: http://www.edcom.org/Files/Admin/EdComBookletFinalApril805.pdf (accessed 13 November 2009); American Association of Museums Curators Committee, *A Code of Ethics for Curators*, 2009. Online. Available HTTP: http://www.curcom.org/_pdf/code_ethics2009.pdf (accessed 13 November 2009).

32 American Association of Museums Curators Committee, *Code of Ethics for Curators*, p. 3.

33 Ibid., p. 5.

34 Association of Art Museum Curators, *Professional Practices*, p. 6.

35 Committee on Education, *Excellence in Practice*, p. 6.

36 Ibid., p. 8.

37 Edson, *Museum Training*, p. 40; Glaser and Zenetou, *Museums: A Place to Work*, p. 81. "Although curators have many duties and responsibilities, their primary value to the museum lies in their specific expertise. Curators are historians engaged in scholarship with a special emphasis on physical objects." Association of Art Museum Curators, *Professional Practices*, p. 6.

38 Association of Art Museum Curators, *Professional Practices*, p. 12.

39 Committee on Education, *Excellence in Practice*, pp. 6, 8.

40 L. C. Roberts, "Educators on Exhibit Teams: A New Role, a New Era," in Hirsch and Silverman (eds.) *Transforming Practice* (essay originally appeared 1994), pp. 89–97, quote p. 93.

41 Munley and Roberts, "Are Museum Educators Still Necessary?" p. 30; L. C. Roberts, *From Knowledge to Narrative: Educators and the Changing Museum*, Washington, DC, and London: Smithsonian Institution Press, 1997, p. 159. Jennifer Wild Czajkowski and Shiralee Hudson Hill, seeking to establish the educator's role today, find "the future of museum educators in interpretation" as one of challenging and resisting museum hierarchies, particularly those of the curator and a focus on art historical content. Czajkowski and Hill, "Transformation and Interpretation," pp. 259, 261. In contrast, de Montebello

criticizes the diminishment of the curator and calls for a public premium on expertise, the primary value of curatorial practice. Acknowledging the public as "key to the precious colloquy engaged by the principal players on the museum stage: the art, the curator, and the visitor," he urges public "confidence in the critical framework curators use in the selection of the art on view." De Montebello, "Art Museums, Inspiring Public Trust," in Cuno (ed.) *Whose Muse?* pp. 167, 168, 155.

42 Roberts, "Educators on Exhibit Teams," p. 99.

43 Responding to the tensions arising from the changing roles of curators and educators in the late 1980s, Danielle Rice locates their differences in ethical terms. She claims a special significance in the "moral duty" of the educator. "For the task that falls to the educator is to navigate through institutional contradictions in order to bridge the gaps between the value systems of the scholars who collect and exhibit art and those of the individual visitors who come to the museum to look at, and perhaps to learn about art." Following Roberts, we would argue that museums workers *together* "bridge the gaps" between different value systems. D. Rice, "On the Ethics of Museum Education," *Museum News* 65: 5, 1987, pp. 13–19, quote p. 17.

44 Lowry, "A Deontological Approach," p. 129.

45 Museum of Modern Art, "Director of Interpretation and Research," posted 19 October 2009. Online. Available HTTP: http://www.jobtarget.com/c/job.cfm?site_id=8712&jb= 6328540 (accessed 21 October 2009).

46 Roberts, *From Knowledge to Narrative*, p. 151. Acknowledging the "turf battles" between curators and educators, Jeanette Toohey and Inez Wolins claim: "Turf battles arise when staff members from different departments lack shared goals or values or lose sight of complementary skills or expertise and when divisions of labor create barriers to cooperation. The most notorious turf battles arise between curators and educators when both claim the interpretation and presentation of collections as major aspects of their job responsibilities." Their article outlines ideas to develop "effective partnerships" as a means to achieve a museum's commitment to the public through shared responsibility for audiences. J. M. Toohey and I. S. Wolins, "Beyond the Turf Battles: Creating Effective Curator–Educator Partnerships," in Hirsch and Silverman (eds.) *Transforming Practice* (essay originally appeared 1993), pp. 98–103, quote p. 98. In contrast, Hein observes that "the endeavor to achieve pluralism has a flattening effect that diminishes individual accountability. Nowhere is this more evident than in the demotion of curatorship to bureaucratic status. Denied their traditional authority and devoid of the passionate connoisseurship of the independent amateur, curators must now be client-oriented team players, harnessed to exhibition teams as 'resource persons.'" Hein, *The Museum in Transition*, pp. 142–3.

4

Museums and the end of materialism

Robert R. Janes

Introduction

It is common knowledge that the planet earth and global civilization now confront a constellation of issues that threatens the very existence of both. These issues range from climate change to the inevitability of depleted fossil fuels, not to mention the bewildering array of local concerns pertaining to the health and well-being of myriad communities throughout the world. There is nothing new about these challenges and there is a burgeoning literature which offers dire warnings and solutions for their resolution.[1] Surprisingly, museums are rarely, if ever, mentioned or discussed, causing one to conclude that the irrelevance of museums as social institutions is a matter of record.

I submit that the majority of museums, as social institutions, have largely eschewed, on both moral and practical grounds, a broader commitment to the world in which they operate. Instead, they have allowed themselves to be held increasingly captive by the economic imperatives of the marketplace and their own internally-driven agendas. Whether or not they have done this unwittingly or knowingly is immaterial, as the consequences are the same. It is time for museums to examine their core assumptions.

In making this sweeping assessment, I am, of course, generalizing, and I accept this liability as the starting point for reconsidering the underlying purpose, meaning and value of museums. These questions are rarely, if ever, truthfully examined in the museum literature or thoughtfully discussed at museum conferences. On the contrary, museum practitioners and academics are seemingly preoccupied with method and process – getting better and better at what they are already doing well.

Nonetheless, there are some essential questions worth considering, such as – if museums did not exist, would we reinvent them and what would they look like? Further, if the museum were to be reinvented, what would be the public's role in the reinvented institution? It has been noted that "the great challenge to our time is to harness research, invention and professional practice to deliberately embraced human values." The fateful questions, according to scientist William Lowrance, are "how the specialists will interact with citizens, and whether the performance can be imbued with wisdom, courage and vision."[2] None of these questions have been articulated by the majority of museums, much less addressed by them, despite there being no more important questions than these for both museums and society at large.

I have not set out to support or disclaim a particular theory, as the meaning of social engagement for museums is not only deep, varied and untested but it is also too unwieldy to be subsumed under a particular intellectual model. This potential variability is akin to the concept of the biosphere, where the diversity of life is the key to ecological health. So should it be with museums, where individual and organizational approaches to social relevance can be as diverse as the communities which spawned the museums themselves. Although my approach lacks a theoretical stance, I have drawn on various theoretical perspectives as both stimuli and counterpoints to my own thinking, including modernism, postmodernism, positivism and materialism. While theory plays an important role in any well-reasoned proposition, my bias is toward practicality.

If this chapter can be said to reflect any particular aspect of modern thought, it would be in the realm of the civil society, or the so-called public sphere. Simply put, the civil society is that part of society lying between the private sphere of the family and the official sphere of the state, and refers to the array of voluntary and civic associations, such as trade unions, religious organizations, cultural and educational bodies, that are to be found in modern, liberal societies. Museums belong in this sphere, yet have received little or no attention as fundamental agents in advancing the collective good, other than in the realms of education and entertainment. Although I have no theory to espouse, other than an abiding interest in social capital and the civil society, I also intend to debunk the imposition of free market ideology on the museum sector. I will do so by interpreting a collection of empirical observations and data based on my professional experience, the literature and my belief that it is incumbent upon us to question ourselves about where the future is leading – all in an effort to demonstrate that museums have far greater value than is currently being realized.

The turning point

Museums have inadvertently arrived at a metaphorical watershed where it is now imperative to ask broader questions about why museums do what they do, to confront a variety of admittedly unruly issues, and to forge some new choices. After decades of museum self-help manuals and collections of papers on museum studies, it is not enough for museums to do their work better – they have to ask once again what their real work should be. This metaphorical watershed is not unlike Peter Drucker's concept of a "divide." In his words, "Within a few short decades society rearranges itself – its worldview; its basic values; its social and political structure; its arts; its key institutions. Fifty years later, there is a new world."[3] Drucker noted that we are currently living through the transformation to a post-capitalist society, with knowledge being the real and controlling resource, not capital, land or labour.

In reassessing the purpose of museums, I have no intention of judging the conduct or commitment of individual museum workers. I ask the reader to recognize that there is an underlying paradox at work here, and resist the urge to dismiss many of these observations as judgemental. The inherent paradox is the widespread disconnection between individuals who work in a museum and the manner in which the museum functions as an organization. Individual staff members can be insightful and innovative, yet these qualities may never be translated into institutional reality. With this in mind, my purpose is not to challenge the commitment of any museum worker, especially in light of the multifarious and often contradictory requirements of museum work. These challenges include notoriously low salaries, high professional standards and governing authorities who lack relevant expertise, not to mention fickle funding agencies that encourage mission drift through their insistence upon short-term, project funding.

An ecological metaphor for museums

An ecological metaphor is useful here in pondering the role of museums in contemporary society, as ecology is about the relationships between organisms and their environments – including dependent, independent and interdependent relationships. Museums have predicated their survival on being both dependent and independent, as exemplified by commonplace comments such as "give us the money; we know what to do." In the process of overlooking the meaning of interdependence, museums have contributed greatly to their own marginalization. It is time to forge an ecology of museums that recognizes that a broad web of societal relationships is the bedrock of successful adaptation in a complex, and increasingly severe, world. The lack of interdependent relationships among most museums is an increasing liability, and being valued for ancillary educational offerings and often ersatz entertainment is no longer sufficient to ensure sustainability.

It is also no longer sensible to ignore the web of these relationships by claiming some sort of benighted status for museums as innocent beneficiaries. Can we not expect more deliberate reflection from museums about their societal role – as organizations that pride themselves on their historical acuity and their objective frame of reference? This means that the museum enterprise has an inordinate amount of rethinking to do, as the era of museum privilege begins to decline. By privilege I mean that paradoxical mixture of societal respect and indifference which has allowed museums to stand sedately on the sidelines in the service of their own self-interest. The decline in privilege is inevitable for the unprecedented reason that various social, economic and environmental issues have now transformed into a critical mass that can no longer be ignored by government, corporatists and citizens. In comparison, no such urgency attaches to the purpose and goals of the vast majority of museums, despite the fact that the status quo for museums is arguably even more brittle and beleaguered than it is for society at large.

The tyranny of the marketplace

One of the most significant challenges to heightened consciousness among museums is the rise of marketplace ideology and museum corporatism, whose uncritical acceptance by museum practitioners has created a Frankensteinian phenomenon that is unravelling or enfeebling a host of otherwise competent museums. There is no doubt that museums and galleries worldwide are struggling to maintain their stability in response to the complex challenges facing the non-profit world. These challenges range from declining attendance for many, and over-attendance for some, to finding the appropriate balance between public funding and earned revenues. Many of these challenges are inescapably economic, and originate in the belief that unlimited economic growth and unconstrained consumption are essential to our well-being. Indeed, capitalism and the lure of the marketplace have become inescapable for all of us.[4] The dominant ideology of capitalism and the decline of public funding for museums have combined to produce a harmful offspring – a preoccupation with the marketplace and commerce, characterized by the primacy of economic interests in institutional decision-making.

Corporatism

The other face of marketplace ideology is corporatism – based on "our adoration of self-interest and our denial of public good," to quote the Canadian essayist, John Ralston Saul.[5] He notes that corporatism also results in individual passivity, conformity and silence, because the corporatist system depends upon the citizen's desire for inner comfort. Instead, Ralston Saul argues that our individual and collective responsibilities in a democracy hinge upon participation and the psychic discomfort which inevitably accompanies active engagement in the public sphere. In his view, "the acceptance of psychic discomfort is the acceptance of consciousness."[6]

Contrary to "active engagement in the public sphere," many museums see no other way but to consume their way to survival or prosperity, failing to recognize that this is increasing their vulnerability as social institutions. This trend, in combination with the free-market worship of the consumer's supreme power, has made things very difficult for museums. This is all the more reason why museum boards and staff must seriously ponder a critically important distinction. That is, while we can acknowledge that the market is the key element in economics and in wealth creation, we are not bound to accept a free-market society where everything is to be achieved through the pursuit of private interest.[7] Corporations are second only to governments in their influence on public policy and have clearly demonstrated time and again that the common good can be an inexhaustible arena for private gain. It is obvious that the marketplace is incapable of addressing the collective good, while museums are potentially key agents in doing so. It is essential that museums become more conscious of the market forces they are embracing, in an effort to avoid the consequences described below.

Complex portfolios

The inappropriateness of unthinking adherence to the marketplace lies in the complexity of museums as institutions because every museum, in the language of the marketplace, is a mixed portfolio. Some museum work is clearly subject to market forces, such as restaurants, shops and product development, while other activities such as collections care, scientific research and community engagement are not. The latter bear no relation to the market economy and, in fact, require a safe distance from the marketplace and corporatist influence.

Market ideology and corporatism have failed to demonstrate any real ability to deal with the complexities of a competent museum and are, instead, homogenizing the complex portfolio with a stultifying adherence to financial considerations. The tyranny of quantitative measures, such as attendance numbers and shop revenues, is a clear indication of this reality. The failed relationship between museums and the marketplace goes beyond the clash of nonprofit and for-profit values, however, and includes several other embarrassing and injurious consequences. These afflictions include short-term thinking, money as the measure of worth, conspicuous consumption and business tribalism, each of which is discussed below.

The short-lived corporation

Recognizing that short-term thinking is the foundation of marketplace ideology, it is appropriate to note that the average life expectancy of multinational corporations is between 40 and 50 years, a discovery that provoked such alarm that an inquiry was undertaken to determine why.[8] The author of this work, Arie DeGeus, a senior planner at Royal Dutch Shell, concluded that the exclusive focus on the production of goods and services has doomed the vast majority of companies to rapid extinction. Most importantly for this discussion, DeGeus concludes that

> The twin policies of managing for profit and maximizing shareholder value, at the expense of all other goals, are vestigial management traditions. They no longer reflect the imperatives of the world we live in today. They are suboptimal, even destructive – not just to the rest of society, but to the companies that adopt them.[9]

Yet, these twin policies continue to grow in status and influence, and have now entered the museum boardroom in the guise of quantitative measures, earned revenues, excess consumption, hollow imitation and "the customer is always right" mantra.

Money as the measure of worth

Underlying the pervasive power of short-term thinking is the new orthodoxy of money as the measure of worth, and herein lies another significant clash in values. As difficult as it is to concede, the marketplace now provides much of our ostensible happiness and sense of worth, and museums are not immune. This has not gone unnoticed in museums, and there is concern about the advent of money as the measure of worth. Veteran museum executive Tom Freudenheim writes that "The money worm has burrowed into museum foundations in the last five decades, weakening structures already challenged by power politics, relevancy issues, and contemporary anxieties."[10] He further notes that "the idea of a museum … as a money-making machine is frighteningly pervasive."[11]

Similar anxieties are also emerging from the United Kingdom (UK), where the Museums Association (MA) notes that more and more museums are adopting the short-term, money focus characteristic of business. The MA's landmark report questions the sustainability of museums that occupy energy-hungry buildings, have expanding collections, and continually destroy old exhibitions with little reuse or recycling, while also promoting international tourism that involves energy-consuming travel.[12]

The so-called "Bilbao Effect"

The global museum community is currently enamoured with the "If you build it, he will come" syndrome, and this infatuation is heralded by the "Bilbao Effect." The "Bilbao Effect" refers to the Guggenheim Museum Bilbao (GMB), the architectural monument designed by Frank Gehry and rumoured to be the transformative agent in revitalizing the depressed industrial economy of the Basque region of Spain. In short, for urban planners, politicians, museum directors and trustees, the "Bilbao Effect" means "the transformation of a city by a new museum or cultural facility into a vibrant and attractive place for residents, visitors and inward investment."[13] Alas, the "Bilbao Effect" might well be an illusion, now that the boosterism is being replaced by evaluation and reflection.

In a recent article by Beatriz Plaza, an economist in the Faculty of Economics at the University of the Basque Country (Bilbao, Spain), we learn that the "Bilbao Effect" is not the magical solution so fervently hoped for by those in search of painless museum renewal. Contrary to the ardent believers who credit the GMB with transformative powers, Plaza writes that the GMB was part of a much larger economic redevelopment strategy which included a new subway line, new drainage and water systems, an airport, residential and business complexes, a seaport and industrial and technology parks. In Plaza's words, "The icing on the cake was the construction of the GMB and additional cultural investments, such as a concert hall and a centre for young artists to promote art and cultural tourism as a means of diversifying the economy and reducing unemployment."[14] Plaza's quantitative and qualitative analysis is in blunt contrast to the simplistic coronation of the "Bilbao Effect" – much heralded by directors, trustees, governments and consultants, as well as the celebrity architects themselves, as the solution to irrelevant museums, urban blight and economic renewal.[15]

There is no doubt that bold and creative buildings attract visitors and can provide meaningful visitor experiences, but these inducements are increasingly suspect and maladaptive, in a world beset by a host of social and environmental pressures – ranging from global warming to endemic poverty. The superficial truisms of the marketplace have proven to be not only inadequate as solutions, but also the source of many of our present difficulties.

Business tribalism

In addition to short-term thinking, money as the measure of worth, and culture as consumption, there is another feature of the marketplace that imbues it with considerable control and influence – the culture of business. This culture underpins the clash of values discussed earlier and is a dominant factor in blinding museums to a sense of their own worth and well-being. The origin of much of this difficulty lies in the tribal nature of business. By tribal, I mean a particular reference group in which individuals identify with each other through common language, ritual and legend.[16]

This tribalism sets values that orient the behaviour of individuals around common interests. Clearly, the culture of business and business literacy contribute much that is essential to our collective well-being, but that is not my concern here.

Business tribalism has several faces, including the celebrity worship of business leaders; in-group thinking that excludes non-business people; immature corporate governance which has created a litany of scandals, and narcissistic notions of personal worth as measured by obscenely high salaries and bonuses. Although museums have mostly avoided governance scandals and overpaid executives, many have nonetheless come to resemble corporate entities, with revenues and attendance being the predominant measures of worth. Many museum boards are increasingly indistinguishable from their corporate counterparts, with too many directors being chosen for their business, legal or accounting experience.

The market values and tribalistic traits discussed above are ideological, and remain alarmingly unexamined by the museum community. The trouble with ideology, according to writer and philosopher, Robert Grudin, is that it "enables us to pass judgments on a variety of issues while lacking adequate information or analytic skill or commitment to discovering the truth."[17] Museums cannot consciously evolve without analyzing their assumptions, no matter how deep and well protected these beliefs may be. Organizational self-knowledge requires that the ideology that governs purpose and values, both individually and organizationally, be made explicit.[18] It is imperative that museums embark on this journey of self-knowledge, not only to make practical sense of a beleaguered world, but also to define a meaningful contribution to an increasingly troubled world.

Methods aren't values

The distinction between methods and values recalls the characteristics of long-lived companies, which were also identified by DeGeus in his landmark study. These characteristics include sensitivity to the environment, organizational cohesion and identity, tolerance and decentralization, and conservative financing.[19] None of these defining factors have anything to do with commercial dogma or business literacy – they are values. It would seem that in the pressure cooker called the marketplace there is little or no time for values, even though values are the essential and enduring beliefs that articulate how an organization will conduct itself. Instead, values are replaced by imperatives – more visitors, more earned revenues, more collections, etc. I suggest that DeGeus' characteristics of long-lived companies could also serve as qualitative performance measures for museums.

In addition, classical economic theory and commercial dogma do not allow for the needs of future generations, because marketplace decisions are based on the relative abundance or scarcity of things as they affect us, now. Jeremy Rifkin, the economist and social critic, wrote: "No one speaks for future generations at the marketplace, and for this reason, everyone who comes after us starts off much poorer than we did in terms of nature's remaining endowment."[20] The marketplace notion that "the present is all there is" is antithetical to the very nature of museums, whose existence is predicated on the stewardship of posterity. A respectful sense of the future is required in museum planning and strategy, aided and abetted by business literacy, but not beholden to the values of the marketplace.

Museum renewal for a new age

The warning signs of our collective vulnerability continue to accumulate. These include population stress arising from differences in population growth rates between rich and poor societies; energy stress from the increasing scarcity of conventional oil; environmental stress from worsening damage to our land, water and forests; and economic stress due to instabilities in the global economic system (including the widening gap between the rich and the poor), as well as climate stress.[21]

All of these complexities can be distilled into a rather simple model of what could transpire as these events unfold. Jeremy Rifkin notes that "our modern economy is a three-tiered system, with agriculture as the base, the industrial sector superimposed on top of it, and the service sector, in turn, perched on top of the industrial sector."[22] Each sector is totally dependent on more and more non-renewable energy – fossil fuels. Rifkin posits that, as the availability of this energy diminishes, the public and private service areas will be the first to suffer, because services are "the least essential aspect of our survival." In short, an economy with limited energy sources will be one of necessities, not luxuries or inessentials, and will be centred on those things required to maintain life. Where do tourism, edutainment, museum shops, permanent collections and blockbusters fit in this looming adaptive model?

Museums are a public service, and the extent to which they will weather the above scenario is difficult to predict. In addition to the willpower required to reduce consumption, is the greater need to transform the museum's public service persona (defined by education and entertainment) to one of a locally-embedded problem-solver, in tune with the challenges and aspirations of the community. In a world of pressing local and national issues, it is commonsensical to expect that public funding will eventually go to environmental, social and economic priorities. Those museums that remain committed to consumption, edutainment and ancillary education will no longer be sustainable in this context. Many are not sustainable now.

Decline is not inevitable

What alternatives do museums have as the combined tyranny of traditional practices and the marketplace conspire to undo them? Renewal – rethinking, replacing and rejuvenating – is the only alternative, despite the hackneyed use of this concept. There is much lip service paid to this ageless and vital concept in organizations, but very little actual renewal. This is because authentic renewal is a tough and burdensome process, not a silver bullet. In effect, all people, organizations and societies start slowly, grow, prosper and decline.[23] Organizational decline, however, is not inevitable if museum boards and staff are willing to challenge assumptions and conventional practices, because this kind of thinking is the precursor to renewal. Renewal is also profoundly paradoxical, because it requires change at a time when "all the messages coming through to the individual or the institution are that everything is fine."[24] The fact that most museums think that everything is fine is the most salient reason for widespread renewal. As uncertain as the future is, there are at least six ways of framing museum renewal in this declining age of materialism.

Museums are free to choose and act

Museums, unencumbered with the public policy responsibilities of government and the destructive bottom lines of corporations, are agenda-free at the moment – with the exception of their tacit commitment to mainstream consumer society. The time has come for a particular "museum agenda," predicated on greater awareness of the world and the social responsibility that accompanies this awareness. Museums are some of the most free and creative work environments in the world, and there are few organizations which offer more opportunities for thinking, choosing and acting in ways that can blend personal satisfaction and growth with organizational goals.

For those boards and executives who claim a lack of autonomy with which to chart a course of greater awareness and social responsibility, there is no doubt that addressing the litany of social and environmental issues will require both courage and a leap of faith. Not surprisingly, society is not even cognizant of the museum's unique potential, much less demanding its fulfilment. This is ideal, for it permits museums to engage in deliberate renewal of their own design, but the time to do so grows short. Marketplace ideology, capitalist values and corporate self-interest are clearly not the way forward, having conclusively demonstrated their financial fragility and moral bankruptcy with the global meltdown of capital markets in 2008–2009.

Museums are seed banks

The technological present persists in disavowing much of the scientific, traditional and local knowledge that chronicles our species, and modernity has led to the loss of knowledge of sustainable living practices that have guided our species for millennia. Museums are the repositories of the evidence of our adaptive failures and successes, not to mention the chroniclers of our creativity and pathos. In this sense, museums are akin to the biological seed banks that store seeds as a source for planting, in case seed reserves elsewhere are destroyed.

If seed banks are gene banks, then museums are tool, technology and art banks – curating the most distinctive trait of our species – the ability to make tools and things of beauty. And to this priceless legacy we must add the trove of natural history specimens housed in the world's museums. Richard Fortey, a prescient paleontologist at London's Natural History Museum, has suggested that "Museums might now be considered the conscience of the world." He notes that their permanent collections "will be the only way to understand and monitor what we're doing to the world."[25]

The need to revisit this cumulative knowledge and wisdom may come sooner than expected, as the destruction of the biosphere renders industrial technology increasingly malevolent. The record of material diversity contained in museums may have a value not unlike biodiversity, as we seek adaptive solutions in an increasingly brittle world. Collections will be the key to examining the relevance of this material diversity in contemporary times, and will distinguish museums as the only social institutions with this perspective and the necessary resources. In this respect, museums are as valuable as seed banks.

Museums are diversity personified

The meaning of the word "museum" enjoys explicit name recognition everywhere, irrespective of language, and museums populate the world. There are 22,500 museums in Canada, the USA and the UK alone, and the World Bank estimates there are about 40,000 museums worldwide, although this strikes me as an underestimate.[26] Museums come in all shapes and sizes, with collections and mandates as diverse as human existence. It's as if there is a global museum franchise, only it is self-organized, has no corporate head office, no board of directors, no global marketing expenses, and is trusted and respected. Is this not the dream of every marketplace ideologue?

This informal network exists by virtue of the apparently universal need for museums, and museums are a significant antidote to the globalized homogenization that is the by-product of hyper-capitalism.[27] This homogenization is overpowering much of what was once unique and diverse in the natural and cultural worlds. With a global presence grounded in specific communities and cultures, yet united in purpose and tradition, the vast network of museums has untold potential for nurturing the diversity that underlies the integrity of the biosphere. The challenge will be for museums to collectively acknowledge that they are capable of defining the limits of homogeneity, and then embarking upon this task. Resistance and independence of thought will be essential to this renewal.

Museums are the keepers of locality

No one would dispute the fact that most of the world's museums are expressions of locality and community, and the world is full of museums because they are spawned by individual communities. The ubiquity of museums and the familiarity they enjoy are the building blocks of renewal, especially as the need increases to seek ingenuity and solutions on a smaller scale – in communities.

Wendell Berry writes that "the real work of planet-saving will be small, humble and humbling" and that problem solving will require individuals, families and communities.[28] The UK's Department for Culture, Media and Sport consultation paper, *Understanding the Future: Museums and 21st Century Life*, noted that, while globalization brings new opportunities for travel, cultural diversity and access to information, it also disperses communities and erodes traditions. This creates a greater need for community roots and values, and enhances the role of museums "by virtue of their unique ability to connect the local to the global and ... place personal beliefs within more general and universal truths, and historical settings."[29]

Museums are the bridge between the two cultures

The persistent fissure between the humanities and science, both symbolic and pragmatic, is an increasingly destructive tension in Western societies. It was brought to the attention of the world in two famous essays by C.P. Snow entitled *The Two Cultures: And a Second Look*, wherein Snow described the dangerous split between the humanities and the scientific community.[30] Snow argued in 1959 that Western society had become seriously fragmented, with scientists and non-scientists failing to communicate and working at cross-purposes, with no place where the two cultures could meet.[31] Canada's public intellectual, John Ralston Saul, also condemns the cult of expertise and specialization, and writes that "Such intellectual splintering explains some of academia's passivity before the crisis of the society they ought to be defending."[32]

Intellectual splintering also underlies museum passivity when, in fact, museums are one of the few knowledge-based institutions equipped to bridge the divide between the two cultures that continues to fragment our world-view. Although museums have borrowed the disciplinary boundaries of the academy, they are not bound to them for purposes of institutional identity and advancement. The very nature of any human, natural history, science or art museum demands inter-disciplinarity and holistic thinking, because they embrace multiple subjects and points of view, all of which are intimately interconnected.

Herein lies another opportunity for renewal – the possibility of museums becoming the meeting place for the two cultures. In the process, museums might well create a "third culture," along with other mindful individuals and organizations, by parting company with academic convention and offering a less splintered understanding of human presence in the biosphere. Museums are not only particularly suited for this renewal – the troubled world and its citizens are crying out for this leadership.

Museums bear witness

Wendell Berry writes, "One thing worth defending, I suggest, is the imperative to imagine the lives of beings who are not ourselves and are not like ourselves: animals, plants, gods, spirits, people of other countries and other races, people of the other sex, places – and enemies."[33] I am indebted to Marjorie Schwarzer, Chair of Museum Studies at John F. Kennedy University, for cementing the connection between Berry's aspirations and the relevance of museums. I can do no better than quote Schwarzer, who wrote:

> If not for the museological impulse, there would be NO memorials, NO resources and NO caretakers of the remnants of the kinds of history that our society's more evil impulses seek to destroy ... I'm saying all of this because I do raise this question: despite all of the missed opportunities perpetuated by poor and unethical museum practice, would the world be a better place without museums?[34]

Berry and Schwarzer are talking about bearing witness – an unsung role for museums but one that is unmistakably present. One need only consider the work of the International Coalition of Sites of Conscience as a powerful reminder of the need to remember past struggles for justice and to address their contemporary legacies.[35] The scope for bearing witness has expanded exponentially in recent times, however, and now includes an increasingly damaged biosphere, as well as the seemingly infinite catalogue of human rights conflicts and issues. Are not museums founded on "imagining the lives of beings who are not ourselves"? All museums specialize in assembling evidence based on knowledge, experience and belief, and in making things known – the meaning of bearing witness.

In search of resilience

Resilience means "the ability to recover from or adjust easily to misfortune or change," and suggests a frame of mind that is not bound by deadening routine, habit, or traditional practices.[36] Resilient systems are supple, agile and adaptable, and resilience is enhanced by "loosening some of the couplings inside our economies and societies," in the words of Homer-Dixon.[37] For museums, this means a serious appraisal of the current growth model based on building expansions, expensive exhibitions, growing collections and increased operating costs – coupled with the relentless imperative of visitor consumption in order to augment the earned revenues that are required to support the increased costs. This vicious cycle is unsustainable as discussed earlier, and decoupling may be the only solution.

The strength which ensues from a mix of sound business practices and social responsibility is qualitatively no different than the strength which emerges from species diversity in an ecosystem. For a museum to judge its performance on attendance and/or collection growth is analogically identical to monoculture food production, where only one crop is grown. This is not resilient; it's a high-risk strategy because that one crop may fail – just like blockbuster exhibitions commonly do. Yet, everyday we see museum boards, executives, troops of consultants and architects decreasing resilience by promoting more growth, bigger buildings and increased costs. This is brittleness, not resilience,

Our collective well-being requires enhanced resilience, and that all organizations (private, public, nonprofit and for-profit) contribute concepts, ideas, plans and alternatives for a better and more stable world, not to mention assistance in coping with the fears, constraints and issues that already exist. A surge of innovation, creativity and experimentation is urgently needed, and to assume that the majority of museums may somehow sit this one out is the embodiment of self-deception. The "long emergency" is now well underway, and will require no less than the shift from our "high-entropy culture" (the purpose of which was to create material abundance and satisfy every human desire) to a "low-entropy world" that minimizes energy flow.[38]

In our high-entropy culture, we have celebrated material progress, efficiency and specialization, and joined this with an unalloyed hubris that places our species at the centre of the universe. Fossil fuels have allowed this spectacular florescence of technological growth, but these days are numbered.[39] In contrast, the inevitable low-entropy world will recognize that excessive materialism and consumption are maladaptive and constitute an unacceptable assault on the biosphere. What role will museums play in expanding this awareness?

Assuming responsibility

Are museums up to this task? How many have actually contemplated their role and responsibilities as the world moves from energy consumption to energy frugality? Nearly three decades ago, Jeremy Rifkin made an observation that could serve as a touchstone for the strategic future of museums. He wrote:

> After a long, futile search to find out where we belong in the total scheme of things, the Entropy Law reveals to us a simple truth: that every single act

that occurs in the world has been affected by everything that has come before it, just as it, in turn, will have an effect on everything that comes after. Thus, we are each a continuum, embodying in our presence everything that has preceded us, and representing in our own becoming all of the possibilities for everything that is to follow.[40]

Is this not the eloquent mission statement of a competent museum? As self-professed keepers of the continuum and "all those acts that preceded us," can museums not be the harbingers of an adaptive future? The high energy paradigm, currently the foundation of our existence, must be dismantled deliberately and quickly, taking into account its social ramifications and indecipherable complexities. Are museums to wait for passive bureaucracies and faltering politicians, at all levels, to point the way? If museums are reluctant to assume these responsibilities in the absence of any authority to do so, then they must ask themselves from what source they think their authority will come.[41] Because museums will never be in control of society or their communities, waiting around for the authority to act responsibly is both heedless and fraught with risk.

There are simply no better social institutions than museums to help define a sustainable future, grounded as they are in a diachronic view of humankind's successes and failures. The current preoccupation of museums with growing collections and audiences, while confronted with the choice of outmoded tradition or renewal, heralds the metaphorical watershed discussed earlier. Museums have arrived at Peter Drucker's "divide," or that point in history "when society rearranges itself – its worldview; its basic values; its social and political structure; its arts; its key institutions."[42] Are museums to be active participants as these events unfold, or victims of an indecipherable myopia?

In praise of museums

This chapter has sampled the growing complexity in biospheric affairs and the seeming reluctance of the museum community to muster the will and innovation to address the issues and challenges that relate directly to them. The fundamental question is – what social institutions exist to address these challenges, recognizing the growing ineffectiveness of government bureaucracies and the wreckage of the corporate profit agenda? Even universities are becoming the handmaidens of corporatists, with science in the interests of consumerism driving many university research budgets. Museums, it is argued, are one of the few social institutions with vast potential for proactive and effective community engagement.

This challenge is not about a new business model for museums, however. Instead, it requires going beyond business models to reappraise the museum mission itself. Business models are about processes and the means to the end, including collecting, preserving and exhibiting. The contemporary challenge for museums is ultimately about the ends. In fact, the endless preoccupation with business models has become tiresome and harmful. This preoccupation with the "how"' is diverting museums from the real task at hand, which is to ask "why?", and become mindful of what is actually going on in the world around them, and then redefining their missions to reflect this new sensibility and purpose in appropriate ways.

Long live the museum

Paradoxically, museums have survived for thousands of years, unlike the bulk of corporate enterprises. In the process, museums have evolved from the elite collections of imperial dominance, to educational institutions for the public, and now to the museum as "mall."[43] The mall is the culmination of marketplace dominance, over-merchandised and devoted to consumption and entertainment. There is an important lesson in this historical trajectory, and it resides in the ability of museums to learn and adapt as circumstances require, however slowly. This ability is one of the characteristics of the long-lived companies discussed earlier, and can be described as organizations remaining "in harmony with the world around them" and reacting in a "timely fashion to the conditions of society around them."[44]

Now, and together with the rest of the developed world, museums have arrived at the dead end of materialism. This turning point for museums has evolved slowly, in the manner of the cabinet of curiosities becoming educational resources, but there is now much greater urgency to hasten renewal. Remarkably, museums have retained their core work of collecting, exhibiting and interpreting, irrespective of all of these historical iterations – a clear demonstration that core practices need not be relinquished as the environment changes. The sustainability that museums require cannot be achieved through education, entertainment and connoisseurship, but by sustained public benefit through the quality of the work they do, sustained community support through the commitment of the local community and an appropriate degree of financial commitment by the main financial stakeholders.[45]

In conclusion, the world is in need of intellectual self-defence as an antidote to the mindless work of marketers, the self-interest of corporatists and money as the measure of worth. Museums, as public institutions, are morally and intellectually obliged to question, challenge or ignore the status quo and officialdom, whenever necessary. With the exception of museums, there are few, if any, social institutions with the trust and credibility to fulfill this role.

It is time to honour this trust and broaden the purpose of museums to encompass critical thinking, mindfulness and social responsibility. Human adaptation lies at the heart of the current global challenges and all museums can help. Judging by the state of the troubled world and the urgent need for community organizations of the highest order, museums are positioned to realize their societal potential in a manner that truly reflects their inherent worth.

Acknowledgements

This article is based on Robert R. Janes' recent book *Museums in a Troubled World: Renewal, Irrelevance or Collapse?* (London and New York: Routledge, 2009). The author wishes to thank Matthew Gibbons, Editor for Classics, Archaeology and Museum Studies at Routledge, for permission to use this material. I am also indebted to Richard Sandell, Joy Davis and James M. Bradburne for their generous assistance and support throughout the research and writing of this book. I also want to acknowledge Priscilla Janes for her editorial assistance with this chapter. Janet Marstine invited me to contribute to this volume and I thank her for her initiative, commitment and unflagging support.

Notes

1 For several powerful overviews of the world's challenges, the reader should see T. Homer-Dixon, *The Ingenuity Gap*, Toronto: Vintage Canada, 2001; T. Homer-Dixon, *The Upside of Down: Catastrophe, Creativity, and the Renewal of Civilization*, Toronto: Alfred A. Knopf, 2006; B. McKibben, *The End of Nature*, New York: Random House, 2006; and E.O. Wilson, *The Future of Life*; New York: Vintage Books, 2003.

2 W.W. Lowrance, *Modern Science and Human Values*, London: Oxford University Press, 1986, p. 209.

3 P.F. Drucker, *Post-Capitalist Society*, New York: HarperCollins Publishers, 1994, pp. 1–8.

4 M. Kingwell, *The World We Want: Virtue, Vice, and the Good Citizen*, Toronto: Viking, 2000, p. 184.

5 J. Ralston Saul, *The Unconscious Civilization*, Concord, Canada: House of Anansi Press, 1995, p. 2.

6 Ralston Saul, *The Unconscious Civilization*, p. 190.

7 E. Hobsbawm, *On the Edge of the New Century*, New York: The New Press, 2000, p. 106.

8 A. DeGeus, *The Living Company: Habits for Survival in a Turbulent Business Environment*, Boston: Harvard Business School Press, 1997, p. 1.

9 DeGeus, *The Living Company*, pp. 15–16.

10 T. Freudenheim, 'Fifty museum years, and then some', *Curator: The Museum Journal* 50: 1, 2007, pp. 55–62, quote p. 55.

11 Ibid., p. 60.

12 M. Davies and H. Wilkinson, *Sustainability and Museums: Your Chance to Make a Difference*, London: Museums Association, 2008. Online. Available HTTP: <http://www.museumsas-sociation.org/asset_arena/text/al/sustainability_web_final.pdf> (accessed 2 July 2008).

13 G. Lord and M. Sabau, 'The Bilbao effect: From poor port to must-see city', *The Art Newspaper* 184, 2007, pp. 32–3. Online. Available HTTP: <http://www.lord.ca/Media/TheArtNewspaper32–33Museums.pdf > (accessed 7 July 2008).

14 B. Plaza, 'On some challenges and conditions for the Guggenheim Museum Bilbao to be an effective economic re-activator', *International Journal of Urban and Regional Research* 32: 2, 2008, 506–16, 507.

15 <http://www.lord.ca/Media/TheArtNewspaper32–33Museums.pdf>.

16 R.B. Lee and I. DeVore (eds.), *Man the Hunter*, Chicago: Aldine Publishing Company, 1968, p. 188.

17 R. Grudin, *The Grace of Great Things: Creativity and Innovation*, New York: Houghton Mifflin Company, 1990, p. 220.

18 Grudin, *The Grace of Great Things*, pp. 220–1.

19 DeGeus, *The Living Company*, p. 9.

20 J. Rifkin, *Entropy: A New World View*, New York: The Viking Press, 1980, p. 134.

21 T. Homer-Dixon, *The Upside of Down*, pp. 11–12.

22 J. Rifkin, *Entropy: A New World View*, pp. 217–18.

23 C. Handy, *The Age of Paradox*, Boston: The Harvard Business School Press, 1994, pp. 50–55.

24 C. Handy, *The Age of Paradox*, pp. 51–9.

25 Quore, R. Fortey, in J. Allemang, 'Save museums, they're the conscience of the earth,' *The Globe and Mail – Science and Ideas*, 20 September 2008, p. F8.

26 Canadian Heritage Information Network, 'World Museums', email (September 2008).

27 E. Hobsbawm, *On the Edge of the New Century*, p. 66.

28 W. Berry, *Sex, Economy, Freedom and Community*, New York and San Francisco: Pantheon Books, 1992, pp. 24–33.

29 Department for Culture, Media and Sport, *Understanding the Future: Museums and 21st Century Life*, p. 11. Online. Available HTTP: <http://www.culture.gov.uk/images/consultations/UnderstandingtheFuture.pdf> (accessed 26 January 2009).

30 C.P. Snow, *The Two Cultures: And a Second Look*, New York: Cambridge University Press, 1959 and 1963.

31 Snow, *The Two Cultures*, pp. 9–26.

32 Ralston Saul, *The Unconscious Civilization*, p. 174.

33 Berry, *Sex, Economy, Freedom and Community*, p. 82–83.
34 M. Schwarzer, email (July 2008).
35 International Coalition of Sites of Conscience. Online. Available HTTP: <http://www.site-sofconscience.org/about-us/en/> (accessed 5 July 2008).
36 *Merriam-Webster's Collegiate Dictionary*, 10th edn, Springfield, MA, USA: Merriam-Webster, Incorporated, 2002, p. 993.
37 T. Homer-Dixon, *The Upside of Down*, pp. 281–7.
38 The 'long emergency' is the phrase used by J.H. Kunstler to describe the decades ahead and the consequences of peak oil, climate change, epidemic disease, habitat destruction and so forth. See J.H. Kunstler, *The Long Emergency: Surviving the End of Oil, Climate Change, and Other Converging Catastrophes of the Twenty-First Century*, New York: Grove Press, 2005. The shift from a high-entropy world to a low-entropy world is taken from J. Rifkin, *Entropy: A New World View*, New York: The Viking Press, 1980, pp. 205–23.
39 Kunstler, *The Long Emergency*, pp. 22–60.
40 Rifkin, *Entropy*, p. 256.
41 R.R. Janes and G.T. Conaty, 'Introduction'. In R.R. Janes and G.T. Conaty (eds.), *Looking Reality in the Eye: Museums and Social Responsibility*, Calgary, Canada: The University of Calgary Press and the Museums Association of Saskatchewan, 2005, p. 12.
42 P.F. Drucker, *Post-Capitalist Society*, p. 1.
43 A. Gopnik, 'The mindful museum', *The Walrus*, 4 June, 2007, p. 89. This article is adapted from the 2006 Holtby Lecture at the Royal Ontario Museum in Toronto, Canada.
44 A. DeGeus, *The Living Company: Habits for Survival in a Turbulent Business Environment*, p. 6.
45 Foundation for Heritage and the Arts, *Annual Report*. Halifax, Nova Scotia, Canada: Foundation for Heritage and the Arts, 2000–2001, pp. 6–7.

5

Changing the rules of the road

Post-colonialism and the new ethics of museum anthropology

Christina Kreps

Introduction

Richard West, former director of the Smithsonian National Museum of the American Indian (NMAI), summed up the impact of post-colonialism on museum anthropology with this simple line: "the rules of the road have changed."[1] West was referring specifically to how research and scholarship on Native cultures at NMAI would be different from previous anthropological approaches, but his words carried much broader implications. They signaled a profound shift in the power relations vis-à-vis museums and source communities, or, "communities from which museum collections originate,"[2] and whose "voice" would be dominant in the museum. For West, it was not so much that the anthropological enterprise had been wrong, but, more so, was incomplete because it had not included the Native voice to any sizable degree.

This chapter examines changes that have taken place in museum anthropology[3] over the past thirty years or more as a result of the post-colonial critique of museums, and how these shifts have been engendering a stronger sense of ethical responsibility toward source communities as indigenous peoples have asserted greater control over how their cultural heritage is studied, interpreted and curated in museums. It considers several key developments: the process of decolonizing museums in Europe (specifically, the Netherlands) and settler nations like the United States and the passage and implementation in the US of both the National Museum of the American Indian Act (1989) and the Native American Graves Protection and Repatriation Act (1990). I discuss how these developments have fostered collaborative relationships between museums and source communities, giving rise to more culturally appropriate and ethically responsible museological practice. This is especially evident in new attitudes and approaches toward the treatment and repatriation of human remains and culturally sensitive objects as well as toward the revision of professional museum codes of ethics. Such trends mark a radical shift in the museum world from a primary focus on objects and material culture, to an emphasis on people and their relationships to tangible and intangible culture. As Besterman writes, "ethics defines the relationship of the museum with people, not with things."[4]

Taken together, these trends mark a humanistic turn in museum anthropology that places cultural and human rights at the center of museological discourse and practice.

They also signal a dramatic rethinking of museological ethics. It is now apparent that what has been considered ethically appropriate in one historical period and cultural context may not be in others. Museums should be concerned not only with "best practices," but also how practices need to be continually reassessed in light of new perspectives and ethical concerns.

Post-colonialism and the Post-colonial Critique of Museums

The term post-colonial has come to mean many things and encompass a broad range of topics, disciplines and theoretical approaches. For some, post-colonial simply refers to the period which begins with the withdrawal of Western colonial rule in overseas territories and during which former colonies became independent, roughly the 1940s and 1950s. However, others use post-colonial to describe all aspects of the colonial process from the beginning of colonial contact onward, emphasizing how post-colonial societies continue to be subject to neo-colonial forms of dominance. Hence, post-colonialism can be seen as a continuing process of resistance and reconstruction. The point of departure for post-colonial studies is the historical fact of European colonialism, and the diverse material and ideological effects to which the phenomenon gave rise.[5] Postcolonial theory and studies address the experiences of "migration, slavery, suppression, resistance, representation, difference, race, gender, place and responses to the influential master discourses of imperial Europe."[6] They also critically examine the effects of imperialism within "settler/invader" societies such as those of the Americas, Australia, New Zealand and other Pacific island nations.

Post-colonial theory has now permeated many fields, including anthropology and museology, although it initially was associated primarily with literary criticism. In the literary context, the term post-colonial described a body of work on the persistence of colonial representations of the non-European "other" and has largely concerned the critical analysis of discursive practices and cultural strategies of imperial institutions. The field was influenced most notably by Edward Said's seminal work *Orientalism* (1978). For Said:

> Orientalism is a style of thought based upon an ontological and epistemological distinction between 'the Orient' and (most of the time) 'the Occident' ... Taking the late eighteenth and nineteenth century as a very roughly defined starting point Orientalism can be discussed and analyzed as the corporate institution for dealing with the Orient—dealing with it by making statements about it, authorizing views of it, describing it, by teaching it, settling it: in short, Orientalism as a Western style for dominating, restructuring, and having authority over the Orient.[7]

Not surprisingly, post-colonial theory has had a significant impact on anthropology in general, and museum anthropology in particular, given the fields' colonial legacy and historical preoccupation with collecting, studying and representing "others." The post-colonial critique of museums coincided with the "reflexive turn" in anthropology in which anthropologists turned their gaze on their own work to interrogate power relations embedded in their discipline. Literature covering the post-colonial critique of museums as well as reflexive anthropology began to emerge in the 1980s, and is now extensive.[8] The post-colonial critique of museums problematizes the museum concept and museological practices, revealing their Eurocentric epistemological biases and assumptions; and how museum collections, as products and tools of colonialism, are embedded in power relations. Postcolonial museum theorists have been exploring questions like:

> What impact did the imposition of colonial power have on indigenous societies and on cultural production within them? How have objects imported or appropriated from colonies been displayed at the imperial centre? What impact do the power relations of colonialism have on the interpretation of objects? What are the possibilities for the display of 'colonial' objects in the present day and how can contemporary museum practice address the inheritance of colonialism?[9]

In addition to the scholarly community's critique of museums, source communities have also "encouraged an assessment of the positionings of museums within Western colonial culture."[10] As Nicks has pointed out, contemporary relationships between museums and source communities, "which can range from contestations over the interpretation and ownership of collections to the possibility of collaboration and shared authority, make sense when seen against the background of colonial histories."[11] Over the past several decades, source communities have challenged basic premises of conventional museological and anthropological paradigms. Most of the dramatic changes that have taken place in museums of anthropology over the past few decades directly linked to these challenges. Today, museums are urged to establish "on-going dialogue and partnerships with indigenous communities and to define a framework for respectful collaboration in the restoration of that inherent human right—the right to be the custodian of your own culture."[12]

Decolonizing Museums

The post-colonial critique of museums and the ensuing changes in ethics can be seen, on the whole, as part of an on-going process of decolonizing Western museums, defined here as a process of acknowledging the historical, colonial contingencies under which collections were acquired; revealing Eurocentric ideology and biases in the Western museum concept, discourse and practice; acknowledging and including diverse voices and multiple perspectives; and transforming museums through sustained critical analysis and concrete actions. The decolonization of museums has taken distinct forms and has been carried out at varying paces in different historical, national and sociocultural contexts. In several European countries some museums began to undergo decolonization some fifty or more years ago while in the Americas the process did not really get underway until the 1980s.

The Tropical Museum, or Tropenmuseum, in Amsterdam, for instance, was a product and tool of Dutch colonialism that, beginning in the 1950s, was transformed into an institution dedicated to increasing cross-cultural awareness and international cooperation. The Tropenmuseum's transition from a colonial to a post-colonial museum mirrored changes taking place in Dutch society as it confronted its colonial past and the changing nature of its relationships with former colonized people.

The forerunner of the Tropenmuseum was the Colonial Museum founded in Haarlem (1864) by the Society to Stimulate Trade and Industry. The Society promoted commercial interests in Dutch colonial territories, such as the Dutch East Indies, now the Republic of Indonesia. The Colonial Museum was designed to give the Dutch public a view of life in the colonies, both that of native populations and of the colonizers. Nineteenth- and early twentieth-century museum exhibits represented the production processes of export products such as coffee, sugar, rubber, textiles and so forth as well as ethnographic information on the people who made them. Exhibits highlighted native people's "simple" technology in contrast to the more "sophisticated" technology of the West. The ideology behind the exhibits was clear: colonialism could be justified on the basis of how it was bringing progress, civilization and development to the colonies. In short, how and why the museum exhibited non-Western people's cultures reflected colonial interests and ideology. Tony Bennett, in his often cited piece "The Exhibitionary Complex," describes how this was a common strategy of imperial displays:

> The effects of these developments were to transfer the rhetoric of progress from the relations between stages of production to the relations between races and nations by superimposing the associations of the former on the latter. In the context of imperial displays, subject peoples were thus represented as occupying the lowest levels of manufacturing civilization. Reduced to displays of 'primitive' handicrafts and the like, they were represented as cultures without momentum except for that benignly bestowed on them from without through the improving mission of the imperialist powers.[13]

In 1910 the Colonial Museum was moved to Amsterdam and merged with the Colonial Institute, which was primarily dedicated to research and training colonial civil servants, missionaries and others working in the colonies.[14]

After World War II and the loss of Dutch colonies, the Colonial Museum had to reorient its mission since its former mandate was no longer relevant. The Colonial Museum was renamed the Tropical Museum and became part of the Royal Tropical Institute (Koninkijk Instituut voor de Tropen) in 1950.[15] At this time, the museum's ethnographic purview expanded to include regions beyond former colonial territories such as Africa, the Middle East, South America and Southern Asia. During the 1960s, the museum also had to reassess its audience because, through television, print media and travel, museum visitors were becoming more aware of the economic, social and political realities of people living in so-called developing areas or the "Third World." Furthermore, people who were represented in the museum as colonial subjects in the past were now members of Dutch society. Consequently, the museum was pressured to bring its exhibits up to date and present a more realistic, contemporary and socially relevant picture of people's lives. Throughout the 1970s, the museum's exhibits and programming focused on the theme of development and exhibits took on an "emancipatory" and consciousness-raising approach, covering topics like poverty, education, agriculture, human rights and international cooperation.[16] The Dutch Ministry of Foreign Affairs/Development Cooperation became the museum's main source of financial support as it continues to be.

Over the decades, the Tropenmuseum has remained dedicated to working in the reflexive mode, periodically stepping back to reassess its mission, programs and exhibitions in light of its colonial past. In December 2008, the museum celebrated the completion of a ten-year, large-scale renovation project with an international symposium called "Tropenmuseum for a Change." Speakers from the Netherlands and abroad discussed the role and relevance of an ethnographic museum with such a prominent colonial legacy in the twenty-first century, and in the multicultural, globalized country the Netherlands had become.[17]

Two new, permanent exhibitions at the Tropenmuseum also address its history and the Dutch colonial past in general. "Netherlands East Indies" takes visitors through 350 years of Dutch colonial history, beginning with the activities of the Dutch East Indies Company, proceeding to the final years of colonial rule and the independence of the East Indies. The exhibition "Eastward Bound: Art, Culture, and Colonialism" focuses on the history and culture of Southeast Asia and Oceania, and, according to the museum's website, "contributes to today's debate on national and cultural identity and the relevance of colonial history to today's society."[18]

In sum, the Tropenmuseum continues to undergo decolonization by facing up to its past and taking a moral and ethical stance. It exemplifies how museums as social institutions and part of public culture do not exist as isolated entities in society, but evolve in response to shifting social values, mores and ethics. But the Tropenmuseum has not merely reflected these trends, it has also helped shape them as an agent of social change and consciousness raising—to many, an increasingly important role for twenty-first century, post-colonial museums.[19]

The decolonization of museums in the United States did not gain momentum until the late 1980s, although the Civil Rights movements of the 1960s and 1970s set the process in motion as African-Americans, Latinos, Native Americans and other ethnic minorities, as well as women's rights organizations, began to pressure museums to be more inclusive. The turning point for museum anthropology came with the passage of the National Museum of the American Indian Act (NMAIA) in 1989 and the Native American Graves Protection and Repatriation Act (NAGPRA) in 1990 by the United States Congress.

The Impact of the NMAIA and NAGPRA on Museum Anthropology

The NMAIA and NAGPRA are laws enacted to redress wrongs committed against Native Americans after centuries of contact with Western civilization and under conditions of internal colonialism.[20] Despite the many pitfalls and criticisms of both NMAIA and NAGPRA,[21] their passage and implementation has had a profound impact on museums and anthropology, and were a catalyst for decolonizing museums in the United States.

Although a formal apology and reparations have yet to come from the United States government for the genocidal policies inflicted on Native peoples, the NMAIA and NAGPRA can be seen as symbols of cultural restitution and a step in that direction. Cultural restitution is a process in which the historical conditions under which objects and remains were acquired are acknowledged and rectified through concrete actions.

The NMAIA's objectives were fivefold. In addition to authorizing the repatriation of Native American human remains and sacred and ceremonial objects held specifically in Smithsonian collections, it authorized the purchase of the collections of the Museum of the American Indian, located in New York City. The museum was founded by George Gustav Heye, a wealthy New York banker who amassed some 800,000 objects over sixty years of collecting. The collection was considered the largest body of Native American material ever accumulated by one person, and contained objects representing indigenous cultures from Tierra del Fuego to the Arctic.

The Act provided for the construction of a new museum in New York to house part of the Heye collection, plus a library of 40,000 volumes related to the archaeology, ethnology, and history of Native American peoples. This new museum opened in November 1994. The Act also funded the construction of a Cultural Resource Center in Suitland, Maryland, which opened in 1998. It functions as the museum's research and collections storage facility. The final component, and some would say the centerpiece of the Act, is the museum located on the National Mall in Washington, D.C. It is the first national museum solely devoted to the study, preservation and exhibition of the life, languages, history, arts and cultures of Native Americans.

The NMAI has been described as a "post-colonial," "decolonized" museum that offers a new paradigm for the interpretation and representation of Native peoples.[22] Opening on 21 September 2004, the museum was the culmination of some fifteen years of planning. For Rick West, founding director and member of the Southern Cheyenne and Arapaho tribes, it represents an opportunity for reconciliation and the recognition of the legitimate place of First Nations in the histories of the Americas. Facing the United States' Capital building alongside other Smithsonian national museums, the NMAI occupies a profoundly symbolic space. West saw the museum as a cultural and spiritual marker on the mall—a long overdue monument to the first nations of this hemisphere that celebrates their achievements and continual vitality. Certainly, one of the museum's goals is to dispel images of the "vanishing Indian" and other stereotypes of Native peoples, past and present, and to impress on visitors that Native cultures are still very much alive. Showing how the histories of Native peoples and Euroamericans are intertwined is also central to the Museum's mission.

The post-colonial museum is fundamentally about inverting power relations and the voice of authority. In the post-colonial museum the voice of authority is no longer that of anthropologists, art historians and professional museum workers, but the voices of the people whose cultures are represented in museums. At NMAI "Native voice," worldviews and philosophies have shaped nearly every aspect of the museum. In the following passage, West describes what Native voice means in the museum:

> Native people possess important and authoritative knowledge about themselves and their cultures, past and present, and deserve to be at the Museological table of interpretation and representation ... Exhibitions at the National Museum of the American Indian are developed in partnership with Native people. This practice is based on the belief that indigenous people are best able to teach others about themselves. Their understanding of who they are and how they present themselves to the world is what the museum calls 'Native voice.'[23]

Shannon, an anthropologist who conducted ethnographic research on the collaborative process behind the creation of the museum's exhibitions, states that "community curating is the method through which NMAI constructs 'Native voice' ... and gives the museum its legitimization as a Native museum, one which ethically presents Native voice."[24] In the process of planning the museum, staff met with more than 500 Native people from approximately 300 communities across the Americas to determine the design of the various facilities as well as the contents of exhibitions and programming.

In addition to presenting alternative ways of interpreting and representing Native cultures, the NMAI has been a leader in establishing guidelines for curating Native materials in culturally appropriate ways. These guidelines suggest how objects, especially those considered sacred or culturally sensitive, are to be handled, stored, conserved and displayed in accordance with Native protocols. Particularly significant is how Native methods of traditional care are being integrated into the management and care of collections through its "Culturally Sensitive Collections Care Program."[25]

At the Cultural Resource Center in Suitland, Maryland, one can see examples of how the philosophy behind traditional care is put into practice.[26] For example, objects may be arranged and stored on the basis of Native classification systems, which reflect traditional values and customs associated with the use and meaning of particular objects. Some are organized according to their gender or status while others are aligned to the cardinal directions, depending on specific tribal dictates.

To many Native peoples, certain objects are animate, living entities, imbued with a life force that must be appropriately cared for. Special provisions are made for these objects such as the construction of customized containers that allow them to breathe or be taken out periodically for ritual cleansing. To accommodate these practices, NMAI has created a space for the ceremonial feeding or smudging of objects and the performance of other rituals. This perception of objects as alive stands in sharp contrast to how objects have been conventionally perceived and treated in mainstream museums. It also shows how traditional care methods are intended to protect not only an object's material integrity but also its spiritual integrity, reflecting a particular community's religious and cultural protocols regarding the use and treatment of certain kinds of objects.

Access to some objects is restricted in keeping with tribal traditions and wishes. For some tribes, certain objects were never intended to be seen by all tribal members. Some can only be viewed or touched by men, others by women, while others only belong to the domain of particular clan members, societies, families, and so on. In this case, the museum may post signs to alert staff to the object's status. Similarly, knowledge about certain objects may also be restricted due to its sacred or secret nature. Only those who have earned or inherited rights to this knowledge are allowed to possess it.

Following NMAI's model of culturally appropriate and ethical curatorship, many museums, professional organizations and universities in the United States now have published guidelines for curating culturally sensitive, ceremonial and sacred objects, such as the Association of Art Museum Director's Report on the *Stewardship and Acquisition of Sacred Objects* (2006), *Stewards of the Sacred* published by the American Association of Museums and Center for the Study of World Religions at Harvard University (2004), and the Minnesota Historical Society's *Caring for American Indian Objects. A Practical Guide* (2004).[27]

In some museums, culturally sensitive materials as well as human remains are now separated from general collections and stored in areas where access is restricted to tribal representatives and designated museum staff. In many museums, human remains and culturally sensitive and sacred objects have been removed from public display as a requirement of NAGPRA and out of respect for Native wishes.[28]

The passage of NAGPRA was the culmination of decades of struggle on the part of Native American tribal governments, activists, lawyers and their supporters to protect graves against desecration, repatriate thousands of ancestral human remains and return stolen or improperly acquired property to Native Americans. According to Trope and Echo-Hawk, who were both involved in deliberations leading up to the passage of the Law, NAGPRA was landmark legislation because it represented fundamental changes in the attitudes toward Native peoples by the museum and scientific communities as well as the public. Although some see NAGPRA primarily as cultural property law, others, like Trope and Echo-Hawk, assert that "NAGPRA is, first and foremost, human rights legislation. It is designed to redress the flagrant violation of the 'civil rights of America's first citizens.'"[29]

The Act constituted a compromise among the different ethical principles, values and interests of the museum, scientific and Native American communities. And although the concessions made by the different parties can certainly be debated, the processes it created and actions it facilitated have taught us much about how to reconcile what can at first seem like irreconcilable differences. This is largely because the Act emphasized face to face consultations and negotiation, measures that have inadvertently opened doors to many unanticipated but fruitful outcomes such as greater dialogue, engagement and collaboration between museums and source communities.

Under NAGPRA, museums receiving any form of federal funding are required to comply with the law. In addition to protecting burial sites, it provides a process for museums and Federal agencies to repatriate Native American human remains, funerary objects, sacred objects or objects of cultural patrimony to lineal descendants and culturally affiliated tribes, as well as Native Hawaiian organizations.[30] NAGPRA also requires museums to make inventories of Native American and Hawaiian human remains and materials in their collections, and in consultation with tribal representatives and federal agencies to determine their "cultural affiliation." Museums are then required to make these inventories, as well as any pertinent information, available to respective tribes. Once tribal affiliation and appropriate ownership rights are proven, tribes may make a request for repatriation. As of 2006, 31,995 individual human remains, 787,781 funerary objects, 3584 sacred objects and 1045 objects of cultural patrimony had been repatriated to tribal communities.[31]

A number of museums had been working in partnership with Native communities on repatriation claims for years prior to NAGPRA and increasingly sought their input on exhibitions, educational programming and so on. However, there was no consensus within the American museum and scientific communities on repatriation nor laws to dictate practice. In fact, NAGPRA was enacted largely because of the perception that the American professional museum and scientific communities had not done enough to recognize the rights of Native people. As Richard Hill observed, "some museums, mainly smaller ones, responded immediately to the claims of Native peoples without requiring the force of law to compel them. But the Native American Graves Protection and Repatriation Act came about because many of the major museums would not address our concerns."[32] Thus, NAGPRA is an example of how a professional body's code of ethics can be inadequate in dealing with particular concerns, and how a law, in turn, can stimulate new ethical agendas. "The law is sometimes the last resort for those confronted by unethical acts."[33]

One of the many outcomes of NAGPRA is the growing presence of Native American curators, traditional scholars and advisors in museums. Native points of view are increasingly being heard and challenging conventional museological paradigms and practices. Greater collaboration between museums and Native American communities and the co-curation of collections and exhibitions has increased our knowledge of indigenous curatorial methods, or how communities have traditionally cared for, perceived, valued and interpreted their cultural heritage. These practices are expressions of a particular community's religious beliefs and cultural protocol pertaining to the use, handling and treatment of certain classes of objects and human remains.[34]

The practice of restricting access to and use of Native American human remains and culturally sensitive objects, for example, in research and exhibitions, has been one of the most contentious aspects of NAGPRA. Some believe restricted access goes against the idea of the museum as a public and democratic institution whose resources and collections are ideally accessible to all. Restricting access to collections as well as repatriating them to indigenous communities is disturbing to some who see these practices as anti-science and against academic freedom. To these constituencies, museums engaging in such practices are placing Native American religious beliefs and values above the values and ethical codes of the scientific community in addition to the public interest. But the public nature of museum collections and curatorial work, in general, is unsettling to many Native communities. For some, the whole concept of collecting objects to be seen, studied, cared for and displayed by people outside their community is inconsistent with tribal traditions.[35]

While some members of the professional museum community have opposed NAGPRA on legal and scientific grounds, others have embraced the opportunities it has opened to forge new partnerships with source communities. Collaboration between source communities and museums and the co-curation of collections has led to more culturally appropriate ways to manage and care for collections as well as a deeper understanding and respect for the values and meanings museum objects can hold for source communities.[36] Today, repatriation and the respectful treatment of human remains and culturally sensitive materials no longer revolve around questions about the ownership of cultural property. They are now largely viewed as moral and ethical issues that are increasingly being seen as part of people's cultural and human rights.[37] The key is continued interaction and dialogue through which all parties may discover shared ethics, values and responsibilities, or, if the case may be, come to an understanding that cultural differences exist and need to be respected.

Post-colonialism and International Museum Ethics

The decolonization of American museums and museum anthropology in the form of the developments described above has also been occurring in other settler nations such as Canada, Australia and New Zealand. Due to the physical presence and activism of indigenous communities, museums, government agencies and other organizations in these countries have been on the forefront of movements to create more ethical policies and culturally appropriate approaches to cultural heritage management.[38] The process of decolonization manifests itself differently in each country based on its historical relationships with indigenous communities; national, regional and local legislation; professional codes of ethics; individual museum policies and procedures; and the particularities of their own museum cultures. Similar to the situation with Native Americans, indigenous populations have been particularly concerned with the treatment and repatriation of human remains and culturally sensitive materials. In response, museums have developed policies and procedures under pressure from and in cooperation with indigenous communities.

European museums as well have been questioning the ethics of past practices regarding the treatment of human remains and culturally sensitive material. The Tropenmuseum, for instance, published Bulletin 375 *Physical Anthropology Reconsidered: Human Remains at the Tropenmuseum* in 2007. The Bulletin discusses the Tropenmuseum's collection of human remains as well as objects made with human remains based on an inventory of the Museum's physical anthropology collection acquired from 1914 to 1964. "The aim of this publication is to contribute to the debate about the significance of the physical anthropology collections around the world, taking the Tropenmuseum collection as an example."[39] By publishing an inventory of the collections the Museum hopes to "find a final resting place for these human remains because they no longer have any significance for us as an ethnographic museum."[40]

Debates within the international museum community on repatriation and the treatment of culturally sensitive materials have motivated professional museum associations to revise their codes of ethics to acknowledge changing attitudes and to provide guidelines for museums workers to follow. The 2006 Code of Ethics of the International Council of Museums (ICOM)[41] makes reference to human remains and culturally sensitive materials in Sections 2, 3, 4 and 6 regarding how these collections should be acquired, displayed, used and returned if a museum is requested to do so. For example, Section 2.5, "Culturally Sensitive Material," recommends that:

> Collections of human remains and material of sacred significance should be acquired only if they can be housed securely and cared for respectfully. This must be accomplished in a manner consistent with professional standards and the interests and beliefs of members of the community, ethnic or religious groups from which the objects originated, where these are known.

Section 6.2 suggests that "Museums should be prepared to initiate dialogues for the return of cultural property to a country or people of origin," and, in general, cooperate with source communities through the sharing of knowledge, documentation and other resources.

The American Association of Museums also includes in its Code of Ethics for Museums, adopted in 1993, a clause pertaining to the treatment of human remains in its section on Collections. It states: "The unique and special nature of human remains and funerary and sacred objects is recognized as the basis of all decisions concerning such collections."[42]

Codes of ethics are intended to guide behavior and set standards of ethical practice. They are not laws, and, in fact, generally call for standards of conduct higher than those set by laws. Professional codes of ethics are also considered living documents because they continue to evolve in response to changing values, situations and social movements. For instance, both the ICOM and AAM codes have been revised several times. In this respect, we can see how ethical codes are relative to particular historical, social, national and cultural contexts, just like ethical principles in general. As a case in point, ICOM makes clear in its Code that each ICOM member or member institution has the right to participate in ICOM according to their own national committees and standards. Implicit in this statement is that members are not necessarily bound to ICOM's Code of Ethics.

Conclusion

The rules of the road are certainly changing for the anthropological museum world. The post-colonial critique of museums and challenges from source communities have generated new paradigms for museological practice. But while much progress has been made over the past few decades in decolonizing museums and cultivating a greater sense of ethical responsibility toward source communities, the process has been uneven in both time and place as well as in the degree to which a museum is decolonizing. Some question if it is even possible for Western, mainstream museums to ever truly become decolonized, given their colonial legacies and their location in the power structure of dominant societies.

Lonetree contests the assertion that the NMAI is a "decolonizing museum" on the grounds that it does not present a clear and coherent understanding of colonialism and its on-going effects in its historical exhibits. The exhibits "fail to tell the hard truths of colonization and the genocidal acts that have been committed against

Indigenous peoples."[43] In this regard, NMAI stands in contrast to the Tropenmuseum which has been problematizing its colonial roots and legitimacy for decades through exhibitions, symposia, publications and international development aid and projects.

It is also important to keep in mind that what to some is a progressive development to others is old wine in a new bottle. Collaboration and "partnering" for some source communities are just alternative words for cultural appropriation and forms of neo-colonialism. As in all "contact zone" situations we have to consider what the terms of collaboration and partnership are and who is setting, defining and managing them.

Museum anthropology is still a politically charged arena, and perhaps this is how it should be because it is only through sustained critical analysis that the field can be continually transformed and reinvented to meet the challenges of the day. Despite the fact that Indigenous peoples have been a primary force in transforming and decolonizing museums, as well as moving us toward more ethical practice, they remain significantly under-represented in both the scholarly and public discourse on museums and in the professional museum and anthropological communities.[44] Full participation and inclusivity remain an ideal to which we continue to aspire.

Galla argued in his chapter "Indigenous People, Museums, and Ethics," published in Edson's *Museum Ethics*, that museums have lagged behind other social institutions in addressing social justice and human rights issues.[45] Recent developments are reversing this tendency, however. In the spirit of reconciliation and cultural restitution museums are grappling with our need to respect cultural diversity with the concomitant need to reach consensus on what constitutes ethical behavior and practice.

What we are witnessing is a humanistic turn in museum anthropology in which a history of detached scientific objectivity and aversion to politics is giving way to advocacy and engagement. This trend represents nothing less than a new sense of ethical responsibility to our core subject—humanity.

Acknowledgements

An earlier version of this paper was presented at the Indian Arts Research Center of the School for Advanced Research 2009–2010 Speaker Series "Intersections: Native Collections, Curation, and Museums" March 18, 2010, Santa Fe, New Mexico. I want to thank Cynthia Chavez Lamar for the invitation to speak and to audience members for their helpful comments. I am also grateful to my many colleagues at the Tropenmuseum, Amsterdam, for the opportunity to follow their remarkable work over the years and to participate in the December 2008 symposium "Tropenmuseum for a Change." Finally, many thanks to Janet Marstine for her steadfast work on moving ethics into the forefront of the museum profession, and for her vision and editorial guidance.

Notes

1 R. West, "Research and Scholarship at the National Museum of the American Indian: The New 'Inclusiveness,'" *Museum Anthropology* 17: 1, 1993, pp. 5–8.

2 L. Peers and A. Brown, *Museums and Source Communities: A Routledge Reader*, London: Routledge, 2003.

3 "Museum anthropology" is used here to refer to the subfield of anthropology devoted to the study, collection, interpretation and representation of material and visual culture, as well as the visual and performing arts, cross-culturally. It also refers to anthropological work in and about museums, including research, curatorial work and education. "Museum of anthropology," "anthropology museum," and "ethnographic museum" can mean any type of museum, i.e., art, history, natural history, ethnographic and so on that houses collections and materials (historic or archaeological) primarily from non-Western cultures. A concise definition is difficult because anthropology museums take different forms in different contexts. For example, in Europe "ethnological" or "ethnographic" museums, or museums entirely devoted to ethnology, are common. However, this museum type is less common in the United States (except perhaps at universities) where ethnographic and archaeological collections can be housed in history, natural history and art museums.

4 T. Besterman, "Museum Ethics" in S. Macdonald (ed.) *A Companion to Museum Studies*, Malden: Blackwell Publishing, 2006, pp. 432–441.

5 B. Ashcroft, G. Griffiths and H. Tiffin, "Introduction" in B. Ashcroft, G. Griffiths, and H. Tiffin (eds.) *The Post-Colonial Studies Reader*, London and New York: Routledge, 1995, pp. 1–4.

6 Ibid.

7 E. Said, *Orientalism*, New York: Vintage Books, 1978.

8 See M. Ames, *Cannibal Tours and Glass Boxes: The Anthropology of Museums*, Vancouver: University of British Columbia Press, 1992; T. Barringer and T. Flynn, *Colonialism and the Object: Empire, Material Culture, and the Museum*, London and New York: Routledge, 1998; T. Bennett, "The exhibitionary complex," reprinted in D. Boswell and J. Evans (eds.) *Representing the Nation: A Reader. Histories, Heritage and Museums*, London: Routlege, 1991, pp. 332–461; M. Bouquet, *Academic Anthropology and the Museum: Back to the Future*, New York: Berghahn Books, 2001; S. Butler, *Contested Representations: Revisiting Into the Heart of Africa*, Amsterdam: Gordon and Breach, 1999; J. Clifford, "Museums as contact zones" in J. Clifford (ed.) *Routes: Travel and Translation in the Late Twentieth Century*, Cambridge: Harvard University Press, 1997; J. Clifford, *The Predicament of Culture: Twentieth Century Ethnography, Literature and Art*, Cambridge: Harvard University Press, 1988; J. Clifford, "Objects and selves: an afterword" in G. Stocking (ed.) *Objects and Others: Essays on Museums and Material Culture*, Madison: University of Wisconsin Press, 1985; J. Clifford and G. Marcus (eds.) *Writing Culture. The Poetics and Politics of Ethnography*, Berkeley: University of California Press, 1986; E. Hooper-Greenhill, *Museums and the Interpretation of Visual Culture*, London and New York: Routledge, 2000; I. Karp and S. Lavine (eds.) *Exhibiting Cultures: The Poetics and Politics of Museum Display*, Washington, D.C.: Smithsonian Institution Press, 1991; C. Kreps, *Liberating Culture: Cross-Cultural Perspectives on Museums, Curation, and Cultural Heritage Preservation*, London and New York: Routledge, 2003; C. Kreps, "Decolonizing anthropology museums: the Dutch example," unpublished M.A. thesis, University of Oregon, Eugene, Oregon, 1988; C. Kreps, "Decolonizing anthropology museums: The Tropenmuseum, Amsterdam," *Museum Studies Journal* 3: 2, 1988, pp. 56–63; H. Lebovics, *Bringing the Empire Back Home: France in the Global Age*, Duke University Press, 2004; S. Macdonald and G. Fyfe (eds.) *Theorizing Museums: Representing Identity and Diversity in a Changing World*, Oxford: Blackwell Publishers, 1996; J. Marstine (ed.) *New Museum Theory and Practice: An Introduction*, Malden: Blackwell Publishers, 2006; Peers and Brown, *Museums and Source Communities*; M. Simpson, *Making Representation: Museums in the Post-colonial Era*, London and New York: Routledge, 1996; G. Stocking (ed.) *Colonial Situations: Essays on the Contextualization of Anthropological Knowledge*, Madison: University of Wisconsin Press, 1992; N. Thomas, *Colonialism's Culture: Anthropology, Travel and Government*, Princeton: Princeton University Press, 1994.

9 Barringer and Flynn, *Colonialism and the Object*, p. 1.

10 T. Nicks, "Introduction," in Peers and Brown, *Museums and Source Communities*, p. 20.

11 Ibid., p. 30.

12 E. Arrinze and A. Cummins (eds.) *Curatorship: Indigenous Perspectives in Post-Colonial Socie-ties*. Directorate Paper no. 8, Canadian Museum of Civilization, the Commonwealth Association of Museums, and the University of British Columbia, 1996, p. 7.

13 Bennett, "The exhibitionary complex," pp. 353–354.

14 See J. Ave, "Ethnographical museums in a changing world" in *From Fieldcase to Showcase*, W. Van Gulik and H. Den Straaten (eds.), Amsterdam: J. C. Grieben, 1980, pp. 11–58; H. Frese, *Anthropology and the Public: The Role of Museums*, Leiden: The Netherlands, 1960.

15 The museum is just one component of the Royal Tropical Institute, which conducts research in the field of international development and offers advisory and consultancy services; provides training and offers courses; and houses one of the world's largest libraries specializing in the tropics.

16 Material presented here on the Tropenmuseum is based on research conducted in the Netherlands in 1987 on the history of Dutch ethnographic museums. This research cul-minated in my thesis *Decolonizing Anthropology Museums*. Follow up research was carried out in subsequent visits in 1999, 2005 and 2008.

17 See the museum's website for video presentations and more information on the sympo-sium. Online. Available HTTP: www.tropenmuseum.nl (accessed 2 May 2010). See also D. Van Dartel (ed.) *Tropenmuseum for a Change! Present Between Past and Future: A Symposium Report*, Bulletin 391. Amsterdam: KIT Publishers, 2009. I was invited to participate in the symposium based on my long-standing research on the museum and its historical devel-opment. Thus, I participated in the symposium discussions and visited the exhibitions described in the text.

18 Online. Available HTTP: http.www.tropenmuseum.nl (accessed 23 July 2009).

19 See R. Janes, *Museums in a Troubled World. Renewal, Irrelevance or Collapse?* London: Routledge, 2009; R. Sandell (ed.) *Museums, Society, Inequality*, London: Routledge, 2002.

20 J. Trope and W. Echo-Hawk, "The Native American Graves Protection and Repatriation Act" in D. Mihesuah (ed.) *Repatriation Reader: Who Owns Native American Remains?* Lincoln: University of Nebraska Press, 2000, p. 21.

21 For critical analysis of the NMAI and NAGPRA see K. Fine-Dare, *Grave Injustice: The American Indian Repatriation Movement and NAGPRA*, Lincoln: University of Nebraska Press, 2002; C. Fluehr-Lobban (ed.) *Ethics and the Profession of Anthropology. Dialogue for Ethically Conscious Practice*, Walnut Creek: AltaMira Press, 2003; A. Lonetree and A. Cobb (eds.) *The National Museum of the American Indian: Critical Conversations*, Lincoln: University of Nebraska Press, 2008; T. McKeown, "Considering repatriation legislation as an option: The National Museum of the American Indian Act (NMAIA) and the Native American Graves Protection and Repatriation Act (NAGPRA)" in M. Gabriel and J. Dahl (eds.) *Utimut. Past Heritage-Future Partnerships.* Copenhagen: IWGIA/NKA, 2008; S. Sleeper-Smith (ed.) *Contesting Knowledge: Museums and Indigenous Perspectives*, Lincoln: University of Nebraska Press, 2009; J. Watkins, "Who's right and what's left on the middle ground?" in M. Gabriel and J. Dahl (eds.) *Utimut*, pp. 100–107.

22 C. Smith, "Decolonising the museum: the National Museum of the American Indian in Washington, D.C.," *Antiquity* 79: 2005, pp. 424–439.

23 Quoted in J. Shannon, "The construction of native voice at the National Museum of the American Indian," in S. Sleeper-Smith (ed.) *Contesting Knowledge*, pp. 232–233.

24 Ibid., pp. 219, 222.

25 See L. Sullivan and A. Edwards (eds.) *Stewards of the Sacred*, Washington, D.C.: American Association of Museums in cooperation with the Center for the Study of World Religions, Harvard University, 2004, p. 129.

26 G. Flynn and D. Hull-Walski, "Merging traditional indigenous curation methods with modern museum standards of care," *Museum Anthropology* 25: 1, 2001, pp. 31–40; N. Rosoff, "Integrating Native views into museum procedures: hope and practice at the National Museum of the American Indian," *Museum Anthropology* 22: 1, 1998, pp. 33–42; L. Sullivan and A. Edwards, *Stewards of the Sacred*.

27 It is important to note, however, that there is no standard way of curating Native Amer-ican materials because each tribe has its own methods of traditional care and cultural protocol, making consultation an essential element of the curatorial process.

28 See V. Cassman, N. Odegaard and J. Powell (eds.) *Human Remains: Guide for Museums and Academic Institutions*, Lanham, MD: AltaMira Press, 2007.

29 J. Trope and W. Echo-Hawk, "The Native American Graves Protection and Repatriation Act," p. 22.

30 For definitions of terms see the National Park Service website. Online. Available HTTP: http:www.nps.gov/history/nagpra (accessed 2 May 2010).

31 Online. Available HTTP: http:www.nps.gov/history/nagpra (accessed 25 July 2009).

32 R. Hill, "Regenerating identity: repatriation and the Indian frame of mind" in T. Bray (ed.) *The Future of the Past: Archaeologists, Native Americans and Repatriation*, New York: Garland Publishers, 2001, p. 315.

33 G. Edson, "Ethics" in G. Edson (ed.) *Museum Ethics*, London and New York: Routledge, 1997, p. 27.

34 See C. Kreps, *Liberating Culture*.

35 See P. Parker, *Keepers of the Treasures: Protecting Historic Properties and Cultural Traditions on Indian Lands*, Washington, D.C.: National Park Service, United States Department of the Interior, 1990.

36 C. Kreps, "Appropriate museology in theory and practice," *International Journal of Museum Management and Curatorship* 1: 23, 2008, p. 23.

37 See M. Gabriel and J. Dahl, *Utimut*.

38 M. Clavir, *Preserving What is Valued: Conservation and First Nations*, Vancouver: University of British Columbia Press, 2002; A. Herle, "Objects, agency and museums: continuing dialogues between the Torres Strait and Cambridge" in Peers and Brown, *Museums and Source Communities*, p. 194; T. Hill and T. Nicks, "The task force on museums and First Peoples," *MUSE* 10: 2-3, 1992, p. 81; H. Morphy, "Sites of persuasion: Yingapungapu at the National Museum of Australia" in I. Karp and C. Kratz (eds.) *Museum Frictions. Public Cultures/Global Transformations*, Durham, North Carolina: Duke University Press, 2006, p. 469; R. Phillips, "Commemoration/(de)celebration: super-shows and the decolonization of Canadian museums, 1967-92" in B. Gabriel and S. Ilcan (eds.) *Post-Modernism and the Ethical Subject*, London: McGill-Queen's University Press, 2004, pp. 99–124; M. Simpson, *Making Representations*.

39 D. Van Duuren et al., *Physical Anthropology Reconsidered. Human Remains at the Tropenmuseum*, Bulletin 375, Amsterdam: Koninklijk Instituut voor den Tropen, 2007.

40 Ibid., p. 9.

41 The International Council of Museums (ICOM) operates under the auspices of the United Nations Educational, Scientific, and Cultural Organization (UNESCO). It is an international, non-governmental organization of professional museum workers dedicated to the improvement and advancement of the world's museums, the museum profession and museological interests. ICOM's headquarters is located in Paris, France.

42 American Association of Museums Code of Ethics for Museums 2000, p. 8. Online. Available HTTP: http://www.aam-us.org/museumresources/ethics/upload/Code-of-Ethics-for-Museums.pdf (accessed 29 April 2010).

43 A. Lonetree, "Museums as sites of decolonization. truth telling in national and tribal museums" in Sleeper-Smith, *Contesting Knowledge*, pp. 322–337.

44 See P. Smith, *Everything You Know about Indians is Wrong*, Minneapolis: University of Minnesota Press, 2009.

45 A. Galla, "Indigenous peoples, museums, and ethics" in Edson, *Museum Ethics*, pp. 142–55.

6

"Aroha mai: Whose museum?"

The rise of indigenous ethics within museum contexts: A Maori-tribal perspective

Paul Tapsell

Introduction

This essay is written primarily from a Maori-tribal (kin-accountable) position for an academic/scholarly audience. It remains cognizant of other disciplinary views and perspectives, not least a wider indigenous readership. It provides a discussion of the rise of indigenous ethics (principles) and associated tensions within an Aotearoa/New Zealand museum context. I offer a three-way hybrid perspective[1] based on my identities as: indigenous community member (kinship); academically trained museum professional (museology); and former museum executive (office).

In 2009, I returned to full-time academia after eight years at the Auckland Museum/Tamaki Paenga Hira (AWMM).[2] This change in focus provided me the opportunity to comment reflexively upon practices and principles within New Zealand's two major museums and take stock of current directions.[3] In particular, I was interested in the key principles that are apparently driving the relatively new practice of formalized indigenous collaboration in nation-spaces. National museum projects in other colonized nations (for example, the National Museum of Australia and the National Museum of the American Indian) have observed the development/redevelopment of New Zealand's two international museums: Te Papa (the national Museum of New Zealand in the capital city of Wellington, which reopened in 1998 in a new building) and Auckland Museum (opened in 1852, but revitalized in 1996 under new legislation: AWMM Act 1996). They have established very different approaches to engaging with *Maori* (the indigenous peoples of New Zealand). As these key nation-space institutions of memory resettle into their third decade of (re) displaying Maori culture to the world, it appears timely to examine critically how inherently indigenous principles associated with material culture are being maintained, valued and ethically integrated into wider museum governance and operations. This essay draws on Maori values and experiences using the above two museums as a platform from which wider indigenous ethics in post-colonial museum contexts – nationally and internationally – may be discussed. What crisis/critical event(s) triggered the inclusion of Maori values in museums? And who (insiders/outsiders) is defining and maintaining associated boundaries? How are these boundaries being (re)negotiated to continually remain relevant and to whom?

This essay begins by discussing the relationship between source communities and their associated values, especially in museological terms. By way of example, it then provides a general overview of the Maori knowledge system to assist the development of cross-cultural understanding within museum contexts. This is followed by a Maori perspective on values relating to their museum-held ancestors, then a discussion of the triggers that brought Maori into museums in the 1980s. The paper finishes by considering an example of a recent Maori touring exhibition and exploring what role indigenous ethics (kinship) might yet play in the future of museum governance (office).

As this essay provides a uniquely Maori-tribal perspective it inevitably draws on the Maori language from time to time, as understood by my Ngati Whakaue-Te Arawa relations at home (see Figure 6.2), to better describe particular values that symbolically capture the essence of underlying principles being discussed. A glossary of terms is provided at the end of the essay for easy reference.

Source communities: source values

Within the professional practice of museology, the concept and use of the term "source community" appears to have become widely adopted.[4] This recognition seems to indicate museums' general willingness to develop collaborative relationships with the indigenous groups from which museum-held objects originated, especially regarding ongoing care, research, publication and exhibition. In particular, community-led exhibitionary projects have been developing to a sophisticated level in Australia and North America. Curators have successfully activated source community engagement, taking on the role of knowledge facilitators, rather than authoritative experts,[5] and radically shifting museums from colonial disengagement to "cooperative museology".[6] Through this more transparent, inclusive approach, knowledgeable community elders have become empowered and recognized as co-producers *or* co-researchers,[7] directly involved in reviewing museum-controlled knowledge and actively participating in the redistribution of authority.[8] Out of this exhibitionary interpretation of the indigenous "other" has emerged the idea of cross-cultural contact zones,[9] or what Nicks has more recently coined trans-cultural spaces.[10]

Not yet fully explored in museological discourse is the equally important ancestral relationship by which museum-held objects are "valued" within their respective source communities. By becoming more aware of underpinning source values (ethics/principles) that originally governed any particular object, item or thing,[11] museums are more likely to curate exhibitions built on purposeful source community engagement. The New Zealand Museums' Code of Ethics has come some way in recognizing the importance of developing operational partnerships with Maori communities, especially concerning access, use, loans, ownership, human remains, staff employment, *koha* (cultural presents) and visitation.[12] However, the crossroads at which museums in New Zealand appear to have arrived is whether they are really prepared to share their exhibitionary power from the ground up with *tangata whenua* (local Maori communities) on which each institution stands. Is *office* (ownership; museum values) willing to accommodate *kinship* (belonging; indigenous values) so each may co-exist and complement one another within museums' overall governance and operations?

Whakapapa: philosophy of kinship

This essay opens with an illustration of *Te Kaoreore* (Figure 6.1), who rests in the Auckland Museum. He represents my tribal peoples' great ancestor, Ngahue, and, when performed[13] in appropriate kin-contexts, he has the almost magic-like ability of collapsing generations of time so that it is Ngahue himself who is standing before my tribal community, Ngati Whakaue-Te Arawa. For them, *Te Kaoreore* is the tangible embodiment of Ngahue's momentous event that occurred some 30 generations ago, enabling tribal survival. To better understand how such moments are recreated, and why, it is important to provide a brief overview of the indigenous (kinship) value system, called *whakapapa*, a philosophical system of ordering the universe that originated out of an ancient Pacific voyaging culture.[14]

In a museum context, my experience and observations since 1990 suggest that, if a curator comes to understand well Maori source values, then s/he has a far better chance of successfully engaging source communities or *tangata whenua* and co-producing a uniquely Maori-museum experience that all audiences – including the community itself – can appreciate. A good understanding of source values encapsulated by the concept of *whakapapa* is also important to ensure appropriate representation of both the physical items and the values ascribed by their creators and communities.

Whereas the museum perceives an audience in 'the now', it is highly likely that the community elders they are engaging are equally motivated by the cultural need to address a perceived audience of future descendants, but with care to what precedents have transpired in their tribally-maintained past. In other words: ancestral accountability, meaning any actions in the present, need to remain in alignment with past generations' leadership decisions, while maintaining continuity into the future.

The Maori tribal view of the universe is ordered according to *whakapapa*, the genealogical layering (weaving) of knowledge, both vertically – *mana* (exclusive ancestral authority or what anthropologists would describe as descent) and horizontally – *whakawhanaungatanga* (inclusive familial ties or kinship). However, *whakapapa* is more than vertical or horizontal memory lists of ancestors. It is the way by which tribal Maori systematically order themselves and their relationship to customary estates (for example, their lands, forests and waterways) in distinction to all others. Over time, prestigious ancestors, descendants and estates become genealogically fused as one identity, which is symbolically expressed by tribal name and *marae* (ancient ritualized space at the heart of Maori tribal communities). For example, my tribal community, *Ngati* Whakaue, translates as *"the people of the ancestor named* Whakaue" and our 600 hundred-year-old marae *Te Papa-i-Ouru* (see Figure 6.2 below) symbolically focuses our (Whakaue's) ancestral authority over the surrounding estates of Lake Rotorua.

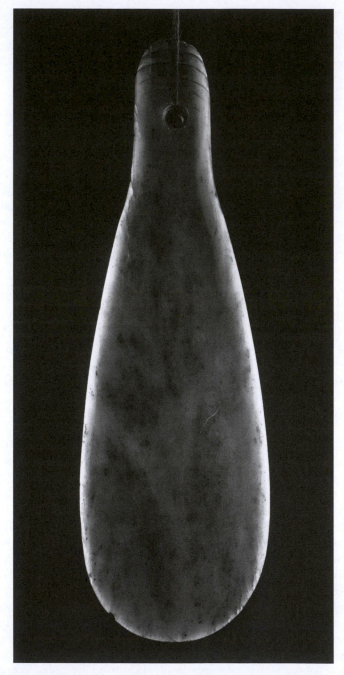

Figure 6.1 Te Kaoreore. Prized Ngati Whakaue weapon shaped from an ancient slab of *pounamu* (greenstone: nephrite). This slab was fetched by Ngahue on his voyage of discovery to Aotearoa (New Zealand) some 30 generations ago and taken back to the ancient home island of Ra'iatea (Near Tahiti). Photograph, Krzysztof Pfeiffer, Auckland Museum.

Figure 6.2 Tama te Kapua. Ngati Whakaue-Te Arawa in front of their carved ancestral house, Tama te Kapua, welcoming visitors onto Te Papa-i-Ouru marae (courtyard) in the centre of Ohinemutu village, Rotorua. Photograph, Krzysztof Pfeiffer, Auckland Museum.

In Figure 6.3 and Figure 6.4 (below), the narrative explaining these *whakapapa* derives from private writings and discussions of Ngati Whakaue's late tribal leaders Pateriki te Rei, Hamuera Mitere and Hikooterangi Hohepa.[15] From a Maori tribal worldview, they saw *whakapapa* as the accepted Maori way by which time is ordered, beginning with *Te Kore* (the infinite epoch of nothingness) through to the emergence of consciousness itself represented by *Io Matua Kore* (the parentless one). From that point many more vast epochs passed, out of which energy evolved into light, giving birth to the father of heavens, *Rangi Nui* (Sky Father). Evolving in parallel was the potential to create, by which darkness became night, manifesting herself as *Papa tu a Nuku* (Earth Mother). With their union the many elements of life were conceived, culminating in the elder son, *Tane* (creator of trees, biosphere and the first humans; and fetcher of divine knowledge), thrusting apart his parents, *Rangi* and *Papa*, to enable light to enter our world (*Te Ao Marama*). *Tane's* many siblings also became *atua* (gods, supreme beings) responsible for generating 70 distinct elements of existence, constituting the whole universe. Through another of *Tane's* deeds, two descent lines of consciousness evolved, one line representing *hapu atua* (celestial descent) under the care of *Rangi* and the other being *hapu oneone* (earthly descent) under the protection of *Papa*. From time to time, these two flows of conscious thought met and begat demi-gods such as *Rua, Tawhaki, Rata* and *Maui* who emerged as moral 'heroes'. These ancestral 'heroes' provide narrative-driven life lessons and codes of behaviour concerning respect for ancestors and the environment

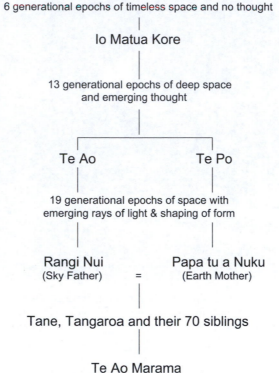

Figure 6.3   Abbreviated *whakapapa* of creation according to Ngati Whakaue-Te Arawa traditions.

(*heritage*), balanced by the need to continually seek out new benefit for wider kin (*opportunity*), to ensure cross-generational survival – continuing access to resources.[16]

From the time of *Maui*, another thirty or more generations passed before a new period of exploring ancestors came to dominate the Pacific (Figure 6.4). The adventures of these more recent heroes originate out of Taputapuatea, located on the island of Ra'iatea (west of Tahiti). Taputapuatea is one of the oldest and most important of all *marae*, or ritual tribal courtyards that can be found in various forms throughout the Pacific. Heroes including Nukutawhiti, Kupe and Ngahue departed Taputapuatea and came to provide the founding layers of *waka* (canoe)-voyaging narratives that remain embedded in today's Eastern Polynesian culture. Ngahue explored further south than his contemporaries, retrieving the famous slab of nephrite (*pounamu*/greenstone) from Te Wai Pounamu (South Island of New Zealand), which back in Ra'iatea was shaped into the great *toki* (axe), *Tutuaru*, and was eventually used to carve the *Arawa waka*. Also created from the same slab were *Te Kaoreore* (see opening Figure 6.1) and a number of other famous ancestral treasures

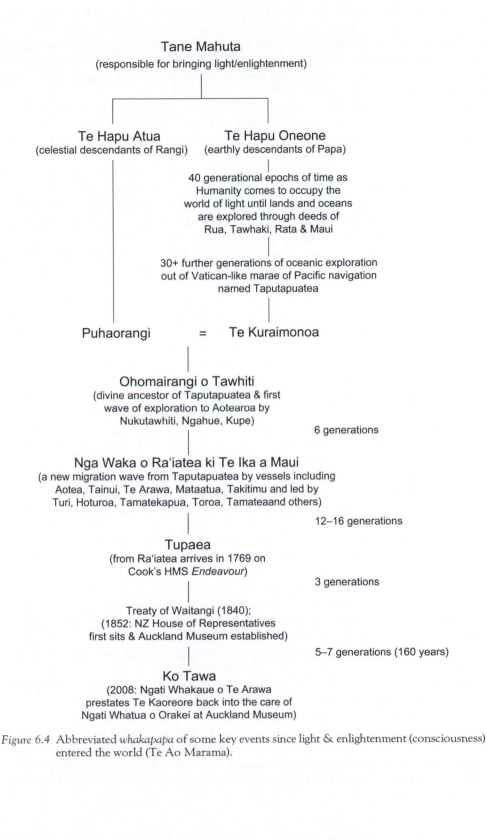

Tane Mahuta
(responsible for bringing light/enlightenment)

Te Hapu Atua
(celestial descendants of Rangi)

Te Hapu Oneone
(earthly descendants of Papa)

40 generational epochs of time as
Humanity comes to occupy the
world of light until lands and oceans
are explored through deeds of
Rua, Tawhaki, Rata & Maui

30+ further generations of oceanic exploration
out of Vatican-like marae of Pacific navigation
named Taputapuatea

Puhaorangi   =   **Te Kuraimonoa**

Ohomairangi o Tawhiti
(divine ancestor of Taputapuatea & first
wave of exploration to Aotearoa by
Nukutawhiti, Ngahue, Kupe)

6 generations

Nga Waka o Ra'iatea ki Te Ika a Maui
(a new migration wave from Taputapuatea by vessels including
Aotea, Tainui, Te Arawa, Mataatua, Takitimu and led by
Turi, Hoturoa, Tamatekapua, Toroa, Tamateaand others)

12–16 generations

Tupaea
(from Ra'iatea arrives in 1769 on
Cook's HMS *Endeavour*)

3 generations

Treaty of Waitangi (1840);
(1852: NZ House of Representatives
first sits & Auckland Museum established)

5–7 generations (160 years)

Ko Tawa
(2008: Ngati Whakaue o Te Arawa
prestates Te Kaoreore back into the care of
Ngati Whatua o Orakei at Auckland Museum)

Figure 6.4 Abbreviated *whakapapa* of some key events since light & enlightenment (consciousness)
entered the world (Te Ao Marama).

now either held by the Ngati Whakaue community or resting in museums around the world.[17] Ancient items such as *Te Kaoreore* embody ancestral narratives transmitted down through the generations, personifying spectacular explorative adventures across the whole Pacific.[18]

A second and much larger wave of migration voyages, like those led by Turi, Hoturoa, Tama te Kapua, Toroa, Tamatea and others, left from Taputapuatea for Aotearoa six generations later. On board the *Arawa waka* was Ngahue's *Te Kaoreore*. In time, after the people had populated themselves across claimed territories, the vessels themselves came to symbolize the powerful fusion of ancestors, people and the lands settled, as one identity. Upon their arrival in Te Ika a Maui and Te Wai Pounamu (North and South Islands of Aotearoa / New Zealand) some 20–30 generations ago, it appears that the navigational knowledge of these ancestors and their originating island *marae* diminished. The early Maori settlers shifted from an oceanic existence (realm of *Rua*) to one rooted within ancestrally relevant landscapes (realm of *Tane*) that came to be represented by dominating *pa*-complexes (engineered/sculptured volcanic cones and hills).[19]

Up to this time, *whakapapa* had provided the epistemological framework on which the highly ritualized navigational knowledge of the Polynesian ancestors was developed and maintained from one generation to the next for over 100 generations of Pacific exploration. Priestly navigators literally mapped genealogical recitations onto the Pacific night sky – linking star pairs with particular ancestral island groups, enabling continuous and very successful oceanic exploration over millennia.[20] *Marae* complexes, like the 2000+-year-old Taputapuatea in Ra'iatea, evolved throughout the Pacific as a direct response to the deep-sea navigational culture of the Proto-Polynesians, providing ritual spaces where critical knowledge was transmitted by specialists down the generations.[21] *Marae* also provided the leadership fora by which the *atua* (divine ancestors) could commune with *tangata* (earth-bound humans), eliciting the *marae* principles of chiefly engagement we recognize today as *rangatiratanga* (trusteeship), *manaakitanga* (service) and *kaitiakitanga* (custodianship). Through association with 30 generations of leadership, *Te Kaoreore* is seen as the embodiment of these chiefly principles. Ngati Whakaue's ritualized presentation of him to Tawa (Capt. Gilbert Mair) in 1866 was in recognition of the receiver understanding these principles and the obligations inherent in accepting *taonga* (ancestral Maori treasures).[22]

In 1890, Tawa placed *Te Kaoreore*, along with 246 other *taonga* (Maori ancestral treasures),[23] in the Auckland Museum's former Princes Street building that stood on an ancient *pa* site[24] of the local tribe, Ngati Whatua, only 200 meters from the current Auckland Art Gallery in Albert Park. Ngati Whatua's dominant *pa*, however, was Hikurangi, situated on the tallest volcanic peak of the Auckland Isthmus named Maungakiekie.[25]

Many hundreds of similarly engineered multi-terraced earthwork *pa*-complexes like Hikurangi still exist today, reflecting former Pacific *marae* structures but on a much grander scale. Central to these *pa*-complexes was the *marae atea*, the public space of encounter that ancestrally focussed the wider landscape. Although the disruptive forces of colonization resulted in strategic relocation of *marae*-communities to better access new resources within home territories,[26] *pa*-complexes still symbolically represent local kin-authority over surrounding estates and continue to be referenced today by local *marae* elders as powerful markers of identity in counter-distinction to all other tribes.[27]

With the assistance of powerful *taonga* such as *Te Kaoreore*, the founding voyages of Maori to Aotearoa have been recounted thousands of times across hundreds of *marae* for many generations. These great voyages, undertaken over 600 years ago, probably only took about 30 days at most, yet the experiences are still ceremonially recited and sung by elders in first person, up and down our islands, as if they occurred yesterday. *Waka*-voyaging narratives have remained powerful markers of ancestrally-organized kin identity, especially among wider tribal regions. Up to 40 of these epic narratives represent general boundary-markers that may unite or differentiate home kin from visiting outsiders, whether from another Maori tribe or the other side of the world. Belonging to a particular ancestrally-defined kin group validates an individual's rights of access and custodial responsibilities to customary land/s and waterways from one generation to the next. Thus, *whakapapa* is in itself the vehicle of kin-validation, reaching back 100 plus generations by which eventful ancestral journeys through space and time are formally structured, memorized and selectively narrated in the public domain of *marae*. Each name more than celebrates a real person linking the present with the celestial realm of creation. They also mark critical moments in time when crises were ameliorated, perhaps by war, marriage, gift, oratory, sacrifice or bravery in order for the tribe to survive and continue as a distinct social, political and economic identity.[28]

The politics of leadership back then was every bit as complex as today, but with very high stakes: one poor decision might not only result in your own death, but also precipitate the annihilation of your community. *Marae* remain the preferred forum of astute kin-qualified leaders (*whakapapa* of descent) when formally confronted with internal or external constraints or opportunities. These leaders frequently draw on ancestral precedents represented by *taonga* to explore the genealogical legitimacy of any *kaupapa* (political, social or economic agenda) challenging their community. Astute marae elders are always on alert, differentiating underlying principles (*whakakapa* of knowledge) from self-serving beliefs (*whakapapa* of indoctrinations & misaligned patterns of behaviour) and, through this *taonga*-guided process, identifying useful strategies that may strengthen and enhance cross-generational continuity of their tribe.

Taonga: ancestral trajectories

Maori carefully (re)perform their past by way of *taonga* from one generation to the next on appropriate occasions across 800 plus *marae* throughout Aotearoa. The power of *taonga* is perceived by descendants in terms of *mana* (ancestral authority), *tapu* (ancestral restriction, respect and discipline) and *korero* (ancestrally ordered narratives and ritual), complementing the *wairua* (spiritual presence), *ihi* (awe inspiring), *wehi* (spine tingling fear), *wana* (artistry of the *atua*) and *mauri* (life-force) contained within.[29] *Taonga* were carefully passed down particular descent lines and would be purposefully selected for *marae*-focussed performances, joining kin under one very powerful ancestral identity. *Taonga* might take the form of oratory, song, dance, incantations, weavings, carvings, art or weapons (such as *Te Kaoreore*) and be performed according to the audience and the requisite genealogical knowledge required, upholding kin-identity. Such *marae*-framed recounting of past events through *taonga* performance is always being tested, verified or corrected by wider kin elders. With each performance, *taonga* provide the vehicle by which leadership might skilfully (re)negotiate, maintain, shift or dismantle ancestral boundaries of identity and associated rights to access or control particular landscapes and resources.[30]

As a direct result of colonization many of these powerful symbols of kin-identity became separated from their source *marae*-communities and were launched on trajectories beyond their originating *marae*-based value system. Some were *marae*-associated *prestations* (ceremonial gifts carrying inherent obligations of reciprocity) like *Te Kaoreore*,[31] *Murirangaranga*[32] and *Pareraut*[33] (Figure 6.5), while others exited by less honourable means, as was the case for *Te waka huia o Te Teko*.[34] Like their originating landscapes, they, too, were all eventually captured by a foreign (monetary/fiscally-measured) value system, transforming them into commodities (objects of curiosity or trade) of which many thousands ended up in museums worldwide. For 100 plus years, museum-held *taonga* became servants to another culture's ideological representation of "otherness" without recourse to originating *marae* and their kinship-maintained values.

Figure 6.5 Pareraut123 and Murirangaranga. Descendants bring their ancestors home to Rotorua region. Te Papa-i-Ouru Marae, 29 April 2008, Photograph, Krzysztof Pfeiffer, Auckland Museum.

In 1984 certain events compelled Maori people to consider more deeply the historical purpose of museums and the custodial issues in respect to their museum-held *taonga*. Source community interaction occurred in museum contexts with the development of *Te Maori*, a major New Zealand Government-supported international Maori Art exhibition that toured the United States and New Zealand between 1984–87. Although the government attempted to prescribe elders' involvement to one of veto, the elders nevertheless found a way to initiate the re-emergence and re-emphasis of Maori (source) values of *taonga* within previously unfamiliar museum contexts.[35] While others have commented on the contributing role of *Te Maori* to the development of a bicultural nation,[36] not so apparent in museological discourse has been the catalytic role of *taonga*. The performative release of *whakapapa*, awakening the *mana*, *tapu* and *korero* that had otherwise lain dormant within prestigious museum-held *taonga* like *Pukaki*, *Tiki* and *Uenuku*, affected a nation searching for new identity in the wake of economic instability during the 1970s.[37]

The *Te Maori* exhibition was the turning point in New Zealand for how Maori engaged with museums. Up until then, Maori were generally not involved in museum practices concerning their *taonga*. Despite the *taonga* that museums contained, Maori generally did not feel any sense of "belonging" or inclusiveness that gave requisite cause or inclination to enter foreign, urban-located museums in New Zealand, unless invited.[38] There are, of course, exceptions; one notable case concerns the Rotorua Museum where Te Arawa have been encouraged to store many of their ancestral treasures on long-term loan since the late 1960s. Generally, however, Maori viewed museums as curious, if not alien, monuments built by the "Other" for reasons beyond their own cultural frames of comprehension. *Taonga* within museums were on trajectories of their own destiny to which many elders of a former generation believed should be left alone.

I still vividly recall Te Arawa elder Kuru o te Marama Waaka's briefing, prior to a meeting between Ngati Whakaue (travelled from Rotorua) and the Auckland Museum Trust Board on the afternoon of 4 April 1997. Pointing his finger at the younger members of my tribe, he sternly said: "I do not want to hear any one of you say give *Pukaki* back! It is for *Pukaki* to decide to come home. He is our father, we are his children. He will decide, not us!" A line was clearly drawn and some of the group were still in shock as supporting elders of the home Auckland tribe, Ngati Whatua – standing beside the museum's leadership – ceremonially welcomed us into the alien heart of museum culture, the boardroom. Thereafter, Museum governance and officials could only politely look on in bewilderment as customary tribal host (Ngati Whatua) converted boardroom into tribal *marae* and warmly engaged their tribal visitors (Ngati Whakaue) on behalf of the museum, each speaking their respective tribal dialects. No one dared speak out of turn or even hint that *Pukaki* should be returned. The first words of English eventually spoken after 30 minutes of *whakapapa*-guided interchange were from the Director: "The Auckland Museum acknowledges Ngati Whakaue as still the owners of *Pukaki*". Kuru, sitting in front of me, rocked back in his chair and I gently pushed him forward. He replied: "then it is settled, *Pukaki* has decided"; with that, we all stood and Ngati Whatua led the Auckland Museum in the *hongi* (ritual sharing of the breath of life by pressing of noses, completing the welcoming ceremony) with their Ngati Whakaue guests. *Pukaki* had revealed his trajectory. We belonged to him and the time had come to prepare for his homecoming. Within six months, a comet-like *Pukaki* travelled back across our tribal horizon to be with his Ngati Whakaue-Te Arawa grandchildren on Te Papa-i-Ouru *marae* again.[39]

Museums: repositories of national identity

Generally, Maori source communities seek to formally engage museums on purposeful occasions, taking care, as in the case of *Pukaki*, to honour the trajectory of ancestors to whom they "belong". Conversely, *Pakeha* (New Zealanders of British descent)[40] continue to believe they "own" museums and have shaped them to referentially symbolize monumental representations of their own British transplanted cultural heritage. Until the 1980s, museums in New Zealand provided evidential substantiation of perceived western-world order – capturing the whole world in miniature[41] – and interpreting with feigned objectivity spiritually endowed objects like *Pukaki* and *Te Kaoreore* as "primitive curios" that (re)presented the "native other".[42] Thus, any formal Maori interaction with the museum was generally on the institution's terms, be it via visiting curators on collecting expeditions;[43] commissions for new work;[44] contracts for services;[45] institutional openings;[46] or launching Maori-related exhibitions.[47]

Te Maori was not the only catalyst that encouraged a new form of engagement between Maori and museums. During the 1970s and 1980s, a number of not insignificant events turned museums' engagement with Maori on its head. Major political milestones such as the 1975 Maori land march and protests;[48] the 1976 Olympic boycott by 26 African nations due to New Zealand's ongoing sporting contacts with South Africa;[49] the 1977–78 Bastion Point occupation;[50] the 1970s rise of urban-led radical Maori activism;[51] the 1981 Springbok rugby tour protests;[52] wage freezes, high inflation and record unemployment;[53] police dawn raids on immigrant Samoan communities;[54] and, not least, the 1985 Rainbow Warrior bombing[55] combined to contest white-New Zealander's mono-cultural national identity. These events created a sense of national unease, bordering on crisis, and a heightened public consciousness of the place of Maori (among other issues) in New Zealand society. The Waitangi Tribunal was established in 1975 (with a significant broadening of its jurisdiction in 1986). It enabled Maori to present grievances against the Crown where their claims showed that breaches of the Treaty of Waitangi – 1840 treaty that gave Britain sovereignty over New Zealand – had occurred. Leading up to the 1970s, the rural/urban boundary had been dismantled as a developing post-World War II nation-state lured thousands of young opportunity-seeking rural Maori[56] into city workforces to help build modern British-like centres, but with little consideration for the home tribal people.[57]

Britain's 1960s–70s realignment toward the European Economic Community was also an economically painful reality check for New Zealand. Underpinning the national insecurity was the escalating racial tension as a new and very vocal urban-raised ethnic Maori identity began publicly polarizing society[58] and agitating for their share of access to once Maori-controlled but now *Pakeha*-dominated resources, as prescribed in the Treaty of Waitangi.[59]

A decade of challenging events cumulatively awakened the nation from its 100-year myopic, British-like state of mono-cultural identity. New Zealand was no longer able to perpetuate a façade of racial harmony, especially now that upwards of 80 per cent of Maori shared the same urban spaces as *Pakeha*[60] once almost exclusively the domain of British colonial-settler culture. Maori were re-ascribing a new and more competitive ethnic self-identity to better access perceived opportunities and resources. In this developing environment, Maori were strongly asserting themselves, publicly and politically. This was the situation from which the *Te Maori* exhibition arose and Maori began front-footing their concerns in relation to museum and *taonga* issues.

After twenty painful years of British "economic decolonisation",[61] New Zealand, with its bruised national pride, sought rejuvenation by developing new trade partners in Asia and the United States to break the recession of the 1970s and early 1980s.[62] New ideas of post-colonial nationhood,[63] couched in terms of bicultural uniqueness, simultaneously began emerging, too, especially in the context of exhibiting "primitive" Maori art to a discerning US audience.[64] Despite being a monoculturally curated exhibition,[65] *Te Maori* was immediately recognized as a watershed event, taking all of New Zealand by surprise.[66] The nation's shift away from being Anglo-centric, especially on the return of *Te Maori* to New Zealand (*Te Hokinga Mai – The Return Home*), was proportional to the increased Maori interaction with museums.[67] Tens of thousands of New Zealanders were enthusiastically hosted by young, mostly urban-raised *kaiawhina* (Maori guides) who personally introduced them to their tribal ancestors as revered Maori art pieces or *taonga* of national importance.[68]

It appears that the emotional impact of *Te Maori* also directly contributed to the white population's wider sense of "indigenized" belonging within New Zealand's unique bicultural nation-space, evoking a growing acceptance of the Maori-ascribed ethnic-label, *Pakeha*.[69] The nation began evolving toward this new more bi-culturally framed South Pacific identity, especially as it would apparently lead to economic recovery. By the end of the US leg of the tour, the government had already begun linking *Te Maori* to a newly proposed National Museum project.[70] The homecoming tour of *Te Maori* became the vehicle by which the new bicultural ethos was introduced, enabling the existence of an indigenized settler identity to occupy an ideological space of ethical merit in the Pakeha national imagining.[71] In essence, *Te Maori* conversely validated *Pakeha* rights of difference – in Maori terms – within a new and emerging treaty-framed New Zealand and the term *Tangata Tiriti* (New Zealanders by right of the Treaty of Waitangi) arose in distinction to *Tangata Whenua* (First peoples of New Zealand).[72]

As written elsewhere, not all of the *Te Maori* interactions were positive.[73] The first hint of unchecked inter-Maori friction, which was to manifest in New Zealand's major museums over the next decade, became observable at the final *Te Maori* venue – Auckland Art Gallery – when urban Maori-fuelled inter-tribal rivalry transformed into un-*marae*-like angry scenes, due to the absence of local tribal elders.[74] Wider tribal observers began to question the polarizing ideology resting behind government-led (mono-cultural) Treaty of Waitangi-framed boundaries of difference (two people, one land) and what effect this might begin to have on *marae*-communities which, after all, were the source of *Te Maori taonga* in the first place.[75]

In the post *Te Maori* years (1980s–1990s), the full effect of homogenized (ethnic identity) boundary contestations – Maori versus Pakeha – were to erupt time and again, revolutionizing museum-Maori engagement, operationally and at governance levels.[76] It appears that the new generation of urban-raised Maori had become politically conscious of the critical roles that New Zealand's two largest museums, in particular, were providing. In the 1990s, academic commentators began questioning the centrality of New Zealand museums as bicultural edifices by which "Maoriness" was being construed in terms of its difference from Pakeha,[77] without recourse to communities of origin.[78] Critical media-heightened events[79] provided political fora by which urban-based Maori publicly confronted museums' rights to own and control ancestral remains[80] and *taonga*.[81] The exclusive right of museums to exhibit *taonga* deemed too *tapu*[82] was under question, as, too, were the multiple image appropriations of ancestors being marketed within and beyond museums,[83] taking advantage of the emerging cultural tourism market.[84]

In general terms, by the 1990s, the unexamined nineteenth-century ethic representing capture and control of the Maori "other" that had ruled New Zealand museums had run its course. The colonial context out of which museums arose gave way to the sheer weight of Waitangi Tribunal reports, Appeal Court & Privy Council findings and legislative accommodation of Treaty principles[85] and to the principles of *mana*[86] and *tapu*.[87] Finally, the actualities of New Zealand's previously mono-cultural history were being redressed, not just in textbooks, but also in museums. *Te Maori* provided a timely museum-activated vehicle by which New Zealand transformed into a post-colonial bicultural nation-state.[88] *Taonga* that activated the *Te Maori* phenomenon remain central to museums' ability to maintain this biculturalism. But who might accurately translate associated source values (*kinship-belonging*) into museums' governance and everyday operations (*office-ownership*) and create an inclusive space of co-existence?

Ko Tawa: a model for coexistence

140 years after *Te Kaoreore* was gifted by Ngati Whakaue to Captain Gilbert Mair (also known as Tawa), he ceremonially reappeared back on his home *marae* of Te Papa-i-Ouru in Ohinemutu, Rotorua. *Te Kaoreore* was one of 28 *taonga* that were central to the Auckland Museum's international touring *Ko Tawa* Exhibition Project (2005–2008).[89] The project was named *Ko Tawa* to honour equally *taonga* and collector as an inseparable collision of tribal autonomy and settler colonial government, represented by their two mutually exclusive values systems within the museum context – kinship/belonging and office/ownership. These collisions climaxed as boundary contestations over key resources, resulting in a decade of civil war (1863–1872), legislated confiscations and state implemented atrocities. Throughout this period, Maori leadership used their most prized *taonga* to continually petition the settler government to take heed of its Treaty of Waitangi. Tawa was trusted by many tribal leaders as a worthy government advocate, and received time and again Maori society's greatest *taonga*, like *Murirangaranga*, *Pareraututu* and *Te Kaoreore*. These crisis-heightened moments appear to represent some of the earliest on-the-ground interactions out of which ideas of Treaty-bound nationhood beyond being British were conceived. However, the omnipresent colonial agenda of New Zealand's settler government was immune to Mair's attempts of advocacy; any ideas of twin streams

of cultural identity coexisting in one nation-space remained unrealised until over 100 years later.

As its curator I was thus compelled to ensure *Ko Tawa* was designed to provide an ethical and compelling, multi-experience[90] exhibitionary vehicle by which a new generation of at-risk urban-raised Maori youth[91] might be effectively introduced to their museum-held *taonga* and associated ancestral land-based identity in controlled home-community contexts. Almost without comparison, Tawa, a gifted Maori orator in his own right, carefully recorded *taonga*-associated *korero* (kin-ordered narratives) at time of receipt. These, along with the inevitable trajectories of dispossession both *taonga* and land suffered during New Zealand's turbulent nineteenth century, were made available to youth and wider visitors alike. It was most important that these powerful narratives were safely released under the customary control – *rangatiratanga*, *manaakitanga* and *kaitiakitanga* – of local community elders or *tangata whenua*, thus preventing any possibility of a *Te Maori*-like inter-tribal incident reoccurring. From one venue to the next, the *tangata whenua* ritually provided a protective mantle or *mana o te whenua* (exclusive ancestral authority of the land; from the land; and over the land, symbolically represented by the tribal *marae*) over the *taonga* and under which all visitors, contributing source communities and supporting museums were equally empowered as honoured guests on home lands.

From the outset (16 April 2003), the elders of all 18 tribes involved in *Ko Tawa* were as equally keen as the Auckland Museum's mostly Maori exhibition team[92] to use *taonga* to reconnect their urban-raised relations with home-*marae* communities. They became co-producers as each party committed time and energy to ensure the project's success in youth outreach. *Ko Tawa* functioned as a uniquely South Pacific application of Hooper-Greenhill's post-museum in which the Auckland Museum was able to move "as a set of processes into the spaces, the concerns and the ambitions of the communities".[93] Each of the *taonga* selected from the Gilbert Mair Collection carried rich narratives (oratory, song, genealogy and image),[94] effectively linking landscapes, ancestors and living descendants as one identity. *Ko Tawa* was designed so that the *taonga* (objects, items or things ancestrally represented by a multitude of carvings, weavings, oratory, songs and photographic images, both still and moving) were made central – metaphorically and physically – to the exhibition space. Conversely, the arrangement sought to push visitors back toward the gallery walls, providing them an opportunity to spatially experience what it might feel like to be subordinate to the objective gaze of ancestors. Under the guidance of a leading Maori architect and me as curator, the exhibition was totally Maori (*whakapapa*-concept) in its design (Figure 6.6), including unorthodox dramatic elements of height and light, and absence of glass cases or distracting labels. A floating canopy subtly resembled the ancestral rafters of a meetinghouse and a plinth suggested a voyaging *waka*. The 28 *taonga* were displayed in a genealogical order that mirrored the central north island landscape – *mai Maketu ki Tongariro* (from Maketu on the coast to the great inland volcanoes of Tongariro) – and cloaked in a multi-audio visual experience of lingering ancestral images, narrative, song and landscapes, simulating a voyage through ancestrally collapsed time/space to which the visitor was provided a once-in-a-lifetime glimpse. To borrow from Phillips,[95] *Ko Tawa* enabled the Auckland Museum to become a participant in the Maori tribal community as much as the Maori tribal community became a participant in the museum.

Figure 6.6 Ko Tawa. International touring tribal Maori exhibition, 10 June 2005–29 April 2008. Photograph, Krzysztof Pfeiffer, Auckland Museum.

The source community pride *Ko Tawa* created became most apparent at the time of transfer from one venue to the next, totalling 12 ceremonies in all. These rituals of exchange were the climax to three previous years of intense source community engagement in home-*marae* contexts. Key to discussions was setting up a three-way relationship between Auckland Museum, source community elders and their local *Pakeha* community museums. Auckland provided the curatorial, conservation and technical expertise; local elders oversaw appropriate implementation of customary obligations and the local museum supplied a secure venue. On the arrival of *Ko Tawa* in each tribal region, the local elders invited their local museum to assist in welcoming all the ancestors represented in *Ko Tawa* onto the local *marae* under the escort of the previous hosting tribal group and with Auckland Museum's exhibition team in attendance. In particular, special greetings would not only be made to the *taonga* of local origin, as was the case with *Te Kaoreore* in Rotorua, but also to Auckland's home tribal people, Ngati Whatua, whose elders had (a) spiritually safe-guarded their ancestor(s) since first arriving in the Auckland Museum some 140 years earlier;[96] and (b) supported the *Ko Tawa* Project team of mostly Maori in making such a homecoming possible. Thereafter, the chiefly *marae* duty of *rangatiratanga*, *manaakitanga* and *kaitiakitanga* associated with *Ko Tawa* was ritually passed over to the new hosting kin group which then took charge of the exhibition's transfer into their local museum venue.

The kin-obligations inherent in accepting such a chiefly duty over powerful *taonga* from many different tribes were exceptional. At every venue, tribal-*marae* elders worked alongside their local museum to ensure their customary responsibility of spiritually and physically safeguarding all 28 *taonga* would be successful from time of *marae*-ritual receipt through to their ceremonial passage to the next *marae*-community host. In one particular case (Whangarei), the museum and local community even shared security with local-kin (Maori Wardens) who slept on site and maintained 24-hour guard and hosting duties over the ancestors for eight weeks. Each museum venue rose to the challenge, providing necessary resources to support the local community in the very serious business of welcoming and guiding thousands of visitors through *Ko Tawa*. As hoped, many of the 100,000+ visitors[97] were Maori youth, who entered museums to engage ancestrally important *taonga* for their very first time. *Ko Tawa* also provided local *Pakeha* communities with a unique opportunity to better understand and value the underlying regional heritage from their Maori neighbours' perspective and see Maori objects in a whole new light. *Ko Tawa* demonstrated that, even in the most racially polarized of communities, two value systems (kinship and office) could equally coexist within a museum operational context and provide multiple benefits to all involved.[98]

On 29 April 2008, the exhibition's support team packed up *Ko Tawa* for the final time and the journey from Tauranga back to Auckland began under the escort of local elders from Ngaiterangi and Ngati Rangi. Tauranga happened to be where Tawa himself had died in 1923 before being carried by Ngati Whakaue-Te Arawa back to Te Papa-i-Ouru *marae*, Rotorua, where he remains buried today. In a similar vein, *Ko Tawa* the exhibition followed the same route. On arriving at Te Papa-i-Ouru, the Tauranga elders ceremonially passed the *taonga* and the *mauri* (the life-force stone that represented Tawa (Mair) himself) into Ngati Whakaue's custodianship. At every venue since leaving Auckland the *mauri* had rested on a *whaariki* (fine woven mat) made by Ngati Whakaue's female ancestors. On taking receipt of the *mauri*, Ngati Whakaue completed the *marae* rituals by ceremonially placing it on Gilbert Mair's grave, ritually symbolizing the end of *Ko Tawa*. Thereafter, for some of the *taonga*, like *Murirangaranga*, *Pareraut018* and *Tiki o Te Roro*, the journey was over and they returned into the care of Rotorua Museum and Ngati Whakaue.

Four hours later, 100 plus Ngati Whakaue arrived at the Auckland Museum's doorstep, after having escorted the remaining *taonga* north. It was now time for the final ritual of placing them back into the care of Ngati Whatua o Orakei and their Auckland Museum. On arrival, the most senior *taonga*, *Te Kaoreore*, was released from his crate and placed into the hands of Ngati Whakaue's senior elder in readiness to symbolize the ceremonial return passage of *rangatiratanga*, *manaakitanga* and *kaitiakitanga* to local kin. The elder, Alfie McRae, was a direct descendant of the nineteenth-century leader who had prestated *Te Kaoreore* to Tawa in 1866. Everyone gathered and a hush enveloped the crowd as ancestor and descendants fused into one powerful identity of common origin. Eventually, Ngati Whatua's female elders ritually called for Ngati Whakaue-Te Arawa to enter the Maori Court, their melodic cries of ancestral welcome echoing off the many *taonga* that once used to stand in the Rotorua region. Led by Alfie brandishing *Te Kaoreore*, Ngati Whakaue erupted into *haka* (war challenge), recounting the ancient arrival of the *Arawa waka* as if happening now. In time everyone took their seats but, before the speechmaking began, Ngati Whatua called on the Maori officer in charge, firmly requesting he release the *taonga* from their crates so they might properly participate in their final ceremony before being recommitted to the darkness of storage. Thereafter, the exchange of *whakapapa*-laden speeches and songs commenced as one elder after another paid homage to genealogical links embodied in the *taonga* resting before everyone. In turn, the visitors honored Ngati Whatua's custodianship within Auckland Museum and their vision to support the *Ko Tawa* Project Team in customary terms. The ceremony seemed to climax when Ngati Whatua brought me forward, presenting me back to my people eight years after having ceremonially received me when I first took up Auckland Museum's Director Maori position.[99] But this was eclipsed by Ngati Whakaue stepping forward in return and prestating *Te Kaoreore* to hosts, Ngati Whatua o Orakei, thus symbolizing completion of the *Ko Tawa* journey; all the *taonga* were now ritually cleared to return to storage.

My time of continuously balancing museum *office* with tribal *kinship* values had come to an end. *Ko Tawa* was a testament to the museum world that a post-museum is achievable, demonstrating that two value systems could equally co-exist and provide mutual benefit to source communities, local hosting kin and museums in and beyond their four walls. My many aunties present stepped forward and protectively wrapped themselves around me. My *tuahine* (female cousin), who had worked alongside me for many years, also joined the enveloping embrace of our aunties. Together, we bid farewell to our many ancestors, including *Te Kaoreore*, and exited the museum via the front door.

Conclusions

This essay opened by suggesting that New Zealand's two international museums appear to be at a crossroads. At an operational/curatorial level, at least, they have paralleled international trends of providing interpretation of the indigenous "other", especially within exhibitionary contexts, or what Nicks calls trans-cultural spaces.[100] But are these museums really prepared to share power of interpretation over nation-spaces, enabling indigenous values as understood by their indigenous people to coexist at governance, decision-making levels? In Auckland, the Maori Advisory Committee (Taumata-a-Iwi) has a representative sitting on its Museum Trust Board, but he remains acutely aware that the legislation stipulates the Board need only "take due regard of the advice given" by its Maori advisors.[101]

From a Maori perspective, what Nicks was describing resembles the ancient but highly effective *marae*-space. The most observable evidence of these dialogically-bounded interactions is the apparent shift of operational policies and procedures to enable museums to better engage indigenous voices.[102] But, overall, have museum-governing legislation, principles and policies in these same institutions kept pace with international museum-academic thinking? It appears that those who govern national museums, especially in North America, Australia and New Zealand, are struggling to align to or take account of curators' new and evolving approaches to accessing indigenous knowledge within post-museum contexts. In the early 1990s, curators at anthropologically-orientated museums, in particular, came to realize the academic/curatorial importance of accessing and controlling vitally important customary knowledge in order to secure their discipline's long-term survival. Paradoxically, museum boards (governance) have sought to counter or at least slow this move toward professional (operational) collaboration with the native "other"[103] by revalidating their institution's moral – (post) colonial – authority to control any curatorial-driven democratizing models of engagement that appear to empower source communities beyond historically entrenched boundaries.

As *Ko Tawa* came to an end, the then newly appointed director received a clear mandate from her Trust Board to lead the Auckland Museum in a new direction that might better leverage apparent opportunities to increase attendance and popularity.[104] However, a number of nation-wide controversies were to challenge the Museum and its Board, including the disestablishment of ten dedicated Maori positions, resulting in a nation-wide Maori outcry,[105] and the Sir Edmund Hillary archive controversy, pitting his family against the museum and eventually culminating in the director's early resignation.[106] During those two years since the conclusion of *Ko Tawa*, the *tangata whenua*-led ethic of kin-accountability enshrined within Auckland Museum Trust Board's Guiding Principles and its Maori Advisory Committee's *Kaupapa*[107] – each reflecting AWMM legislation by acknowledging five key principles of Maori engagement and the customary right of the local kin community to provide leadership – was tested, especially concerning Maori employment and repatriation.[108]

As AWMM demonstrates, leadership in any national museum will come and go, but it is hoped that ethically developed principles, policies and procedures will weather seasonal agendas and museums' governing authorities will maintain a steady course through turbulent times, especially from the perennial storms that continually challenge indigenous authority. Global redress of museums' code of ethics, led by internationally recognized museum-academics, would provide such shelter, but these efforts must be nationally specific to encourage and protect much-needed policy reform of nation-space institutions at governance level. Successful integration of source values at national code of ethics level will guide normalization of emerging post-museum approaches and encourage museum policy-makers to align with their national peers by proactively engaging source communities within and beyond nation-spaces as equals.

For now, (post) colonial museums may continue to be reluctant to change, but ultimately they cannot have it both ways. Since the opening of *Te Maori*, museums in New Zealand, Australia and North America have repeatedly sought to replicate the unique power of indigenous engagement first demonstrated by *taonga* within exhibitionary contexts, but all the while remaining reluctant to accommodate underpinning kin-values from the ground up. What new crisis needs to occur before *office* will willingly accommodate *kinship* so each value system may respectfully co-exist and complement one another within museums' overall governance and operations? Will nation-space museums come to accept and acknowledge that the landscapes on which they stand remain under the customary governance of enduring local kin communities? As national museums promote indigenized settler identities, like being Pakeha in Aotearoa/New Zealand, will they also provide the space for local kin communities to tell their story? Over the past two centuries museums throughout the (post) colonial world have ignorantly subjected local kin to a spiritual burden of incredible proportions. Hundreds of thousands of ancestors have been acquired and then placed in museums on their customary landscapes without their customary sanction. Today, as source communities throughout the world seek to engage with (post) colonial museums, they will inevitably first seek audience with the local kin community (*marae*) to appropriately honor them for providing cross-generational trusteeship (*rangatiratanga*), service (*manaakitanga*) and custodianship (*kaitiakitanga*) over their museum-held ancestors (*taonga*). By supporting the local kin community to lead-host such ceremonies within their four walls, museums will be taking their first and most crucial step toward developing ethically sustainable source community relationships.

Today, it appears that the Auckland Museum Trust Board is again willing to commit to the very sound indigenous principles its predecessors developed over the past decade. I, for one, hope it has the courage to reopen the promising pathway of post-museum engagement *Ko Tawa* has already forged. Governance commitment to post-museums will empower operational action in New Zealand's oldest museum and give effective meaning to the two world views embodied within our nation's founding treaty. Perhaps the looming crisis of local tribe exclusion from having any authority within the new amalgamations of regional urban centres like Auckland and Wellington to form "Super Cities" will yet be a catalyst for New Zealand's museums to have an ethical rethink concerning indigenous engagement in a newly evolving urban-clustering nation-space. Will New Zealand's museums become captive of yet another political belief system based primarily on economically framed values of ownership and rights? Or perhaps museum governance will follow their curators' lead and seek a more enduring principled approach to interpreting the twin streams of culture that far more accurately represent New Zealand's still emerging ideas of nationhood beyond bicultural ideology. As the late Michael Ames so succinctly noted, and which I constantly remind myself:

> museums do change, often ahead of other public agencies, and their short-comings in cross-cultural encounters may be due less to ignorance or lack of integrity than to their taken-for-granted embeddedness in a different ('Enlightenment' or 'Eurocentric') paradigm of integrity – that is, in their own cultural tradition – which has, however, become somewhat out of step with the times.[109]

A new horizon beckons. Museum-indigenous partnerships at a governance-kin leadership level are the next frontier. If indigenous values (kinship/belonging) might one day come to co-exist equally within legislation, principles and policy (office/ownership), they will constructively permeate throughout museum operations to serve the good of a nation. This will require (post) colonial museums' power-brokers (governance/trust boards) to be prepared to take that extra step of recognizing more formally the ethical importance of developing equitable indigenous partnerships with appropriate local kin elders: leader to leader. Thereafter, our industry's ability to deliver a wider co-produced authentic indigenous-lived exhibitionary experience of belonging – post museum – will be dramatically increased, keeping museums vital in our rapidly re-indigenizing world.

Glossary

atua	divine ancestors
haka	war challenge
hongi	ritual sharing of the breath of life by pressing of noses, completing the welcoming ceremony
ihi	awe inspiring
Io Matua Kore	the parentless one
kaiawhina	Maori guides
kaitiakitanga	custodianship
kaupapa	political, social or economic agenda
Ko Tawa	Auckland Museum Exhibition Project (2005–2008)
koha	cultural presents
korero	ancestrally ordered narratives and ritual
mai Maketu ki Tongariro	from Maketu on the coast to the great inland volcanoes of Tongariro
mana	exclusive ancestral authority or what anthropologists would describe as descent
mana o te whenua	exclusive ancestral authority of the land; from the land; and over the land, symbolically represented by the tribal marae
manaakitanga	service
Maori	the indigenous peoples of New Zealand
marae	ancient ritualized space of Pacific tribal communities that remains central to Maori identity
marae atea	the public space of encounter that ancestrally focussed the wider landscape
Maui	demi-god, trickster, Polynesian folk hero who was last born in his family
mauri	life-force
Ngati.	*The people of.*
Pa	village, fortified hilltops, engineered/sculptured volcanic cones and hills
Pakeha	New Zealanders of British descent
Papa tu a Nuku	Earth Mother

rangatiratanga	trusteeship
Rangi Nui	Sky Father
Tane	creator of trees, biosphere and the first humans; and fetcher of divine knowledge
tangata	earth-bound humans
Tangata Tiriti	New Zealanders by right of the Treaty of Waitangi
tangata whenua	local Maori communities; people of the land
taonga	ancestral Maori treasures
tapu	ancestral restriction, respect and discipline
Taputapuatea	famous marae in Ra'iatea (west of Tahiti)
Tawa	Capt. Gilbert Mair
Te Ika a Maui and Te Wai Pounamu	North and South Islands of Aotearoa / New Zealand
Te Kaoreore	Greenstone hand weapon of great antiquity and prestige: see Figure 6.1
Te Kore	the infinite epoch of nothingness
Te Maori	a major New Zealand Government-supported international Maori Art exhibition that toured the United States and New Zealand between 1984–87
tuahine	female cousin
wairua	spiritual presence
waka	canoe/sailing vessel
wana	artistry of the *atua*
wehi	spine tingling fear
whaariki	fine woven mat
whakapapa	a philosophical system of ordering the universe
whakawhanaungatanga	inclusive familial ties or kinship

Notes

1 With reference to R. Phillips, 'Community Collaboration in Exhibitions: toward a dialogic paradigm – Introduction', in L. Peers and A. Brown (eds.) *Museums and Source Communities: A Routledge Reader*, London: Routledge, 2003, p. 166.
2 Auckland Museum is also officially known as Auckland War Memorial Museum – AWMM and in Maori: *Tamaki Paenga Hira*.
3 Cf. M. Kawharu, 'Indigenous Governance in Museums: a case study, the Auckland War Memorial Museum' in C. Fforde, J. Herbert & P. Turnbull (eds.) *The Dead and their*

Possessions: Repatriation in Principle, Policy and Practice, London: Routledge, 2003, pp. 293–304; P. Tapsell, 'From the sideline: Tikanga, Treaty Values and Te Papa', in M. Belgrave, M. Kawharu & D. Williams (eds.) *Waitangi Revisited: Perspectives on the Treaty of Waitangi*, Melbourne: Oxford University Press, 2005, pp. 266–282.

4 See Peers and Brown, *Museums and Source Communities*, for a range of academic discussions on this emerging museological approach.

5 T. Nicks, 'Museums and Contact Work – Introduction' in Peers & Brown, *Museums and Source Communities*, pp. 19–27.

6 J. Clifford, *Routes: Travel and Translation in the Late Twentieth Century*, London: Harvard University Press, 1991, p. 224.

7 P. Tapsell 'Beyond the Frame: An Afterword' in Peers & Brown, *Museums and Source Communities*, p. 245.

8 M.M. Ames, 'How to Decorate a House' in Peers & Brown, *Museums and Source Communities*, pp. 171–180.

9 Clifford, *Routes*, pp. 100–101.

10 Nicks, 'Museums and Contact Work – Introduction', 2003, p. 24.

11 Building on discussions previously presented by A. Appaduri, *The Social Life of Things: Commodities in Social Perspective*, Cambridge: Cambridge University Press, 1986; and M. Strathern, 'Artefacts of History: Events and the Interpretation of Images' in J. Siikala (ed.) *Culture and History in the Pacific*, Helsinki: The Finnish Anthropological Society Transactions 27, 1990, pp. 25–44.

12 *Code of Ethics for governing bodies of museums and museum staff*, Wellington: Museums Aotearoa Te Tari o Nga Whare Taonga o te Motu, The Museums of New Zealand Inc., 2003.

13 P. Tapsell, 'The Flight of Pareraututu', *Journal of the Polynesian Society* 106: 4, 1997 (December), pp. 323–374.

14 P. Tapsell, 'Footprints in the sand: Banks's Maori collection, Cook's first voyage 1768–71', in M. Hetherington & H. Morphy (eds.) *Discovering Cook's Collections*, Canberra: National Museum of Australia Press, 2009, pp. 92–111.

15 Similar interpretations can be found in published sources, for example, P.T.H. Jones, *King Potatau: an account of the life of Potatau Te Wherowhero, the first Maori king*, Wellington: Polynesian Society, 1959.

16 P. Tapsell & C.R. Woods, 'Potikitanga: indigenous entrepreneurship in a Maori context', *Journal of Enterprising Communities: People and Places in the Global Economy* 2: 3, 2008, pp. 192–203.

17 For example, *Kaukaumatua*, presented to George Grey and now in the British Museum: G. Grey, *Maori Mementos being a series of addresses, presented by the native people, to His Excellency Sir George Grey, K.C.B., F.R.S. Governor and High Commissioner of the Cape of Good Hope, and Late Governor of New Zealand; with introductory remarks and explanatory notes, to which is added a small collection of laments, &c. By Charles Oliver B. Davis, translator and interpreter to the general government*, Auckland: Williamson and Wilson, 1855, p. 15.

18 Some other examples being *Matuatonga*: G. Grey, *Ko nga Moteatea, me nga Hakirara o nga Maori*, Wellington: Robert Stokes, 1853; *Marutuahu*: P. Tapsell, *Ko Tawa: Maori Ancestors of New Zealand – Gilbert Mair Collection*, Auckland: David Bateman Ltd., 2006, p. 41; and *Korotangi*: Major Wilson, 'On the Korotangi, or Stone Bird', in *Transactions and Proceedings of the Royal Society of New Zealand* 22, 1889, pp. 500–518.

19 See, for example, P. Tapsell, 'Papamoa Pa', in M. Kawharu (ed.) *Whenua: Managing Resources in Aotearoa New Zealand*, Auckland: Reed Publishing, 2002, pp. 272–286.

20 S. Low, 'Nainoa Thompson's path to knowledge: How Hokule'a's navigator finds his way', in K. Howe (ed.) *Vaka Moana: Voyages of the Ancestors*, Auckland: David Bateman Ltd and Auckland Museum, 2006, pp. 23–53.

21 Tapsell, 'Papamoa Pa'; and 'Footprints in the sand', for wider discussion.

22 Tapsell, *Ko Tawa*, for in depth discussions on *taonga* and Gilbert Mair.

23 Tapsell, *Ko Tawa*, pp. 182–185.

24 The site still carries the name, *Te Horotiu*.

25 M. Kawharu, *Tahuhu Korero: The sayings of Taitokerau*, Auckland: Auckland University Press, 2008, pp. 19, 21.

26 For instance, Ngati Whatua relocated themselves within their customary territory to Orakei in 1841 to better support the British Government, which the tribe had successfully invited to come to Tamaki to develop Auckland as the nation's capital.

27 See, for example, Ngarimu Blair profiled in 'A Voice to Move Mountains', in *New Zealand Herald*, 20 February 2010, p. B1.

28 See also M. Kawharu, *Whenua*, for multiple discussions on the role of ancestors concerning identity and relationship to land.

29 Tapsell, 'The Flight of Pareraut018', p. 330.

30 Ibid, pp. 331–333; 350.

31 Tapsell, *Ko Tawa*, pp. 115–126.

32 A human bone flute. Ibid, pp. 95–114.

33 A dog skin cloak. Ibid, pp. 51–62.

34 Carved treasure box taken during the 1860s government raids as war-booty; Tapsell, *Ko Tawa*, p. 183.

35 S.M. Mead (ed.), *Te Maori: Maori Art from New Zealand Collections*, New York: Abrams, 1984, for catalogue; and S.M. Mead, *Magnificent Te Maori: Te Maori Whakahirahira*, Auckland: Heinemann, 1986, for exhibition venue commentaries.

36 'Nga Taonga o te Motu: Treasures of the Nation, National Museum of New Zealand Te Marae Taonga O Aotearoa, a Plan for Development', *Report of the Project Development Team*, Wellington, 1985; N. Thomas, *Colonialism's Culture: Anthropology, Travel and Government*, Cambridge: Polity Press, 1994; and B. Dibley, *Museum, Native, Nation: Museological Narrative and Postcolonial Nation Identity Formation*, unpublished M.A. thesis, Department of Sociology, University of Auckland, 1996.

37 K. Jackson, 'The New Zealand preoccupations – politics, sport and trade' in *The Round Table* 72: 285, 1983, pp. 34–44 for a summary of causal effects of New Zealand's identity shift through the 1970s.

38 Mead, *Magnificent Te Maori*.

39 P. Tapsell, *Pukaki: a comet returns*, Auckland: Reed Publishing, 2000, for full account.

40 See M. King, *Being Pakeha Now: Reflections and Recollections of being a White Native*, Auckland: Penguin, 2004, for full discussion on this ethnic identity marker within a New Zealand context.

41 T. Bennett, *The Birth of the Museum: history, theory, politics*, Oxon: Routledge, 1995, p. 84.

42 M.M. Ames, *Museums, the Public, and Anthropology*, Vancouver: University of British Columbia Press, 1986.

43 See, for example, proceedings and curatorial files of Canterbury and Auckland museums, documenting multiple visits to Rotorua by agents and/or curators in the late 1800s.

44 For instance, R. Neich, *Carved Histories*, Auckland: Auckland University Press, 2001, pp. 215–17, documenting works for the 1906 Christchurch International Exposition by the Colonial Museum.

45 Ibid, p. 212, documenting Tene Waitere re-carving elements of the meeting house *Rangitihi* in Auckland Museum in 1906.

46 See, for example, R. Wolfe, *A Noble Prospect: 75 Years of the Auckland War Memorial Museum Building*, Auckland, 2005, documenting the 1929 Maori opening of AWMM.

47 See *Exhibition of Cook's South Seas*, New Zealand Herald 22 Nov 1969, p. 1, documenting the opening of *No Sort of Iron – Culture of Cook's Polynesians* at AWMM; and Mead, *Magnificent Te Maori*, documenting 1984–85 openings in the US.

48 R.J. Walker, *Nga Tau Tohetohe: Years of Anger*, Auckland: Penguin Books, 1987.

49 C.W. Mason, 'The Bridge to Change: The 1976 Montreal Olympic Games, South African Apartheid Policy, and the Olympic Boycott Paradigm', in G.P. Schaus & R.W. Wenn (eds.) *Onward to the Olympics: historical perspectives on the Olympic Games*, Canada: Wilfred Laurier University Press and The Canadian Institute in Greece/L'Institut canadien en Grece, 2007, pp. 283–296.

50 R.J. Walker, *Bastion Point*, Auckland, s.n. University of Auckland Library, 1979.

51 R.J. Walker, 'The Treaty of Waitangi as the Focus of Maori Protest', in I.H. Kawharu (ed.) *Waitangi: Maori & Pakeha Perspectives of the Treaty of Waitangi*, Auckland: Oxford

University Press, 1989, pp. 263–279; and R.J. Walker, *Ka Whawhai Tonu Matou: Struggle Without End*, Auckland: Penguin Books, 1990.

52 R. Shears, *Storm out of Africa: The 1981 Springbok Tour of New Zealand*, Auckland: Macmillan, 1981.

53 Jackson, *The New Zealand preoccupations*, pp. 34–44.

54 Ibid, pp. 34–44.

55 Multiple web sites document this event. Online. Available HTTP: <http://www.nzhistory. net.nz/search/node/Rainbow+Warrior> (accessed: 25 July 2010).

56 See E. Schwimmer (ed.), *The Maori People in the Nineteen-Sixties: A Symposium*, Auckland: Blackwood and Paul, 1968, for numerous perspectives on this phenomenon.

57 I.H. Kawharu, 'Urban Immigrants and Tangata Whenua', in Schwimmer, *The Maori People in the Nineteen-Sixties*, pp. 174–186.

58 H. Greenland, 'Ethnicity as Ideology', in P. Spoonley, C. MacPherson, D. Pearson and C. Sedgwick (eds.) *Tauiwi: Racism and Ethnicity in New Zealand*, Palmerston North: The Dunmore Press Ltd, 1984, pp. 86–102.

59 Walker, *Ka Whawhai Tonu Matou*, pp. 248–284.

60 I. Pool, *Te Iwi Maori: A New Zealand Population, Past, Present, and Projected*, Auckland: Auckland Univeristy Press, 1991.

61 Jackson, *The New Zealand preoccupations*, pp. 41.

62 Ibid, pp. 34–44.

63 Dibley, *Museum, Native, Nation*, p. 10.

64 Mead, *Magnificent Te Maori*; P. Tapsell, *Taonga: A Tribal Response to Museums*. Unpublished D. Phil. dissertation, School of Museum Ethnography, University of Oxford, 1998.

65 B. Kernot, 'Te Maori Te Hokinga Mai: Some Reflections', in *AGMANZ: Art Galleries and Museums Association of New Zealand Journal* 18: 2, 1987, p. 4; and G. McManus, 'The Question of Significance and the Interpretation of Maori Culture in New Zealand Museums', in *AGMANZ* 19: 4, 1988, p. 10.

66 Tapsell, *Taonga: A Tribal Response to Museums*, pp. 168–171.

67 Ibid.

68 Ibid.

69 Thomas, *Colonialism's Culture*; and Dibley, *Museum, Native, Nation*, for wider discussion on Pakeha identity within New Zealand's nation-space context.

70 *Nga Taonga o te Motu: Treasures of the Nation*.

71 Dibley, *Museum, Native, Nation*, p. 59.

72 W.L. Renwick, *The Treaty Now*, Wellington: GP Books, 1990, p. 146; also see *Tuhinga: records of the Museum of New Zealand Te Papa Tongarewa*, Wellington: Museum of New Zealand, 1995, p. 62.

73 P. Tapsell, 'From the sideline: Tikanga, Treaty Values and Te Papa', in M. Belgrave, M. Kawharu & D. Williams (eds.) *Waitangi Revisited: Perspectives on the Treaty of Waitangi*, Melbourne: Oxford University Press, 2005, pp. 266–282.

74 Ibid.

75 See, for example, S. Jones, 'Museums and the Treaty of Waitangi', in *A Framework for Funding and Performance Measurement of Museums in New Zealand: A Project of the Museum Directors Federation of Aotearoa New Zealand and Taonga o Aotearoa National Services of the Museums of New Zealand*, Wellington: McKinlay Douglas Limited, 1995, p. 14.

76 M. Ames, 'Biculturalism in Exhibits', in Mark Lindsay (ed.) *Taonga Maori Conference New Zealand. 18–27 November 1991*, Wellington: Internal Affairs 1991; Ames, *Museums and Source Communities*; Tapsell, *Taonga*; and Tapsell 'Beyond the Frame', pp. 242–251.

77 For instance, Thomas, *Colonialism's Culture*, pp. 184–5.

78 Tapsell, *Taonga*, pp. 156–261.

79 See, for example, *New Zealand Herald* 21 February 1998, p. A3 and 23 February 1998, p. A4, documenting Sotheby New York sales of two Tainui greenstone weapons or *mere*; *New Zealand Herald* 14 November, 1999, documenting Auckland Museum's hosting of APEC leaders, p. A1.

80 See B.F. Leach, *The Wakatupapaku from Waimamaku*. Waitangi Tribunal. Wai 38 – Te Roroa. Doc. #D17. 1990.

81 See *Hotonui Protocol*, Taipari Whanau Incorporated and Auckland Institute & Museum, Auckland Museum, 15 May 1996. Also see Tapsell, *Taonga*, pp. 229–230.

82 See, for instance, 'Museum bows to ultimatum from tribe', *New Zealand Herald*, 9 February 2006, p. A5, concerning waka koiwi (burial chests) of Ngati Hine origin.

83 See Tapsell, *Pukaki*, pp. 116–121; N. Thomas, *Possessions: Indigenous Art/Colonial Culture*, London: Thames & Hudson, 1999; Treaty of Waitangi Tribunal Claim 262, concerning protection of Cultural and Intellectual Property rights over indigenous fauna and flora and to other taonga. Online. Available HTTP: www.med.govt.nz/templates/Page_____1207.aspx (accessed 25 July 2010).

84 B. Kirshenblatt-Gimblett, *Destination Culture: Tourism, Museums, and Heritage*, Berkeley: University of California Press, 1998, p. 157.

85 M. Durie, 'Tino Rangatiratanga' in Belgrave, Kawharu & Williams, *Waitangi Revisited*, pp. 3–19; M.S.R. Palmer, *The Treaty of Waitangi in New Zealand's Law and Constitution*, Wellington: Victoria University Press, 2008.

86 See, for example, *Auckland War Memorial Museum (AWMM) Amendment Act 1996*, Wellington: Government Printer, New Zealand, 1996.

87 See *Resource Management Act 1991*, Wellington: Government Printer, New Zealand, 1991; *Pukaki Trust Deed*, New Zealand Cabinet, 2001.

88 Thomas, *Colonialism's Culture*; Dibley, *Museum, Native, Nation*; Tapsell, 'From the sideline', pp. 266–282.

89 Tapsell, *Ko Tawa*, for full narratives, commentaries and inventory associated with the exhibition of the same name.

90 28 exhibited *taonga* supported by ten independent multimedia presentations of archival and contemporary recordings/ images of tribal landscapes, ancestors and elders, including live and recorded narratives, songs, academic essays, publications, catalogue, web-packages and visitor-accessible public commentary (taped broadcast).

91 T. Bradley, J. Tauri & R. Walters, 'Demythologising Youth Justice in Aotearoa/New Zealand', in J. Muncie & B. Goldson (eds.) *Comparative Youth Justice*, London: Sage Publications Ltd., 2006, p. 81, states Maori youth are three times more likely to offend and dominate New Zealand Youth Courts by between 50 per cent and, in some districts, up to 90 per cent; Also see V. Owen, 'Whanake Rangatahi: Programmes and Services to address Maori Youth Offending', in *Social Policy Journal of New Zealand* 16, 2001 (July), pp.175–190, for a government overview.

92 For background on *Ko Tawa* exhibition project, led by its curator and author of this essay, Paul Tapsell, see: Online. Available HTTP: www.kotawa.co.nz (accessed 25 July 2010).

93 E. Hooper-Greenhill, *Museums and the Interpretation of Visual Culture*, London: Routledge, 2002, p. 153.

94 For Auckland Museum *Ko Tawa* database website, see: Online. Available HTTP: http://tekakano.aucklandmuseum.com/am_kotawa/home_maori.asp (accessed 25 July 2010).

95 R. Phillips, 'Community Collaboration in Exhibitions: toward a dialogic paradigm – Introduction', p. 161.

96 As per the Taumata-a-Iwi Kaupapa explained in M. Kawharu, 'Indigenous Governance in Museums', pp. 298–300.

97 AWMM's conservative estimation of *Ko Tawa* attendance was: Auckland 27,000; Wellington 40,000; Sydney 35,000 and the total for five tribal region venues: 40,000.

98 For example, on the *Ko Tawa* exhibition at the Whakatohea-led Opotiki venue, see Tapsell, *Ko Tawa*, pp. 28–35 for background to *taonga* associated with the source communities.

99 Tapsell, *Taonga*, pp. 240–242, for the Ngati Whakaue discussion on customary principles behind presenting kin for employment in Maori contexts.

100 Nicks, 'Museums and Contact Work – Introduction', p. 24.

101 *AWMM Amendment Act 1996*, section 12(2)(g).

102 M. Kawharu, 'Indigenous Governance in Museums', pp. 293–304; also see Phillips, 'Community Collaboration in Exhibitions: toward a dialogic paradigm – Introduction', p. 167.

103 Phillips, 'Community Collaboration in Exhibitions: toward a dialogic paradigm – Introduction', pp. 163–167, for a full discussion concerning these two general typologies of collaboration.

104 *Auckland Museum Annual Plan July 2008–June 2009*, Auckland Museum Trust Board.

105 'John Key offers mediation to solve 'sad' Hillary-Museum situation', *New Zealand Herald*, 15 May 2008, p. A1.

106 'Showdown at city's museum', *New Zealand Herald*, 9 December 2009, p. A1; 'Bad PR for Museum', *New Zealand Herald*, 21 February 2010, p. 36; and 'Museum can learn from Vitali's exit', *New Zealand Herald*, 18 March 2010, p. A12.

107 *Auckland Museum Annual Plan July 2003–June 2004*, Auckland Museum Trust Board.

108 For example, *AWMM Governance Policy Human Remains December 2008 C.17*, compared to previously tangata whenua-led 'Ancestral Human Remains' policy adopted in *Auckland Museum Annual Plan July 2003–June 2004*, thereby removing Ngati Whatua o Orakei's customary responsibility to directly guide returning of over 1000 Auckland Museum-held Ancestral Human Remains back to source communities.

109 Ames, 'How to Decorate a House', p. 179.

7

The responsibility of representation

A feminist perspective

Hilde Hein

Origins

Ethical restrictions apply to both individuals and social institutions. Ethics, however, is not simply constraint; it also enables the discovery and creation of value. Individuals and institutions differ in the specifics of the ethics they live (or fail to live) by, but they are all guided by ethical conditions of which they may be more or less cognizant. I will argue that museums are uniquely empowered by the nature of what they do to bring about positive change in the world that would benefit all its inhabitants.

My point of departure is feminist theory, which originates in women's experience, but is not confined to the study of women or their exclusive advancement. I have argued elsewhere in defense of theory, and specifically feminist theory, as a guide to reconceive the museum.[1] There I point out that proposals to modify museum practice are usually provoked by currently identified problems such as inadequate disability access or racial insensitivity. While solutions to such problems sometimes turn out to benefit all museum users, they are as frequently unwieldy, incompatible with one another, and ultimately unhelpful. I argue that theoretically based planning is more coherent and adaptable; and, although feminist theory is not yet mature, its foregrounding of relations and openness to pluralism address the very weaknesses that critics of the prevailing museum system consistently underscore.

I favor appealing to feminist theory because it most conspicuously addresses the binarism at the heart of Western philosophy that, in turn, is the basis of the historic museum. On my view, this base is deeply flawed and morally compromised. The philosophy contains the central tenet that consciousness is the bedrock of world-making. The universe, according to that doctrine, is accessible to us only and exclusively through the portals of our understanding. Their limits define our capacity to know and interact with the world. Therefore, the skills and devices we develop to represent the world determine what we can do in it or hope to control.[2] Entailed within that position is the radical denigration of the pliable *object* of consciousness. Whether that be conceived as of lesser stuff – mere matter, for example, or insubstantial ideas, the theory supposes a profound inequality between the active *subject*, or agent, and whatever it proposes to itself as object. Given the culture and politics that gave birth to modern philosophy and their perpetuation well into the present, a residual dualism persists today between genders, races, human attributes (e.g. minds versus bodies), social identities and more. Museums are among the propagators of that dualism. They are the offspring of a flawed philosophy. In its place, I propose a theoretical approach to the museum that addresses the primacy of its ethical identity. I derive that from its central function of representation.

The philosophy that I hope to displace has been a source of worldwide discontent, largely among persons and groups systematically excluded from the superior status of subjecthood. Since subject agency is realized in practice in the form of power and authority, those denied it suffer material disadvantage, and their ideas receive limited attention. There is, however, widespread resistance to the prevailing doctrine and a growing fund of creative theoretical discourse initiated from "outside" the privileged center. Feminist theory makes common cause with these marginalized perspectives and is one source of such philosophical innovation. Feminists converge with theoretical movements such as postcolonialism, critical race theory and queer theory in rejecting the dualistic polarization intrinsic to the mainstream Western tradition. While the dominant philosophy's operative subject/object inequality is offensive to many of its critics, dismantling the dualism that underlies it is a fundamental mission for feminist theory because the discrimination between mind and body invariably assigns inferior status to the incarnate female.[3] I view the radical commitment to resolving dualism as a promising point of departure from which a coalition politics might grow. The proliferation of alternative theories, feminism among them, is the result of individual and collective experience differently understood and of realities differently conceived than that declared by the modernist paradigm. Those who advance the alternatives do not presume their universality. Feminist theorists do not insist upon a single correct mode of apprehending the world; they welcome collaborative efforts among the outsiders that could generate novel ideas and lead to more equitable power distribution everywhere.

Representation is a common practice indulged in by all people as a means of navigating the world. It is the museum's vocation to develop expertise in multiple types and techniques of representation, to explore the variety of their expression and histories, and to reveal how we and our ancestors have constructed what we take to be the universe. No matter a museum's type or area of specialization, it is committed to depicting aspects of the world as filtered through some human consciousness. That endeavor is presumed to be a cognitive enterprise, primarily assessed in terms of truth and accuracy; and so museums are classified along with educational institutions, libraries, laboratories and the like, as epistemological purveyors and preservers.[4] I will argue, however, that representation is ethically freighted in both its origin and termination. It derives out of and fixes value, hence bears a moral burden that, arguably, exceeds epistemic correctness. On my view, museums, at the core of their being, are ethical entities. This is not a consequence of their social activism nor of their endorsement of specific moral causes; it is, rather, entailed by the museum's historic essence. Museums may elect one or another vision or focus, but they cannot elude the ethical impulse that animates all representation.

The institution developed within a tradition that reveres abstract ethical ideals that dictate monochromatic uniformity of behavior. Like a single truth, a singular ideal of rightness and goodness is assumed. The imperatives proclaimed by this system are not directed at particular instances or persons: They are general, but they arise from within the moral community and social environment of which the conventional philosopher is a part. Albeit in very impersonal, schematic terms, the ethical rules and prohibitions are addressed to likeminded agents and for the instruction of subordinates. Philosophical discourse is abstract – it does not prescribe specifically contextualized behavior, but it is meant to influence individual conduct and to affect individual lives. There is no doubt that it has done so. I believe, however, that its façade of neutral universality and its implicit normativity have fostered the radical misallocation of both privilege and blame, and have sanctioned a multitude of repugnant abuses. Under the cover of supposedly dispassionate philosophy, such (mis)conduct becomes normalized and is perpetuated, even among those it injures.

Many museums are now engaged in self-appraisals that reassess the inherited values of their origin. They are attending with interest to challenges from sources they previously discounted. The ethical dilemmas the museums face are lodged in current, real-life quandaries, but as they strive to reform themselves and realize innovative goals, they risk offending the sources that gave them birth. At the same time, their attention bewilders newly designated beneficiaries, many of whom were heretofore inclined to view the museum diffidently or to pass it by with indifference.

Long gone is the self-assured composure and elitism of the nineteenth-century institution. Today's museums are reflexive and wracked with the anguish of self interrogation. Instead of preaching to their audience, they hold focus sessions and welcome public opinion. Where formerly they relied on the ethical instincts (or certainties) of their wealthy patrons and amateur curators, they now submit to impersonal professional standards and are sworn to accountability and transparency. Social responsibility, dialogue, diversity and empowerment of the marginalized are today's explicit priorities.[5] Yet, history is adhesive; in the eyes of the public, museums retain the aura of their past authority. They take their tenure of the public trust seriously – and rightly so.[6] They worry about retaining it, and so must weigh the comfort of conformity against adventurous innovation. I do not underestimate the museum's aspiration to the moral high road, but I find a contradiction between the overt expressions of that endeavor and the mission that is vested in the museum's philosophical foundation. And so I look to the balm of theory – specifically feminist theory – to ease a way to a solution.

Identity

Museums are institutions. As such, their character differs from that of individual human beings, but museums, like people, exercise agency and are no less morally responsible for what they do. Some people maintain that only individuals, not social collectives, can be held accountable for their actions; but institutions are able to compound and multiply personal efficacy. Arguably, their responsibility is, therefore, proportionately greater insofar as their authority and influence exceeds that of most ordinary individuals. Certainly, their ethical impact is no less. Yet, typically, the primary duty of museums is described as the protection of the objects they preserve. Of course this does not exclude further obligations, to people – living, dead, and unborn – and abstractly, to their heritage. As public servants, museums are charged with collecting, harboring, studying, exhibiting, teaching and sometimes entertaining. They must do so without falsification or dissemblance: Like any corporate entity, they are legally liable. But, apart from such requirements of legal and moral conformity, museums are chiefly expected to please and enlighten us, to expand and perpetuate the means of our intellectual growth and sensuous gratification.

Obviously, museums are composed of people as well as objects, and these people – from the board of directors to security guards, kitchen staff, designers, curators and maintenance crews – are individually bound by the conventional moral standards that, independently of institutional setting, govern all ethical intercourse. Just as all persons are accountable for their conduct, museum-related people must not steal, lie, intentionally injure or endanger others. No one is absolved of such obligations merely in virtue of being part of an organization: We all function on several tracks that do not invariably coincide and can sometimes conflict. My discussion here is not about ethical obligation in general, however, but specifically as it pertains to the institutional entity that is the museum. This exists over and above the individual people that work there or are in charge. It must be understood that such identities interlace insofar as the museum's decisions and agency take the form of human beings thinking, deciding, and acting in concert. Clearly, heads will fall and some individuals will bear the blame for any improprieties ascribed to the museum, but this is often a matter of deferred responsibility. The agency attributed to the institution is a sort of fiction. It derives from multiple behaviors exhibited by distinct persons, but is not reducible to the sum of their actions. It is not identifiable as collective behavior, for it is singular – the performance of the museum.[7] The human components cannot be eliminated in practice, but my reference here is to the emergent museum entity and to its uniquely ascribed responsibility. Except in the case of extremely small museums or those with very autocratic leadership, the museum does not express the will of any single individual, but is a complex composite of legacies of originators, bequests of donors, applicable civic constraints and endorsements, the aptitudes and attitudes of trustees, directors and current staff. These intersect the limitations of the physical premises, economic resources and the disposition of collections.

All personnel must execute responsibilities according to their skills and assignments, but the sum of their performances does not add up to the museum's fulfillment of its moral function. Neither does its ethical persona merge with theirs. The museum's persona is sometimes articulated in terms of an aspiration or a mission. The National World War II Museum, for example, promises to tell "the story of the American Experience in the war that changed the world – why it was fought, how it was won and what it means today – so that all generations will understand the price of freedom and be inspired by what they learn."[8] The Museum of Tolerance, in Los Angeles, declares its dedication "to promoting respect and mutual understanding, through education, community partnerships, and civic engagement."[9] Not everyone who works in the museum must be personally motivated by its professed objective – the ethical persona of the museum and that of its affiliated personnel remain distinct – but all are obligated to foster the ends of the museum.

What differentiates the museum from the other benevolent, public or private institutions to which it is often compared? Educational, religious, preservationist, scientific, health-related and charitable organizations similarly serve the public by means of the staff they employ, the work they do and the objects they own and use. None is exempt from ordinary moral conventions; all involve specific professional duties and prohibitions appropriate to their particular fields of specialization (e.g. to do no harm, to fulfill fiduciary responsibilities, to engage in open publication, to respect client confidentiality). A simple answer might be that the service of these other agencies is more direct and more explicitly articulated than that of museums. But that is arguable: A probe of their precise duties might find them equally obscure. I suggest that the ambiguity and ephemerality of the museum's content distinguish it from these other institutions. Hospital beds and school desks can be moved or replaced without incident (apart from cost), but substituting one museum object for another invites controversy because it affects the significance of every object.[10] While, to a certain extent, hospitals, banks, libraries and schools can regard their property as fixed assets, museums thrive on the very mutability of their hold-ings' meaning. Museums, indeed, cherish the multiple potentiality of their objects much as parents embrace the unpredictable diversity of each of their children.

Museum objects have more than utilitarian or mere monetary value. That is also true of libraries that preserve "precious" manuscripts or botanical gardens, aquaria and zoos that shelter and study rare species. Hence these institutions are effectively considered museums when serving in such curatorial capacities. But their primary responsibilities – such as loaning books or developing new species – are non-museal. However aesthetically enchanting a piece of laboratory equipment might be to the scientists who use it, their first responsibility is to the experiments for which the apparatus is required. Hospitals, likewise, value the costly materials on which they rely primarily for the practical functions they serve and not for other accrued sig-nificance. In contrast, museum objects are effectively divested of their worldly applications prior to collection.[11] Once in the museum, their meaning shifts within diverse contexts and they are perceived to play a variety of parts.

Some museums explicitly commit to a moral vocation, for example to bring dis-puted social issues such as alternative energy use, genetically modified agriculture or healthcare legislation to the center of public notice. Where traditional object-centered museums might state their case didactically, newer experiential museums are inclined to deploy the aesthetically charged capabilities of the museum to address a various public variously with a view to eliciting dialogue. Instead of approaching their audi-ence as receivers of a predetermined product, they count on the permissive space of the museum to enable visitors to achieve conclusions autonomously. This strategy repudiates the notion of a single museum community that shares a common body of axioms or aspires to preordained ends. Diversity is assumed, not as an obstacle to be overcome; neither is it to be simply celebrated. Rather, it individuates people and qualifies their perceptions. It is therefore to be approached with serious interest and learned from. I applaud such expansion of the museum's purview, but I have reser-vations about the museum's transparency as mediator. I believe that in the absence of a thoroughgoing reappraisal of the museum's inherited identity its success will be confined to condoned alternatives – those sanctioned within a preexistent scheme. I advance a feminist analysis in hopes of evading the rigidity of such "permitted" disjunctions.

Knowing and representing

Museums take part in the business of representation alongside media agencies such as print, film and electronic services. Each of these addresses fluctuating audiences by means of specialized languages, rituals and materials. However performed or embodied, representation is denotative. It involves a quality of "aboutness," a reference to something that need not exist in reality, and is invariably mediated.[12] One thing – a word, sound, square of cloth, sequence of numbers – "stands for" another: A canvas bag represents first base, a will represents someone's wishes concerning the distribution of her property, a congresswoman represents the interests of her constituents, a portrait represents an actual person. Museums employ objects assembled in various combinations to represent ideas. They also use texts, performances, sounds, living creatures (including people), arrangements in space and abstract structures and policies to that end. Representation is always intentional, but not necessarily successful. I may fail in my attempt to convey an idea to you if my representation is inadequate or you do not take notice of it: I may also misrepresent something in error or by deception.

Museums use a vast array of objects, often including works of art, for the purpose of representation, but not all art is representational. There is an abundance of representational systems, each characterized by rules and conventions that prescribe what is representative of what within that system. A given thing can represent within one system, but not another. Cowrie shells, for example, work as currency in some contexts, but not in others; so do rectangular slips of paper with specific numerical markings and pictures of prominent people. Thus cowrie shells and bills with a picture of George Washington might coexist in a museum or exhibition on money or commerce. Only the cowrie shell would be displayed in a natural history collection, while Washington's image might be included in a portrait gallery or history exhibition. Representation invariably entails a sort of doubling (suggested by "re"presentation) – something that stands in the place of something else – possibly, but not necessarily, by way of resemblance – as in a photograph; or, in the case of political representation, as a proxy chosen to act on behalf of other people.[13]

If, as I maintain, representation is the essence of the museum's business, and what its resources equip it to do, surely museums bear enormous responsibility. That seems self-evident when expressed in terms of "getting it right," i.e. eliciting correct belief, or having the desired answer. As long as we think of the museum in purely epistemic terms as a truth teller or dispenser of information, we obviously demand that it conform to relevant requirements of evidence gathering, fact checking, citing the proper authorities, establishing authorship and provenance and observing due diligence and appropriate scholarship. But these are cognitive virtues. Adherence to them does not establish worth. Why know these things, and why this rather than that? What is the merit of one representative system over another? What values are furthered by that choice? What values are denied?

I have indicated that representation is capable of both deliberate and unintended falsehood. Its truthfulness may be a trivial asset. A "correct" representation is sometimes of little or no interest; or worse, it can be harmful! An idealized portrait or a grim passport photo might correctly represent the sitter at different moments, and could evoke very different consequences. Is she a crazed killer? A job candidate? A Pulitzer Prize winner? Representations may be misleading or misled. Political regimes have, for centuries, employed artists' visions to extol themselves and revile enemies. Indeed, no one understood this principle better than the Nazis whose legendary Ministry of Popular Enlightenment and Propaganda, led by Joseph Goebbels, implanted ideology into the hearts and souls of German citizens as effectively as their minds.[14]

Museums design exhibitions that affect how people think, and what they value and do. They frequently employ means whose persuasiveness has less to do with truth or accuracy than with emotive force and aesthetic potency. Representation sometimes achieves its ends by seduction, a covert form of violence. Hence its moral relevance.[15] Because it shapes our conception of and accommodation to reality, representation distributes power – and does so unequally. Because representation both limits and enables action, it is political. It defines possibility, opens and closes options. Under the guise of description representation is normative: Sometimes the certainty it induces is simply an effect of withholding alternatives. I argue that representation restricts reality and is therefore ethically problematic.

To whom, on the part of whom, and to what end do museums represent? The artfully prepared objects in their collections embody and convey ideas to an audience. Many promote the ambitions of a founder. Napoleon decreed the Louvre a public museum and filled it with the trophies of war in order to generate pride of citizenship among a previously unenfranchised populace. Frank Oppenheimer initiated the Exploratorium to extend the excitement and curiosity that motivates scientific inquiry to a broad public. The Bob Jones University Art Museum is intended to inculcate belief in fundamentalist Christianity. Wilhelmina Cole Holladay created the National Museum of Women's Art to reverse the underrepresentation of art by women in other museums. Most contemporary museums are less univocally ideated. Their missions may change with new leadership incentives, or demographic shifts in their environment – but, invariably, they do impart cultural ideology. My claim is that, beyond the criteria of intellectual integrity that apply to all institutions committed to the pursuit and transmission of knowledge, and beyond the demands of honest commerce, museums must be measured by another standard.

Museums are answerable, I hold, for (1) their choices of what to represent, including the means by which they do so; (2) their non-representations that add up to exclusions, whether or not intentional, and, most problematically, (3) what they do not choose to – but nevertheless do – represent, by indirect means. My concern is thus less with "misrepresentation" that results from willful or inadvertent error in ascertaining truth and falsity than with the institution's *de facto* preemption of reality.

Museums have grown self-aware of their evocative capacity. Open-ended exhibitions and programs that invite audience response have increased exponentially in the past several decades and are meant to enlarge the museum's own vision. There is genuine interest in public engagement, in gaining visitor collaboration, and correlatively in enlisting diversity. Expanded modes of aesthetic presentation testify to the will of the museum to address different publics differently.[16] Too often, however, the motivation seems largely practical – to get the public in the door. Once inside, visitors must adapt to an alien subjectivity or comply with an estranging means of "talking back." In effect, representation conditions consciousness. It determines what we apprehend, and shapes how we experience, diminishing some inclinations and activating others. Museums play an eloquent part in that enterprise. Clearly museums are not alone in performing that identity-forging function. We are surrounded by cultural lesson mongering. However, museums have an extraordinary variety of resources at their disposal and have acquired dexterity in their manipulation: Their ethical responsibility for deploying them must therefore be assessed accordingly. I take the current pressures for change in the museum world as reflective of widespread discontent, but also as recognition of the mutability of representation. Agitation tends to follow a glimmer of hope that present conditions are not inevitable. Feminists join others in registering dissatisfaction with the prevalent construction of the world, and feminist theory offers an approach to understanding and alleviating that condition.

Resisting representation

Rebellious voices – feminist, postcolonialist, poststructuralist, racialist, queer theoretical – are rising up against the subject/object, self/other orientation that purports to describe the world and fix "our" place within it. Whether framed as knowing, naming or domesticating, that aggressive epistemic stance aspires to conquest and dominion. Historic sexism, couched in the terms of pure and blameless objectivity, represents women as mentally, physically and spiritually inferior to men. For centuries, men and women the world over have been indoctrinated with that "truth" which has legitimized the treatment of women as fecund beasts of burden. In the same vein, a licensed curiosity justified the voyages of exploration in the Renaissance[17] and still rewards rapacious pursuit of discoveries carried out in the name of new knowledge with prizes, fame, wealth – and representation by the museum. This "impersonal" quest warrants search and seizure of "specimens," animate and inanimate, living and dead, and their removal from wherever they are found to sanctuaries of study – including museums. Here, torn from their environment of origin, they are reduced to ultimate "objecthood," severed from prior social affinities and refused the subjectivity their scrutinizers cherish in themselves. Whether living creatures, inanimate objects, commodified experiences or intellectual property, they have become irretrievably "other." Notwithstanding its confounding scientific designation, a "subject" of inquiry (interest, research, or investigation), having been degraded to the status of specimen, is objectified.

The Western tradition of modern philosophy puts consciousness, unfettered by embodiment, at the center of the world, thereby elevating the individual ego above everything it surveys and aspires to dominate.[18] This unencumbered, obtusely gendered subject, devoid of emotion, sex, color, desire – let alone mass or location – yet driven by curiosity and the will to power, confronts a (frequently feminized) universe perversely resistant to understanding. The museum is but one of the units mustered to subdue that hapless adversary. Their weapons are the instruments of selection and representation that ensnare and appropriate their catch to conform to the vision of the seekers. But that vision is peculiarly blinkered, and much is overlooked by its scrutiny. A feminist approach questions this construction of "otherness" and of the items so designated. But, as I have indicated, the issue at issue is less their "misrepresentation" than the determination to represent them as object at all, and so to force them into a mold that diminishes them – like "a patient etherized upon the table."[19]

The inclusion of ceremony and festivals among museum displays stretches the common understanding of "museum objects" and helps us approach them not as static things, but performatively as process.[20] Things are unmoored to become temporal passages. Feminist theory has liberated the performative, enlivening the strangely fixed vacuity of the object, heretofore viewed as a "surface awaiting signification" by a superior mental agent. Replacing such reductive rendition of sex and gender as "regulatory fictions that consolidate and naturalize ... power regimes," the feminist theoretician Judith Butler describes gender as "a performatively enacted signification" that can subvert the classical status reification.[21] Bodies, on Butler's view, are simply "styles of the flesh." There is no preexisting identity, no true or false gender, but only that "congealed through sustained social performances."[22] So, too, I suggest, the objects that fill museums are enacted scenes of temporal performances. Let us consider how freeing objects from their relegation to fixed "objecthood" parallels the enfranchisement of persons who have suffered a similar fate. Entire genders and populations, together with their customs, possessions and creations, are diminished as quaintly (or dangerously) subhuman according to a code they had no part in constructing. Museums have not been innocent bystanders to this injury. Simply by carrying out their designated function and executing the objectifying activity for which they are eminently qualified, they have perpetuated the practice – whether or not with malicious intent. Feminist theorizing clarifies its wrongfulness and can help find a way to its correction.

In an essay on museum ethics, Ivan Gaskell describes the fate of tribal basketry regalia formerly used in annual renewal ceremonies of the northern California Hoopa Indians. These spiritually animated items are functional vehicles whose historic and aesthetic vitality is derived from their production and use within their culture. This is lost upon their subjection to the "ethnographic gaze" that classifies them according to categories of knowledge. Gaskell asks how objects that partake of the numinous in the precincts of their origin might be transferred respectfully into the neutralizing environment of the museum.[23] I am pressing beyond his query to question the museum's entitlement to define reality at all. I suggest that the museum's ethical service should lie not, as Gaskell proposes, in affirming alternative answers to issues of identity – although that would at least pluralize the bases for respect – but in breaking the circuit of authority by calling its self-acclaimed historic judgment to account. The adulation of knowledge degenerates easily into prurient curiosity, and pursuit of scientific inquiry can yield abominations. Consider the infamous abuse of the "Hottentot Venus." It included her display, caged and nude, as a living specimen and its post-mortem dissection by the famed anatomist Georges

Cuvier.[24] The reduction of all experience to collectible nuggets of (potential) knowledge sculpts it pragmatically according to the language and parameters of the already known. In effect, it does not even engage the other as truly other – and therefore beyond comprehensibility – but renders it by negation to familiar categories of the presumed known. Indeed, the other is conventionally defined in terms of its non-conformity to the familiar. Effectively, this procedure assimilates all unknowns to one another (in light of their difference from the known) and precludes their accessibility on any terms. It might also warrant their collaborating amongst themselves – as some proclaimed "others" have done.

I venture to think that our only plausible relation to the wholly other must be ethical, and that this must be a precondition of any human interaction. Respectful forbearance should also be the essential posture of decency that museums adopt in their representations of the world. That stance precedes understanding, tempers it and relieves its excesses. It makes no sense to anticipate otherness with animosity, nor to consider it as of purely cognitive interest – a temptation to guarded curiosity. Yet, we are conventionally trained to mistrust what we perceive as alien and so to subdue it as representation. Saatjie Baartman would probably have elicited no more attention in her own environment than would a man with a bulbous nose in our own.

The belief that everything must be judged in relation to "my" universe and must be comprehensible within it is not everywhere shared. Feminists join with other "others" in pointing out just how parochial and how debilitating that conviction is. The philosopher Charles Mills, citing Ralph Ellison's novel *Invisible Man*, observes that oppression leaves no doubt in its victims of the reality of others, but casts considerable uncertainty on one's own existence.[25] Mills portrays this state of consequential non-being as a pitiable artifact of adversity. Various feminist theorists have described a similarly pathological erasure of self among veterans of such trauma as rape, torture, or confinement in concentration camps. However, these examples implicitly adhere, by obversion, to the egocentric Cartesian model. They elucidate the negative consequences (for those objectified) that follow from their "othering," but offer no alternative to it. They illustrate how its victims aspire to reverse or rise above their status, indeed to achieve the subject preeminence of their tormentors. This reveals how represented "objects" can collude, however unwillingly, in perpetuating the system of objectification. But it does not show a way out of that dilemma.[26]

One alternative adopted by many feminist theorists and common to communitarian societies is to deny the reality of the individual ego apart from its significant community. Patronymics such as the Icelandic gendered endings (Petursson, Magnusdottir) are a familiar device indicating parental lineage, and many cultures use more elaborate verbal or decorative signs – tattoos, hairstyles, conventional dress – that convey who belongs where and to whom. These are instantly recognizable features where kinship is the key to identity. No one stands individually alone as a subject: Instead, relatedness anchors the person. Physical, emotional or spiritual separation from the whole diminishes and objectifies the severed part. An isolate, bereft of its nested being, is without meaning, lost even to itself as a limb amputated from the whole ceases to be functional. In opposition to the prevailing philosophy that glorifies autonomy, feminists affirm that relatedness is no defect. On the contrary, they defend it as an enabling capacity that enhances understanding. Ethically, relatedness relieves the isolation of the unencumbered Cartesian subject.[27]

I am compelled to admit that, thus far, feminist theory has not displaced the harsh binarism of the subject/object:self/other dyad – but only questioned its preeminence. The language and metaphysics, indeed the entire dismal heritage of "the egocentric predicament," still seem inescapable.[28] It is tempting to suggest that, precisely because of the wealth of non-linguistic and non-cognitive resources at their disposal, museums might come to the rescue and find a better way.

The prospect for museums

There is no lack of critics who charge the modern European museum with "grasping the world" and intervening in its national and secular affairs.[29] Some observers credit the museum with softening the ferocity of that grasp, but few can overlook the aggressive dualism entailed by representation altogether.[30] At best, the proponents of pluralism strive to enlarge the scope of what is representable, and to render it reciprocally, not as a one-way process. It is a refreshing lesson in humility to encounter ourselves and our cultural practices depicted through the expressive artifacts of others. Totem poles by First Nations peoples of the Northwest Coast comically adorned with top-hatted white men, Chinese paintings of hairy white traders with big noses, incredulous tales by African storytellers of European missionaries who celebrate their faith by drinking the blood and eating the body of their god: White commentators refer to these as crude caricatures crafted by primitive natives. But to their makers and primary audience, the features depicted may accurately represent the most memorable (and shocking) aspects of their foreign visitors

Observing these helps us to become more self aware, less exclusive and less credulous of what are pronounced universals. More egalitarian interaction within the museum that permits ideas to percolate throughout the institution also helps detach ideas from specific egos – protective of their ownership and interests – and so further deconstructs the foundations of selfhood and subjectivity. Museums took a great step in this direction when they shifted from exclusively curator-initiated exhibitions to filtering them through design teams that include staff members with regular public interaction. Pressures from within and without, however, tie the museum to its historic roots. I do not think that museums can evade their commitment to representation altogether, but I believe they can rebalance its ethical merit against the encumbrance of epistemological pretension.

I have noted that moral responsibility is usually assigned individually, not institutionally, but that institutions are also ethically freighted. The effects of their misconduct are borne over time by multitudes of unknown individuals, who ignore the origin of their misery and have few options for its alleviation. Racism is an instance: Its sources are institutional, though perpetuated by individuals who usually are unacquainted with their victims, toward whom they may bear no personal malice. This is no less true of sexism, which is perpetuated by the complicity of well-meaning women as well as men. One reason why a racist or sexist environment is hard to eliminate is that moral blame is commonly associated with specifiable acts that are carried out by identifiable persons.[31] Moral blame, moreover, is rarely assigned to the passive beneficiaries of such acts. Thus, whoever prospers at the expense of those who bear the burden of historic racism, sexism and other collective injuries enjoys dubious innocence. Having "done nothing wrong," they bristle at the suggestion that they are, nonetheless, ethically culpable. Why hold them responsible for something they did not "do"? What should they have done differently?

Assuming that museums are not active perpetrators of identifiable wrongs – and this is not invariably the case – they are nonetheless institutionally implicated in passing along and so endorsing systemic wrongs. They can be charged with the failure to prevent or oppose wrongdoing, but we have limited practical means to deter wrongdoing *in general*. Our ethical, like our legal structures, are designed to address one specifiable offense at a time, and not to take note of their cumulative effects. We cannot, therefore, expect that museums do battle against all wrongdoing, but it is not unreasonable to ask that they recognize and restrict their own special proclivity toward it.

This, I maintain, derives from the mixed blessing of their unparalleled provision for representation. I do not dispute the superior ability of various new technologies to convey us to possible, probable and wholly imaginary worlds; but museums are extraordinarily equipped to evoke a powerful conviction of reality. They do this by way of their disposition of objects, texts, sounds and a multitude of sensory and suggested presences. All museums – whatever their orientation or the nature of their holdings – are dedicated to representation. They are training us to think, see, understand or imagine the universe in one or more specific ways. We may come away indifferent or unpersuaded, but we will have been invited to entertain possibilities that, now rendered plausible, could be transformative. Surely that is a powerful ethical calling.

No doubt there is legitimate disagreement as to which visions of the world are most convincing or deserve explicit representation. Not everyone endorses the same causes; neither is that necessary. Personally, I would welcome an end to the depiction of women in a manner that both mystifies and normalizes them as perennial "others," chiefly as sex objects, idealized maternal figures, helpmeets in the affairs of men and creatures of male fantasy. But, more importantly, I want it recognized that these *are* representations, maybe misrepresentations, that there are (or might be) alternatives to them, and that their reiteration, whether intentionally or not, reinforces their hold on common belief. It is in this regard that museums have been shortsighted about acknowledging their moral responsibility. Portraying themselves in light of their epistemic function, they claim the status of truthtellers, but ignore the selective bias of that enterprise. Indeed, they follow, too well, the path of the universities in cultivating a passive clientele that consumes prepackaged cultural products and leaves little initiative for dissent.

It has been argued that the museum is just one of many decentered and dispersed microcenters of domination. I have some quarrel with that analysis, but my concern here is not the generalized (mal)distribution of power. It is, rather, with the tactical expertise of representation that the museum deploys so efficiently and well, but with nary a glance to its ethical potency. Let me reemphasize that I do not advocate the elimination of all representation. So far, there is no alternative route to understanding, and representation is, in addition, an indisputably potent source of aesthetic and emotional gratification. Perhaps, one day, there will be other avenues to knowledge, but I have no idea what these might be. My aim, meanwhile, is simply to underscore the crucial role that representation plays in constituting the world and fixing our place within it. This is too weighty a task to be entrusted to a self-selected few who willfully ignore the ethical impact of what they do.[32]

The world cannot be collected in all its particulars, and if collected, not everything in that collection can be understood, and if understood, not rightly so. Museums make ethical choices at every point and with every interpretive judgment. In this chapter, I focus on the ethics of representation because it is so fundamental that it is commonly overlooked. However, its invisible force is augmented by the political structure and organization of the museum institution as a whole – by its hierarchical employment ladder, its economic dependency, its social history and by the clientele it typically aims to gratify. All of these, working in concert, conspire to naturalize and neutralize ethical presumptions that are dubious at best.

Finally, I urge that we cease to depict the museum chiefly in epistemic terms because that route is self-limiting and resistant to criticism. It precludes unorthodox thinking. We need, instead, to ask how the museum might transform what has been represented as true and actual to make the world a better place.

Notes

1 H. Hein, "Redressing the Museum in Feminist Theory," *Museum Management and Curatorship*, 2007, 22: 1, pp. 29–42.

2 Philosophical modernism reputedly begins with the seventeenth-century ideas articulated by René Descartes (1596–1650), although he was by no means their only source.

3 Judith Butler points out that the mind–body distinction is generally drawn out of theological contexts that assign the signifying role to the immaterial element, which is automatically assigned higher status. J. Butler, *Gender Trouble: Feminism and the Subversion of Identity*, London and New York: Routledge, 1990, p. 152.

4 Even museums whose emphasis appears to be non-cognitively experiential or aesthetic ultimately justify their existence in terms of learning – whether to reconcile the past or assimilate the present. Conceivably this is a practical survival mechanism.

5 Individual museums, in conversation with peer institutions, fellow professionals and their patrons, are continuously redefining themselves, drawing upon their own immediate circumstances and experience. This is a departure from the abstract orientation and code-determined conduct to which they aspired a half-century ago. See accounts of specific contemporary instances in this volume and further discussions on the web site of the Institute of Museum Ethics, Seton Hall University, Online. Available HTTP: http://www.museumethics.org/content/about (accessed January 31, 2009).

6 James Cuno reports that, according to a survey taken by the American Association of Museums in 2001, "Museums were judged trustworthy by 87 percent of the respondents, while books were judged trustworthy by only 61 percent and television news by only 50 percent." J. Cuno, *Whose Muse? Art Museums and the Public Trust*, Princeton, NJ, and Oxford: Princeton University Press, 2004, p.18.

7 Like a nation or a university, the entity is a composite of people, buildings and other concrete objects, as well as non-tangibles such as systems of law, traditions, reputation and conferred status.

8 Online. Available HTTP: http://www.ddaymuseum.org/ (accessed 12 August 2009).

9 Online. Available HTTP: http://www.museumoftolerance.com/site/c.tmL6KfNVLtH/b.4865925/k.83A7/Whats_ Happening_at_the_MOT.htm (accessed 12 August 2009).

10 This may be a matter of degree. Experiential museums often have replicable exhibits designed to provoke an experience in the observer. The material stuff of the equipment in that instance is purely instrumental, but its replicability diminishes where the object is neither a specimen (of a kind) nor a generic means to an end. Notwithstanding its uniqueness, however, an irreplaceable object is subject to unlimited interpretation.

11 This is not invariably the case. Precious objects such as dishware and jewelry were sometimes removed from princely collections to be used on stately occasions. Collections of Native American materials, even now, include ceremonial items that may, by arrangement, be "borrowed" back for tribal use.

12 Arthur Danto develops the notion of "aboutness" as a feature of art (among other things) that does not merely point to or identify a content but also comments upon it. A. Danto, *The Transfiguration of the Commonplace: A Philosophy of Art*, Cambridge, MA: Harvard University Press, 1981.

13 There is dispute within electorates regarding the proper role of representatives. Ought they to act according to their own best judgment or in accordance with the will of their constituents?

14 Recognizing the efficacy of restraint and at least the appearance of "objective" accuracy, Goebbels compared subtle persuasion to a gas: "The best propaganda is that which, as it were, works invisibly, penetrates the whole life without the public having any knowledge of the propagandistic initiative." Cited in C. Koonz, *The Nazi Conscience*, London and Cambridge, MA: Belknap Press of Harvard University, 2003, p. 13.

15 There is an established literature on the ethics of Holocaust representation. See, for example, B. Kaplan, *Unwanted Beauty: Aesthetic Pleasure in Holocaust Representation*, Urbana, IL, and Chicago: University of Illinois Press, 2007; B. Lang, *Holocaust Representation: Art within the Limits of History and Ethics*, Baltimore, MD, and London: Johns Hopkins University Press, 2003; United States Holocaust Memorial Museum, *After Representation: The Holocaust, Literature, and Culture*, New Brunswick, NJ: Rutgers University Press, 2009.

16 My own observation is that the impact is mostly on conventional museum audiences. Their number has increased, and they seem to enjoy their experience. Those to whom the museum has been an alien concept continue to ignore it.

17 "[W]ith particular reference to the 'artificial curiosities' obtained on the voyages of Captain James Cook in the Pacific, it is sometimes argued that science justified imperialism, but it would seem closer to the mark to suggest that imperialism legitimated science." N. Thomas, "Licensed Curiosity: Cook's Pacific Voyages," in J. Elsner and R. Cardinal (eds.) *The Cultures of Collecting*, Cambridge, MA: Harvard University Press, 1994, p. 116.

18 Arguably, the tradition originates in Greek philosophy with Socrates' admonition to "know thyself" and Plato's (unfulfilled) quest for knowledge of the Good.

19 Quoted from T. S. Eliot, "The Love Song of J. Alfred Prufrock," in *Collected Poems, 1909–1935*, New York: Harcourt Brace, 1936, p. 111.

20 Barbara Kirshenblatt-Gimblett, in a discussion of the Smithsonian Institution's Folklife festivals, points out that the presentation of these celebrations is usually a reenactment or representation of such events, thereby removing them to some degree from their original performative condition. B. Kirshenblatt-Gimblett, "Objects of Ethnography," in I. Karp and S. D. Lavine (eds.) *Exhibiting Cultures: The Poetics and Politics of Museum Display*, Washington, DC: Smithsonian Institution Press, 1991, p. 424. This is correct, but their processual or event-like quality is still conveyed, suggesting that what we are confronting is not reducible to "mere" object status.

21 Butler, *Gender Trouble*, pp. 33–34.

22 Ibid. p. 141.

23 I. Gaskell "Ethical Judgments in Museums," in G. Hagberg (ed.) *Art and Ethical Criticism*, Malden, MA: Blackwell, 2008, pp. 229–242.

24 This was the popular title given to Saatjie Baartman, a South African Khoi woman who was brought to Europe under false pretenses. Once arrived, she was abused and displayed as a carnival freak. After her death in 1817, Dr. Cuvier performed an autopsy on her cadaver to compare her genitalia with those of apes. He thus advanced racist scientific theories on African women's oversexed and subhuman state which continued to circulate

for more than a century. In March 2002, the French Senate finally agreed to return Baart-man's remains – including her preserved organs – for burial in her homeland. N. Bancel et al. (eds.) *Human Zoos: From the Hottentot Venus to Reality Shows*, trans. Teresa Bridgeman, Liverpool: University of Liverpool Press, 2009; D. Willis, *Black Venus 2010: They Called her "Hottentot,"* Philadelphia: Temple University Press, 2010.

25 C. Mills, *Blackness Visible: Essays on Philosophy and Race*, Ithaca, NY: Cornell University Press, 1998, p. 7.

26 S. J. Brison, "Outliving Oneself: Trauma, Memory, and Personal Identity," in D. T. Meyers (ed.) *Feminists Rethink the Self*, Boulder, CO: Westview Press, 1996. These authors suggest that self-imposed invisibility might serve a therapeutic function, providing a condition conducive to a survival of sorts, i.e. one that permits the eventual reclaiming of subjectivity.

27 A residue of the kin-identifying tradition remains, of course, in married women's assumption of their husband's name. Regrettably this has been interpreted as her con-tractually alienated ownership (by him). The custom of assigning children the names of living or dead relatives derives from a similar will to establish linkage, if not possession, in our own culture.

28 Ralph Barton Perry, an American Realist philosopher, coined the expression, observing that, although there is no direct introspective intuition of a self, it must be presupposed hypothetically as a condition of any thought. R. B. Perry, "The Ego-centric Predicament," *Journal of Philosophy, Psychology, and Scientific Methods*, 1910, 7, pp. 5–14.

29 In their introduction to the anthology that bears this title, the editors hark back to an ancient and medieval understanding of the concept that assimilates "to grasp" or "seize" with the mental processes of comprehending the world. I believe, however, that their observation must be taken with a touch of postmodern irony.

30 "The persistence of the museum *idea* can aid us in not reducing the past to a form of the present, and the other to a form of the same." D. Preziosi and C. Farago (eds.) *Grasping the World: The Idea of the Museum*, Aldershot: Ashgate, 2004, p. 8. I would add that we must also steer clear of assimilating the present to a past that we can reconstruct but never recover.

31 In such environments the culpable acts are generally not viewed as "wrongdoing" outside of the offended community precisely because they are commonplace and do not seem objectionable to those who routinely practice or condone them.

32 Without conceding to the charge of essentialism, I share the feminist conviction that "the interpretive screen through which the world is viewed cannot be underestimated" (*sic*). See L. Alcoff, "Philosophy Matters: A Review of Recent Work in Feminist Philosophy," in *Signs*, 25: 3, 2000 (spring) pp. 841–882.

Part II
ETHICS, ACTIVISM AND SOCIAL RESPONSIBILITY

8

On ethics, activism and human rights

Richard Sandell

In 2007 and 2008, interpretive experiments appeared in nine different museums and galleries across the UK, each drawing on different kinds of collections and deploying diverse modes of interpretation, but nevertheless sharing the same purpose – to offer ways of seeing which subvert dominant (discriminatory, oppressive, stereotypical) representations of disabled people and engage a wide range of visitors in contemporary debates linked to disability rights. These nine interventions – displays, exhibitions, films and education sessions for schools – were the result of an experimental action research project[1] that sought to explore new ways of representing disabled people and constructing disability-related narratives which resisted prevalent (medicalised, tragic, dehumanising) interpretive frames found in popular and news media, literature, advertising and film. Ultimately, we hoped to challenge, inform and enrich visitors' perceptions and broader public understandings of disability.

This project can be seen as part of a broader resurgence of interest, at the start of the twenty-first century, in museum philosophy and practice which emphasises the social responsibilities and potential value of museums. More museums than ever now express support for the principle of 'access for all' (within their mission statements and strategic plans) and employ staff with specific responsibility for engaging communities previously excluded from visiting. Similarly, there is renewed interest in the potential for museums to respond, in creative ways and with their unique resources, to wide-ranging social inequalities and environmental concerns and there are exciting instances of innovation and experimentation in this field.[2]

However, these trends towards more democratic, socially engaged and responsible forms of practice have not gone unchallenged. Indeed, there are worrying signs that competing views on museum purposes and responsibilities – including some which threaten to undermine the ethical bases of museums – appear to be gaining ground in many parts of the museum world. I shall return shortly to these worrisome trends but they are one reason why a renewed commitment to exploring ethical practice is both a timely and important project.

Firstly, it is appropriate in a book, which seeks to define and champion ethical practice, to make my intentions in this chapter explicit and transparent. I begin by reviewing the increasingly trenchant backlash against the trend towards professional concern for accessibility, inclusion and social responsibility, which has emerged in recent years, including the often heated debates regarding the social purposes (and concomitant moral obligations) of publicly funded museums and galleries. My intention here is to argue for a museum ethics that positions contributions to social well-being, equity and fairness as an integral part of museum work; that acknowledges the obligations which follow from the unequal patterns of participation that characterise the majority of museums' visitorships; and, more particularly, recognises the imperatives to actively dismantle the multiple barriers which continue to deny less advantaged communities access to museum experiences. In the second part of the chapter, I return to look in more detail at *Rethinking Disability Representation* – the project with which I began this chapter – to examine the complex ethical challenges bound up in attempts to inform public opinion and to engage visitors in debates about human rights. Despite a marked resurgence of interest in recent years in museum thinking which prioritises social relevance and value, this purposefully activist approach to museum work is on an uncertain footing. A number of high-profile public controversies in which museums have been attacked for their ('unbalanced', 'impartial') treatment of morally charged and rights-related issues[3] have, in some countries and contexts, operated to erode professional confidence, inhibit risk-taking and stifle further attempts to engage with challenging contemporary issues. My aim here is to defend and lend support to activist museum practice as an entirely legitimate and increasingly important (albeit challenging) approach to museum work – an approach which acknowledges both the opportunities and the obligations museums have to contribute to greater social good.

Competing visions and values

Ethics is an undeniably messy business. Indeed, there would be little need for debate and deliberation if the ethical dilemmas museum practitioners faced involved choosing between clearly delineated notions of right and wrong, of good and bad. Ethical codes of conduct exist to offer guidance and principles with which practitioners might navigate contested moral territory,[4] but some of the most challenging dilemmas inevitably arise when we are faced with competing visions of what constitutes ethical practice. In such circumstances, which sets of values, beliefs, practices – each with their own apparently seductive and convincing logic – offer the most appropriate way forward and how might we choose between them?

Access for all?

The last twenty-five years have seen what some have called a paradigmatic shift in the museum away from a primary focus on acquiring, preserving and researching objects towards a much greater concern for enabling a more diverse body of visitors to access and experience museums.[5] Although the extent to which this shift has been real, rather than merely rhetorical, remains open to question,[6] it has nevertheless been highly significant for the profession and for professional practice. It has been codified in museum ethics documents and inspired bodies such as the American

Association of Museums, the UK's Museums Association and the International Council of Museums (ICOM) to develop new definitions of the museum which give emphasis to the value of enhancing access.[7] It has enabled a much deeper understanding of the ways in which visitors engage with, and learn within museums, and it has created a climate in which at least some organisations have begun to move away from a passive approach to their audiences ('the doors are open and everyone is welcome') to one in which greater responsibility is taken for identifying and dismantling the wide-ranging barriers which have operated (with considerable effectiveness) to exclude many groups from participation.

Some thirty years ago, programmes aimed at broadening museum audiences by engaging groups who, traditionally, have not participated in museum visiting, were the preserve of a minority of pioneering community-focused museums. Today, most institutions have made at least some efforts to appeal to groups under-represented in their visitorships. The effects of this widely documented 'turn to the audience' on patterns of visitation are, however, highly uneven in character. Whilst a few organisations have undoubtedly made radical transformations to their missions, priorities and to the allocation of their resources (and, as a result, have succeeded in engaging and sustaining more diverse audiences), others have responded in a much more cosmetic fashion with little alteration to their core values and priorities. In the majority of cases, attempts to engage non-traditional audiences are generally confined to education and outreach departments, or short-term projects with limited resources and power to change experiences for the everyday visitor.

Alongside increasing professional concern for greater equity in opportunities for participation has been a growing interest in representing – through collections and displays – the lives, cultures and contributions of more diverse communities. The new social movements of the latter part of the twentieth century and the global influence of human rights, accompanied by demographic shifts arising from transnational migration, have, over the past three decades or so, given rise to increasing calls for women, indigenous and minority ethnic communities (and, to a lesser extent, faith groups, sexual minorities and disabled people) to be represented in more equitable and fair ways which affirm their rights. Against a backdrop of widespread interest in representing more culturally pluralist narratives, a minority of organisations have adopted an explicitly activist position and purposefully sought to engage audiences in debates about equality and social justice.[8] These socially purposeful museums very often seek to engender support for the human rights of different communities whose lived experiences of disadvantage and marginalisation have often been reflected in their exclusion from, or misrepresentation, within existing museum narratives.

These significant shifts in thinking have, not surprisingly, generated a powerful backlash and, more worryingly, there are signs of a decreasing emphasis (within policy and practitioner discourse) on access and inclusion as continuing priorities for the sector. Criticism rarely challenges the value of broadening audiences or the validity of constructing more diverse narratives *per se*. More commonly, critics focus on what are seen as misguided attempts to impose museums on individuals who have no interest in culture; they make assertions that museums are losing their way and mount assaults on the ways in which governments and other funders and policy makers are directing attention towards the need to broaden access, arguing that such

131

approaches inhibit creativity and risk-taking in cultural organisations. Perhaps the most widely used mode of attack is to invoke the notion of 'dumbing down' through which – it is argued – museums have been required to communicate in overly simplistic and unscholarly ways in order to meet the needs of an uneducated (and uninterested) audience.[9]

The following is just a sample of recent comments from the fierce debates that have taken place, in both the museum profession and in the mainstream media, concerning the fundamental purposes and obligations of museums and what should be collected and displayed, for whom, by whom, and to what end.

In 2004 Josie Appleton of the Institute of Ideas wrote:

> Over the past ten to fifteen years, the face of museums has changed beyond recognition. Out has gone the focus on the collection, study and display of artefacts. Instead, we've seen museums reinvent themselves as social missionaries, getting involved in building communities, improving mental health and educating children. Other museums have reposed themselves as businesses, developing a 'brand' and working to give the 'customers' what they want. Rows of stuffed animals have been replaced by interactive machines, and scholarship has given way to outreach work.[10]

The Turner Prize-winning British artist Mark Wallinger wrote in the *Observer* newspaper in 2002:

> I think the enemy of creativity is society's obsession with accessibility and education in museums and galleries; there's a kind of desperate notion that somehow you've got to meet people half way. Art can be very difficult, and why shouldn't it be?[11]

In a newspaper article in May 2000 entitled 'No, you can't come in: you're the wrong colour' the journalist Minette Marrin expressed her outrage at attempts by government to encourage nationally funded museums and galleries in England to address marked inequities in levels of participation between white and minority ethnic populations:

> With quite astonishing arrogance, the Department of Culture, Media and Sport has just issued a truly shocking threat to this country's leading art galleries and museums ... if they don't increase their numbers of 'ethnic' visitors in line with strict quotas, they may lose their funding ... [12]

James Cuno, President and Director of the Art Institute of Chicago, wrote in 2003:

> How can we direct [visitors'] attention to the art with just enough assistance to help them, but with not so much that we limit their responses? ... I would suggest that we could begin by clearing away some of the clutter in our museums, the many distractions we have introduced into them – the commercial, the alimentary, the promotional, the entertaining, even – to the extent that it comes between the viewer and the work of art – the educational.[13]

In 2001, in a publication featuring a range of perspectives on museums' relationships with their publics, Josie Appleton stated:

> While the core function for which museums were created is downgraded to an ancillary activity, a vast range of spurious functions are loaded onto them for which they are entirely unsuited. For the new orthodoxy, museums must reflect the concerns and experiences of our society and of everyday life. They must become relevant, and inclusive, and should talk to 'real people' ... Museums should stick to what they do best – to preserve, display, study and where possible collect the treasures of civilisation and of nature. They are not fit to do anything else.[14]

Journalist and writer James Delingpole made the following comments in a British newspaper in 2006:

> Arts funding that might once have been spent acquiring a particularly fine Stubbs or a rare medieval manuscript, is now diverted towards fashionable campaigns to coax more ethnic minorities up the steps of the National, or on community projects to help the homeless or the mentally ill feel better about themselves ... Greater 'access' and 'education' may not in themselves be unworthy aims, but to emphasise them at the expense of museums' core function is to miss the point completely. Without the stimulus of new collections, museums become moribund. Who will want access to a museum that's dead?[15]

Efforts at greater inclusion, as several of these critics and commentators argue, are necessarily at the expense of other, more important, activities. Museums, it is implied, must make a choice between collections and visitors, between scholarly, collection-based research and social engagement; between offering experiences of awe and wonder and presenting objects in narrowly didactic ways which close down and delimit visitor responses. Such oppositions are false and misleading. The most powerful and successful examples of inclusive practice are those which draw on the unique power of collections; which combine curatorial expertise with other sources of knowledge and experience; and which are underpinned by rigorous research into both collections and visitors.

Minette Marrin's statement reflects concerns over the ways in which measures of performance have been increasingly used by governments in the UK to influence museum priorities. It is, of course, true that some performance targets are crude and that more sophisticated means of capturing the personal, social and cultural value of museums (and advocating this to government and other funders) is needed, along with the recognition that some forms of value cannot be reduced to a set of econometric measures. Arguments such as Marrin's, however, are undermined by their underlying resistance to any frameworks of accountability designed to ensure museums pay attention to the make-up of their audiences. In a similar vein, Mark Wallinger's plea to keep art 'difficult' conflates the obligations placed on individual artists with those of the museums and galleries which show their work, implying incorrectly that the proponents of inclusion call for accessible *art* as well as accessible *institutions* and *institutional practices*.

Several of these statements deploy language that makes the thinking and motivation that underlie them appear seductively benign. Who would wish to pursue activities that curtail organisational or artistic creativity? The idea of foisting museums on those who are avowedly uninterested or coaxing reluctant visitors into galleries is surely manipulative? The rhetoric also strongly suggests that the removal of 'clutter' from galleries can only serve to enhance the visitor experience, perhaps even make it more accessible. The idea that museums should 'stick to what they do best', meaning their apparently core functions of collection, preservation, research and presentation, is a further common feature in these debates. Critics of the inclusive museum often imply that the use of museums to achieve broader social, civil and educational aims is something entirely new – an argument that conveniently ignores the historical roots of public institutions in the nineteenth century.[16]

Underlying each of these statements is an assumption that museums are discretely *cultural* organisations and should be free to operate autonomously in ways which take no account of social, political, educational and cultural inequalities. For many critics of access and inclusion, biases in patterns of participation are explained solely by the individual tastes and preferences of groups that choose to visit and those that don't. Similarly, they would argue that biases in the kinds of material and artworks collected and displayed by museums have no relationship to broader patterns of inequality and no discernible social effects and consequences. These assumptions support the view that museums have no obligation to acknowledge and take account of these inequalities in the ways in which they are managed.

Whilst some in the museum sector highlight the widespread shift in rhetoric and practice over the past two or three decades to suggest that 'the battle has been won', the statements shown above reflect a worrisome counter-trend and do not support the claim that access, diversity and inclusion have entered the mainstream of museum thinking and practice. The philosophy and practices they argue for have very real effects. They deny the many complex ways in which museums are complicit in broader social inequalities and they resist the notion that museums play a significant role in shaping social values and understandings of difference. This is a position which, as we shall see, is increasingly untenable in the face of a growing body of empirical evidence exploring the ways in which visitors perceive, engage with and make use of museums. More fundamentally, those who challenge the trend towards more inclusive practice effectively seek to restrict museum visiting to those with the resources (material, educational, cultural) to take advantage of them. As Mark O'Neill has powerfully argued:

> Resistance to targets and access often extends beyond staff to Board members, regular users and Friends organizations who, while they may indeed enjoy the cultural experience for its own sake, also relish the experience of exclusiveness. The outrage they feel about facilities required to orient and welcome novice visitors (a.k.a. dumbing down) may be due to a fear that people may think the implied lack of knowledge or appreciation applies to them, or that the museum may communicate that just about anyone can visit without passing what Kenneth Hudson has referred to as the 'secret exam'.

Social inclusion is not about simplifying difficult things. It is about pro-viding points of entry for people whose education and background has not equipped them to approach difficult works that they might in fact be interested in. It is not about determining a response but about sharing an enriching experience.[17]

These competing viewpoints, briefly reviewed here, reflect differing opinions on the extent to which museums might be accountable, and to whom. Indeed, the issue of accountability and the challenges posed by attempts to accommodate the needs and interests of diverse stakeholders is a central concern of museum ethics. As Tristram Besterman[18] highlights, the multiplicity of interests that museums must seek to balance means that they are inevitably faced with competing demands which, in turn, generate challenging ethical dilemmas. At the same time, Besterman is clear that this 'ethics of accountability' should not limit museums to responsive modes of practice. In contrast, he argues that 'Museums are places of creative interaction, in which traditional values and orthodoxies can and should be challenged. An ethical museum should be free to surprise and to do the unexpected.'[19]

It is to this idea of the museum as a creative space in which certain sets of values and ways of thinking can, and should, be challenged, that I wish to now turn.

Museums and moralities

Over the past two decades, the view that museums are socially constitutive and that they construct and communicate realities which function to reshape (not simply reflect) social relations, moral codes and conventions is one which has gained wide-spread support, not only within museum studies but also in sociology, cultural stu-dies and anthropology. Historical analyses of the museum's agency have tended to highlight their capacity to control, to civilise the citizenry and to exclude, marginalise or silence minority groups through representational practices which operate to pro-duce oppressive and discriminatory effects. More recently, however, interest amongst researchers in empirically investigating the social effects and consequences of representational practices has been fuelled by growing practitioner interest in representing previously excluded communities in more respectful and equitable ways which attempt to shape and engender visitors' support for more egalitarian understandings of difference. These studies have revealed the complex ways in which visitors respond to, and engage with, the representations they encounter. Museums offer conceptual and material resources that are taken up by visitors in various ways and which, along with other media resources and individuals' prior experiences and beliefs, help to shape their interpretations of cultural difference.

Although audiences are undoubtedly highly active in the construction of the meanings they produce out of the exhibition encounter (as demonstrated by their capacity not only to endorse and take up the messages they perceive within displays but also to resist, appropriate, recode and outrightly reject them), the narratives which museums construct and present nevertheless play a part in shaping normative truths and social relations, as well as in framing the ways in which visitors and society more broadly view and discuss contemporary social and moral issues.[20] Museums emerge from this analysis as agents in the broader mediascape, their displays potentially competing with resources generated by other media. Whilst many other media forms (newspapers, television, online media and so on) are undoubtedly more ubiquitous and pervasive, the particular qualities – veracity, authenticity, credibility – with which audiences very often endow museums, secure them a relatively authoritative and potentially highly influential position in the media hierarchy.[21]

Increasing engagement with politically and morally charged contemporary issues has played a part in opening the museum up to more diverse audiences, to more democratic and collaborative modes of practice, and to a greater sense of their responsibilities to their publics. At the same time, however, as Gary Edson[22] has argued, these new forms of practice have exposed museums to greater public scrutiny and the expectations that they will maintain ethical standards.

The conception of the museum as a site of moral activism – as an agency that does not simply reflect and reinforce dominant moralities[23] and widely supported positions on rights issues, but is increasingly concerned to actively challenge and reconfigure them – generates a set of vexing questions and ethical challenges with which museum practitioners and researchers are increasingly grappling. What moral frameworks might practitioners draw upon for guidance in negotiating this contested terrain? What modes of interpretation are most likely to engender support amongst visitors for principles of equity and fairness, but at the same time resist an approach which is didactic, tendentious and which closes down visitor responses?

These are difficult questions for which there are, of course, no easy answers and no simple formulae exist which can be universally and straightforwardly applied across different circumstances and contexts. My intention is to focus in on a particular context and to return to the project with which I began this chapter, as a means of highlighting principles, sources of ethical guidance and interpretive strategies that might be deployed to navigate pathways through the challenges such work entails.

Rethinking Disability Representation

Rethinking Disability Representation was initiated by the Research Centre for Museums and Galleries (RCMG) at the University of Leicester. It grew from prior research which had investigated the reasons behind the paucity of disability-related narratives and representations of disabled people in museums and galleries in the UK. Why, at a time when museums were increasingly concerned to research and present hidden histories pertaining to women, indigenous peoples, minority ethnic communities and other social groups, was disability rarely, if ever, considered?[24]

The research identified a wealth of material in collections of all kinds. This was not confined to medical and history collections, where material might have been expected, but also to social history, fine and decorative art, military, archaeological and ethnographic collections. However, much of this material was in store, not on display. Where objects and artworks were displayed, their connection with disability was rarely made explicit or interpreted to visitors. Representations of disabled people, though relatively few in number, most often conformed to prevalent stereotypes found in other media – in film, literature, television and charity advertising.

These stereotypes include disabled people as freaks, defined by their physical unconformity and presented as objects of pity or amusement; as passive and dependent recipients of charity, care or biblical miracle cure; and as heroes who somehow transcend disability by overcoming the challenges presented by their impairments.[25] Depictions of disabled people in everyday life were practically non-existent.[26]

The paucity of representations of disabled individuals, combined with an absence of disability-related narratives, appeared to the research team to be worthy of further investigation. At a time when museums were increasingly concerned to represent minority communities and to address contemporary identity-related issues in their programmes, why were disabled people so markedly absent?

This question was at least partly answered through interviews we conducted with curators. Many interviewees revealed an openness to engaging with disability in exhibitions and displays, but also noted a set of concerns which operated to restrict experimentation in this relatively uncharted area of practice. A number of curators invoked the nineteenth-century freakshow to express their anxieties over presenting depictions of disabled people which might invite disrespectful or otherwise unwelcome forms of looking. Others raised concerns about 'outing' a person as disabled who might not want, or have wanted, to be known, in this way, for example, imposing a disabled identity on a historical figure who might have gone to great lengths to conceal his or her impairment. Our study identified an abundance of material which lent itself to celebratory narratives, countered prevalent stereotypes and highlighted disabled people's diversity, their humanity and their many contributions to society. However, some curators also drew our attention to material in their collections which evinced more challenging, dark and painful stories linked to disability. What place, they asked, did material which told stories of pain, loss, oppression and disempowerment play in addressing the absence of disabled people from cultural narratives; how might it be interpreted and how would audiences (disabled and non-disabled) respond to it?[27]

To explore and test potential pathways through this challenging array of questions, RCMG developed an action research project that, through collaboration, experimentation and evaluation, could begin to move practice forward.[28] A critical feature of the project was the establishment of a 'think tank' comprised of disabled activists, artists and cultural practitioners who would play a leading role in shaping the content and tone of different interpretive interventions that eventually appeared in nine different museums in 2007 and 2008. These interventions took a variety of forms and were tremendously diverse in theme and approach. Colchester Castle Museum, for example, developed a temporary exhibition which used objects, personal testimonies, films and artworks to reveal the lives of disabled people in the city, past and present. The exhibition, *Life Beyond the Label*, sought to challenge negative stereotypes by presenting rich and diverse life experiences of disabled people. Tyne and Wear Museums also produced a temporary exhibition, the title of which – *One in Four* – referred to the proportion of people living in the Tyne and Wear region today who qualify as disabled (as opposed to one in five in the UK as a whole).[29] Birmingham Museums and Art Gallery took paintings from their fine art collections that featured depictions of disabled people and invited disabled artists in the region to record, through a series of audio commentaries, their responses to the paintings which visitors could access alongside the more customary curatorial inter-pretations. These personalised responses, drawing on the lived experience of dis-ability, very often used the ways in which disabled people were represented in the paintings to reflect on contemporary issues and debates pertaining to disability rights and related issues of prejudice and discrimination. The Imperial War Museum, London, developed a series of educational sessions for pupils in secondary schools which drew upon collections to shed light on the complex relationships between conflict and disability and to encourage participants in the sessions to question, and perhaps reassess, their own attitudes towards disabled people.

Ethical and moral challenges

Not surprisingly, these purposeful attempts to challenge and reshape visitors' understandings of disability generated a multitude of thorny ethical challenges, some specific to the context of disability, but many that are likely to resonate with an array of similarly activist projects designed to purposefully inform, challenge and reshape visitor opinions and understandings of difference.

Adopting a moral standpoint

What sources of ethical guidance might then exist to assist museums in the undeniably difficult task of shaping the ethical standpoints they take up and for which they attempt to engender support? The search for moral and ethical frameworks which could steer and strengthen our initially fuzzy ideas around disability led us initially to the disability rights movement.

Interestingly, over the last two decades, the influence of human rights in the field of culture has been pronounced, not least in the museum and gallery sector, where there has been an extraordinary proliferation in the number and type of projects internationally that have, in varied ways, deployed a discourse around human rights, equality and social justice to frame their approach to (and interpretation of) wide-ranging contemporary and historic events and subjects. Although aware of the fierce debates that have characterised the field of human rights (not least surrounding the comparative merits of universalist and cultural relativist positions on rights issues which have dominated the field of anthropology during the latter half of the twen-tieth century),[30] we nevertheless turned to the disability rights movement and the field of disability studies for a source of guidance during the formative stages of *Rethinking Disability Representation*.

The disability studies literature inevitably contains a diversity of opinions and viewpoints but there is nevertheless a degree of consensus around certain principles and conceptual approaches to understanding disability. In particular, the social model of disability has been widely recognised as a key conceptual tool for the advancement of the rights of disabled people. The social model rejects an individu-alist, medicalised understanding of disability and instead locates the issue and the need for action, not with the body, the individual and their impairment, but with society and the barriers which restrict and oppress disabled people. The basis for what has become the social model of disability was a document produced in 1976 by

The Union of Physically Impaired against Segregation (UPIAS) entitled the *Fundamental Principles of Disability*.

> In our view, it is society which disables physically impaired people. Disability is something imposed on top of our impairments, by the way we are unnecessarily isolated and excluded from full participation in society.[31]

There is a large body of literature discussing the emergence and significance of the social model and, whilst its contemporary relevance is increasingly debated,[32] there nevertheless remains widespread consensus on its value as a means of articulating a progressive understanding of disability (as bound up in the social context) and the implications this model has for advancing the rights of disabled people. The social model of disability was taken as a starting point for framing the wide-ranging interpretive approaches used in each of the nine museum projects and repeatedly drawn upon – as the projects evolved and developed – to steer the choice of objects displayed and the tone of accompanying interpretation.

Didacticism or dialogue?

A further dilemma that inevitably arises within initiatives underpinned by activist ambitions concerns the manner in which the moral positions adopted by the museum are presented to visitors. Activist philosophies and practices are characterised by a desire to elicit support for a particular (fixed) moral viewpoint. This immovability or fixedness implies a lack of negotiation, perhaps an unwillingness to accommodate and engage with competing or alternative views, which sits uncomfortably with much contemporary museum thinking. Recent years have seen a move away from didactic modes of communication within museums towards more dialogic relationships with visitors. Research suggests that visitors can construct wide-ranging meanings from a museum visit – meanings that are mediated and informed by their own values, experiences and prior knowledge – and that effective learning and communication seeks to acknowledge and validate these diverse meanings. But what if these personal meanings are ones which exhibit prejudice or which express opinions that stand in opposition to human rights and social justice? Surely there are some issues on which it is reasonable to unequivocally adopt, and attempt to unambiguously communicate, a particular moral standpoint that leaves little room for opposition?

Museum practitioners are understandably uncomfortable with the idea of moralising to visitors, aware that overly prescriptive messages are likely to be rejected as patronising, politically correct or otherwise unpalatable. How then can museums articulate – with clarity, power and honesty – the positions they seek to engender support for, whilst simultaneously resisting interpretive approaches which close down possibilities for engagement and understanding?

Whilst developing *Rethinking Disability Representation*, one project we drew upon to assist us in achieving this balance came from the United States Holocaust Memorial Museum. To accompany their exhibition, *Deadly Medicine: Creating the Master Race*, which examined the history of eugenics and 'euthanasia' in Nazi Germany, they invited disability rights activist Harriet McBryde Johnson to bring a rights perspective to the issues the exhibition raised. The following extract is taken from the Museum's web site, where the live interview with Johnson turns to the contemporary issue of 'cure'.

> *Ringelheim.* Can we talk about cure?
>
> *Johnson.* Okay.
>
> *Ringelheim.* I would think that most people who, in the audience, who are not disabled would say there's something important about medicine developing cures for certain diseases. Do you think that's true?
>
> *Johnson.* I have no interest at all in a cure for my disease. And there again, the community is by no means monolithic. Christopher Reeve really and truly cared deeply about cure. He was sincere. Nobody was forcing him to do the work that he did, and that's legitimate. That came from his experience. But to me my disability is, I mean, it is part of my DNA. It's in every, every, will you say molecule of me? I don't know enough about the biology. But, you know, at the tiniest level, the disability is part of who I am. And, you know, I really have no interest in changing that. It seems to be much more interesting to figure out what to do with this kind of body and this kind of life. Now, when my mother got breast cancer, I was very glad that there were some good treatments for her, and maybe that doesn't make sense. But maybe it does. I don't know. Does that make sense? Anybody?

On the Museum's web site, Johnson's concluding statement – Does that make sense? – is used to invite visitors to share their own thoughts and experiences. Those of us working on *Rethinking Disability Representation* found this approach tremendously helpful, enabling us to see that a commitment to rights and social justice did not require museums to tell their visitors what to think. In contrast, engagement with a rights perspective could provoke, stimulate debate and expose visitors to alternative perspectives and ideas which challenge the interpretive frames that underpin dominant understandings of disability and disabled people.

Contestation and conflict

Museum interpretation that engages directly with questions of rights and equality will inevitably generate instances in which the interests of different groups are, or are perceived to be, in conflict. In such instances, to what extent are museums required to arbitrate or mediate between conflicting positions?

At Birmingham Museums and Art Gallery, several of the paintings to which disabled artists in the region were invited to respond were historic works of biblical scenes or with otherwise religious content. These paintings elicited strong feelings from some members of the group who expressed their views regarding the role of religion and the part that religious followers have played in the oppression of disabled people. In his personal response to William Holman Hunt's *The Finding of the Saviour in the Temple*, for example, artist and broadcaster Paul Darke cited his recent experiences whilst out shopping and linked these to the treatment of the disabled characters in the painting.

Recently, I was sitting in my wheelchair in Boots the Chemists patiently waiting to be served at the 'Pay Here' desk and an elderly woman approached me: nothing unusual there I thought. I am often the recipient of witticism about being in a wheelchair. This was different. The elderly woman put her hand on my head and said: *'I shall pray for you and your father: a father's sins have made you this way'*. She took her hands off my head and sauntered away.

I was neither surprised nor baffled. After all, I had been to a special school for people with spina bifida: a Christian faith school where we had to read, and were read, the Bible daily. No TV on a Sunday: only Church. My religious schooling has often made me feel that disabled people are exploited by 'ordinary' people in the furtherance of their own religious beliefs. The school was a Lord Shaftesbury school – a man who could have seen this painting as he died in 1885.

Holman Hunt's 'The Finding of the Saviour in the Temple' explores Christian faith through its symbols, signs and metaphors. The painting, for me, symbolises the relationship between Christianity and disability. I feel disability is seen in two ways. Firstly, as something that can be healed by faith. And secondly, that it can be exploited as a route into heaven by 'helping' disabled people – just like it was in my childhood. This view sees me, my body, my self, as little more than a metaphor or an example of God providing an opportunity for believers to become closer to Him. Within this view, I – the disabled – have little merit or worth as a whole human being in myself: I am, as the blind and the crippled are in Holman Hunt's painting, peripheral to the real drama of normal life. I have to endure the denial of disabled people's value as extraordinary human beings.

I like the painting because it explains to me the history of this view of disabled people. But it depresses me, at the same time, because it suppresses me. I take away from the painting the message that there is no future for disabled people outside of the oppressive practice of charity. I am not anti-religion of any kind. I merely object to religions' uncritical exploitation of disability. I feel this painting reinforces to a non-disabled audience the righteousness of the dominance of the normal over the abnormal. It indicates the place of disabled people as second class citizens and the rightness of seeing me as less than you.

This very personal response (and indeed other responses which related to different religious themed paintings) generated considerable discussion amongst museum staff who were committed to the project's underpinning philosophy, but were also anxious not to offend Christian visitors.

Such conflicts are not always easily resolved and there are no clear-cut formulae museums can apply in the process of arbitrating between competing perspectives. However, the lens offered by a human rights or social justice perspective is undoubtedly a helpful starting point, enabling museum practitioners to ask, 'whose lives are enriched by certain representations and whose are damaged?'[33] Paul Darke's interpretation of Holman Hunt's painting was ultimately included within the project.

Unsettling narratives

The final dilemma I wish to highlight concerns the representation of objects and material that deal with challenging stories of oppression, pain and disempowerment. The project's think tank of disabled activists, artists and cultural practitioners were unanimous in their view that these should be included, where appropriate, alongside the more celebratory stories that emerged from museum collections.

The Royal London Hospital Museum and Archives worked with filmmaker David Hevey to produce *Behind the Shadow of Merrick* – a short film about Joseph Merrick (more commonly known as the Elephant Man) which blended curatorial accounts of aspects of Merrick's life with highly personalised responses from three disabled people – Tina, Rowan and Tim – for whom his story had particular resonance. Their powerful reactions to objects and material linked to Merrick's life revealed experiences of stigma, discrimination and the everyday experience of being stared at. In this brief extract, a description of Merrick's hat and veil is interspersed with Tina's responses to this object.

> *Jonathan Evans (archivist, Royal London Hospital Museum and Archives).* The hat's made of felt and the bottom – the veil – is made of linen. It's got a single eyehole and the hat's got a peak, as you can see.
> *Tina.* When I had long hair I used to hide my face a lot with my hair. I used to love it – it was a security blanket and I felt protected by it. He was literally thought of as a thing, an animal, and people actually think that now sometimes about disabled people ... and I guess he just had to hide away from it through that hood to protect himself against the harsh comments and stares.
> *Jonathan Evans.* The hat is the size, the circumference of a man's waist and it indicates just how large Joseph's head was. It caused him great difficulty throughout his life; the overgrowth of bone and flesh on his head ...
> *Narrator.* But what is it like to be stared at and isolated this way?
> *Tina.* Oh ... public property! You know, I, like many other people, we're public property. We get on a bus, we're a spectacle. From the moment we open the front door we're a spectacle. You have to be prepared for that, be prepared for the onslaught.

This unconventional approach to interpretation that combined curatorial and community voices – the former factual and measured, the latter personal, emotional and unsettling –proved to have a powerful effect on audiences. Indeed, our evaluation of audience engagement with each of the nine projects revealed a wide variety of audience responses. Whilst some were cautious and expressed discomfort at their perceptions and values being challenged during their visit, many more were supportive and expressed an openness to the sometimes difficult and provocative material they encountered.

Activism in the museum

The conception of the museum as a site of activism is, as we have seen, both fraught with challenges and likely to generate fierce opposition from those who maintain that museums should take no account of broader social and political inequities in the ways in which they operate. These challenges, I would argue, should not deter progress towards the development of more socially engaged, responsible and ethically informed museum practice.

There will always be competing visions of the museum's purpose and different views on the social and moral responsibilities incumbent on practitioners. However, a much broader and deeper understanding of the social agency of museums, and the nature of the relationships between institutions and visiting and non-visiting communities, makes opposition to approaches that promote access and inclusion increasingly untenable. Although visitor profiles and broad patterns of visitation remain stubbornly biased towards the more advantaged sectors of society, some museums have nevertheless succeeded in engaging, over a sustained period of time, audiences that are much more representative of society at large. A large body of research with both visitors and non-visiting communities has pointed the way towards more accessible practice. In short, the knowledge required to make museum experiences more accessible exists, although most organisations remain reluctant to transform their practices. Similarly, the idea that museums are culturally generative, authoritative and highly trusted sites of knowledge, constructing and communicating narratives which have social consequences beyond the museum – which play a part in shaping (as well as reflecting) social relations – can no longer be easily dismissed as the opinion of a few leftist practitioners. A growing body of empirical research supports the view that the decisions museums make regarding their collections, displays and interpretation have social effects and consequences. It is this enhanced understanding of the museum's agency, I argue, which supports the case for activist ethical approaches to museum work to move from the margins to the mainstream of practice.

Notes

1 *Rethinking Disability Representation* was initiated and developed by The University of Leicester's Research Centre for Museums and Galleries (RCMG). I gratefully acknowledge the work of Jocelyn Dodd, co-Director of the project, and members of the research team, Ceri Jones, Debbie Jolly and Jackie Gay.

2 R. R. Janes, *Museums in a Troubled World: Renewal, Irrelevance, or Collapse?* Abingdon and New York: Routledge, 2009.

3 See, for example, D. Casey, 'Museums as Agents for Social and Political Change', *Curator* 44: 3, 2001, pp. 230–237; T. W. Luke, *Museum Politics: Power Plays at the Exhibition*, Minneapolis, MN, and London: University of Minnesota Press, 2002.

4 T. Besterman, 'Museum Ethics', in S. Macdonald (ed.) *A Companion to Museum Studies*, Oxford: Blackwell, 2005, pp. 431–441.

5 S. E. Weil, 'From Being about Something to Being for Somebody: the Ongoing Transformation of the American Museum', *Daedalus* 128: 3, 1999, pp. 229–258.

6 J. Marstine, 'Introduction', in J. Marstine (ed.) *New Museum Theory and Practice: An Introduction*, Malden, MA, and Oxford: Blackwell, 2005, pp. 1–36.

7 Besterman, 'Museum Ethics', pp. 431–441.

8 For a discussion of the emergence of these kinds of organisation see R. Sandell, *Museums, Prejudice and the Reframing of Difference*, London and New York: Routledge, 2007.

9 See M. O'Neill, 'The Good Enough Visitor', in R. Sandell (ed.) *Museums, Society, Inequality*, London and New York: Routledge, 2002; M. O'Neill, 'Commentary 4. John

Holden's *Capturing Cultural Value*: How Culture has become a Tool of Government Policy', *Cultural Trends* 14: 1, No. 53, 2005, pp. 113–128; J. Barr, 'Dumbing Down Intellectual Culture: Frank Furedi, Lifelong Learning and Museums', *Museums and Society* 3: 2, 2005, pp. 98–114.

10 J. Appleton, *The Object of Art Museums*, 2004. Online. Available HTTP: http://www.spiked-online.com/articles/0000000CA502.htm (accessed 19 October 2009).

11 M. Wallinger, 'Creativity', *Observer*, 22 September 2002. Online. Available HTTP: http://www.guardian.co.uk/theobserver/2002/sep/22/features.magazine147 (accessed 19 October 2009).

12 M. Marrin, 'No, you can't come in: you're the wrong colour', *Daily Telegraph*, 26 May 2000, p. 28.

13 J. Cuno (ed.) *Whose Muse? Art Museums and the Public Trust*, Princeton, NJ, and Woodstock: Princeton University Press and Harvard University Art Museums, 2003, p. 73.

14 J. Appleton, *Museums for 'the People'*, Conversations in Print, London: Institute of Ideas, 2001, pp. 21–26.

15 J. Delingpole, 'The Last Chance to See? A Museum', *Telegraph*. Online. Available HTTP: http://www.telegraph.co.uk/comment/personal-view/3624988/Last-chance-to-see-a-museum.html (accessed 19 October 2009).

16 M. O'Neill, 'Museums, Professionalism and Democracy', *Cultural Trends*, special issue: *The Consequences of Instrumental Museum and Gallery Policy*, 17: 4, 2008, pp. 289–307.

17 O'Neill, 'John Holden's *Capturing Cultural Value*', pp. 113–128.

18 Besterman, 'Museum Ethics', pp. 435–436.

19 Ibid.

20 See E. Hooper-Greenhill, *Museums and the Interpretation of Visual Culture*, London and New York: Routledge, 2000; S. Macdonald, *The Politics of Display: Museums, Science, Culture*, London: Routledge, 2002; Luke, *Museum Politics*; Sandell, *Museums, Prejudice and Reframing*.

21 See F. Cameron, 'Moral Lessons and Reforming Agenda: History Museums, Science Museums, Contentious Topics and Contemporary Societies', in S. J. Knell, S. MacLeod and S. Watson (eds.) *Museum Revolutions: How Museums Change and are Changed*, Abingdon and New York: Routledge, 2007, pp. 330–342; Sandell, *Museums, Prejudice and Reframing*.

22 G. Edson (ed.) *Museum Ethics*, London: Routledge, 1997.

23 The term 'moralities' is purposely used to suggest plurality: different moral discourses, values and practices coexist in a given context (S. Howell, *The Ethnography of Moralities*, London: Routledge, 1997). Those which enjoy widespread support might then be considered normative or dominant whilst alternative, perhaps competing, moralities might be considered resistive or counter-hegemonic.

24 RCMG, *Buried in the Footnotes: the Representation of Disabled People in Museum and Gallery Collections: Phase One Report*, Leicester: Research Centre for Museums and Galleries, 2004.

25 A. Delin, 'Buried in the Footnotes: the Absence of Disabled People in the Collective Imagery of our Past', in Sandell, *Museums, Society, Inequality*, pp. 84–97.

26 R. Sandell, A. Delin, J. Dodd and J. Gay, 'Beggars, freaks and heroes? Museum collections and the hidden history of disability', *Journal of Museum Management and Curatorship* 20: 1, 2005, pp. 5–19.

27 Sandell, *Museums, Prejudice and Reframing*.

28 This £0.5 million project was funded by the Heritage Lottery Fund and the National Endowment for Science, Technology and the Arts with additional support from the University of Leicester and the nine partner museums.

29 RCMG, *Rethinking Disability Representation in Museums and Galleries*, Leicester: Research Centre for Museums and Galleries, 2008.

30 From the 1950s and 1960s onwards, anthropological debate tended to side with a relativist position, arguing that respect for cultural differences was undermined by universalising conceptions of rights which could, more accurately, be understood as an attempt to naturalise and legitimise Western liberal democratic norms and to impose them on non-Western cultures. Since the 1990s, however, the ways in which anthropologists approach the subject has fundamentally changed, fuelled, at least in part, by the growing global influence of human rights discourse and increasing concern for (and interest in) notions of

global justice (R. Wilson and J. P. Mitchell, eds., *Human Rights in Global Perspective: Anthropological Studies of Rights, Claims and Entitlements*, Routledge, 2003). Culturally relativist perspectives on rights have come under increasing attack from those who have argued that adopting such a position 'has morally nihilistic, politically conservative and quietist consequences' and that 'the noble anthropological goal of seeking to understand others in their own terms cannot be employed as an excuse to avoid making moral and ethical judgments' (N. Rapport and J. Overing, *Social and Cultural Anthropology: The Key Concepts*, London and New York: Routledge, 2000, p. 166). More recently there have been helpful attempts to move beyond the conception of human rights in purely binary terms and calls to view universalism and relativism not as 'irreconcilable worldviews' but rather to view the tension between them 'as part of the continuous process of negotiating ever-changing and interrelated global and local norms' (J. K. Cowan, M. B. Dembour and R. A. Wilson, *Culture and Rights: Anthropological Perspectives*, New York: Cambridge University Press, 2001, p. 6).

31 The Union of Physically Impaired against Segregation, *Fundamental Principles of Disability*, 1976, quoted in T. Shakespeare, *Disability Rights and Wrongs*, Abingdon and New York: Routledge, 2006, p. 12.

32 See, for example, Shakespeare, *Disability Rights and Wrongs*, p. 12.

33 J. Eichstedt, 'Museums and Social (In)Justice', in H. H. Genoways (ed.) *Museum Philosophy for the Twenty-first Century*, Lanham, MD, and Oxford: AltaMira Press, 2006, pp. 127–138.

9

Collaboration, contestation, and creative conflict

On the efficacy of museum/community partnerships

Bernadette T. Lynch

The world today seems to be conspiring against trust … Trust has been sentenced to a life of frustration.

Zygmunt Bauman[1]

If we want to increase trust, we need to avoid deception.

Onora O'Neill[2]

There is, as Freud reminded us, much revealed in the inadvertent verbal 'slip'. In this case, the word was 'privilege'. The circumstances? A meeting in 2007, around a table in a room within the depths of an old institution, the Manchester Museum, a university museum in the north of England. A group of museum staff members, with one or two from senior management (myself included), were having a meeting with some community partners. The group assembled comprised the planning team for an upcoming 'co-produced' exhibition on the sensitive subject of race. The intention was that the exhibition should take place at the Museum, and be co-curated by staff and interested community members.

At this meeting there was a good deal of tension and frustration. Staff members were worried about schedules slipping and community members were feeling pressurized, let down by the institution apparently making its own decisions, despite the avowed intention to co-produce the exhibition. In such 'collaborative' situations between museums and community partners, decisions frequently tend to be rushed through on the basis of the institution's agenda or strategic plan, thereby manipulating the illusion of consensus.

There is growing discomfort and dissonance about the perceived benefits of 'participation' in a number of areas, for example international development studies, when in many cases participation actually turns out to be manipulation. Development theorist Uma Kothari points out that participation can reinforce 'a normative discourse that reflects a group consensus … while the complexities and "messiness" is filtered out'.[3] Laclau adds the reminder that 'Everything depends, as Lewis Carroll would put it, on who is in control.'[4] In cases such as the co-produced exhibition above it is, incontrovertibly, the museum.

The community participants in the Manchester situation were coming to realize a few hard lessons, which they may or may not have suspected at the outset. Being included in what Nancy Fraser, the noted critical theorist concerned with notions of justice, memorably calls 'invited spaces'[5] is no guarantee of participation. Similarly social anthropologist Andrea Cornwall reminds us that simply

> having a seat at the table is a necessary but not sufficient condition for exercising voice. Nor is presence at the table [on the part of institutions] the same as a willingness to listen and respond.[6]

What is becoming clear is that expanding democratic engagement in museums calls for more than invitations to participate. In the case of Manchester's collaboration it is possible that the institution's academic discourse overrode the contributions of participants. If so, what institutional values were at work that influenced the attitudes and behaviour of museum staff towards the participants?

Participation in museums can be understood as shaped by the individual's position in relation to the other individuals present and, through them, with the museum institution. Associated with this perspective are different concepts of power. In transactions between museums and participants, because of the challenges of different perspectives that such encounters will inevitably generate, issues of power and coercion become central. Yet, such processes remain largely invisible to all concerned, frequently due to a lack of awareness about the ethics of these relations within the museum's public engagement work. There is therefore an imperative to make such processes visible, in order to illuminate the relational complexities within the messy and contradictory work of participation in museums.

Developing a reflexive practice in museums would significantly help clarify the subtle nature of the power relationships and levels of participation on offer that are too often hidden within these transactions. As Gaventa notes:

> Participation in invited spaces is generally on the terms set by those who create and maintain those spaces. What gets on to the agenda and what remains off limits for discussion, may be implicitly rather than explicitly controlled by those doing the inviting.[7]

A museum curator in Hackney acknowledges the power relationship even more overtly, demonstrating an admirable level of self-awareness when commenting:

> I think we held the reins pretty tightly all the time because it was easier and less time consuming and less stressful to do that. I wouldn't say we co-produced – we involved loads of people but we held onto the power![8]

How power works in museums: 'clients' and 'beneficiaries'

'Invited spaces' in museums, as elsewhere, are ostensibly devices for dialogue, but remain forever permeated with the power effects of difference. Indeed, as international development theorists Sam Hickey and Giles Mohan point out, in writing about social inclusion and citizenship, all discourses of participation offer a limited number of positions for participants that delineate the available level of inclusion and agency, sometimes in very subtle ways.[9] Welcomed into the 'invited space', participants are deftly encouraged to assume the position of 'beneficiaries' or 'clients'. This in turn influences what they are perceived to be able to contribute or entitled to know or decide. To make use of invitations participants need to understand what is going on, what is at stake and over what it is possible to press demands.

This particular meeting at the Manchester Museum took place at a late stage in the exhibition planning process, when pressure was high to resolve and implement decisions. Some community members voiced dissatisfaction with the process, and what they perceived as the museum exercising a veto based on its power to make decisions off-agenda, outside of the meetings. It is entirely likely that staff members had little or no awareness of the subtle ways in which such a 'veto' operated. As a recent study on power and community participation in Britain comments:

> One of the more powerful resources ... is the power to set the agenda and the terms of consultation/power sharing ... Determining what is on and what is off the ... agenda are not necessarily the result of a people working intentionally to prevent the consideration of certain courses of action (though, of course, that happens), but are often the product of deeply engrained mindsets.[10]

The unintentional use or abuse of power in these relations was groundbreakingly explained in the context of public policy by the political and social theorist Steven Lukes in his classic *Power: A Radical View*.[11] Lukes distinguishes three different dimensions or 'faces' of power: the public face, the hidden face and an 'insidious' third face. These dimensions are described as the ability to get one's way despite opposition or resistance; the ability to keep issues off the political agenda in the first place; the shaping of the public domain through beliefs, values and wants that are considered normal or acceptable; and the process through which the relatively powerless come to internalize and accept their own condition, and thus might not be aware or act upon their interests in any observable way. The awareness of a level of coercion or manipulation may thus lie just below the surface and remain unspoken, unless something, some inadvertent verbal slip creates an opening for its expression. This, it seems, is what occurred at the Manchester Museum.

Can museums 'unlearn' their privilege?

At the meeting in Manchester, the growing tension in the room led to a discussion on the role of community members in this type of project. At one moment, a community member took particular offence at something inadvertently said by a couple of museum staff members regarding the word, 'privilege', and focused all of his anger on this word, with the subsequent decision to end his part in the discussion and pull out of the project.

The use of the word 'privilege' in this context was technically a 'misunderstanding', according to all the staff members present. It was used in context of remarking what a privilege (as in 'lucky') these two staff members felt, to have had the privilege of a university education and be able to work with access to wonderful collections in a museum – noting, with regret, that this was not something available to the majority. One community member, however, heard this as an ill judged, ill timed boast from white, middle-class, well-paid professionals to a black unpaid volunteer, giving his time to help on the project – that these staff members were boasting that the museum's staff has power and privilege unavailable to those others present.

What had the Museum staff members understood or intended by using the word 'privilege'? Was it somehow to be divested of privilege by showing their awareness of it, by giving it a name? Sara Ahmed questions the benefit of revealing or admitting to privilege in such a context, and asks:

> Whether learning to see the mark of privilege involves unlearning that privilege? What are we learning when we learn to see privilege? ... We cannot simply unlearn privilege when the cultures in which learning takes place are shaped by privilege.[12]

She continues, 'We need to consider the intimacy between privilege and the work we do, even in the work we do *on* privilege.'[13] She finally suggests that one step might be 'the recognition of privilege *as* privilege'.[14] Yet this revelatory word that sparked an emotional response to the museum's authority over what was to be included or left out of the exhibition, led to participants' views, and more importantly, their anger, being 'managed', sidelined, diverted and ultimately dismissed. The museum staff members recognized the privilege that existed in their positions in relation to the community members present, yet they somehow appeared to feel that this awareness exempted them from its consequences. As Trinh T. Minh-ha said of anthropologists, but could equally apply to museum staff in such a context, ' ... once more *they* spoke. *They* decide who is "racism-free or anti-colonial", and they seriously think they can go on formulating criteria for us.'[15]

Thus, at the meeting in Manchester, there was little serious attempt to listen, discuss or debate the views of this angry community member, or indeed the revealing word that inadvertently sparked them. This was mainly because the staff members, with a degree of professional distance but no vestige of malice, simply did not understand why the emotive word 'privilege' mattered so much in that instance, and what it actually revealed. In a public debate entitled 'Are Museums Racist?' that was organized by the Museum following the opening of the exhibition, one member of the CAP (Manchester Museum's long-established Community Advisory Panel) commented:

> I'm not an academic, but sometimes my problem is with academia ... . It's like people who don't talk about racism but the symptoms of racism. Racism is about human beings – it's not about analysing it in an exhibition. It's the feelings we have inside, the hatred, the palpable feelings – that's the racism I'm interested in.[16]

Empowerment-lite in the museum as contact zone

Is it a fear of loss of control that is the central undermining flaw within well-meaning attempts at democratizing museums, so that such expressions of anger are deliberately contained? By using their power to control and demarcate the limits of these 'invited spaces' have museums simply succeeded in delivering, at best, what Andrea Cornwall, a Research Fellow in the Participation, Power and Social Change Team at Sussex University, calls 'empowerment-lite'?[17]

There were explicit references to these tensions and inequalities in anthropologist Mary Louise Pratt's original concept of the 'contact zone'.[18] Clifford's later application of the term to museums[19] went on to adapt Pratt's definition by emphasizing the potential for conflicting views in the interpretation of museum collections. Nonetheless, in much engagement work in museums today, there seems to be little realization of what such contact actually entails, and how fraught with suppressed anger and emotion it can be.[20]

Clifford makes evident the power imbalance in the contact zone, and yet sees the potential for the active agency of all concerned, brought about through proximity:

> By using the term 'contact' I aim to foreground the interactive improvisational dimensions of colonial encounters so easily ignored or suppressed by diffusionist accounts of conquest and domination. A 'contact' perspective emphasizes how subjects are constituted in and by relations to each other. [It stresses] co-presence, interaction, interlocking understandings and practices, often with radically asymmetrical relations of power.[21]

Yet Clifford's enthusiasm for the potential of this contact somehow disregards the museum's fear of others that flows like an undercurrent beneath these encounters. It underestimates the museum's need to exercise control, and its even greater fear of change.

Within Clifford's idealized 'contact zone', the relationships can quickly turn to anger when the promise of collaboration and mutual respect is apparently withheld by the museum, as seen in the following case reported with admirable candour by the Hackney Museum in London:

> ... there was a feeling of weariness, of disappointment, of frustration from the community members and the museum staff (two of whom had left). One member of the community embarked on an almost fanatical vitriolic series of complaints and criticisms – that the museum had no real understanding or knowledge of the community, that it lacked commitment and experience, that it was misappropriating the funds, that it was not transparent in its dealings with the community, that it was unprofessional and exclusive, that it was only concerned with completing the project for its own aims and not for any benefit to the community and finally, and most damning, that the museum encouraged (and I quote) 'subterfuge, distrust and competition' within the community.[22]

When museums are faced with what the sociologist Zygmunt Bauman calls these 'strangers',[23] they respond, as in Manchester and Hackney, and many other instances in museums, by closing ranks. Reading Bauman suggests that, despite a commitment to the contact zone ideal, our institutions in the West continue to face the Other with fear, and work hard to exercise control, because engagement will always serve to 'unmask the brittle artifice of division'.[24] Yet despite Bauman's scepticism is there potential for Clifford's contact zone to exist in the museum? What conditions would have to be realized for such mutually beneficial engagement to take place?

What ethical values must inform the museum as 'contact zone'?

Let us return to the conditions that had led up to the confrontation in that room at the Manchester Museum, a museum well known and well reputed for innovation in community engagement, that spoke widely of its 'contact zone' commitment. During the years in which it was my overall responsibility, the Manchester Museum's engagement work was influenced not only by idealized notions of Clifford's contact zone, but increasingly by the complementary writing of the philosopher, Emmanuel Levinas.[25]

Levinas claimed that, as relational beings, humans can only successfully learn about themselves through engagement with another. If we apply this to museum practice as a reciprocal process, museum staff and community members, despite different backgrounds and experiences, will inevitably develop understanding and respectful relationships through working together in 'proximity' (another Levinas theme) and thus become increasingly aware that they are each ultimately dependent upon and responsible for each other.[26] Levinas writes:

> The unique other is bound to me socially. That person cannot be represented and given to knowledge in his or her uniqueness, because there is no science but that of generality ... It is in proximity, all the novelty of the social; proximity to the other, who eluding possession, falls to my responsibility.[27]

What was the moral obligation the Museum entered into at that moment of first encounter, towards this 'other' who is, as Bauman puts it, the 'stranger [who] is neither friend nor enemy ... because he may be both ... we do not know, and have no way of knowing which is the case ... '?[28] Levinas responds, 'I am to the other what the other is to me ... '[29] This is the relationality of human existence, and with it the responsibility, one for the other, with no expectation of a return. This is *reciprocity* in action in the exchange.

In terms of museums, it seemed that if we began our engagement work with an awareness of this mutual responsibility, we could next move to a negotiation of an actual exchange. Thus, in Manchester, an ethics of responsibility and reciprocity was taken into the museum as contact zone as we developed the practicalities for a negotiation of an exchange specific to a museum – in other words, related to collections. New ways of working were created, aimed at tackling the central, thorny issues of shared knowledge and the interpretation of collections. Fundamental to this approach was the establishment, in 2000, of the Museum's Community Advisory Panel (CAP) primarily made up of Diaspora community members drawn from Manchester's many diverse communities, whose origins and journeys reflected those of the collections. The CAP collectively agreed to the express aim that it should challenge the Museum's traditional Eurocentrism through a process of ongoing dialogue and debate related to the interpretation of the museum's collections.

Though by now long established, the relationship with the CAP has over the years often run into difficulties, highlighting increasingly troubling flaws in the Museum's philosophy and practice of reciprocity. In retrospect, differences of opinion were frequently diffused by the museum staff's intervention, and, as in the case cited at the beginning of this chapter, potential conflict was usually contained, circumvented or completely bypassed. At the *Are Museums Racist?* debate, held at the museum in August 2007, a member of the CAP described the problem in the following way:

> We're here to challenge and I fear that others may not challenge us back. It's not for you to just listen to us being angry and *just* listen. The point is the dialogue. The point is that we could be totally wrong. I don't personally believe I am wrong – but I am willing to listen to somebody who totally disagrees with me.[30]

Over the years of operation, there was an ever-increasing sense that the CAP existed simply to rubber-stamp museum policies and projects, however 'liberal' and risk-taking these projects may have seemed to museum staff at the time. This often resulted in both 'sides' feeling frustrated and dissatisfied and ultimately disillusioned, all the while maintaining a more and more hopeless commitment to the process, *in principle*. Those who disagreed with the process (not even always, with the project itself) simply left the CAP, sometimes in anger. Those who stayed increasingly adopted a more passive role.

One of the founding members of CAP, a Nigerian woman, resigned in 2002, along with the community group that she led (made up of local women from Diaspora communities). Her action was made in protest at the Museum's refusal/inability (depending upon one's standpoint) to allow full voting membership for a representative of the Community Advisory Panel on the Museum's University-controlled governing board. With her parting words she demonstrated full awareness of the government's social inclusion targets, as tied to funding for the museums. Her parting statement: 'You need us more than we need you'.[31]

In east London, Hackney Museum, well known and respected for its long-term commitment to community engagement, similarly experienced difficulties with participation, when the Museum's efforts were met with anger from participants. Yet as one of the Hackney Museum curators stated unapologetically, or pragmatically, depending on your point of view:

> I wouldn't hand over [control] completely unless I'm absolutely sure of my ground and of the people I'm working with. I'd make it clear that the museum has the final say or overall editorial control – if that's the way I think it needs to be.[32]

Instead of revealing a pragmatic approach, does this stand-off position conceal a greater institutional fear? Robert Chambers (coming from an international development perspective on participation) notes the institutional fear of losing control that occurs worldwide, reminding us that 'any professionals need the solid structures of their realities, their prisons'.[33] These structures and rules are not necessarily explicit; power is frequently expressed through the implicit understanding of 'how things work'.

Collective Conversations: contact zone or comfort zone?

Increasingly uneasy about the seeming inescapability of the stand-off (or worse, passive collusion) between museum and community 'partners', but with a continued commitment to relationships and a policy of 'reciprocity' and intercultural dialogue, we proceeded at the Manchester Museum to further embed the formal foundations of the Community Advisory Panel. We went on to develop a unique, accredited community volunteer training programme and, building on extensive, long-term work with refugees, a video-based oral history process contributing to the interpretation and documentation of collections.[34] Inspired by the affective impact of objects, through working with refugees in object-handling programmes[35] we created something called Collective Conversations.[36]

The 'Collective Conversations' programme at the Manchester Museum is in many ways unique. It is based on the idea of offering opportunities for inter- and intra-cultural dialogue through developing an expanded 'community of interpretation' with participants from local (mainly Diaspora) communities. The participants are invited to negotiate the interpretation of the museum's collections. (There is a particular focus on using the museum's large, underused collections in store.) It is a way of working that provides opportunities for interested individuals or mixed groups to actively engage with museum collections (including handling them), telling stories and discussing them with museum staff and others. Thus, the museum's avowed intention for the programme is that, through the opening up of the museum's interpretative processes, significant contributions can be made to museum documentation of collections (the round-table conversations are usually filmed by museum staff, and added to the museum's website or available on YouTube). The specially constructed studio space where the conversations take place is literally called the 'Contact Zone'.

On the surface, the Collective Conversations programme in Manchester appears to offer innovative opportunities for the negotiation of collections' interpretation, but in reality it limits the access and choice of collections available for discussion, and similarly offers limited opportunity for debate and contestation with the institution.

Linda Tuhiwai Smith, the internationally renowned researcher in Maori and indigenous education, notes that, in partnerships with museums, 'negotiations are also about respect for the opposition'.[37] In such cases as the Collective Conversations programme, the actual 'negotiation' is questionable as there is little real interaction between museum interpretations and those of the participants, and the hierarchy of interpretation remains unchallenged in favour of the museum. In addition, the experience for the Diaspora participant may be very different than that of the museum, with a very different motivation for participating. As Tuhiwai Smith notes, 'Some knowledges are actively in competition with each other.'[38] She speaks of the Maori motivation behind sharing oral histories with museums, which may be at odds with the museum's purpose. For most Maoris, she says:

It is not simply about giving an oral account ... but a very powerful need to give testimony to and restore a spirit, to bring back into existence a world fragmented and dying. The sense of history in these accounts is not the same thing as the discipline of history, and so our accounts collide, crash into each other ... The need to tell our stories remains the powerful imperative of a powerful form of resistance.[39]

Although Collective Conversations pushes the boundaries of museum interpretation in creating an opening for intercultural dialogue and the sharing of knowledge, it still deftly avoids sharing authority, and does not actively promote the facilitation of conflicting points of view.

The problem with the liberal consensual museum

What is wrong with the engagement work described above? The work is innovative and genuinely committed to establishing long-term relationships with community partners. Yet, some central flaw consistently undermines these relationships within the work of a host of similarly committed museums.

The political theorist Chantal Mouffe,[40] whose work focuses on issues of democracy, blames the influence of those like Levinas and Bauman who, she accuses, ignore the political nature of such encounters with the 'stranger' for whom they claim we are 'responsible'. Thus, any potential opposition is effectively silenced. Mouffe claims that an idealized, consensual form of democracy permeates such work, promoting a view that is profoundly mistaken and bound to fail. The emphasis on 'reciprocity' and 'consensuality' inherent in such so-called partnerships is, according to Mouffe, conceptually fraught with dangers because it produces the opposite effect, exacerbating the antagonistic potential existing in society. Liberal-minded, 'contact zone'-type museum projects, such as Collective Conversations or co-produced exhibitions, inevitably create resentment and antagonism simply because they ignore issues of power and, most importantly, the *political dimension* within these encounters and relationships, and prevent any opposition from being articulated or acted upon.

For Mouffe, the task is to 'envisage the creation of a vibrant public sphere of contestation where different hegemonic political projects can be confronted'.[41] In contrast to Hackney Museum's dismay at the volatility of their community partners, for example, such passion and partisanship might be understood as essential, and fostered within these relationships.

While holding back and controlling antagonism, liberal-minded museums may continually encounter an unbridgeable chasm between the museum and its community participants, based on the simple, but fundamental misunderstanding of antagonism as a destructive rather than an essential force within the public space of the museum. The political theorist Ernesto Laclau helps to further clarify why antagonism is an essential part of democratic dialogue:

Antagonism and violence do not play either a positive or a negative role ... a radically democratic society is one in which a plurality of public spaces, constituted around specific issues and demands, and strictly autonomous of each other, instils in its members a civic sense which is a central ingredient of their identity as individuals .... Not only is antagonism not excluded from [such] a democratic society, it is the very condition of its institution.[42]

A very recent and still painful experience of antagonism, for which they were unprepared, hit UK museums during the 2007 bicentenary of Britain's abolition of the Slave Trade Act. Due to expectations of the Black and Minority Ethnic communities of full collaboration in developing programmes on this subject matter, it brought museums face to face with the challenges of participation and co-production and the everyday politics and realities of racism, conflict and community activism. Yet, despite heightened black community expectations, one museum professional summarized the views of many when she said that 'consultation' was not an accurate description of what took place in their museum during the bicentenary year.[43] Another museum staff member commented, 'There was a sense at certain levels that the [consultation] process would be there to avert the risk of a backlash by not having it in place.' She concluded, 'It was not really about true collaboration.'

This view was echoed by a colleague in a national museum who added, 'The gallery objects had been chosen and the design had commenced by the time the consultation panel had been invited in, so many of the things that would have made the gallery collaborative and facilitated a greater "buy in" were no longer available for discussion'.

Mouffe's work suggests that antagonism, such as that experienced during the bicentenary year, could be dealt with more productively. If we understand the relationship between the museum and its community partners as no longer simply one of 'responsibility' for the other, in a patronizing way, nor one of 'enemies' in a stand-off situation, we could begin to understand it as a respectful relationship between 'adversaries' or 'friendly enemies'.[44]

These two sides thus share a common symbolic space – the museum – despite their very real differences. According to this view, the symbolic space of the museum-as-contact zone could be understood as the political space of encounter between adversaries, where the power relations which structure these encounters are brought to the fore, creating a liberating effect for museums and their community partners.

Developing a practice for active citizens in the museum

If we begin to see museums as civic sites for dialogue, debate and democratic communication between friendly adversaries, we must next consider how museums might be in a position to help people develop the skills necessary for such an exchange. As one Maori activist put it, 'I lack imagination, you say? No, I lack language. The language to clarify my resistance to the literate.'[45]

I have found it useful to go back to ideas of critical pedagogy, to the writings of Paulo Freire, the educational theorist, and to the methodologies of Augusto Boal, the Brazilian theatre director, writer and politician who, inspired by Freire's *Pedagogy of the Oppressed*,[46] created the *Theatre of the Oppressed*.[47]

Boal's techniques use theatre as means of knowledge exchange and transformation of reality in the social and relational field. In the *Theatre of the Oppressed* the audience becomes active, so that as 'spect-actors' they can explore, show, analyse and transform the reality in which they are living. In another Boal technique, the joker as facilitator (the joker – or, one could say, the *wild card* – is not tied down to a particular value, or interpretation of events) invites the spectators to replace the protagonist at any point in the scene that they can imagine an alternative action that could lead to a solution. The scene is replayed numerous times with different interventions. This results in a dialogue about the 'oppression', an examination of alternatives, and a 'rehearsal' for real situations.

It began to be clear that Boal's methods could be usefully applied in the museum-as-contact-zone. They could offer participants the potential to develop the confidence to bring their individual experiences to bear in debating opinions, ideas, and beliefs, in relation to collections.

Working with *Theatre of the Oppressed* through museum objects is unusual, but has already proven to be extremely effective. The technique I am working with is based on the notion that participants need to develop alternative communication skills in order to gain sufficient confidence to challenge the museum's 'knowledge-based' power in the interpretation and contextualization of collections. It means that people can begin to clearly and confidently express their views without being dependent upon Eurocentric academic language or forms of communication. Applying Boal's participatory theatre techniques through the catalyst of contested museum objects allows for museum collections to become the starting point for dialogue and debate that can implicate lived experience far beyond the confines of the museum.

Museums are uniquely well placed to offer such opportunities through negotiating the interpretation of objects, in which all may take a view. I have written elsewhere,[48] borrowing from the British psychoanalyst D.W. Winnicott,[49] on the 'transitional' or amenable museum object. The museum object is 'amenable' to symbolism; acting as symbol, it can unlock experience and thus become an immensely useful device as the focal point for projective imagination in storytelling and memory work, for discussion and debate and for participatory drama. The object helps unlock experience and becomes the catalyst for communication, for intercultural understanding and, sometimes, resistance.

'Talking Objects', which I helped initiate at the British Museum, was the first experiment in using these methods. It aims to create opportunities to discuss and debate museum objects by using the Boalian method.[50] The primary aim was for the young people to spend a week developing a dialogue with museum staff on the interpretation of one iconic object from the British Museum's collections (in this case, the Rosetta Stone). Through the use of forum and playback theatre techniques the young people developed the confidence to use the object as a means to open discussion on a host of issues related to contemporary experience, and, most important of all, became unafraid of expressing differences of opinion in a process I like to call 'creative conflict'.[51]

The best part of the process, as later reported by the young people, was in feeling free and confident enough to argue their opinions with the Museum staff. Consequently, they developed a new interest in the Museum's collections. Interestingly, the young people also demonstrated a great deal of respect for the curator's knowledge. By the culmination of a week's intensive work researching, examining, questioning and acting out versions of the story of the object, a process of projective identification began to emerge.

There was a great deal of emotion expressed in relation to the object biographies, in particular, the turbulent journeys the objects had taken to get to the British Museum. There were differences of opinion about the consequences of these histories. Powerful feelings were evoked relating to the young people's own experiences and identities. In the roundtable debate on the last day, two young Africans, male and female, from different parts of the continent, engaged in an intense debate on the legacy of colonialism in their own lives (Figure 9.1). The young woman spoke eloquently of self-determination and political and economic independence, and the symbolic importance of heritage in the powerful form of objects, that should, she felt, be returned as part of nation-building to her particular country of origin. She felt that these collections had been in 'exile' long enough.

In contrast, the young African man argued that in not only his country, but across much of Africa, people were in no position to have these collections returned, because, he said, 'we are still colonized in our minds'. He was afraid that people in his country would not know how to look after these objects – that the objects would be sold or destroyed. The young woman replied that these objects were their inheritance, and that, whatever happened, it was the prerogative of their African nations, not the former colonial power, to decide the fate of the objects. The lively and involved debate continued, with input from the other young people and museum curators, and culminated, without need for consensus, in the enthusiastic wish expressed by some of the young people to become further involved by volunteering in the Museum's interpretation programmes.

Boal speaks of 'catharsis' within the process of *Theatre of the Oppressed*. According to all involved, this project was a cathartic experience, affecting both the British Museum staff members and the young people in a profound way. It taught the young people 'active agency' in consulting with 'power', an experience of possible use to them outside of this particular project. The original idea was to develop an effective model that could be applied in any museum – it has effectively demonstrated that this can be the case.[52]

Organizations unlearning privilege

Such learning plainly cannot be restricted to community participants alone. Museums staff members need to foster a reflective practice and begin to learn about their 'privilege', if only, as Gayatri Spivak, the literary critic and theorist, memorably put it, to begin to 'unlearn' it.[53] Moving upstream towards this institutional self-awareness and transformation is the next, most important frontier. There is, in my view, a role here, too, for Boal's dynamic methods.

It was such an impetus that led to the Paul Hamlyn Foundation's research project, 'Engagement' at the heart of museums and galleries, completed in May 2010. This project used the Boal methods to help twelve leading museums and galleries across the United Kingdom critically reflect on their engagement and participation

Figure 9.1 Aurelie Lolingo, one of the 'Talking Objects' participants, debates the interpretation of museum collections at the British Museum, August 2008. Photograph, Benedict Johnson, on behalf of the British Museum.

practices. Working with participant groups comprised of staff and community partners in each of the twelve institutions, the project focused on creating opportunities to critically reflect on the power relationships within each of the museums' or galleries' engagement work.[54]

Museums must begin to develop a repertoire of such reflective and dialogical skills and techniques, if they are to build trust and learn from their own practice.

Conclusion

There is often a disconnect between Western academic theory and practice that exist in the realm of the abstract, and the real-life emancipatory struggles that an emotional event like the bicentenary or an exhibition on the subject of race inspire in communities affected by these subjects as part of their everyday reality. Yet, at the first sign of trouble, institutions like museums run away from the fight, as was the case with many museums in the UK after the bicentenary experience. Too often institutions, as Bauman remarks, 'look for a reliably heavy door to lock behind them'.[55]

Museums, wherever they may be located, have not yet been freed from their paternalism. Russell Bishop, a researcher who is a member of an indigenous minority, the Maori people of Aotearoa, New Zealand, while writing about Maori attempts at collaborating with cultural and academic institutions, notes that such institutions continue 'exercising intellectual arrogance or employing evangelical and paternalistic practices'.[56] This was also evident in the Manchester Museum's Freudian slip in the use of the word 'privilege' identified at the beginning of this chapter.

If we in museums are willing to accept differences, to let go some control and work to develop respectful solidarity between adversaries in the museum, then we may be able to exercise the moral courage required to change. However, as Laclau reminds us, change is never easy:

> Any reform involves changing the *status quo* and in most cases this will hurt existing interests. The process of reform is a process of struggles, not a process of quiet piecemeal engineering. And there is nothing here to regret.[57]

The French philosopher Jacques Rancière realistically reminds us that 'unequal society does not carry any equal society in its womb'.[58] Museums cannot fix society's ills. Nonetheless museums can seize upon the opportunity to collaborate in order to share experiences and collectively think through the difficult and urgent issues facing civil society today. They can help people articulate their resistance to inequality. They can help people negotiate the meaning of citizenship and active agency. Through placing a value upon the potential role of dialogue, museums may help tackle some of the questions and issues arising in civil society. This is 'active citizenship' in practice, with its rights and responsibilities. The museum is ideally placed to offer such opportunities, using the past to reflect on the present and collectively prepare for an uncertain future. We might even begin to think of this as the museum's primary responsibility. As Cornwall puts it:

> Participatory sphere institutions are spaces for creating citizenship, where through learning to participate, citizens cut their teeth and acquire skills that can be transferred to other spheres – whether those of formal politics or neighbourhood action.[59]

There is much to gain, for, if museums assume the role of providing (or becoming) such participatory spheres, they may begin to discover their relevance at the heart of civil society. Furthermore, it is becoming clear that museums cannot learn to change *without* the help of their community partners.

The aim of the democratic, participatory museum must be to practise trust – a radical trust in which the museum cannot control the outcome. As Bauman puts it, 'uncertainty is the home ground for the moral person, and the only soil in which morality can sprout and flourish'.[60]

I do not believe it necessary to renounce the liberal philosophy of responsibility and reciprocity inspired by Levinas and Bauman, or to stop pursuing the ideal of the museum-as-contact-zone, as suggested by Clifford. The point is that within each contact, we in museums must begin to understand and remain mindful of the dynamics of engagement. Most importantly, conflict must be allowed to be central to democratic participation if museums are to view participants as *actors* rather than *beneficiaries*.

Cornwall calls for 'a push to go beyond the comfort zone of consultation culture'.[61] This means recasting the role of participants, 'from users and choosers to makers and shapers', as Cornwall and Gaventa memorably put it in the title of their 2001 publication,[62] and understanding the democratic, dialogic space as always contested and political. For us in museums, it means being unafraid of the conflicts within our own practice and facing up to them. We must therefore return the sense of the 'political' to these exchanges in museums, subverting the requirement for consensus and establishing a dynamic of 'conflictuality' within the range of otherwise progressive and exemplary practice currently taking place in museums. The task, therefore, is to create a reflective practice and an institutional space that allows for conflict, and, *hence*, builds trust. To engage with such a courageous museum would indeed be a privilege.

Acknowledgements

While Deputy Director of the Manchester Museum I was responsible for leading a talented, risk-taking team of museum professionals, whose commitment, creativity and reflective practice informed these ideas. I'd like to thank them and other colleagues and friends, inside and outside the museum profession, who have been willing to debate – and argue – the ideas reflected in this chapter. Of note in this respect is Jaya Graves of the Manchester-based Southern Voices organization, to whom I will always be grateful for her graciousness in our on-going 'heated debates'. Special appreciation to Emma Poulter and John Ornstein of the British Museum for their dynamic collaboration, and the Institute of Development Studies (IDS) (in particular, Jethro Pettitt and Andrea Cornwall) at the University of Sussex, who so hospitably welcomed me on a six-month Visiting Fellowship (2008–09), while working on ideas on participation, power and social change. I hope the discussion may continue with all of these valued colleagues and expand to other courageous museum professionals yet to join in this 'collective conversation'.

Notes

1 Z. Bauman, *Does Ethics have a Chance in a World of Consumers?* Vienna Lecture Series, Institute for Human Sciences, Vienna, Cambridge, MA: Harvard University Press, 2008, p. 64.

2 O. O'Neill, Newnham College, Cambridge, speaking on *A Question of Trust*, BBC Reith Lectures, Cambridge and New York: Cambridge University Press, 2002, p. 72.

3 B. Cooke and U. Kothari (eds.) *Participation: the New Tyranny?* London: Zed Books, 2001, p. 147.

4 E. Laclau, *Emancipation(s)*, London and New York: Verso, 1996, p. 118.

5 N. Fraser, 'Rethinking the public sphere: a contribution to the critique of actually existing democracy', in C. Calhoun (ed.) *Habermas and the Public Sphere*, Cambridge, MA: MIT Press, 1992, pp. 109–42.

6 A. Cornwall, *Democratising Engagement: What the UK can Learn from International Experience*, London: Demos, 2008, p. 13.

7 J. Gaventa, 'Towards participatory governance: assessing the transformative possibilities', in S. Hickey and G. Mohan (eds.) *Participation: From Tyranny to Transformation? Exploring new Approaches to Participation in Development*, New York: Zed Books, 2004 p. 28.

8 As reported by a curator of the Hackney Museum at the Museums Association conference discussion 'Can Museums Really Co-create Everything with the Public?' Liverpool, 7 October 2008.

9 Hickey and Mohan, *Participation*.

10 'Carnegie UK Trust Power Moves: Exploring Power and Influence', Carnegie UK Trust, 2008, pp. 3, 8.

11 S. Lukes, *Power: A Radical View*, Basingstoke: Palgrave Macmillan, 2nd edn, 2005.

12 S. Ahmed, 'Declarations of whiteness: the non-performity of anti-racism', *borderlands* e-journal 3: 2, 2004, pp. 8–9. Online. Available HTTP: http://www.borderlands.net.au/vol3no2_2004/ahmed_declarations.htm (accessed 1 August 2010).

13 Ibid.

14 Ibid.

15 T. T. Minh-ha, *Woman, Native, Other*, Indianapolis, IN: Indiana University Press, p. 59.

16 Zahid Hussain, Manchester Museum Community Advisory Panel member, writer and Manchester-based social enterprise developer, speaking at the 'Are museums racist?' debate at the Manchester Museum, August 2007.

17 Cornwall, *Democratising Engagement*.

18 M. L. Pratt, *Imperial Eyes: Travel Writing and Transculturation*, London: Routledge, 1992.

19 J. Clifford, *Routes: Travel and Translation in the late Twentieth Century*, Cambridge, MA: Harvard University Press, 1997.

20 Clifford's adaptation of the term 'contact zone' to museums was a way of developing ideas on the meaning of museum encounters from the point of view of both sides. He saw contact as an ongoing negotiation, 'an ongoing historical, political and moral *relationship*, a power-charged set of exchanges, of push and pull' (p. 192). He pointed out the limits of consultation in museums when engagement continues to be based on a centre–periphery model. This had been Pratt's main concern. She had used the term 'contact zone' precisely to get away from the colonialist centre–periphery model. The point is that, for both Pratt and Clifford, it was clear that the 'contact zone' was a place of conflict between different interests and experiences involving implicit or explicit *struggle*. Clifford noted the 'push and pull', emphasizing the fact that the two 'sides' engaged in the 'exchange' are plainly not equal, as clearly demonstrated in the Manchester example above, in which one 'side' has the power to control not only the terms but the outcome of the engagement.

21 J. Clifford, *The Predicament of Culture: Twentieth Century Ethnography, Literature, and Art*, Cambridge, MA: Harvard University Press, 1988.

22 As reported by a curator of the Hackney Museum at the Museums Association conference discussion 'Can Museums Really Co-create Everything with the Public?' Liverpool, 7 October 2008.

23 Z. Bauman, *The Quest for Order*, 1991, cited in P. Belhartz (ed.) *The Bauman Reader*, Cambridge, MA: Harvard University Press, 2001.

24 Ibid., pp. 291–2.

25 E. Levinas, 'Substitution', in S. Hand (ed.) *The Levinas Reader*, Oxford: Blackwell, 1989.

26 Here Levinas and Bauman intersect in this notion of 'reciprocity' when they claim that ethics begins when one acts upon the moral imperative to freely and willingly take

responsibility for the other facing them at this moment: I address them as someone to whom I owe something and, importantly, *who owe something to me*. Bauman is in concert with Levinas in the need to search for an ethical commitment to developing a 'responsibility for the other' and a philosophy and practice of 'reciprocity'.

27 Levinas, 'Substititution', p. 225.
28 Bauman, *The Quest for Order*, pp. 290–1.
29 E. Levinas, *Alterity and Transcendence*, London: Athlone Press, 1991, p. 100.
30 Z. Hussain, Manchester Museum Community Advisory Panel member, writer and Manchester-based social enterprise developer, speaking at the 'Are museums racist?' debate at the Manchester Museum, August 2007.
31 Anonymous former member of Manchester Museum's Community Advisory Panel, 2002.
32 As reported by a curator of the Sue McAlpine, Hackney Museum at the Museums Association conference discussion, 'Can Museums Really Co-create Everything with the Public?', Liverpool, 7 October 2008.
33 R. Chambers, *Whose Reality Counts? Putting the First Last*, London: Intermediate Technology Publications, 1997, p. 235.
34 Collective Conversations is led by Gurdeep Thiara, the 'In Touch' volunteering programme is led by Adele Finley and community exhibitions are led by Andrea Winn. For further information on the Manchester Museum's continuing innovative programmes with collections and communities, inside and outside the museum, see the Museum's web site. Online. Available HTTP: www.museum.manchester.ac.uk (accessed 1 August 2010).
35 B. Lynch, 'A psychoanalysis of touch with diaspora communities', in H. Chatterjee (ed.) *Touch and the Value of Object Handling in Museums*, London: Berg, 2007.
36 I have spoken extensively on this programme, which won an award from the Museums, Libraries and Archives Council and was cited for excellence in 'Sharing Diversity: National Approaches to Intercultural Dialogue in Europe', a study for the European Commission, commissioned by ERICarts, the European Institute for Comparative Cultural Research, March 2008. Online. Available HTTP: http://www.ericarts.org (accessed 1 August 2010).
37 L. Tuhiwai Smith, *Decolonising Methodologies: Research and Indigenous Peoples*, London and New York: Zed Books, 1999, p. 159.
38 Ibid., p. 43.
39 Ibid., pp. 28, 35.
40 C. Mouffe, *On the Political*, Oxford and New York: Routledge, 2005.
41 Ibid., p. 3.
42 E. Laclau, *Emancipation(s)*, London and New York: Verso, 1996, p. 201.
43 This comment (and other comments in this article relating to bicentenary issues) were made to me in my capacity as chair of the 'Revealing Histories: Remembering the Slave Trade' consortium of eight museums and galleries in the UK's north-west. During the bicentenary year, I was asked to meet with staff from several museums around the country to discuss their problems with community collaboration. I asked if I could reveal their identities, or that of their institutions. However, all the museum professionals interviewed, without exception, elected to remain anonymous. Nonetheless, they agreed to have their comments reproduced for publication. I subsequently organized a special session on the institutional impact of the bicentenary at the British Museums Association conference in Liverpool, October 2007. Of the various evaluative reports on the impact of the bicentenary, the most thorough and revealing research produced on the subject is the '1807 Commemorated' project, led by Laurajane Smith and Geoff Cubitt of the University of York, UK. Online. Available HTTP: www.history.ac.uk/1807/commemorated (accessed 1 August 2010).
44 C. Mouffe, *The Democratic Paradox*, London: Verso, 2000, p. 13.
45 C. Moraga, 'Speaking tongues: a letter to Third World women writers', in G. Anzaldua (ed.) *This Bridge called my Back*, Harmondsworth: Penguin, 1983, p. 166.
46 P. Freire, *Pedagogy of the Oppressed*, Harmondsworth: Penguin, 1972.
47 A. Boal, *Theatre of the Oppressed*, London: Pluto Press, 1979, reprinted 2000.
48 Lynch, 'A psychoanalysis of touch'.
49 D. W. Winnicott, *Playing and Reality*, London: Routledge & Kegan Paul, 1971.

50 Originally called 'Objectively Speaking', the pilot project began in summer 2008. The project, led by Emma Poulter, was initially a collaboration between Museum staff, the 'New Londoners' group of young people from south London's diaspora communities, their youth leaders and the Hi8us South community video project.

51 The project was filmed by the young people with the help of Hi8us South.

52 The 'Talking Objects' project was by no means unproblematic and challenged a number of Museum systems and processes, but as an experiment it demonstrated how such work could be transformative and transferable. It has gained further support and is continuing to work with groups of young people across London. The 'Talking Objects' project continues to be led and further developed by Emma Poulter from the British Museum's staff. At present (spring 2010), the project is continuing at the British Museum. See project web site for more information. Online. Available HTTP: http://www.britishmuseum.org/the_museum/ museum_in_london/community_work/talking_objects1.aspx (accessed 1 August 2010).

53 G. Spivak, *In other Worlds: Essays in Cultural Politics*, London: Routledge, 1985.

54 Engagement at the heart of Museums and Galleries research project was led by the author, Dr Bernadette Lynch.

55 Z. Bauman, *Does Ethics have a Chance in a World of Consumers?* Vienna Lecture Series, Institute for Human Sciences, Vienna, Cambridge, MA: Harvard University Press, 2008, p. 70.

56 R. Bishop, 'Initiating empowering research?' *New Zealand Journal of Educational Studies* 29: 1, 1994, pp. 175–88.

57 Laclau, *Emancipation(s)*, p. 114.

58 J. Rancière, *Hatred of Democracy*, London and New York: Verso, 2006, p. 96.

59 A. Cornwall and V. S. P. Coelho, 'Spaces for change? The politics of citizen participation in new democratic arenas', in A. Cornwall and V. S. P. Coelho (eds.) *Spaces for Change? The Politics of Citizen Participation in new Democratic Arenas*, London: Zed Books, 2007 p. 8.

60 Bauman, *Does Ethics have a Chance?* p. 63.

61 Cornwall and Coelho, *Spaces for change*.

62 A. Cornwall and J. Gaventa, *From Users and Choosers to Makers and Shapers: Repositioning Participation in Social Policy*, Working Paper 127, Brighton: Institute of Development Studies, University of Sussex, 2001.

10

An experimental approach to strengthen the role of science centers in the governance of science

Andrea Bandelli and Elly Konijn

Science centers and science engagement

In the last decade there has been growing interest in Europe concerning the role that science centers and museums play in the governance of science. Science centers, in fact, have the potential to be one of the most effective platforms for the discussions and debates that enable citizens to inform and participate in the democratic development of science.[1] Exhibitions and programs often offer learning opportunities and resources on the ethical, legal and social issues of scientific research in contemporary science and technology. Citizen science programs, science cafés, workshops, discussions and festivals are just a few examples of the wide variety of programs and activities in this direction that have emerged in the field.

Two of the largest museums in Europe, the Science Museum and the Natural History Museum, both in London, went so far as to build whole new facilities for this purpose: the Dana Centre at the Science Museum and Darwin Centre at the Natural History Museum have been established precisely with the goal of creating dialogue opportunities among visitors and between visitors and the scientists, researchers, museum staff and other players in the many fields in which these museums are active.

Many other European science centers and museums include similar activities in their programs and exhibitions; nowadays, it is virtually impossible to find a science center which is not active in the field of science engagement, opening up mechanisms and opportunities for their visitors not only to learn about science and technology, but to "play a role" in the ways science and technology are shaping our society.

Projects funded since the late 1990s by the European Commission have seen science centers and museums developing a variety of activities to tackle the most important issues and topics in the "science in society" agenda: from gender gap to responsible research, from climate change to stem cells to nanotechnology. In parallel, significant attention is given to participatory approaches and methodologies for the public engagement with science at meetings for practitioners and scholars in the field, such as the annual Ecsite conference.[2]

Participation and engagement pervade nowadays all aspects and activities of science centers: from the training of museum explainers, who are the first and most important interface between the public and the institution, to the design of new facilities and infrastructure; some institutions, such as the Natural History Museum in Trento, Italy, for example, make participation the core element of their mission, positioning their approach as an "invitation" for the public to engage in the dialogue between science, nature and society.[3]

The invisibility of science centers and museums

However, despite all this activity, the harsh reality is that policy makers engaged in discourse on the governance of science fail to consult science centers and museums; it's as if these profoundly democratic institutions are somehow "invisible" or irrelevant to those in power. Portuguese Minister for Science, Technology and Higher Education José Mariano Gago spoke in these precise terms in his 2007 address to the Ecsite conference.[4]

Science centers and museums are still largely absent from the policy documents and reports that shape and define European policy on science governance. When they are mentioned, science centers and museums are seen as communicators and disseminators of existing knowledge, rather than as instruments that feed back into decision making. Typical is the characterization by the EU Group MASIS (Monitoring Activities of Science in Society in Europe), "Even though they play a minor role compared to schools or the media, they still reach large numbers of diverse people in society, and are supported due to the expectation of their professional approach to the popularization of science and their role as agents for successful dissemination to a broader audience, engaging more citizens in science in the process."[5] In comparison, science festivals and other ad hoc initiatives are considered more effective and engaging opportunities to anticipate and open up the discussion on the role of science and technology in society and innovation.[6]

There have been, of course, efforts to address this "invisibility", at least at the European level; for example, Ecsite organized a full day at the European Parliament in February 2009 to present the activities of science centers and museums to the members of Parliament and of the European Commission, and some museums organize formal presentations of the results of their projects to policy makers.

But the real issue is not in raising the profile of museums in the opinion of policy makers, but in deeper self-reflection on the social relevance of the mechanisms and activities that science centers develop and implement. Science centers still have a "fear of engagement" – not of the public with science, which they actually and honestly advocate for – but of themselves with the public. Their role as platforms for dialogue, or, as stated in a declaration signed in Toronto by representatives in the field, of "safe places for difficult conversations",[7] remains timidly conceptualized and advanced; science centers seem to have no clear strategy yet for defining how civic discourse about science and technology at their institutions could inform and shape the governance and policy making of science.[8]

One of the issues that underpins this situation is the conventional wisdom among many practitioners that science centers and museums are "neutral" places that present science in an objective and balanced way. Among these practitioners, the thought of taking a political stance or an activist role in society is rejected in fear that it would compromise the aura of impartiality that science centers claim for themselves. The factual information presented in museums can certainly be unbiased: but the meaning-making process that characterizes museums depends on many social and personal factors, and it has been argued convincingly by Sharon MacDonald, among others, that science centers, as all museums, do, in fact, carry political meanings in their exhibitions and programs.[9] This idea that the museum should remain "neutral" often becomes a shield to avoid the consequences of the "difficult conversations" that science centers host. These consequences are defined by a much tighter relationship between science centers and policy decision makers. Enzo Lipardi, former president of Ecsite, explains the situation:

> We want to show to the European decisions makers that science centers are not only places to visit exhibitions, but instruments to implement policies – European ones in this case. We don't want to be instruments of political propaganda; but in situations like the European union, which needs to strengthen its concepts of scientific citizenship, a stronger relationship between science centers and policy makers and decision makers could be very beneficial. I think that this relationship isn't there yet.[10]

Stuck in shallow waters?

Museums have great potential to facilitate the political engagement of citizens, not in the sense of taking part in "party politics", but as full participants in the systems that define and shape society. An institution that has taken on this issue at its core is the Science Museum of Minnesota (SMM), which developed a new mission statement in 2008: "Turn on the science: realizing the potential of policy makers, educators, and individuals to achieve full civic and economic participation in the world." In the past, SMM had minimal interaction with policy makers, limited to seeking biennial funding and hosting occasional events. But, through actualizing this new mission, SMM has become a convener for policy makers in Minnesota; the museum's work with policy makers has shifted from passive and reactive to proactive and strategic. Consequently, the museum has become a place where policy makers come and do their work. However, at the moment, the SMM is rather an exception to the rule among science museums; it is very rare to find references to social or civic values in the mission statements of science centers and museums, let alone to policy making.

Instead, what is common in the field is a certain ambiguity, or tension, in the social and political role of science centers: on the one hand, they express a strong willingness to be "agents of change"; on the other hand, they fear compromising their assumed impartiality.[11]

In reality what is at risk when this ambiguity is not addressed and understood is not the neutrality of science centers, but rather their relevancy and meaningfulness.

Science centers risk becoming stuck in what James Wilsdon, Director of the Science Policy Centre at the UK's Royal Society, calls "the shallow waters" of science engagement, a situation characterized by a "well-meaning, professionalized and busy field, which never quite impinges on fundamental practices, assumptions and routines."[12]

Are science centers able to effectively interface with the public concerning policy making? Are museums "safe places for difficult conversations" because they care about the outcomes of these conversations or because the context in which these conversations take place is sterile and adverse to risk (and therefore "safe," at least from the institution's point of view)?

The challenge for science centers today is how to balance the social and, to some extent, political agendas necessary to contribute to the democratic development of science, with the requisite humility to become more embedded and relevant in the social structure within which they operate.[13] Rather than providing a role for the public in participatory processes and mechanisms designed from the top, science centers today ought to gain ownership of these processes, becoming part of and contributing to the dynamic governance that sustains knowledge and innovation in our society.

This means they need to investigate the ways in which they can directly support the civic engagement of the public through the activities, programs and exhibitions they produce;[14] it also necessitates the development of an institutional culture which includes the public in the decision-making process and, therefore, the governance, of the museum itself.[15]

We believe that a stronger and more responsible role for the public is necessary if science centers want to leave the "shallow waters" mentioned above – a role that is played as much inside the institution as outside, with activities and programs that effectively enable and empower public engagement with science and technology. While every museum or science center can implement actions and processes to reach these goals on their own, a systemic change can be achieved only if these actions are shared and implemented across the field. We think it is important therefore to identify, discuss and learn from those participatory experiences that easily spread across organizations and foster institutional ownership for the methods they use; experiences characterized by qualities such as replicability, adaptability and "contagiousness".

"Decide": an experiment in empowering civic and social action

In this regard, one of the projects that has gained considerable popularity and widespread attention among European science centers is "Decide – Deliberative Citizens' Debates." The project started in 2004 with a grant from the Scientific Advice and Governance unit of the European Commission to better understand the role of science centers in the democratization of science, and it has since then demonstrated how the public can effectively be in charge of the science engagement actions developed by science centers. This role of the public is manifest not only when visitors contribute their knowledge to museum activities, but especially when the public offers the opportunity to increase the relevance and the value of science engagement for policy and governance issues.

It is important to note that "Decide" is a network project rather than an institutional one; the strategy for the project comes from a collaborative effort that involves several institutions and organizations, many of which are museums and science centers, but also associations, advocacy groups and non governmental organizations.

The benefits of this approach are twofold. On the one hand, the collaboration distributes the risk of its activities. Rather than being driven by one institution and its agenda, network projects reside on the "edge" of the institution's activities; they are often treated as experiments and allow for more flexibility and innovation than projects that follow an internal development process. On the other hand, network projects allow for continuity in time across different funding sources and institutional commitments. The leadership is shared among the participants and the project adapts itself in response to the opportunities, needs, goals and possibilities of the participants, rather than following a strict strategic line set by one organization and increasingly more often heavily dependent upon a source of funding.

Projects organized like "Decide" function like jazz bands, as opposed to conventional museum structures which operate more like orchestras: all players have crucial roles in both, but while the orchestra plays under the leadership of a conductor, a jazz band shares that leadership and shifts it among its members.

When "Decide"[16] began in 2004, it had three goals: to raise awareness among the public and science center professionals of the potential of participatory and deliberative consultations; to collect data from debates and discussions on contemporary and controversial science issues; and to create an affordable and easy instrument to be made available as a downloadable kit to conduct debates and discussions in science centers.

The New Economics Foundation, an organization based in London, had developed between 2001 and 2003 a card game called "Democs", which allowed small groups of citizens to conduct discussions and deliberations on controversial topics.[17] "Democs", based on visual thinking and participatory methodologies, was very easy to use and it represented a perfect starting point for "Decide". The partners of "Decide" teamed up with the New Economics Foundation and adapted the original "Democs" game, making it possible to translate the kits and distribute them online.

A "Decide" kit is a PDF file which contains cards and instructions to set up a group discussion for up to eight people. The topic of each kit is of a controversial nature, where there is no easy agreement on the policies to regulate the issues at stake. For instance, the first "Decide" kits developed included topics such as nanotechnology, employing stem cells in research, the criminal liability of people with HIV, climate change, genetic testing and neuroscience. Participants use cards that contain facts, issues and stories to discuss their point of view about a topic. Then, with the same cards, they develop a group response to diverse policies and, if they wish, they can also develop their own alternative policies.

"Decide" encompasses three main phases. In the first phase players clarify their personal position about an issue. By reading the different cards on the table, participants ask themselves questions such as, "What aspects are more interesting to me? Which facts do I already know, and which ones are new? What issues seem more problematic than others?" This phase is helpful to create a common ground among the participants, to "seed" equal starting points for further discussions among them. Regardless of previous knowledge about the topic, this phase, in the words of one participant, "gives people permission to talk". It is an effective definition for a very important process, which we could also call empowerment of the public, in the sense that it allows people who might normally avoid a conversation because they think they have nothing to say, to instead meaningfully engage in discourse, bringing their own perspective and experiences to themes that are discussed and shared by the whole group.

The second phase is a group discussion where the participants identify those issues upon which they can converse and deepen their mutual knowledge, focusing on their common concerns, rather than differences. This is the moment when participants consider their personal values in relation to social values in a process of listening and talking that involves the whole group. The cards on the table act as a catalyst to start the discussion; they represent common items of concern for the group. During this phase it is not unusual for the discussion to open up in new directions: for example, during a "Decide" event on the use of stem cells in research, one group's position was to create a policy that would include biodiversity, and not only human health, as a goal for stem cells research – a radical departure from the usual debate that revolves around the use of stem cells from human embryos or cloning.

The third phase of "Decide" is the deliberative part of the game. On the basis of the discussion, participants arrange the cards used during the game in clusters that represent common areas of concern and interest for the group. A cluster can be, for example, the role played by developing countries in the research field, or alternatives to the proposed research, or its impact on the environment. This process helps the group to reduce the issues that have so far been identified to a manageable number, and it represents an important process in policy making, the fact that at a certain point it is necessary to discard options in order to reach a shared conclusion. After the clustering process, the participants vote on a set of pre-defined policies, and are encouraged to create their own policies if they wish.

Between 2005 and 2006, "Decide" was basically a tool: an instrument by which any organization could set up the process described above. The institutions that organized "Decide" events advertised the activity as a special event for adults, and they usually attracted twenty to thirty people who registered in advance for the event. In these two years about 300 debates were organized, mostly by science centers in Europe.

Most of the time, however, the discussions that it sparked were disconnected from actual policy making. "Decide" was a good way to introduce deliberation; people enjoyed discussing the different topics, but there was obviously a very weak link, if one at all, between the engagement of the participants with the subject and the relevancy of the discussion in actual, social terms. "Decide", just as its aims stated, was good at raising awareness for deliberation as a method to present and discuss contemporary science and technology.

Then, starting in 2007, we noticed a radical development.

Several of the users of "Decide" became developers and broadened considerably the purpose for which "Decide" was used. Museums and other organizations began to create their own "Decide" kits to tackle local and pressing issues such as urban garbage disposal or immigrants and social integration, working in collaboration with the local authorities and institutions responsible for those issues. Others adapted and modified the existing kits for use in a local context: for example, homeless shelter organizations in Vienna worked with the Austrian science center network to adapt the HIV kit and used it to "give a voice" to the homeless in regards to HIV/ AIDS policy at the shelters. Several schools and universities used "Decide" as a training tool for young researchers to address the social implications of their work. Teachers used them in the classroom with students.

The most significant example of this development is the collaboration that Eurordis, the European network of rare diseases, established with Ecsite to use "Decide" in more than 800 debates across Europe that bring together patients of rare diseases, families, care takers and health providers.[18] The goal is to strengthen the argumentative skills of patients and their families through the debates that take place in museums and other venues in the course of 2010 and 2011, and, at the same time, to shape and inform the policy recommendations and advice that Eurordis and the national patients' organizations bring to the European Parliament.

Considering these developments, we recognized that a shift was taking place: "Decide" was changing from a project in which museums made available a tool that users could employ for their own purposes, to a process of much more meaningful and relevant civic action that relied on the co-development by users themselves. We also realized the limits of the approach taken so far. The kits were released with a Creative Commons license that allowed free distribution for non-commercial use,[19] but their content was still "protected" by the institutions that developed it: according to the license, users were actually not allowed to modify the kits, in order to protect the validity of the content.

But a review of the many initiatives that evolved from "Decide" made it clear that this was an unfounded fear. The strength of "Decide" lies in the centrality of its purpose: although it is a playful activity, it is a "serious game"; it requires time and commitment, and encourages participants to develop expectations that their action has been valuable. When it fails (and there have been, of course, instances where players and organizers were both unhappy about "Decide"), it is not because the content is not up to certain standards, but because the institution offering the game does not allow the purpose to emerge, for instance, by not clearly stating what will be done with the results of the discussions and deliberations of the public. The purpose drives the content, not the other way around.

Moreover, the network strategy on which "Decide" relies is built on mutual trust among the participants – institutions and communities; measures to protect the integrity of the game through licensing carry a high risk of diminishing this trust, setting rules that come in conflict with the needs of the users. In a similar way to what happens on the web with sites like Wikipedia, with "Decide" a small community of active developers, loosely connected with each other but trusting their mutual work, create products that are enjoyed by a much larger group of users.

In light of this trend, in 2009 we made three major decisions to steer the development of "Decide" towards greater democracy. The first was to use a more relaxed open source license that allows for modification, distribution and even for commercial derivatives of "Decide", provided that the source is acknowledged and that the products are released with the same open source license.[20] This gesture, in fact, represents relinquishing the control on "Decide" and sharing it with the public. The rationale is that, in order to sustain the purpose of "Decide" and foster innovation in how the public participate in policy and decision-making about science, we need to open up the epistemological and creative process and allow for unplanned and unanticipated uses and developments of the game.

The second was to create a series of "micro-grants" of about €2,500 each to support users to become "brokers", allying local organizations, networks and institutions to strengthen the relevance of their activities creating collaborative projects which address broader publics and innovate on the "Decide" format to better suit specific applications. The purpose of the micro-grants is to embed the use of "Decide" in local issues, where participation connects with policy and decision-making processes. The micro-grants are catalysts to encourage cost-effective innovation.

The third was to provide training and professional development resources to staff of museums and other organizations using "Decide" in order to internalize a culture of dialogue and participation and start a process of organizational change, aligning institutional internal practices with external actions.

These three actions,[21] combined with the availability in 2010 of an online system that allows anybody to create a full "Decide" kit (integrating the design, layout and editing tools), based on specific needs, are at the moment an experiment for the science centers of Europe to implement a devolved and networked approach to civic action, and to share with their publics the authority they traditionally held for themselves.

Radical trust

These initiatives are happening at the "fringe" of the institutions that participate in "Decide", and are currently supported by Ecsite, the network organization of science centers in Europe, as an experiment to broaden the role of science centers and museums in science governance. Very often innovative activities like "Decide" can only begin as special or temporary projects involving a limited number of staff and without too much visibility inside and outside the museum. External support is therefore essential at the beginning. This situation, however, helps to avoid many of the institutional barriers to innovation, allowing a risk-taking attitude which eventually becomes integrated within the institution once the results of the project are visible.

The development of "Decide" in the last six years has been driven mostly by listening, observing and reflecting on the actual use that people made of the game, rather than by pushing a certain institutional attitude; and by being flexible when practice conflicted with the initial rules and policies that we established for ourselves (for example, by not enforcing the first and more restrictive license that governed the kits).

Although "Decide" is a specific example that concerns science centers, parallel developments are occurring in other kinds of museums as well. An open source approach that allows users to take social, cultural and educational action, not only using the resources and know-how of the museum, but also sharing ownership of their actions, is already being implemented by collection-based museums. The Powerhouse Museum in Sydney, for instance, released all its collection documentation under Creative Commons licenses[22] and is expanding their photographic collection on the Flickr Commons.[23] The Brooklyn Museum has implemented access to its collection so that anyone can build applications that make use of their data.[24] These are just a few examples of implementations of the open source approach.

This deeply collaborative process requires museums to develop a certain degree of "radical trust"[25] that the public will not abuse this new openness. With this level of trust the museum effectively empowers the public to take a stronger social and civic role, even beyond the context of the museum; it shares the authority over its content with the public; and it relinquishes part of the control over the meaning and the purpose that museum activities represent for the public (see also Chapter 16). Initially, this relationship concerns a limited part of the museum audience, those who are more committed and acquainted with the museum.

Over time, however, this approach enables museums to enter into networks and collaborations that gradually break down the "fear of engagement" by distributing the risks and by attracting brokers that connect the museum to purposeful and committed audiences and users who do not always overlap with the typical museum audience. The Nanoscale Informal Science Education network,[26] for example, one of the largest initiatives for public engagement with science in the United States, is built on the premise of museums acting as brokers between civil society organizations and the public.

In this context, it is not difficult to see how the social responsibility of the museum means, in fact, becoming comfortable with the concept that the activities and the actions of the public will be meaningful and socially relevant. It means realizing that the museum needs the collaboration of the public in order to achieve its civic and social goals; and that the trust at the basis of this collaboration cannot be established if it is not supported in an integral way throughout the institution. It needs to be implemented not only at the level of the activities, but also in the governance model of the museum, creating clear channels and methods for the public to interact with the decision-making process of the museum. This kind of radical trust is not an ambition, willingness or aspiration, but rather the fundamental factor for science centers to achieve social relevance.

Notes

1 A. A. Einsiedel and E. F. Einsiedel, "Museums as agora: diversifying approaches to engaging publics in research," in D. Chittenden, G. Farmelo and B. V. Lewenstein (eds.) *Creating Connections: Museums and the Public Understanding of Current Research*, Walnut Creek, CA: AltaMira Press, 2004, pp. 73–86.

2 Ecsite is the European network of science centers and museums. Online. Available HTTP: http://www.ecsite.eu (accessed 27 May 2010).

3 Museo Tridentino di Scienze Naturali. Online. Available HTTP: http://www.muse2012.eu/en/ (accessed 27 May 2010).

4 Reported in the Ecsite newsletter, No. 74, spring 2008, p. 4. Online. Available HTTP: http://www.ecsite.eu/wp-content/uploads/2009/06/ecsite-newsletter-74-spring-2008-dialogue.pdf (accessed 27 May 2010).

5 "Challenging Futures of Science in Society: Emerging Trends and Cutting-edge Issues," report of the MASIS expert group set up by the European Commission, Luxembourg, 2009, p. 24. Online. Available HTTP: http://ec.europa.eu/research/science-society/document_library/pdf_06/the-masis-report_en.pdf (accessed 27 May 2010).

6 "Challenging Futures of Science in Society: Emerging Trends and Cutting-edge Issues," Report of the MASIS expert group set up by the European Commission, Luxembourg, 2009, p. 24. Online. Available HTTP: http://ec.europa.eu/research/science-society/document_library/pdf_06/the-masis-report_en.pdf (accessed 27 May 2010).

7 As mentioned in the 2008 Toronto Declaration, endorsed by all the science center networks worldwide. Online. Available HTTP: http://www.5scwc.org/TheTorontoDeclaration/tabid/133/Default.aspx (accessed 27 May 2010).

8 There are of course exceptions: for instance, the advocacy role of the Monterey Bay Aquarium as reported in "Aquariums as a Force for Change: New Roles in Conservation and Social Impact," by Julie Packard, published in *ASTC Dimensions*, September–October 2009, *Taking a Stand: Science Centers and Issues Advocacy*, Washington, DC: ASTC. For more on the potential of science museums to impact policy making, see L. Bell, "Engaging the public in technology policy: a new role for science museums," *Science Communication* 29: 3, 2008, pp. 386–398.

9 This discussion can be found in S. MacDonald, "Exhibitions of power and powers of exhibitions," in S. MacDonald (ed.) *The Politics of Display: Museums, Science, Culture*, New York: Routledge, 1998, pp. 1, 24.

10 Personal communication, January 2009.

11 F. Cameron, "Contentiousness and shifting knowledge paradigms: the roles of history and science museums in contemporary societies," *Museum Management and Curatorship* 20: 3, 2005, pp. 213–233.

12 "Public Engagement in Science: Report of the Science in Society Session of the Portuguese Presidency Conference 'The Future of Science and Technology in Europe,' Lisbon, 8–10 October 2007," European Commission, 2008, p. 20. Online. Available HTTP: http://ec.europa.eu/research/science-society/document_library/pdf_06/public-engagement-081002_en.pdf (accessed 27 May 2010).

13 E. Koster and J. Falk, "Maximizing the external value of museums," *Curator* 50: 191, 2007, p. 6.

14 G. Black, "Embedding civil engagement in museums," *Museum Management and Curatorship*, 25: 2, 2010, pp. 129–146.

15 A. Bandelli, E. Konijn and J. Willems, "The need for public participation in the governance of science centers," *Museum Management and Curatorship*, 24: 2, 2009, pp. 89–104.

16 "Decide" was originally developed by Ecsite, the European Network of Science Centers and Museums and four science centers: Explore at Bristol, in Bristol, UK; Heureka, in Vantaa, Finland; La Cité des Sciences et de l'Industrie in Paris, France; and Città della Scienza, Fondazione IDIS, in Naples, Italy. A. Bandelli has been the director of the project since its beginning.

17 P. Walker and S. Higginson, *"So you're using a card game to make policy recommendations?" The Evolution of DEMOCS*, October 2001–January 2003, London: New Economics Foundation, 2003.

18 Online. Available HTTP: http://www.eurordis.org/content/polka-patients-consensus-preferred-policy-scenarii-rare-disease (accessed 27 May 2010).

19 Online. Available HTTP: http://creativecommons.org/licenses/by-nc-nd/2.5/ (accessed 27 May 2010).

20 Online. Available HTTP: http://creativecommons.org/licenses/by-sa/3.0/ (accessed 27 May 2010).

21 These actions are supported by a grant from the European Commission in the framework of the project "FUND." Online. Available HTTP: http://www.playdecide.eu/about (accessed 27 May 2010).

22 Online. Available HTTP: http://www.powerhousemuseum.com/collection/database/ (accessed 27 May 2010).

23 Online. Available HTTP: http://www.flickr.com/commons (accessed 27 May 2010).

24 Online. Available HTTP: http://www.brooklynmuseum.org/opencollection/api/ (accessed 27 May 2010).

25 Online. Available HTTP: http://www.ideum.com/2006/08/radical-trust/ (accessed 27 May 2010).

26 Online. Available HTTP: www.nisenet.org (accessed 27 May 2010).

11

Peering into the bedroom

Restorative justice at the Jane Addams Hull House Museum

Lisa Yun Lee

Introduction

In the spring of 2009, I found myself the lone museum professional tagging along with a group of Chicago lawyers on an excursion to South Africa. The tour of Johannesburg and Cape Town was led by Prexy Nesbitt, who had been cajoling me ever since I became the Director of the Jane Addams Hull House Museum (JAHHM) to join him on one of his educational trips to learn from activists and politicians engaged in the hard work of tending to the scars and ravages of apartheid and transforming South Africa to a democracy. Prexy is a well-weathered warrior for social justice, and respected around the globe as an activist, educator and international human rights advocate. His work has spanned a staggeringly wide range of activities from supporting liberation struggles from the newly independent Tanzania in 1965–1966 to working as a program officer at the John D. and Katherine T. MacArthur Foundation. In addition, Prexy happens to be a so-called "Hull House kid." His mother worked at Hull House Settlement as a teacher, and Prexy participated as a youth in the Bowen Country Club, the open-air camp that Hull House established in a Chicago suburb in order for urban city kids to escape the squalor of the city and to have the opportunity to swim, play, make art and make friends in desegregated spaces.[1]

Prexy also serves on the JAHHM's Advisory Board, a group charged with helping the Museum expand our audience and to become more inclusive and responsive to as many diverse communities of people in Chicago as possible. The Museum complex consists of the two remaining buildings of Hull House Settlement, the house built in 1856, which is a National Historic Landmark that served as the home and workplace of several Progressive era reformers including Jane Addams, and an Arts and Crafts building called the Residents' Dining Hall, which is a Chicago Landmark. We are a hybrid house museum – both a museum in a house and a house museum – and we contain exhibits that interpret objects related to both the reformers who worked at Hull House and the predominantly immigrant communities that participated in activities that ranged from citizenship classes, labor organizing, theater productions, sex education, painting, music and literature classes. The Residents' Dining

Hall also serves as a site for the Museum's public programming, and we host vibrant film series, lectures, book readings, dance programs and a weekly soup kitchen in this space. Through public programming, we have reinvigorated our legacy as a progressive site for debate, dialogue and organizing. Activists like Prexy have become reacquainted and reengaged with Hull House, but this time through our work as a museum.

One rainy afternoon while in Johannesburg, we visited the Apartheid Museum, which is an arresting granite and glass building on over seven acres of arid land designated as Freedom Park. From the moment a visitor crosses the threshold into the museum, by choosing either the "Whites Only" or "Colored" entrance, one has an unforgettably visceral and uncomfortable experience of the policy of apartheid that turned 20 million people into second-class citizens, and condemned them to political and cultural humiliation and abuse. It was a difficult and inspiring visit that ended with a lecture and conversation with George Bizos in an exhibition hall that bluntly displayed on floor to ceiling panels the police records that documented the arrest, torture and murder of the anti-apartheid activist Steven Biko. It was at this public program that I was introduced to a dynamic definition of truth that provided me with a critical insight into the emancipatory potential of museums and the capacity of cultural institutions to create a more just world. This understanding of truth is something that I have returned to over and again as we curate and create new exhibits at the Hull House Museum.

Bizos is the legendary lawyer and human rights advocate, who in addition to being a long-time member of Nelson Mandela's legal team[2] and counsel to many families of those who died in detention, was also the principal legal activist involved in drafting the Truth and Reconciliation Bill and parts of the interim constitution, which guaranteed fundamental human rights to all citizens of South Africa. He described the challenges of the truth and reconciliation process in creating a new society in which the victims of apartheid were now to live side by side with their oppressors. The Truth and Reconciliation Commission (TRC), established by the newly democratic and newly elected government, consisted of investigators and tribunals that examined the horrors perpetrated on both sides in the name of apartheid *or* equality. Bizos described four categories of truth that were recognized in the TRC. *Forensic truth* established the minutiae and facts of what happened, the when and how. *Personal truth* added the individual interpretation of events and included the stories we tell ourselves in order to make sense of events. *Social truth* placed the individual's story within a broader social dialogue and context and attempted to weave the perspective with other members of the group. And, finally, the fourth truth was a *restorative truth* aimed toward a form of national reconciliation by re-establishing a sense of justice.

It was a "Eureka!" moment for me. What if the JAHHM engaged in the democratic work of these four truths? We were already tasked with balancing our multiple identities as a National Historic Landmark, a public museum that preserves and collects artifacts and a unit of the College of Art and Architecture at University of Illinois–Chicago. This sometimes requires us to negotiate various forms of truthtelling (sometimes contradictory) between national collective memory, our collection of oral histories and contemporary narratives by Hull House Settlement participants, the "stories" our artifacts tell and the scholarly work of historians and other academics. Instead of homogenizing these trajectories and seamlessly presenting them as a coherent whole, what if we revealed the messiness of history and its contradictions? What if we made a commitment to becoming a more democratic space by incorporating multiple voices, encouraging dissenting opinions and dialogue? And, finally, what if we were to take on the considerable responsibility of working toward restorative truth?

One of the first steps in this process is recognizing that museums are places in which to encounter the past, as well as windows through which to contemplate the conditions of possibility for the future. Their instructive and educational value lies not only in the simple storehousing of beautiful or ancient objects and the telling of a set of facts, but also in the opportunity to imagine what could have happened and what might come to be. The JAHHM is not alone in this belief in the potential of museums to help create a more just world. We are a member of the International Coalition of Sites of Conscience, a group of historic sites around the globe that have committed our efforts to not only preserving the past, but to also looking forward to the future. The Gulag Museum at Perm-36 in Russia, the National Civil Rights Museum in the United States and the Work House in England are some of the cohort of institutions "dedicated to remembering past struggles for justice and connecting them with today's most pressing issues."[3] Belonging to this group has enabled us to see how linking our history to the continuing fight for justice is not simply a *choice* that some historic sites and museums make, but rather an *obligation* and *responsibility*. This distinction is absolutely critical because it creates a ground for us to understand our work as an ethical imperative. Instead of thinking about the participation in creating a more socially just world as an option or preference, the JAHHM as a cultural institution and interpreter of history understands it as a duty.

Although we are united in our commitment, each museum and historic site must find a unique way of doing this work within the particularities of our mission, our collections of artifacts and our particular history. And the quest for restorative justice depends on the particular set of "truths" we are negotiating at our sites. For the JAHHM, we celebrate the historic role Hull House played as a site for resistance and recognize the Museum's role in providing "counter" and "oppositional" space that challenges the dominant narrative. Critical to our identity is the continuing commitment to the creation of a "counterpublic" space that might enable a different world and public to come into being.

I am borrowing this term and idea from the work of queer theorist Michael Warner, whose writings on public sphere theory are particularly useful. Warner's scholarship explores how we might create a more vibrant public sphere – one that exists to foster debate, discussion and dissent rather that existing solely to police the private sphere. His analysis of the ideological divide between the public and private revolves around a central question: What is a public? Among his illuminating insights is the provocative thesis that a public is the social space created by the reflexive circulation of discourse. In other words, this means that the public, or more accurately stated as "publics," are not singular or homogeneous, and not timeless, but rather historical and constituted by virtue of their imagining and by forms of address.[4]

Warner's work also shows how traditional liberal procedures of public deliberation often give rise to the expression of a collective interest that often silences the ideas of marginal interests and obscures certain voices. Subordinated groups – women, workers, people of color, gays, and lesbians – have found the need for safe space in order to contest their disadvantage in the official public sphere. The creation of a so-called "counterpublic sphere" provides an alternative site for discourse and can make the predominant public sphere more inclusive and open to dissent. It is important to distinguish counterpublic space from separatist space. While the former seeks to create change by operating within the mainstream, all the while engaging and challenging the normative public sphere by disseminating its discourse to ever widening areas, the latter chooses to disengage and radically sever relationships to the other and reconstitute itself as a discrete entity.

Lofty rhetoric and jargon aside, the practice of doing this work is extremely difficult. Interrogating the nature of what constitutes the public necessarily includes a reconsideration of what is private. This often touches upon sensitive issues that we are not used to debating, discussing and deliberating in public. Furthermore, creating a counterpublic, by definition, goes against mainstream ideas and discourse.

The following is my account of what happened in one exhibit at the JAHHM as we attempted to create a counterpublic space through one of the most ubiquitous forms of public address – the museum label – and how we worked to restore justice within the parameters of our particular history. Because the creation of a counterpublic involves the blurring of the boundaries between the public and private, historic house museum offers a unique site of resistance. The act of peering into bathrooms and bedrooms of other people's houses crosses over the limits and borders of what is normally considered private or public and this trespass into the most intimate areas of someone's residence has the potential of being a transgressive act.

Jane Addams and Mary Rozet-Smith

One of the most captivating historic objects in our collection is a portrait of Mary Rozet-Smith, painted in 1898 by the accomplished artist and teacher Alice Kellogg Taylor (Figure 11.1). This painting hung out of public view for much of the museum's history because it was considered potentially too provocative for visitors and because of the difficulties in describing this work of art in a concise museum label.

The issue of concern was how to identify the portrait's subject. The history books, scholars and public opinion have offered wide-ranging interpretations of Rozet-Smith and Addams's relationship. Sometimes described as a prominent Hull House patron, and at other times as Addams's companion, lesbian lover or lifelong partner, Mary Rozet-Smith is conspicuously absent from the dominant narrative about Jane Addams. This is in part due to the fact that intimate relationships between women during the Victorian era were manifold and complex, and there are problems of ahistoricity when applying current understandings of words such as "lesbian" or "life partner" to historic periods that did not use these terms. Jane Addams's own complex relationship to sexuality and desire might also be considered. But perhaps more significantly, as a beloved historical icon, Addams has been sterilized and sanitized for public consumption. Many people are surprised to find out that *Jane Addams*, who we celebrate as America's first woman to win the Nobel Peace Prize, was also considered at one point in history to be "Public Enemy

Figure 11.1 Mary Rozet-Smith, by Alice Kellogg Taylor, 1898, oil on canvas. Permission of the Jane Addams Hull House Museum, University of Illinois at Chicago.

No. 1" and also "The Most Dangerous Person in the United States." Addams was considered "dangerous" because she was an unwavering peace activist in a time of war and a suffragist who agitated for equal rights for women. But the crucial reason she was under FBI surveillance was simply because she opened Hull House Settlement doors, where she lived and worked, to people who did not always have popular or mainstream views. Addams created opportunities for people to assemble and discuss controversial ideas. Hull House Settlement was the place where social reformers, scientists, artists and others were able to unleash their imaginations and envision a different world. This commitment to radically democratic and inclusive public space challenged power and authority and made some people consider her "dangerous." Her FBI file is on display in the museum, along with an excerpt on the wall text from the FBI file of her friend and fellow suffragette Carrie Chapman Catt:

> Jane Addams is probably a member of more organizations international, socialistic or communistic in character than any other one individual in the United States ... It is Jane Addams who is directly responsible for the growth of the radical movement among women in America. It is Jane Addams who is in the forefront of the battle in the attempt to disarm our nation. It is Hull House, the institution of Jane Addams, that has time and again been the scene of radical meetings where Communists, IWWs [International Workers of the World], anarchists, socialists and all subversive breeds have found shelter.[5]

Yet another and unspoken reason that Jane Addams was considered so "dangerous" was due to the fact that she unabashedly chose Mary Rozet-Smith as her closest confidante and partner. The hushed debates that erupt into public uproars now and again about whether Jane Addams "was or wasn't" reflect legitimate intellectual interest in the cultural evolution of language and the history of sexuality, but more often than not are a manifestation of homophobia expressed as a pathological anxiety about our most important historical icons and what is appropriate and acceptable at any particular historic moment. This uneasiness manifests itself in the all too common symptom of selective historical amnesia.

Though Rozet-Smith had been effectively written out of history, the painting was an artifact that had the potential to become a "site of conscience"[6] and an opportunity to resist an erasure. However, there were multiple "truths" to consider. Not only did historians differ in their naming of the relationship, but also, while most of Mary Rozet-Smith's family members publicly described their love as lesbian, many of Jane Addams's family did not. We decided to create an alternative labeling project that consisted of three different wall texts that gave expression to forensic, narrative and dialogic truth. After consulting with historians and descendants, and re-examining our oral histories and artifacts – all of which had nuanced and complex pieces of the story to tell – we crafted three different museum labels and displayed them next to the painting.

They read as follows:

- Mary Rozet-Smith was Jane Addams's companion for decades and one of the top financial supporters of Hull House. Alice Kellogg Taylor's relationship with Hull House began in 1890. She taught, lectured and exhibited here until her early death in 1900. A teacher at the Art Institute of Chicago, Kellogg Taylor received many honors for her work.

- Mary Rozet-Smith was Jane Addams's life partner and one of the top financial supporters of Hull House. Given the emotional intimacy that is expressed in their letters to one another, it is hypothesized that they were lesbians. It is, however, difficult to determine this for sure, particularly considering the differences in sexual attitudes of the Victorian era in which she lived and Jane Addams's own complex reflections on the ideals of platonic love.
- Mary Rozet-Smith was Jane Addams's partner and one of the top financial supporters of Hull House. They shared a deep emotional attachment and affection for one another. Only about one half of the first generation of college women ever married men. Many formed emotional, romantic and practical attachments to other women. In letters, Addams refers to herself and Rozet-Smith as 'married' to each other. Hull House women redefined domesticity in a variety of ways. Addams writes in another letter to Rozet-Smith, "Dearest you have been so heavenly good to me all these weeks. I feel as if we had come into a healing domesticity which we never had before, as if it were the first affection had offered us." Jane Addams burned many of her letters from Mary Rozet-Smith.

In addition, we asked visitors to let us know what label they found most meaningful and to attach their comment to a large public response board placed next to the painting. We hoped the project would inspire visitors to think more critically and broadly about the history that is represented at the museum and to reflect on what was at stake – the determining of the meaning of history and who gets to decide. Labels on artifacts are the most direct form of communication that we have with our visitors. Beverly Serrell and others have demonstrated the rhetorical power of labels and the occasion these missives present to either captivate, disengage or repel visitors.[7] Yet labels, for the most part, remain a lopsided form of engagement with the public. The most common style of labels, referred to (not without irony) in museum jargon as the "tombstone," appears like a small headstone on the right side of an artifact and bears its most vital statistics. These labels tend to inscribe a static meaning to objects when the sense of an artifact can change over time and context.[8]

Drawing inspiration from the history of Hull House Settlement, where dialogue, dissent and discussion fostered a participatory democracy, we hoped our alternative labeling project would help transform our institutional practices and address visitors as citizens engaged in the process of creating meaning.[9] We live in a culture where we have grown accustomed to being addressed like consumers in every instant of our lives. Labels become yet another form of consumption that permeate the museum. The value of human life and our significance as sentient, sensuous human beings has been eclipsed by our ability to shop and our purchasing power. This is also the case in many museums, where the gift store has become a seamless extension of the exhibit. Labels in museums are yet another manifestation of a consumptive practice when visitors are expected to "buy wholesale" what we tell them happened at our sites or what the significance of a particular artifact is. By inviting visitors to step out of their prescribed role as consumers, we are also required to relinquish our identities as simple purveyors of knowledge. We hoped that this project would create a space for mutually illuminating interplay and usher in the possibility for us to become co-producers of knowledge with our visitors. Surrendering control over the dominant narrative and creating a public space for discourse and dissent such as the one we talk about on the tours has been one of the most exhilarating parts of this process.

Almost immediately, the response board began to fill with comments that revealed a hunger for information beyond the "forensic" truth that labels often provide. The visitors' desire both to "talk back" to us and to have a democratic forum in which they might converse with one another about substantive issues in the museum was apparent by the lengthy responses and comments to one another on the board. In addition, their responses also confirm my belief that looking at ways that sexuality and marginality function in society provides valuable clues to the quality of our common life together.

Some visitors disapproved of the project (even as they almost always let us know their preference for one label over another). Many of the negative responses dismissed the painting and considered Rozet-Smith insignificant in relation to other "more important" issues we should be addressing as a museum. Others also believed that we were violating Jane Addams's private life by making her sexual orientation public. Press articles in the *Chicago Tribune* and elsewhere that characterized the project as "Outing Jane Addams" fueled the sense that we had done something indiscrete and violated Addams's confidentiality. And yet another group of visitors believed that this was an inappropriate issue for the public to weigh in on and would better be left to "experts."

Although I concede that Addams's relationship to Mary Rozet-Smith should not be given any more prominence over Addams's many accomplishments and work, I would argue that it should unambiguously be a part of the historical record. Dismissals of the role that Rozet-Smith played in the life of Jane Addams reveal a bias against same-sex partners and the erroneous belief that, because we are considering the relationship between two women, we are talking about "sex!" This immediate association and linkage of lesbian or gay partners to sex rather than love, support, companionship or any other aspects of our most intimate and important relationships is a characteristic of homophobia. Consider if the painting were of a heterosexual partner or of a husband; visitors would undoubtedly not feel that we were just discussing sex, but that we were providing a relevant aspect of Addams's life story. The work for restorative truth in this case demanded that we overcome normative ideas of what we should be discussing in public, acknowledging that they were functioning as an ideological restraint that privileged heterosexuality.

Responses that conveyed an anxiety about the museum relinquishing our expertise and opening the floodgates to the opinions of the "public" are particularly revealing. This idea of the museum as a rarified institution is at odds with the potential role that museums play in the public sphere as sites that empower communities and champion civic engagement and democracy. Museum labels have often played a role in negotiating these contradictions. The earliest examples of labels appeared with objects of natural history, art and other oddities in so-called *Wunderkammers* – or cabinets of curiosity – to help wealthy collectors keep track and remind themselves of their private possessions. In the invention of the mass museum open to and for the public, the label we think of as a tombstone was developed as a democratizing educational tool and even functioned as an equalizer in class distinctions. In 1857, for example, the British House of Commons passed a rule that required national museums to accompany objects of art, science and historical interest with "a brief description thereof, with the view of conveying useful information to the Public and of sparing them the expense of a Catalogue."[10] This democratizing instinct is part of the history of the label's coming into being.

The personal is political

Many people assume that being a public institution means being more or less apolitical and presenting a so-called "fair and balanced" point of view. But once again, the JAHHM draws its inspiration from the history of Hull House Settlement, which is a constant reminder that the public sphere is something that is and has always been historically constructed, creatively imagined and the result of struggle. Being public is not simply being popular or the voice of the majority, but being a space where active dissent can take place. On closer analysis, the concerns about the public nature of our alternative labeling project can be understood as a gentle yet insistent demand for the maintenance of the distinction between the private and public sphere. As an ideological construct, the insistence on that which is considered appropriate for the public does not contribute to a participatory democracy, but is instead heavily invested in a public that exists only to surveil the private, all the while asserting that people are "free" to do as they like as long as they keep it to themselves or stay within the acceptable normative boundaries. The famous slogan "The personal is political" that acted as a rallying call for many second-wave feminists blurred these borders and gave expression to the critical understanding that the social structuring of private life, such as household labor, intimacy and sexuality are not disinterested, neutral nor immutable, but rather emblematic of relations of power and therefore subject to social transformation and change.[11]

Historic house museums offer a potential site of struggle against the ideological maintenance of this divide. The trespass into the most intimate areas of someone's residence has the potential of being an act of resistance. This potential needs to be activated, however, if it is to be anything other than a voyeuristic experience. Interpretation that mines the collection, explores the built environment and tells the stories of the home owners, visitors or domestic staff that lived and worked in those spaces provides a dynamic opportunity for interrogating issues of class, race, ethnicity and gender.

At the JAHHM, dissolving the bonds of normative distinctions between the private and the public has always been a part of the history of our site. In 1889, Addams stormed the public sphere and co-founded Hull House Settlement with her best friend Ellen Gates Starr in Chicago's Nineteenth Ward – one of the most impoverished areas of the city and home to the majority of the city's immigrant population. As part of the first generation of college-educated white women in the United States, Addams, like many Hull House reformers, blurred the lines between her private life and public efforts. Social movements including abolition, temperance, labor, suffrage and antiracism challenged the prevailing sense of public and private. The collective living conditions at Hull House Settlement included apartments, public kitchens and communal dining halls that allowed the reformers to talk about legislation they were working on over dinner and then read to one another in bed. The reformers' demands for progressive public policy concerning issues traditionally seen as "private" and "domestic" opened up society to public health and housing and progressive school systems regulated by the state. Jane Addams's dictum, "A city is enlarged housekeeping," used language that expressed a vision for the expansion of the welfare state that would continue to allow women a central role in this work, both recognizing and pushing against the prevailing stereotypes. They politicized the domestic economy and turned the division of public and private on its head.[12] The over 9,000 immigrants who came to Hull House each week to mix, mingle, drink coffee, take classes and organize their life and labor contributed to the creation of a richly textured public space at Hull House that was political, engaging, challenging and supportive and managed to expand the notion of family beyond ethnic, cultural and social boundaries.

At the JAHHM, we use this history as a lens through which to understand and approach contentious topics and to engage the public on critical social issues that are too often evaded and avoided in "polite society." We believe that our mission at the museum includes not only preserving and collecting artifacts and telling the exciting stories of Hull House reformers and the neighborhood immigrants, but also preserving this space as a site for radical democratic practices.

Even as I have spent undue time analyzing the negative responses to the project, in part because they were so revealing, it should also be said that there was an overwhelming number of respondents that reacted positively to the project. Many visitors, including gay and lesbian youth on school tours, thanked us for not shying away from this topic and for finally acknowledging something that they felt was all too often a subject of shame and silence in other public institutions. An overwhelming majority of visitors encouraged us to consider alternative labeling with different artifacts throughout the museum.

Although we were convinced that the project did in some small way democratize our museum practices by presenting forensic, narrative truth and providing opportunities for social truth, the question remained how we intended to create the fourth and final restorative truth that works to ensure a more socially just society. The prospect of doing this presented itself when we were awarded a "We the People" grant from the National Endowment for the Humanities. This endeavor, on the sesquicentennial of Jane Addams's birth, includes the historic implementation of a new core exhibition in the two remaining buildings of Hull House Settlement that make up the JAHHM. We will double our square footage for displays and expand the museum to encompass more voices and stories. We will also include architectural encounters that explore our largest artifact – the historic house itself – and link the building to the social ideals of Hull House reformers. The staff began almost immediately the deliberative process about how to move the alternative labeling project into the realm of restorative justice.

Addams's famous quote rang true to us: "Social advance depends as much upon the process through which it is secured as upon the result itself."[13] Our research for the alternative labeling project had included conversations with friends, family, co-workers and lovers, as well as the opportunity to befriend strangers and conduct productive, although at times contentious, discussions with visitors, including senior citizens, Girl Scouts and Catholic school tour groups, about issues that are often perceived as taboo. Our politics, our activism and our commitment to making the world more just were not something that could be kept discrete or separate from our "normal" working lives and public identities in these interactions. This project allowed us to introduce what might normally be understood as our "private opinions" into our institutional work. This refusal to separate schizophrenically our desiring, political selves and everything we care so deeply about from other parts of our daily lives, including the work that we do, does not mean that we are in favor of collapsing the differences between public and private or erasing the distinction between work and leisure, but, instead, that we recognize how these issues are already completely ideologically linked with one another.

Public institutions have missions, but in order for them also to play a meaningful role in society as a site for restorative truth, they need to be informed by a sense of truth, morality and personal ethics which comes from the individuals who inhabit these spaces. This includes both staff and visitors. While organizational missions are crafted in such a way to be lasting and enduring, the nature of social justice is to challenge, change and extend the horizon towards a better future. In fact, looking back in history, we see that society's prevailing notions of morality and responsibility have proven time and again to be inadequate. Restorative truth demands a continuous process of inquiry because the present is a continuous moving ground.

"Truth," like "beauty," is an intimidating term. Both are words that we often shy away from in the museum world because they seem like abstract notions better left to poets or transcendental philosophers, but the reality is that truth and beauty can and should be integral parts of our everyday museum work. Studies have repeatedly shown that visitors trust museums and the material they encounter in them more than any other source, believing the information shared in exhibitions over that in books, newspapers or the internet.[14] This corresponds with a dazzling opportunity for museums to encourage critical thinking and questioning and to cultivate the emergence of a new political agent. This would require the nurturing of curiosity and inquisitiveness, and a commitment to creating exhibits and spaces for the visitor not simply to consume history as objectively presented, but to engage actively in history as a subject and participate in the making of meaning.

In the new exhibition, we will open for the first time to the public Miss Addams's bedroom in the original Hull House Mansion. The room will be furnished with period pieces and breathtakingly beautiful William Morris wallpaper original to Hull House. It will include numerous personal artifacts from her youth, spent at her father's farm in Cedarville, her college days at Rockford Seminary and her life at Hull House. Addams's clothing, travel mementoes, writings, letters and photographs in this space will provide visitors with an intimate glimpse into the personal and political life of Jane Addams and explore how her extraordinary accomplishments continue to enthrall and inspire us. The painting of Mary Rozet-Smith will be moved into this room, where it had historically hung across from Addams's bed (except for when she traveled with the painting when she missed Rozet-Smith). We will place on the mantelpiece below the portrait numerous photographs (Figures 11.2–3) that span the time of their life spent together, and train our museum educators to introduce Jane Addams as a lesbian.

Figure 11.2 Mary Rozet-Smith with Jane Addams, circa 1898, Jane Addams Memorial Collection, Department of Special Collections, The University Library, The University of Illinois at Chicago.

From our experience, we know that this will anger some members of the public, and might even be considered inappropriate for a mainstream National Historic Landmark. But we also celebrate the historic role Hull House played as a site for resistance and recognize the Museum's role in providing "counter" and "oppositional" space that challenges the dominant narrative that has silenced the relationship between Jane Addams and Mary Rozet-Smith. Our ambition is to create a "counterpublic" space that might enable a more just world and public to come into being.

This work of challenging oppression, creating spaces for democracy and dissent and politicizing visitors is the JAHHM's work toward restorative truth and social justice. Returning once more to my experience at the Apartheid Museum in South Africa, an exhibit there inspires me whenever I feel either extremely depressed or extremely hopeful about social change. There is a vast wall filled with text presenting all the laws passed over a short period of time in order to enforce the policies of apartheid. This includes an almost comical, if not so despicable, series of anti-miscegenation laws that attempted to criminalize and prevent love between "Whites and Natives," "Whites and Asians" and "Whites and Blacks." As a visitor, one is simply overwhelmed by the sheer magnitude of effort and resources required to enforce inequality and injustice. This is, however, good news to those of us who are working for social change (and by definition necessarily optimistic). It means that maintaining injustice requires a tremendous amount of work. Whether it is racism, sexism and any other form of oppression, these discriminatory systems need to be constantly re-presented and re-inscribed in culture and society on all different levels and at all times. This presents a tremendous opportunity for us to break through, resist and oppose oppression – even with something as small as a museum label.

Figure 11.3 Mary Rozet-Smith with Jane Addams, circa 1930, Jane Addams Memorial Collection, Department of Special Collections, The University Library, The University of Illinois at Chicago.

Notes

1 On Prexy Nesbitt, see the riveting account of his anti-apartheid work in W. Minter, G. Hovey and C. Cobb, Jr. (eds.) *No Easy Victories: African Liberation and American Activists over a Half Century, 1950–2000*, Lawrenceville, NJ: Africa World Press, 2007. For an oral history of Prexy's reminiscences about his Bowen Country Club experiences and how they contributed to his activism, see the JAHHM web site. Online. Available HTTP: http://www.hullhousemuseum.org (accessed 10 May 2010).
2 Bizos was a part of the team that defended Nelson Mandela, Govan Mbeki and Walter Sisulu in the Rivonia trial in 1963–64 that sentenced the defendants to life in prison.
3 Online. Available HTTP: http://sitesofconscience.org/en/ (accessed 10 May 2010).

4 M. Warner, *Publics and Counterpublics*, Cambridge: Zone Books, 2005.

5 Online. Available HTTP: www.catt.org/ccabout2.html (accessed 10 May 2010).

6 The term 'site of conscience' is a reference to the International Coalition on Sites of Conscience, a worldwide network of historic sites that is dedicated to remembering past struggles for social justice and addressing them in their contemporary legacies. As defined in their mission, a 'site of conscience' does the following four things: interprets history through historic sites; engages in programs that stimulate dialog on pressing social issues; promotes humanitarian and democratic values as a primary function; shares opportunities for public involvement in issues raised at the site. Online. Available HTTP: http://www.sitesofconscience.org.

7 B. Serrell, *Exhibit Labels: An Interpretive Approach*, Lanham, MD: AltaMira Press, 1996.

8 For more on museum labels, transparency and engagement, see P. Z. McClusky, "'Why is this here?' Art Museum Texts as Ethical Guides," this volume.

9 I. M. Young, *Inclusion and Democracy*, Oxford: Oxford University Press, 2002, p. 22. In this work, Young presents the possibilities for "deep democracy" in the context of ongoing structurally unequal power relations. She replaces the ideal of consensus with one of contestation and theorizes inclusion as a central goal for deep democracy.

10 Quote, I. Schaffner, "Wall Text," in P. Marincola (ed.) *What Makes a Great Exhibition*, Philadelphia: Philadelphia Exhibitions Initiative, 2006, p. 157.

11 C. Pateman, *The Disorder of Women: Democracy, Feminism, and Political Theory*, Stanford, CA: Stanford University Press, 1989, p. 118.

12 See S. Jackson, *Lines of Activity, Performance, Historiography, Hull House Domesticity*, Ann Arbor, MI: University of Michigan Press, 2002, and D. Hayden, *Grand Domestic Revolution*, Cambridge, MA: MIT Press, 1982.

13 J. Addams, *Peace and Bread in the Time of War*, New York: Macmillan, 1922, p. 133.

14 See J. M. Griffiths and D. W. King, "Interconnections: The Institute of Museum and Library Services National Study on the Use of Libraries, Museums and the Internet," February 2008. Online. Available HTTP: interconnectionsreport.org/reports/ConclusionsSummaryFinalB.pdf (accessed 9 May 2010).

12
Being responsive to be responsible
Museums and audience development

Claudia B. Ocello

When museums respond to their communities, they attract a larger and more diverse audience that sees their value in a broader context. But can a museum[1] step over the line to become overly responsive, and turn into something it is not – a social service provider? How can this delicate balance between reaching new audiences – often the job of the museum education staff – and serving as a social service organization, be achieved without compromising the mission of the museum?

In this chapter I explore several case studies of museums in the United States and Europe, each serving a relatively small, specialized population with programs and services based around the museum's strengths. These examples will show how museums embrace these programs, sometimes after overcoming staff reservations, how target communities are served and how the larger museum community applauds these efforts. Together, the models will demonstrate that not only are these museums *doing* social service work using the museum's resources, but that the long-term gains of such social service efforts for both the museum and its audiences outweigh a perceived diversion of resources. However, in order for programs such as these to gain widespread acceptance and become the norm rather than the exception, the museum field requires a professional standard or code of ethics regarding museums and social responsibility, as Lois Silverman has observed in *The Social Work of Museums*. According to Silverman, museums today should be helping to "foster cultures of caring" as well as "caring for culture."[2] In the current economic climate, I argue that museums – if they are willing to accept this challenge and are poised for change – should embrace this expanded vision to become more responsive and relevant to society, consequently encouraging sustainability – both as a way to keep the doors open as well as fulfill their mission.

Attitudes towards expanding audiences

The idea of being responsive with programs that engage diverse audiences is not new. John Cotton Dana, the founder of the Newark Museum, wrote in 1920 about the Newark Museum, "We are trying to find a type of museum which demonstrably pays its community fair interest on its investment."[3] While Dana made this statement rebelling against contemporaneous museums which he thought were temple-like, intimidating and not for "the people," also inherent in his statement is the idea that, by serving the local community, the museum "pays" a return on the community's financial support of the physical structure and collections. He explains, "A museum is good only in so far as it is of use."[4] How do we define that use? Is it limited only to the audiences we consider "regular" museumgoers, or can it, should it, include those populations that do not typically visit our museums? And what types of programs best serve these proposed audiences?

Engaging an underserved audience is one important kind of social work, defined by Lois Silverman as "a process of planned change in which a social worker and client(s) develop and implement a close, empowering relationship that enhances the client(s)' well-being, social functioning, and personal influence."[5] Museum programs, especially those that involve multiple visits, sometimes develop a similar relationship with their participants.

Museums have a long history of social work, according to Silverman. She notes, "From fighting politicized battles to contesting the status quo to working with 'undesirable people,' museums themselves have, throughout their history, ventured into social work both knowingly and unknowingly."[6] Silverman compares the social work of museums today to the work of settlement houses and other charitable organizations in the time of John Cotton Dana and earlier. As she demonstrates, museums use many social work techniques or "interventions," from education and facilitation to social action and activism, in their efforts to serve individuals, communities and society at large.[7]

As they have professionalized, museum educators have increasingly exerted influence on the changing role of museums over the last three and a half decades, championing the idea of serving their communities. After a group of educators threatened to secede from AAM in 1973, in 1976 the organization granted them a role in the association's governance through a change in the constitution. Publications such as *Museums for a New Century* (1984) and *Excellence and Equity* (1992) asserted that education is a "primary" purpose of museums and that a commitment to public service is "central to every museum's activities." The International Council of Museums (ICOM) took a strong stance in the 1970s on the active public-service role of museums.[8] I assert, however, that this public service role is not articulated clearly enough for museums to fully embrace their potential – or their directive – as sites of social work. Given the financial pressures that museums face today, with institutions fighting for funding and looking for new communities to serve in their efforts to stay relevant, it is no longer sufficient for institutional missions to profess to "collect, preserve and interpret." I believe that a museum's mission statement should articulate their vision of institutional responsibility toward community. Change toward community at the philosophical level has barely advanced in most museums, as Elaine Heumann Gurian contends, "I have been eagerly awaiting signs that most museums – aside from responding to certain high-profile events – have made it clear that nothing much has changed [in their public service role]."[9]

"What makes a Museum? It's not as Easy as it Sounds" is the aptly named title of Harold Skramstad's 2008 article in *Informal Learning*. Skramstad acknowledges some of the major cultural and sociological shifts which, he warns, are leading museums to see themselves in a new light and take on additional responsibilities. He notes:

> ... there has been an exponential explosion of unmet desires in contemporary American society and museums have tried to come to the rescue. And that is a good thing. There is however a danger that in the process of trying to address every potential new claim on our museums, we will further erode our distinctiveness as institutions.[10]

Skramstad believes that, in trying to address social concerns, museums will no longer be unique institutions (that "collect, preserve, and interpret"), instead morphing into community or social service agencies.

Skramstad's solution is for the museum to become a distinctive "community of choice," which he defines as diverse, mobile and constantly changing, and based upon shared need, mutual obligation, intergenerational support, entertainment values and spiritual belief:[11]

> Individuals have the ability to pick and choose the costs and benefits of being a member of any particular community of choice. In this kind of world, the word "community" is no longer a useful descriptor. The new reality is that the relationship between any organization (such as a museum) and the many 'communities' it serves is complex and contradictory – and always changing.[12]

Skramstad's use of the word "relationship" is significant, as social work is defined by relationships – among people and between people and society.

Skramstad articulates that, to be part of a community of choice, museums need to keep to their mission (to remain unique organizations) but simultaneously be responsive to the changing environment. In my opinion, this is not possible without a change in mission that would expand and articulate the role of the museum in the public eye. Skramstad suggests creating "programmatic strategies that connect the museum's mission, vision and resources to people."[13] Gurian furthers this argument, putting forth the following query to the museum field:

> How do we expand our services so that we make the[se] museum assets [mission, point of view, three-dimensional evidence, and instructional mandate] into relevant programs that reach all levels of community, and are rated by many more as essential to their needs and their aspirations for their children?[14]

Gurian suggests that museums welcome more, share more and control less – which she acquiesces may be particularly challenging for object-based and narrative-based institutions.[15] Gurian explains how some other kinds of museums (often smaller in size and thus more flexible), such as client-centered, community-focused, and national,[16] are taking the lead to become more like active community centers and hubs.[17]

What caused this increased need for reaching out to new audiences and communities? Janet Pieschel, Executive Director of the Calgary Police Service Interpretive Center, notes that, in the early 1990s, due to debt and deficits, both the local and national Canadian government withdrew support from healthcare, social services and education. At the same time, in my view, it appears that the United States became more interested in addressing social issues such as child neglect, teen pregnancy, violent crimes, substance abuse, poverty and dropout rates. Museums seem to have picked up on this heightened concern and stepped in to help fill the gap.[18] This would support Silverman's view that museums are indeed doing social work, since they are responding to the needs of society in a socio-economic and political context. As she explains, "[Social work is] a contextual profession, strongly influenced by its social environment and by the political and economic context within which it is practiced."[19]

In this chapter, I argue that museums could be doing this work to fill a need in society that falls short, due to funding cuts at all levels, today, as in the 1990s. Many museums have already changed their perspective and embraced the idea of "social work" even though they may not call it such, or refined their mission statements to reflect this perspective. In 1999, Stephen Weil noted in his groundbreaking work that museums were shifting "from being about something to being for somebody."[20] He asserted that many museum workers are sympathetic to this transformation, and:

> From that moderate position, they nevertheless share with this author [Weil] the vision of an emerging new museum model – a transformed and redirected institution that can, through its public-service orientation, use its very special competencies in dealing with objects to contribute positively to the quality of individual human lives and to enhance the well-being of human communities.[21]

Museums in the United States and Europe have taken this to heart and are serving new communities in new ways through new collaborative programs.

Case studies

There are many examples across the globe of museums serving a small population with an ambitious and costly education program.[22] The few I have included elucidate a larger phenomenon, and I believe serve as models for practice.

The Sterling and Francine Clark Art Institute in Williamstown, Massachusetts, articulates their mission as "dedicated to advancing and extending the public understanding of art."[23] Within this broad framework, and thanks to a chance discussion at a girls' soccer match in 2006 between the Museum's Coordinator of Community and Family Programs and a local juvenile court judge, a collaborative program providing an alternative sentence for juvenile offenders in the museum galleries took flight. The collaboration began by both parties being in the right place at the right time.

With juvenile sentencing in the Massachusetts court system shifting in the 1990s from a punishment model to an educational model, it would seem the museum acted on a community need for more arenas for "education." The program 'Responding to Art Involves Self Expression' (RAISE) is held twice yearly and involves approximately eight participants, ages thirteen to seventeen, who are on probation with the state. Instead of doing time in juvenile detention, the young men and women are required to attend five carefully designed two-hour sessions at the Clark, learning to look at, engage with and respond to art. Program goals include "using art as a vehicle for thinking, talking, and writing about the human experience and to consider their own connection to the larger social world in more constructive ways."[24] Group leaders and museum staff noted a higher level of self-esteem in participants upon completion of the program. Fostering introspection is one of the areas in which museums are practicing social work, as explained by Silverman.[25]

Initially, many Clark staff members expressed ambivalence about the venture; they worried that the museum placed priceless art in jeopardy with these youthful offenders, that these "unusual visitors" might make other audiences uncomfortable and that change – any substantive change – brings uncertainty.[26] Unarticulated was the unspoken belief that the museum was *not* a social service organization, and the fear that the RAISE program would lead the Clark Art Institute into an arena heretofore unbreached and perhaps inappropriate for a museum.[27] With the museum director's complete support of the initiative, special training helped mitigate some staff apprehension, as did the hiring of an outside instructor to assist with teaching the offenders. Involvement in the program convinced the institute that the risk was well worth taking.

The Clark's Head of Education Programs runs the program, with the support of other staff and the outside instructor. Clark employees who were initially hesitant about RAISE now "love the program."[28] Members and patrons seem pleased that the Clark has created this collaboration. Anecdotal evidence from parents of the offenders also indicates they are appreciative that the Clark and the courts have undertaken this joint effort.[29] The museum community, as a whole, which celebrates innovative partnerships and programs with awards, named the Clark's program winner of the 2010 Excellence in Programming award from the Education Committee of the American Association of Museums (EdCom) and the 2009 runner up for the Brooking Prize for Creativity.

With school budgets being slashed and the demands of student testing eliminating time for field trips, Ronna Tulgan Ostheimer, Head of Education Programs at the Clark Art Institute, believes this type of program – a collaboration that responds to a community need – may be the way to go. "Museums have acted like cloistered organizations," she noted, harkening to Weil's 1999 article, "and they have been treated that way [by communities]. The way museums see themselves, and the way culture sees them is shifting."[30] Museums need to make this shift in order to change the public perception of being elitist; in this case, the museum resources were conducive to acting as an agent of social change and, in the public's eye, expanded their usefulness to the local community.

Other museums have also looked at the justice system as a new arena for programming. The Salt Lake Art Center in Utah uses fine arts as rehabilitation in their twice weekly, six-week-long program, 'Art and Creative Expression' (ACE).[31] While their goals include "increasing visual literacy to process the constant stream of visual stimuli in our culture and dealing with a multitude of cultural, economic, political,

and social issues," the program also aims, much like the Clark's, to elevate participants' self-esteem.[32] The South East Museums, Libraries and Archives Council in
the UK (SEMLAC) "wanted to prove the contribution that museums and galleries in
the region could make to breaking the cycle of re-offending" through their 2002
program 'Black Box', which created personal "museums of the imagination."[33] Both
of these programs take place in the prisons themselves, whereas the Clark's program
occurs in the museum. This difference in venue does not seem to have an effect on
the programs' success, however, because each program starts with creating a "relationship" between the museum objects and the participants. What helps all these
programs succeed is the chance to work through *several* visits to build and expand
relationships and to evaluate change and progress among program participants and
museum staff.

Despite their success, each of the three groups has served only between eight and
twenty-four participants per program cycle. The Salt Lake County Sheriff's Office
covers the costs for the ACE Program at the Salt Lake County Metro Jail while the
Black Box program is funded by the British government, through the Department
for Education and Skills (DES). The Clark has recently assumed program costs as
part of their operating budget, although initially RAISE was grant-funded. Is it ethical
putting so much staff time, institutional resources and grant funds towards programs
serving such small numbers?

The New Jersey Historical Society (NJHS) believed that doing programs that met a
profound community need, even though participant numbers were small, was a
worthwhile direction for the organization. NJHS's "Partners in Learning" program
started in the late 1990s when the institution's education department desired to
expand their audiences by developing programs for teenagers, an audience that was
not visiting NJHS at that time. Partners in Learning evolved into a program that met
the needs of a particular segment of the community – the non-traditional, sometimes
marginalized audience of adolescent parents. While I was Curator of Education at
NJHS, we approached a high school in the urban center of Newark, New Jersey,
in the late 1990s to see about working with teenagers. The director of the Infant–
Toddler Center at Barringer High School, where many teen mothers would leave
their children in day care while they completed classes during the school day, noted
that her required program teaching child development and healthy baby care to these
young parents lacked a "cultural component." Clearly, while NJHS was not in the
business of teaching how to switch babies to solid food or how to discourage use of
a pacifier, they could encourage these young mothers to pull their child away from
the television and take them to a cultural institution – and, importantly, interact
with their child to promote effective learning before, during and after their visit
there. NJHS took on this challenge to create an eight-visit program for twenty to
thirty young mothers (and some fathers) and their children which won the 2002
Award for Excellence in Programming from the Education Committee of the
American Association of Museums.

Using outcome-based evaluation developed in partnership with the Infant–
Toddler Center, NJHS demonstrated the difference the program made in the lives of
these young parents. Comments from the participants, indicating a successful learning experience, included, "The program helped me communicate with my child
without getting or showing him the belt" and "I thought I knew everything about

parenting. But they showed me more."[34] In fact, the originally grant-funded program was so effective that it was folded into NJHS's general operating budget and later expanded to include several more organizations serving teen parents in the state. Buy-in from NJHS leadership and national recognition through the award encouraged the program's survival beyond the grant funds. Most importantly, the Historical Society's vision statement provided justification and focus that buttressed the program and helped it to thrive for several years until its end in 2008:

> Through the history of New Jersey – a quintessentially American place – the Historical Society promotes exploration of our cultures, past and present. As we challenge and inspire people to grow as learners and thinkers, we strive to make a difference in their lives.

The "difference" that the Historical Society makes is not assessed solely through how much history one learns but also how quality of life is improved, in this case through the development of parenting skills including the ability to use cultural institutions as a resource vis-à-vis their children. The community's well-being – that of teen parents and their children as well as the greater community in which they reside – is prioritized and enhanced by participation in this program.

"Partners in Learning" brought NJHS's programs to a new level, what Silverman calls "social work interventions using museum resources."[35] However, it didn't appear to me to be a stretch for the museum to do so. We were simply filling a need within the community. Similarly, children's museums in the United States have also begun serving families with social work-influenced programs, some of them collaborations with social service agencies. In 2005, a new Department of Health and Human Services (DHHS) Welcome Center housing eight agencies under one roof and serving individuals and families in Nassau County, New York, was constructed less than a ten-minute walk from the Long Island Children's Museum (LICM). DHHS staff and a family court judge approached the Museum on how they could work together to support families.[36] This initial meeting led to the formation of a joint local planning committee and national advisory committee to model a collaborative effort that resulted in the founding of a center of community engagement for families and a related program taking place within that space. With the program now in its second year, the museum is committed to its continuation and has applied for additional funding. Its long-term outcomes are being evaluated by the Institute for Learning Innovation.[37]

In this example, the community approached the museum and was already viewing the LICM as a "center for community engagement" for families. Children's museums may have that advantage, as they cater specifically to a family audience. However, this audience may not have always included families that are part of Child Protective Services or Family Court. While a similar program, "Families Together," at the Providence Children's Museum, in Rhode Island, served as a model for the LICM collaboration, the Providence program distinguishes itself as "an innovative therapeutic visitation program for court-separated families in need of special guidance."[38] The judge engaged in the Long Island collaboration believes that parents involved in Child Protective Services cases or Family Court should "learn how to play with their children and, through that process, to be better able to understand

and care for them."[39] His outlook is similar to one of the outcomes in the NJHS "Partners in Learning" Program, "Teens will enhance their parenting skills."[40] While the two programs at the children's museums were direct collaborations with social service agencies, the NJHS program partnered with a school that was providing, in essence, a social service. In this sense, museums are not setting up their own centers to practice social work, but rather exploring the boundaries of their mission statements and collaborating with providers that can bring the audience and the requisite social service background skills to assist museum educators in reaching the desired population.

But, in Gurian's eyes, museums are not going far enough. Gurian proposes that museums go beyond

> 'business as usual' – museums cloaked in the name of social good, justifying their pent-up need – but rather transforming currently less than useful local institutions into dynamic and community-focused 'clubhouses' for building social cohesion, and incorporating social services usually delivered elsewhere, such as job retraining, educational enhancements, and public discourse – in addition to their classic role of collections care, interpretation, and exhibition.[41]

In fact, I believe that many museums of all genres today are working to prove that they are doing more than short-term "social good." The programs cited all claim to help participants sharpen family interaction skills like patience, listening, cooperation, positive communication, role enactment and non-verbal involvement behavior. Recent interviews with caseworkers who observed supervised visits at LICM noted "a difference [more child-driven and more positive interactions] in the level of family engagement."[42] NJHS has proven results through teens both making statements about and demonstrating better skills of talking with their child within a cultural context such as a museum. During the fourth visit of the young parents in "Partners in Learning," staff and aides completed behavioral observation checklists for the parents as they observed them in the NJHS galleries practicing what they learned about visiting museums with their children. This yielded such remarks from the staff working with the young parents as "he acts very mature when he brings his child into public places. I have even seen a positive change in his attitude in my classroom."[43] From these examples, museums are making a difference in the lives of participants, responding to needs and working within their missions.

In some cases, museums responded to a community need first and their community partners followed. Reports from the European Union in 2000 and the Organization for Economic Cooperation and Development (OECD) in 2005 reveal that more than 15 percent of each age group of youth in the EU had not achieved a satisfactory basic education by age twenty. This fact prompted the EU to make programs for lifelong learning a priority for 2007–13.[44] In response, the Jamtli Museum and the State Regional Archives in Sweden initiated a program, "Xpress on Track," to twelve young people, aged twenty to twenty-five, who lacked a basic education and were unemployed; funded by the Östersund Municipality and the Employment service, the "Xpress on Track" program is designed to encourage participants to return to school and/or find a job and curb their dependency on welfare. Multiple visits expose participants to diverse career paths including bookbinding, research, writing, photography and other jobs in the museums and archives context, which helped them see options for work. While trying their hand at the skills and tasks of these jobs, the young people are exposed to professional staff who can serve as mentors in the field.

Social work, according to Silverman, can help participants improve their relationships with society.[45] In the "Xpress on Track" program, the museums involved function as a conduit for representatives from area high schools and employment services who help participants get to the point "where the idea of acquiring the necessary qualifications [for jobs] is both possible and feasible."[46] Results to date show that about one-third of participants have begun basic education, one-third have found employment (mostly short-term) and the other one-third are either still with the project or have left it for a variety of reasons.

The program benefits the community by saving welfare money the government would otherwise have to contribute; it benefits the participants by improving their lives as they return to school or work; and it sustains the museum/archives by utilizing the collections and opening them up to a new audience. Is this exploitation of the museum for social welfare's sake? Is this exploitation of participants to show the museum is serving a diverse audience? It could be viewed as such – but with a population that is marginalized and viewed as a "burden" on society, the museum is responding to a societal need with appropriate learning resources in which it has strengths. In turn, one hopes that the museum sees how their collections and mission can be relevant to a more broadly defined community. Funding from alternative sources such as the state or the Federal Department of Labor could be part of the new paradigm for museums; as museums respond to community needs, they could seek out new funding sources accordingly.

Many museums today are working with refugee communities, populations that both historically and currently are, like at-risk youths, also served by social workers.[47] At the Walters Art Museum in Baltimore, a staff member's personal interest volunteering for a non-profit serving the refugee community was the catalyst for the Museum's service to this population. Out of this interest grew the institution's "Refugee Museum Project," a partnership between the Walters and the Refugee Youth Project (RYP), an after-school program run through Baltimore City Community College (BCCC). The program also partners with Maryland Institute College of Art's (MICA) Master of Arts in Community Arts Program (MACA), which provides an artist/teaching fellow to integrate art and the museum into the after-school program curriculum and plan museum visits for youth. The museum started by doing what it does best – engaging people with works of art. Such work also helps develop language skills, foster self-esteem and encourage a sense of community among these young children who have been displaced from their homelands.[48] Most importantly, the program provides a safe space for youth to express themselves and work out their new identities in the diaspora – a space that may be lacking in their lives at school or at home.[49]

The mission of the Walters Art Museum states that it "brings art and people together for enjoyment, discovery, and learning."[50] Broadly viewed, the program fits the mission; but is it a museum's place to teach English? In New York City, the Lower East Side Tenement Museum attempted to respond to that community need but failed, partially because their educators were not trained in how to teach ESL.[51]

The Walters staff receives training in teaching ESL through BCCC, and has come to realize that many teaching strategies used to overcome language barriers for ESL students, such as providing information in more than one medium, and appealing to many senses in exploring an idea, are strategies of successful museum education practices. Lindsay Anderson, Senior Coordinator for Community Outreach at the Walters, noted that the methods from which staff draw to work with refugee populations utilize their training and expertise as museum teachers.[52] Because the museum has created an environment that is non-judgmental, visual and multi-sensory, stimulating curiosity and imagination, the kids are willing to take a risk to speak, write and improve their communication skills in their second language.

National Museums Liverpool also serves refugees with its project "Engaging Refugees and Asylum Seekers."[53] Nine young people worked with an artist to create stone sculptures not directly related to issues surrounding asylum or refugee-seeking, yet the projects had a social impact, with participants gaining a strong sense of pride in the result. Here is an example of a program in which museums can take part in social issues, "doing what they do best" with art, history or whatever discipline is involved, and help manage – not necessarily solve – some of the issues within their communities. In this way, museums are, as Weil noted, "contributing positively to the quality of human lives."[54]

Reflections

If a museum's mission suggests that the institution is committed to making itself "accessible to diverse audiences," then *all* the aforementioned programs fall within that purview. Broadly stated, a museum collects, preserves and interprets for the good of everyone. Ethically, that includes populations that may only visit the museum in small numbers, due to the low ratio of staff to participants that the programs bringing them into the museum demand. Explicitly stating that museums should act as social service agents – per a field-wide standard of excellence and/or code of ethics that incorporates language and principles of social work – should be, as Silverman recommends, the field's next step.[55] I think this move towards social service should be optional for museums, since not all organizations are ready and/or willing to make this commitment. Yet, as Silverman points out, to remain sustainable, relevant and viable in the next age (and in this age, I would argue), museum professionals and social workers must help the human community, including themselves, to "evolve new strategies for beneficial coexistence."[56]

The large-budget but small population-serving programs detailed in this study bring about a chain reaction of positive consequences: museum serves group with special program; museum staff feel they are making a difference and learn more about diverse communities; museum staff enjoy job satisfaction; satisfied staff results in productivity and low staff turnover. The Community Programs Coordinator at NJHS expressed great pride in being part of the "Partners in Learning" project and she remains a loyal employee of the NJHS education department.

Another chain reaction occurs in the larger museum context with these special programs: museum serves group with special program; museum receives notice from community for this program; word spreads about program and museum;

museum gets good press; museum gets increased visitation from "regular" museum goers as well as non-traditional visitors. The Museums and Galleries Lifelong Learning Initiative (MGLI) noted that, as participants change their attitudes towards museums, they are more likely to visit museums and galleries in their own time with their families and friends.[57] Finding an entirely new audience that is not reached by traditional marketing techniques can – and most likely will – have a long-term effect on a museum's bottom line.

Are we using these populations and the programs that serve them to create a more stable staff with better morale and/or as means to improve community relations? All the museums cited seem to have partnered with communities to create these programs with the intention to serve *audiences*, not the museum itself. The by-products, which have added benefit to museums, are what *keep* these programs going. For example, after the end of the grant period, NJHS made the Partners in Learning Program an integral part of the Education Department, including it in the operating budget, because the Development Department recognized that the program enhanced and strengthened the institution's educational offerings. The Development Department assured us this was an easy program to fund.

Doing a cost analysis will not put these programs out on top in the short-term. However, studies of learning outcomes and the sustained effects of education programs are slowly becoming the norm in grant-funded projects. Long-term studies have been completed in the UK[58] and the LICM has received preliminary reports from the Institute for Learning Innovation on their project, demonstrating that evaluation is both proving the worth of these programs and seen as an integral part of their design.[59]

According to Hannah Gould's report *Where Are They Now?* some of the projects that were part of the MGLI have strengthened advocacy for the museum. Many local governments in the UK now see the museum and art gallery as "having a community purpose, capable of contributing to its [the local government's] policy on social inclusion."[60] Some projects have also helped museums to recognize the necessity of more staff training on the learning needs of diverse populations, and to more fully appreciate the complexity of these new audiences.[61]

One striking commonality among these seemingly disparate programs is their multiple-visit format. No matter the population, longer-lasting results require a longer-term commitment. None of these programs were undertaken to the detriment of other public programs serving "conventional" audiences. Yet these specialized programs may have more impact on participants, museums and society itself than the "bread and butter" school and adult programs that museums depend on to keep up their attendance figures and, in many cases, their revenue. While they are not moneymakers, these programs leave a broader social footprint that ultimately contributes to the greater good in a way that helps museums to re-imagine and reinvigorate their sense of purpose. More long-term, multi-year studies need to be performed to determine the impact of these innovative programs serving small but atypical populations.

Creating change in society is not a quick process, as Skramstad acknowledges:

> The result will not be overnight civic renew, solving the problems of the
> poor, or transforming human nature – but it will have played a small part in

cultivating a richer society – and one in which museums continue to have a very special and distinctive role.[62]

The special role of museums, being responsive to be responsible, can be in keeping with the mission, and is an ethical use of time, staff and funds. As Stephen Weil concludes his musing on "the ongoing transformation of the American Museum":

> In the emerging museum, responsiveness to the community – not an indiscriminate responsiveness, certainly, but a responsiveness consistent with the museum's public-service obligations and with the professional standards of its field – must be understood not as a surrender but, quite literally, as a fulfillment.[63]

Museums provide a safe, alternative space for learning, where children and adults can step outside of their usual ways of acting and interacting in more formal learning settings. Perhaps that makes museums *more suitable* than the classroom or the justice system to change people's lives and impact positively on society. We strive to challenge the assumptions of diverse communities concerning art, science, history and other museum disciplines. Museums should equally be responsive to social needs of communities, even if it means redefining themselves through mission and ethics codes. Being responsive is the most responsible way to stay relevant, sustainable and to demonstrate the worth of the museum to communities and society at large.

Notes

1 I am broadly defining museums to include all types of museums – those with collections of art and historical objects; those with living collections, such as arboreta and zoos; and those with "no" collections, such as children's museums.
2 L. H. Silverman, *The Social Work of Museums*, New York: Routledge, 2010, pp. 37 and 149.
3 J. C. Dana, "A Plan for a New Museum: The Kind of Museum it will Profit a City to Maintain," in W. Peniston (ed.) *The New Museum: Selected Writings by John Cotton Dana*, Newark: The Newark Museum Association and Washington, DC: American Association of Museums, 1999, p. 68.
4 Ibid., p. 109.
5 Silverman, *Social Work of Museums*, p. 38.
6 Ibid., p. 26.
7 Ibid., pp. 144–145.
8 American Association of Museums, *Museums for a New Century*, Washington, DC: American Association of Museums, 1984; American Association of Museums, *Excellence and Equity: Education and the Public Dimension of Museums*, Washington, DC: American Association of Museums, 1992, in S. Weil, "From Being about Something to Being for Somebody: The Ongoing Transformation of the American Museum," *Daedalus*, 1999 (summer), Washington, DC: American Academy of Arts and Science, pp. 234, 237.
9 E. H. Gurian, "Museum as Soup Kitchen," *Curator* 53: 1, 2010 (January), pp. 71, 75.
10 H. Skramstad, "What Makes a Museum? It's not as Easy as it Sounds," *Informal Learning* 91, 2008 (July–August), p. 6.
11 Ibid., p. 6.

12 Ibid., p. 6.
13 Ibid., p. 7.
14 Gurian, "Museum as Soup Kitchen," p. 82.
15 Ibid., p. 73.
16 Ibid., pp. 74–75.
17 Ibid., p. 81.
18 J. Pieschel, "Telling it Like it Is: The Calgary Police Service Interpretive Center," in R. R. Janes and G. T. Conaty (eds.) *Looking Reality in the Eye: Museums and Social Responsibility*, Calgary, Alta: University of Calgary Press, 2005, p. 175.
19 Silverman, *Social Work of Museums*, p. 29.
20 Weil, "From Being about Something to Being for Somebody," p. 229.
21 Ibid.
22 R. Sandell (ed.) *Museums, Society, Inequality*, London: Routledge, 2002; Silverman, *Social Work of Museums*.
23 The Sterling and Francine Clark Art Institute mission statement. Online. Available HTTP: http://www.clarkart.edu/about/content.cfm?ID=37 (accessed 25 June 2009).
24 R. T. Ostheimer, "The Clark in the Courts," paper submitted for the Brooking Prize for Creativity in Museums for the American Association of Museums, 2009, p. 3. Online. Available HTTP: http://www.aam-us.org/getinvolved/nominate/brooking.cfm (accessed June 4, 2009).
25 Silverman, *Social Work of Museums*, p. 45.
26 R. T. Ostheimer, personal interview with author, 22 June 2009.
27 Ibid.
28 Ibid.
29 Ibid.
30 Ibid.
31 J. Heuman, "Looking for program examples," e-mail, personal communication with author, 15 June 2009.
32 Ibid.
33 H. Gould, "What Did We Learn This Time? The Museums and Galleries Lifelong Learning Initiative (MGLI), 2002–2003", p. 5. Online. Available HTTP: http://www.cultureunlimited.org/pdfs/WDWL2.pdf (accessed 30 April 2010).
34 C. B. Ocello. "Institute of Museum and Library Services Final Grant Report on the *Partners in Learning* Program," unpublished report, Newark, NJ, 2000.
35 Silverman, *Social Work of Museums*, pp. 144–147.
36 Long Island Children's Museum, "Be Together, Learn Together: A Partnership of the Long Island Children's Museum, the Nassau County Department of Health and Human Services and Nassau County Family Court," unpublished grant proposal, 2009.
37 Ibid.
38 Providence Children's Museum *Families Together* Program. Online. Available HTTP: http://www.childrenmuseum.org/familiestogether.asp (accessed 15 June 2009).
39 Long Island Children's Museum, "Be Together, Learn Together."
40 Ocello, "Institute of Museum and Library Services Final Grant Report on the *Partners in Learning* Program."
41 Gurian, "Museum as Soup Kitchen," p.76.
42 C. Kessler, *Be Together, Learn Together*, caseworker interviews, unpublished Quick Response Memo, July 2009, pp. 1–3.
43 Ocello, "Institute of Museum and Library Services Final Grant Report on the *Partners in Learning* Program."
44 H. Zipsane, "Cultural Learning in the Transition from Social Client to Learner," paper presented at Scotland Museums conference, 2007.
45 Silverman, *Social Work of Museums*, pp. 53–54.
46 Zipsane, "Cultural Learning."
47 See K. Goodnow, *Museums, the Media and Refugees: Stories of Crisis, Control and Compassion*, New York and Oxford: Berghahn, 2008; P. Carter-Birken, "On a Roll: Mobile Art Program aids Refugee Community," *Museum*, 2010 (March–April), pp. 31–33.

48 Walters Art Museum, Susquehanna Proposal, (unpublished Grant proposal), Refugee Museum Project, 2008.

49 N. Madigan, "Child Refugees' Hope and Fear Show through their Art," *Baltimore Sun*, 15 June 2009. Online. Available HTTP: http://www.baltimoresun.com/news/maryland/baltimore-city/bal md.ci.refugees15jun15,0,1084572.story (accessed 23 July 2009).

50 Walters Art Museum mission statement. Online. Available HTTP: http://thewalters.org/museum_art_baltimore/themuseum_mission.aspx (accessed 6 July 2009).

51 S. Pharaon, personal interview with author, 15 April 2009.

52 L. Anderson, personal interview with author, 2 July 2009.

53 D. Fleming and C. Rogers, "Museums, Young People, and Social Justice" in K. Bellamy and C. Oppenheim (eds.) *Learning to Live: Museums, Young People and Education*, London: Institute for Public Policy Research and National Museum Directors' Conference, 2009, pp. 78–79.

54 Weil, "From being about Something to being for Somebody," p. 229.

55 Silverman, *Social Work of Museums*, pp. 37, 149–150.

56 Ibid., p. 139.

57 H. Gould, "Where Are They Now? The Impact of the Museums and Galleries Lifelong Learning Initiative (MGLI)," 2005, p. 17. Online. Available HTTP: http://www.culture-unlimited.org/pdfs/WATN.pdf (accessed 4 June 2009).

58 Ibid.

59 Jeanmarie Walsh, personal interview with author, 19 June 2009.

60 Gould, "Where Are They Now?" p. 15. In 2003, the UK Department for Culture, Media and Sport (DCMS) issued a policy on DCMS-funded and local authority museums, galleries and archives in England. The policy acknowledges that museums, galleries and archives funded by DCMS have an important role to play in the combating of social exclusion. See Richard Sandell's 2003 article "Social Inclusion, the Museum, and the Dynamics of Sectoral Change," *Museums and Society* 1: 1, 2003 (March). Online. Available HTTP: http://www.le.ac.uk/ms/m&s/issue%201/mands4.pdf (accessed 24 July 2010).

61 L. Anderson, personal interview with author, 2 July 2009.

62 Skramstad, "What makes a Museum?", p. 8.

63 Weil, "From Being about Something to Being for Somebody," pp. 254–255.

13
Ethics and challenges of museum marketing

Yung-Neng Lin

> Everyone has the right to freely participate in the cultural life of the community,
> to enjoy the arts and to share in scientific advancement and its benefits.
> Article 27 of the Universal Declaration of Human Rights, United Nations

The biggest challenge that museums need to address is their function as resources for education and learning. Most museum professionals today regard museums primarily as educational institutions, where people can be encouraged to develop their imagination, and offered opportunities for meaningful learning experiences. Museums hold and care for collections which are invaluable potential learning resources for millions of people. They not only serve school children but also support lifelong informal learning for people of all age groups, ethnic backgrounds and levels of interest.

This viewpoint – that museums are educational institutions – is supported widely by communities, including individuals who are not direct consumers. This has been shown in many surveys. Looking at one UK study (conducted in Lincolnshire in 1988), for example, David Prince argued that conceptions of museums were remarkably consistent; the Lincolnshire study showed that about 98 per cent of respondents, including both visitors and non-visitors, expressed similar notions of museums as sites of learning.[1] A study conducted at the Powerhouse Museum in Sydney also indicated that museums professionals and the wider public share a common view of the fundamental role of museums as educational.[2] It is important for museums to enhance access to and public understanding of their collections. Eilean Hooper-Greenhill argues that, in fulfilling this educational function, museums should take into account the diverse needs of all parties – both actual and potential visitors.[3]

Unlike museums in the United States, which are heavily dependent on market forces, museums in countries such as the UK and Taiwan have historically been funded to fulfil educational, cultural and social functions within the community; up until the 1980s, they did not have to give much thought to issues such as marketing. Marketing first appeared in America after the Second World War, as the supply of goods grew more quickly than consumer demand. It was increasingly applied in the non-profit sector, including museums, throughout the late 1980s in the UK and 1990s in Taiwan.[4] But marketing was seen as something of a dirty word in the museum sector. When the Victoria and Albert Museum (V&A) adopted a marketing campaign in 1988 branding the V&A as an "ace café with quite a nice museum attached", there was fierce debate about whether it should be adopted.[5] Some museum professionals argued that marketing has nothing to do with preservation, exhibition, research and education while others saw it as a powerful tool for achieving their missions.[6] Since the 1990s, however, museums have had to contend with an increasingly turbulent financial environment. As funding has declined and competition for visitors has grown tougher, museums have been forced to become more interested in marketing strategy.[7]

Museum professionals face a number of ethical challenges concerning marketing. The first is to address the inequality of opportunity which exists in regard to museum visiting – most visitors are drawn from higher socio-economic groups – and broaden access to collections. The second is to consider which of the diverse products and services offered by museums should take priority in order to meet the needs of target audiences when resources are limited. The third is to ensure that promotional tools are aligned with the needs, objectives and ethical purview of museums. Finally, pricing policy is a contested issue. Pricing in the museum sector is never easy and museums often face an ethical dilemma over charging. Lack of inclusion or access remains a major concern for many in the museum sector. It is the aim of this chapter to examine these challenges and their ethical repercussions more closely, looking at several case studies along the way, in the hope that this might assist museum and marketing professionals to find ways of making museums more accessible to a broader range of people.

Access to museums

Despite the efforts of museum marketers working in conjunction with educators, curators and directors to tackle the imbalance of participation, museum audiences still tend to be people of higher socio-economic status. The participation rate and the percentage of the general population (over the age of fifteen) who visit museums or galleries at least once a year are strongly related to educational background, income and occupational status. Well-educated and more affluent people are more likely to visit museums than other groups. In its report 'Understanding the Future', the Department for Culture, Media and Sport (DCMS) in the UK states that visitors to museums do not reflect the makeup of the population; they are not representative of the audiences that museums are intended to serve.[8] In general, inequality of opportunity in museum visiting results in under-representation by those on lower incomes, the less well educated, older people and the unemployed. The participation patterns above are consistent with findings from surveys conducted around the world. For example, according to the EU's compilation of cultural statistics for 2007, 41 per cent of respondents stated that they had visited a museum or gallery at least once in the twelve months prior to the research. The findings below indicate that older people (aged fifty-five and over, 34 per cent), the less well educated (those ending their education at the age of fifteen years, 21 per cent), and the unemployed (27 per cent) are under-represented – they show much lower participation rates than other groups (Table 13.1).[9]

Table 13.1 Participation in museums or galleries at least once in the previous twelve months, EU–27, 2007

	% visiting
All adults	41
Age group	
15–24	48
25–39	42
40–54	45
55+	34
Level of education	
End of education at the age of 15 years	21
End of education at the age of 16–19 years	38
End of education at the age of 20 years or more	59
Occupational status	
Unemployed	27
House persons	30
Retired	31
Manual workers	35
White-collar workers	47
Self-employed	47
Students	60
Managers	68

Source: European Communities, *Cultural Statistics, Eurostat Pocketbooks 2007*. Edition, Luxembourg: Office for Official Publications of the European Communities, 2007.

In Taiwan, audience participation follows the same pattern. In a participation survey conducted in Taipei City in 2004, 64.8 per cent of interviewees stated that they had visited a museum or gallery at least once in the twelve months prior to the research. Table 13.2 illustrates that older people (aged sixty-five and over, 56 per cent), the less well educated (those ending their education at junior high school or below, 44.6 per cent), the unemployed (52.1 per cent), and people on lower incomes (£5,000 or below, 62 per cent) are all under-represented.[10]

Access to collections

Museums provide a public service. The collections in museums belong to everyone; they are held in trust for society as a whole. This fundamental principle means that, ethically, museums must ensure equality of opportunity. It has also led to greater political recognition of what museums can achieve in terms of social inclusion.

The principle of equality reflects the fundamental belief that every individual should have opportunities to participate in the arts and culture. Expanding access has been an important part of the work of the museum sector in Anglo-American countries such as the UK, Australia and New Zealand, and in some Asian countries such as China and Taiwan. Even so, there are still some who argue that, although natural history, science and children's museums might achieve a more diverse audience, in general, museums and galleries are highbrow cultural activities that can only

Table 13.2 Participation in museums or galleries in Taipei City at least once in the previous twelve months, Taiwan, 2004

	% visiting
All adults	64.8
Age group	
15–19	66.4
20–24	62.6
25–34	65.7
35–44	67.9
45–54	65.2
55–64	63.6
65+	56.0
Level of education	
Junior high school or below	44.6
Senior high school	62.3
University/College	69.0
Postgraduate or above	75.4
Occupational status	
Unemployed	52.1
Retired	58.5
Parent/Carer	63.5
Working (full-time)	67.7
Student	72.1
Personal income	
£5,000 or below	62.0
£5,001–£10,000	62.9
£10,001–£15,000	68.3
£15,001–£20,000	72.6
£20,001+	73.5

Source: Y. N. Lin, 'Admission Charges, the Representative Audience, and Public Museums', Leicester: unpublished thesis, Leicester University, 2006.

be appreciated by relatively small, elite, well-educated, affluent social groups.[11] There is abundant research to support this view.[12] Evidently, lack of inclusion or access remains a major area of concern in the museum sector.

At the same time it has been argued that museums have the potential to address social inequality. Once a museum has attracted a more diverse audience through the door, it can engage these various communities and help bring about social change. Several micro level studies have demonstrated how museums can help increase social interaction and improve individuals' quality of life.[13] At the macro level, a number of museum services have had encouraging results in their attempts to be inclusive. For example, the Tyne and Wear Museums Service (TYMS) in England has been striving to create an inclusive museum service since 1990. They are committed to the idea of museums as agents of social inclusion. With limited resources, TYMS has made its exhibitions more attractive and created new social history exhibitions designed to appeal to local people. The service has used more effective marketing and publicity strategies to gain widespread news coverage.[14] The results can be seen in the visitor figures. In 1990, only 20 per cent of visitors came from C2, D and E social groups (these indicate the economically disadvantaged, including skilled manual workers, unskilled manual workers and state pensioners, widows or long-term unemployed), while the other 80 per cent were from economically privileged groups A, B and C1 (including those working in managerial positions). However, within a decade, C2, D and E social groups accounted for 52 per cent of visitors, four per cent higher than the A, B and C1 groups.[15] Being socially inclusive means attracting a diverse audience, one which includes people from the full range of socio-economic groups; the measure of social equality in museum visiting is how closely the visitor profile of a given museum reflects the profile of the population in the region. A sound marketing strategy, which includes museum products and services, promotion tools and pricing, can help museums to achieve this aim.

Offering attractive products and services

The second challenge that museums face is which products to offer their audiences. Product is the core element of the marketing mix. It is anything that can be provided for the audience's attention, acquisition or consumption; and it includes both physical objects and intangible services. A museum's products and services comprise many elements; many researchers argue that different kinds of visitors enjoy different elements. For example, Marilyn Hood identified six factors which individuals consider when choosing how to spend their leisure time. Frequent museum visitors (those visiting museums more than three times a year) value the learning opportunity, the challenge of new experiences and the chance to do something worthwhile. On the other hand, non- and occasional visitors (those who visit museums less than twice a year) share the same values. They care about social interaction, they want to feel comfortable in their surroundings and they want to be able to participate actively.[16] Thus, it is important for museum marketers to examine the whole range of their products and services and to cater to all these different groups if they want to be more inclusive.

Challenges for developing offerings

A museum's products and services include a bundle of elements, extending beyond the collections and exhibitions with their associated labels, programmes and museum settings, to include seating, shopping, catering and staffing. It is not always easy to decide which products should be allocated resources first when the aim is to attract a more diverse audience. In recent years, museums have not only faced funding cutbacks, they have also had to compete for audiences with other leisure activities. In this context, it is especially important that museums allocate their limited resources to those areas where performance improvement is likely to promote a more inclusive museum. Audience surveys help museums ascertain visitors' opinions of their offerings. These evaluations place increasing emphasis on identifying: those products and services that make visits more enjoyable, overall visitor satisfaction, visitors' perceptions of museums, their motivations for visiting and their insights on the museum experience as related to museum services.

Museum marketers recognize the importance of visitor satisfaction, and many museums assess visitor satisfaction with regard to the services they offer. The Smithsonian Institution conducted a Smithsonian-wide visitor survey in 2004 to examine what did satisfy their visitors, and to what extent. In the survey, 68 per cent of visitors rated their overall experience as either superior (19 per cent) or excellent (49 per cent). Three in five stated that the most satisfying aspect of their visit was seeing the real thing, followed by gaining information or insight (40 per cent) and spending time with friends/family (35 per cent).[17] A number of researchers have also examined factors that would encourage more frequent attendance among non- and infrequent visitors. In the UK David Prince, using a questionnaire survey, ascertained that workshops, better catering, attractive gift shops, interactive exhibitions, films and videos would make infrequent visitors and non-visitors more likely to visit museums.[18] Research conducted in Taiwan nearly twenty years later yielded similar results; qualitative interviews with thirty non-visitors revealed that events and workshops, better restaurants, interactive and multimedia displays, and leisure facilities would encourage non-visitors to visit museums.[19] Similar factors have been identified in large-scale participation surveys such as that conducted by Market and Opinion Research International (MORI) in England in 1999, where 61 per cent of visitors said interactive computer games would encourage more people to visit museums. Fifty-eight per cent of respondents suggested providing internet access and allowing visitors to handle the objects on display.[20]

According to the above research, visitor studies conducted around the world have indicated that museums everywhere are facing similar problems. Over the last two decades, museum managers have allocated energy and resources to products and services on the basis of such findings. But the same issues continue to show up in audience surveys. This begs the question: are these managers in fact misdirecting their efforts? Consumer behaviour researchers argue that visitor satisfaction is determined by the relationship between visitors' expectations before their visit and the perceived service performance.[21] But the above studies do not reveal the gap between visitor expectations and perceived services. Their findings may not discover the degree of visitor satisfaction, since most only examine either attribute importance or performance.

Getting the products and services right

Getting the products and services right is the most important task for museums wanting to be more inclusive. The surveys mentioned above suggest that non-visitors and occasional visitors value the same attributes; museums should therefore allocate their resources to areas which will have most appeal to these groups of visitors. Importance–performance analysis (IPA), first introduced by John Martilla and John James,[22] can help museums to achieve this aim.

By identifying the strengths and weaknesses of museum services, IPA can provide insights into which services should be allotted more resources, and which may be downgraded. IPA involves evaluating a museum's output in terms of visitors' perceptions of performance in certain key products and services, and in terms of the perceived importance of each of these performance areas.

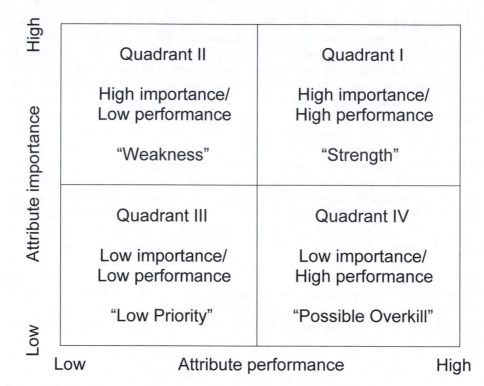

Figure 13.1 Importance–performance analysis. Courtesy of Yung-Neng Lin.

In IPA analysis, museum product and service attributes are separated into four categories aligned with the level of their importance and performance as perceived by museum visitors. IPA utilizes a matrix to examine those attributes which are most critical to museum visitors and have the highest impact on overall visitor satisfaction but which are perceived as showing low performance. The usefulness of IPA will be limited if key service factors are neglected. Thus, a range of qualitative and quantitative research can be examined in order to identify key service attributes. A questionnaire survey instrument can then be developed to assess visitor satisfaction with museum services. Visitors are asked to rate importance and satisfaction on a five-point Likert scale. By calculating scores of mean importance and performance and pairing them, each attribute can be assigned to one of the quadrants of the importance–performance matrix.

In Figure 13.1, the vertical axis indicates perceived importance and the horizontal axis shows the performance of the attributes. The quadrants may be described as follows:

- *Quadrant I (strength)*. Attributes evaluated by visitors as high in both importance and performance show strength and indicate that the museum should keep up the good work. Visitors value this service attribute and are satisfied with the museum's performance.
- *Quadrant II (weakness)*. Visitors value this service attribute but show low satisfaction with the museum's performance. Museum managers should further develop

these attributes to meet visitors' expectations without delay in order to improve overall satisfaction.

- *Quadrant III (low priority)*. Museum visitors rate the attribute as low in performance; however, they do not perceive this attribute to be important. Attributes located in quadrant III are of low priority and require no additional action when resources are limited.
- *Quadrant IV (possible overkill)*. Attributes in quadrant IV are rated low in importance but high in performance, indicating that museum resources committed to these attributes might be better allocated elsewhere.

Museum marketers can use the findings from importance–performance analysis to help them determine a marketing strategy to promote inclusion. For example, weaknesses in quadrant II should be made top priorities and targeted for immediate improvement action, while those attributes in quadrant I, the museum's strengths, should be heavily promoted to the target audience.

A research project conducted at the Yingge Ceramics Museum (YCM), Taiwan, during 2009 applied IPA to analyse the museum's products and services. The instrument was created to evaluate perceived attribute importance and performance across a range of products and services at the YCM, and to measure overall visitor satisfaction.[23]

A questionnaire was drafted to evaluate YCM services on fourteen items (Table 13.3). Five hundred and twenty-seven visitors to the YCM were asked fourteen questions about their expectations and perceptions of products and services. They were asked to rate importance on a five-point Likert scale (1, not at all important, to 5, very important); similarly, satisfaction was measured on a five-point scale rating from 1, very unsatisfied, to 5, very satisfied. The YCM's products and services were rated as at Table 13.3. The table indicates a mean importance attribute of 3.85 and a mean performance attribute of 3.66.

Table 13.3 Importance–performance rating of museum services

No.	Attributes	Importance (mean)	Performance (mean)
1	Themes of the exhibition	3.73	4.05
2	Reputation of artist	3.13	3.83
3	Display techniques	3.91	4.05
4	Well-designed visitor pathways	4.06	3.92
5	Well-designed exhibit labels	4.11	3.99
6	Guides with good communication skills	3.88	3.31
7	Interpreting facilities	3.93	3.54
8	Learning sheet	3.58	3.09
9	Workshops	3.62	2.90
10	Comfortable surroundings	4.23	4.31
11	Helpful museum staff	4.22	4.34
12	Sufficient parking spaces	3.85	3.06
13	Decent catering services	3.49	2.78
14	Sufficient and clean toilets	4.23	4.08
	Total	3.85	3.66

Measuring YCM's product and service importance generated the following results. 'Comfortable surroundings' and 'sufficient and clean toilets' (4.23) were rated as the most important factors, followed by 'helpful museum staff' (4.22), 'well designed exhibit labels' (4.11) and 'well designed visitor pathways' (4.06). The least important factor was 'reputation of artist' (3.13). On the other hand, when visitors were asked to evaluate the performance factors, 'helpful museum staff' was the highest (4.34), followed by 'comfortable surroundings' (4.31), 'sufficient and clean toilets' (4.08), 'display techniques' and 'themes of the exhibition' (4.05). 'Decent catering services' (2.78) was the lowest-rated performance attribute. From the results, we can see which products and services are most important to visitors, and therefore where resources should be prioritized in budgeting.

Attributes in quadrant I are those valued by visitors and with which they are satisfied. YCM is obviously succeeding here. Six attributes are located in this quadrant: comfortable surroundings, helpful museum staff, display techniques, well designed visitor pathways, well designed exhibit labels and sufficient and clean toilets (Figure 13.2).

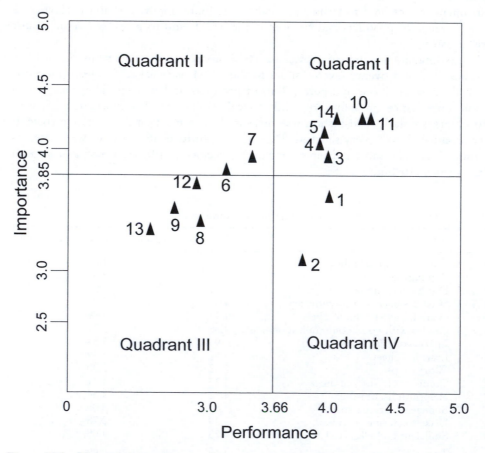

Figure 13.2 Visitors' importance–performance scoring of service attributes. Courtesy of Yung-Neng Lin.

Quadrant II shows the weaknesses of the YCM, where visitors value attributes but show low satisfaction with the museum's performance. The YCM should focus on these products and services immediately in order to improve visitor satisfaction. Two attributes are located in quadrant II: guides with good communication skills, and interpreting facilities.

Attributes located in quadrant III are of low priority and need no additional action when the resources are limited. Visitors rate these attributes low in performance but do not regard them as important. Four attributes are located in quadrant III: workshops, learning sheet, decent catering services and sufficient parking spaces.

Attributes in quadrant IV are rated low in importance but high in performance, indicating that resources committed to these attributes might be better allocated elsewhere in principle. The YCM was judged to be doing a good job of mounting exhibitions, and of showcasing popular artists. Although visitors perceived these features as less important, the museum should maintain a high standard in these areas since they are core services of a museum.

According to the above findings, astonishingly, there were no statistically significant differences between the evaluations of respondents from different age groups, educational backgrounds and personal income brackets, with three exceptions. Firstly, female visitors valued the 'reputation of artist' and 'workshops' more than male visitors did. Secondly, frequent visitors cared more about 'comfortable surroundings' than infrequent visitors. This challenges existing assumptions.[24] Thirdly, less-well-educated visitors valued 'comfortable surroundings' less than well-educated visitors. Although these differences do not affect the positioning of the attributes in the matrix, the findings do highlight ways in which the YCM might amend its marketing strategy to appeal to a more diverse audience. Every museum is different; by applying IPA, museum marketers can target resources to their audience with more confidence.

Providing the right products and services is vital if museums are to meet the needs of a diverse audience, and it is up to museum marketers to identify the critical service performance attributes that generate satisfaction among different visitor groups. Visitors are satisfied when a museum's performance matches their expectations. However, many traditional visitor studies have evaluated either visitor expectations or actual service performance in isolation, rather than looking at the two together. The lack of systematic study into the relationship between visitor expectations and museum performance is making it more difficult for museum marketers to develop a sound marketing strategy for achieving inclusive museums. Importance–performance analysis is not only an efficient way of assessing visitor acceptance of museum products and services; it may also indicate where resources are being wasted. Many museums have dedicated resources to providing services such as workshops and catering services, but the findings in the case study above suggest that managers have been directing their efforts to the wrong products and services. The frequent and first-time visitors in this case did not appreciate these services. Professionals believe more support services will please communities, but the audience did not rate these products and services as important. The case study shows that using IPA can help museums to allocate their resources more effectively and to meet the need of diverse audiences.

Promoting the museum

In order to be more representative, museums should use different promotional tools to reach diverse audiences effectively. Promotion has a strong relationship with the rest of the marketing mix. Museums use various promotional tools to communicate with target audiences. How effectively museums use promotion to be more inclusive depends on both the quality and quantity of information available to them. No amount of good promotion will create a triumph if the exhibition is not attractive or the admission charge is too high, and not even an excellent exhibition will achieve its targets without a careful promotion plan.

Promotion plays a vital role in the marketing strategy of any museum. In order to achieve effective promotion and to be more inclusive, marketers must be familiar with a range of promotional tools suited to the needs of both museums and their audience; they must also be aware of their proportion of the marketing budget.

The Museums, Libraries and Archives Council and Arts Council England suggest that the marketing budget should be about 9 per cent of an arts organization's total income.[25] However, most museums and galleries in the UK spend less than 4 per cent on marketing.[26] Taiwanese museums follow the same pattern of low spending. As the financial pressure on museums grows, it is vital for them to identify the most effective promotional tools for reaching a more diverse audience. Advertising, for example, is not only the most expensive way to promote museums, but it mainly appeals to frequent/repeat visitors. It is not a good promotional tool for attracting non- and infrequent visitors.[27] Word of mouth and public relations are better for this.

Word of mouth and public relations

Word of mouth is one of the most frequently cited reasons for visiting a museum, and it is the best and cheapest promotional tool available to museums.[28] Word of mouth is also the most persuasive form of personal communication, attracting infrequent visitors, including people of disadvantaged socio-economic status, to museums; visitor surveys repeatedly show that word of mouth is the most important source of information for these groups. Donald Adams's research identified word of mouth as the principal motivation behind visitors deciding to visit museums. In his case studies of the Henry Ford Museum (HFM) and Greenfield Village (GV), conducted between 1980 and 1988, between two-thirds (64 per cent) and three-quarters (74 per cent) of visitors said that they heard about HFM and GV through word of mouth.[29] Adams's findings indicate the significant influence of word of mouth among people from marginalized socio-economic groups and first time visitors.[30] Taiwan follows the same patterns even today. Although only half of the visitors (43.6 per cent) to the Yingge Ceramics Museum (YCM) cited word of mouth as their information source, this was nevertheless the most popular way for visitors to hear about the museum. The YCM survey confirms that first time visitors (46.8 per cent), those who left school at junior high school level or below (60 per cent), and people aged fifty-five and over (64.3 per cent) were more heavily influenced by word of mouth than were other groups; word of mouth was cited by all these groups as their principal source of information about the YCM.[31]

Because of its cost-effective nature, many museums try to stimulate word of mouth exposure by reaching opinion leaders or by encouraging testimonials from satisfied visitors. For example, the National Museum of History in Taiwan often organizes open evenings before special exhibitions, to which it invites key opinion leaders in the hope of spreading word of mouth from an early stage. Word of mouth can be a double-edged sword, however. Both positive and negative word of mouth communication will affect people's decision whether to visit museums or not, but positive experiences are likely to have less impact than negative ones, and negative word of mouth may even reduce the effectiveness of other promotional tools. Nevertheless, museums should endeavour to take advantage of word of mouth, as it is a key way of attracting a more diverse audience to the museum sector.[32]

Another effective and inexpensive way for museums to attract a more representative audience is through public relations (PR). Effectively, this is also a kind of word of mouth. PR is an extremely important promotional and communications tool for museums. It is, in effect, the planned and sustained effort to establish goodwill between a museum and its public, and can have a tremendous impact on public awareness.

Press coverage is probably the most important form of PR for museums. A good media editorial can be extremely helpful to an exhibition. The key to success is to maintain a good relationship with news reporters and provide a good press release, even though the museum will not have ultimate control of the content of the press coverage. Unlike advertising, the most costly and least cost-effective promotional tool, PR is employed by many arts organizations as a cheaper option. Because of the nature of PR, museums assume that they do not need to pay for it, but both PR and advertising need time and money to be done properly, albeit in different proportions.

Confusing the roles of public relations and advertising may lead to false expectations of what either can do. Museums do not need to pay for the time or space acquired from the media, but they must pay the salaries of staff involved in PR events and coordinating press coverage. Unlike advertising, which is more appealing to existing audiences, PR, which aims to create word of mouth and influence attitudes and behaviour, can play a major role in attracting non-users.[33] It is a good way of raising awareness among the public.

Admission prices in museums

Within the marketing mix, pricing is probably the most sensitive issue. Deciding pricing policy in the museum sector is never easy, and museum marketers often face an ethical dilemma over charging. The debate about whether or not to charge is long standing; it has been intensively discussed in the sector for the last two decades. Where admission charges have been introduced, visitor numbers have slumped by between 20 per cent and 80 per cent, though there are a few exceptions.[34] Moreover, it leads to a disproportionate fall in attendance among lower socio-economic groups.[35]

Museum professionals in favour of charges primarily focus on financial necessity and management pragmatism. On the other hand, arguments against admission charges are predominantly based on the principles of equality of opportunity and free access. Despite this polarity in views on the imposition of admission charges, there is considerable consensus amongst museum professionals concerning the educational function of museums and the importance of expanding public access to their collections. With this in mind, any museum that introduces admission charges should endeavour to offer some form of free access to those who need it.

In favour of charging

Perhaps the strongest argument in favour of charging is economic necessity: admission charges provide additional income for museums. However, admission charges may be a major reason why disadvantaged socio-economic groups are under-represented. According to the research conducted by Stephen Bailey et al., this view is strongly held in all types of museums in England.[36]

There was a time when pricing was not an important issue for museums in Taiwan. There was no need for them to seek other financial support. However, this situation has begun to change. As governments cut grants to arts organizations, they are facing increasing financial pressure. Museums recognize that charging for admission limits access, especially for disadvantaged people; on the other hand, without income from ticketing, and faced with inadequate public funding, most will inevitably have to restrict access in other ways, such as closing galleries, eliminating special exhibitions, reducing opening hours and cutting programmes.

Although some museums gain additional income from admission charges, others might actually lose income once they start to charge admission. It seems that the revenue provided by admission charges comes at the cost of lost income opportunities elsewhere, for example in the gift shop, café, programmes and private donations. Conversely, abandoning entry fees may lead to increased income in these areas. The income from admission also needs to be weighed against the cost of losing a great number of visitors. Those national museums in the U.K. that charge admission claim these fees raise additional revenue;[37] however, in some cases, the results have been different. When visitors pay an admission charge, other income obtained from museum cafés, gift shops and donations is reduced.[38] Catherine McDonald describes how, in the first five years after the Auckland Museum, one of the most visited museums in New Zealand, imposed a $5 admission-by-donation fee in January 1999, annual visitor figures dropped from one million to 447,215 visitors. More important, in the same period the museum was unable to meet its revenue targets.[39] Even today, visitor numbers have failed to reach pre-admission charge levels. According to a press release issued by the Auckland Museum in October 2009, annual visitor numbers had exceeded 700,000 for the first time in more than ten years.[40]

On the other hand, a loss of admission revenue can be made up for from other sources because of the resulting increase in visitor figures. For instance, when five major regional museums in Taipei County, Taiwan (the Yingge Ceramics Museum, Shihsanhang Museum of Archaeology, Gold Ecological Park, Danshui Historic Sites and the Lin Mansion and Garden) abolished admission fees in January 2008, visitor numbers increased by 78 per cent, compared with the same period in 2007. When admission fees were removed, gift shop revenues increased by 60 per cent at the Yingge Ceramics Museum (YCM) and by 47 per cent at the Lin Mansion and Garden.[41] Moreover, YCM received more first-time visitors (people who had not visited any museum in the previous twelve months – from 29.1 per cent to 37.1 per cent), more visitors aged fifty-five and above (from 4.7 per cent to 8.0 per cent), and more unemployed/retired visitors (from 3.0 per cent to 7.7 per cent) between 2007 and 2009.[42]

Another major argument in favour of charging is that, when admission fees are imposed, the duration of visits tends to increase and the satisfaction of visitors improves. Most charging museums assert that the introduction of admission charges raises visitor satisfaction levels because visitors are more determined to secure value for money, and therefore stay longer and pay more attention to the exhibitions. Charging museums also argue that admission fees may discourage uninterested people from visiting. These comments appear to echo elitist sentiments expressed over a century ago by John Ruskin, who suggested that a small entry fee would prevent museums from being encumbered by the idle, or disgraced by the disreputable.[43] Researchers believe that people make a value judgment about how much a museum experience is worth in terms of the return it gives. Thus, value for money is more important to visitors than the actual cost.[44] This is confirmed by Dickenson who states that, even today, the implementation of admission charges in French museums is still considered to encourage respect for the collections and to discourage those who are not interested.[45] A study conducted by Rene Goudriaan and Gerrit Jan Van't Eind in four museums in Rotterdam echoes this finding. It shows that visitors stayed longer when admission charges were raised;[46] they reacted by reducing the monetary visiting price per unit of time.

Another major reason cited to justify charging is the commonly held view that cost-free means low quality, and that charging improves visitor satisfaction for this reason. Keith Diggle argues that people tend to undervalue services provided for free; non-charging museums are thought to be of less value than charging museums.[47] A study carried out by the Research Centre for Museums and Galleries (RCMG) at the School of Museum Studies, University of Leicester, also confirms that some non-visitors think free admission means low quality.[48]

It is perhaps surprising then that, according to evidence provided by the DCMS, visitor satisfaction has improved significantly in certain UK national museums since admission charges were abolished in 2001.[49] Fifty-one museums and galleries are classified as National Museums and Galleries (NMGs) in the UK. These are directly funded by the DCMS. About 58.8 per cent of them (thirty NMGs) charged for admission in 1998. According to the claims of the charging museums, when admission charges are removed, visitor satisfaction declines because visitors pay less attention to the, now free, exhibitions.[50] However, the DCMS's research indicates differently. It shows the percentage of visitors going to DCMS-sponsored museums (including the Tyne & Wear Museums) between 1999 and 2003 who thought they were good or very good. Only three in ten (32.11 per cent) of visitors thought the museum services were good or very good in 1999/2000. However, this figure had more than doubled, to 67.64 per cent, by 2002/03. In other words, the majority of visitors were highly satisfied with these free museums, not to mention that the free for all policy attracted more visitors from lower socio-economic groups.[51]

Against charging

One of the most important arguments against the introduction of admission charges is the claim that admission fees lead to a disproportionate fall in attendance among marginalized socio-economic groups.[52] Museums have a duty to broaden access to their collections. The argument against the introduction of admission charges in museums primarily rests on the allegation that admission charges result in a significant decrease in visitor figures and deter people of marginalized socio-economic status from visiting. Yet, many studies show that even when museums are free of charge, the typical visitor profile is skewed towards higher-income and well-educated groups. It is likely that the imposition of admission charges exacerbates this situation and makes museums less accessible to those people with lower incomes.[53]

Museum collections, which are held in trust for society, belong to everyone. They should be accessible to every individual. Even people who do not visit should still feel that public museums belong to them, their children, grandchildren and neighbours, and that they can use those museums if they wish. However, a charging museum cannot proclaim this principle in the same way as a non-charging museum: these museums are unable to reach out to the entire population, as their benefits are limited to those who are able and willing to pay for entry. It is an unethical policy to make the cultural heritage contained within our museums available only to the economically advantaged members of the population. The imposition of an admission fee undermines one of the main rationales for the existence of museums – to provide a free educational resource to the population. Ultimately, the decision whether or not to go to a museum should be based on the visitor's interest, not their financial capacity.

Where admission charges have been introduced, visitor numbers have slumped by between 20 per cent and 80 per cent, though there are a few exceptions.[54] Research conducted in Taipei, Taiwan by the author indicates that admission charges are likely to deter people on lower incomes. In the research, 7.1 per cent of respondents who had not visited a museum in the previous twelve months said that this was because admission charges are too high. This equates to approximately 2.5 per cent of the general population aged fifteen or over in Taipei. Moreover, the results showed that there is a significant relationship between the attitude towards charging and income. Thus, admission fees may lead to a disproportionate fall in attendance among lower-income groups. 8.1 per cent of respondents who had an income below £5,000 and who had not visited a museum in the previous twelve months (approximately one per cent of all respondents) cited high admission charges as the reason. This was followed by a figure of 6.2 per cent in the £5,001–£10,000 group and 3.6 per cent in the £10,001–£15,000 group. On the other hand, no one who had an income of more than £20,001 cited charges as a reason for not visiting museums. The results imply that people who are interested in visiting museums but who earn a low income are much more likely to be affected by entry fees; these are the very people whom socially engaged museums most want to serve. The introduction of charges violates the principle of equality of opportunity. It is partly responsible for the homogeneity of museum visitors, and makes museum audiences less diverse.[55]

Although the fundamental belief in the principle of equality is deeply rooted, when museums face cutbacks in funding and efforts to win central and local authority support for free access have failed, then charges are inevitable. Even when faced with this action, however, consideration should still be given to how to offer some form of free access. It is vital to arrive at a pricing policy that does not discourage a fully diverse public from accessing the collections. If admission charges are levied, the revenue should be reinvested in the museum. Free admission should be offered at least one day a week; moreover, concessions should be given to school children, the disabled and the elderly. For example, Taipei Fine Arts Museum (TFAM) in Taiwan opens its gates freely to disabled and elderly (over sixty-five years) visitors, and students are allowed free entry on Saturdays. The results are encouraging. In 2007, TFAM received about 400,000 visitors, approximately half of whom were students, disabled or senior citizens.[56] This approach may help to break up the homogeneity of museum visitors.

Conclusion

Museums exist to serve the public; their mission is educational, aesthetic and historical. As non-profit organizations, they have in the past enjoyed protection from the buffeting of the free market system in some countries such as the UK and Taiwan, but this is changing. Not only are they are under increasing financial pressure, but they must also compete for their audience in an expanding leisure market. In other words, it is commercially as well as socially desirable that they learn to serve a more diverse audience. Museums have traditionally believed that if they focused on their core functions such as education and learning, visitors would come, but this attitude has only ever drawn a select group of visitors. They are now realizing that they must proactively identify audience expectations and desires and set about meeting these. Consequently, marketing is becoming an increasingly important feature of the museum sector.

This chapter highlights four critical areas of ethical debate in museum marketing: the need to broaden and diversify audiences, the importance of evaluating museum products and services, the effectiveness of various modes of promotion and the arguments surrounding pricing policy. Museum audiences tend to be drawn from elite social groups; a key task facing museum and marketing professionals is to find ways of making museums more accessible to a broader range of people. As the pressure on resources grows, managers need to be able to evaluate effectively the relative importance and perceived performance of the wide range of elements which comprise a museum's products and services in order to meet the needs of diverse audiences. The above discussion illustrates the usefulness of IPA here. Again, where there are limited resources available, it is even more important that marketers are familiar with the range of promotional tools at their disposal, and their relative effectiveness at attracting target audiences. The issue of charging is highly contentious and one that goes to the heart of what we want our museums to be. It is argued here that, if they are to continue to serve the social and educational function for which they were established, any museum that introduces charges should still endeavour to offer some form of free access to those who need it.

Notes

1 D. R. Prince, 'Factors influencing museum visits: an empirical evaluation of audience selection', *Museum Management and Curatorship* 9: 2, 1990, pp. 149–68.

2 C. Scott, 'Measuring social value', in R. Sandell (ed.) *Museums, Society, Inequality*, London: Routledge, 2002, pp. 41–55.

3 E. Hooper-Greenhill, *The Education Role of the Museums*, London: Routledge, 1994.

4 For example, see E. Hill, C. O'Sullivan and T. O'Sullivan, *Creative Arts Marketing*, Oxford: Butterworth Heinemann, 1995.

5 F. McLean, *Marketing the Museum*, London: Routledge, 1997.

6 Ibid.

7 T. J. Hannagan, *Marketing for the Non-profit Sector*, London: Macmillan, 1992.

8 Department for Culture, Media and Sport, *Understanding the Future: Museums and Twenty-first Century Life: The Value of Museums*, London: DCMS, 2005.

9 European Communities, *Cultural Statistics, Eurostat Pocketbooks 2007 Edition*, Luxembourg: Office for Official Publications of the European Communities, 2007.

10 Y. N. Lin, 'Admission Charges, the Representative Audience and Public Museums', unpublished Ph.D. thesis, Leicester: University of Leicester, 2006.

11 For example, see N. Merriman, *Beyond the Glass Case: The Past, the Heritage and the Public*, London: University College London, 2000.

12 European Communities, *Cultural Statistics, Eurostat Pocketbooks 2007 Edition*.

13 For example, see J. Dodd and R. Sandell, *Building Bridges: Guidance for Museums and Galleries on Developing New Audiences*, London: Museums and Galleries Commission, 1998.

14 D. Fleming, 'Positioning the museum for social inclusion', in Sandell, *Museums, Society, Inequality*, pp. 213–24.

15 *Renaissance in the Regions: A New Vision for England's Museums*, London: Resource, 2001.

16 M. G. Hood, 'Staying away: why people choose not to visit museums', *Museum News* 61: 4, 1983, pp. 50–7.

17 Smithsonian Institution, *Results of the 2004 Smithsonian-wide survey of museum visitors*, Washington, DC: Smithsonian Institution, 2004. Online. Available HTTP: http://www.si.edu/opanda/Reports/Reports/SI2004_Survey_Booklet.pdf (accessed 6 May 2009).

18 Prince, 'Factors influencing museum visitors', pp. 149–68.

19 Y. N. Lin, 'Leisure: A function of museums? The Taiwanese perspective', *Museum Management and Curatorship* 21: 4, 2006, pp. 302–16.

20 Market and Opinion Research International, *Visitors to Museums and Galleries in the UK*, London: Market and Opinion Research International, 2001.

21 A. Parasuraman, V. A. Zeithaml and L. L. Berry, 'A conceptual model of service quality and its implications for future research', *Journal of Marketing* 49: 4, 1985, pp. 41–50.

22 A. J. Martilla and J. C. James, 'Importance–performance analysis', *Journal of Marketing* 41: 1, 1977, pp. 77–9.

23 W. L. Lin and Y. N. Lin, *An Investigation into the Audience at the Yingge Ceramics Museum*, Taipei: Research report to the Yingge Ceramics Museum, 2009 (in Chinese).

24 Hood, 'Staying away: why people choose not to visit museums,' pp. 50–7.

25 S. Runyard and Y. French, *Marketing and Public Relations Handbook: For Museums, Galleries and Heritage Attractions*, London: Stationery Office, 1999.

26 McLean, *Marketing the Museum*.

27 Ibid.

28 J. H. Falk and L. D. Dierking, *The Museum Experience*, Washington, DC: Whalesback, 1992.

29 G. D. Adams, 'The process and effects of word-of-mouth communication in a museum setting', *Visitor Studies* 3: 1, 1991, pp. 165–79.

30 G. D. Adams, 'The Process and Effects of Word-of-mouth Communication at a History Museum', unpublished M.A. thesis, Boston, MA: Boston University, 1989.

31 H. F. Chiu, 'A Study on Visitors' Satisfaction on Exhibition Environment of the Yingge Ceramics Museum, Taipei', unpublished M.A. thesis, Taiwan: National Taiwan University of Arts, 2009.

32 McLean, *Marketing the Museum*.

33 Adams, 'The process and effects of word-of-mouth communication in a museum setting', pp. 165–79.

34 S. Davies, *By Popular Demand: A Strategic Analysis of the Market Potential for Museums and Art Galleries in the UK*, Lincoln: Museums and Galleries Commission, 1994.
35 Merriman, *Beyond the Glass Case*.
36 S. Bailey et al., *To Charge or not to Charge? Full Report*, London: Museums and Galleries Commission, 1998.
37 Ibid.
38 G. Savage, *Charges Dropped! Admission Fees to Cultural Attractions*, Sydney: Environmetrics, 2001. Online. Available HTTP: http://www.environmetrics.com.au/resources/entryfees.pdf (accessed 3 May 2010).
39 C. McDonald, 'Charging for Access for Non-residents to the Art Gallery and Museum', unpublished report, 2005. Online. Available HTTP: http://www1.ccc.govt.nz/council/proceedings/2005/june/cnclcover23rd/chargingforaccess.pdf (accessed 3 May 2010).
40 See press release of Auckland Museum, 29 October 2009. Online. Available HTTP: http://www.aucklandmuseum.com/site_resources/library/Top_Menu/Media/2009_Media_Kit/Spring_2009/Auckland_Museum_Sees_Big_Jump_in_Numbers.pdf (accessed 10 March 2010).
41 See press release of the Taipei County Government, 1 June 2009.
42 Lin and Lin, *An Investigation into the Audience at the Yingge Ceramics Museum*.
43 J. Ruskin, 'Letters to Leicester Museum Subscribers', *Art Journal*, new series, 19, 1880.
44 PLB Consulting, 'Developing New Audiences for the Heritage: Research Study for Heritage Lottery Fund', unpublished report, London: PLB Consulting, 2001.
45 V. Dickenson, 'The economics of museum admission charges', in K. Moore (ed.) *Museum Management*, London: Routledge, 1994, pp. 104–14.
46 R. Goudriaan and G. J. Van't Eind, 'To fee or not to fee: some effects of introducing admission fees in four museums in Rotterdam', in V. L. Owen and W. S. Hendon (eds.) *Managerial Economics for the Arts*, Akron, OH: Association for Cultural Economics, 1985, pp. 103–9.
47 K. Diggle, *Guide to Arts Marketing: The Principles and Practice of Marketing as they Apply to the Arts*, London: Rhinegold, 1984.
48 Research Centre for Museums and Galleries, *Developing Audiences and Promoting Social Inclusion: National Museums and Galleries of Wales*, Leicester: RCMG, 2002.
49 S. Matty (ed.), *Overview of Data in the Museums, Libraries and Archives Sector*, London: MLA, 2004.
50 Bailey et al., *To Charge or not to Charge?* p. 47.
51 Matty, *Overview of Data in the Museums, Libraries and Archives Sector*.
52 Merriman, *Beyond the Glass Case*.
53 V. Kirchberg, 'Entrance fees as a subjective barrier to visiting museums', *Journal of Cultural Economics* 22: 1, 1998, pp. 1–13.
54 For example, see Davies, *By Popular Demand*.
55 Y. N. Lin, 'Admission charges and public museums', *International Journal of Arts Management* 10: 2, 2008, pp. 56–67.
56 W. L. Lin and Y. N. Lin, 'To charge or not to charge? A study on admission policy of national museums', *Museum Quarterly* 22: 3, 2008, pp. 55–71 (in Chinese).

14

Memorial museums and the objectification of suffering

Paul Williams

For memorial museums – the fast-expanding cluster of institutions that commemorate and interpret modern mass atrocities – ethics sits squarely at the center of their mission and educational and social goals. In contrast to more established, mainstream museum genres where ethics is largely understood in terms of professional practice, in memorial museums ethics, morality and human deeds occupy the very heart of the topics on display, and correspondingly involve especially careful considerations of representation and reception.[1] Extending Timothy P. Brown's caution that it becomes "a matter of ethics for museums to consider how dangerous they can be if they are not attuned to their complicity in the use and abuse of culture," we can anticipate how acutely partial accounts and false or unfaithful museological practices could affect still contested violent histories where life and death – especially death – are involved.[2]

With a common mission to prevent future horrific suffering – the "never again" imperative instigated by Holocaust remembrance – memorial museums attempt to mobilize visitors as both historical witnesses and agents of present and future political vigilance. This chapter explores the practices and issues involved in eliciting these responses, and considers questions of reception at the visitor level. Several overlapping topics organize this inquiry. These include: (1) responsible use of victims' and perpetrators' images and artifacts; (2) the physical experience of being at authentic sites of destruction; (3) issues of personal identity, culpability, responsibility and victimhood for the visitor; (4) the larger political question of what is, and should be, commemorated. As memorial museums emerge as increasingly popular sites of heritage tourism, the tension between the competitive desire to attract visitors and the need to meaningfully connect to local communities of interest also becomes more pressing. In forging an understanding of these issues, the politically and morally sensitive case of the memorial museum can be used as a lens through which to understand the politics of heritage tourism more generally.

Objects, images and precarious representation

The combination of the calamity of a violent event, its political and existential gravitas and the scarcity of material traces normally left behind means that the objects that *are* displayed in museums become especially crucial. While the generic history museum provides a container for a wide variety of topics, the relationship between the memorial museum and its event is intimately entwined. A marked feature of memorial museum collections is that they are defined by what the violence in each event *produced*. Institutions must decide how to incorporate and frame the output that the calamity generated, knowing it will come to symbolize the event. While the Holocaust is notably associated in object form with the industrial machines that effected the disappearance of bodies (such as boxcars, gas chambers and ovens), it also produced, as terrible "by-products," clothing, jewelry, eyeglasses, watches and hair. These copious items are emblematic for Holocaust museums worldwide, along with keepsakes and diaries hidden by victims, Nazi regime equipment and insignia, and civilian artifacts that help to evoke 1930s and 1940s mise-en-scène.

Focusing on this last category, we might examine the qualities that make an object "belong to" an event. Consider, as one case, the fracas over artifacts acquired by Berlin's Jewish Museum for its 2001 opening. A flashpoint was the modest living room furniture that the Scheuers, a German-Jewish family expelled from Staudernheim in 1938, took with them to the U.S. Museum spokeswoman Eva Söderman stated that the furniture represents "the exile of the little people."[3] Chana C. Schütz, deputy director of Berlin's Centrum Judaicum, challenged the choice of acquisition, asking, "Can you tell me one Jewish object that is not a Holocaust object that can be that impressive? They shouldn't think buying furniture of people who emigrated to the United States makes a good object. It's still old furniture."[4] For members of the Jewish Museum's curatorial staff, the point *was* that it was typical. As one exclaimed, the point is "to show people that these things exactly looked like everything else. They're not *Jewish*."[5] Yet, for Schütz, this justification masks a fascination with the idea that the objects were actually there – that any object has gravitas through connections to the Shoah. For Schütz, this perpetuates a vision of Jewish history that is maudlin and reactive rather than strident and self-affirming; the furniture acts as a signifier of evacuation and loss and avoids harder political condemnation. Instead of producing exhibits based around, for instance, personally naming Jewish wartime collaborators (something the Centrum Judaicum has done), "everything at the Jewish Museum will be politically correct because they are very afraid of making any mistakes."[6]

The framing of objects as "too safe" or "risky" understands the ethics of display principally in terms of visitor sensitivities. Yet, given that victims suffered the actuality of horrific acts, is it a cop-out to consider its mere emblems too uncomfortable to view? Further, are exhibition designers, advisors and curators the rightful gatekeepers of what we should see? Ethical issues surrounding respect for privacy may give us pause. Take the example of the "Women in Prison" gallery at the Memorial of the Victims of Communism and Anti-Communist Resistance in Sighet, Romania. It showcases the story of women detained for their political views and separated from their families. In a case, visitors see a bar of soap sent from a husband at home that bears the carved words *I love you*. Should we be privy to objects intended to be so intimate, and which possess such pathos? Or, to take a hypothetical case: should the publicly broadcast recordings of those who made phone calls to loved ones moments before dying on 9/11 be included at the forthcoming National September 11 Memorial and Museum? If they are received as either an expressive illustration of the deep value of a real human life, or a gratuitous exercise in pure emotional affect, does such interpretation lie simply in the way objects are framed, or are ethical issues imbued in the intrinsic qualities of the object itself?

As memorial museums seek to fully represent the lives that were lost, not just as victims but as fully embodied individuals and members of communities, the personal story has come to the fore as a dominant narrative construct. The personalization of mass atrocity has precedents. Undoubtedly, the most famous figure, Anne Frank, has had her diary translated into more than fifty languages, and produced as a film and Broadway play. She has also been awarded her own memorial museum – Amsterdam's popular Anne Frank House. While some visitors may struggle to remember the details of complex political histories, individual lives have stirring notes of detail that inevitably find ways to intersect with our own. As someone who we come to know, Anne Frank may be considered a "screen memory" for our understanding of the Holocaust. Marita Sturken uses the concept of screen memories to conceptualize how societies use mnemonic aids – people, icons, phrases, and parables – to block out other larger memories and historical facts that are too difficult to conceive and articulate. The theory of screen memories derives from Freud, who used the term to describe certain recollections that function to screen out those the subject wants to keep at bay.[7] While coming to know one person intimately has the advantage of bringing us closer to the emotion of human experience, as an exhibition tactic, it could be charged with allowing us to draw away from comprehending the terrible dimensions of mass killing. How could we, as visitors, absorb the repetitive yet unique details of six million individual deaths?

Taking themes of privacy, empathy and alienation to their logical conclusion, museums as a general rule find the display of human remains from modern atrocities untenable. According to the Director of External Affairs at the U.S. Holocaust Memorial Museum, for instance, "it must be assumed that objects such as hair, bones, and ashes will not be considered as potential accessions ... They do not belong in an American setting, where no concentration camps stood and which was not the primary arena for the Holocaust."[8] He continued: "At any standard, the display of human hair and/or ashes and bone is offensive to the memory of the dead." Such displays would "offend, repel, and sicken many visitors physically, emotionally and spiritually."[9] Questions of sensitivity similarly account for why both Cambodian and Rwandan genocide memorial museums now choose to display human remains less starkly than before. Chea Sopheara, director of Cambodia's Tuol Sleng Museum of Genocidal Crimes, said of its "skull map" display (a three-dimensional map of the country comprised of victims' skulls): "By removing the skulls, we want to end the fear visitors have while visiting the museum."[10] Ildephonse Karengera, director of Rwanda's Kigali Memorial, also sees the display of remains as unproductive: "We want the memorials to be centers for the exchange of ideas, not collections of bones."[11] Others argue that the remains should stay in place as evidence of what happened, in order to defy those who would doubt or deny genocidal acts. However, as both Cambodians and Rwandans traditionally bury their dead, their display is spiritually and ethically problematic. A practical compromise has emerged in the Rwandan case. "For those who say it is undignified to show bones, we're burying them, in a sense, behind dark glass," said Dr. James Smith, who runs the Aegis Trust, an organization working with the Rwandan government to refurbish several of its memorials. "For those who say it is necessary to see the death, we're accommodating them, too."[12] Clearly, memorial museum collections are *evidence* in a sense that is greater than simply "attesting to history." They can also help support cases of international law – such as files of victims found stored at Tuol Sleng that were used in the Cambodia Tribunal trials against Kaing Guek Eav (Duch), who was chief of the prison torture and murder site.

The visitor response to the explicitness of emotionally affecting objects typically depends on how authentically the museum frames the encounter. For instance, the use of lifelike mannequins depicting slain women and children at the Nanjing Massacre Memorial Museum is jarring, not so much for its graphic appearance, but because efforts to artificially create horror suggest a crass kitsch. Yet questions of taste in displays can be critiqued for bowing before aesthetic values of judgment and technique that risk stylizing an event for maximum public appeal. Precisely because the high stakes associated with the content of memorial museums can produce drama more easily than other types of museums, they are now at the forefront of the "performing museum" paradigm.[13] Over traditional interpretive museum practices, the performing museum layers theatrical tropes based on reality effects. These include, for instance, architectural views that highlight historically authentic spaces through exposed walls or glass floors that display archaeological finds, stage set-like scenes and rooms (such as reconstructed officers' quarters or torture cells), and the use of personal testimony (where, using a handheld device, a witness virtually accompanies the visitor as he or she moves through galleries). In the performing museum, the total physical environment becomes the attraction as the visitor is encouraged to re-enact the drama in a kind of empathetic walk-through. Hence, rather than viewing museum spaces in principally intellectual terms, as theatrical environments they are as equally concerned with the visceral, kinesthetic, haptic and intimate qualities of bodily experience.[14] The strength of experience at memorial museums may mean that what we "never forget" as visitors is our own experience of an event's *representation*. That is, without a direct conduit to the event itself, we remember our own sensory engagement, and value it especially when we feel it holds authenticity.

Moving from the display of objects to images, different questions about authenticity and evidence come to bear. One involves authorship. While memorial museums sometimes contain images taken by photojournalists and known perpetrators and witnesses, non-attributed photographs are more common. They arguably possess greater cachet, both because one may imagine them as having been taken by a concerned witness (a viewing position the museum visitor can comfortably share), and since pictures of restive events seem more authentic when amateurish in composition. Susan Sontag has noted that pictures taken by military amateur photographers at Bergen-Belsen, Buchenwald and Dachau concentration camps at the time of their liberation have been widely regarded as more valid than those by professionals like Margaret Bourke-White and Lee Miller.[15] With their lack of technical prowess, anonymous shots may be preferred precisely because they are not normally designed to arouse compassion.

Even when photographers are credited, the immersive power of an historical scene can make them forgotten. Viewers easily forget the invisible mediating camera, instead focusing on what is visually made available:

What is seen in the picture was there – not only in the sense coined by Roland Barthes (that is, as testimony that what is seen in the photograph was present facing the camera) but in the sense that the time lapse makes present the gap between a seemingly stabilized object seen in the camera and the photographer's apparently external point of view. Thus, the spectator is liable to plunge into what's seen in the photograph and forget that a photographer had been there when it was taken.[16]

If the act of taking a picture is fleeting, the depicted subject may have been even less aware of the moment. Consider, for example, Figure 14.1, a photograph displayed at the Museum of Occupations, Tallinn, captioned "Ingers being repatriated to Finland."

What is happening here? Who are these people? Who took the picture? We learn from the museum that the Ingrian are rural peasant Fenno-Ugric people who lived in the Leningrad oblast. We see, pictured, a case of their forced evacuation in 1942 or 1943 as they are overseen by a Finnish and a Nazi officer. Victims of the 1939 Molotov–Ribbentrop pact, these anonymous people were displaced to Estonia and eventually on to Finland. Many others were executed, deported to Siberia or forced to relocate to other parts of the Soviet Union. In the process, they were persecuted to the extent that their language and culture are now largely extinct.[17] While the Museum of Occupations frames this photograph to argue that forced evacuations should be understood as partial justification for the regained independence of the Estonian state, the anonymous evacuees could never have known the narrative that their actions would be held to represent.

Figure 14.1 Ingers being repatriated to Finland. Copyright the Museum of Occupations, Tallin.

While as museum visitors we bring with us the hindsight of history's judgment, what is the level of consciousness captured at the time by such images? Does it allow us to gauge the degree of trepidation and angst experienced by the Ingers depicted above? As viewers, we understand the ramifications of their situation – its historic magnitude and bearing – and yet each subject in this photograph took the particulars of their own experience with them. In searching for historic meaning in photographs, viewers may emotionally overcompensate, imputing more to the split second of facial expressions and body language than either the subject or photographer could have intended. As Ulrich Baer notes:

> Empathetic identification can easily lead us to miss the inscription of trauma because the original subjects themselves did not register the experience in the fullness of its meaning ... The viewer must respond to the fact that these experiences passed through their subjects as something real without coalescing into memories to be stored or forgotten.[18]

While neither one's memory nor the camera are especially good at recording the completeness of an experience, we continue to turn to them both as evidence of historical atrocities, owing to our persistent cognitive connection between visual reconstruction and truth.

That photographs can be dubious as evidence was ably demonstrated by the example of the "Verbrechen der Wehrmacht" (Crimes of the German Wehrmacht) exhibition. Organized by the Hamburg Social Research Institute, the exhibition toured museums in thirty-three cities in Germany and Austria between 1995 and 1999, drawing almost 900,000 visitors.[19] It was comprised primarily of previously unknown photos sourced from private collections of German soldiers depicting war crimes in Eastern Europe. Impassioned arguments broke out at the venues displaying the exhibition. There were large demonstrations in Munich and Dresden, the exhibition was vandalized in several cities and, in Saarbrucken, right-wing extremists attempted to firebomb it.[20] While the exhibition organizers anticipated restive demonstrations, in October 1999 a different kind of disaster struck. An historian challenged that photographs of Wehrmacht soldiers in Tarnopol, Poland, apparently standing over the bodies of recently slaughtered Jews, were in fact Ukrainians murdered by Stalin's retreating army before the Wehrmacht arrived. The ensuing scandal over the authenticity of the pictures (seized on by right-wing groups) forced the organizers to close the exhibition, pending a report by an independent commission. The commission concluded that the original thesis was correct, but that the photographs had been carelessly sourced and sloppily used. The retitled pictures appeared as part of a new, critical, self-reflexive mini-exhibition called "Photos as Historical Sources," which was shown at the German Historical Museum in Berlin from 2000. The charges of falsity were disturbing not least because they raised questions in viewers about their trust in museums and the potential for manipulation. Moreover, it showed that while a historical photograph captures something that was "really there," it cannot pass context on to us. Since memorial museum images (and objects) are potentially *evidence* in a politico-legal sense, the need for diligent context-based research becomes especially pressing.

Visitor presence and physical place

Moving from indoor to outdoor spaces, we arrive at a significant distinction; visitors to memorial museums on sites of destruction are almost certainly more attuned to environmental perception (the air, wind, and earth, the ineffable aura) than those to indoor museums, which are principally organized around sight and, occasionally, sound. The theme of bodily awareness, little investigated in museum studies, is important for memorial museum interpretation. As Monika Langer writes: "It has become necessary to reconsider the nature of sensing and to tackle the problem of describing it is 'that vital communication with the world,' that 'intentional tissue' which underlies and sustains all thought."[21] Memorial museums increasingly attempt to provide evocative common spaces that engage our "intentional tissue." On the grounds of the Bergen-Belsen Memorial, for instance, visitors find the House of Silence, an architecturally sparse, diamond-shaped room with wooden pews and a table at one end, on which tributary pebbles are laid. Standing at the rear of the space and gazing upwards, visitors look through the semi-transparent roof skyward. In terms of its evocation of enriched communal experience, the encounter shares much with churchgoing. In each case, people may come not simply to learn information (such as historical facts, or details of scriptures), but because they wish to be in a total environment that affirms a sense of being in place. Both the memorial museum and church make concrete the notion of sacred ground and congregate people around a single topic. Attention to an individual's quality of feeling that stems from being in a charged environment, amongst others interested in exercising the same moral concern, is consistent with the idea that we remember most vividly those experiences that are related to the bodily and visceral. This is especially pertinent when relating to the themes of memorial museums centered on physical discomfort, pain and alienation.

Of the various sites of destruction converted into memorial museums, including schools, fields, churches and government offices, the most common is probably the former prison. Museums that commemorate political prisoners generally focus on a combination of harsh claustrophobic conditions and contextual information, refusing the drama of re-enactment and theatricality that characterizes tourist prison museums. Tours of Robben Island Museum, for instance, highlight the "elite" Section B (containing Nelson Mandela's cell), and decorate other sections differently to display the contrast in living conditions over the years – from the spartan, single blanket quarters all political prisoners endured until the 1970s, to the addition of beds and newspapers, and even a radio supplied after 1980. The size and physical condition of the cells provide a material and spatial dimension to visitors' indignation at apartheid injustice. Prison space is similarly made appreciable at the Memorial of the Victims of Communism and Anti-Communist Resistance in Sighet, but in a different form. Beneath the original watchtower, the prison courtyard features a dozen or more naked sculpted bronze "prisoners" in various kinetic poses. The visually arresting sculpture provides an embodied sense of scale to an otherwise desolate prison courtyard. By occupying the site with permanent figures, the museum reinforces the immutability of the site's current interpretation; its aesthetic historicization aims to nullify the possibility of the re-emergence of the building – and by extension, Romania – as an actively violent and intolerant place.

Conceiving life as a political prisoner is obviously a difficult projection for everyday museum visitors. In the process of making a prohibitive space accommodating as a tourist facility, other forms of identification (personal objects, photographs and recorded testimony) are added to make the suffering of prisoners more readily available, giving the prison greater historical context and emotional texture. Such exhibition spaces give voice to the – normally silent – body in pain that is central to all forms of violence and trauma. The tactic of combining both alienating and empathetic interpretive devices forces together competing registers. This makes visitors reconcile the private, confined pain associated with imprisonment and torture with the public "lesson" facilitated by curatorial "show and tell" techniques.

Since visitors are seldom made aware of the techniques and technologies of preservation that maintain sites of destruction in suspended decay, they tend to imagine they are seeing them "as they were." Recent debates over how, and whether, to renovate or preserve the sinking Auschwitz-Birkenau gas chambers call attention to how the evolving physical nature of a site colors how we feel: what quality of remembrance does its renovation to resemble a 1940s killing center – albeit emptied and sanitized – help to elicit? Does it help to communicate that "it could be now," or do we see it as a staged heritage installation? Alternatively, does natural decomposition contribute to a sense that the event was a tragic but receding aspect of the past? While, on the one hand, we might anticipate that it would be natural decay that would soften the harsh reality of camps like Auschwitz-Birkenau, it may be that, "in order to frame the camp 'furniture,' which the museum authorities are so painstakingly reconstructing, their managed ecology of tidiness and order has a tendency to tame the horror of the place."[22] By displaying a site and its artifacts with no or little reference of how the exhibition came to be, the museum risks perpetuating the belief that what we see is what was. It may be that while physical surroundings appear to draw us closer to the reality of an event, their chief function is to provide a spatial-geographic frame for our own memories as visitors.

The identity-bearing historical witness

As the memorial-museum compound suggests, key institutional messages typically exist in tension: the respect awarded to memorials, and the interpretation favored by contemporary museums. At a time when interactive, opinion-driven experiences are favored by museums all over, memorial museums continue to be associated with both one-way communication and thoughtful respect as the order of behavior. Accounts of actions such as tourists posing for photographs beneath the infamous main gate at Auschwitz, carefree teenagers sitting on Dachau bunk beds or visitors to Tuol Sleng Museum of Genocidal Crimes touching the skulls on the skull map, are common. At Berlin's Memorial to the Murdered Jews of Europe, discussion over proper behavior began immediately after opening in 2005. "Stop Disgracing Ourselves," the *Berliner Kurier* said in one headline. The *Tagesspiegel* complained about some of the visitors' "strange customs" like kissing and sunbathing around the pillars. Some younger people played on the slabs, leaping from one to another.[23] Understandably, officials are reluctant to enhance security measures, such as adding to the two existing guards, erecting a fence or adding security cameras. The association of the Holocaust with forms of policing and bodily control makes such actions symbolically thorny; the memorial's director reaffirmed that "the basic concept is tolerance."[24] It was similarly not uncommon in the period after 9/11 to hear complaints about manners at New York's Ground Zero. As one onlooker commented: "I could hardly believe it. I was there at Ground Zero to pay my respects. But while I stood in tears reading 'rest in peace' messages scrawled on the walls encasing the platform, a pack of tourists clambered around me to get the best view of the mass grave. What had gotten into these people?"[25] In these situations, as in many war memorial and pilgrimage sites, tourism and commemoration exist in tension. This is partly because they are based around incompatible behaviors – bodily pleasure versus punctiliousness, or mental escapism versus application. Yet, as the opening of a new memorial site increasingly emerges as a highly publicized media event, it may be supercilious to criticize the tourist who displays behavior associated with more spectacular forms of entertainment.

The gravity of what occurred on sites of destruction tends to produce self-consciousness about one's movements and actions. How swiftly should I move between galleries? Can I take photographs? Ask questions? Could the staff member who greeted me be a survivor? Memorial museums offer a vivid experience in apprehension and diffidence for all kinds of visitors. Comparing the viewing of museum displays of atrocities to the British tendency to avoid staring at street accidents, John Taylor suggests that ethical awkwardness rests with *being seen* to be inspecting the anguish of others:

> Apart from sexual or morbid perversity, another reason why staring and gawping are abhorred, and why there are many attempts to regulate, or at least guide the act of looking, is that meeting eyes opens the possibility of obligation. The "I–it" relation becomes "I–thou," and identification may lead to complications.[26]

The sense of prohibition in memorial museums reflects doubts about whether one should have the right to intimately observe the suffering of others. While the act of visitation is ostensibly about learning and paying respect, it is situated in an exchange marked by an utter disparity in life experiences. As I described my own experience at Choeung Ek Genocidal Center, a Cambodian "killing field" outside Phnom Penh:

> Fragments of human bone and cloth are scattered around the disinterred pits. The embankments separating them serve as haphazard paths. After only a few minutes of walking, taking care not to let my footing slip, it became apparent that the identical hollows would yield few revelations. I noticed a cluster of children standing under a tree with a sign that reads: "Chankiri tree against which executioners beat children." "Picture, sir?" the children solicited, as they gathered around, their heads lining up against the small red target that has been attached four feet up its trunk.[27]

Brooding about the purpose of any memorial museum visit can generate conflicted feelings. Visiting Auschwitz and Israel's Yad Vashem Holocaust memorials,

Moris Farhi found himself confronting discordant emotions that clash with desired institutional messages:

> In none of my visits did my courage to face what had happened to members of my family give me the strength to brave the world. Instead, I was gripped by despair. I felt the loss of my resolve to do everything within my abilities to prevent such atrocities happening again. In fact, I felt murderous – and righteous for feeling murderous ... I felt the need to unleash yet another holocaust, one which would be directed against the perpetrators of holocausts and one in which I myself – a demented self – would take part as a purveyor of justice.[28]

Involuntary, solipsistic feelings of inadequacy, guilt, anger or dismay may not be easily led towards remembering and resolving "Never again." While surveys about museum services are routinely conducted, much less common are those that seek qualitative information about visitors' emotions. One rare instance asked Israelis exiting Yad Vashem to summarize their feelings by choosing one or more responses from a list. The results were dominated by sadness (56 percent), thoughtfulness (50 percent), and anger (43 percent), and, to a lesser extent, by melancholy (13 percent) and revenge (8 percent).[29] Whether these feelings were already formed or changed as a result of the museum visit is unknown. Moreover, it is difficult to determine whether such sentiments stayed with the person and came to bear on later ideas and actions. Indeed, memorial museums, founded on the ethical link between visitor response and social action, are attempting to shape and sway a set of ideas that are often rooted in deep cultural frameworks. In this, visitors are not simply learning about a topic, but are negotiating the museum's attempt to shape their moral worldviews.

The politics of remembrance

The connection between a historical event and its institutional memorialization is not simply an objective outcome of its size or scope. Instead, it depends on its ability to *support a ritual encounter* with the past. There are many events that lack the temporal or spatial boundaries (memorials for third world poverty, perhaps) or politically organized nature (global violence against women) that would make them a likely topic for a memorial museum. The question of what deserves representation, on what scale, and in which locations, is one that will never be decided through some appeal to the historical record, but instead depends on both how it appears and is narrated in collective memory (itself highly influenced by media industries like television and print), and on the power of political and economic will.

A sense of global ethics also pervades discussions about which events are deserving. This is especially pertinent where the line separating perpetrators from victims is blurred. An example that highlights this conundrum is the proposal for a National Memorial Center Against Expulsions to be situated in Wroclaw, Poland.[30] At the end of World War Two, some 12 million ethnic Germans living in ex-German Eastern Territories and Eastern Europe were forced to abandon their homes and move to Allied-occupied Germany, despite sometimes having family histories in those places going back centuries. Civilian casualties during the exodus were high, with estimates that range from one to two million. While major German political parties agreed on the proposal for a museum, troubled German–Polish relations have stalled plans.[31] The fear that such a museum could relativize the legacy of German Holocaust guilt is clearly a major point of difficulty for Poles, Jews and others. A 2003 petition signed by dozens of European historians declared that "A Centre Against Expulsions would not contribute to a critical examination of the past. Rather, it would tend to pit one people against another, exacerbate national antagonisms and therefore retard the process of European integration."[32] A differing view might suggest that the proliferation of museums with incompatible or conflicting views of the past might help to produce a more nuanced understanding of common suffering and moral ambiguity.

The issue of which individuals to remember in any memorial can be as vexed as that of who to blame. At Madrid's poignant cupola-shaped 11-M Memorial, which memorializes the victims killed in the Atocha rail station terrorist attack, this question came to the fore. The bombings by an Al-Qaeda-inspired group that killed 192 people were far from Spain's first experience with terrorism. Attacks by ETA, the Basque separatist group, have claimed more than 800 lives over the past thirty years, and yet there was no national memorial to commemorate those losses. José Alcaráz, president of Madrid's Association for the Victims of Terrorism, wished to address this discrepancy, stating that "there are more than 460 families in Madrid alone who have been affected by ETA's terrorism. We believe that [the memorial] should include them as well."[33] Others resisted linking the attacks, instigated by distinct groups with very different political aims. In its finished form, the memorial listed only those killed that day, raising certain questions: is the basic fact of tragic, unwarranted death at the hands of terrorists enough to unite those killed (and, as importantly, their families) in shared experience? If not, does distinguishing victims according to the circumstances of their deaths serve to define them chiefly through the machinations of killers?

A related issue concerns the organization of the names of the dead to be inscribed around the walls of the World Trade Center's "Reflecting Absence" memorial. Should they be ordered alphabetically, making them easily located – so as not to force families to perform another search of sorts? Should they be listed randomly, in order to reflect the arbitrariness of those killed? Or should they be sorted by profession to demonstrate the primary sacrifice of those in uniform? This last proposal has proven especially contentious, as families of victims who worked in the buildings largely oppose the affiliation-based scheme favored by police and fire department officials, arguing that special designations would create a hierarchy of victimhood.[34] In cases like Madrid and New York, where violent death occurred in public at the hands of a political faction, it is seen as suitable to shift commemoration out of the private mourning associated with cemeteries and into public spaces. In such instances the topic of "proper" remembrance also becomes public property, as victims become part of a debate about representation that easily sees their individual lives eclipsed.

The question of how prominently a memorial museum should feature perpetrators in the midst of victims is also quite contentious. Speaking at the dedication of the Oklahoma City National Memorial, President Clinton stated, "there are places in our national landscape so scarred by freedom's sacrifice that they shape forever the soul of America – Valley Forge, Gettysburg, Selma. This place is such sacred ground."[35] By associating the loss of life through an act of domestic terrorism with that of sites of nation building and freedom, the Oklahoma City bombing is narrated as a noble national sacrifice. It is difficult to find reference inside the museum to Timothy McVeigh or Terry Nichol. McVeigh is pictured only once, being led away handcuffed by FBI officers. Of the museum's ten thematic galleries, the first begins with "chaos" (the moment of the blast) and the last is "hope" (the city's rehabilitation). In between, there is little attention to motives for the bombing, persons responsible, nor the history of homegrown terrorism. The museum's youth-focused public outreach programs also abstract the nature of the violence. "The Hope Trunk," lent out to schools for a two-week period, holds artifacts and class-room exercises that "use the story of the bombing to educate students about the senselessness of violence and the need to find more peaceful means to solve our differences."[36] The setting aside of questions of who and why makes the institution a memorial in its pure, depoliticized sense. Perhaps out of a sense that to depict ter-rorists is to lend them selfhood, perspective or reason, victims are almost the sole frame of reference.

If the blast at 9:02 a.m. represents the decontextualized moment of instigation that is nonetheless the tragic raison d'être for the Oklahoma City National Memor-ial, the colossal explosion at 8:15 a.m. fulfills an analogous function at the Hiroshima Peace Memorial Museum. Specific attention to the motives and rationale of the American military leadership and the greater wartime context are similarly given minor attention in the permanent exhibition. The diminishment of discussion about *why* the bombs came may be a legacy of the institutional origins of the Hiroshima Peace Memorial Park. The 1948 Peace City Construction Law approved by local referendum expressed the spirit of Hiroshima's postwar reconstruction as the "Peace Memorial City." As Lisa Yoneyama argues, the real impetus came from American-led Allied powers, which "welcomed the proposal to convert the field of atomic ashes into a peace park, while simultaneously enforcing censorship on Japanese publications concerning the bomb's devastating effects on human lives and communities."[37]

The museum has been sharply criticized for the way that, in positioning itself as a "peace city," questions of its own historical acts in the Pacific War are severed from the "last act." The Nanjing Massacre is the only atrocity (briefly) cited. As Benedict Giamo notes, there is no other mention of, for instance, the 1941–42 Rural Pacifi-cation Campaign in China, which reduced the population in Communist areas by 19 million via death and expulsion, the execution of 5,000 Chinese in Singapore in 1942, or the death of some 40,000 Filipinos and 5,000 Americans during the Bataan Death March in that same year.[38] Instead of references to Japanese militarism and imperialism against Asian nations, discussion of wartime is largely limited to the hardship of domestic conditions.[39] The product is a curiously ahistorical memorial, best captured by the engraving on the Park's central cenotaph, which reads (trans-lated): "Please rest in peace; for we shall not repeat the mistake." The elegy is ambiguous in two regards: who are "we," and what was the "mistake"? The favored interpretation is the universalist we and the global mistake of our human willingness for atomic annihilation. A more deliberate interpretation, of course, would make either the Japanese or the Americans the "we," and either side's military actions the "mistake."

The potential controversy of any memorial museum is typically shaped by the prevailing attitudes towards the event in question in their home nation. Has the nation made a decisive break from the conditions of the event depicted by the museum, or do they linger? At one end of the spectrum there are pasts widely considered settled. In this context, where an historic break has been made, the memorial museum can represent triumph over adversity; the struggle is vindicated by the eventual beneficial outcome. Such museums – I have in mind the apartheid-themed District Six Museum in Cape Town or the Hiroshima Peace Memorial Museum – can be characterized as *offering lessons*. At the other end of the spectrum there are nations where elements of the violence being represented by memorial museums are felt to continue to threaten (such as the various 9/11 memorials, or the Memorial Center Srebrenica – Potocari, where thousands of slaughtered Bosnian Muslims are buried). In these situations, where the museum exists in the midst of the event's ongoing repercussions, the institution can be characterized as *staging an intervention*. In an area in between, there exist a variety of "unmastered pasts" in nations like China, Cambodia, Rwanda, Armenia, Argentina and Chile. Working with the premise that a painful history cannot remain safely buried, for fear it might re-emerge in politically catastrophic ways, museums in these nations aim to establish the veracity and visibility of the event, and might be characterized as *bringing to light*.[40] Given these various roles, we should recognize that the ethics of representation is not a one-size-fits-all situation, but depends on the sensitivities and restrictions of each context.

In conclusion, memorial museums face an insurmountable test of ethics, insofar as they are judged as a preventive educational bulwark against real world outcomes (the "never again" standard). This formidable test reveals the possibilities for positive intervention, but also speaks to the practical limitations of the work of cultural institutions as they might impact mighty political changes. Beyond this question, the key issue – who has the clearest claim to "own" the memory and interpretation of tragedy? – is being fought along lines that acknowledge that museum effects, such as the display of often confrontational objects and images, exhibition design and architectural preservation, and levels of patronage from governments, community leaders or NGOs, have significant political utility.

Compared to other history museums, ethics at memorial museums have a greater attachment to current day politics – both in a general sense of bringing difficult pasts into a contemporary frame and, in a more specific sense, via their relation to the judicial-legal context of legal evidence. Concrete political attempts to establish – and partially recover – what history has damaged have been guided by the Holocaust, which acts as the standard and model for reparative justice.[41] Political attempts to correct aspects of the past include the establishment of special courts and national and international truth and reconciliation commissions. Actions might be focused on the material-economic, in the form of financial payments to individuals and groups or the return of land. Importantly, reparations can also be symbolic. Along with, for instance, the issuance of diplomatic apologies from current or former leaders, or the provision of a proper burial ground for exhumed corpses, support for the creation of memorials and museums forms a significant symbolic act. In these situations, detrimentally affected communities increasingly come to assert public representation of their suffering as a key moral and political expectation.

Memorial museums have an unusually important place among civil institutions. Rather than conceive them as a byproduct or subsidiary educational arm of concrete political actions, they should be understood as a vital means to challenge museums to be pushed towards initiating public awareness about past events that is newly required or overdue. As Andreas Huyssen has put it:

> ... discussions about how to remember the past have morphed into an international debate about human rights, restitution, and justice, replete with NGOs (nongovernmental organizations), extradition requests, and prosecution across borders. This debate depends on the recognition of specific pasts as much as it is really concerned with the future.[42]

Atrocities now occur within a memory culture in which "national patrimony and heritage industries thrive, nostalgias of all kinds abound, and mythic pasts are being resurrected or created."[43] Memorial museums are especially politically useful in the way they concretize and distil an event. By providing a tangible sense of a topic that would lack a physical place, existing only in personal memories, and in disparate books, films, websites and so on, political activism is projected onto and interpreted through the shape of the physical memorial museum. Hence, they serve as surrogate homes for debates that would otherwise be placeless. While courts and truth commissions are other spaces that support historical re-examination, they are chiefly involved in direct, high-level legal questions concerning prosecution, amnesty, compensation and suchlike. Somewhat fuzzier and perhaps underrecognized aspects of the event, such as the experiences and memories of everyday people, or the quality of emotional hurt, often now find themselves translated into the architecture and exhibition design of memorial museums. In this, memorial museums potentially serve a valuable social role as spaces that can provide a public forum for discussion: it is their very ability to stand for unpopular ideas, to be battered by and absorb criticism, and to weather the storm of political sea-changes, that makes them suitable vessels for histories that, due to their severity, will likely remain essentially contested.

Notes

1 See International Council of Museums, ICOM Code of Ethics for Museums, 2006. Online. Available HTTP: http://icom.museum/ethics.html#introduction (accessed 9 August 2009).
2 T. P. Brown, "Trauma, Museums and the Future of Pedagogy," *Third Text*, No. 18, 2004, p. 249.
3 Quoted in J. M. Klein, "From the Ashes, a Jewish Museum," *American Prospect* 12: 3, 2001. Online. Available HTTP: http://www.prospect.org/cs/articles?article=from_the_ashes_a_jewish_museum (accessed 9 August 2009).
4 See http://www.prospect.org/cs/articles?article=from_the_ashes_a_jewish_museum.
5 Ibid.

6 Ibid.

7 M. Sturken, *Tangled Memories: The Vietnam War, the AIDS Epidemic, and the Politics of Remembering*, Berkeley, CA: University of California Press, 1997, p. 45.

8 E. T. Linenthal, *Preserving Memory: The Struggle to Create America's Holocaust Museum*, New York: Columbia University Press, 2001, p. 213.

9 Ibid., p. 213.

10 AP, "Cambodia Skull Map Dismantled," *CNN World*, 10 March 2002. Online. Available HTTP: http://archives.cnn.com/2002/WORLD/asiapcf/southeast/03/10/cambodia.skulls/index.html (accessed 29 July 2009).

11 Quoted in "The Dead are Ever Present," *New York Times*, 26 February 2004, p. A8.

12 "The Dead are Ever Present," p. A8.

13 See V. Casey, "The Museum Effect: Gazing from Object to Performance in the Contemporary Cultural History Museum," paper given at International Cultural Heritage Informatics meeting: *Proceedings from ichim03*, Paris: Archives and Museum Informatics, 2003.

14 B. Kirshenblatt-Gimblett, *Destination Culture: Tourism, Museums, and Heritage*, Berkeley, CA: University of California Press, 1998, p. 194.

15 S. Sontag, *Regarding the Pain of Others*, New York: Farrar Straus & Giroux, 2003, p. 77.

16 A. Azoulay, *Death's Showcase: The Power of Image in Contemporary Democracy*, Cambridge, MA: MIT Press, 2001, p. 285.

17 This interpretation is provided by the Director of the Museum of Occupations, Tallinn. H. Ahonen, "Occupations Question," e-mail, 6 April 2006.

18 U. Baer, *Spectral Evidence: The Photography of Trauma*, Cambridge, MA: MIT Press, 2002, p. 13.

19 Hamburg Institute for Social Research, "Crimes of the German Wehrmacht," 1995. Online. Available HTTP: http://www.verbrechen-der-wehrmacht.de/ (accessed 26 May 2009).

20 S. Madievski, "The War of Extermination: The Crimes of the Wehrmacht in 1941 to 1944," *Rethinking History* 7: 2, 2003, pp. 243–54.

21 M. M. Langer, *Merleau-Ponty's Phenomenology of Perception: A Guide and Commentary*, London: Macmillan, 1989, p. 15.

22 A. Charlesworth and M. Addis, "Memorialization and the Ecological Landscapes of Holocaust Sites: the Cases of Plaszow and Auschwitz-Birkenau," *Landscape Research* 27: 3, 2002, p. 246.

23 Cited in *F.A.Z. Electronic Media*, "Is it a Memorial or a Playground?" 20 May 2005. Online. Available HTTP: http://www.faz.net/s/Rub9E75B460C0744F8695B3E0BE5A30A620/Doc~E5F6F57D35B0D4BE588433252BEF12242~ATpl~Ecommon~Scontent.html (accessed 26 May 2009).

24 Ibid.

25 Quoted in D. Lisle. "Gazing at Ground Zero: Tourism, Voyeurism and Spectacle," *Journal for Cultural Research* 8: 1, 2004, p. 11.

26 J. Taylor, *Body Horror: Photojournalism, Catastrophe and War*, Manchester: Manchester University Press, 1998, p. 40.

27 P. Williams, "The Atrocity Exhibition: Touring Cambodian Genocide Memorials," in L. Wevers and A. Smith (eds.) *On Display: Essays in Cultural Tourism*, Wellington, NZ: Victoria University Press and Fergus Barrowman, 2004, p. 203.

28 M. Farhi, "Courage to Forget," *Index on Censorship* 2, 2005, pp. 23–24.

29 Cited in S. Krakover, "Attitudes of Israeli Visitors towards the Holocaust Remembrance Site of Yad Vashem," in G. Ashworth and R. Hartmann (eds.) *Horror and Human Tragedy Revisited: The Management of Sites of Atrocity for Tourism*, New York: Cognizant Communication Corporation, 2005, p. 112.

30 H. Süssner, "Still Yearning for the Lost *Heimat*? Ethnic German Expellees and the Politics of Belonging," *German Politics and Society* 22: 2, 2004, p. 1.

31 C. Hawley, "Is the World Ready for German Victimhood?" *Der Spiegel* (English edn), 4 November 2005. Online. Available HTTP: http://service.spiegel.de/cache/international/0,1518,383263,00.html (accessed 31 January 2009).

32 H. Henning Hahn et al., "For a Critical and Enlightened Debate about the Past," *Bohemistik*, August 2003. Online. Available HTTP: http://www.bohemistik.de/zentrumgb.html (accessed 31 January 2009).

33 Quoted in L. Abend and G. Pingree, "Spain's Path to 3/11 Memorial," *Christian Science Monitor*, 4 July 2004, p. 7.
34 D. W. Dunlap, "Alphabetical, Random or Otherwise, Names are a Ground Zero Puzzle," *New York Times*, 2 April 2006, p. 7.
35 Quoted in E. T. Linenthal, *The Unfinished Bombing: Oklahoma City in American History*, Oxford: Oxford University Press, 2001, p. 234.
36 Oklahoma City National Memorial, "Education and Programs," *Oklahoma City National Memorial*, 2005. Online. Available HTTP: http://www.oklahomacitynationalmemorial.org/educ.htm (accessed 27 October 2008).
37 L. Yoneyama, "Remembering and Imagining the Nuclear Annihilation in Hiroshima," *Getty Conservation Institute Newsletter* 17: 2, 2002, p. 17.
38 B. Giamo, "The Myth of the Vanquished: The Hiroshima Peace Memorial Museum," *American Quarterly* 55: 4, 2003, p. 705.
39 D. Seltz, "Remembering the War and the Atomic Bomb," in D. Walkowiz and L. Knauer (eds.) *Memory and the Impact of Political Transformation in Public Space*, Durham, NC: Duke University Press, 2004, p. 131.
40 See T. W. Adorno, "What does Coming to Terms with the Past Mean?" in G. H. Hartmann (ed.) *Bitburg in Moral and Political Perspective*, Bloomington, IN: Indiana University Press, 1986, p. 128.
41 J. Torpey, *Making Whole What has been Smashed: On Reparation Politics*, Cambridge, MA: Harvard University Press, 2006, p. 37.
42 A. Huyssen, *Present Pasts: Urban Palimpsests and the Politics of Memory*, Stanford, CA: Stanford University Press, 2003, p. 95.
43 Ibid.

Part III

THE RADICAL POTENTIAL OF MUSEUM TRANSPARENCY

15
Cultural equity in the sustainable museum

Tristram Besterman

The recognition of the need for both personal and political responsibility and accountability leads people to the realization of the importance of democratic governance.

Wangari Maathai[1]

Museums and accountable stewardship

Across the world, people are experiencing the effects of living unsustainably. From climate change and environmental degradation to irrational money markets and corrupt regimes, what is unsustainable seems self-defining and increasingly predictable. Opinion on what constitutes a sustainable alternative, however, is divided. Regardless of how it is defined, living sustainably means that humanity will be held to account by future generations for the responsible stewardship of the planet and its resources.

Museums are manifestly not in the business of saving the planet. But they are in the business of stewardship: of tangible cultural resources (scientific, technological and artistic) for the benefit of humankind. This chapter explores the ethical, political and social aspects of the sustainable stewardship of a global resource: the collections in Western museums. I focus on the museum's cultural footprint and how this contributes to a just society, reflecting values of international accountability and transparency.

The vast imbalance between those who benefit from the exploitation of the finite natural and cultural capital of the world and those who suffer its consequences fuels a resentment towards the West and gives a moral edge to the politics of sustainability. It is unsustainable, I argue, for Western museums to act as though they are above the maelstrom: they are part of it and should act as beacons of *cultural equity* to mitigate the deep divisions in society that they may otherwise represent.

Cultural equity describes the values of the sustainable museum, reflected in the transparency and democratic accountability of its conduct. Equity in this context means both "fairness; recourse to the principles of justice to correct or supplement the law,"[2] and a share interest in an enterprise. To the extent that it supplements the law, cultural equity lies precisely in the purview of ethics; as Gary Edson puts it, "Laws restrict activities and define methods or means of compliance. They serve as the minimum standards of social behavior. Ethics defines and describes correct actions for persons working in a specialized profession."[3]

Cultural equity embodies a democratic principle of universal entitlement, of citizens participating in the museum, which does not presume to a monopoly on knowledge and authority, and is concerned with the accountable exercise of power. Cultural equity is conceived as an alternative to the ethic embodied in the *Declaration on the Importance and Value of Universal Museums*.[4] The challenge for museums with encyclopaedic collections is to go beyond the polemic of inter-cultural aesthetics and to open a more democratic debate around trans-cultural accountability.

Cultural capital: a sustainable global resource

In Europe and the United States, many museums possess collections that transcend the boundaries of the modern nation-state and reflect aspects of diverse cultures. Such diaspora collections, possessed by museums in developed nations of increasingly diverse ethnicity today, challenge traditional notions of personal and corporate accountability, as ideas of representation and cultural identity are debated in a fragile world of increasing volatility and global interdependence.

Historically, the extended frontiers of empire from the eighteenth to the mid-twentieth centuries provided rich pickings for institutions and individuals, be they curator, private collector, scholar, colonial administrator, traveller, entrepreneur or the merely curious. The resulting collections by various means became concentrated in a range of museums maintained within Western democracies. Today, the disproportionate wealth of individuals and institutions continues to render the borders of the modern nation state selectively permeable to the flow of cultural objects, long after the geopolitical frontiers of the colonial era retreated. The traded transfer of cultural patrimony from nations rich in art and antiquities into museums with buying power in the developed world has become the subject of intense debate within the museums community and by journalists and cultural commentators outside that community.[5]

The museums whose democratic credentials I consider here are those that are part of the public realm, instituted under a legal instrument of trust (regardless of how reliant they are on support from the public purse). All such museums have fiduciary obligations to society, on whose behalf they hold collections and for whose benefit they make those collections publicly available. As with all forms of public trust, transparency of process is the strongest guarantor of probity.

Crossing frontiers of accountability

A museum is accountable to many constituencies, some residing beyond the frontier of the democratic state that maintains the museum. In Brighton, a small city on the south coast of England in 2009, I am present as an invited co-facilitator at a meeting between museum staff and an indigenous claimant group, the Ngarrindjeri people from South Australia. The latter have come to Brighton to negotiate the return of the skull of an ancestor, modified for use as a water-carrier by their people in the nineteenth century, when it was collected and taken to England. With the assistance of expert colleagues in Oxford and London, the museum has prepared a well-researched written statement on the historical context and cultural significance of the skull, which cites published observations of European travellers of the time. The museum's report[6] concludes that the skull is "spiritually inert" and that, having been subjected to a funerary ritual prior to modification, "the idea of relatives then performing a further, supplementary, funerary ritual for the cranium seems very unlikely." The Ngarrindjeri elders confide to me an oral tradition of re-burial, whose existence would not normally be shared beyond the appropriate people within the community, hence the lack of documentation relating to these practices in the written record. They allowed an edited version of their statement to be presented as written evidence[7] to the museum's governing body, which then agreed to repatriate the skull.

The divergent narratives from museum and claimant group come from people who act in good faith and care about the meaning of something culturally important. Nonetheless, a scholarly account is challenged and found to be partial, in the sense of being both incomplete and inclining in a particular direction. Furthermore, emotions and beliefs demand recognition as legitimate criteria for our understanding of material culture. There is no parity of authority or entitlement: the Ngarrindjeri people live outside the scope of English law, and in reclaiming their own they come as outsiders. Whilst the museum holds not just the Old Person but also all the legal cards, the indigenous source nation wields nothing more potent than the force of moral argument. Both parties must follow a procedure[8] developed by British curators and scientists in resolving the claim, whose criteria work against the values of cultural equity.[9] The museum is accountable to local councillors and residents, visitors, colleagues and the source nation; in deciding to privilege one group's interests over another's, the museum weighs evidential, legal and ethical criteria of British manufacture. Transparency, in this process, may be compromised by the conventions of scholarship and by cultural sensitivities.

Accountability and the passage of time

"The past is a foreign country": the opening words of L. P Hartley's *The Go-between* provide an apt title to Lowenthal's deconstruction of Western attitudes to heritage.[10] Echoing the distancing effect of geopolitical borders in relation to democratic structures of accountability and control, museums face ethical boundaries of accountability over time. Cultural equity, and the burdens of accountability and transparency that it demands of the museum, is inter-generational: " ... museums and their collections embody human relationships across the four dimensions of space and time. Museums uniquely occupy a contemporary, historic and future place ..."[11] The borders of accountability appear increasingly blurred the more distant they are from the present. It is as though an ethical as well as a legal statute of limitations has become embedded in attitudes to cultural equity. We can measure this accountability gradient in human lifetimes of sixty-two years, a metric devised by Toffler.[12]

In our present lifetime, an antiquity looted and illicitly trafficked since 1970 falls foul of the UNESCO *Convention*[13] to which state governments in Europe and North America, *inter alia*, are signatory. Consequently, any member of museum staff or board who is party to such activity can be prosecuted, as a number of U.S. museums have discovered to their dismay.[14] National standards, professional codes of ethics for museums and institutional policies typically cite and endorse the UNESCO *Convention*.[15]

Just over one lifetime ago, art acquired by museums that was spoliated – taken forcibly from their legal owners by the Axis powers in the Nazi era (1933–45) – is not covered by the UNESCO *Convention*. A conference held in Washington in 1998 acted as a catalyst for action and generated internationally agreed principles[16] on restitution. Since then, governments, museums' professional bodies and museums have met the challenge variously with supervisory structures, policies and changes in statute law to facilitate restitution.[17] All agree that any work that entered a museum after the Second World War, with incomplete or absent documentation for the period 1933–45, should be the subject of careful research. The onus is on the museum to establish ethical possession: an important principle and precedent.

However, the retentive mindset of some museum practitioners can make museums deaf to the human story beyond the contested artefact. Anne Webber, Co-chair of the Commission for Looted Art in Europe, reports[18] conversations with individuals whose relations were murdered by the Nazis. Their experience of some European museums that possessed property looted from their family was of institutions focused exclusively on ownership of objects; whereas, behind the object the human stories that mattered to the family were apparently of no concern to the museum. In some cases, acknowledgement of the human suffering was all that was sought, and its denial by the museum created a sense of continued violation, echoing, in its absence of empathy, the brutal, institutionalised and officially sanctioned attitudes of the era in which the looting occurred.

The British Museum found itself to be in possession of art works that were undoubtedly spoliated.[19] However, to return them to the rightful heirs would have entailed a breach of parliamentary statute: "Objects vested in the Trustees as part of the collections of the Museum shall not be disposed of by them … "[20] Recognising the wrong that the law inadvertently perpetuated, Parliament intervened. In 2009, a Bill[21] was passed unopposed, which allows seventeen named museums to transfer objects from their collections under prescribed conditions. When the Bill was debated in the House of Lords, Baroness Deech observed that the museum visitor is tainted by association:

> Art is an ethical issue. Displaying looted art, once it is known to be such, is not just an invasion of privacy … it is also putting on show something that the owners never meant to be seen in such circumstances. It has ceased to be an object of beauty and one that museums can be proud of or use for educational and aesthetic aims. The spectator cannot look at it without seeing the pain and betrayal that led it to be situated there in a national museum. It taints the spectators who knowingly take advantage of the presence of the picture there and it speaks to them of loss and war, not creativity and insight.[22]

By contrast, Norman Rosenthal, former exhibitions secretary at the Royal Academy in London, believes that

> ... history is history and you can't turn the clock back or make things good through art ... grandchildren or distant relations of people who had works of art or property taken by the Nazis do not now have an inalienable right of ownership ... [23]

The fact that the British Parliament has had to intervene to find a statutory remedy to injustice stored in its national museums is not in itself remarkable. That is, after all, how a democracy should work. What could well undermine public trust in these museums is that the necessary legislative changes have been brought about despite, rather than because of, the lead given by the national museums concerned.[24] Placing the need to keep the museum's collections intact above all other considerations is not a defence of integrity but its betrayal. Behaviour that might seek justification within the retentive dogma of universalism is exposed as an unedifying derogation of ethical leadership.

Turn the clock back a mere two lifetimes to 1897 and we enter a truly "foreign country" with the British army's "punitive" expedition to Benin City in what is now Nigeria. The brutality of this invasion has been compared with Hitler's advance into the Ukraine.[25] Apart from the carnage caused by British machine guns, the palace of the *oba* (king) was burnt to the ground. The British looted some 3,000 cultural objects, including 900 cast brass plaques and sculptures which decorated the palace. These examples of the sophisticated art of an African people are today to be found mainly in museums in Britain and Germany. No one denies the historic circumstances of their acquisition, though museums are less than transparent about explaining them publicly.

Three lifetimes ago, in the first decade of the nineteenth century, Lord Elgin caused his agents to remove a large group of sculptures from the Parthenon in Athens, many of which were sawn off the building itself. These were destined to decorate the country house he was building in his native Scotland. Elgin claimed to have the authority of a firman, a kind of licence, issued by the Ottoman administrator in Athens. The original document has never been found; only an Italian translation survives, which permits Elgin's men to do no more than draw, measure and take casts of sculpture located *in situ*, and to remove fallen material they found around the temple. Shipped back to Britain, the sculpture made by Pheidias in the fifth century BC was sold in 1816 to the British Parliament by Elgin, who had run out of funds. From Parliament's purchase derives the British Museum's claim to legal title to the Parthenon sculptures today. Classicist Mary Beard quotes the observation of a contemporary eye-witness, who, she points out, shared with Elgin a sufficient understanding of

> the crucial nexus between art, collecting and patriotism to concede grudgingly that " ... while we indignantly reprove and deeply regret the irreplaceable damage that has been done to the Athenian monuments, we must not overlook that advantage which the fine arts in our country will derive from the introduction of such estimable specimens of Grecian art."[26]

Patriotism – accountability to the national interest – was recognised as a worthy motive for importing cultural property from overseas. Today, that same motive by nations wishing to reclaim what they consider to be theirs, is challenged by the philosopher, Kwame Appiah, on the grounds that " ... a great deal of what people wish to protect as 'cultural property' was made before the modern nations came into being, by members of societies that no longer exist."[27]

These cases seem to illustrate a kind of temporal relativism in the ethics of accountability. Go back more than a single lifetime, and the glass of the museum's moral compass loses transparency, though the principles point in the same direction.

Museum collections in the public realm

In teasing out ethical strands of accountability and responsibility, we should distinguish between challenges to the museum's stewardship which may result in the removal of material from the public domain and those which don't. In the former category we can place an indigenous group that reclaims one of their forebears for reburial and the family that re-possesses a painting looted by the Nazis. Arguably, such items entered the public domain illegitimately, so the museum's overriding responsibility is to remedy that injustice. In the latter category, many claims are made by or on behalf of museums, where repatriation would merely transplant cultural objects to another part of the public domain.

When we consider cultural equity in the public domain, we should also distinguish content from tangibility, as the philosopher James O. Young points out:

> Perhaps certain items of intellectual property may belong to all humanity, but the suggestion that tangible property belongs to everyone is not helpful ... . The artistic commons is composed of those artistic elements (styles, motifs, general plots and so on) that anyone is free to appropriate. If we are dealing with tangible property such as individual works of art, the situation is different. All of humanity can share some item of intellectual property in a way that they cannot share a sculpture or a stele. Even if we say that something belongs to humanity, the question of who ought to have custody of it still remains.[28]

Similar issues arise with what one might call the scientific commons. All of humanity has a share in scientific discovery, but that doesn't equate to communal ownership of scientific evidence. Humankind's understanding of vertebrate evolution has gained immeasurably from published research on Cretaceous fossils found in Liaoning, which nonetheless remain the property of the Chinese state.

In 2005 I was invited to work with colleagues in Buenos Aires. I took a day out to go to Plaza Huincul in Patagonia to give to the Museo Carmen Funes some fragments of dinosaur eggshell. These fossils had come to light in the palaeontological collections of the Manchester Museum, of which I was then Director. The specimens had been exported illicitly from Argentina and purchased by the Museum after 1970, so their presence in the Museum's collections was unethical and against its own policy. The financial value of the fossils was negligible and the Museo Carmen Funes already had a large research collection of such material. However, the repatriation was front page news in Argentina,[29] the Culture Minister in person thanked me and the mayor of Plaza Huincul hosted a press conference when I arrived. What galvanised politicians, media and local people was the idea that a museum in a distant, rich and powerful European nation should concern itself with the restitution of their cultural patrimony. It was a humbling experience and brought home to me the significance that can be attached to a modest gesture of ethical accountability. Science, too, was well served by an act of restitution that has kept objects in the public domain. A research partnership between palaeontologists in Patagonia and Manchester, based on the principles of cultural equity, has flourished to the benefit of scientific and local communities.

In a discussion of museum ethics framed within the context of cultural equity, placing the focus on the relational aspects of the museum's purpose raises the suspicion that its role as steward of collections is sidelined. However, for all museum practitioners and trustees, regardless of their views on the primary purpose of the museum, the legitimacy of title to objects entrusted to their care must be a matter of fundamental concern, for it goes to the heart of the legitimacy of the museum itself. That is where the true integrity of the collections can be debated.

Authenticity, transparency and context

As Harold Pinter argued, "There are no hard distinctions between what is real and what is unreal, nor between what is true and what is false. A thing is not necessarily either true or false; it can be both true and false."[30] The playwright's observation may smack of moral relativism and be couched within the context of theatre, but Pinter was a man who "forces entry into oppression's closed rooms."[31] His message has resonance for the social *locus* of the museum, which can exclude people from its "closed rooms" in a way that recollects and conserves past oppression.

The British Museum's "world under one roof" was established, the Director informs us, to enable "the truth to emerge" from "the study of things gathered together from all over the world"; moreover, this is "not one perpetual truth, but truth as a living, changing thing, constantly remade as hierarchies are subverted, new information comes, and new understandings of society emerge."[32] MacGregor's recognition that truth is mutable, evanescent and often relative – my truth may be different from yours – runs counter to museum orthodoxy.

In their eagerness to interpret material evidence, museums should be humble about their capacity to "represent" peoples or environments, be they contemporary or from the past. From fragments that emerge into the public gaze through a typically capricious, arcane and opaque selection process, museums can at best provide splintered glimpses of art or nature, reflections of a particular set of ideas at a particular time. Yet, museums seldom disclose the sequence of chance events and calculated decisions that result in the display of a particular sculpture, picture, fossil, flint tool or jet engine. Nor is the source of authority of the voice in its interpretation discussed. In this most essential part of the museum's relationship with society there is a conspicuous lack of transparency in museum presentation. Pinter's ghost has its place, but the encouragement of a willing suspension of disbelief on the part of the observer belongs in the theatre, not the museum.

The socially astute museum is keenly aware of the need to diversify the authorial voice, and is willing to cede control of the narrative. By transparently dismantling the traditional structures of editorial control, the museum redefines the terms of its accountability to society and creates new forms of engagement between audience, object and museum.

Handing over galleries and collections to the sometimes subversive curatorship of contemporary artists has become relatively commonplace over the last twenty years. Reflecting on the run-away success in 2009 of an invited "invasion" by the street artist Banksy, Bristol Museum and Art Gallery exchanged the safe role of editor-in-chief for the risk-taking one of facilitator:

> We took the risk and managed it, we prepared the ground by developing values that stressed new approaches and doing things differently ... Giving up control is anathema for an organisation such as ours. Museums have built their reputations on their reliability and authority ... The rewards for giving up control were that we had lots of new visitors, and even our regular visitors seemed to appreciate a new-found freedom, seeing the museum and its collections in a new light.[33]

Making it up? The challenge to transparency

In allowing voices from beyond the museum's sphere of control to influence the interpretation and disposition of collections, to what extent is it acceptable for the museum to be absolved of responsibility for narrative "truth"? Is it enough to encourage in the visitor a more questioning approach to the voice within the museum, or is the museum still ultimately accountable to the visitor for the evidential reliability of the information with which it is associated? This is an issue with the transparency of the museum's role as interlocutor at its core.

The resolution of the claim by the Ngarrindjeri people to the museum in Brighton raised precisely these issues. In their research, the museum drew on the published observations of white, European visitors to South Australia in the nineteenth century.[34] These describe contemporary cultural practices through white man's eyes.[35]

The museum should be vigilant to ensure such testimony is untainted. Angas, an artist who became director of the Australian Museum, did indeed depict Ngarrindjeri platform burials. But he would have been aware that such Indigenous burial sites were, as Hemming and Wilson report, "a systematic target for looting and 'collecting', as there was a growing demand for the remains of 'Aboriginal people'."[36]

The sceptic might argue that it's all very well for the Ngarrindjeri elders to claim oral tradition as their authority, but how do we know they are not making it up, or at the very least putting a convenient spin on the story to support their claim? Just such issues of "cultural falsification" surfaced when the so-called Hindmarsh Island affair was debated in the press, and fought in the courtroom and the political arena over the "truth" of Aboriginal claims.[37]

In 1994 a group of Ngarrindjeri women halted a proposed commercial development when they claimed that it would violate a secret, sacred women's site on Hindmarsh Island, in the Murray River in South Australia. A second group of Ngarrindjeri women came forward a year later and denied the existence on the island of secret sacred women's business. The conclusions of a Royal Commission that the claim of sacredness had been fabricated were subsequently ruled in court to have been unsound. In the dispute between parties, the judge characterised the anthropologists as acting as advocates, akin to lawyers.[38]

The national debate around Hindmarsh Island transplanted Aboriginal fragmentation into the body politic of Australia. Simons[39] regards it as emblematic of a fractured society, dysfunctional academe, environmental degradation and just how elusive objective truth can be, especially when the quest is pursued by a deeply flawed process, in which evidence was selectively suppressed and spun.

The implications for museum practitioners are daunting. Among the many lessons to be learned from Hindmarsh Island is that a claim from an Indigenous community from the other side of the globe is likely to have a context that is both contemporary and historical, many-layered and subtly nuanced: in other words uncomfortably challenging to neatly packaged Western notions of verifiable truth.

Transparency and language

There is an uncertain kind of scholarly museum language, characterised by such phrases as "thought to have been" or "there is evidence to suggest" or "it is likely that," which serves to detach the authorial voice but also distances the reader from narrative engagement. It is a linguistic form that is transparent in communicating the distinction between what is known and what is conjectural. This is defensible in the interpretation of, say, the excavated antiquities of an ancient people or the intentions of a long-dead artist. In the case of communicating the culture of a people who are still around, it is inexcusably opaque: the museum can and should lift the epistemic veil and elicit first-hand testimony from those in the know. Otherwise, from the perspective of the source community, as Wangari Maathai puts it, "It is like we have looked at ourselves through another person's mirror – and seen only cracked reflections and distorted images."[40]

The Western-educated curatorial voice short-changes the public and perpetuates cultural misappropriation by denying the source community a voice in the dialogue mediated through the object. The presence of diaspora communities in Western society provides a resource for the museum to invite participation in a conversation in which objects from the collection act as prompts to recall narratives based on personal experience. In the process, a creative alchemy takes place, transforming the object from something mute and out of time into a vital cultural resonator, and the museum into a "contact zone," the term coined by Mary Louise Pratt.[41]

Take, for example, Mohammed El-Bahari, who is from southern Sudan, now living in Manchester. Out of a group of objects from Sudan in the Manchester Museum, he picks up a spear about a century after it was collected. Beginning with an explanation of its precise tribal affiliation and use for self-protection and hunting small animals, a more personal story emerges as he describes a land dispute in his village before he left Sudan. During an argument, tempers flare and in the ensuing mêlée one of the protagonists is killed instantly when "a spear like this" goes through his heart. A relic of the colonial encounter is transformed into something contemporary, personal and compelling. El-Bahari's story is accessible to the museum's users across the globe through its posting on YouTube, along with several hundred other "Collective Conversations" to which viewers can add their comments.[42]

The Manchester experience precisely reflects Clifford's observations of what transpired with the Tlingit at the Portland Museum of Art in Oregon, where the exchanges

> did not primarily illuminate or contextualize the objects of the [collection]. Rather, the objects provoked (called forth, brought to voice) ongoing stories of struggle. From the position of the collecting museum and the consulting curator, this was a disruptive history which could not be confined to providing past tribal context for the objects. The museum was called to a sense of its responsibility, its stewardship of the clan objects.[43]

In Oxford University's Pitt Rivers Museum, there is a collection of thirty-three photographic portraits of the Kainai First Nation taken by an anthropologist in Alberta, Canada in the 1920s. Today, anthropologists Laura Peers and Alison Brown describe a process in which authority over the narrative voice is restored to the source community:

> Some eighty years later, copies of these photographs have been returned to the Kainai Nation, through a visual repatriation project that considers the contemporary meanings of the images to Kainai people ... This project has demonstrated that research methodology is crucial to uncovering knowledge, meanings, and discursive formations surrounding artefacts, especially those which were acquired in circumstances of intellectual and political colonial control. Over the years, many Aboriginal people have talked to us about the legacy of mistrust of museums and anthropologists amongst their communities ... We have also been told of the misinterpretations and errors within ethnographic texts and archival sources that are still drawn upon by researchers, Native and non-Native. It has been patiently explained to us that communities need to reinterpret historical documents and photographs in their own way, for their own purposes, and to ensure that their histories are presented in their own words.[44]

Cultural legacy in source communities today: are museums accountable?

Within many source communities the colonial era is no distant reverberation, but the cause of an all too present and keenly felt social dislocation in the here and now. The appropriation of indigenous culture by Western collectors started four centuries ago and reached its peak in the nineteenth and early twentieth centuries. This activity disrupted systems of belief and oral traditions that typically spoke of the relationship of a people with the land. Authority, dignity, responsibility and self-determination drew sustenance from a long-established order of things. Cultural artefacts – and human remains – are emblematic of those collective values. When removed to Western museums, it is not only the object that is de-contextualised, but also the makers and users of the object. Continued possession and representation in the Western museum may impede the source community's ability to take back responsibility for its own destiny. Wangari Maathai expresses the same principle:

> Culture is the means by which a people expresses itself, through language, traditional wisdom, politics, religion, architecture, music, tools, greetings, symbols, festivals, ethics, values, and collective identity ... Whether written or oral, the political, historical, and spiritual heritage of a community forms its cultural record, passed from one generation to another, with each generation building on the experience of the previous one.
>
> Culture gives a people self-identity and character. It allows them to be in harmony with their physical and spiritual environment, to form the basis for their sense of self-fulfilment and personal peace. It enhances their ability to guide themselves, make their own decisions, and protect their interests. It's their reference point to the past and their antennae to the future. Conversely, without culture, a community loses self-awareness and guidance, and grows weak and vulnerable. It disintegrates from within as it suffers a lack of identity, dignity, self-respect and a sense of destiny.[45]

If repatriating cultural identity and control is key to African peoples taking responsibility for their lives today, the same is true elsewhere. In parts of Australia, Aborigines live at or beyond the margins of society in a self-destructive spiral of abuse and addiction. In her account of the death of an Aboriginal man in 2004 in police custody, Chloe Hooper describes the dysfunctional context of some Aboriginal communities. She suggests a cause of the cycle of abuse that goes down the generations "must be people being forcibly taken from their parents, who had in turn been taken from their parents, who'd been taken from theirs."[46] The programme of state-sponsored Indigenous assimilation, now referred to as the Stolen Generation, involved some 100,000 aboriginal children who were taken from their families to be raised in institutions or adopted by white families between about 1880 and 1960. Tom Tevorrow, an Elder of the Ngarrindjeri nation, makes the connection with the grave-robbing that supplied museums with the bodies of his nation's Old People in the nineteenth century:

> The "First Stolen Generations" were torn from their country and resting places in much the same way as Indigenous children were stolen from their families ... For Ngarrindjeri people, the pain and suffering caused by these acts of racialised power has been handed down through generations.[47]

The discussion about the stolen generations is really a debate about cultural diversity in contemporary Australian society. The museum that engages equitably with an Indigenous source community mediates a process that can contribute, however infinitesimally, to the restoration of a measure of authority, dignity and control to a dispossessed source community. These issues concern the museum's accountability to peoples today as much as to the past, a point lost on the curator who observed, "We are not in the business of redressing historic wrongs."[48] Compare that attitude with the words of Aunty Ida West, a Tasmanian Aborigine, reflecting on the continuing sense of violation caused by the near extirpation of her people by the British in the previous century: "Where the bad was, we can always make it good."[49] In terms of an ethically sustainable position, the museum must decide which set of values shows a greater sense of accountability to humankind.

Enlightenment, access and accountability

Museums that are encyclopaedic in scope are immeasurably enriching and should be valued for celebrating the human spirit in all its diversity of creative expression. In analysing the ethic of the encyclopaedic museum, two propositions need to be separated. The first concerns the benefits to humankind derived from the study and enjoyment of many cultures in one place. The second, which tends to get muddled with the first, concerns the issues raised by the possession of cultural material whose provenance is demonstrably tainted. Alan Howarth, former UK arts minister, extols the cultural benefits that the refurbished British Museum provides to the world, when he quotes David Attenborough:

> " ... we will once more be able to view superb golden jewels made for the kings of East Anglia, and others, equally astonishing, made for the emperors of the Andes. We will be able to compare delicate textiles woven in China with others made in the forests of Borneo ... we may admire the superb statuary of ancient Egypt, then walk a few yards and be astonished and moved by the great masterpieces of sculpture from sub-Saharan Africa."
>
> This universal museum, this place of big ideas, cannot be reconciled with the narrow claim that because a thing was made in a particular geographical place, it should be returned to it. Modern nationalism seems small-minded in an institution which embraces the world.[50]

That description captures the undeniable pleasures and enlightenment experienced by those who can get there when they wander through well-lit galleries in London, Paris, New York and Madrid. After all, "The British Museum's collection is world-wide in origin and is intended for use by the citizens of the world."[51] But as the independent commentator and strong advocate for restitution, Kwame Opoku, points out, the Director of the British Museum "does not appear to be embarrassed that Kenyans, Ghanaians, Nigerians, Ethiopians and others have to come to his museum in London in order to seek materials for their history."[52] That some citizens are privileged to be able to sample aspects of cultures from around the globe in one place is a social good, particularly if it is a source of creative inspiration, combats prejudice and leads to better understanding between peoples. Bringing ancient Chinese, Persian, Mesopotamian and Nigerian culture to London is a political as well as a cultural act. But the traffic is usually one-way. The 2009 exhibition, *Dynasty and Divinity: Ife Art in Ancient Nigeria*, opened in Santander, toured to New York and London, but was not seen in any African country. The fact that all of the self-appointed universal museums are in Europe and North America is the result of a conflicted history that cannot be unmade. Whilst that is, arguably, not a reason to call into question their legitimacy, it should, nonetheless, be a cause for the encyclopaedic museum to reflect on its obligations to global constituencies and context.

It is too easy to accuse, or worse still to dismiss, encyclopaedic museums for being full of the loot of empire. However, as even one of their staunchest defenders, Alan Howarth, concedes, "there are aspects of the history of the accumulation of the great museum collections that we must deprecate from our twenty-first-century perspective."[53] Whilst the British Museum resists challenges to its possession of looted art and antiquities, its reluctance to open up a public debate on the issues appears increasingly unsustainable. Regardless of how unscientific the self-selected sample of nearly 130,000 votes cast in a poll run by a British newspaper[54] after the opening of the new Acropolis Museum, the fact that 94.8 per cent of respondents said yes to the return of the sculptures to Athens and only 5.2 per cent voted no indicates an issue that should, at the very least, be properly and publicly debated with the museum. Both Parliament and the "fourth estate" challenge and hold the museum to account in expressing the will of the people.

In engaging transparently with their diverse constituencies, museums need to "hone their listening skills and to watch their language."[55] These are key attributes of the mediator. As Opoku patiently explains, "I often feel that many of the controversies regarding restitution could be solved or at least rendered less acrimonious if the holding museums used sensible and less offensive language and behaviour."[56]

Cultural equity and accountability: redefining the encyclopaedic museum

In museums from Cambridge to Götheborg, an alternative, radical and socially reflexive praxis is taking root. In terms of their collections' encyclopaedic scope, these museums could claim the kind of universalism declared by museums elsewhere. That they don't is an expression of an entirely different ethic, one rooted in cultural equity. The author Tom Flynn argues that this kind of approach embodies a new form of enlightenment:

> We have seen, and continue to see, evidence of new visionary thinking among more progressive museum professionals. Many of them do nurture a vision of a more enlightened museology, grounded not in further encyclopaedic accumulation, ownership and confrontation, but in collaboration, co-operation and exchange. This may require replacing the outdated model of the temple with that of the forum in order to account for the museum's changing social function in a rapidly changing world. However, that need not represent a dissolution of its primary responsibility to engage and educate. Instead it could endow the museum with a new function: to use the exchange of material culture to help build social cohesion.[57]

Sweden's National Museums of World Culture put a sustainable relationship with the world at the centre of their mission, which undertakes that "the cultural heritage is used as an active force in promoting sustainable global development."[58] They state that this is a commitment which they share with their government and parliament, to which the museum is accountable.

Historic and continuing imbalances of power and unsustainable consumption that privilege the peoples of the developed world at the expense of the rest of humanity and the environment are recognised as the root causes of many ills that beset humankind. Museums are not to blame for this pathology in global equity, but in recognising that they and their collections derive from, and are emblematic of, such imbalances, the values of cultural equity become a symbolic means of redress. Museums send out a powerful message when they recognise their accountability to peoples, hitherto denied a voice, both within and beyond the borders of the state.

Museums, like the philosophy of Christopher Hamilton, can afford to be "less interested in finding answers than in finding the right questions to ask. We may all be confused in the end, but we can share our confusion in a productive kind of way."[59] The challenge to museum practitioners is to relinquish the comfort of old certainties and embrace the richer, more egalitarian territory of productive confusion, the very antithesis of the taxonomies of knowledge and hierarchies of authority that have been the cornerstones of the Western museum for so long. The dividend will be to bring humanity back into the museum, and the museum more sustainably back to humanity.

Notes

1 W. Maathai, *The Challenge for Africa: a New Vision*, London: Heinemann, 2009, p. 171.
2 H. W. Fowler and F. G. Fowler, *The Concise Oxford Dictionary of Current English*, Oxford: Oxford University Press, 1976, p. 350.
3 G. Edson, 'Ethics', in G. Edson (ed.) *Museum Ethics*, London and New York: Routledge, 1997, p. 9.
4 Cleveland Museum of Art, *Declaration on the Importance and Value of Universal Museums*. Online. Available HTTP: http://www.clemusart.com/ASSETS/37CD35CFA0F6454EAFE2-C5EAA2714919/UniversalMuseums.pdf (accessed 3 June 2009).
5 See, for example, J. Cuno (ed.) *Whose Culture? The Promise of Museums and the Debate over Antiquities*, Princeton, NJ: Princeton University Press, 2009; T. Flynn, 'The Universal Museum: A Valid Model for the Twenty-first Century?' Online. Available HTTP: www.tomflynn.co.uk/UniversalMuseum.html (accessed 3 July 2009); K. Opoku, 'When will everybody finally accept that the British Museum is a British institution? Comments on a lecture by Neil MacGregor'. Online. Available HTTP: http://www.modernghana.com/news/203507/1/when-will-everybody-finally-accept-that-the-britis.html (accessed 16 July 2009); K. Opoku, 'Whose "Universal Museum"? Comments on James Cuno's *Whose Culture?*' Online. Available HTTP: http://www.modernghana.com/news/212197/50/whose-universal-museum-comments-on-james-cunos-who.html (accessed 2 June 2009); C. Renfrew, *Loot, Legitimacy and Ownership*, London: Duckworth, 2006; M. J. Reppas, 'Empty "International" Museums' Trophy Cases of their Looted Treasures and Return Stolen Property to the Countries of Origin and the Rightful Heirs of those Wrongfully Dispossessed', *Denver Journal of International Law and Policy* 36: 1, 2007, pp. 93–123; L. Rothfield, *The Rape of Mesopotamia: Behind the Looting of the Iraq Museum*, Chicago: University of Chicago Press, 2009.
6 Brighton and Hove Museums, 'Claim for the repatriation of a water vessel made from a human cranium', report prepared by the World Art section for the Human Remains Working Group, Royal Pavilion and Museums, November 2008, unpublished; the original documentation can be examined on application to the Head of Collections and Interpretation at Brighton and Hove Museums, Royal Pavilion Gardens, Brighton, East Sussex BN1 1EE, United Kingdom.
7 M. Sumner and G. Trevorrow, 'Claim for the repatriation of a Ngarrindjeri Old Person (modified as a water vessel)', commentary by Ngarrindjeri Representatives, 15 May 2009,

unpublished; the original documentation can be examined on application to the Head of Collections and Interpretation at Brighton and Hove Museums, Royal Pavilion Gardens, Brighton, East Sussex BN1 1EE, United Kingdom.

8 UK government, *Guidance for the Care of Human Remains in Museums*, London: Department of Culture Media and Sport, 2005.

9 T. Besterman, 'Why the British Museum should give back Maori human remains if it wants to take a truly enlightened approach', *Museums Journal*, July 2008, p. 17.

10 D. Lowenthal, *The Past is a Foreign Country*, Cambridge: Cambridge University Press, 1985, p. xvi.

11 T. Besterman, 'Museum ethics', in S. Macdonald (ed.) *A Companion to Museum Studies*, Malden, MA: Blackwell, 2006, p. 432.

12 A. Toffler, *Future Shock*, London: Pan Books, 1971, p. 22.

13 UNESCO (1970) *Convention on the Means of Prohibiting and Preventing the Illicit Import, Export and Transfer of Ownership of Cultural Property*, 1970. Online. Available HTTP: http://portal.unesco. org/en/ev.php-URL_ID=13039&URL_DO=DO_TOPIC&URL_SECTION=201.html (accessed 15 July 2009).

14 Cuno, *Whose Culture?* p.13.

15 See, for example, ICOM, *Code of Ethics for Museums*, 2006, section 7.2. Online. Available HTTP: http://icom.museum/ethics.html#section2 (accessed 6 June 2009); Museums Association, *Code of Ethics for Museums*, 2008, p. 10, section 5.10. Online. Available HTTP: http://www.museumsassociation.org/ma/10934 (accessed 19 May 2009); Museums, Libraries and Archives Council, *The Accreditation Scheme for Museums in the United Kingdom: Accreditation Standard*, 2004, p. 33, section 4.1.3. Online. Available HTTP: http://www.mla. gov.uk/what/raising_standards/accreditation/accreditation_application (accessed 10 July 2009); American Association of Museums, *Standards regarding Archaeological Material and Ancient Art*, 2008, pp. 1–2. Online. Available HTTP: http://www.aam-us.org/museumresources/ethics/standards_ancientart.cfm (accessed 4 September 2009); University College London, *Cultural Property Policy*, 2009, p. 10. Online. Available HTTP: http://www.ucl.ac. uk/cultural-property/policy.shtml (accessed 25 October 2009).

16 United States Department of State, *Washington Conference Principles on Nazi-confiscated Art*; released in connection with the Washington conference on Holocaust Era assets, Washington, DC, 3 December 1998. Online. Available HTTP: http://www.state.gov/ www/regions/eur/981203_heac_art_princ.html (accessed 16 September 2009).

17 Canadian Jewish Congress Charities Committee, webography, *A Compilation of Links to Resources and Research Sites pertaining to Looted Art*. Online. Available HTTP: http://www. cjccc.ca/holocaust/nazi_looted_art_link4.html (accessed 5 September 2009).

18 Anne Weber, personal communication with the author.

19 D. Hirst, *Report of the Spoliation Advisory Panel in Respect of Four Drawings now in the Possession of the British Museum*, London: House of Commons, 2006. Online. Available HTTP: www.culture.gov.uk/images/publications/HC1052_SAPreport.pdf (accessed 8 June 2009).

20 UK Parliament, *British Museum Act*, 1963, p. 2. Online. Available HTTP: www.britishmuseum. org/PDF/BM1963Act.pdf (accessed 24 June 2009).

21 UK Parliament, *Holocaust (Stolen Art) Restitution Bill* [changed to *Holocaust (Return of Cultural Objects) Bill*], 2009. London: UK Government. Online. Available HTTP: http://www. publications.parliament.uk/pa/cm200809/cmbills/111/09111.i-i.html (accessed 17 June 2009).

22 UK Parliament, *Holocaust (Return of Cultural Objects) Bill*, second reading, House of Lords debates, 10 July 2009, 11:45 a.m. Online. Available HTTP: http://www.theyworkforyou. com/lords/?id=200-0-10a.902.1 (accessed 16 July 2009).

23 N. Rosenthal, 'The time has come for a statute of limitation', London: *The Art Newspaper*, 2008. Online. Available HTTP: http://www.theartnewspaper.com/article.asp?id=16627 (accessed 10 June 2009).

24 P. Steel, 'NMDC fights back spoliation legislation', *Museums Journal*, October 2008, p. 9.

25 R. Gott, 'The looting of Benin', *Independent* newspaper, 22 February 1997, reproduced by Africa Reparations Movement. Online. Available HTTP: http://www.arm.arc.co.uk/ lootingBenin.html (accessed 8 September 2009).

26 M. Beard, *The Parthenon*, London: Profile Books, 2004, p. 92.

27 K. A. Appiah, 'Whose culture is it?' in Cuno, *Whose Culture?* p. 74.

28 J. O. Young, *Cultural Appropriation and the Arts*, Malden, MA: Blackwell, 2008, pp. 66–7.

29 M. L. Picabea, 'Un museo inglés devolvió al país piezas fósiles robadas', *Clarin*, Buenos Aires, 8 September 2004. Online. Available HTTP: http://www.clarin.com/diario/2004/09/08/sociedad/s-03201.htm (accessed 1 September 2009).

30 H. Pinter, 'Art, Truth and Politics', speech on receiving the Nobel Prize for Literature in 2005. Online. Available HTTP: http://nobelprize.org/nobel_prizes/literature/laureates/2005/pinter-lecture-e.html (accessed 30 September 2009).

31 Nobel Prize for Literature, 2005 citation. Online. Available HTTP: http://nobelprize.org/nobel_prizes/literature/laureates/2005/index.html (accessed 30 September 2009).

32 N. MacGregor, 'To shape the citizens of "that great city, the world"', in Cuno, *Whose Culture?* p. 39.

33 T. Corum, 'Giving up control: how Banksy helped us let go', *Museums Journal*, October 2009, p. 17.

34 G. F. Angas, *Savage Life and Scenes in Australia and New Zealand: being an Artist's Impressions of Countries and People at the Antipodes*, London: Smith Elder, 1847, Vol. 1; R. M. and C. H. Berndt, *A World that Was: the Yaraldi of the Murray River and the Lakes, South Australia*, Melbourne: Melbourne University Press, 1993, p. 289.

35 Angas, *Savage Life*, pp. 68, 94.

36 S. Hemming and C. Wilson, 'The first "stolen generations": repatriation and reburial in Ngarrindjeri Ruwe (country)', in M. Pickering, P. Turnbull and H. Morphy (eds.) *The Long Way Home: The Meaning and Values of Repatriation*, Canberra: National Museum of Australia, 2010.

37 K. Gelder and J. M. Jacobs, 'Promiscuous sacred sites: reflections on secrecy and scepticism in the Hindmarsh Island affair', *Australian Humanities Review*. Online. Available HTTP: http://www.australianhumanitiesreview.org/archive/Issue-June-1997/gelder.html (accessed 18 June 2009).

38 F. Merlan, 'Assessment of von Doussa on Anthropology', unpublished address at a seminar given on 31 October 2001 at the Centre for Aboriginal Economic Policy Research, Australian National University, Canberra. Online. Available HTTP: http://www.aas.asn.au/publications/Hindmarsh%202001%20Panel%20Discussion/Merlan.pdf (accessed 2 June 2009).

39 M. Simons, *The Meeting of the Waters*, Sydney: Hachette Australia, 2003.

40 J. Hari, 'I am a daughter of the soil', interview with Wangari Maathai, *Independent* newspaper, *Independent Life*, 28 September 2009, p. 3.

41 J. Clifford, *Routes: Travel and Translation in the late Twentieth Century*, Cambridge, MA: Harvard University Press, 1997, p. 192.

42 Manchester Museum, *Collective Conversations*. Online. Available HTTP: http://www.youtube.com/ManchesterMuseum (accessed 9 June 2009).

43 Clifford, *Routes*, p. 193.

44 L. Peers and A. K. Brown, 'Colonial photographs and post-colonial histories', in A. M. Timpson (ed.) *First Nations, First Thoughts: The Impact of Indigenous Thought in Canada*, Vancouver: University of British Columbia Press, 2009, pp. 123–4.

45 Maathai, *The Challenge for Africa*, pp. 160–1.

46 C. Hooper, *The Tall Man*, Victoria: Penguin Group, 2008, p. 244.

47 Hemming and Wilson, 'The first "stolen generations"'.

48 http://www.arm.arc.co.uk/lootingBenin.html.

49 T. Besterman, 'Returning a stolen generation', *Museum International* 241/242, 2009 (May), p. 110.

50 A. Howarth, 'The Elgin marbles should stay', *The Guardian* newspaper, 5 February 2002. Online. Available HTTP: http://www.guardian.co.uk/education/2002/feb/05/artsandhumanities.highereducation (accessed 17 June 2009).

51 http://www.modernghana.com/news/203507/1/when-will-everybody-finally-accept-that-the-britis.html.

52 British Museum, 'Museum in the World'. Online. Available HTTP: http://www.britishmuseum.org/the_museum/museum_in_the_world.aspx (accessed 2 June 2009).

53 http://www.guardian.co.uk/education/2002/feb/05/artsandhumanities.highereducation.
54 A. Edemariam, 'How G2's Parthenon marbles poll went global', *The Guardian*, 18 July 2009. Online. Available HTTP: http://www.guardian.co.uk/artanddesign/2009/jul/08/parthenon-marbles-guardian-poll (accessed 14 July 2009).
55 Besterman, 'Returning a stolen generation', p. 108.
56 K. Opoku, 'Your latest offering', e-mail (12 July 2009).
57 www.tomflynn.co.uk/UniversalMuseum.html, p. 24.
58 Statens Museer för Världskultur (National Museums of World Culture), mission statement. Online. Available HTTP: http://www.etnografiska.se/smvk/jsp/polopoly.jsp?d=148 (accessed 8 December 2009).
59 J. Walsh, 'Christopher Hamilton: I'm not the man I was', *The Independent*, 13 April 2009. Online. Available HTTP: http://www.independent.co.uk/arts-entertainment/books/features/christopher-hamilton-im-not-the-man-i-was-1668201.html (accessed 20 October 2009).

16

'Dance through the minefield'

The development of practical ethics for repatriation

Michael Pickering

The title of this chapter, 'Dance through the minefield',[1] derives from a comedy sketch broadcast on Australian television in the 1970s. In it, a flamboyant colonel, confronted with a minefield, instructs his men to form pairs. Then, to appropriate music, he dances his embarrassed and confused men through the minefield, avoiding all the mines. One soldier is left. Pleading that he can't dance, the soldier nonetheless makes a half-hearted effort, proceeds into the minefield and is blown up. The colonel goes on to develop a new school of military training based on choreography.

The scene is appropriate to the discussion of the repatriation of human remains by museums (although I'm sure this was not the intention of the writers). The mines represent the ethical and legal codes of various professions, institutions, governments and, indeed, individuals, usually discovered only in the transgression. The dancers are the practitioners – their lives spared despite a naive and random engagement in the task at hand. The lone soldier/victim, someone bound by a single dogmatic code of conduct, is unable to deviate from the role. The future lies in redirection and somewhat unconventional initiatives.

Life for the practitioner of repatriation of Indigenous remains can be similarly hazardous. Repatriation involves extensive engagements with internal and external stakeholders, including employers, governments, professional interest groups, legislation and the applicants. It is an intensive and emotional engagement, often beyond the conventional experiences of many museum professionals. Because of the multiplicity and intensity of engagements, there is rarely a single guiding principle that the practitioner can follow or which protects the practitioner. For every ethical code that might be read to support repatriation, there is another that opposes it. Ethical behaviour is very much in the eye of the vested-interest holder.

In this discussion, any use of the word 'repatriation', unless otherwise noted, refers to the issue of *repatriation of Indigenous human remains*. Of course, repatriation debates also apply to a wide array of other forms of collections and materials. However, circumstances, codes, laws and conventions applicable to these materials may differ considerably to those applicable to Indigenous human remains.

Ethics

Ethics .... . A system of moral principles, by which human actions and proposals may be judged good or bad, or right or wrong.[2]

All ethical codes are developed within, encapsulate and reflect the particular social and cultural milieus of their creators. As will be shown, the Australian experience is that repatriation can be supported as the most ethical behaviour by one audience, and condemned as the most unethical by another. Who will be the arbiters of what is best ethical practice? This is a very real concern as professional, institutional, national and personal reputations depend upon an answer. Who or what determines what ethical values are appropriate? Are ethics to be legitimated by the legal codes of the administering state? By the museums industry? Or by a discipline-focused professional body? What support is there for the agent who disobeys one applicable code of ethics in favour of another? What if the agent is not aware of a code of ethics that may condemn their actions? These are real questions based on real experiences in repatriation.

What this chapter does not consider in any detail are the ethical codes of Indigenous stakeholders, the people with biological, social or cultural affiliations to remains. This is an argument best presented by Indigenous representatives. Nonetheless, it must be a key consideration in the development of non-Indigenous ethics for repatriation. There is no one-size-fits-all cross-cultural code of ethics. Not all Indigenous groups will apply the same criteria. For some, the return of remains may be unimportant, for others, it is a crucial cultural responsibility. What happens when a claimant bases a claim on criteria that may conflict with other claimants or prevailing knowledge of that claimant's cultural background? How are Indigenous criteria to be evaluated? *By whom?* Academic and philosophical debates on applicable ethics can become irrelevant in the engagements between the repatriation officer and the Indigenous claimants. Whatever 'we' determine as appropriate, our ethics will eventually be judged by the Indigenous stakeholders – present and future.

The curator

For many years, the primary source of new social history curators was professionals in a particular field, employed because of achievements in their disciplines, becoming curators through a lateral career change. More recently, we see the development of the professional curator, with the growth of museum studies departments offering immersive academic training in museology. Both strands of curator enter the professional museum world with ethical codes formed by their different educational engagements. The laterally moving professional brings the pluralist ethical codes of professional associations representing the discipline, as well as the codes/laws of external agencies, whereas the vertically moving professional brings the more constrained and abstract ethical codes of museological theory and practice. I belong to the older 'seasoned campaigner' school of curators, becoming a curator mid-way in my career. For twenty years previously, I had been active in Indigenous social and cultural heritage-based organisations throughout Australia. My work required familiarity not only with the ethical codes of anthropology and archaeology, but also with state and territory legislation, as well as the codes of Australian Indigenous cultures. This experience now informs my practice as a curator. My 'applied' engagements left little time for anything but cursory engagement with intellectual disciplinary debates; jobs had to be completed on time. My experiences in repatriation have been similarly driven by strategic and logistic considerations – completing work effectively, on time and in budget. Spare time for open-ended academic engagement and research has been limited. Indeed, museology students probably get to read and digest more of the literature on repatriation theory and practice than I do.

As an outcome of my diverse professional engagements, I am often stunned by the dogmatic ethical codes applied by many disciplines, be they anthropology, history or museology. Often a result of debates within the 'academies', such codes are commonly poorly informed by the reality of practice, or by concurrent debates and codes of other disciplines and legislations. Repatriation is a microcosm of museum practice, producing engagements that repeatedly highlight the disparities between the ethical, legal and occasionally commercial codes of various stakeholders.

This chapter is, therefore, pragmatic. It does not so much address the philosophical construction of an ethical code but rather identifies some of the problems of working in an environment where ethical and legal codes are varied, disparate and sometimes contradictory.

Repatriation in Australia

This chapter is based on Australian experiences in the repatriation of Indigenous human remains, both from domestic collections and from overseas collections. There are, of course, other items of repatriation, including sacred and secular objects and materials from both Indigenous and non-Indigenous origins. However, the ethical issues around the repatriation of these items have much in common with the issues raised in repatriation of remains. Similarly, Australian experiences will have analogies with overseas experiences.

The museum-based repatriation officer in Australia faces a seemingly overwhelming array of potentially applicable domestic ethical and legislative codes. Broadly, they can be categorised as those that directly affect repatriation, including government, industry, institutional, professional, stakeholder and individual, and those which more indirectly affect it, such as federal, state and territory legislation and heritage management policies. Together, these include not only explicitly written 'codes of ethics' but also policies, legislation, protocols and guidelines.

Government

The Australian federal government is committed to the repatriation of Australian Indigenous remains.[3] Although a 'code of ethics', or equivalent (e.g. repatriation legislation) specifically relevant to repatriation does not exist at a federal level, the government's policy commitments to repatriation impose a duty on the federal public servant (i.e. me). Thus, as a public servant – a curator in the federally funded National Museum of Australia (NMA) – I am required to act in accordance with the

Commonwealth Public Service 'Code of Conduct'.[4] This requires employees to, amongst other things, comply with Australian laws, comply with lawful directions and *'disclose, and take reasonable steps to avoid, any conflict of interest (real or apparent) ...* '[5] (my emphasis).

Note the last point, ' ... *conflict of interest ...* '. In writing this, did the public service identify that many professionals will have obligations to discipline-based associations and their codes of conduct or ethics? Museum professionals can find themselves between two or more competing responsibilities. What if, in carrying out the instructions of my employer, I breach an ethical value of my discipline or industry, or vice versa? Fortunately, many organisations, particularly those that manifest at an international level, include a get-out-of-jail-free clause that the requirements of the institution come first. For example, the Code of Ethics of Museums Australia states that 'Museum officers must faithfully discharge their responsibilities to the employing authority' and ' ... with due regard to the performance of their duties and the interests of their institution, act loyally towards their professional colleagues, director and governing body'.[6]

Industry

The Australian museum industry supports repatriation. Its professional body, 'Museums Australia', provides a 'Code of Ethics'[7] as well as guidelines as to recommended museum practice with regard to Australian Indigenous cultures.[8] These guidelines reflect and guide prevailing industry views. While not binding on museums or unaffiliated museum professionals, they do reflect an expected ethical code that would be noticed in the transgression. For example, any major Australian museum that opposed repatriation would most likely be, formally or informally, marginalised by the others.

Membership of Museums Australia is optional, for both institutions and individuals, with one of the criteria for membership being that individuals or organisations must ' ... support the objects of the Association and the Association's code of ethics'.[9] The Code of Ethics of Museum Australia also officially recognises ICOM, and other external and social, disciplinary ethics, stating, 'Museum officers have obligations not only to museum objects but also to the owners and/or custodians of those objects and *to their institution, to their colleagues and their profession*, and to the public as a whole ... '[10] (my emphasis).

The Code also acknowledges other Commonwealth, State and Territory legislations, as well as its own policies and guidelines for the care and management of indigenous material. Through these documents, Museums Australia explicitly supports repatriation, stating:[11]

1.4.4   Museums are to seek out the rightful custodians of ancestral remains and ask them whether they wish the remains to be repatriated to the community or held by the museum on behalf of the community.

1.4.5   If rightful custodians ask for the return of ancestral remains museums should agree. All requests for the repatriation of Aboriginal and Torres Strait Islander ancestral remains should be promptly and sensitively dealt with by museums ...

1.4.6   Museums must not place conditions on communities with regard to the repatriation of ancestral remains.

This is a very strong and unambiguous statement of support for repatriation by Australia's peak museums industry representative body.

Institutional

The National Museum of Australia also has its own Code of Conduct Guidelines.[12] Based upon the Australian Public Services (APS) Code of Conduct, the Museum's code explicitly requires museum employees to adhere to the rules of the public service, the professional codes of ethics and conduct published by Museums Australia and the International Council of Museums, and by professional organisations relevant to the work of the museum.[13]

As well as endorsing the ethical codes and conduct of these organisations and professions, the NMA is also an institutional member of both ICOM and Museums Australia. Further, the Museum has an 'Ethics Statement' that, in its first clause, states that the Museum ' ... affirms its commitment to the repatriation of human remains and sacred/secret material in liaison with Aboriginal and Torres Strait Islander peoples'.[14]

The Museum's commitments to repatriation are further evident in its policies.[15] The 'Aboriginal and Torres Strait Islander Human Remains Policy', for example, explicitly states: 'The Museum will return human remains to appropriate communities on request ... ' and 'The Museum shall not place conditions on communities with regard to ancestral remains that are repatriated.'[16]

The National Museum has enthusiastically committed itself to the unconditional return of Australian Indigenous human remains with considerable success. The Museum has been returning remains and objects since its inception in 1980 and is recognised nationally and internationally for its repatriation work. The remains of more than 1000 individuals have been unconditionally returned to Indigenous communities.[17] This activity demonstrates an unambiguous statement of support for repatriation, through both philosophy and practice, by Australia's pre-eminent national museum.

A recap: ICOM, and a problem?

Thus the Australian government, Museums Australia and the National Museum of Australia all support repatriation, either through policy, philosophy, actions or a combination of the three. All also concede that activities must be in accordance with the Australian Public Service Code of Conduct. However, Museums Australia and the National Museum of Australia also endorse the Code of Ethics of the International Council of Museums (ICOM). But does ICOM support repatriation? This is discussed further in the 'International' section below.

Professional

As well as industry-focused professional bodies, such as ICOM and Museums Australia, every museum professional can also identify a discipline-focused professional body to which they are accountable. Again, membership of such organisations is not essential for the ethical codes of those organisations to be applied in the assessment of an individual's professional character. Whereas a member formally agrees to abide by the ethical codes of the organisation, a non-member may nonetheless find themselves subject to praise or condemnation based on the organisation's code.

The two professional organisations most relevant to repatriation in Australia are the Australian Archaeological Association (AAA) and the World Archaeological Congress (WAC). As archaeological organisations, they have human remains and material culture directly in their ambit. Both have codes of ethics. The AAA Code[18] requires members to:

1.3 ... acknowledge the rights and interests of Indigenous peoples. AAA endorses ... the current guidelines for ethical research with Indigenous parties published by the Australian Institute of Aboriginal and Torres Strait Islander Studies ...

2.4 ... recognise the importance of repatriation of archaeological materials for both Indigenous and non-Indigenous communities of concern ...

3.2 ... acknowledge the special importance ... of ancestral remains ...

while the WAC Code[19] states that members shall:

1. ... acknowledge the importance of indigenous cultural heritage, including ... human remains, to the survival of indigenous cultures ...

3. ... acknowledge the special importance of indigenous ancestral human remains, and sites containing and/or associated with such remains, to indigenous peoples ...

5. ... not interfere with and/or remove human remains of indigenous peoples without the express consent of those concerned.

In 'The Vermillion Accord on Human Remains',[20] WAC further requires '1. Respect for the mortal remains of the dead ... '; '2. Respect for the wishes of the dead concerning disposition ... '; '3. Respect for the wishes of the local community and of relatives or guardians of the dead ... whenever possible, reasonable and lawful'; '4. Respect for the scientific research value of ... human remains ... '; and '5. Agreement on the disposition of ... remains shall be reached by negotiation on the basis of mutual respect for the legitimate concerns of communities for the proper disposition of their ancestors, as well as the legitimate concerns of science and education.'

Superficially, such codes and clauses might be interpreted as providing explicit support for repatriation. However, these statements alone do not constitute support. Indeed, the requirements for respect of scientific importance may be used to cancel out any possibility of repatriation. But they are recognition that Indigenous peoples find repatriation important and this belief must be recognised and respected. However, under such terminology the desires of those indigenous people do not necessarily have to be acceded to. 'To respect' does not mean 'to concede'. In the Vermillion Accord (Clause 5 above) this position is made clearer in that disposition of remains will be reached by negotiation. Further, there are the words 'possible, reasonable and lawful'. Who decides what is reasonable? In short, if the holding institution does not desire to return the remains, and has no legal compulsion to do so, it does not have to.

Moreover, as long as the wording of such codes remains unchanged, even public statements in support of repatriation by executive members of such organisations have a life only while that executive holds the position. For example, in 2003,[21] the AAA's media liaison officer stated that the Association:

> ... supports calls by Indigenous Australians for the immediate repatriation of Aboriginal skeletal remains from a British museum ... The Code of Ethics of the Association ... makes it clear that the primacy of ownership, curation and protection of skeletal remains must ultimately reside with Indigenous Australians.

The President of WAC similarly stated:[22]

> The World Archaeological Congress (WAC) ... supported calls by Indigenous Australians for the repatriation of the bones of ancestors ...
> ' ... Let me be quite clear on this. It is only a matter of time. These ancestral remains will be returned to the care of Indigenous Australians.'

Because of the wording of the codes, any change in executive office bearers could also bring a change in interpretation.

Other Australian professional organisations that have ethical codes that may influence repatriation activities include the Australian Anthropological Society (AAS)[23] and the Australian Institute of Aboriginal and Torres Strait Islander Studies (AIATSIS).[24] The Institute (AIATSIS) is Australia's pre-eminent government institution with regard to professional engagements and research with Aboriginal and Torres Strait Islander peoples. The Institute maintains 'Guidelines for Ethical Research in Indigenous Studies',[25] the principles of which are explicitly ' ... founded on respect for Indigenous peoples' inherent right to self determination, and to control and maintain their culture and heritage'.[26] Typically, most researchers working with Australian Indigenous peoples and heritage will defer to the guidelines of the AIATSIS over professional association codes.[27] The codes of AAS and AIATSIS are less dogmatic than the codes of AAA and WAC, with a stronger focus on the rights of the subject/stakeholder and less of a focus on material culture. Significantly, both codes make explicit reference to the professional adhering to external ethical codes and laws of relevant professional bodies, organisations or states, an important acknowledgement that professional practice is influenced by, and accountable to, other external agencies. Interestingly, however, the AIATSIS explicitly states that it will not fund ' ... returning materials to communities or repatriation of material'.[28] Further, despite more compassionate codes, neither the AAS nor AIATSIS (unlike AAA and WAC) have ever issued a public statement in support of repatriation.

What does all this mean? In my case, it means that, at any one time, as repatriation officer with the National Museum of Australia, I am accountable to at least eight ethical codes or codes of conduct, many of which cross-reference each other.

Certainly, many of these are complementary and, where conflicts exist, concessions are usually made to defer to the prevailing codes of the employer. Nonetheless, these are codes of which I must be aware.

Further, these are the codes that relate directly to day-to-day practice within my profession and within the public service. There are still many other codes that may be applicable. For example, the 'National Statement of Ethical Conduct in Human Research' is an invaluable and thorough document that, although focusing on health and medical research, still addresses issues relevant to repatriation, including a specific section dealing with Aboriginal and Torres Strait Islander peoples.[29] Despite being a national statement by the Australian government, the National Health and Medical Research Council, the Australian Research Council and the Australian Vice-Chancellors Committee, it is not explicitly cross-referenced by any of the previously referred to disciplinary or industry ethical codes.

But wait, there's more. The repatriation officer is also accountable to the legislation of the nation and its component states or territories. This obviously encompasses specific heritage legislation.[30] However, in addition, it includes rather unusual and seemingly obscure legislation, for example, relevant Coroner's Acts, Transplantation Acts and Anatomy Acts.[31] It is, after all, often an offence in Australia to be in possession of human tissue without legislative approval. These laws were usually intended to manage the remains of recently deceased people; however, because the existence of museum collections of remains was never explicitly considered in framing the legislation, it is possible that they could be affected by such legislation. Australian museums with holdings of human remains may well be breaking the law.

Although the National Museum of Australia is a Commonwealth Government institution, its powers and legal authority are no greater, indeed often less, than the authority of major state and territory museums and heritage agencies. Repatriation activities by the National Museum occur across Australia. In each event, familiarity with, and adherence to, prevailing state laws is a prerequisite to working in, and with, those states and territories, regardless of the ethical codes of the disciplines or museum.

The Museum is also contractually engaged by one Commonwealth government department to store and repatriate remains returned to Australia from overseas, while another provides grant funding to support repatriation of remains from domestic museum collections.[32] Both impose contractual conditions on activities that are similarly legally binding on the museum, including the requirement to act in good time.

Nearly all of the above-mentioned codes, contracts and legislation are codes that I **must** work to – either as a professional anthropologist and archaeologist, as a professional curator, as a public servant or as an Australian citizen. All have clauses that make adherence mandatory, either as a condition of membership or employment or as a set of values against which my professional behaviour will be judged. Of those codes identified, very few explicitly identify *repatriation* of human remains as a theme; rather the treatment of remains is the issue. The two exceptions are the NMA's own ethics and policy statements[33] and Museums Australia's principles and guidelines.[34] In the other codes cited, ethical behaviour has to be interpreted as it *might* apply to the subject of repatriation.

International engagements

So far, I have concentrated on Australian domestic engagements. As the title of this chapter suggests, it is a minefield. Nonetheless, it is fair to conclude that, generally speaking, Australia sees repatriation of Indigenous human remains as ethical. Despite the capacity for prevailing professional codes to be interpreted differently, I can be confident that my work reflects this current ethic.

The overseas situation is different, however. In many countries, museums and museum professionals see repatriation of remains as 'unethical'[35] though this position is not always through reference to a written ethical code. The International Council of Museums (ICOM), to which both Museums Australia and the National Museum of Australia Ethical Codes refer, is vague on the subject. The 'ICOM Code of Ethics for Museums'[36] has several clauses relating to the treatment of human remains, with the three clauses of greatest relevance being:

2.5 ... Collections of human remains and material of sacred significance should be acquired only if they can be housed securely and cared for respectfully ...

3.7 ... Research on human remains and ma-terials [sic] of sacred significance must be accomplished in a manner consistent with professional standards and take into account the interests and beliefs of the community, ethnic or religious groups from whom the objects originated, where these are known ...

4.3 ... Human remains and materials of sacred significance must be displayed in a manner consistent with professional standards and, where known, taking into account the interests and beliefs of members of the community, ethnic or religious groups from whom the objects originated. They must be presented with great tact and respect for the feelings of human dignity held by all peoples.

These endorse the concept of 'respect'; however, 'respect' is not defined and does not necessarily translate into endorsement of repatriation. Indeed these clauses primarily concern housing, research and display. The Code further says:[37]

8.4 ... Members of the museum profession should promote the investigation, preservation, and use of information inherent in collections. *They should, therefore, refrain from any activity or circumstance that might result in the loss of such academic and scientific data.* [My emphasis]

This last clause is crucial. No one can deny that the repatriation of human remains constitutes an activity that technically results in the loss of academic and scientific data. It is a 'safe' clause because everything has scientific potential. It must be recognised, however, that the majority of collections of Indigenous human remains originally derived from destructive and unscientific methods of collection. As a result they have limited scientific potential due to the biases in their collection, storage and documentation. The presumed loss that results from their repatriation is more than adequately compensated by the new knowledge that is generated. Further, more ethical, and more scientifically rigorous, alternatives now exist, such as in-situ examination of newly discovered remains in collaboration with Indigenous stakeholders, that allow the acquisition of higher quality information on human remains.[38]

Is the repatriation practitioner/supporter therefore technically in breach of the ICOM Code of Ethics? In February 2008, the Musée du quai Branly in Paris hosted an international symposium on the subject of repatriation.[39] The conference was initiated by, and largely in defence of, the refusal of the French government to allow the return of a tattooed Maori head to New Zealand on the basis that it was no longer a human remain but rather a museum object. Through its representatives present at the symposium, including Christine Albanel, then Minister of Culture and Communication, the French Government and its leading collecting institutions clearly expressed their opposition to the repatriation of Indigenous human remains.[40]

Michel Van Praët, Professor at the Paris Natural History Museum (MNHN) and member of the Executive Council of ICOM (France), reiterated the ICOM ethical code in stating that the process of return cannot result in the destruction of knowledge, it must create something. This reflects the ICOM position that museums should refrain from activities that might result in the loss of scientific data.

Accepting that some international constituencies, supportive of repatriation, may disagree with ICOM's positions, ICOM provides escape clauses under 'Ethics of Professional Conduct', allowing:

8.2 Professional Responsibility
     Members of the museum profession have an obligation to follow the policies and procedures of their employing institution …
8.3 Professional Conduct
     Loyalty to colleagues and to the employing museum is an important professional responsibility …

The fact that there is strong industry resistance to repatriation of indigenous remains in Europe, from which the bulk of ICOM's membership is drawn,[41] suggests that unambiguous policy statements, either supporting or opposing repatriation, are unlikely. Repatriation of remains will be 'tolerated' by ICOM. Whether ICOM endorses it as 'ethical' or 'unethical' awaits further debate.[42]

Increasing numbers of nations have made declarations in support of Indigenous remains. In 2004, Sweden initiated the return of a collection of Australian Aboriginal remains on the basis that the circumstances of their collection were unethical. Museums in the Netherlands and Germany have also recently returned remains, with returns from Italy expected in the near future.[43]

Since 2001, Britain has engaged closely with the repatriation debate, following the British Government's declaration of its support for international repatriation.[44] However, subsequent reviews and legislative changes[45] have not made repatriation mandatory and, while a number of UK museums have willingly returned remains,[46] many continue to oppose repatriation, either in practice or in principle. The British Museum, for example, while having recently returned remains to Australia, nonetheless maintains, 'While the Human Tissue Act 2004 gave the Trustees of the British Museum the power to deaccession human remains, the Trustees generally presume that the Museum's collection should remain intact.'[47] Dr Robert Foley, of Cambridge University, where other remains are held, has similarly stated, 'These collections are central to what we do; if we have to hand some of this material over it will be tragic.'[48]

In the United States, the 'Native American Graves Protection and Repatriation Act 1990' (NAGPRA)[49] guides the repatriation of remains and grave goods. While the existence of this Act would suggest that a philosophy of repatriation prevails, this is not necessarily the case. Certainly, museums return the remains of Native Americans because the legislation compels them. However, in recent years, claims were made for the return of remains collected during the 1948 Australian-American Expedition to Arnhem Land. While a number of remains were eventually returned, some were retained by the Smithsonian.[50] It would seem that the return of remains to Native Americans is ethical, while the return of remains to other non-American Indigenous people is not ethical.

In contrast, there is no legislation in Australia that explicitly compels repatriation, although there is legislation that could facilitate repatriation, if necessary.[51] Australian governments and museums return remains because they want to, not because they have to. It is seen as the right thing to do.

There is a bewildering array of codes of ethics, conduct, legislation and policy that apply to the repatriation practitioner. There is no consensus on repatriation, and thus applicable ethical codes, in the museums industry, or, for that matter, the disciplines and professions that make up that industry. What is considered appropriate in one jurisdiction is considered inappropriate in another.

The repatriation officer is in a delicate position. It is not uncommon for me to be challenged by Australian researchers and accused of unethical behaviour through facilitating 'destruction' of remains and collections. This is despite clear and unambiguous Australian government and museum industry ethics, philosophies and practice that endorse repatriation, and by ambiguous, but still supportive, statements of the key professional bodies. It is questionable whether negative comments by some commentators actually reflect prevailing institutional or industry codes or policies, or just the opinion of the individual.

A characteristic of 'ethical' conduct is that it is often identified only in the transgression. How many people are actually aware of the ethical codes that apply to their professions and industry? How many people are aware of the laws – themselves codes of acceptable, thus ethical, behaviour – that may apply to their duties? Usually it is only with an allegation of wrongdoing that an ethical code is found that might identify the action was indeed 'an offence'. The allegation of unethical behaviour becomes akin to a church pronouncement of heresy. The allegation alone is considered to be sufficient to bring the accused to heel. Indeed, the most common allegations against repatriation practitioners are, firstly, 'that's unscientific', and, secondly, 'It's the destruction of scientific knowledge.' Both are statements driven by disciplinary dogma rather than by impartial investigation. Rarely is reference made to the particular ethical code that identifies a breach of professional behaviour.

Second-class citizens?

Interestingly, 'heated' debate about the ethics of repatriation seems to be reserved for Indigenous remains. Other objects and materials, both secular and sacred, similarly looted from occupied peoples, such as art, money, documents and similar items of heritage and culture, are treated quite differently, with wide in-principle support for their return. There are numerous international conventions on the ethical treatment – including repatriation and/or restitution – of such materials; for example, the 1970 United Nations 'Convention on the Means of Prohibiting and Preventing the Illicit Import, Export and Transfer of Ownership of Cultural Property'[52] and the 1995 'UNIDROIT Convention on Stolen or Illegally Exported Cultural Objects 1995'.[53] Indeed, the history of international conventions, policies, agreements and philosophies supporting repatriation of, or restitution for, cultural objects stolen during war or occupation extends back for well over 200 years[54] (although history also shows that when the shooting starts these conventions are meaningless).

We have yet to see the impact of the 2007 United Nations 'Declaration on the Rights of Indigenous Peoples' which, through Articles 11 and 12, explicitly endorses repatriation and restitution, with Article 12 concisely stating, '1. Indigenous peoples have the right ... to the repatriation of their human remains.'[55]

Why are indigenous human remains treated so differently from other materials of cultural heritage, given that they are the misappropriated remains of Indigenous people, and thus items of significant cultural heritage to associated indigenous peoples? The answer lies partly in that such conventions are not retroactive, and cannot be applied, *as conventions*, to facilitate the return of remains taken before the convention came into force. Further, remains do not have the financial value, or iconic cultural significance, of a painting or sculpture by an eminent artist. Finally, remains are often seen as belonging to the state of the collecting institution, collected from peoples the state was governing at the time. Whatever the reason, Indigenous remains have not been seen as that important until relatively recently.

Nonetheless, while the conventions are not retroactive, and cannot be applied, the philosophies and ethical considerations behind their introduction can be seen as prevailing, regardless of time, and applicable to items and remains taken before the conventions were developed. If a convention derives from a debate and the realisation that the process of acquisition of an item of cultural significance was 'unethical', then surely that philosophy, if not the law/convention, applies to events in the past? It is reasonable to expect that states sympathetic to the return of cultural materials acquired inappropriately in recent years would see that the same philosophy and sympathy could be applied to materials acquired similarly in distant years. Ethical behaviour should not have to be legislated in order to be applied.

Why are the ethics of repatriation of Indigenous remains so confused, especially when compared with the codes applicable to other cultural materials? Part of the problem appears to be that no one was expecting the issue to become as complex as it has. The primary concern has been the management of stolen material culture from neighbouring states. As well as being legal acts, repatriation and restitution were also mechanisms for 'healing' after a century of wars, revolutions and slaughter – local politics, particularly in Europe, demanded it. On the other hand, Indigenous peoples were seen as minorities whose welfare would be managed by the dominant nation-state. Their claims for repatriation were simply not an issue when compared with international politics. However, Indigenous peoples the world over are finding a stronger voice. A potent symbol of their subjugation is the subjugation of their ancestors, even in death. Respect for the dead, evinced by their repatriation, translates as respect for the living.

Another problem with repatriation ethics is that, where any statement on the issue exists, it has usually emerged through a very 'closed shop' engagement; archaeologists determine what is ethical for archaeologists based on the experience of practising archaeology, anthropologists determine what is ethical for anthropologists based on experiences of practising anthropology, and so on through history and museology. Engagements with ethical codes outside of the disciplines are rare. As noted earlier, while Australian archaeological and anthropological associations, museums and museums studies departments have ethical codes, none explicitly refer to the codes applicable to medical and anatomical disciplines.[56] Compared with the ethics applicable in the medical arena, the ethics of the social sciences are quite archaic.

It is also rare that such disciplinary codes refer to prevailing legislation.[57] However, it is in this area that the greatest developments are likely to emerge, and it is legal interpretations that are more likely to define the ethics of practical repatriation than closed-shop disciplinary debates. In recent years, jurists have made significant, if often unintentional, contributions to the development of repatriation ethics. The UK Working Group On Human Remains addressed the distinction in the way the bodies of British subjects and Indigenous peoples were treated after death, determining that there was no valid reason for the inconsistencies and that all remains were entitled to the same respect under prevailing laws. In May 2007, the National History Museum, London, returned remains to the Tasmanian Aboriginal Community. Initially characterised by adversarial positions, the dispute was heading for the UK High Court, when, at the last minute, a negotiated settlement occurred and the remains were returned. Similarly, in France, in 2007, the French Government stopped the return of Maori remains. Then, in June 2009, the French Senate overturned this decision and agreed to the repatriation.

What happened? A hint comes from the events leading up to the National History Museum case. The Tasmanian Aboriginal Centre (TAC) had already established a precedent of being recognised by the Tasmanian Supreme Court[58] as the executors for the remains in question – an interesting precedent in itself. This entitled the TAC to represent the estates of the deceased whose remains were held by the Natural History Museum. The rights and responsibilities of an executor include the authority to arrange appropriate disposal of remains. Does this constitute 'ownership of human remains'?[59] If this case were to go to court, would the common law principle of 'no property in human remains' be overturned? If so, what would be the impact on wider collections? If not, what would be the impact on future applications for repatriation? A similar situation was raised at the 2008 symposium held at the Musée du quai Branly.[60] 'After a sequence of highly polarised opinions from those for and against repatriation, the discussion amongst the jurists[61] suggested that if a claim for the return of remains was to go to court, then existing precedents made it likely remains would be returned to the applicant group.[62] Although details of the in-confidence legal advice received by the National History Museum, the Musée du quai Branly and the French Government are not available to me, I would speculate that such advice might have indicated that applications, through a judicial process, for the return of indigenous remains might be successful, and, as a result, might establish precedents regarding ownership of remains that the dissenting museums and governments may not like.

This encouragement of closer engagement with jurists, amongst others, is not to encourage resolution through litigation but rather to warn of it. Litigation may lead to decisions and precedents that are 'disadvantageous', both to museums and/or claimant groups. That said, there are issues that would be interesting to see tested, in particular whether there can be property in human remains, and whether museum collections of human remains are held legally under prevailing state legislation.

Most of us in the field go to work and do the best we can, often with limited resources. There is little time to keep up with academic developments in the industry. This is unfortunate as it means many museum professionals remains locked in the intellectual era of their graduation date. Debates at the broad national and international levels do not directly affect many of us – the outcomes are filtered down through progressive government, industry and institutional policies. The individual does not feel the need to engage with the codifiers and jurists at a practical day-to-day level; that will be done for them by a sequence of administrative hierarchies. Thus, many individuals will remain unaware of the debates, often trusting to their local professional organisation or employer for direction.

This is dangerous, leading to isolation, polarisation and the development of localised dogma. Individuals need to engage more closely with industry debates and, in particular, with debates in disciplines other than their own. There are two major reasons for this, the first being that it leads to practical and workable ethical codes, the second is that it is fun.

Conclusion

What now? The issue of repatriation of Indigenous human remains is growing. It cannot be ignored and will not go away. It is no longer a question of respectful treatment of remains as 'objects' but an issue of respecting human rights. The time is right for major industry engagements with internal and external contributors, first and foremost, of course, with Indigenous people, but, in terms of policy development, with jurists and medical sciences. What concerns might the future debate address? The issue of whether repatriation is appropriate or not needs to be more fully deliberated. At the moment, speakers seem motivated more by individual opinion rather than sustained arguments. The discussions need to be informed by, and to subsequently inform, prevailing judicial codes. It is no good having a disciplinary ethical code that is illegal under the laws of the state. The philosophies that will apply if repatriation occurs need to be considered. How shall remains be managed? Stored? Handled? Returned? What principles of recognition of 'culture' shall guide the process? For example, should decisions be based on demonstrated biological descent or on cultural affiliation? Should age limits on remains be applied? Should representations at a government-to-government level be acceptable, or should engagements be restricted to claimant groups and institutions? What should happen to remains provenanced only to country? The list goes on. An examination of the array of codes shows that at some time or another at least one institution or another has included conditions that address these and/or other criteria.[63] These disparate institutional and state codes need to be pulled together for consideration and synthesis. As history demonstrates, ethical codes will change over place, time and dominant factions. It is best that this change be managed by informed debate, similarly informed by practical application and experience.

There is a lot to be said for not looking too closely, instead following a single ethical code, either of the employer or of the discipline, and remaining isolated and secure. However, that risks retreat into dogma and only leads to dispute and polarisation, rather than debate and reconciliation. However, despite disparities in different codes, the job is done. The Australian experience in repatriation has been a worthy one, and has contributed to the creation of new knowledge about both past and present Indigenous cultures. It has led to improved relationships between Indigenous groups and the museum industry, as well as the development of ethical codes that are applicable to non-Indigenous issues.[64]

And so we'll continue to dance through the minefield, enjoying both the praise and condemnation of fellow disciplinary and industry professionals, pushing the envelope with other possibly applicable legal codes. We'll be frustrated by codes and protocols developed in isolation, away from the practical day-to-day realities of the repatriation process. Nonetheless, the work will continue. Repatriation work may occasionally be frustrating, but it's never boring.

Notes

1 Australian Broadcasting Commission, 'Colonel Passionfruit leading his men through a dangerous choreographed war with the *Pride of Erin* mine avoidance tactic', 1971–72, from *The Aunty Jack Show Series One 1971–1972*, released by the Australian Broadcasting Commission (ABC) as DVD, 2005. See also online HTTP: http://www.youtube.com/watch?v=AAfB7XtbjdI.
2 *The Macquarie Dictionary*, 4th edn, Sydney: Macquarie Dictionary Publishers, 2005, p. 404.
3 Department of Environment, Water, Heritage and the Arts, *Return of Indigenous Cultural Property*, 2009. Online. Available HTTP: http://www.arts.gov.au/indigenous/return (accessed 15 June 2009); Department of Families, Housing, Community Services and Indigenous Affairs, *International Repatriation Program*, 2009. Online. Available HTTP: http://www.fahcsia.gov.au/sa/indigenous/progserv/repatriation/Pages/default.aspx (accessed 15 June 2009); Cultural Ministers Council, 2008. Online. Available HTTP: http://www.cmc.gov.au/home (accessed 15 June 2009).
4 Australian Public Service Commission, *APS Code of Conduct*, n.d. Online. Available HTTP: http://www.apsc.gov.au/conduct/ (accessed 15 June 2009).
5 Ibid. The Australian Public Service Commission also provides for an 'Ethics Advisory Service' to assist with interpretation of the Code of Conduct.
6 Museums Australia, *Museums Australia Incorporated Code of Ethics 1999*. Canberra: Museums Australia, 1999. Online. Available HTTP: http://www.museumsaustralia.org.au/dbdoc/maethics.pdf (accessed 15 June 2009).
7 http://www.museumsaustralia.org.au/dbdoc/maethics.pdf.
8 Museums Australia, *Continuous Cultures, Ongoing Responsibilities. Principles and guidelines for Australian museums working with Aboriginal and Torres Strait Islander cultural heritage*, Canberra: Museums Australia, 2005. Online. Available HTTP: http://www.museumsaustralia.org.au/dbdoc/ccor_final_feb_05.pdf (accessed 15 June 2009).
9 Museums Australia, *Museums Australia Incorporated Constitution and Rules*, Canberra: Museums Australia, 2008. Online. Available HTTP: http://www.museumsaustralia.org.au/UserFiles/File/MA-Constitution-Rev-20-May-08.pdf (accessed 15 June 2009).

10 http://www.museumsaustralia.org.au/dbdoc/maethics.pdf. See professional conduct: Principles, p. 12.

11 Museums Australia, *Previous Possessions, New Obligations: Policies for Museums in Australia and Aboriginal and Torres Strait Islander Peoples*, Museums Australia: Canberra, 1993, revised 2005 as *Museums Australia 2005 Continuous Cultures, Ongoing responsibilities*. Online. Available HTTP: http://www.museumsaustralia.org.au/dbdoc/ccor_final_feb_05.pdf (accessed 20 June 2009).

12 National Museum of Australia, *Code of Conduct Guidelines*, August 2008, Version 1.4, Canberra: National Museum of Australia.

13 Ibid. See part two, paragraph 6.

14 National Museum of Australia, *Ethics Statement*. Online. Available HTTP: http://www.nma.gov.au/about_us/nma_corporate_documents/ethics_statement/ (accessed 27 June 2009).

15 National Museum of Australia, *Policies*. Online. Available HTTP: http://www.nma.gov.au/collections/repatriation/policies/s (accessed 15 June 2009).

16 National Museum of Australia, *Aboriginal and Torres Strait Islander Human Remains Policy*, vol. 2.1, 24 March 2009. Online. Available HTTP: http://www.nma.gov.au/shared/libraries/attachments/corporate_documents/policies/atsi_human_remains_policy/files/27533/POL-C 011_Aboriginal_and_Torres_Strait_Islander_human_remains_2.1_(public).pdf (accessed 16 June 2009).

17 National Museum of Australia, *Repatriation*, 2009. Online. Available HTTP: http://www.nma.gov.au/collections/repatriation/ (accessed 15 June 2009).

18 Australian Archaeological Association, 2009. Online. Available HTTP: http://www.australianarchaeologicalassociation.com.au/welcome (accessed 15 June 2009).

19 World Archaeological Congress. Online. Available HTTP: http://www.worldarchaeologicalcongress.org/site/about_ethi.php (accessed 16 June 2009).

20 Ibid.

21 P. Veth, Press Release, 2003. Online. Available HTTP: http://www.australianarchaeological association.com.au/node/1925 (accessed 22 June 2009).

22 C. Smith, 'World Archaeological Congress Supports Return of Aboriginal Bones from British Museum', Media Release, World Archaeological Congress, 2003. Online. Available HTTP: http://www.worldarchaeologicalcongress.org/site/news/Repatriation_British_Museum.rtf (accessed 22 June 2009).

23 Australian Anthropological Association. Online. Available HTTP: http://www.aas.asn.au/ (accessed 20 June 2009).

24 Australian Institute of Aboriginal and Torres Strait Islander Studies. Online. Available HTTP: http://www.aiatsis.gov.au (accessed 22 June 2009).

25 Australian Institute of Aboriginal and Torres Strait Islander Studies, *Guidelines for Ethical Research in Indigenous Studies*, n.d. Online. Available HTTP: http://www.aiatsis.gov.au/__data/assets/pdf_file/10534/GERIS_2007.pdf (accessed 27 June 2009).

26 Ibid., p. 2.

27 At time of writing, the Australian Institute of Aboriginal and Torres Strait Islander Studies is advertising for a researcher to undertake a review of its *Guidelines for Ethical Research*.

28 Australian Institute of Aboriginal and Torres Strait Islander Studies 2009 Research Grants. Online. Available HTTP: http://www.aiatsis.gov.au/research_program/grants (accessed 27 June 2009).

29 Australian Government, *National Statement on Ethical Conduct in Human Research*, Canberra ACT, 2007. Online. Available HTTP: http://www.nhmrc.gov.au/PUBLICATIONS/synopses/_files/e72.pdf (accessed 27 June 2009).

30 For example: *The Aboriginal and Torres Strait Islander Heritage Protection Act 1984*. Online. Available HTTP: http://www.austlii.edu.au/au/legis/cth/consol_act/aatsihpa1984549/ (accessed 27 June 2009); *Archaeological and Aboriginal Relics Preservation Act 1972*. Online. Available HTTP: http://www.legislation.vic.gov.au/Domino/Web_Notes/LDMS/PubLaw Today.nsf/95c43dd4eac71a68ca256dde00056e7b/F6BB8C1F1EFF88FCCA256E70001B4B60/ $FILE/72-8273a050doc.doc (accessed 27 June 2009). The latter Act makes it an offence to possess or display Aboriginal remains in the state of Victoria without a permit.

31 For example: *Australian Capital Territory Transplantation and Anatomy Act 1978*. Online. Available HTTP: http://www.legislation.act.gov.au/a/1978-44/current/pdf/1978-44.pdf (accessed 27 June 2009). This Act allows for research on human remains only in a recognised school of anatomy. Further, research can only be performed by a qualified medical officer. *New South Wales Human Tissue Act 1983*. Online. Available HTTP: http://www.austlii.edu. au/cgi-bin/download.cgi/download/au/legis/nsw/consol_act/hta1983160.rtf (accessed 22 June 2009?).

32 Department of Environment, Water, Heritage and the Arts, *Return of Indigenous Cultural Property*, 2009. Online. Available HTTP: http://www.arts.gov.au/indigenous/return (accessed 15 June 2009); Department of Families, Housing, Community Services and Indigenous Affairs, *International Repatriation Program*, 2009. Online. Available HTTP: http://www.fahcsia. gov.au/sa/indigenous/progserv/repatriation/Pages/default.aspx (accessed 15 June 2009).

33 http://www.nma.gov.au/shared/libraries/attachments/corporate_documents/policies/atsi_ human_remains_policy/files/27533/POL-C-011_Aboriginal_and_Torres_Strait_Islander_ human_remains_2.1_(public).pdf; http://www.nma.gov.au/about_us/nma_corporate_ docu ments/ ethics_statement/.

34 http://www.museumsaustralia.org.au/dbdoc/ccor_final_feb_05.pdf.

35 Musée du quai Branly, International Symposium 'From Anatomic Collections to Objects of Worship', 2008. Online. Available HTTP: http://www.quaibranly.fr/fileadmin/user_ upload/pdf/Original_Version_Symposium_Human_Remains.pdf (accessed 9 January 2010).

36 International Council of Museums, *ICOM Code of Ethics for Museums*, 2006. Online. Available HTTP: http://icom.museum/code2006_eng.pdf (accessed 21 June 2009).

37 Ibid.

38 M. Pickering, 'Lost in Translation', *borderlands e-journal* 7: 2, 2008, p. 12. Online. Available HTTP: http://www.borderlands.net.au/vol7no2_2008/pickering_lost.pdf (accessed 21 June 2009).

39 http://www.quaibranly.fr/fileadmin/user_upload/pdf/Original_Version_Symposium_Human_ Remains.pdf. Unfortunately, while the English speakers at the conference were subsequently transcribed into French on the website of proceedings, the same courtesy was not applied in the translation from French to English. I have had to rely on my notes and on a limited web-based translation tool for translation of the French into English. I apologise if meaning and nuances differ from the original.

40 On 28 June 2009 it was announced that France was to return this and other Maori remains to New Zealand. Online. Available HTTP: http://www.news.com.au/story/ 0,27574,25702718-23109,00.html (accessed 28 June 2009). See also R. Sorensen, 2008, 'Demands for repatriation of human remains have forced museums to confront skeletons in the closet'. Online. Available HTTP: http://www.theaustralian.news.com.au/story/ 0,25197,23429019-16947,00.html (accessed 27 June 2009).

41 ICOM's head office is located in Paris. Online. Available HTTP: http://icom.museum/ headquarters.html (accessed 27 June 2009).

42 A dilemma. The Australian Government supports repatriation, the National Museum of Australia employs me to repatriate remains. The NMA is a member of ICOM. I am a member of ICOM. The Director of the NMA is the President of ICOM Australia. ICOM opposes repatriation. Am I employed to do something that my employer should reprimand me for doing?

43 P. Totaro, 'Italy agrees to return Aboriginal remains', *Sydney Morning Herald*, 13 July 2009. Online. Available HTTP: http://www.smh.com.au/world/italy-agrees-to-return-aboriginal- remains-20090712-dhfj.html (accessed 13 July 2009).

44 Department for Culture, Media and Sport, *Report of the Working Group on Human Remains*, 2003, pp. 1–5. Online. Available HTTP: http://www.culture.gov.uk/images/publications/ wghr_reportfeb07.pdf (accessed 2 July 2009).

45 Department for Culture, Media and Sport, *Report of the Working Group on Human Remains*, 2003. Online. Available HTTP: http://www.culture.gov.uk/reference_library/publications/ 4553.aspx (accessed 28 June 2009).

46 For example, Edinburgh University, UK Royal College of Surgeons, Exeter Museum, Manchester Museum, Horniman Museum, the Science Museum, Bristol Museums and

Art Gallery, Torquay Museum, Royal Cornwall Museum, Hancock Museum, Glasgow Museum, University College London, Museums Scotland, Wellcome Trust, Liverpool Museum and Brighton and Hove Museum.

47 The British Museum, *Human Remains*, n.d. Online. Available HTTP: http://www.britishmuseum.org/the_museum/news_and_press_releases/statements/human_remains.aspx (accessed 22 July 2009); *The British Museum Policy on Human Remains*, 2006. Online. Available HTTP: http://www.britishmuseum.org/PDF/Human%20Remains%206%20Oct%202006.pdf (accessed 22 July 2009).

48 J. Amos, 'Science argues to keep bones', *BBC On Line*, 16 May 2003. Online. Available HTTP: http://news.bbc.co.uk/2/hi/science/nature/3032657.stm (accessed 2 July 2009).

49 National Parks Service, US Department of the Interior, *National NAGPRA*. Online. Available HTTP: http://www.nps.gov/history/nagpra/ (accessed 2 July 2009).

50 J. Macklin, 'Indigenous leaders to bring home grandmothers remains', Press Release, Minister for Families, Housing, Community Services and Indigenous Affairs, 26 July 2008. Online. Available HTTP: http://www.facs.gov.au/internet/jennymacklin.nsf/print/indig_leaders_bring_remains_28jul08.htm (accessed 13 July 2009).

51 For example, *Aboriginal and Torres Strait Islander Heritage Protection Act 1984*. Online. Available HTTP: http://www.austlii.edu.au/au/legis/cth/consol_act/aatsihpa1984549/ (accessed 13 July 2009).

52 United Nations Educational Scientific and Cultural Organisation 1970, *Convention on the Means of Prohibiting and Preventing the Illicit Import, Export and Transfer of Ownership of Cultural Property 1970*. Online. Available HTTP: http://portal.unesco.org/en/ev.php-URL_ID=13039&URL_DO=DO_TOPIC&URL_SECTION=201.html (accessed 18 July 2009).

53 UNIDROIT (International Institute for the Unification of Private Law) *Convention on Stolen or Illegally Exported Cultural Objects* (Rome, 24 June 1995). Online. Available HTTP: http://www.unidroit.org/english/conventions/1995culturalproperty/1995culturalproperty-e.htm (accessed 18 July 2009).

54 A. F. Vrdoljak, *International Law, Museums and the Return of Cultural Objects*, Cambridge: Cambridge University Press, 2006.

55 United Nations, *United Nations Declaration of the Rights of Indigenous Peoples Adopted by General Assembly Resolution 61/295 on 13 September 2007*, 2007. Online. Available HTTP: http://www.un.org/esa/socdev/unpfii/en/drip.html (accessed 18 July 2009).

"Article 11 …

2. States shall provide redress through effective mechanisms, which may include restitution, developed in conjunction with indigenous peoples, with respect to their cultural, intellectual, religious and spiritual property taken without their free, prior and informed consent or in violation of their laws, traditions and customs.

Article 12

1. Indigenous peoples have the right … . to the repatriation of their human remains.

2. States shall seek to enable the access and/or repatriation of ceremonial objects and human remains in their possession through fair, transparent and effective mechanisms developed in conjunction with indigenous peoples concerned.

Australia, while not an original signatory state, was nonetheless repatriating Indigenous remains, both domestically and internationally, under internal policies.

56 For example, and as cited above, 'The National Statement on Ethical Conduct in Human Research' and the various Coroners Acts, Transplantation and Anatomy Acts.

57 After working in repatriation for a number of years, and being well-informed in debates and discussions in the Australian archaeology, anthropology and museums industries, it is only in recent years that I have become aware of the work being done by jurists, in particular, Professor Lyndell Prott, Dr. P. J. O'Keefe and Professor Ana Filipa Vrdoljak, Australian experts in international cultural heritage law.

58 M. Denholm and P. Wilson, "Museum Bones Legal Fight 'a Waste' of $1m", *The Australian*, 4 February 2007. Online. Available HTTP: http://www.theaustralian.news.com.au/story/0,20867,21278185-2702,00.html (accessed 30 July 2009).

59 See also M. Duan, 'What Lies Beneath: Should Museums Repatriate Their Collections of Ancient Human Remains'? *The Triple Helix*, 2008. Online. Available HTTP: http://camtriplehelix.com/magazine/Mich08_16.pdf (accessed 30 July 2009).

60 http://www.quaibranly.fr/fileadmin/user_upload/pdf/Original_Version_Symposium_Human_Remains.pdf.

61 http://www.quaibranly.fr/fileadmin/user_upload/pdf/Original_Version_Symposium_Human_Remains.pdf See pp. 5, 70–96, quote p. 5. Session *'The status of human remains from a legal, ethical and philosophical point of view'* "This discussion examined French and international law relative to the treatment and property of human remains, the possible interpretations of the French bio-ethics bill of 1994, the ethical and philosophical questions raised by the extension of the notion of person to human remains."

62 This point was particularly well argued by Marie Cornu.

63 For example, The British Museum 'Policy on Human Remains', states:

> 5.8   In the display of human remains at the Museum … the public benefits of display will be balanced against the known feelings of
>
> 5.8.1   any individual with a direct and close genealogical link to the remains (where they are less than 100 years old); or
>
> 5.8.2   a community which has Cultural Continuity with the remains in question and for whom the remains have Cultural Importance (where they are more than 100 years old).

The British Museum Policy on Human Remains, 2006. Online. Available HTTP: http://www.britishmuseum.org/PDF/Human%20Remains%206%20Oct%202006.pdf (accessed 22 July 2009).

64 The National Museum of Australia's 'Return of Cultural Objects Policy' applies to all cultural material, both Indigenous and non-Indigenous.

17
Visible listening
Discussion, debate and governance in the museum

James M. Bradburne

The question is whether we can really still keep telling the same stories the same way and assume that we can provide lives of decent quality for those who follow us in our places. I think the answer is no. Part of the solution is to find new stories that have new meanings and new value systems implicit in them. I don't know what those stories are. And I don't think it is the job of the historian or the museum to create the story. Our job is to create the context in which people can create those stories and reach some level of consensus around them.[1]

Robert Archibald, Director, Missouri Historical Museum

Who is the museum for?

Ethics is a branch of philosophy which seeks to address questions about the nature of morality, how moral values should be determined, how a moral outcome can be achieved in specific situations, how moral capacity or moral agency develops and what its nature is and what moral values people actually abide by. Much of applied ethics is concerned with just three theories: utilitarianism, in which the practical consequences of policies are evaluated on the assumption that the right policy will be the one which results in the greatest happiness to the greatest number; notions based on 'rules'; and an assumption that there is an obligation to perform the 'right' action, regardless of actual consequences. It is clear that museum ethics is a particular form of applied ethics, and shares with business ethics the idea that institutions, not only individuals, can act morally. This is not an uncontested claim; organisations have often been considered exempt from moral claims, as it is argued that only individuals can act morally, and that an extension of individual morality to a larger entity such as government, non-profit agency or corporate entity is invalid, as such entities lack the coherence of belief to be considered morally accountable. International conventions have wrestled with the notion of moral responsibility for actions from their inception: the Geneva Conventions explicitly proscribe collective punishment, and, conversely, although the Hague Convention clearly held signatory powers responsible for adherence to the provisions of the charter, nowhere were individuals said to be culpable for the policies of their government.

So how can an institution have ethics? Robert Janes has written compellingly about the need for museums to take seriously their responsibility towards global issues, including human rights, sustainability and climate change.[2] Social responsibility has been on the museum's agenda since the first great public museums were born in the early years of the French Revolution. Social responsibility informed many of the innovative museological thinkers of the twentieth century, from John Cotton Dana to Marshall McLuhan.[3] This responsibility has been framed in diverse ways; from the abstract expression of accessibility to cultural resources incumbent upon a democratic society to a concrete and specific responsibility to recognise the ownership of cultural property. Traditionally, museums have espoused a conservative logic of stewardship, in which other people's objects were preserved from harm for future generations for their own and the objects' good. Recently, however, this role of the museum has been called into question, and many now argue that the museum should be a forum for diverse competing voices, not the preserve of the curatorial 'voice of god' enshrined in the museum label. Instead of a place for the museum to tell visitors a story, it should be a place where visitors' stories can be recognised and heard.

Robert Archibald, Director of the Missouri Historical Society, argues that it is time to challenge the hegemony of the curator and of the museum. "Who is the curator? Who defines the meanings of objects? Where are the experts? Who has authority? Every museum visitor is a storyteller with authority. Every evocative object on exhibit is a mnemonic device. Every visitor interaction is story making as visitors fit portions of our collections into personal frames of reference, most often in ways we neither intended nor anticipated. Visitors rummage through our galleries searching for pertinent objects ... We museum professionals can no longer claim ultimate authority in what our artefacts, our collections mean. Nor can we assert interpretative control over the past. We are preservers, facilitators, conveners so that the conversations can take place and the stories be told and, more importantly, shared. This is who we really are, who we must be."[4]

Museums often become locked in the perverse logic of representation. The heart of the problem, it seems to me, stems from an unwillingness to re-examine the way in which museums have traditionally defined their own role, and what is called for is a total reappraisal of the notion that museums can and should have something to do with shaping identity. When confronted with the collapse of the grand narratives, the museum's response to the postmodern dilemma has been to remain firmly 'top down', and to address the content of the narrative, ever seduced by the desire to retain control over the narrative it presents. 'Bad' old grand narratives are to be replaced by 'good' new decentred authorless narratives. Instead of museums of heroes, we now make museums of victims. Instead of museums that celebrate imperial identity, we make museums that trumpet new identities. But even in inviting selected representatives – however legitimate or legitimised – it is still the museum that calls the shots, and shapes the content. So under pressure to affirm new national identities – we create a Scottish Museum as the counterpart to the British Museum, and, who knows, perhaps we will soon need a new Museum of the Isle of Skye, a Glasgow Museum, a Gorbals Museum, a Museum of the three flats next door – as our identity becomes increasingly fragmented. Where we stop if we follow this logic is only a matter of time and entropy. By definition, the notion of nationhood is restrictive, historical and constructed from the top down. It is a part of the legitimisation of political objectives on behalf of those who wield power, and part of the ideological armament of political action. Culture, on the other hand, is fluid, ever-changing, and almost always bottom-up – boundaries are only discovered through exploration. I was born in Canada, a country whose identity is both shaped and distorted by disagreement over which claims to sovereignty take priority. Is Québec a nation? The Dene people? The Inuit? If so, what is Canada? Which museum legitimises what identity? The question would be even more vexed if we took the example of Serbia. Who is a national and who is a minority depends on the definition. A Kosovar is in the minority in Serbia, while a Serb would be in the minority in an independent Kosovo. What would a Kosovar Museum in Belgrade exhibit? Or a Serbian Museum in an independent Kosovo? As museum professionals are we content if our museums are only instruments through which we trumpet jingoistic self-affirmations?

Mine Games: an early experiment

If the museum is to claim moral authority, therefore, it should look to develop opportunities for many voices to be heard instead of writing those stories itself. In 1990 the Canadian anthropologist Drew Ann Wake and I were invited to develop a new gallery on the earth sciences for Science World, a large science centre located in downtown Vancouver.[5] There were two clear alternatives to tackling the subject. On the one hand, the earth sciences could be treated as they have been in traditional science centres. Visitors would learn about geological time, the development of rocks, faulting and continental drift. Following the example of other science centres, we could link geological themes to newsworthy geological events that captured the public's interest – volcanoes and earthquakes. By treating the earth sciences as a subset of geophysics, we would follow a traditional path: separating scientific fact from social issues.

The alternative was clearly more challenging. Instead of an exhibition on the earth sciences, we proposed to look at how the geological sciences are applied in a political and economic context: in short, we suggested an exhibition on mining. The exhibition Mine Games would deal with the issues surrounding the mining industry in the province of British Columbia, issues that had been increasingly the subject of heated debate in the press, on television, in parliament and in the streets. This single change – from earth science to mining – entailed a complete re-examination of the way in which the exhibition would be planned and designed. With a mining exhibition, we could initiate a debate about the future of the province, asking visitors to evaluate any number of competing positions, including those of the First Nations, the mining industry, the government and environmental activists. An exhibition on mining would question the role the science centre should play, suggesting that the role of the science centre is to prepare visitors to participate in the social and political life of their community.

The exhibition was designed as a series of games to enable the visitor to advise a fictitious community – Grizzly, BC – on whether or not to allow a mine to proceed, and culminated in an interactive voting theatre called Hotseat! where visitors debated how best to advise the townspeople. Visitors were given the opportunity to learn a wide range of scientific information, not all of it in agreement. They were invited to explore this information and develop skills that would help them to understand, and to alter, the political process in the province. Once the exhibition opened, it was clear that the visitors quickly understood the excitement of the game structure, and used the clipboards provided at the entrance to record their progress. A comparatively large percentage of visitors stayed in the exhibition for extended periods of time, and many returned regularly to test new ideas and debate different options. A high level of discussion and involvement were observed.[6] The computer games were highly successful in attracting and engaging teenaged users, while the hands-on exhibits and demonstrations kept other user groups actively participating. The Hot-seat! theatre gave visitors a real say in the issues surrounding resource development in the province, and the entire exhibition continued to be a forum for debate about the issue for over four years after the exhibition opened – two years after it was originally scheduled to close.

Whilst this was an exceptional initiative in 1993, this approach has subsequently been explored by several institutions around the world, notably the Ontario Science Centre, the Museu de la Ciencia in Barcelona and the Dana Centre at the Science Museum, London. However, despite superficial similarities, many recent initiatives intended to invite other voices into the space of the museum in the form of community involvement, co-curation by 'facilitator activists' are often merely replacing one voice of presumed legitimacy with another. This phenomenon also accounts for the rash of 'museums of victims' being built to replace the 'museums of heroes' of the nineteenth and early twentieth centuries mentioned above. What makes the Mine Games experiment exceptional is that, rather than being a pulpit from which the newly legitimised voice can be heard, it was intended as a 'piazza' in which competing, dissonant, but equally legitimate voices could be heard and their positions evaluated by visitors.

The current experiment: the Fondazione Palazzo Strozzi

The Fondazione Palazzo Strozzi is an experiment in sustainable innovation. Since its founding in July 2006, the key challenge of the Fondazione Palazzo Strozzi has been to bring an international approach to making culture in Florence, to provide a platform for experimentation, to establish a place for debate and discussion, to create new synergies with other cultural players and to be a catalyst for cultural change. In the past year the Fondazione has found several ways to express its double mission of bringing international level cultural events to Florence, and giving the Palazzo Strozzi back to the city. One of them is the well-known slogan 'Think global, act local'. Another, stressing the importance of seeing the Palazzo Strozzi as a single cultural destination that appeals to diverse interests, is to redefine it as 'not just exhibitions'. This has seen the Fondazione expand its activities to include opening the Centre for Contemporary Culture Strozzina (CCCS) and a permanent exhibition on the Palazzo's history, as well as bringing the Palazzo's courtyard to life with a café, bookshop, seating and wide range of collateral activities, a programme of installations, concerts, fashion shows, lectures and events. The goal of the Fondazione is to awaken the visitor's curiosity, to whet their appetite for culture and to recognise their intelligence.

What is visible listening?

The Palazzo Strozzi is deeply visitor-centred, and its cultural strategy can be described as 'visible listening'[7] – the recognition that culture is made of many voices – and the importance of making different voices visible. This approach was inspired in large measure by the municipal school system of Reggio Emilia, where I worked on several projects with Reggio Children, the non-profit institution responsible for promoting the work of Reggio Emilia's educators. Together we spent a great deal of time thinking about how their educational philosophy of 'making learning visible' could be translated into the very different context of a public exhibition. So what does 'visible listening' mean in an exhibition? At the Palazzo Strozzi we have tried several different strategies. In the exhibition *Cézanne in Florence* (spring 2007), 'visible listening' meant including texts throughout the exhibition written by two young girls, eleven-year-old Anna H. and thirteen-year-old Emily W.[8] Their comments provided a fresh new perspective on Cézanne's masterpieces, completely different than that of the curators. In the exhibition *ControModa* (fall 2007),[9] visible listening took the form of running comments on the exhibition curators' wall texts, written by six of the world's leading fashion critics, including Suzy Menkes, Holly Brubach and Franca Sozzani. In both cases the Palazzo Strozzi signalled its willingness to admit other points of view into the exhibition.

The exhibition *China: at the Court of the Emperors* (spring 2008) had as one of its key goals to understand how Florence could better address the needs of Chinese visitors, both from abroad and from the local Chinese community in Prato, which is one of the largest in Italy. As a consequence emphasis was placed on the Chinese language itself, and all the wall texts in the exhibition – and a selection of well-known Tang poems – were written in Chinese by one of China's leading calligraphers. An initiative with the local milk producer – Mukki Latte – saw millions of milk cartons printed with a short lesson about the Chinese language on one side during the exhibition, linked with an invitation to participate in weekend family workshops. The exhibition's 'visible listening' took the form of special labels, 'Through Chinese Eyes', in which native-born Chinese themselves spoke of how they responded to the objects on display. For the Chinese, a Madonna and Child is exotic but a Boddhisatva isn't, so they were asked to give their opinion on some of the objects in the exhibition. The importance of the Chinese perspective shouldn't be underestimated: for instance, for them, a beautiful dancer represented the ideal of Chinese beauty, of which they say her face is as 'round as a pearl, and is moist as jade' – a startling expression unfamiliar to us. To prepare these labels for the exhibition, three focus groups were conducted with Chinese adults and children of different ages in a Beijing museum to find out what interested them about the objects in the exhibition, because in a way it was 'their' exhibition as much as it was the Palazzo Strozzi's. Given the importance of the Chinese language in the exhibition, the Palazzo Strozzi published a series of seven works in dual language editions: Italian/Chinese and English/Chinese. These included an oral history of the first Chinese to come to

Tuscany in the 1930s; a children's book; a book about the elements China and Tuscany have in common, such as silk, terracotta, porcelain and street food; and a book subtitled 'They all look the same,' examining how native-born Chinese see Western Europeans and Western culture, and how Western Europeans see the Chinese culture.[10] Finally, the 'passport' that accompanies every Palazzo Strozzi exhibition was published in all three languages, and given to every Chinese who received a visa at the Italian Embassy in Beijing in 2008. According to the visitor surveys done during the exhibition (over 1500 surveys as well as interviews with selected visitors), the attention paid to the Chinese language yielded important dividends not only with visitors from China, who appreciated the inclusion of Tang poetry, but also with Chinese community members, who commented favourably on the inclusion of the Chinese language texts in the exhibition.

All major exhibitions at the Palazzo Strozzi express – in one way or another – the Fondazione's commitment to 'visible listening'. In the exhibition *Painting Light* (Summer 2008), visitors were invited to become actively involved as 'art detectives' to solve questions posed by the Impressionist masterpieces in the exhibition.[11] In the exhibition *Women in Power* (Fall 2008),[12] visitors could contribute to a large public artwork, each one helping create a tapestry that grew continuously throughout the exhibition. In every major exhibition, the Fondazione Palazzo Strozzi encourages the design team to find ways in which the visitor can leave a trace of their passage in the space of the exhibition.

The Fondazione Palazzo Strozzi: an experiment in governance

The means by which an institution expresses its corporate morality is through its governance: the administrative framework used to make decisions on behalf of the institution and its stakeholders, and defined in the organisation's Statutes, Code of Ethics and Board Guidelines. In addition to being an experiment in creating sustainable culture, the Fondazione Palazzo Strozzi represents an important experiment in the management of Italian cultural institutions. As a public–private foundation with four founding members, the City of Florence, the Province of Florence, the Florentine Chamber of Commerce and an association of private partners representing some of Italy's leading businesses, it is unique, governed by an independent and autonomous board of trustees nominated by the founders for a period of three years. The trustees, although nominated by the founders, do not represent them, and the Foundation's Statutes give the trustees the authority to function autonomously – at arm's length – from those who nominated them for their three-year term.

The aim is to model the Fondazione upon best management practice in the private sector, while creating a rich cultural programme to serve the needs of the city, province and region's citizens. The Fondazione Palazzo Strozzi is an experiment meant to show that cultural institutions are best managed with a mix of public and private resources and experience; the organisational structure also is intended to demonstrate that independence and autonomy are the most reliable means to ensure that cultural institutions are both sustainable in the long term and responsive to their diverse stakeholders, both public and private. The Fondazione Palazzo Strozzi – even in the difficult economic conditions of 2008 and 2009 – continues to thrive in part because of the attention it pays to 'visible listening' considered as a more democratic approach to governance.

The mission of the Fondazione Palazzo Strozzi is to bring international-level cultural events to Florence, and to open the Palazzo Strozzi up to Florence and its citizens. At the level of governance, this has taken the form of two major initiatives. The first is the Association of Partners of Palazzo Strozzi (APPS). The APPS was created as a framework for the support of the private sector for a project deliberately seen as a model for Italy. The APPS is transversal, and includes competitors in different sectors, such as Ferragamo, Gucci, the wine producers Antinori, Frescobaldi, Folonari and Mazzei, as well as international firms American Express, Saatchi & Saatchi and Boston Consulting Group. In return for a contribution equal to that of the public sector partners, the APPS has the right to nominate two members to the seven-person board of trustees.

The second initiative is the Friends of Palazzo Strozzi. Launched in April 2008, the Friends of Palazzo Strozzi was designed to 'give the Palazzo back to the city'. Both individuals and small businesses were invited to participate in the life of the Palazzo Strozzi, which includes special Friends' events, Family Sundays and meetings with the Foundation's director and staff to discuss future programming. Whereas many museums have friends' associations, this close involvement of the Palazzo Strozzi's supporters – which reflects its commitment to 'visible listening' – is a major step forward in the governance of Italian cultural institutions. At the Palazzo Strozzi, more than just the Palazzo's grand doors are open to the city – its decision-making also takes into account the voices of at least some of its users, who, according to research conducted in collaboration with Boston Consulting Group (as well as the over 1500 surveys of every exhibition), represent a broad spectrum of the local population – not just the cultural elite.

The invitation to the Friends of Palazzo Strozzi to participate – even in a modest way – in the governance of the Foundation highlights some of the ambiguities surrounding governance and museum ethics, in particular with regard to involving the public. Consistent with most museum codes of ethics, the not-for-profit Fondazione Palazzo Strozzi should create value for the public it serves. But how is this public articulated? And how can the voice of the public be expressed in such a way that it can participate? Andrea Bandelli and Elly Konijn in this volume have criticised museums for the lack of genuine public involvement in their governance, but to what extent and in what ways is this critique justified? The difficulty seems to lie in reconciling the notion of an open-ended and undifferentiated 'public' consisting of the institution's real and potential users, and the expression of this public in a form whereby its voice can effectively be heard.

Surely the public – in the form of various levels of government – is already fully involved in the governance of most cultural institutions, at least in the European context. Three of the Fondazione Palazzo Strozzi's founders are public bodies, and can be said to represent the city of Florence, the province of Florence and the city's Chamber of Commerce (in Italy a public entity). Moreover, the region of Tuscany is a key multi-year sponsor of the Palazzo's activities. So the public – at least as defined by the institutions in a representational democracy – already has a strong voice in the governance of the institution. Exceptionally, with the Fondazione, the private sector too has a voice through the APPS, the founder that represents the private sector. So what 'public' is missing? Who should have a voice in the Fondazione's governance who does not already?

When Bandelli and others quite rightly champion the public's right to be part of an institution's governance, they are often talking about those who are not necessarily able to influence the decisions already made on their behalf by their elected representatives. Who is this public? Clearly in the case of the Palazzo Strozzi, this public is represented, in part at least, by its Friends. But even this is problematic, as it is not at all clear what gives a Friends association greater legitimacy than the publicly elected bodies already fully integrated in the governance of the institution. Experience shows that any group that articulates itself 'politically', i.e. by creating internal mechanisms of governance, representation and administration, becomes similar to the others, and excludes the undifferentiated 'public' whose participation is (sometimes nostalgically) desired. Paradoxically, the structure of the Friends of Palazzo Strozzi comes closest to representing the undifferentiated public, as it is not an association, has no statutes, minutes or officers, and organises itself solely around the events to discuss the plans and programme of the Palazzo Strozzi. As the composition of the Friends is continually changing, the profile of the individual members can be surprisingly diverse. The Fondazione is currently working on a series of initiatives meant to ensure that even those who are not frequent visitors to the Palazzo also feel welcome to participate in the discussions. What it lacks in structural legitimacy – representatives, a seat on the Board, a formal voice in decisions – the Friends group makes up for in being permeable, open to new voices, and, in certain ways, at least potentially, a reflection of the public the Palazzo Strozzi serves.

It is important to stress that the 'visible listening' approach is based on a logic of diversity (in the original, not the current American sense of the word), not representation. The frameworks in which constituencies are declared representatives and the legitimacy of that representation often merely replace, rather than fundamentally change, the nature of the museum enterprise, leaving the management structure profoundly top-down, with merely the representatives changed. Creating diversity, on the other hand, makes no claims to legitimise one or another voice, or to privilege one voice over another. Loris Malaguzzi, one of the key figures in the municipal schools of Reggio Emilia, speaks of the '100 languages of children', and calls for a respect for the countless different ways children see the world, regardless of whether they represent a constituency other than the speaker herself. The very act of inviting different – even random – voices into the space of the museum, and of giving any and every visitor the possibility of leaving a trace of their presence, is a very different – and in some ways more powerful – cultural strategy, as it remains bottom-up, fluid, and constantly open to change. It is not the role of a fundamentally non-democratic institution such as the museum to legitimise this voice or that, a task for which it is ill suited and ill equipped. The role of the museum is to create a space in which many competing voices can be heard, and to find ways in which the voices of its many and diverse users can remain visible in order to contribute to the conversations of future users.

The real challenge: governing in the raw

Transparency is at the heart of ethical governance. As Maxwell Anderson points out, transparent leadership requires the disclosure of information that has traditionally been seen as sensitive, such as how the institution attracts support and spends it, who it has succeeded in serving and how it measures success. Transparency reveals not only the mechanics of the institution's operations, but also its philosophy of management.[13] In this regard the Fondazione Palazzo Strozzi is exemplary in Italy. Already all the Fondazione's Statutes, its Code of Ethics, Board Guidelines as well as the audited accounts and Annual Report are all available on the Fondazione's web site, www.palazzostrozzi.org.

In Indianapolis, Maxwell Anderson, CEO of the Indianapolis Museum of Art and former director of the Whitney Museum of American Art and Toronto's Art Gallery of Ontario, has made key data about the institution available to the public with what he calls the 'IMA Dashboard'. "In 2007 the Indianapolis Museum of Art launched the IMA Dashboard – a visual display of various data about the museum and its activities. Updated regularly, the IMA Dashboard offers online visitors access to current statistics about attendance, art collections, finances and other areas important to the daily operation of the museum. Visitors and stakeholders can use these changing facts and figures to better understand how the museum operates as a public institution with a responsibility to its community. The resource also serves as a management tool for museum staff members to measure their own performance relative to how effectively the museum is pursuing its mission and its strategic priorities. Statistics are organised and sorted both by topic and department to enable easy updating and navigation. Information such as attendance and web usage is generated on a weekly basis while other statistics are generated monthly."[14] Audited year-end financial statistics on the Palazzo Strozzi are currently available online and exhibition attendance figures are published weekly – so what's left? If the provisional financial performance of the foundation were also made visible on a monthly or weekly basis, the public – and the foundation's key stakeholders – would be in the position to comment on the ongoing financial situation of the institution in real time. Even if such disclosure would be allowed by the Statutes (which requires that financial data be audited and approved prior to being made public), whether this would enhance – or undermine – the trustees' autonomy and their ability to govern is a question that besets the debate about proposals for democracy by online referendum and deserves more consideration than can be offered in this chapter.

Conclusion

Nelson Goodman wrote in 1980 that 'the museum has to function as an institution for the prevention of blindness in order to make works work. Works work when, by stimulating inquisitive looking, sharpening perception, raising visual intelligence, they participate in and ... the making and remaking of our worlds'.[15] The ethics of an institution are expressed by its actions, which, in turn, are shaped by its governance and its leadership. For an institution to behave ethically – to respect and recognise diversity, to be accessible, generous and welcoming, to be a place where 'the life of the mind is a pleasure'[16] – it must be able to act autonomously. It must also be transparent and provide the means for scrutiny by its stakeholders, which in the case of most cultural institutions also includes the public, in one form or another. The Fondazione Palazzo Strozzi is not the first institution committed to hearing and understanding its various constituencies, nor are all its initiatives unique. What makes the foundation exceptional, especially in the European context, is its robust governance by an autonomous board comprised of both public and private stakeholders committed to management best practice. This, in turn, allows the foundation to be a laboratory for culture – a place to experiment with how to best make the voices of its many users visible. When all the stakeholders have the means to participate in the life of the institution, and a voice in shaping its future, they also participate – in a small way – in the making and remaking of the world.

Notes

1 R. R. Archibald, transcribed from an untitled lecture presented at the conference Time, Space and Learning, St Louis, MO, March 2006.

2 R. P. Janes, *Museums in a Troubled World: Renewal, Irrelevance or Collapse?* London: Routledge, 2009.

3 J. C. Dana, *The New Museum*, Woodstock, VT: ElmTree Press, 1917; M. McLuhan and Q. Fiore, *The Medium is the Message*, 1st edn 1967; Berkeley, CA: Gingko Press, 2001.

4 R. R. Archibald, 'Touching on the Past', unpublished keynote lecture written for the seminar series 'The Museum as Social Laboratory: Enhancing the Object to Facilitate Social Engagement and Inclusion in Museums and Galleries', King's College, London, December 2006.

5 J. M. Bradburne, 'Mine games', with Drew Ann Wake, *Revue des Arts et Métiers* 10, spring 1995, pp. 30–37.

6 J. M. Bradburne, *Interaction in the Museum*, Hamburg: Alibris, 2000.

7 The approach of visible listening owes a huge debt to the pedagogy developed by the renowned Italian children's author Gianni Rodari and the Italian educators Loris Malaguzzi and Carlina Rinaldi.

8 J. M. Bradburne and L. Sebregondi, *Amore a prima vista*, Florence: Maschietto, 2007.

9 K. D. Spilker and S. Takeda, *ControModa*, Milan: Skira, 2007.

10 J. M. Bradburne, L. Sebregondi, A. Fiorentini and R. Bargelli, *Reflections; Correspondences; Encounters; Discoveries*, Milan: Skira, 2008.

11 C. Bucci and C. Lachi, *The Mystery of the Dead Impressionist*, Milan: Skira, 2008.

12 R. Piumini and K. Eisenbeichler, *The Divining Eye*, Florence: Mandragora, 2008; R. Palumbo, *EternArtemisia*, Bologna: Comma 22, 2008.

13 M. L. Anderson, 'Prescriptions for art museums in the decade ahead', *Curator: The Museum Journal* 50: 1, 2007, pp. 9–18.

14 P. Sacco and A. Zorloni, 'Achieving Excellence: Investigation into the Use of Performance Indicators in Museums', unpublished paper, 2009.

15 N. Goodman, speech to a joint meeting of the Canadian Museums Association and the American Association of Museums, Boston, MA, 1980, quoted in S. Weil, *Rethinking the Museum: and other Meditations*, Washington, DC: Smithsonian Institution Press, 1990, p. 173.

16 J. Miller, private verbal communication, February 1997.

18

Ethical, entrepreneurial or inappropriate?

Business practices in museums

James B. Gardner

When the economy suffers, museums suffer. Earned revenue, fund raising, invest-ments and endowments – all are critical to the continued viability of our museums and indeed our jobs, and all are vulnerable to the vicissitudes of the economy. Indeed museums have long operated so close to the edge financially that even the smallest change in the economy has direct and significant impact. We welcome good times but with the knowledge that the rewards may be few and short-lived, and we dread any economic slowdown or downturn, certain that the impact on our institu-tions will be severe and sustained.[1] In such a context, we must be entrepreneurial – we have to come up with creative solutions to our problems, not wait for larger economic changes to trickle down. But tenuous financial situations do not give us carte blanche to do whatever we feel necessary. No matter what the circumstances, we operate in the public trust, and unethical activities are never justifiable. We must draw the line between appropriate entrepreneurial initiatives and unethical business practices.

Museums have long struggled to maintain attendance and revenue levels in the face of more and trendier competitors for the public's time and money, and over the years we've found ourselves depending more and more on philanthropy and busi-ness revenue as public support has failed to keep up with needs. Many of us have tightened our belts by cutting back on public hours, canceling new exhibits and paring down programs and other offerings. Some museums have had to downsize – the National Museum of American History, for example, has not been able to fill most vacated positions and, as a consequence, lost over a third of its curatorial and collections management staff between 1999 and 2009, with significant impact on collections stewardship. Even more painfully, other museums have furloughed or laid off staff, asking remaining staff to stretch themselves and take up the slack. A few have even had to face the worst case scenario – the prospect of closing down for good. The situation became so alarming that the American Association for State and Local History held annual meeting sessions and developed a white paper in 2006 on "When a History Museum Closes."[2] For evidence of the reality of this state of affairs consider, for example, the closures of the City Museum of Washington, DC, the Robert E. Lee Boyhood Home in Alexandria, VA, and America's Black Holocaust Museum in Milwaukee, WI, not to mention the prolonged rollercoaster rides of the New York Historical Society and the American Textile History Museum.[3] We are all vulnerable.

Faced with a more competitive economic environment, museums have adopted different strategies, ranging from entrepreneurial to unethical. There's a fine line between the former and the latter – it doesn't take much to end up compromising your institution's integrity. No one ever intends to do that, but too often that's been the case. Marie Malaro argues that museums and other nonprofits in recent years have become less mission-oriented and more market-oriented: "They have failed to make choices that demonstrate sensitivity to why they are nonprofits." She warns that when museums and other nonprofits "appear to have lost sight of their public purpose, or appear too entrepreneurial or self-serving, or are unwilling to account for their activities, or merely give lip service to ethical standards, then the public reacts and questions privileged status."[4] Beginning in 2002, the Smithsonian, my own institution, came under fire for business practices undertaken to address critical resource needs. We were criticized in the press and in Congress for confidential business contracts, problematic relations with donors, and questionable expense reimbursements for senior managers brought in from the for-profit sector – and the reputation of the nation's museum suffered as a consequence.[5] At that time, in a discussion about ethical standards in regard to donor relations, a colleague from outside the Smithsonian suggested, tongue in cheek, that the most direct statement might be "Whatever the Smithsonian does, don't do it." Our reputation has clearly taken a beating since the days when the field looked to the Smithsonian and more specifically to people like Marie Malaro, then Smithsonian General Counsel, for leadership and best practices. With new management and oversight, we have reformed our business practices and are working hard to rehabilitate our reputation, but the Smithsonian should never have gotten itself in such a situation. While the ethics of business practices may be a bit complicated in some areas, I would argue that the issue is not whether there are appropriate standards but whether we as museums operate within them. We basically know what we should and should not do – we cannot claim that we do not. Responsibility for maintaining those ethical standards rests with each of us. There are no vehicles for enforcement in our field (compliance with the law and financial accounting standards are different issues), so the only thing standing between ethical and unethical behavior is our recognizing our obligation to the public trust, to maintaining public confidence, not just for today but for the long term.

The Smithsonian's problems may be, perhaps, the most visible and widely discussed in the museum community, but we are, unfortunately, not alone in our transgressions. Too many museums today, of all kinds and sizes, seem to use "whatever's necessary" as a guide for decision making, arguing that the bottom line is what's critical, that survival has to take priority over the niceties of museum ethics. Let's not kid ourselves – even when we invoke "protecting the collections" as our justification, such behavior is usually rooted in more practical concerns about paying bills and meeting payroll. While not dismissing the anxieties of cash-strapped museums and their staffs, I would argue that little is achieved in saving a museum if doing so means abandoning its mission and violating the public trust. Museums are about more than us and our jobs. But we all know that. The problem is not the absence of a professional consensus on ethical standards but our tendency too often to look the other way, to choose the expedient over principle.

I approach this topic not as an expert in business or legal matters – I'm a historian from the curatorial side of the house, with little direct responsibility for business matters on a day-to-day basis. But I work in a context shaped by such decisions and do not have the luxury of curatorial isolation. More directly, I was involved in the development of the Smithsonian's first institutional ethics statement, one of the governance reforms that followed the resignation of Lawrence Small in 2007, and I was appointed as the first chair of its Ethics Advisory Board, responsible not only for advising the Institution's Secretary and its Regents but also for fostering discussion across the Smithsonian community on our individual and collective responsibilities.[6] My interest is less in the responsibilities we face as individuals (for example, conflict of interest, use of employment, and the like, which are important but not my focus here) and more in our larger obligations as museums. While business practices are arguably the actions of individuals, it is in our collective responsibilities and decision making that we seem to fail most often. What follows is not a comprehensive survey of business practices and ethical issues but rather an exploration of key issues and challenges. While my specific focus is museum practice in the United States, the basic principles are applicable anywhere – they are based on professional standards, not the laws of specific jurisdictions.

Governance

In *Museum Governance*, Marie Malaro convincingly argues that every board of trustees should recognize the importance of ethics to their governance responsibilities, not only enhancing "the public's perception of the integrity of the organization" but also constituting "prudent risk management."[7] For most museum trustees, this often boils down to simply avoiding conflicts of interest – in other words not putting personal interests ahead of duty or loyalty to the museum. While that will always be a governance issue and the standards can get a bit complicated when distinctions are made between core and subsidiary functions, it doesn't concern me too much – I believe we all basically know what's at stake and how such problems should be handled.[8]

What worries me more is when a governing body is simply "asleep at the wheel," not taking seriously their governance responsibilities. How can a board claim to operate consistent with its mission and responsibilities when it gives only cursory review to business practices, and then only within the context of information provided by the CEO? Too often, Marie Malaro notes in *Museum Governance*, "It is easier for boards to drift along without too much thought until a crisis occurs. ... When the executive director of an organization is a strong personality who prefers to set the pace, a board often allows itself to be led. ..."[9] In the furor that led to the resignation of former Secretary Small, the Smithsonian's Regents certainly learned the hard way that they do indeed have fiduciary responsibility and must take it seriously, not simply go through the motions and rely on the CEO.[10] Too many boards delegate too much responsibility, assuming we're all in this together, sharing the same values and goals. By the time they realize that that is not the case, it's too late, and the damage is done. I'm not arguing for micromanagement by boards but for reaffirming and following through on the respective roles and responsibilities of board and staff in our joint enterprise. According to Malaro, a prudent board should be able to show that it reviewed and discussed appropriate information before voting on a matter, and that the "decision can be supported by the information presented (i.e., reasonable people could come to that conclusion based on the information presented)."[11] That is not a high standard – any board that fails to meet it is not taking its responsibilities seriously. While board training may help, it doesn't always – this is less about training than about the board's engagement in its responsibilities.

Financial management

Whenever the economic situation worsens, whether locally or on a larger scale, too many museums turn to creative accounting. Perhaps the most problematic accounting solution in the United States is ignoring the difference between restricted and unrestricted assets and deciding to capitalize collections. While the American Association of Museums has avoided taking a clear stand on this, AASLH states unequivocally that "Collections shall not be capitalized or treated as financial assets," and the Association of Art Museum Directors similarly argues that "collections should not be capitalized."[12] Yet too many museums see capitalization as an option. Part of the problem is the guidelines established by FASB (Financial Accounting Standards Board) and GASB (for state and local governments), which allow and even encourage capitalization. The fact that they do not require it gets lost in the discussion, and too many museums end up capitalizing their collections. Some establish monetary values for their collections for insurance purposes and others as a strategy to document the investment in their collections (and hence to claim a continuing need), but too frequently capitalization is frankly nothing more than the first step toward using the collections as collateral or selling them to address financial needs, actions which are clearly unethical.

Even more problematic, in 1993, the New-York History Society came under public and professional criticism for using part of its collection as collateral to secure a loan during difficult financial times. More recently, in 2003, Hancock Shaker Village in Massachusetts pledged its assets, including its collections, to secure a loan. While neither collection may ever have actually been at risk of being liquidated to cover debts, the museums' decisions to use their collections as collateral arguably converted them from restricted assets held in the public trust to capitalized financial assets to be managed along with other unrestricted property. In a white paper on capitalization of collections, AASLH states flatly that such practice "puts the institution's (and public's) collections at risk" and is "unacceptable in meeting the institution's fiduciary obligations." More eloquently, Robert McDonald, then director of the Museum of the City of New York, charged that the NYHS had "jeopardized its soul."[13]

One of the worst examples of the use of collections as unrestricted assets was the 2002 sale by the Museum of Northern Arizona of twenty-one works of art in order to fund payroll and other operating costs.[14] And in 2005, the Rhode Island Historical Society became the focus of public and professional outrage over its plans to sell off part of its permanent collection in order to address deficits caused by the erosion of its endowment, the consequence of a questionable decision to handle ongoing budget needs through heavy draws on the endowment. The Society essentially proposed an unethical use of restricted assets (the collections) as the solution to a situation rooted in the unethical use of other restricted assets (the endowment).[15] Then in 2008, the decision of the National Academy Museum and School of Fine Arts to sell two paintings from its collection in order to meet operating costs led to an acrimonious public debate about the institution's mission and survival. Such situations become more complicated when a museum's parent body is from outside the field and does not hold the same professional ethical standards. For example, in 2007, Randolph College, despite arguments from museum staff about ethical obligations, decided to sell pieces of art held by its Maier Museum in order to address financial needs. Or consider Brandeis University's proposal in 2009 to close entirely, for financial reasons, the Rose Art Museum and sell its collections.[16] And then there's the problem of historic houses and properties – while a historic house or property may arguably be a museum's most important object, it is too often treated as an unrestricted asset and used in ways contrary to accepted standards.[17] Unfortunately those examples are just the visible tip of the iceberg – for every high profile situation, there are *many* more museum professionals quietly trying to convince their boards not to take this route. Somewhere along the line, too many museums are panicking and losing sight of the fact that collections are restricted assets, held in the public trust, that cannot be used to address financial problems, for the short term or the long.

In a time of tightening resources, I'm also concerned about the ethical side of budgeting and resource allocation, a subject too rarely discussed. How are museum budget priorities set? How is it ethical to claim to be an educational institution and then turn around and cut the education budget first? And when there is funding for educational programs, what are our obligations as a public trust to underserved audiences relative to core constituencies? Those are not just programmatic decisions – they are rooted in how we define ourselves and in our ethical obligations to the public we serve. Or what about collections – if we define our museums as collecting institutions, how do we justify the relatively meager allocation of resources to collections stewardship that we see in so many museums today? One of the purposes of a joint American Association of Museums–National Museum of American History collections planning initiative launched in 2002 has been to better position collections within the business plans of museums, recognizing the "radical" notion that collections stewardship requires financial support.[18] Museums need to pause and consider whether continuing to collect is ethical if they cannot provide the financial support to appropriately care for existing collections, let alone new collections. Museum budgeting today is too frequently detached from mission, lurching from project to project without providing the sustained support for the core activities for which we were established.

Earned income

As public support tightens, museums rely more and more on earned income and fund raising. The former includes not only admission charges but also shop revenue, special event fees and other proceeds from business activities. Too often we come dangerously close to crossing the line in such activities. As we try to dodge unrelated business income tax, we end up making tenuous claims of educational value for gift shop products. And we develop products based on our collections that in too many instances seem to cheapen the very reason we exist. Is commodification of the collections appropriate, given that we hold them in the public trust, not as revenue sources? AAM, AASLH and ICOM assert that such revenue-producing activities should not compromise a museum's integrity and mission, but what constitutes "compromise"?[19] Is there ever a point when business activities become inappropriate or have we become so income needy that we'll do anything for money? Malaro finds that too often today "Mission gets blurred or is so elastic it can be construed to accommodate whatever might be the latest income-producing technique."[20]

Some argued in 2006 that this was the Smithsonian's problem – that it had become so focused on developing new revenue sources that it had lost its way. In insisting on the confidentiality of the terms of a partnership with Showtime Networks Inc., the Smithsonian opened itself to widespread criticism for "under the table" arrangements of questionable benefit to the Institution. But is it realistic to expect the corporate world to enter into contracts with museums without some level of confidentiality? Can we address both our responsibilities as museums and the needs of the businesses we partner with? While the Smithsonian's relationship with Showtime in the development of a Smithsonian television channel has yielded impressive products, the process itself – the secrecy surrounding the contract and the exclusivity of the relationship – has remained problematic.[21] And, unfortunately, while developing the various television programs has taken time away from core responsibilities, the arrangement has not provided the participating Smithsonian museums much in the way of new revenue. I would argue that, in this case, the ends have not justified the means. But is that an appropriate calculation in any case? Do the potential benefits to the public trust ever justify questionable practices? I would argue "no" – we are ethically bound to be conservative in such activities, always cognizant of our responsibilities. Malaro agrees: "… before going down a commercial world path, a nonprofit should keep its eye on its mission, should be ready to explain openly what it is doing, and should be reasonably assured that its constituency will find its actions appropriate for an organization devoted to such a mission."[22] While the Smithsonian can argue that the relationship with Showtime is mission appropriate and that at least some of its constituents found the arrangement appropriate, it is difficult to claim transparency in either the negotiation or the implementation.

A business activity that is attracting greater scrutiny is what Marie Malaro terms "lending for profit" – some critics more bluntly call it "renting" collections. While some museums charge other museums high fees to borrow objects – the Whitney Museum of American Art and others have reportedly charged substantial fees in order to secure revenue for their museums – I'm more concerned when museums lend collections to for-profits in order to generate revenue.[23] While arguably the motive is the same and the differences inconsequential, I am at least willing to look the other way when the loan is to another institution that meets appropriate standards and has a public mission, even if at heart the purpose of the loan is generating income. But I find it highly problematic when a museum loans collections held in the public trust to a commercial operation, as did the Phillips Collections, the Museum of Fine Arts, Boston, and the Museum of Contemporary Art, San Diego, all to the Bellagio Gallery of Fine Art in the Bellagio hotel-casino complex in Las Vegas. While each museum strongly defended its decision in populist language about taking art to the people, none denied the importance of the revenue these deals brought in. To make the situation even more problematic, the first two arrangements were handled by art dealers, which should strike anyone as a conflict of interest.[24] Marie Malaro finds this trend so troubling that she devotes an entire chapter in *Museum Governance* to it, suggesting that it is not "a stretch of the imagination to say that 'lending for profit' looks very much like utilization of collections for financial gain." She laments that "in focusing so much attention on earning income, we are forgetting what we are all about, and every day it seems to bother us less."[25] Indeed, such activities diminish us all.

But what about when the business activity is actually bringing an exhibit to our museum – a "blockbuster" developed by a commercial operation? The popularity and profitability of touring exhibitions of plasticized human bodies made museums across the United States eager to book them, despite the ethical concerns raised and protests that erupted at various tour stops (see Chapter 22). Are such exhibits indeed educational or are they actually exploitative? Do the record-breaking crowds paying special admission charges justify museums' looking the other way?[26] Doubtless the revenues from such exhibits enable the booking museums to fund more mission-focused activities, but is that sufficient justification? Some defenders argue that such exhibits draw new audiences to museums, but I've yet to see evidence that those new audiences are sustained. And the reverse may actually be the case: John Walsh, former director of the Getty Museum, has argued that blockbuster exhibitions, regardless of who organizes them, "have changed the audience's expectations about the purpose of a museum visit. The audience more and more comes to think of art as an event – if there is no show, why go to the museum?"[27] Perhaps most importantly, do market-oriented traveling exhibitions compromise the integrity of the sponsoring museums, diverting scarce resources from other responsibilities for only short-term gains? Again, I question whether the ends justify the means or even should.

While the financial challenges we face require innovative responses and some complicated juggling acts, we must not lose sight of our unique roles and larger responsibilities as museums, mission-centered and operating in the public trust. And we must not put our museums in deeper jeopardy with risky business propositions. As the Association of Art Museum Directors states in "Revenue Generation: An Investment in the Public Service of Art Museums," new revenue streams must not only be consistent with a museum's mission but must be good business and manageable, with a sufficient return on investment and protection against financial loss.[28]

Marketing

One of the justifications for the Smithsonian's Showtime contract has been increasing outreach and enhancing the visibility of the Institution. But when do the costs of visibility and outreach outweigh the benefits? Because the goal of marketing is to increase visitation and visibility for the museum, it too often focuses on quantity rather than quality – "any publicity is good publicity" rules when you're measuring a museum's success mainly in terms of the number of visitors rather than the quality of their experiences. In discussing the responsibilities of the nonprofit sector in *Museum Governance*, Marie Malaro asks: "Can a cultural organization really focus on quality when it has placed itself in a position where drawing capacity alone determines its fate?" She warns museums that mission rather than marketability must be the focus of decision making.[29]

Coming at this issue from the curatorial side, I'm particularly concerned about the use of collections for marketing purposes. While collections are certainly at the core of our brands, I do not support their use for whatever museum marketing purpose might be dreamed up. The museum must always show respect for its collections and the stories that they represent and avoid situations that seem exploitative. Moreover, no matter what the visibility, it is not appropriate to take an object to an event for publicity purposes if a curator or a conservator feels it puts the object at risk. While we all know curators and conservators can be unnecessarily fearful, that does not mean that it is acceptable to overrule their professional judgments because of our marketing goals or expectations.

At the same time, a curator should not be pressured to acquire an object because the museum wants to have a high-profile press event. Collecting should never be marketing driven – it should always grow out of the museum's mission.[30] In 2009, the Smithsonian learned first-hand how badly such collecting can turn out when a *Washington Post* article by Philip Kennicott criticized the Institution's decision to collect the desk used on the *American Idol* television program. Kennicott linked the acquisition of the desk to the marketing of the new movie *Night at the Museum: Battle of the Smithsonian* – both *American Idol* and *Night at the Museum* share a single corporate parent, News Corp. Decrying the commercialism of the relationship, he declared "The main hall of the Smithsonian Castle is now a cluttered and not-quite-wholly-owned subsidiary of News Corp." His concern was not just with the marketing arrangement but also with the way that this relationship had distorted collecting priorities, blurring the lines between "the values of popular culture ... and the values of museums."[31] This gets us back to the fundamental point made by Malaro – that museums must not stray from their missions in the face of marketplace pressures.[32]

Fund raising

While others might argue to the contrary, I'm including fund raising under the rubric of business activity – after all, it is a form of financial transaction. Perhaps the most troubling recent example of what not to do was the fund raising for the exhibition *Sensation: Young British Art from the Saatchi Collection* at the Brooklyn Museum of Art in 1999. Despite initial statements from officials to the contrary, the museum eventually admitted that Charles Saatchi, the owner of the works exhibited, was himself the single largest financial contributor for the exhibit, and that other under-writers included Christie's auction house and other gallery owners who could expect to benefit from future sales of the artists represented in the show. The private and commercial interests of the exhibit funders clearly constituted conflicts of interest, contrary to the museum's insistence that their actions were no more problematic than that of other museums. Efforts to cover up the sources of support only made a bad situation worse, suggesting that the museum did indeed have something to hide. The museum's image was tarnished even further when memos and emails were released revealing that Saatchi not only provided funding for the exhibition but also was allowed to weigh in on curatorial matters.[33] In the wake of that controversy came new guidelines from AAM in 2000 on exhibiting borrowed objects, which pointedly call for a museum to "make public the source of funding where the lender is also a funder of the exhibition. If a museum receives a request for anonymity, the museum should avoid such anonymity where it would conceal a conflict of interest (real or perceived) or raise other ethical issues."[34]

In 2001 and 2002, AAM issued new guidelines regarding developing and managing business and individual support. While the guidelines are relatively straightforward (emphasizing accountability and transparency), managing donors still remains a tricky enterprise for museums.[35] Museums must, for example, carefully consider whether a prospective corporate donor is an appropriate partner. In "Managing the Relationship between Art Museums and Corporate Sponsors," the Association of Art Museum Directors warns museums to keep in mind that "Some corporations may engage in unfavorable or unethical business practices, or may market con-troversial products or services. Others may seek to showcase products or services within the museum context or attempt to exert undue influence over the content of museum programming." Museums must take care to ensure that corporate donors are respectful of their mission and values and that their integrity is not compromised by the donors' interests.[36] And that can be difficult to accomplish – too many of us approach potential corporate donors with hat in hand, not as equals. When we defer to the interests of financial capital, we undervalue our own cultural capital.

I'm less concerned here about issues of conflict of interest, donor recognition or even confidentiality, and more about protecting the integrity of the museum in the face of donor influence. In return for their support, donors increasingly appear to expect undue input into exhibitions and programs. While it is always important and appropriate to listen to different perspectives, even those of donors, at what point are we jeopardizing the museum's integrity by allowing unethical donor influence over content? How do we define "influence"? Will we know it when we see it? Is listening appropriate as long as we don't implement? Or does listening legitimate the donor's input and put the museum's integrity at risk? When does this relationship or transaction cross the line from appropriate to unethical? Of course, all donor relations are not created equal. At the National Museum of American History, we know that, when a prospective donor puts money on the table first and we develop concepts in response, it nearly always goes badly for us – as opposed to when we seek funding for concepts we've developed. No matter how difficult fund raising is or how much other sources of revenue shrink, we must not compromise our commitment to the public trust.

Conclusion

The above does not constitute a comprehensive inventory of the ethical issues related to museum business practices – the issues I've identified are a better reflection of my own experiences and perspectives than of the challenges of the larger field. But they provide a good start to a topic of growing importance. While much of the field's attention remains on ethical matters related to collections and exhibitions – what we think of as "museum business" – it's the business side of museums that consumes more and more of our time and poses more and more challenges to our integrity, and ethical lapses in business practices can put all that the museum does in disrepute. We don't need new ethical standards, but we do need a clearer articulation of their application to business practices. And we need a stronger commitment to principle over expediency – even in difficult economic times, we must remain committed to our mission and the public trust in all our business practices.

Notes

1 For a discussion of cost-cutting activities by museums in the context of the economic downturn that began in the fall of 2008, see J. Seligson, "Now What? The Upside of Cutting Down," *Museum*, September–October 2009, pp. 52–57.
2 American Association for State and Local History, "When a History Museum Closes: Ethics Position Paper 2," 2006. Online. Available HTTP: http://www.aaslh.org/documents/EthicsPositionPaper2-WhenaHistoryMuseumCloses.pdf (accessed 11 September 2009).
3 J. Trescott, "City Museum Moves Up Closing Date to November 28," *Washington Post*, 10 November 2004, p. C10; A. O'Hanlon, "'Sold' Sign on Lee House Jarring; Foundation Sells General's Boyhood Home to Private Owner," *Washington Post*, 7 March 2000, p. B1; "Black History Museum Closing in Milwaukee," 31 July 2008. Online. Available HTTP: http://www.blackwebportal.com/wire/DprA.cfm?ArticleID=4004 (accessed 11 September 2009); K. Guthrie, *The New-York Historical Society: Lessons from One Nonprofit's Long Struggle for Survival*, San Francisco: Jossey-Bass, 1996; and L. Bassett, "Textile Museum Threatened with Closure," *CSA e-News*, May 2005. Online. Available HTTP: http://www.costumesocietyamerica.com (accessed 11 September 2009).
4 M. Malaro, *Museum Governance: Mission, Ethics, Policy*, Washington, DC: Smithsonian Institution Press, 1994, pp. 37, 113.
5 For examples of the news coverage regarding the Smithsonian's activities, see B. Thompson, "History for $ale: Larry Small Wants to Remake the National Museum of American History, and He's Banking on a Set of Big-time Donors to Help. Will They End Up Privatizing the American Past?" *Washington Post*, 20 January 2002, p. W14; R. Roberts, "Where Cash and Culture Go Hand in Hand," *Washington Post*, 7 February 2002, p. C1; J. Trescott, "Smithsonian Deal Was Not Made in Secret, Small Says," *Washington Post*, 9 May 2006, p. C1; J. Grimaldi and J. Trescott, "Controversial CEO to Leave Smithsonian Business Ventures," *Washington Post*, 17 May 2007, p. A1; P. Eisenberg, "Same Old Smithsonian: After an Appalling Year of Scandal, an Appalling Lack of Action," *Washington Post*, 14 January 2008, p. A21; J. Trescott and J. Grimaldi, "Smithsonian Makes Changes at Troubled Business Unit," *Washington Post*, 21 June 2008, p. C7; and J. Trescott, "Smithsonian Lends Name to Tour Operator; Competing Travel Agents Call No-bid Deal Unfair," *Washington Post*, 27 August 2008, p. C1.

6 Smithsonian Institution, "The Smithsonian Institution Statement of Values and Code of Ethics," 2007. Online. Available HTTP: http://www.si.edu/about/policies/values-code-of-ethics.asp (accessed 11 September 2009).

7 Malaro, *Museum Governance*, pp. 18–19.

8 For a discussion of conflict of interest and core and subsidiary activities, see Malaro, *Museum Governance*, pp. 11–13.

9 Malaro, *Museum Governance*, p. 71.

10 See "The Regents' Reckoning; The Smithsonian Board, AWOL for Too Long, Is Back," *Washington Post*, 22 June 2007, p. A18; J. Grimaldi and J. Trescott, "Secrecy Pervaded Smithsonian on Small's Watch; Independent Panel Also Faults Regents and Others for Lack of Spending Scrutiny," *Washington Post*, 21 June 2007, p. C1; J. Grimaldi, "Report Slams Small's Tenure; Smithsonian Had 'Ill-suited' Leader," *Washington Post*, 20 June 2007, p. A1; and J. Trescott and J. Grimaldi, "Museum's Deputy Secretary Resigns; Smithsonian Board Raps Own Knuckles," *Washington Post*, 19 June 2007, p. A1.

11 Malaro, *Museum Governance*, p. 32.

12 American Association for State and Local History, "Statement of Professional Standards and Ethics," 2002. Online. Available HTTP: http://www.aaslh.org/ethics.htm (accessed 11 September 2009); and Association of Art Museum Directors, "Professional Practices in Art Museums," 2001. Online. Available HTTP: http://www.aamd.org/about/documents/ProfessionalPracticies2001.pdf (accessed 11 September 2009). See also American Association for State and Local History, "The Capitalization of Collections: Ethics Position Paper 1," 2003. Online. Available HTTP: http://www.aaslh.org/pos.pap.htm (accessed 11 September 2009).

13 W. Honan, "The Historical Society is Criticized for Using Artworks as Collateral," *New York Times*, 28 January 1993. Online. Available HTTP: http://www.nytimes.com/1993/01/28/arts/the-historical-society-is-criticized-for-using-artworks-as-collateral.html?scp=1&sq=The%20Historical%20Society%20Is%20Criticized%20for%20Using%20Artworks%20as%20Collateral&st=cse (accessed 13 April 2010); "Why Risk It?", *Maine Antique Digest*, June 2003. Online. Available HTTP: http://maineantiquedigest.com/articles_archive/articles/jun03/ed0603.htm (accessed 11 September 2009); and AASLH, "Capitalization of Collections." Online. Available HTTP: http://www.aaslh.org/pos.pap.htm (accessed 11 September 2009).

14 B. Bruner, "Museum on the Rebound," *Arizona Daily Sun*, 24 June 2007. Online. Available HTTP: http://www.azdailysun.com/news/article_ef8af97d-c148-5266-8d72-07564fccdf1f.html?mode=story (accessed 13 April 2010).

15 C. Crowley, "Critics Say Auction Isn't Necessary," *Providence Journal*, 4 March 2005. Online. Available HTTP: http://www.projo.com/news/content/projo_20050304_money04.24bf965.html (accessed 13 April 2010); and B. Van Siclen, "Sale of Rare Desk Challenged," *Providence Journal*, 4 March 2005. Online. Available HTTP: http://www.projo.com/news/content/projo_20050304_desk04.24c0334.html (accessed 13 April 2010).

16 R. Pogrebin, "National Academy Revises its Policies," *New York Times*, 14 March 2009. Online. Available HTTP: http://www.nytimes.com/2009/03/14/arts/design/14acad.html?_r=1&scp=1&sq=National%20Academy%20Revises%20Its%20Policies&st=cse (accessed 13 April 2010); C. Desrets, "Maier Museum Art Controversy Boils," *Lynchburg News Advance*, 3 October 2007. Online. Available HTTP: http://www2.newsadvance.com/lna/news/local/article/maier_museum_art_controversy_boils/2340/ (accessed 13 April 2010); G. Edgers and P. Schworm, "Brandeis to Sell School's Art Collection," *Boston Globe*, 26 January 2009. Online. Available HTTP: http://www.boston.com/ae/theater_arts/articles/2009/01/26/brandeis_to_sell_schools_art_collection/ (accessed 13 April 2010); and R. Kennedy and C. Vogel, "Outcry Over a Plan to Sell Museum's Holdings," *New York Times*, 28 January 2009. Online. Available HTTP: http://www.nytimes.com/2009/01/28/arts/design/28rose.html?scp=1&sq=Outcry%20Over%20a%20Plan%20to%20Sell%20Museum%92s%20Holdings&st=cse (accessed 13 April 2010).

17 For a discussion of the complications regarding historic houses, see American Association for State and Local History, "Repurposing of a Historic House/Site: Ethics Position Paper 3," 2009. Online. Available HTTP: http://www.aaslh.org/pos.pap.htm (accessed 11 September 2009).

18 See J. Gardner and E. Merritt, *The AAM Guide to Collections Planning*, Washington, DC: American Association of Museums, 2004.

19 American Association of Museums, "Code of Ethics for Museums," 2000. Online. Available HTTP: http://www.aam-us.org/museumresources/ethics/coe.cfm (accessed 11 September 2009); AASLH, "Statement of Professional Standards and Ethics." Online. Available HTTP: http://www.aaslh.org/ethics.htm (accessed 25 April 2010); and International Council of Museums, "Code of Ethics for Museums," 2006. Online. Available HTTP: http://icom. museum/ethics.html#intro (accessed 11 September 2009). The Museum Store Association is more concerned with authenticity and misrepresentation of products, see "Code of Ethics," 1984, revised 2000. Online. Available HTTP: http://www.museumdistrict.com/ membership/EthicsCode.cfm (accessed 11 September 2009).

20 Malaro, *Museum Governance*, p. 113.

21 See J. Trescott, "Smithsonian Deal with Showtime Restricts Access Filmmakers," *Washington Post*, 4 April 2006, p. C1; J. Trescott, "End Smithsonian–Showtime Deal, Filmmakers and Historians Ask," *Washington Post*, 18 April 2006, p. C2; J. Trescott, "Historians Protest Smithsonian's Deals," *Washington Post*, 26 April 2006, p. C1; J. Tres-cott, "Capitol Hill Joins Criticism of Smithsonian Film Deal; Key Congressmen Call for Review of Showtime Pact," *Washington Post*, 29 April 2006, p. C1; J. Trescott, "Smithso-nian TV Contract Spurs Panel to Cut Funds; House Subcommittee Bans Exclusive Deals," *Washington Post*, 5 May 2006, p. C1; J. Trescott," Smithsonian Deal Was Not Made in Secret, Small Says," *Washington Post*, 9 May 2006, p. C1; and B. Craig, "Historians Again Protest Smithsonian's Showtime Deal," *Historians in the News*, 29 November 2006. Online. Available HTTP: http://hnn.us/roundup/entries/32382.html (accessed 11 September 2009).

22 Malaro, *Museum Governance*, p. 77.

23 Ibid., p. 109.

24 G. Edgers, "MFA's Monets: Dicey Deal?" *Boston Globe*, 25 January 2004. Online. Available HTTP: http://www.boston.com/news/local/massachusetts/articles/2004/01/25/mfas_monets_ dicey_deal// (accessed 13 April 2010); G. Edgers, "Art Fans Take a Vegas Vacation," *Boston Globe*, 15 February 2004. Online. Available HTTP: http://www.boston.com/news/globe/ living/articles/2004/02/15/art_fans_take_a_vegas_vacation/ (accessed 13 April 2010); T. Green, "Museum Ethics, Part Three," Modern Art Notes blog, 16 September 2004. Online. Available HTTP: http://www.artsjournal.com/man/2004/09/museum_ethics_part_ three.html (accessed 11 September 2009); F. Bernstein, "Borrowings: A Loan That Keeps On Paying," *New York Times*, 30 March 2005. Online. Available HTTP: http://query.nytimes. com/gst/fullpage.html?res=9500E0DF1E3CF933A05750-C0A9639C8B63&scp=1&sq=Borrowings: %20A%20Loan%20That%20Keeps%20on% 20Paying&st=cse (accessed 13 April 2010); T. Green, "Privatizing Fine Arts," *Boston Globe*, 4 July 2005. Online. Available HTTP: http://www.boston.com/news/globe/editorial_opinion/ oped/articles/2005/07/04/privatizing_fine_arts/ (accessed 13 April 2010); and T. Green, "MCASD Rents Collection Works to Las Vegas," Modern Art Notes blog, 25 February 2009. Online. Available HTTP: http://www.artsjournal.com/man/2009/02/the_latest_collection_ rental_m.html (accessed 11 September 2009).

25 Malaro, *Museum Governance*, pp. 116–17. For a larger discussion of the issues, see "Lending for Profit," in Malaro, *Museum Governance*, pp. 108–17.

26 For an example of the discussion surrounding *Bodies: The Exhibition*, see J. Roach, "Cada-ver Exhibition Draws Crowds, Controversy in Florida," *National Geographic News*, 29 August 2005. Online. Available HTTP: http://news.nationalgeographic.com/news/2005/08/ 0829_050829_human_bodies.html (accessed 13 April 2010); for an example of the discussion surrounding *Body Worlds*, see "Museum Exhibit of Human Bodies Draws Record Attendance, Controversy," Institute for Global Ethics, 27 November 2006. Online. Available HTTP: http://www.globalethics.org/newsline/2006/11/27/museum-exhibit-of-human-bodies-draws-record-attendance-controversy/ (accessed 11 September 2009).

27 Quote, J. Walsh, in M. Feldstein (ed.), *The Economics of Art Museums*, Chicago: University of Chicago Press, National Bureau of Economic Research Conference Report, 1992, p. 29.

28 Association of Art Museum Directors, "Revenue Generation: An Investment in the Public Service of Art Museums," 2001. Online. Available HTTP: http://www.aamd.org/papers/documents/RevenueGeneration_000.pdf (accessed 11 September 2009).

29 Malaro, *Museum Governance*, pp. 7, 113.

30 The "Code of Ethics for Public Relations" of the Public Relations and Marketing Committee of AAM focuses on conduct and conflicts of interest.

31 P. Kennicott, "Artifact or Artifice? If Simon, Randy and Paula's Desk Sits in the Smithsonian, Is the Institution Performing its Proper Role in Chronicling Our Culture?", *Washington Post*, 30 August 2009, p. E1.

32 Malaro, *Museum Governance*, p. 7.

33 D. Barstow, "Brooklyn Museum Recruited Donors Who Stood to Gain," *New York Times*, 31 October 1999. Online. Available HTTP: http://www.nytimes.com/1999/10/31/nyregion/brooklyn-museum-recruited-donors-who-stood-to-gain.html?scp=1&sq=Brooklyn%20Museum%20Recruited%20Donors%20Who%20Stood%20to%20Gain&st=cse (accessed 13 April 2010); "Virgins No More: What Saatchi's 'Sensation' Really Exposed," *Commonweal*, 19 May 2000. Online. Available HTTP: http://findarticles.com/p/articles/mi_m1252/is_10_127/ai_62655935/?tag=rbxcra.2.a.11 (accessed 13 April 2010); H. Suda, "Civic Engagement or 'Censorship': The Brooklyn Museum's *Sensation* Exhibit," Graduate Student Symposium, Graduate Program in Art History and Museum Studies, City College of New York, December 2003; and New York Foundation for the Arts, "The Brooklyn Museum: A Chronology of a Controversy," *NYFA Quarterly*, winter 2000. Online. Available HTTP: http://www.spiderschool.org/archive_detail_q.asp?fid=1&year=2000&s=Winter (accessed 11 September 2009).

34 American Association of Museums, "Guidelines on Exhibiting Borrowed Objects," 2000. Online. Available HTTP: http://www.aam-us.org/museumresources/ethics/borrowb.cfm (accessed 11 September 2009).

35 American Association of Museums, "Guidelines for Museums on Developing and Managing Business Support," 2001. Online. Available HTTP: http://www.aam-us.org/museumresources/ethics/bus_support.cfm (accessed 11 September 2009); and "Guidelines for Museums on Developing and Managing Individual Donor Support," 2002. Online. Available HTTP: http://www.aam-us.org/museumresources/ethics/indiv_support.cfm (accessed 11 September 2009).

36 Association of Art Museum Directors, "Managing the Relationship between Art Museums and Corporate Sponsors," 2007. Online. Available HTTP: http://www.aamd.org/papers/documents/CorporateSponsors_clean06-2007doc.pdf (accessed 11 September 2009).

19

"Why is this here?"
Art museum texts as ethical guides

Pamela Z. McClusky

The initial questions

I hope you've all been there. Standing in front of a sculpture, a painting or display, and wondering, "what on earth is this, why is it here, how do I make sense of it?" With exhibits featuring sharks in formaldehyde to masks with embedded shark teeth, art museums can evoke confusion and disorientation. After an initial reaction, some visitors challenge themselves to figure out what the shark or its teeth are doing in a presentation under spotlights. However, for less confident viewers, the guidance system offered is often a blunt text on a label. Such texts often seem as if a mallet has pounded flat the ideas behind the art or released a smoke bomb of complex notions that hover in a foggy haze.[1] Then there are the labels that gush with superlatives or what one critic has called a "mass of linguistic strutting."[2] Hanging in thousands of museums, labels may leave many ideas bruised or ignored, neglected or maligned.

For those who aren't sure what I'm talking about, here I am. On an art museum label, I'd first get what is known to many museum writers as a tombstone–the name alone is ominous. Mine would read:

> *Female*, 21st century
> Bones, flesh and blood, wearing multimedia clothing and accessories
> American, b. in San Francisco
> On loan from the Seattle Art Museum Curatorial Division

In some galleries, that's it. You are on your own after the tombstone. Contemporary galleries often rely on minimal texts as a standard practice–the museum hangs a single string across a room, displays fingerprints embedded in beeswax or suspends ten cars upside down, and it's up to the audience to figure out why. Such situations become a test of critical thinking and (hopefully) inspire the reflective perceptions that come of creative encounters. Viewers who are familiar with the tools of interpretation often value this shock of the unknown artist who leads them to begin a search for further references. However, for audiences that want more immediate guidance, the tombstone is followed by a chat, which in my case might read:

> A long-standing member of the staff, this person has a distinct penchant for scrutinizing routine solutions that museums abide by. Her requests to alter

the format for wall texts have become unbearable to all who work with her. It is rumored that she is again plotting to undermine the rules which are applied to text panels and wall labels.

Just as this chat reduces my career to three sentences, so an artist's life work or a culture's most important icon may receive a blunt assessment. Write your own tombstone and chat and see what you can fit in. It's a difficult task, but, given the need to provide equal wall or case space for every object in a museum, and the desire not to presuppose artistic impressions, the choice is made to leave many observations out. Some are deemed too volatile for discussions with a public audience, others are sacrificed for brevity and most steer clear of personal opinion. Yet, as one other critic assessed them, "There is a lack of both rigor and regard paid exhibition wall text, which has become, like wallpaper, something of a dreary necessity, taken for granted even by the curators that write them."[3] All too often, art museums seem to proliferate with what could be termed ILDS or innocuous label domination syndrome. Why does this syndrome so often prevail?

The curatorial writing challenge

When art museum curators write, they often rely on art historical training as a baseline of analysis. This background is not the best model for short, pithy prose. Indeed, as James Elkins has described art history in his work *Our Beautiful, Dry and Distant Texts*, it is deemed "a rambling conversation or a kind of fiction that does not move in any single direction," and he cites the "metaphor of meandering as a way to describe how art history drifts from topic to topic in an unhurried, directionless, and yet not entirely uncontrolled manner." He also admits that "Art history is not usually radical thought, though it is often confrontational and not infrequently catty. It 'muses,' 'shines' and 'doubts,' to use words that Mallarmé chose to express the randomness of all thought."[4]

Take a devoted art historian who is enamored of their field, full of meandering insights and intimate observations, and then ask them to write one short paragraph that answers audience needs. It is a misfit assignment for many art museum curators, and, yet, most don't want to hand it over to others, so they try to make their case. Over decades of curatorial work, I've probably written thousands of labels and wince as each one is put on the wall. For those who haven't had this experience, here's an example of the dilemma that comes up.

A mask is chosen as an anchor for a display, partly because it has proven to be extraordinarily compelling and confusing for audiences. Entitled *Gela* (The Ancient one) from the Wee people of Liberia and Côte d'Ivoire, it is composed of a multitude of defensive animal parts (teeth, tusks and horns), all drawn together on to a facial form (Figure 19.1). In my meandering art historical mind, this mask evokes a multitude of associations. As a teenager, I was present when a mask of this type appeared in a village where I was visiting. Given my age, I was not able to witness its appearance but was kept inside a house for several hours while it made its way through the village. I listened, surrounded by other women and children, as the mask uttered inhuman sounds and an intense drumming orchestra accompanied it. Women

Figure 19.1 Gela Mask (The Ancient One), 20th century. African, Ivorian, Wee culture. Wood, raffia, cloth, teeth, horn, feathers, hair, fiber cord, cowrie shells, mud, and pigment. 45.7 x 27.8 cm. Seattle Art Museum. Gift of Katherine White and the Boeing Company, 81.17.193.

whispered to me about how dangerous it was, what might happen if I sneaked out to look at it and how long it might keep us confined.

The memory was triggered suddenly when I saw this mask for the first time at a collector's home in Los Angeles. She had heard that I'd been in Liberia, so she placed the mask on the pillow of the bed that I was to sleep in. I couldn't tell her how horrified I was to have to move it, let alone look directly at it. Placing it carefully in a closet for the days that I was in residence, I felt a lot of conflict in my mind about whether and how to explain the circumstances of my first encounters with the full character of *Gela*.

Several years later, the museum acquired the mask from the collector and it came time to handle it. I asked male staff members to take care of all the movement and preparation for display and mentioned that it wasn't appropriate for women to handle it. Not explaining more than that, I was later surprised when I heard a story circulating around the staff about how this mask had the power to sterilize women. Where that notion came from was not clear, but it brought up the dilemma of displaying art that once had such power in its original context and yet was deemed dangerous for different reasons in another. Realizing the potential for public outrage about perceptions of art meant to sterilize, I then made sure to talk about the background and significance of the mask as a means of establishing order through its powerful appearance. With a face submerged by an arsenal of animal parts, *Gela* could look into difficulties that no mere human could.

On another level, I was also faced with a dilemma of conscience about what was happening where *Gela* came from. News about the extreme conditions of life under a siege of warfare that prevailed in Liberia during the last generation has been devastating. The descendants of the Wee people who created an intensive cycle of masquerade leaders were suffering from waves of violent anti-leadership that was hard to comprehend from a distance. Most of my friends and extended family had fled the country, but a few remained to send occasional messages about how war lords prevailed with ruthless tactics and corrupt armies of child soldiers. Would anyone want to know what was happening to the men who made the mask?

But, wait, this is a mask now safely housed in a beautifully designed space where people come to see wondrous objects and may prefer not to read about the horrors of war in a place far away. Most don't want to hear what my experiences of it are, and want to have their own experience. So, eventually, I turn off all the channels of meandering thought, dismiss any intimate revelations, distance myself from the process of summation and write a tombstone and chat that fit.

> Gela mask (The Ancient One)
>   Wee culture, Côte d'Ivoire/Liberia
>   Wood, raffia, cloth, teeth, horns, feathers, hair, cowrie shells
>   Gift of Katherine White and the Boeing Company, 81.17.193
>   Like a magnet, this face has attracted a mass of animal parts to cover its
>   core. Exploding into sight, the Gela is required to dodge a vast array of
>   physical challenges–sharp nails, daggers or other obstacles that might cause
>   the masquerader to stumble and fall. Full of forceful elements from the
>   forest, the Gela reminds people that he is capable of absorbing their worst
>   thoughts and taking them back to the forest with him

Just as James Elkins said, the dry and distant text prevails. The label presents a severe abbreviation of a deeply conflicted terrain for interpretation. An immensely complex art form has been made simple. One can hope that viewers who are inspired to know more about the art on display realize that this is not, by far, a complete account and that many other sources for reflection on Wee masquerades exist. Whether it is just a hope is not known. Audience retention and the conundrums of understanding that occur during museum visits are understudied areas of museological inquiry. Among museums themselves, very few ever offer footnotes or caveats about the limitations of interpretative texts and their propensity for ILDS.

Interpretation ethics

In fact, there are no hard and fast rules to guide the writer of museum texts. Each museum develops their own editorial regimen, with manuals that specify word counts and styles for layout and punctuation. In the latest "Code of Ethics for Museums" issued by the American Association of Museums in 2000, there is no direct mention of interpretive texts. "Intellectual integrity," "providing access to information" and "respecting pluralistic values, traditions and concerns" are referred to as essential values. In the ICOM "Code of Ethics for Museums," issued in 2006, clause 4.2, *Interpretation of Exhibits*, states: "Museums should ensure that the information they present in displays and exhibitions is well founded, accurate and gives appropriate consideration to represented groups or beliefs."

Finding an ethical backbone, one that looks at how texts provide audiences with pluralism and accuracy at the same time, requires a search for precedents.

Models of text experimentation

There are models for texts that take on tough subjects and invite audiences to consider them in galleries. While blunt texts in a neutral tone may prevail, several artists and curators have enacted installations that mitigate ILDS. Such invigorated texts can ignite interest in ethical issues that are implicated in collecting and interpreting art from around the world. Among the issues that are often avoided, but stand out as points of intrigue, are: conflicts about collecting practices, judgments cast on objects that are controversial, differing opinions about what qualifies as art, consultation and credit being given to cultural advisors and sensitivities to religious practices. To start off, I'll cite two examples that highlight the power of brevity and of conflicting opinions—one at the Brooklyn Museum of Art and another at the Museum of Fine Arts, Boston. A discussion of a few experimental case histories at the Seattle Art Museum will follow.

Joseph Kosuth, a conceptual artist with a strong reputation for interrogating museum conventions, was invited to stage an installation in 1992 for the Brooklyn Museum. Kosuth's *The Play of the Unmentionable* became a milestone in confrontational collection display. It was formulated in response to a volatile time in museum history. In the previous two years, the National Endowment for the Arts had refused to give grants to museums whose proposals contained works that it had decided were immoral or pornographic. Simultaneously, the Corcoran Gallery of Art in Washington, DC, had cancelled a Robert Mapplethorpe exhibition and the director of the Cincinnati Contemporary Arts Center (CAC) was on trial facing obscenity charges over seven out of 175 photographs in a Robert Mapplethorpe show. In a move designed to head straight into this storm and invite public response, the Brooklyn Museum curators all agreed to turn over their Grand Lobby to Kosuth. He combed through holdings from every department of the museum's vast collections in a search for objects that might be or have once been considered obscene or controversial. To dissolve the usual categories of display, Kosuth placed ancient and modern, well-known and obscure objects in a seeming scramble that required careful observation to discern relationships. Large texts unified the installation, offering diverse opinion statements by people as varied as Adolf Hitler, George Bernard Shaw and Ruth Benedict (Figure 19.2). Audiences had to work to understand the connections between objects and texts, underscoring that it takes time to construct meanings even if large quotations are made available in a standard museological gray silkscreen. How do you make sense of an array of Bauhaus chairs and porcelain containers with the following quote above them?

> The artist does not create for the artist: he creates for the people and we will
> see to it that henceforth the people will be called in to judge its art.
> Adolf Hitler[5]

Smaller labels led the way through an exchange by the Nazi SS with Mies van der Rohe in Berlin about how Professor van der Rohe needed to fire his leading

Figure 19.2 Joseph Kosuth, American, born 1945, *The Play of the Unmentionable*, 1992, Installation at the Brooklyn Museum of Art. Varied museum collections with text. Photograph courtesy of Ken Schles and Joseph Kosuth.

instructors and change the curriculum before he would be allowed to reopen the Bauhaus. What a visitor might assume to be a ubiquitous modern chair Kosuth placed back in the center of a struggle over the path of modernist design. This was just one wall of a dense installation that gave audiences a lot of conflicts and questions to sort out. The Brooklyn staff reported that "to see the museum filled with virtually thousands of people every day, some casual museumgoers and some artists, art historians and other professionals was the greatest reward to all of us."[6] *The Play of the Unmentionable* unveiled the potency of placing objects in a strident interpretive framework and letting audiences see the messiness of their past.

The Label Show: Contemporary Art and the Museum, a 1994 exhibition at the Museum of Fine Arts, Boston, curated by Trevor Fairbrother, took an intensive turn away from label conventions. To explain ten thematic groupings of art, Fairbrother introduced each theme with a wall text, but then stepped back as he invited sixty-five different individuals to write their own labels. Each object was accompanied by a highly varied sequence of texts. Among the authors who contributed were the artists themselves, relatives of the artists, staff of the MFA, a playwright, a filmmaker, professors, high school students and a feminist theory reading group. Instead of a voice of institutional authority as a guide, visitors had a choice of voices which ranged from the technical to the freely imaginative in their response to objects. The following three labels for a light bulb lit by a lemon-powered battery by artist Joseph Beuys, entitled *Capri Batterie*, 1985 (Figure 19.3), provide an example of the bold shifts in perspective that this exhibition offered:[7]

> On one level, Beuys' composition is a sardonic persiflage on a poem by Goethe universally known in Germany with the opening lines:
>
> > Kennst du das Land wo die Zitronen bluh'n
> > Im dunklen Laub die Goldorangen gluh'n?
>
> > Have you seen the land where the lemon trees bloom,
> > Where gold-oranges glow in dark foliage?
>
> The poem expresses nostalgic longing for Italy and for the harmony between nature and art that Goethe (and Beuys) discovered there. The "glowing gold-oranges" of Goethe's poem give rise to a visual/verbal pun in Beuys' assemblage. The word for "light bulb" in German is "Gluhbirne" which, as in Beuys's whimsical sculpture, presents a commercial mechanism in the guise of fruit while *gluh* again links it to the Goethe poem.
>
> Fred Licht, Professor of Art History, Boston University

> When 'Capri-Batterie' is on exhibit, my colleague Kathyrn Potts and I share the responsibility of changing the lemon once each week. I take this task very seriously. If, for instance, the lemons are shriveled and sickly-looking at one market, I head for another, and so on, until I find a fresh, photogenic lemon. Next, wearing cotton gloves, I unplug the week-old fuzzy green lemon and plug in the new one, at which point the light bulb turns on. Hint: Lysol Spray helps to keep the citrus battery charged by slowing down mold growth.

Figure 19.3 Joseph Beuys, German, 1921–1986, *Capri-Batterie*, 1985. Lightbulb, socket and lemon. 18.4 x 17 cm. Museum of Fine Arts, Boston. Gift of Lucio Amelio, 1986.531. Photograph © 2010/Museum of Fine Arts, Boston.

The signed certificate that accompanies the object includes Beuys' instruction: 'Nach 1000 Stunden Batterie auswechsein' (Change the battery after 1,000 hours). With sincere apologies to the late Mr. Beuys, I fear that, after forty-one days on view, the stench of the rotting lemon would drive most visitors out of the Foster Gallery, and therefore we change it every 168 hours.

Kathy Drummy, Operations Coordinator, Department of Contemporary Art, Museum of Fine Arts, Boston

Research Laboratory Condition Report:

Contact with the acidic lemon has produced considerable corrosion on the copper ends of the plug. The slits had completely filled in with corrosion product and the ends had begun to be etched. The paper baseplate has accretions of organic debris from the lemon and there is iron corrosion covering the tack (?) nailed through the paper. The plastic casing has lemon residue on all areas that contacted the lemon.

Carl Zahn, Director of Publications, Museum of Fine Arts, Boston, MA

The Label Show also subjected other classic museum conventions to scrutiny and near parody. Fairbrother placed labels from the Museum Shop, which offers its own form of informational texts, on display and juxtaposed original works of art with the shop reproductions. He arranged various photographs of a Donatello marble relief that had been taken between 1917 and 1986 in a sequence next to the original sculpture. Vast differences in the photographs provided a glimpse of the power of the photographer to frame a vision of art through their lens. As an exclamation point in a museum known for its Anglo-American period rooms, a contemporary living room was concocted with objects from the collections and tacky furnishings taken from the staff lounge and the museum shop. One reviewer stated that "the aggressive awfulness of its décor was itself a reminder that museums can no more replicate the reality of everyday life than zoos can portray the natural life of animals." As a response, the curator of American decorative arts added a long label to explain why this room was a mock effort designed for didactic purposes. Texts have rarely been so loaded with personal opinions and questions about what museum labels should provide.

The Label Show put up texts that exposed their prominence in museum work. It involved audiences in the ethics of selecting art, selling reproductions of art, inventing contexts for art, like period rooms, and determining how meaning can come from a work of art, the artist, the viewer or all of them combined. This choice to expose so many of the pitfalls of curatorial decision-making and destabilizing the unqualified platform for high art led to a wide range of reactions. The curator shared one letter from a patron of the MFA who asserted, "it was an exhilarating experience–despite the fact, of course, that the show itself was dismal."[8]

At the Seattle Art Museum, the goal of mitigating ILDS and asking audiences to consider ethical choices in museum work has led to several experiments with texts. Four case histories are offered here for review. Each case aims to expose an ethical situation that is often hidden from sight–how stories of collecting derived from personal experience don't follow expected acquisition policies, how cultural advisors can be upset by past representation, how public audiences are not encouraged to advocate for what enters the museum's holdings and how private collectors collect on their own terms and in their own ways.

The ethic of disclosure: "Why is this here?" texts

Case No. 1. The Untold Story[9] offered a literal response to the question "Why is this here?" In it, objects were selected based on the often perplexing manner in which they were collected. Stories that are usually left behind in object files, as part of the records that the public doesn't see, became the focus. Every label was treated as if it were a short story, with a title to match. Galleries contained an intentionally eclectic diversity of objects from the museum's African and Oceanic collections (Figure 19.4). Labels included the following:

Figure 19.4 *Cow Figure*, 20th century. African, Burkina Faso, Mossi culture. Wood and pigment. 54.8 x 63.5 cm. Seattle Art Museum. Gift of Katherine White and the Boeing Company, 81.17.123.

The world's longest straw?

A pizza box arrived at the museum. When it was opened, this fragile curving element was found inside. It is an exquisite example of a straw, meticulously made out of tiny wrapped reeds and quills. One end is hollow, while the other has a miniature basket for straining beer as you sip. The collector acquired it in Uganda in the 1970s and brought it back to Portland, Oregon where it sat well preserved in a box with a perfect fit.

Death on display

No one here quite knows how this works or if it has ever been used. The collector was thrilled to find it and put it in a national exhibition about Household Objects that she was organizing in 1978. It is a rat trap constructed by the Giriama people of Kenya out of wood, twine and a large pick. Never on view at this museum before, whether the trap actually belongs in an art museum is a valid question that has no absolute answer.

Pompidou's Christmas pulley

This sculpture was given to the museum by a donor with the following note: 'I first noticed African sculptures when I had tea with Georges Braque in 1960. He had a treasured small sculpture on a table in front of his Fauve paintings. I couldn't wait to find a similar piece. This piece was given to me one Christmas by Mrs. George Pompidou. It had belonged to her husband and I had always admired it.'

Buying animals in Burkina

While on a trip to Burkina Faso in 1969, Katherine White wrote about how she bought these animals in a busy market: 'In the midst of the flurry came a man with a heavy burlap bag out of which he pulled a massive boa constrictor, maybe twelve feet long, with which he danced, winding the snake around his neck like a scarf. Another man came with a tiny little deer, dik-dik size, which he tethered to his ankle. Obviously they intended to feed the snakes then and there. They were shooed away–perhaps it was going to take too long. I was relieved–I sided with the deer.

There were stalls of fine Arabic leatherwork, and some wood carvers with marvelous animals. I finally got a bull and found I could make a path by saying "moo, moo" and everyone, chuckling, made way for me. Many of the Peul clicked their tongues as if I were doing something naughty. I had quite a gang follow me to the car, even after it was locked inside they stood there, looking at the bull through the windows.'

A rare survivor

An eccentric uncle left this cloak to a family who had no idea what it was. It once belonged to their great-grandfather, an Irish miner named Paul Corcoran who went to Johannesburg, South Africa, in 1889. He moved to Idaho and became a national hero when he was wrongly convicted of murder in a union-busting effort. Paul gave the cloak to the uncle, who lived alone in a small cabin. South African museum officials are captivated by this unusual garment–made by Tswana for a chieftain from the pelts of hydraxes and a serval cat–since they are mostly known only from pictures and sketches from the late nineteenth century.

The Untold Story texts exposed the choices that collectors make, some of which are not exactly in the realm of professional practice, and how the museum works with their legacy. Such texts can prompt viewers to compare notes on what they have done or might do, as they collect objects and stories about them. Would they send something to a museum in a pizza box with a note? Is it important to know that a President of France once gave away a heddle pulley? Is one culture's rat trap another culture's sculpture? This approach to texts led to many revealing tours, particularly with young audiences, who responded most positively to the notion of reading short stories with titles such as "A festival of insults," "Mars attacks," "Portrait of a dying prophet," "A pole never before seen in public," and to the varied accounts of how objects were acquired.

The ethic of cooperation: who curates who?

Case No. 2. Maasai collects Maasai[10] is a model for collecting objects and their meanings as an ethical exchange. This interaction was engineered by a student who was appalled by what art he found in Museum storage from his culture. Kakuta Maimai Hamisi, a Maasai from the Merrueschi community of Kenya, came to the Seattle Art Museum as an intern from Evergreen State College. His summer assignment was to review the Maasai art in storage and its documentation. In preparation, he was given stacks of books about Maasai that often featured their photogenic nature without considering their names, opinions or whether they had granted their permission to take the photographs. Kakuta was livid, and literally wouldn't speak to me for a couple of weeks. Then he just asked, "Shouldn't a Maasai collect Maasai art?" At the end of his internship, he presented a proposal to the trustees–if they would fund a project in his community, he would acquire Maasai art for the Museum in return. It was the first time the committee had considered an abstract proposal–there was nothing but a possibility of something to come if they would help build a one-room school.

When Kakuta arrived at home he called a meeting to announce that this place they call a museum was giving money to build a school to be run by Maasai teachers. He had to explain what a museum was. "I called it a place where *wazungu* [white people] keep things from all over the world." Some couldn't understand it, but when building of the school began, it spread a powerful and emotional message of enabling children to be educated near by, instead of having to be sent away to boarding schools. He said, "I think my community was shocked, confused, and amazed by what we did."

In return, everyone was asked to bring what they thought would represent them best. Elders provided their finest authority staffs, warriors contributed a full assembly of garments and implements and women assembled a bride's outfit which consists of twenty layers of beadwork, each with intrinsic messages attached. Kakuta documented the process with video interviews, narration and written records. For each object, the creator or owner's name is noted and his or her words about the transaction are recorded. A Maasai collection devised by Maasai and documented by Maasai now stands for a new type of partnership that is based on an exchange of art and ideas. It has led to more exchanges between Seattle and the Merrueschi community that can be seen in a website, http://www.Maasai association.org.

Kakuta Hamisi's actions enable the museum to move from the vague past to the very lively present. Instead of a ubiquitous attribution to art "from Maasai culture," the museum records reflect layers of knowledge about the artists and their intentions. For example, a bull necklace was created by Naleop ene Matini in 1999. In a video interview, she explains why her necklace is named and why she chose the colors she did. Through this exchange, vague sources from another continent are replaced with specifics that are equivalent to the standard for documentation expected with an American artist.

The ethic of public service: who wants it?

Case No. 3. Passion for Possession invited visitors to become involved in the process of buying art for a museum collection.[11] Usually, what curators, directors and trustees choose to collect involves a closely guarded decision-making process that takes place behind tightly closed doors. Armed with $10,000 raised from deaccessioning fifty-eight African artifacts (that were of low quality or duplicates), I asked the director and Committee on Collections for permission to experiment with a transparent process.

The gallery displayed nine different options for the money to be spent such as on: a single mask; documentary photographs of Cameroon; a recent print from a South African artist; a return visit by artist Fred Wilson; a historic rickshaw driver's outfit from Cape Town; and an assemblage by local artist Marita Dingus. A label accompanied each choice, explaining what the object or project could do for the museum (from my point of view). Every visitor was invited to spend our $10,000 by filling out a ballot and justifying their vote with a written rationale. Tallies of votes were accumulated, and the commentaries offered for other visitors to read.

Ballots are blunt texts, but imply trust in the public process. In this case, most visitors took their newfound influence seriously. People talked about what it is like to choose something, not for you, but for everyone else to see. Arguments flared up about different ways to collect ethically, and the discourse gave me a chance to convince a few collectors to buy some of the objects that didn't win the vote, but still would be valuable additions to the collections. Ultimately, however, the public vote surprised the staff because it was for the last work I mentioned which one could not comprehend without reading the label. It is an installation that moved people to write strong statements of advocacy (Figure 19.5). Since then, whenever this piece is up, I still see people flinch when they read this text. Here's the label that explains the artist's intent that won the prize for purchase:

Four hundred headless bodies made out of rags may seem playful. Zipper tops, Christmas tree light bulbs and dangling threads are casual, but their repetition here is conscious. In fact, *400 Men* was inspired by the artist's visit to Elmina Castle, a fort in Ghana where slaves were stored and loaded into ships. She walked into rooms where 400 men were kept often for months. They were small, stuffy and claustrophobic. Marita Dingus spent every day for a year and a half on this assembly. It twists a playful first impression into a serious reminder of a disturbing historic episode.

As the votes accumulated, so did ballots full of arguments on behalf of *400 Men*. Among the most moving were:

> Its color, size and scope drew me in and then the message hit me right between the eyes.
>
> I think we find it difficult to comprehend tragedy on a massive scale. This piece of art helps us look at each person, to imagine who they were, what they felt, and what would have been were they not slaves.
>
> Presents a complex issue to be contemplated. We need more of this.
>
> Makes a statement without preaching.
>
> Much like the Vietnam wall, but nameless, faceless, forgotten, dismembered.

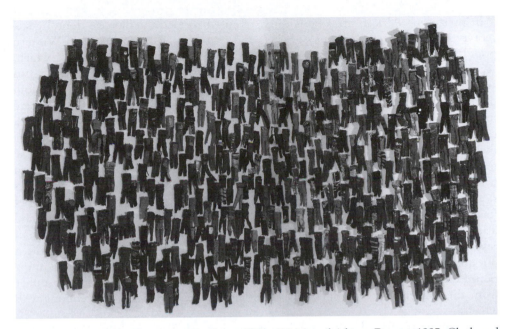

Figure 19.5 Marita Dingus, American, born 1956, *400 Men of African Descent*, 1997. Cloth and mixed media, Varied dimensions. Seattle Art Museum. African Art Acquisition Fund, 98.43. Photo: Susan A. Cole.

It seems, at first, funny and trivial. I overheard a young girl say something about Barbie dolls. But when you look closer and when you read the explanation, the power of it and the tragedy of it strike you strongly.

Because the slave trade is something that profoundly affected the history of the entire western hemisphere. Slavery is a worldwide issue.

Reading the description made my stomach flip.

The artist who created *400 Men*, Marita Dingus, took on a very difficult subject and exposed it in a way that enabled audiences to respond emotionally and intellectually. Ballots offered them a chance to contribute to the museum's decision making, and suggest the value of tailored public involvement in what has been a guarded museum secret. What if every label was turned into a ballot for the art to come or go? It was telling to see audiences vote by the thousands, but also write moving statements on behalf of the art they preferred. That the resulting selection was by far the most challenging was a conclusion that surprised many staff, but is revealing of the potential for this kind of democratic process in a museum.

The ethic of shared expertise: whose voice is heard?

Case No. 4. Art from Africa: Long Steps Never Broke a Back is based on the assertion that labels are not always the best choice for an exhibition. This led to another experiment, this time substituting labels with conversations.

In presenting African art, one is often required to face the damage done by stereotypes and misinterpretations of beliefs and traditions, as perpetuated in Western
popular culture. Perhaps the most egregious case is that of the *Nkondi*, which,
recontextualized without acknowledgement of its history and intended function, can
automatically trigger the term fetish. In fact, the *Nkondi* originated from a kingdom
that converted to Christianity, saw images of the crucifixion and, over several centuries, evolved with the creation of a sculpture that has a unique role. When a
resolution or agreement is reached, litigants take a nail and lick it to offer saliva as
their signature and pound it into the figure as a visual record for all to see. The
museum created an ad campaign using the slogan, "imagine a civilization where you
hammer out your differences without attorneys." Explaining the context of this
slogan and allowing its implications to sink in is difficult to accomplish in the brief
format of a label. In such cases, one hopes the label acts as an opening door, and
leads visitors to take home a catalogue to read as they digest deeper points of
research. However, the very people who I've found wanting to know more are often
not able to afford this next step, either financially or in terms of time. In this situation, I wanted to provide direct access to the original source–the leading philosopher
from this culture who has spent years explaining the truths and conventions with
which he grew up.

This commitment led to the exhibition *Art from Africa: Long Steps Never Broke a
Back*.[12] In it, I asked African advisors and artists each to curate a section that they
could explain through recordings of their personal experiences. The exhibition
included profiles of each of them, alongside kiosks where each advisor narrated the
art on view through audio recordings. Visitors were encouraged not only to stand
and walk through the galleries, but also to sit and listen to hear directly from a philosopher from the Kongo, a musician raised in the palace of the leader of the Asante
of Ghana, two extremely successful contemporary artists living in London, a
member of the Cameroonian royal family and masquerade organizers from Nigeria
and Liberia. How many times do Americans have direct access to such voices and
personal accounts in museums? The absence of labels encouraged visitors to reorient
themselves from literary to aural culture and to approach the objects from another
perspective.

The sign of success for me occurred during the last week, when I was observing in
the galleries without my badge and a woman just came up and said, "Aren't you sad
to see this go?" She proceeded to tell me that she had come eight times and still
wanted to hear more. The sign of failure for me revealed itself when this exhibition
traveled and, at one venue, in a cost-cutting measure, the entire audio component
was eliminated. Written labels were posted that never mentioned the source of
insights as derived from distinct individuals, but instead gave authorship to the great
unknown of museum authority. When one of the advisors and I went to see the
show at this other institution, we were both aghast at the crush of convention and
how heavy the feeling of ILDS was. ILDS prevailed in galleries without voices, music
and an alternative placement of objects. Art tagged by anonymous text encourages a
singular experience for the audience. Recordings of interviews and projections of
performances not only showcase the senses overlapping, but people too. Crowd
interaction with art takes the object out of solitary confinement and into active
engagement. One of the advisory groups involved with this exhibition was a

performing troupe from Nigeria whose title *Ayan Agalu* translates as "May the Spirit of Drumming Carry one Aloft." Finding ways for museums to create a social space where being aloft and receptive to long conversations about art and ethics and collecting and exchanging is an ongoing endeavor.

The ethics of public versus private: who owns it?

Case No. 5. A Bead Quiz introduces a form of text that throws down a gauntlet, challenging visitors to engage in participatory learning about what is on view. Instead of relying on labels alone, it asks why not offer a quiz?

This question came about when I was installing a textile gallery, showcasing the extreme difference between how an individual and an institution collect. The gallery installation, entitled *A Bead Quiz*[13] pays homage to the fact that beads are the earliest portable art form, and act as magnets pulling people into networks that span continents and centuries. How this magnetism is reflected in an institutional path and how it is manifested in one person's quest became a way to organize a display of contrasting methods of collecting. In searching through the Museum's holdings of art that utilized beads, I came across many objects that had never been exhibited before, partly because they don't fit into our more established categories of display which are largely defined by geography–the art of China, Japan, Australia, America, Native America, and so on. With the Museum's holdings representing nearly every continent on one side of the gallery, on an opposite wall, I countered with art from one collector's closet. This world traveler and photographer with an eye for ornament had a closet filled with at least a thousand necklaces. We borrowed nearly 200 and amassed a wall that gives a sense of what the museum hasn't done, and why. Beads, in their diminutive way, cross over so many boundaries that they don't belong in any single department. For a public audience, they offer a perfect chance to test one's knowledge of world trade. By every case, labels were treated as beads and strung for easy access to check whether audiences could recognize where, how old and what materials the beads were made out of. It provides a self-guided test that no one is forced to take, but for those who aspire to lifelong learning, why not consider some displays as open book exams?

This face-off of public and private collecting arenas also offered an illustration of the differences between what an institution and an individual do with their holdings. In the label texts for the objects owned by the museum, there were details of interpretation derived from consultation with local artists, with advisors from the Tibetan community, with visiting artists from the Ndebele of South Africa and from accumulated research. For the objects owned by the individual, who happens to be a constant world traveler with a keen eye for photography, the form of documentation relied on photographs taken during her travels. Beaded objects in the museum are surrounded by a vivid trail of connections that generations of scholars can keep adding to and refining. Following the code of ethics established by the AAM, "stewardship of collections entails the highest public trust and carries with it the presumption of rightful ownership, care, documentation, accessibility and responsible disposal." Beaded objects in a person's closet are cared for in another manner.

Cosmic ethics

Kwame Anthony Appiah cites museums as places that can help us envision our role as cosmopolitans, or as "citizens of the cosmos," because they "allow us to take pleasure in cultures with which we don't have the connection of identity, they permit us to engage with cultures to which our connection is just our connection as human beings."[14] Being cosmopolitan is defined as being at home in all parts of the world, as distinct from being metropolitan which is defined as relating to cities and home territories of imperial or colonial states. He describes the cosmopolitan as one who revels in the range and variety of the ways people live and the things they do, and doesn't endeavor to change others to fit into a mold.[15] In many ways, museums are perfect reflective ponds for the "citizen of the cosmos" and their texts can lead the way for us all to be better equipped to deal with strange and unexpected creativity.

Notes

1 Example of a text panel from an Anish Kapoor exhibition at the Haus der Kunst, 2007: "In Kapoor's work, material plays a central role, although always in conjunction with an idea of presence and spirituality that transcends the superficial 'actuality' of the object. In Kapoor's words: 'In a certain way matter always leads to something immaterial.' He sees this as the fundamentally paradoxical yet complementary proviso of the material world. Terms like lightness, slowness and growth seem to be the inspiration and driving force for Kapoor's new kinetic objects and special objects shown in this exhibition. At the root of them all is Kapoor's expression of anxiety through unabashed emblems and formal reference to sexuality and violence: the unspeakable is given voice."

2 C. Demand, "Inflated Phrases," Signandsight.com, 28 May 2008. Online. Available HTTP: http://www.signandsight.com/features/1703.html (accessed 21 June 2010).

3 I. Schaffner, "Wall Text, 2003/6," in Paula Marincola (ed.) *What Makes a Great Exhibition?* Philadelphia: Philadelphia Exhibitions Initiative, 2006, p. 156.

4 J. Elkins, *Our Beautiful, Dry and Distant Texts: Art History as Writing*, London and New York: Routledge, 2000, pp. xv, 176.

5 *The Play of the Unmentionable: An Installation by Joseph Kosuth at the Brooklyn Museum*, exhibition catalog, New York: Brooklyn Museum of Art and New Press, 1992, p. 115.

6 C. Kotik, "Introduction," in *The Play of the Unmentionable*, p. xv.

7 Trevor Fairbrother provided label copy from the exhibition he curated entitled "The Label Show: Contemporary Art and the Museum," Museum of Fine Arts, Boston, MA, 1994, to me with personal correspondence. There was a small brochure published for the exhibition, but it did not include actual label copy.

8 Ibid. For a review of the exhibition, see A. Solomon-Godeau, "The Label Show: Contemporary Art and the Museum," *Art in America*, October 1994, pp. 51–55.

9 "The Untold Story" was installed at the Seattle Art Museum from November 2003 to November 2004.

10 "Maasai collects Maasai" has been shown in numerous ways since the collection was formulated in 2000 but was most extensively displayed in *Long Steps never Broke a Back: Art from Africa in America*, which was on view at the Seattle Art Museum in 2001 and then toured to the Philadelphia Museum of Art, the Wadsworth Atheneum, the Frist Art Center and the Cincinnati Art Museum.

11 "Passion for Possession" was installed at the Seattle Art Museum from June 1997 to June 1998.

12 See *Long Steps* above.

13 "A Bead Quiz" was installed at the Seattle Art Museum from October 2008 to February 2010.

14 K. A. Appiah, *The Politics of Culture, the Politics of Identity*, Eva Holtby Lecture on Contemporary Culture No. 2, Toronto: Institute for Contemporary Culture at the Royal Ontario Museum, 2008, pp. 6, 15.

15 Ibid., p. 16. See also K. A. Appiah, *Cosmopolitanism: Ethics in a World of Strangers*, New York: Norton, 2006.

20

Transfer protocols

Museum codes and ethics in the new digital environment

Ross Parry

A decade can be a long time in computing. Indeed, if we were to identify the key milestones, inventive steps and innovations that, over the last ten years, have taken place in the area of digital heritage (that complex of professional practice and subject research at the juncture between cultural heritage and digital media), we would not be short of candidates. After all, our sector has watched its online (Web-based) visitation in many institutions tip over its on-site footfall; evermore, the museum pushes content into 'the cloud', as much as it pulls visitors into the venue. Likewise, from wireless networking to movement sensing, and from high definition screens to large-scale projectors, the sector has created successful ways to embed digital inter-activity seamlessly into its exhibition spaces and interpretive interventions. With continually more intuitive and ambient design solutions, the more the museum uses the new media (innately) within its exhibitions, the more, today, that same media – from the visitor's perspective – effectively disappears.[1] Internally, within the organisation of the museum, the changes have been just as overt and expansive. The start of the twenty-first century has witnessed the specifications of recruitment and human resource management rearticulated to accommodate a phalanx of staff posts without precedent – e-learning curators, new media managers, Web editors, digital archivists – many of whom find a place in restructured institutions, replete with 'new media units' and 'digital programme departments'.[2]

There is, however, another shift that has taken place, a development that has been just as meaningful and impactful. Yet, it is a change that is perhaps more subtle, and possibly requires more circumspection to comprehend. For, this is not a change conjoined to the release of a particular application or software, nor does it hang on the production of a new type of physical technology or hardware. Although undoubtedly influenced by these sorts of progresses, this change is, instead, about our professional language. More specifically, it is about a modification in the vocabulary that figures more prominently in the sector's discourse. It is, in short, about digital heritage looking more to *experience* and *emotion*. It is about a community of practice whose former (and enduring) priorities and conclusions on technical operation are, today, being joined poignantly by a set of new reference points orientated around social responsibility and trust. This, in other words, is about the rise of *compassionate computing*.

A helpful demonstration of this shift in discourse can come through analyses of key outcomes and 'take homes' from digital heritage congresses over this last decade. Consider, for instance, a typical example, the 'UK Museums on the Web' conferences – a key forum for practitioners and researchers who work with digital media, convened annually by the Museums Computer Group (MCG), a national curators group formed back in the early 1980s at the outset of the personal computing revolution. At the close of its 2004 conference (entitled 'Web Enabled'[3]), delegates were asked to contribute to a round table discussion led by heads of new media of five national cultural heritage organisations in the UK. The conclusions of this session (titled 'The strategic development of on-line provision') leaned heavily on the need for a 'coordinated national strategy' and 'joined up thinking' in the provision of new technology. A year later, the conclusions of the MCG's 2005 conference ('The Digital Object'[4]) were shaped by both a discussion on 'Best and future practice in digital object management and recording' and, with respect, again, to digital strategy, a plea for the sector to engage with 'the challenges facing small museums'. Similarly, the key 'take homes' identified by the conveners of the 2007 conference ('Web Adept'[5]) gravitated towards both the 'standards' and 'legal requirement' that would make possible the 'interoperability' described in several of the key presentations.

These outcomes reflect a dominant discourse in the first half of the decade, a discourse that gathered in equal measure around procedural challenges and technical processes. Here was a sector still working out how to make these exciting new technologies work reliably, which to opt for and how to sustain them, according to wider technical standards and guidelines. Here, in other words, was a community of practitioners that observed the principles of good digital preservation and storage.[6] Here was a community that was adhering responsibly to established standards for data management.[7] Here was a community that also worked professionally within the legal frameworks of digital rights management.[8] In each case, these (often hard won) principles, protocols and parameters would remain firm and important for the sector; they would continue to provide a vital infrastructure within which quality could be maintained, best practice shared and efficiencies met. And, to this extent, each protocol spoke importantly to the sector's ethical responsibility with digital media. However, characteristically, these protocols were orientated around process and procedure, the emphasis on conduct, propriety, functionality. They were much less (overtly at least) about values.

It was poignant, therefore, that the 2007 conference was marked also by a change of emphasis in a number of the papers presented. These were authors and commentators who sought to express themselves using another set of terms and with their focus fixed upon another set of priorities. As well as looking at the likely technical requirements for a semantically enabled cultural Web,[9] and the applications required to wire together 'mash-ups' of museum content on-line (both of which were highly consistent with the prevailing machine-orientated discourse of these events and this group), this community of professionals – for the first time in that particular forum – engaged with questions of its 'ethical obligation'[10] to ensure its Web-based content was accessible to users of all abilities, and (perhaps most challengingly of all) to address the 'ethical questions' that arise for museums when they choose to display sacred images on the Internet.[11] Here, in other words, was the community of digital heritage practitioners and researchers looking to the social, cultural and spiritual implications and accountability of their actions with digital media. Here were the developers and deliverers of the new media provision attempting publicly and collegially to form a more nuanced social understanding of their work.

Strikingly, in the two years of conferences that followed ('Integrate, Federate, Aggregate' in 2008,[12] and 'The Everyday Web' in 2009[13]), we see this same community of practice continuing to locate some of its main conclusions and priorities within a very different (less technocratic, and more experiential) context. Conveners at both events highlighted a new vocabulary. The watchwords of 'standards', 'usability' and 'interoperability' that had become mainstays of earlier discussions had (by 2008) been joined with reference to the 'beauty' of museums' digital offer and the 'delight' it might now engender in users. Again, in 2009, within its discussion on the sociality of the Web, comment now dwelled upon the new forms of 'relationship' museums were building with their audiences, how they might 'care' for these new audiences, treating people with 'respect', whilst considering the 'trust' between the individual and the organisation, and being 'sympathetic' to their personal circumstances and needs.[14]

It is to this apparent shift in values, this new conception of a wider horizon of professional responsibility, that this chapter will look. This choice illustration of the evolution in language and priorities of one professional community may be specific and limited, but it, nevertheless, reveals the key idea at the heart of our discussion here – that digital heritage is no longer (just) about making systems technically work, knowing what equipment to procure and learning to evaluate impact. That, rather, it is beginning to confront the implications of a swathe of new socio-technological outcomes: the implications of fostering social, personal and participatory communities through this media; the effects of these means of interaction being embedded in audiences' everyday lives; the repercussions of being able to use computers to support highly believable experiences that may interact with the user's body in a number of sensory channels; and the consequences of not just involving a wider community of interest in the interpretation (and perhaps documentation) of museum objects and collections, but also of allowing the online collections to be distributed and recontextualised beyond the institution's own website into a much wider matrix of inferences, cross-references and 'linked data'.

Our discussion here will suggest four specific directions in which the digital heritage community might usefully look in order to allow its existing ethical framework to negotiate and reflect key challenges and changes that have emerged over the last decade with new media, namely: the new 'situated media' (where content can be location-specific, and where users can be not just distant but itinerant); the new 'sensory media' (where computer-generated displays become believable and delightful, and act upon the body of the visitor in unprecedented ways); and the new 'semantic media' (where content is recontextualised and inferences generated in potentially less predictable ways). We begin our discussion, however, with a consideration of 'social media', and a reminder that our evolving computer networks are full of people – and not just machines.

The ethics of social media

Just as in the last decade of the twentieth century, when the sector was transformed by the affordances of the Web, so, in the first decade of the twenty-first century, museums have seen their opportunities for social interaction with these new online audiences diversify at an exponential rate. Initially the Web presented itself as a medium where pages containing predominantly text and image were not just viewable to anyone with a connection and the skills to find the museum's domain, but were also connected through predetermined links to other points of interest or relevance. In terms of making resources available (be it collections data or educational material), or for advertising key organisational information (be it opening times, entrance fees or current programming), the Web presented museums with a channel of communication that (eventually) resonated well with existing commitments to publishing, outreach and marketing.

The Web then evolved – and the sector (like the rest of the modern digital age) quickly grew comfortable referring to 'Web 2.0', as if now it was in a second iteration, differentiating its current functionalities from what had come before. More specifically, as both the (software) browser capability and the (human) design proficiency developed, not to mention (hardware) connectivity quickened, the metaphor of the 'page' was joined by many other spatial strategies for organising on-screen content. This content was now just as likely to be sound, video and three-dimensional model, as it was text and static image. Perhaps the most defining change for the Web (and the sector) in that second decade was the levelling of the means of publication and production. With the rise of blogging and social networking media, the barriers to participation were significantly reduced. The Web was now something audiences 'used', rather than simply 'browsed'. It had become as much a communications device as a reference tool.

The ethical challenges presented to museums by the 'social Web' are far from simple, probably not all yet apparent, but certainly highly contingent. Any attempt to begin to frame a sense of positive and constructive ethical responsibilities with the new social Web needs to be predicated upon the sheer range of variables that exist within it as a medium. For example, there are (first) instances where the museum will initiate interaction, but other scenarios where it is the user or community of users that initiate. It is probable, in each case, that questions of responsibility and ownership are answered differently. Second, these social interactions do not take place in just one type of on-line place; they may be within the 'walled garden' of the museum's website, or they may potentially be in the user's (or community's) domain, or even within a third party application (such as, for instance, a social networking or microblogging site). Again, the location of the interaction has a bearing on not just how the protocols for behaviour are set (and by whom), but where accountability for the interaction ultimately resides. Third, the duration of these interactions may vary considerably. Some may be fleeting (a passing posting, a brief tagging act), others may be project-bound (around an on-line event, tracking an on-site exhibition), whereas others may represent a commitment by either the institution or the user to a longer-term relationship and interaction. Fourth, owing to the rich media content of the social Web, the formats of the content around which this interaction pivot could vary considerably. The new social media allow for museum and individual (or community) alike to participate and contribute through image as well as text, video as well as sound. Each of these media carry with them their own set of agencies, some of which may be culturally contingent. Finally, it is also prudent to resist generalisation about the motivations and aims for these types of interaction. Some interactions, after all, may be systematic (a methodical, planned survey or contact), other interactions may, instead, be highly serendipitous (a chance visit to a website or an unplanned introduction through a third party).

There are, in other words, myriad points of calibration on these various axes related to *who* initiates, as well as *where*, *when*, with *what* and *why* they initiate this interaction through social media. Despite this difficulty and complexity, there are several specific areas that are already revealing themselves as points worthy of ethical attention. It is already apparent, for instance, that owing to the distributed nature of the new social media, museums are now having interactions with users and audiences in locations that are either less predictable or outside of the places in which these institutions have traditionally intervened. At this juncture, it is a simple (but helpful) point to keep in mind that, with social media and the Web, it is the museum that does the visiting. The traditional centralised model of the 'visit act' involves the visitor choosing to enter the museum precinct, stepping from the everyday to a liminal space, at the threshold of the real and the imaginary. On the Web (with social media), it is the museum, instead, that does the visiting, with the dynamic switched to a localised model. Here, conversely, the visitor ('user') chooses to receive part of the museum's provision. At that point, the museum, used to enveloping the visitor within an experience, is itself enveloped – this time into that user's chosen locality.

As well as presenting a set of new design and interpretive challenges (for how long will these visitors dwell on this on-line content, what resources do they have around them, are they alone or part of a group?), the museum, on the Web, is confronted with a new array of responsibilities and considerations. Unlike the controlled and knowable environment of the gallery space, the user on-line may be in many types of settings (domestic and professional, public and private), in many types of cultural and geographical contexts, bound in each case potentially by different legal jurisdictions as well as diverse paradigms of what is considered acceptable and what might be thought to be transgressive behaviour. Furthermore, in their new social media exchanges, museums may well be presenting a different proposition, as well as implying a different type of transaction, to their audiences. At that point (when the museum chooses to 'tweet' within the indiscriminate mêlée of a microblogging community, when it allows itself to be contextualised within the cross-references and referrals of an extensive social networking site and when it commits to hosting or joining an on-going dialogue with a set of on-line users), then the institution has entered into a substantially different ethical landscape than it has occupied before. And it is here that the sector has perhaps only just begun to unpick the new sets of responsibility that it carries into such spaces.

On-site, within the physical familiarity of the gallery, or even within the recognisable spaces of outreach, the museum might, for example, frame with the utmost care the parameters of a reminiscence session (highly vigilant to how those participants contribute and react).[15] Likewise, it might observe with the utmost respect the display of a religious object (highly deferential to fulfilling a sacred rite).[16] Such considerations are established parts of best practice within the orthodoxies of museums' on-site provision. However, in the space of social media, it becomes harder (or, at least, at first it seems harder) for the museum to predict and deploy these same sensitivities that it might show within its own venue, within its own jurisdiction, according to its own protocols and cultures of visiting and propriety. In short, when it comes to social media, the sector is still in the process of defining these parameters of how to observe, how to moderate, when (and how) to react and intervene and where the limits of responsibility might be. It is here where the ethics of social media are still absent or, at best, only emergent.

The ethics of situated media

The new social media have challenged us to imagine (if, at first, counter-intuitively) types of museum experience that can take place outside of the museum. Over the last decade, this network has helped to reprogram not just the rules by which a museum encounter might occur, but also the type of data that is required to measure the impact of this experience. Many institutions today, consequently, are alert to 'IP addresses', 'dwell time', 'landing pages', 'unique visits' and 'key referrers' – the digital footprints and clues to where in the world these users could be, why they might be accessing museum Web content and what path they take through this online provision. Yet, just as the museum has begun to develop evaluation processes and metrics that might evidence the impact and value of the new social media,[17] there have at the same time been some other key diversifications and extensions in the delivery channels open to users.

In particular, it has been with the advent of mobile media and location-based services (that is, digital content that is sensitive to and configured for users' geographical position) that the museum's online audience (and *potential* online audience) has become not just distant, but also now itinerant. This brings with it a new challenge: not just for planning where a user might be, but to where that user might be moving. The new distance users and learners of the museum are no longer tethered; they (like the new access technology they hold) are mobile. Moreover, their growing expectation may be for content that is not just mindful of the fact that they are not in a museum, but is also tailored to their current location. Therefore, just as once the distributed network of the Web presented the museum with a technology that was as much alluring as it was anomalous to established practice, so now, with the rise of 'situated media' (a useful term to capture this mobile, pervasive, location-specific and context-aware set of hardware and services), museums are being tested yet again – this time to accommodate not just the on-site visitor, and not just the online user, but now also the in-transit *flâneur*.

Museums have, for some time, reflected upon the implications of locative media. In terms of 'in-gallery' provision, commentaries have centred upon the relative merits of different hardware specifications and platforms, the respective consequences of mobile devices being supplied by the institution or brought by the visitor, as well as the impact of 'handhelds' upon interaction amongst visitors and upon engagement with the exhibit.[18] Similarly, in terms of off-site provision, the question of tariffs, connectivity and compatibility have all warranted scrutiny and discussion.[19] And throughout, analysis has raised questions of the function of mobile media; is it there as another dissemination tool, or a genuine two-way communications device? Is it a personalised narrator of a curatorial pathway, or is it a pocket guide to way-finding, or maybe perhaps a portable archive ready to expose supplementary material?

Yet, questions such as these expose only part of the complexity. Beyond these technical requirements and functional uses sit a number of other issues related to the experiential consequences of our new mobile delivery modes. First, there is value in rotating our line of enquiry, and asking who is excluded (as well as who is empowered) by the new situated media. Although mobile media (and smartphone) usage may be very high in some communities and in some of our audience segments, coverage and consumption is still uneven and far from universal. A museum poised to invest valuable resources in a new phone-based resource must think hard about whether it can (ethically) justify the expense to develop an application that a limited proportion of a visiting (or distance) audience has the technology to access. After all, many of the questions we once routinely asked about Web connectivity and usage (for whom exactly were we providing online, and – more important – who were we excluding when we chose to engage audiences through the Web?), have now migrated to mobile media.[20] As with the first generation of Web provision, the museum today is presented with the functional possibilities of the location-based mobile services, but, at the same time, the responsibility of targeting resource (in some cases public funds) to applications that are genuinely accessible to its public.

Alongside these 'ethics of opportunity', sit a series of further responsibilities related to the specific circumstances of these mobile users – as well as the places the museum may be encouraging the user to go. The question is whether a museum that provides mobile content for a specific geographical location (that geo-tags part of its collections or content to a particular map reference) then has any sort of responsibility for the implications of that user accessing that content in that location. After all, a museum would assiduously think through the ethical implications of presenting particular types of content (controversial themes, contested narratives, non-repatriated objects) in its galleries.[21] The question is whether that same institution has a duty to review the implications of displaying certain types of content in certain types of social setting – even if this display is conducted vicariously and at a distance, and even if that display is merely through the limited screen interface of a mobile device. There may, for example, be a political (in)sensitivity (if not an unfortunate unforeseen inference) to attaching that museum content to a given geographical reference point, just as there may be a cultural contravention in making a particular piece of the museum's collection openly visible within a particularly resonant site or venue. The new 'ethics of location' is about that instant when a museum chooses to make its collections not only accessible outside of the museum, but when it chooses to fix an interpretation on a particular place, with the potential that the user may be in that location when they see that interpretation.[22] At that moment, the museum's intervention becomes implicated with (and contextualised by) the social and political contingencies of that location.

There are similar consequences to be worked through when a museum constructs an interactive 'trail' through a city or rural space, or elicits context-specific user-generated interpretation from its locale.[23] In this regard, Arvanitis' notion of the 'museum in the everyday' is a useful case in point. In this model, members of a community use mobile media to capture and generate interpretation about the objects and built heritage 'left behind' by the local museum, and which (to that point) remain under-interpreted amongst the routines of the community's domestic and working lives.[24] A manifestation (if not a media extension) of Hooper-Greenhill's concept of the 'post-museum', the 'museum in the everyday', is a useful illustration of how the boundaries of the institution (as well as the responsibilities for, and definitions of, 'curatorship') can today be blurred. Yet, crucial (and what perhaps goes unsaid in this model) is the question of how these acts of fieldwork and interpretive excavation generate real points of responsibility for the host museum. For, at that point when the institution uses this mobile communication to encourage users to conduct activities outside of the museum, and when they are invited to move independently to specific locations, this presents to the institution a set of questions about its duty to those distant and dispersed participants.

One area where this ethical dimension of the new situated media is already being exposed is in the context of 'alternate reality gaming'. Here, users mesh together the fiction of role-play with the realities of their physical environment, relying on a range of media (including location-specific services and mobile media), typically to work through a series of problem-solving games all set within a framing narrative device.[25] This genre of playful media (with so much potential for heritage sites looking to reach out to alternative audiences and open to multiple uses of their properties and venues) has already found application (if with modification) within museums.[26] Crucially, such activities can contain game-play that subverts the usual protocols and proprieties of museum visiting.

One illustration of this is 'Ego-trap', opened by the Experimentarium (Copenhagen) in 2007 in consultation with a games developer and DREAM (the Danish Research Centre on Education and Advanced Media Materials), to stimulate young people's interest in science.[27] The game invites visitors to use their own mobile phones to trigger and follow a task-based 'digital narrative' through the space of the science centre.[28] The story begins with the user co-operating with an orthodox set of science-based tasks housed in digital interactives around the venue, but then gains an ironic twist and subversive subtext when it is revealed to the user (through a voice-mail message sent to their mobile phone) that a conspiracy (of course, fictitious) may sit behind these tests – if not, indeed, the whole institution. A pivotal episode in the storyline requires the gamer to go through a door clearly marked as out of bounds to visitors. The gamer–visitor is presented, therefore, with the moral dilemma of whether to act in an overtly transgressive way within the site of the museum. However, this level of role play and immersion also exposes just some of the ways in which these new channels of communication, and the new dynamics of interaction they afford, also take the museum into some potentially very different scenarios of visitor engagement. The alternate reality game-play of 'Ego-trap' may be a highly choreographed arch example, but it highlights what can happen (and, indeed, is happening) in the sector when creative cultures of mobile media and museum provision come together. When museum content is delivered to the user through mobile media, the user's surrounds can become augmented by a layer of digital content and interpretation. It is that augmentation that brings with it new conducts and expectations – and, critically, it is there that we need to resolve a new ethics of situated media.

The ethics of sensory media

When the user-gamer of Ego-trap hesitates at that threshold of the Experimentarium (uncertain about whether to cross into an apparently prohibited area), the realms of fantasy and reality begin to compete. Significantly, it is digital technology (in that case, the real-time live updates and intuitive messaging of mobile media) that makes the critical contribution to this believable scenario. Tellingly, it is the presence of the digital media, in that instance, that makes the situation convincing for the visitor. In the context of museum computing, this is a non-trivial development. What we are seeing here (amidst the digital revolution) is the cultural referents of computing being changed. To include digital media in an exhibition today is to include technology from the real world. A presence that for many visitors was once specialist and exceptional is now (increasingly) unremarkable, if not mundane. Where digital media may previously have made a museum experience less like everyday life, now (conversely) it has the very effect of introducing the familiar. As digital media becomes increasingly part of the routine with which we make sense of the world around us, and as we augment our own reality more and more with digital information and services, so digitality's place in museums becomes much less of a 'shock of the new', and much more recognisable and reassuring.

Visual technology is a pertinent example in this regard, raising its own set of issues around belief and trust. For, historically, we have become used to apologising for lack of authenticity in computer media.[29] As much as we have been aware of the extra information its databases can offer to a visitor, and as much as we recognise the value of its graphical expositions, these digital interventions have, in the main, been conspicuously representational. In a sense, the digitality of digital content (the way it was evidently computer-generated) has been obvious. Yet, for many years, computing was tolerated in the exhibition because the unique functionality (and occasionally the novelty) it offered outweighed its patent artifice. However, the high-definition of the new generation of screen technologies, along with the continuing advance of computer processing power, allow us, today, to generate highly realistic heritage representations.[30]

Once plainly simulations, the three-dimensional models and fly-through animations of the modern gallery can now be utterly convincing.[31] This sheer realism and plausibility present the museum with a new (ethical) dilemma; in short, what if the models we build are simply too believable? The polish of these photorealistic, three-dimensional models can run the risk of implying a certainty that is perhaps misplaced.[32] In actuality, there may be contested theories as to the exact composition of a particular architectural space. There may be gaps and interruptions within the documentation and verification that can substantiate the complete formations of certain models and environments. And yet these compelling and persuasive simulations may mask in their professional sheen the doubt and uncertainty (the speculation, the hypothesis) that might, in fact, evidence the model presented to the visitor.

Perhaps for the first time, this high verisimilitude and realism (because it is so apparently genuine and accurate) now requires the museum to reflect upon the implications of building believable simulations. (Consider, for instance, the example of how, through a stereoscopic headset and believable three-dimensional representation of a 1910s street scene, including recruitment poster, the National Archives

(London), in April 2003, immersed a 106-year-old First World War veteran in a virtual space, provoking a powerful, personal emotional response. What is the institution's responsibility at that point?[33]) In other words, just as it has traditionally framed and managed the responsible display of its replicas, casts and copies, so digitality's 'new realism' demands similar consideration and reflection on the ethics of trust.

It is also important to note that, alongside this 'new realism', digitality's new sensory media is also today interacting with the body of the visitor in unprecedented ways.[34] Since its first widespread adoption of networked and in-gallery technology in the mid 1990s, the profession has been mindful of the consequences of conveying meaning and presenting content through specific media and sensory channels.[35] Museums have been aware of (if not always fully compliant with)[36] their responsibility to design 'interactives' that were of value to visitors of all abilities. Furthermore, by building upon an important framework of audit and benchmarking, digital heritage practice has made advances in taking a holistic, sensitive and circumspect view to the accessibility of its digital provision.[37] However, this work is problematised by more recent developments in software and hardware design. These are developments that have broadened (and made more complex) the channels through which digital media interacts with the visitor. For instance, in its first iteration (with its 'pages', 'posts' and 'publishing') the interface of the Web was largely organised around the metaphor of printing and was characterised by its textuality. This has been reflected in the guidelines and standards for best practice in accessible media, with, for instance, their emphasis on 'screenreader' technology, alternative textual tags for images.[38] To make museum Web sites accessible was (it seemed) largely a case of making this published hypertextuality 'readable' to all users. Yet, today, the new sensory Web is an environment defined as much by its sound, moving image, augmented reality and three-dimensionality as it is its text. It is a space full of dynamic, real-time and changing content organised by multiple interface metaphors and strategies. Static, pre-authored 'pages' are being outweighed by content that is syndicated and assembled 'on the fly'.

Here, the museum's challenge (and responsibility) is to make their contributions to this live, multi-media and dispersed environment accessible to all of its users, whatever their ability. However, what is already apparent (particularly in the cases that are being identified by the sector itself as being of inspirational quality[39]) is that some of the most ethically robust approaches to designing digital media with disability in mind are those where the new multi-sensory nature of the technology is a solution rather than a problem. Consequently, it would appear that the new ethics of sensory media is likely to be built around not just remedial changes to existing media, or simply acquiescence and compliance to broad accessibility guidelines on digital design, but rather where these new sensory channels and means of interaction (three-dimensional printing, haptics, movement, video-signing, sonic landscapes) prove empowering and not disabling.

The ethics of semantic media

As well as the *social*, *situated* and *sensory* media that is characterising the new digital heritage landscape, museums are further confronted (although the size of this confrontation is not perhaps yet fully apparent) with the task of constructing an ethical framework that can accommodate the new *semantic* media; a set of new principles and connections are fundamentally altering the way digital content is linked and discovered online. The 'Semantic Web' restructures the Web into a more intelligent and powerful database of connected content. Through the use of 'frameworks' of association (rules for connecting one piece of content logically with another online) and 'ontologies' that define the meanings within these associations, the semantically enabled Web is defined by its network of co-contextual content and inferences.[40]

This can be both a technically and conceptually elusive development to grasp; however, from our perspective in the museum sector, we might usefully distil the Semantic Web down to three discernible functions. First, by building maps of interrelated concepts (in contrast to relying on hard-wired hyper-links) the Semantic Web can support more efficient searching and discovery of content. Rather than just finding direct occurrences and matches of a user's search terms (strings), the Semantic Web, instead, is able to consider other inferences and, perhaps, 'friend of a friend' associations to these terms. (The equivalent of a search engine returning – figuratively speaking – the response: 'You didn't ask for this by name, but we think it's very relevant to what you are looking for.') Second, the Semantic Web might be usefully seen as a collection of co-contextual 'resources', rather than linked and directory-based 'pages'. The result of this is a grinding down of Web-based content and a movement away from simply identifying and visiting 'pages' – but, instead, of discovering and compiling collections of individual elements (pieces of text, images, sound, all kinds of 'logical objects') that may or may not be currently within a page on the Web. In a sense, the Semantic Web has the potential to increase the granularity and resolution of Web-based content, and, consequently, refine the specificity of what can be discovered. (Or plainly put, instead of a search engine returning a list of Web pages, the (figurative) response might be more along the lines of: 'We've found this picture, this news story, this video, this biographical detail and this museum object that are likely to be relevant to your search.') Third (and perhaps most importantly) the Semantic Web is defined by a machine-to-machine automatic linking and processing of data. Data becomes meaningful to machines on the network and logical associations can be made through and across resources and datasets – an image cross-referenced with a biography, tied to a map, linked automatically to other images and other individuals. Rather than relying on pre-existing links and human intervention, the Web, in other words, is enabled to build its own webs of significance for the user. (Or – to continue our example here – a practical example might be the Web (again figuratively) being able to return to the user: 'This book is relevant to your search, and, what's more, the library that holds it is only twenty minutes away from your house. As there are no appointments in your diary this afternoon, you could get there on No. 27 bus that leaves at 14:45.')

For the museum sector, the challenges of building and responding to the Semantic Web have traditionally been seen as technological[41] and procedural,[42] if not also presentational (about what the technology is and what it ought to be called).[43] However, principles have emerged that affirm how 'linked data' (semantic or otherwise) can help to 'reduce inefficiency', to 'improve workflows' and minimise 'duplication of effort'.[44] National standards agencies in information and collections management, such as the UK's Collections Trust, have identified how this more co-contextual, resource-orientated and machine-processable Web of linked data has the power to improve the sector's service to the public; 'connecting the data we hold and curate', it suggests, 'is the best way to achieve Public Value'.[45] Significantly, emphasising an implicit right of reuse by audiences, the new semantic media (and linked data) is also seen as a 'channel through which Culture-sector content can be enjoyed and used by a wider, more diverse public'.[46] And it is here – crucially – that we are alerted to a new set of potential ethical considerations for museums, for the new semantic media raise issues related to ownership, authorisation, control and use.

For instance, if museums' online data is broken up, pushed out and automatically linked to the cloud of other Web-based media, institutions traditionally used to tightly framing, authenticating and contextualising their content have the prospect of negotiating and accommodating a more unpredictable, changeable and potentially even unseen set of contexts into which their content might be integrated. Museums are likely to find themselves increasingly contributing (perhaps even unknowingly) to narratives, rather than just authoring and building them themselves. Collections and interpretation that have customarily been owned and seen to be 'inside' the online presence of the museum will also – with the new semantic media and linked data – appear shared and floating 'outside' of the institution. In such a context (where the position of objects and resources appears more fluid, and where context may be less predictable), the museum will be required to anticipate at which point these contexts and this culture of 'reuse' might be deemed to be insensitive and inappropriate. The new ethics of semantic media will be about anticipating and thinking through the unexpected contexts into which these new 'feral' digital museum resources might find themselves. In short, what the museum sector is yet to confront are the implications of the machine-processable Web automatically building inferences and co-contextuality around museum objects and resources online. We still await the ethics of our new semantic media.

Towards compassionate computing

As the museum moves into new *social*, *situated*, *sensory* and *semantic* media spaces, so its ethical framework needs to adjust and respond to the implications and consequences of these new interactions and interventions. Considering each of these new media in turn, as we have done in this chapter, we are struck not just by the creative (if not transformative) potential that each affords the museum, but also the ethical questions associated to each that are yet to be fully worked through and resolved. We see the new social media, for instance, moving the museum towards building relationships with individuals and communities according to parameters (related to identity, disclosure, care, trust) that are yet to be fully defined. Likewise, we see the new situated media locating museum content in the physical landscape of society, thus being implicated with a horizon of other contexts (political, personal, cultural), the consequences of which are still to be envisaged. Similarly, we see the heightened realism of the new sensory media producing images and simulations that have the potential to hide their artifice and engender belief – and, in doing so, bringing into focus new questions of trust and authority. We also see the same media interacting with the body of the visitor in ways that are more complex and unprecedented – raising new questions of propriety, accessibility and responsibility. And, in the new semantic media, we have seen technology that automatically builds its own inferences and associations, in processes over which the museum may not always have control and with recontextualisations of which it may not always be cognisant – thus foregrounding for the profession new discussions about ownership and authorship online. For all of these reasons, we are minded, therefore, to reflect further upon what an ethical framework for digital heritage might resemble – and, of course, as always, what an opportunity such reflection presents.

Acknowledgements

The discussions set out in this chapter have been informed by two funded research projects on which I have served as principal investigator: a Collaborative Research Training grant awarded by the Arts and Humanities Research Council (which has crucially included reflections on the ethical dimensions of digital heritage research); a Research Networking Pilot grant awarded in 2009 by the Arts and Humanities Research Council in association with British Telecommunications (BT), for a project entitled 'LIVE!Museum' (specifically with respect to the section on situated media). I would also like to offer my thanks to the organisers of DISH2009 (8–10 December 2009, Rotterdam) for their kind invitation to me to think through (in such a public manner as a keynote address) the reflection on the future of digital ethics as set out in this chapter. I am grateful to the American Association of Museums and the convenors of their international conference, 'Museums without Borders', 23–26 May 2010, Los Angeles – where again, the opportunity for me to present on 'digital ethics' served as a vital catalyst for this chapter.

Notes

1 For one attempt at explaining this sense of in-gallery digital media being used more and more, but noticed less and less, see R. Parry and A. Sawyer, 'Space and the machine: adaptive museums, pervasive technology and the new gallery environment', in Suzanne MacLeod (ed.) *Reshaping Museum Space: architecture, design, exhibitions*, London and New York: Routledge, 2005, pp. 39–52.

2 For a brief but helpful overview of the nature and behaviour of this emergent genre of digital heritage professionals, see P. Marty, 'Informational professionals in museums', in P. F. Marty and K. Burton Jones (eds.) *Museum Informatics: people, information and technology in museums*, New York and Abingdon: Routledge, 2008, pp. 269–74.

3 Museums Computer Group, 'Web Enabled: museums, online access and ability', *UK Museums on the Web Conference 2004*, University of Leicester, 22 April 2004. Online. Available HTTP: http://museumscomputergroup.org.uk/2004/04/22/web-enabled-museums-online-access-and-ability/ (accessed 31 January 2010).

4 Museums Computer Group, 'The Digital Object: visualization, interpretation, sustainability', *UK Museums on the Web Conference 2005*, University of Leicester, 21 April 2005. Online. Available HTTP: http://museumscomputergroup.org.uk/2005/04/21/uk-museums-on-the-web-2005-the-digital-object/ (accessed 31 January 2010).

5 Museums Computer Group, 'Web Adept', *UK Museums on the Web Conference 2007*, University of Leicester, 22 June 2007. Online. Available HTTP: http://museumscomputergroup. org.uk/2007/06/22/uk-museums-on-the-web-2007-web-adept/ (accessed 31 January 2010).

6 See Northeast Document Conservation Center, *Handbook for Digital Projects: a management tool for preservation and access*. Online. Available HTTP: http://www.nedcc.org/resources/ digitalhandbook/dman.pdf (accessed 10 March 2010). On preserving web-based resources see University of London Computer Centre, UKOLN and JISC, *The Preservation of Web Resources (PoWR) Handbook: digital preservation for the UK HE/FE web management community*, JISC, 2008. Online. Available HTTP: http://www.jisc.ac.uk/media/documents/programmes/ preservation/powrhandbookv1.pdf (accessed 10 March 2010).

7 See, for instance, the Dublin Core Metadata Initiative. Online. Available HTTP: http:// dublincore.org (accessed 10 March 2010); see also ICONCLASS. Online. Available HTTP: http://www.iconclass.nl/ (accessed 10 March 2010). For a seminal discussion on the necessity for standards in data management, see D. Bearman, 'Standards for networked cultural heritage', *Archives and Museum Informatics: Cultural Heritage Informatics Quarterly* 9: 3, 1995, pp. 279–307.

8 See Collections Trust, *Get to Grips with Copyright*. Online. Available HTTP: http://www. collectionslink.org.uk/get_to_grips_with_copyright (accessed 10 March 2010); N. Korn *et al.*, *Web2Rights*, HEFCE. Online. Available HTTP: http://www.web2rights.org.uk/about. html (accessed 10 March 2010).

9 In his paper 'The Rewired Web', Paul Shabajee drew upon earlier work to explain the coding and logistical challenge of building a semantically enabled cultural web. See D. Reynolds, P. Shabajee and S. Cayzer, 'Semantic Information Portals', *Thirteenth World Wide Web Conference*, New York: ACM, 2004, pp. 290–1.

10 B. Kelly, 'The Accessible Web', paper presented to 'Web Adept', *UK Museums on the Web Conference 2007*, University of Leicester, 22 June 2007.

11 A. Whitfield, 'The Ethical Web', paper presented to 'Web Adept', *UK Museums on the Web Conference 2007*, University of Leicester, 22 June 2007.

12 Museums Computer Group, 'Integrate, Federate, Aggregate: making collections connect online', *UK Museums on the Web Conference 2008*, University of Leicester, 19 June 2008. Online. Available HTTP: http://museumscomputergroup.org.uk/2008/06/19/uk-museums-on-the-web-2008-integrate-federate-aggregate/ (accessed 31 January 2010).

13 Museums Computer Group, 'The Everyday Web: situated, sensory, social', *UK Museums on the Web Conference 2009*, Sackler Centre, Victoria and Albert Museum, London, 2 December 2009. Online. Available HTTP: http://museumscomputergroup.org.uk/2009/11/ 25/uk-museums-on-the-web-2009-situated-sensory-social/ (accessed 31 January 2010).

14 R. Parry, 'Closing Remarks', *UK Museums on the Web Conference 2009*, Sackler Centre, Victoria and Albert Museum, London, 2 December 2009. It is appropriate to note here that, as co-convenor of these conferences, and (since 2008) as chair of the national Museums Computer Group, I was fortunate enough to provide the summarising addresses to these events.

15 G. Kavanagh, *Dream Spaces: memory and the museum*, New York and London: Leicester University Press, 2000.

16 C. Paine, *Godly Things: museums, objects and religion*, London: Leicester University Press, 2000.

17 G. Davies, and D. James, 'Evaluating the on-line audience of a new collections Web site', in J. Trant and D. Bearman (eds.) *Museums and the Web 2010: Proceedings*, Toronto: Archives and Museum Informatics, 2010. Online. Available HTTP: http://www.archimuse. com/mw2010/papers/davies/davies.html (accessed 10 March 2010).

18 See L. Tallon and K. Walker (eds.) *Digital Technologies and the Museum Experience: handheld guides and other media*, Lanham, MD and Plymouth: AltaMira Press, 2008, pp. 35–60.

19 For a useful outline of key requirements for learning with mobile devices, see A. Kukulska-Hulme *et al.*, 'Innovation in mobile learning: a European perspective', *International Journal of Mobile and Blended Learning* 1: 1, 2009, pp. 13–35.

20 For an example of digital heritage practitioners making an evidenced case for engaging with a specific audience segment through mobile phones, see: D. Bressler, 'Mobile phones: a

new way to engage teenagers in informal science learning', in J. Trant and D. Bearman (eds.) *Museums and the Web 2006: Proceedings*, Toronto: Archives and Museum Informatics, 2006. Online. Available HTTP: http://www.archimuse.com/mw2006/papers/bressler/bressler.html (accessed 10 March 2010).

21 See, for instance, S. Macdonald, *Difficult Heritage: negotiating the Nazi past in Nuremberg and beyond*, London: Routledge, 2008; W. Logan, *Places of Pain and Shame: dealing with 'difficult heritage'*, London: Routledge, 2008.

22 For a description of how the Philadelphia City Archive and Philadelphia's Mural Arts Program mapped parts of their collection onto the cityscape (and, with respect to the content of some of its more 'inappropriate' images, not completely without controversy), see M. Heckert, 'Putting museum collections on the map: application of geographic information systems', in J. Trant and D. Bearman (eds.) *Museums on the Web 2009: Proceedings*, Toronto: Archives and Museum Informatics, 2009. Online. Available HTTP: http://www.archimuse.com/mw2009/papers/heckert/heckert.html (accessed 10 March 2010).

23 Perhaps one of the most well-established (and referenced) examples of a museum providing these kinds of narrative and interpretive pathways through a city is the award-winning local history project 'My Brighton and Hove'. Online. Available HTTP: http://www.mybrightonandhove.org.uk/ (accessed 10 March 2010).

24 K. Arvanitis, 'Museums outside walls: mobile phones and the museum in the everyday', in R. Parry (ed.) *Museums in a Digital Age*, London and New York: Routledge, 2010, pp. 170–6.

25 A. Moseley, 'An Alternative Reality for higher education? Lessons to be learned from online reality games', unpublished paper presented to ALT-C 2008, Leeds, 9–11 September 2008.

26 R. Cherry, 'A walk in the park: the Balboa Park Online Collaborative first year report', in J. Trant and D. Bearman (eds.), *Museums and the Web 2010: Proceedings*, Toronto: Archives and Museum Informatics, 2010. Online. Available HTTP: http://www.archimuse.com/mw2010/papers/cherry/cherry.html (accessed 10 March 2010).

27 A. Kahr-Højland, 'Ego-trap: You have no idea … how to extend the learning experience within museums by means of a digital narrative', paper presented to *UK Museums on the Web Conference 2009*, Victoria and Albert Museum, London, 2 December 2009.

28 Ibid.

29 See, for example, F. Cameron, 'Beyond the cult of the replicant: museums and historical digital objects: traditional concerns, new discourses', in F. Cameron and S. Kenderdine (eds.) *Theorizing Digital Cultural Heritage: a critical discourse*, Cambridge, MA, and London: MIT Press, 2007, pp. 49–75; C. Lynch, 'Authenticity and integrity in the digital environment: an exploratory analysis of the central role of trust', in Parry, *Museums in a Digital Age*, pp. 314–31; and J. Malpas, 'Cultural heritage in the Age of New Media', in Y. E. Kalay, T. Kvan and J. Affleck (eds.) *New Heritage: new media and cultural heritage*, London and New York: Routledge, 2008, pp. 13–26.

30 M. Roussou, 'The components of engagement in virtual heritage environments', in Kalay, Kvan and Affleck, *New Heritage*, pp. 225–41.

31 Consider, for instance, A. Law *et al.*, 'Projecting restorations in real-time for real-world objects', in Trant and Bearman, *Museums on the Web 2009: Proceedings*, Toronto: Archives and Museum Informatics, 2009. Online. Available HTTP: http://www.archimuse.com/mw2009/papers/law/law.html (accessed 10 March 2010).

32 R. Parry, *Recoding the Museum: digital heritage and the technologies of change*, London and New York: Routledge, 2007, p. 66.

33 R. Parry and J. Hopwood, 'Virtual reality and the soft museum', *Journal of Museum Ethnography* 16, 2004, pp. 69–78.

34 K. Carey, 'My dream of an accessible Web culture for disabled people: a re-evaluation', in Parry, *Museums in a Digital Age*, pp. 189–92.

35 M. Weisen, 'Barrier-free museums: the quest for inclusive design', *Access by Design* 110 (spring), 2007, pp. 12–15.

36 See N. Poole, *Disability Portfolio Guide 7: Using technology*, Resource, 2003. Online. Available HTTP: http://www.mla.gov.uk/what/support/toolkits/libraries_disability/find_out_about_disability (accessed 10 March 2010); and J. Bell, S. Matty and M. Weisen, *MLA*

Disability Survey 2005, Birmingham: MLA (Museums, Libraries and Archives Council), 2006, pp. 19–20. Online. Available HTTP: research.mla.gov.uk/evidence/view-publication. php?dm=nrm&pubid=256 (accessed 10 March 2010).

37 B. Kelly, L. Phipps and C. Howell, 'Implementing a holistic approach to e-learning accessibility', in Parry, *Museums in a Digital Age*, pp. 193–203.

38 H. Petrie, N. King and F. Hamilton, *Accessibility of museum, library and archive websites: the MLA audit*, London: MLA (Museums, Libraries and Archives Council) and City University, 2006.

39 I think here, in particular, of the recent winners of the 'Jodi Awards'. 'Celebrating practice that inspires', the 'Jodis' are run by the Jodi Mattes Trust and are given annually 'for museums, galleries, libraries, archives and heritage venues which use digital technology to widen access to information, collections, learning and creativity for disabled people'. Online. Available HTTP: http://www.jodiawards.org.uk/ (accessed 10 March 2010).

40 See D. Allemang, *Semantic Web for the Working Ontologist: effective modeling in RDFS and OWL*, Amsterdam: Morgan Kaufmann, 2008; S. Powers, *Practical RDF*, Beijing and Cambridge: O'Reilly, 2003.

41 See, for instance, E. Hyvönen *et al.*, *Publishing Museum Collections on the Semantic Web: The MuseumFinland Portal*, 2004. Online. Available HTTP: http://www.seco.tkk.fi/publications/ 2004/hyvonen-junnila-et-al-publishing-museum-collections-2004.pdf (accessed 10 March 2010).

42 For a consideration of the Semantic Web within the context of museum practice and politics, see R. Parry, N. Poole and J. Pratty, 'Semantic dissonance: do we need (and do we understand) the Semantic Web?' in J. Trant and D. Bearman (eds.) *Museums on the Web 2008: Proceedings*, Toronto: Archives and Museum Informatics, 2008. Online. Available HTTP: http://www.archimuse.com/mw2008/papers/parry/parry.html (accessed 10 March 2010).

43 E. Tonkin, 'If it quacks like a duck … developments in search technologies', *Emerging Technologies for Learning*, BECTA Research Report 3, Coventry: BECTA, 2008, pp. 73–90. Online. Available HTTP: http://partners.becta.org.uk/upload-dir/downloads/page_documents/ research/emerging_technologies08_chapter5.pdf (accessed 10 March 2010).

44 Collections Trust, 'Ten principles for linked data in the culture sector'. Online. Available HTTP: http://www.collectionstrust.org.uk/pdfs/linked_data_principles.pdf (accessed 10 March 2010).

45 Ibid.

46 Ibid.

21

Sharing conservation ethics, practice and decision-making with museum visitors

Mary M. Brooks

Museums and galleries have developed expertise and sensitivity in displaying and interpreting conserved artefacts. However, the same degree of engagement is rarely shown in exploring the conceptual framework – often bundled up under the term 'ethics' – which governs the conservation decision-making process enabling objects to be displayed to the museum visitor. Going beyond the 'wow' factor to address 'why' as well as 'how' is important to engage in a deeper exploration of conservation thinking and principles as well as practice. Conservation will flourish best when conservation practice itself is understood by the public and policymakers alike as not just a means of 'fixing things', vital though that is, but as a means of creating cultural meaning. For this to be achieved, stakeholders and users need to understand the nature of conservation ethics and how these inform the presentation and interpretation of artefacts.

Conservation ethics and practice

Conservation – the preservation of material cultural heritage and the interlinked intangible heritage – is central to creating and maintaining national and individual identity, memories and values. Ethical guidelines or codes[1] are widely accepted as the bedrock of individual practice as well as an important element in defining the profession as a whole and its relationships with the sector and the public.[2] Whether guiding direct intervention with an artefact or a modification of its environment, the ethics underlying conservation approaches are, of course, culturally determined. Necessarily, opinions vary on their interpretation and the status and content of ethical codes change to reflect changing practices and understanding of the goals of these activities.

Conservators' awareness and knowledge of the roots of conservation practice and the intellectual and moral framework for their professional practice have always been important in educating the next generation of practitioners,[3] informing reflection on past practice and enabling positive change. Alison Richmond acknowl-edged this when discussing the revision of the conservation decision-making frame-work known as the Ethics Checklist at the Victoria and Albert Museum (V&A). Not only had the Museum's practice evolved, with a need to work 'across teams and beyond the wall of the Museum', but new concepts in museum practice had become significant.[4] Awareness of different traditions and concerns informing modern con-servation theory and the problematic process of realising theoretical ideals in prac-tice is part of the current discourse of conservation.[5] Curatorial codes have undergone similar processes of revision to acknowledge new approaches and prio-rities.[6] Curators and conservators still tend to operate to distinct but parallel ethical codes[7] although they share common goals and there are areas of overlap.[8] Never-theless, the overarching International Council of Museums (ICOM) *Code of Ethics for Museums* takes a technological view of conservation, rather than seeing it as a means of making and communicating meaning nothing that, 'The principal goal [of conserva-tion-restoration] should be the stabilisation of the object or specimen.'[9] This may not be helpful to conservators seeking to use the museum's traditional mode of com-munication – the exhibition – to explore how the ethics of their own practice both guide and limit the presentation and representation of artefacts in the museum whilst liberating meaning and value.

Sharing conservation ethics and practice

As conservators sought to define themselves as a profession and gain recognition as more than 'fix it' people and distinguish the practice of conservation from the – in some cases dubious – practices of unprofessional 'restoration',[10] their focus was understandably on defining the ethical boundaries of conservation practice rather than communicating such ideas to the public. The stance was intransitive rather than transitive. The important Getty Conservation Institute publication *The Nature of Conservation* (1986) exemplifies this position, observing, 'The welfare of the object takes precedence over all other considerations.'[11] Philippot's thoughtful discussion of the relationship of objects with both their makers and those who now preserve and enjoy them shows how conservators have become increasingly aware of the complexity of such interactions:

> Since the first step towards conservation is to establish an inventory of what should be conserved, criteria that recognise the creative quality, documentary significance and impact of the object on human consciousness must be established. Such criteria will, of course, never crystallise in fixed rules but will reflect the development of each country's culture.[12]

Alongside this awareness of changing ideas about the pre-eminence of the object, conservators have become increasingly cognisant of the importance of engaging with the public. The International Council of Museum's Conservation Committee (ICOM-CC) fourteenth triennial meeting highlighted 'the need to involve the public more in the conservation profession'.[13] The conference newsletter presented many examples of such practice. Simon Cane, then Chair of the ICOM-CC Public Awareness Task

Force,[14] noted that conservators ' ... need to raise our gaze from the objects more ... it's important that we show, as a profession, that we have a role to play.'[15]

Conservators' changed approach was summarised in the resolution submitted to the ICOM-CC fifteenth triennial conference, ' ... the public has increasingly become an essential partner in safeguarding our shared cultural heritage.'[16] To characterise this rather crudely, there is a spectrum of conservation/public relationships. Conservation may be seen as a self-evidently valuable activity which needs no justification; as a public service preserving culturally significant artefacts but which does not require a public interface; as a culturally meaningful activity which engages with the public; or as an activity which creates public value and meaning through the active involvement of the public. Dean Sully has defined this as:

> ... a process of understanding and managing change rather than merely an arresting process; it is a means of recreating material cultural heritage that seeks to retain, reveal and enhance what people value about the material past and sustain those values for future generations ... [17]

The transitive has replaced the intransitive. Openly acknowledging the role of conservators as agents in cultural activities and making an active contribution to contemporary cultural values and social life is potentially a democratising practice.[18]

Conservation ethical codes or guidelines are changing to reflect this new commitment to engagement. The V&A's Conservation Department's *Using the Ethics Checklist* defines 'clients' not only as V& A curators and colleagues but also as 'the public, students, private owners'.[19] However, it is one thing to model engagement with the public as a concept and quite another thing to realise this in practice. This difficulty is echoed in the 1994 American Institute for Conservation *Code of Ethics* in which the conservator is obligated to, *inter alia*, 'the public and to posterity'.[20] Like the jam which the White Queen offers Alice, posterity only ever arrives tomorrow and never today,[21] thus making any dialogue impossible. Significantly, the shift towards engagement has developed most substantially in countries where conservators are grappling with the complex physical heritage of colonialism. The 1986 Australian Institute for the Conservation of Cultural Material *Code of Ethics and Guidance* defined conservators' responsibilities as balancing the cultural needs of society with the task of preserving material.[22]

How far can engagement with stakeholders go – and who makes the ultimate decision? The experience of the Dordrecht Museum, in the Netherlands, is instructive here. The public was asked whether or not an additional strip from Aelbert Cuyp's painting *The Shepherdess* should be removed. The vote was indecisive so the museum staff made the decision based on scientific analysis. As Frans Grijzenhout noted, such public engagement depends on the public being both interested and informed: for him, that is 'the challenge of the next decennia'.[23]

Public perceptions of conservation

Such approaches are a long way from the problematic public understanding of artefact conservation with which many conservators are all too familiar. Rather than making links between ecological and artefact conservation, there may be unhelpful confusion.[24] A quick search of Google images brings up photographs of conservators, often gloved and masked, using mysterious high-tech instruments – and usually absorbed in an intense, exclusive and almost hermetic relationship with the object. At one level, this public relations stereotype is appropriate: conservators are charged with responsibility for the physical well-being of the artefact and this is based on an understanding of its material nature and condition. As Miriam Clavir put it, 'from a conservator's perspective, the objects contain knowledge in their very fabric'.[25] What this stereotype does not show is how conservators contribute to the understanding of the object and hence to the making of cultural meaning. Conservators are rightly aware of the importance of making this 'invisible creativity' accessible and sharing the process of exploration and learning with museum colleagues, researchers, collectors and museum visitors.[26] This can be the basis for exciting discussion and dialogue. There are also implications for museums in revealing, rather than concealing, the fact that most displayed artefacts have undergone treatment before they are presented to the visitor.[27] Concealing this intervention may be necessary for aesthetic appreciation[28] but it also conceals part of the biography of the object.[29] On a more pragmatic but no less important level, communicating the benefits of conservation for people and objects may help persuade decision-makers and funders of its significance.

Communicating conservation ethics and practice in museums

Levels of expertise in 'reading' the cultural code of exhibitions is an important factor in all museum display[30] but initiatives to communicate conservation may have an advantage as they offer the intriguing spectacle of the possibility of slowing the natural decay to which all objects (and humans) are subject. There is also the very real attraction of offering visitors a 'behind the scenes' moment, showing the processes of conservation thinking and doing rather than their (often invisible) product. The interaction between conservator and object may be foregrounded through the presence of an actual person or their representation in some form of media. But any conservation exhibition needs to learn from the principles of museum exhibition and integrate good practice. Visitors' responses will have some commonalities with their responses to other museum exhibitions. There is necessarily a strong element of the subjective, reflecting individuals' own interests and prior knowledge. This is true of any cultural learning experience but the museum visitor is also affected by other factors in the visit experience – individual or group, empty or crowded, rushed or leisurely. However, there may be distinctive differences in visitors' responses to communicating conservation in museums. Often an unfamiliar subject, it may, as noted above, be confused with environmental conservation.

Conservation practice, by its nature, is interdisciplinary, crossing the boundaries of art and science, intellectual and practical. Some visitors may find this intriguing, while others may find it complex and off-putting. Conservation ethics, particularly the complex boundary between conservation and restoration, may seem arcane and sometimes even perverse. Is it enough simply to enable museum visitors to watch conservators work in a public space within the museum or gallery or in the virtual world? Does this mystify or demystify? Is it inspirational or boring? The challenges in developing an effective exhibition on conservation principles and practice include:

- Presenting a technical subject in an accessible way without 'dumbing down'.
- Engaging with the wider issues of the benefits and difficulties of object conservation.
- Enabling visitors to understand conservation principles.
- Giving conservators the necessary confidence and skills to engage with the public.

The point made by Jerry Podany and Susan Maish remains highly pertinent: ' ... it is often difficult to communicate these aspects to fellow professionals within the museum world, let alone to the completely uninitiated visitor'.[31]

Exhibiting conservation

Acknowledging that conservation is a means of making meaning and enriching museum interpretation as a matter of course is the ideal. Sadly, even when conservation is integrated into exhibitions, the effect may be to marginalise rather than centralise the issue of practice and ethics; the 'conservation interpretation panels' in the 2003 display of the Werner Collection of paintings at the Ranger's House, Blackheath, south London, were 'relegated to dark, out of the way corners isolated from the objects on display'.[32]

Most dedicated engagement with conservation issues has been in the form of temporary special exhibitions, sometimes using artefacts from permanent collections, sometimes loans and sometimes pieces which have been treated in a particular conservation laboratory. However, the tradition of exhibiting conservation principles and practice is longer and more established than might have been expected. In 1942 the Istituto Centrale del Restauro, Rome, mounted – as its first public event a year after its foundation – an exhibition of restored paintings called *Mostra dei dipinti di Antonello da Messina*. The aim was to demonstrate 'what a real restoration treatment should be, i.e. a treatment based on full respect of the work's authenticity rather than the capacity to "adjust", complete or beautify, with results that often turned the work into a forgery of itself'.[33] In this exhibition, the radical decision was made to 'reveal the principles, methods and techniques employed for at the time it was common practice to keep all that secret'.[34] The exploration of ethical practice was clearly evident in this exhibition, together with notions of openness, sharing and engagement with stakeholders. The idea of 'civic responsibility' in caring for, and about, shared cultural heritage was central. This theme was also emphasised in the catalogue for *Cleaned Pictures*, another early conservation exhibition held at the Walker Art Gallery, Liverpool, in 1955. The Chairman of Liverpool Libraries, Museums and Art Committee, expressed the hope that the display of restored pictures would 'bring many people into the Gallery for the first time ... we want these pictures to be enjoyed as deeply and widely as possible.'[35] Such exhibitions have continued; for example, the French Service de Restauration des Peintres des Musées Nationaux has reported on the many exhibitions to which they have contributed.[36]

Although the historiography of conservation exhibitions is still to be written, the following typology identifies some different models with distinct, although not necessarily exclusive, characteristics. Conservators often took the curatorial or team leader role in these exhibitions which aimed to present conservation issues and methods in an accessible way using the accepted 'grammar' of museum exhibitions such as text panels, labels and videos. Both their achievements and the strengths and weaknesses of the different models should be acknowledged.

Technological model

In the Walker Art Gallery's *Cleaned Pictures*, the main interest was the paintings rather than the conservation process. Objects were selected because they were 'especially notable or interesting' rather than because of any specific conservation issues.[37] Nevertheless, the Gallery Director clearly saw the potential of conservation in visitor learning:

> ... the technical approach to works of art has unexplored possibilities for interesting the public. The public tends to be mystified by the arts, but it is interested in techniques. Cannot the technical approach break down some of the barrier between the Liverpool public and its splendid collection of pictures?[38]

A similar approach underpinned the highly successful series of exhibitions at the National Gallery, London,[39] which presented the results of conservation to the public.[40]

Transformational/revelatory model

This model depends on the 'wow' factor, modelling conservation as a dramatic intervention which transforms artefacts. Whilst undoubtedly striking – and sometimes spectacular – this approach may not help visitors to gain a broader understanding of conservation ethics and practice and some of conservation's less dramatic but equally important responsibilities. As Podany and Maish observed, 'Too often, people learn about conservation from the presentation of stunning dramatic before-and-after views. This technique is an assured way to attract attention but an ineffective way of keeping it.'[41]

Single object model

This may draw on the transformational model but focuses on one artefact or artefact class. In some cases, such exhibitions may engage with broader issues. The 2006 exhibition *Stories in Stone* was developed by the Getty Conservation Institute, Los Angeles, to explain how Roman mosaics in Tunisia could be cared for in-situ. As well as detailing processes of degradation, the exhibition explained the training programme at the Institut National du Patrimoine including monitoring, documentation, repair and maintenance. Ethics appear to be implicit here rather than explicitly drawn out.

Explanatory/'behind the scenes' model

This model focuses on intriguing the visitor with a glimpse behind the scenes and insights into what is normally concealed. This may involve bringing visitors into the conservation laboratory or recreating the laboratory experience in the museum.

This aim informed the development of the Centre for Conservation at the British Library, London, which offers regular tours to 'take Conservation, Collection Care and the Sound Archive out of the back room and into the public eye'.[42] Despite its obvious attractions, this model raises practical issues in terms of artefact security and also has an impact on the conservators involved in terms of workloads and deadlines. The Liverpool National Museums and Galleries on Merseyside (NMGM)[43] were mindful of these issues when, in 1995, they created the National Conservation Centre, one of the most famous examples of enabling public access to conservation practice. Public access was integrated from the beginning with the goal of reducing barriers between conservators and visitors. An NMGM survey of visitors' interests informed plans for an innovative centre (complete with café and shop) in which visitors would be able to gain an understanding of the scientific processes of conservation which would then enhance their enjoyment of artefacts in the collections.[44] Communication of conservation practice, based on consultation with conservators, was developed with six layers of access:

- A permanent exhibition exploring mechanisms of deterioration and remedial conservation approaches with audio-guides and interactives.
- A video addressing the same topics.
- Live video links at specified times enabling a dialogue between visitors and conservators working in the laboratories, mediated by one of the Centre's demonstrators.
- Pre-booked laboratory tours.
- Hands-on sessions exploring degradation pathways and reconstruction methods facilitated by a demonstrator.
- Pre-booked 'surgeries' to answer questions about visitors' own objects.

This laudable and multilayered commitment to communicating conservation appears to have been process-orientated, rather than engaging in debating the ethics behind decision-making, although doubtless ethical issues were discussed in the live discussions. Based on feedback from both staff and visitors, changes were made by the project team so that the majority of the conservators were happy with the public access to the Centre.[45] The Centre has been refocused as a 'vibrant and contemporary gallery'[46] which 'explores both the memories that objects contain and how science helps us to interpret them' using demonstrators, interactives and multimedia. The name of the permanent exhibition *Reveal: the Hidden Story of Objects* suggests the transformational model.[47]

Many museums have mounted special events to explore and explain museum conservation to their visitors. The British Museum has made a commitment to raising the profile of conservation. Their 2008 exhibition *Conservation in Focus* aimed to showcase 'this often unseen aspect of the Museum's work'.[48] Conservators undertook conservation in the galleries and actively drew visitors into discussions. The

Museum of London has also held public events to 'encourage visitors to understand and learn about conservation within a museum'.[49] The Historic Royal Palaces has made visitor engagement part of conservation practice in their programme called *Ask the Conservators* which aims to embed conservation within the Palace's programming and interpretation.[50]

Science model

Fade: The Dark Side of Light was a 2008 collaboration between the California Science Center and the Getty Conservation Institute, combining 'science and art to explore the destructive effects of light exposure on priceless museum treasures and family photos'.[51] It also sought to raise awareness of the need for conservation under the by-line 'Conservation is Science'. Visitors were introduced to the physics of light which was linked with the destruction of 'personal and collectively held memories' such as photographs, artworks and domestic objects. A similar stress on science informed the exhibition *Conservation: In Safe Hands* held at Wakefield Museum, Yorkshire, England, in 2007. The conserved wheels of an Iron Age chariot were the star of the show which was linked with National Science Week as well as providing inspiration for primary school teaching. A local councillor noted that the exhibition showed 'science being used in unusual and very interesting ways' and expressed the hope that it would inspire schoolchildren to 'consider science as a career'.[52]

Principles and practice model

An increasing number of exhibitions do engage with the complex issues in conservation practice, including ethical decision-making. Conservation education and training programmes are in a good position to highlight the intense engagement between the student and the artefact as well as presenting the students' chosen strategies, the result of investigation, research and significance assessment conducted within the framework of conservation ethics.[53] The exhibition *Verschachtelt und Behütet* ('Nested and Protected') at the Institute for Conservation and Restoration, University of Applied Arts, Vienna, focused on preventive conservation. Most unusually, rather than showing the transformed object, the exhibition poster showed hats prepared for storage – a familiar sight to conservators but one rarely seen by the public. This radical image of the 'hidden' process of preventive conservation makes a striking and dramatic poster (Figure 21.1).

Exhibitions setting out to engage the public overtly in conservation ethics and principles include *Preserving the Past* at the J. Paul Getty Museum (1991), *Stop the Rot* at York Castle Museum (1993–94)[54] and *De Kunst van het Bewaren* ('The Art of Conservation', 2002–2004) at a Dutch museum, the Rijksmuseum Twenthe. All these, as well as exploring the technical and transformative aspects of conservation, aimed to enable visitors to understand the nature – and consequences, both intellectual and practical – of conservation ethics. As well as offering multiple learning routes and making information accessible through videos and interactives, *Preserving the Past* used dedicated facilitators who had received a special introduction to conservation so they could answer questions and thus 'offer visitors one more layer of information by which complex issues could be made accessible'.[55] For visitors who

Figure 21.1 Poster for the exhibition *Verschachtelt & Behütet* ('Nested and Protected'), Institute for Conservation and Restoration, University of Applied Arts, Vienna, 2008–9.

were clearly interested in further information, the facilitators had a handout detailing information on publications, conservation courses and the American Institute for Conservation.[56] *Stop the Rot* culminated in the detailed exploration of ethical decision-making behind the treatment of some show-stopping objects, ranging from full-scale restoration and investigative conservation to minimal treatments. *De Kunst van het Bewaren* involved the public in multiple activities relating to caring for objects, offering schoolchildren the opportunity to learn how to handle art and read radiographs.[57] The curator reported that, although this was a great success, it was labour intensive and required great communication skills on the part of the conservators.[58]

The 2006 exhibition *Mission Impossible? Ethics and Choices in Conservation* at the Fitzwilliam Museum, Cambridge, overtly focused on the complexity of conservation decision-making. The exhibition layout looked like that of many thematic exhibitions, with a dense wall hang and packed cases of objects from the Fitzwilliam's extensive collection of art and antiquities (Figure 21.2). But the text panels sought to engage the visitor in the reasons why the objects in galleries look the way they do. Techniques and treatments were secondary to debating the dilemmas faced by conservators. The presentation of Frans Snyder's large 1620 painting *The Larder*, which has survived without major treatment, demonstrates the strategies used to draw visitors into the ethical debate. The detailed text explored the implications of doing nothing (future treatment may be more difficult) and of intervening (the rare original state is irreparably altered forever), asking the visitor to consider what is the right thing to do by exploring questions such as:

- What action should be taken now?
- How far should we go?
- Will the act of conservation ultimately shorten the life of an object?

Figure 21.2 Visitors at the 2006 exhibition *Mission Impossible? Ethics and Choices in Conservation*, Fitzwilliam Museum, Cambridge, England. Reproduced with permission of the Trustees.

With real courage, the Fitzwilliam conservators opened up to visitors the reality of the decisions and the conceptual framework which has governed the interventions undergone by most artefacts before they were considered 'fit for display'. Text panels and labels explored the role that conservation plays in interpreting artefacts, supplemented by a video showing the painstaking restoration of the notorious broken Chinese vases.[59] The juxtaposition of objects which had received different treatments resulting from different conceptual frameworks demonstrated changing attitudes to finishes, lacunae and previous treatments. The restorations to a Roman statue of Apollo by the eighteenth-century sculptors John Flaxman and Antonio d'Este are valued today because of the artists who carried them out. This was contrasted with our acceptance of losses in a Roman-period Egyptian mummy portrait. This strategy of the contrasting visual impact of actual objects, coupled with careful exploration in text panels, enabled visitors to gain an understanding of the interpretative role of conservation and the ethical frameworks governing such interventions.

Even more important was the way ideas presented in the exhibition permeated interpretation of the museum as a whole. Conservation was not represented as just a 'special case' but a fundamental approach underlying displays throughout the galleries. Placing the *Mission Impossible?* logo beside objects with complex conservation histories enabled visitors to apply the understanding that they had gained in the special exhibition to artefacts in the permanent collection. This is where the central museological dilemma maps onto conservation concerns. How can complex ideas be presented in a way which is accessible to diverse – and often foot-weary – museum visitors, possibly with varying understanding of English and – in many cases – a limited attention span? The importance of 'take-home material' was recognised in the *Stop the Rot*[60] leaflet and the Fitzwilliam's detailed guide.[61] This raises the issue of sustaining this engagement with the public over the long term. Strategies to achieve this at the Fitzwilliam included lunchtime talks by conservators and short courses offering a deeper engagement with conservation decision-making relating to mummy portraits, paintings, papyrus and silver.

The Conservation Science Investigations (CSI) 'exhibition', which left the museum behind altogether, demonstrates this. Located in a shopping centre in Sittingbourne, Kent, southern England, this event invited volunteers and passers-by to clean and conserve finds from nearby Anglo-Saxon burials after preliminary training and under supervision. A survey of the volunteers' attitudes to opinions showed a radical change: 'Before opening, it was thought to benefit academics. Subsequently, people have revised their view: it is for them.'[62] How can museums and other organisations capture this level of engagement? Special exhibitions and activities have a vital role but unless an organisation fundamentally alters its practices, as in the case of the Historic Royal Palaces, these are – albeit exciting and positive – temporary. It is here that the internet may have a role to play.

Virtual exhibitions: conservation on the net

Museums are increasingly using the internet as a means of broadening access and interacting with real and virtual visitors. Cane's 2002 study of the representation of conservation on museum web sites found it to be either absent or deeply buried.[63] This is changing and conservators are using the web as a means of making conservation principles and practice more accessible and understandable. Web-based exhibitions can be accessed at any time by those who have the necessary equipment and skills and can be designed to be highly interactive, challenging and entertaining. The nature of this experience is necessarily different from those in the galleries and there may be concerns that the 'real' object is being supplanted by the virtual. There are also access, cost and sustainability issues; web sites, like museum exhibitions, need maintenance.

Virtual engagement is being achieved in a variety of ways. Sometimes it can be as simple – and dramatic – as following through the conservation treatment of an iconic object as in the Silver Swan Conservation Project which daily charted the intervention into the Bowes Museum's remarkable musical automaton.[64] The basic principles of the investigation and intervention are clearly outlined, together with conservation revelations which revised dating of some parts of the swan.

It is usually only feasible to give a small number of visitors the experience of being in a working conservation laboratory or talking to conservators working in the museum gallery. The web means many more people can share a version of this experience. In 2007, the Statens Museum fur Kunst, Copenhagen, welcomed visitors into the conservation laboratory. During the conservation of Jakob Jordaens' painting *The Ferry Boat to Antwerp* (1623), museum visitors could view conservation in progress while virtual visitors could follow progress through the on-line blog, vastly increasing the numbers of people able to share the experience.[65] Nevertheless, the web image accompanying this innovative approach to communicating conservation was accompanied by the familiar visual trope of a white-coated conservator, wearing a magnifier, focused on surface cleaning the painting.

Others choose to develop content from the issues. Starting with a discussion of the impact of time, the Nelson–Atkins Museum web site *Tempus Fugit* explores the concept of degradation and the conservator's attempt to ameliorate this inevitable process.[66] In 2002, the Canadian Conservation Institute (CCI) launched a new web site, *Preserving my Heritage*,[67] including:

- 'Amazing Facts', which explores the creativity shown by conservators and conservation scientists in preserving artefacts
- 'Preservation Quests', which offers virtual visitors interactive games to test their growing conservation understanding and knowledge. This enables a depth of learning which may be deeper than that which can be achieved in a short exhibition visit
- 'Before and After' Gallery, which highlights the transformative 'magic' of conservation

Visitors are able to take a virtual tour of the conservation laboratories and, for those whose interest has been piqued, there is information about professional education and training. The name of this web site is significant; it is called 'my heritage', not 'our heritage', to make the link between the individual's and the nation's heritage.[68] The site was designed to broaden access and encourage people 'to become engaged in protecting items in their homes and communities'.[69]

Impact assessment

The available evidence to assess the impact of conservation exhibitions, particularly whether visitors have gained a fundamental understanding of conservation ethics, is limited. For example, the impact of the NMGM was measured only in visitor numbers and awards.[70] Unusually, 125 visitors to *Preserving the Past*[71] participated in an informal survey and thirty-eight were interviewed in depth. Ideas about conservation ethics seem to have been understood and remembered. Evaluation indicated that most visitors 'were able to discuss at least one of the principles of conservation highlighted in the exhibition with impressive accuracy'.[72] Results of a questionnaire answered by seventy visitors to *Stop the Rot* showed changed understanding of conservation practice.[73] The exhibition was successful in communicating some of the core ideas about conservation practice although confusion over ecological links remained. No evidence has yet been identified to assess how effectively these initiatives were in communicating conservation ethics to the public or to evaluate conservation web-sites.

Ethical practice and the concept of public value

The concept of public value was first developed by Mark Moore at the Kennedy School of Government, Harvard University, in the mid-1990s. At its heart, the idea is simple if somewhat circular: 'public managers create results that are valued' and public value is that which is valued by the public.[74] Its application in practice as a means to engineer change and justify administrative shifts has been adopted by UK politicians with some enthusiasm – and it has potential as an argument for those of us in the heritage sector who seek to explain that what we do has a value beyond the financial and can be used to define public 'goods' which include cultural, spiritual and economic benefits.[75]

John Holden of the think-tank Demos[76] has been instrumental in introducing the concept into UK cultural organisations as both a process and a performance measurement tool. The Demos report *It's a Material World: Caring for the Public Realm* (2008)[77] applied this argument to conservation, positing that conservation principles and practice are central not only to culture and heritage but also to the well-being of society. Conservation juries were proposed to enable active public engagement in the process of conservation decision-making by 'prioritis[ing] cases for conservation according to public interest, and ... recommend[ing] how the public might be drawn into the process'. Chaired by conservators, the juries would 'reflect the public's rights, responsibilities and interests in relation to conservation'.[78] If implemented, this approach to integrating the values underpinning conservation practice could inform a wide range of activities to reflect not only the past but the diversity of world cultures and their living practices, as well as their material heritage. Conservation exhibitions which communicate conservation principles form part of this engagement.

Drawing conclusions

This chapter has argued that demonstrating the ethical and technical decision-making involved in preparing artefacts for display and study can enhance value and meaning and so enrich the museum visitor's experience and understanding. Xavier-Rowe noted the benefits ensuing from conservators' engaging in communicating 'hidden secrets' while acknowledging the challenges involved:

> ... it can be an uphill battle to include conservation stories alongside conventional interpretation. We need to be persuasive and willing to generate and communicate conservation stories. Through this process we can begin to prove our worth to the core business of interpreting object.[79]

New communication technologies (conservation on Twitter, perhaps?) are offering more ways of communicating conservation ethics and practice but all these demand developing existing skills or gaining new ones. A step change may be all that is needed; from preparing a poster for an exhibition to writing a text panel is not such a big shift. But this also requires a strategic shift in thinking about conservators' relationship to the public and a recognition of a fundamentally changed position within the museum hierarchy so that such engagement becomes possible, not just in one-off special exhibitions but embedded as part of common practice. Such a shift might also have the effect of communicating conservation in a positive way within institutions as well as potentially aligning curatorial and conservation ethics and practices more closely. The glamour and drama of the transformational 'before and after' may attract public attention but going beyond this will enable conservators to demonstrate their unique contribution to the making of meaning in museums and engage the public in a deeper debate on the value and implications of conservation – and museological – ethics and decision-making.

Acknowledgements

Thanks are due to the following for sharing ideas, information and stimulating debate: Simon Cane, Head of Museum Operations, Birmingham Museum and Art Gallery; Julie Dawson, Senior Assistant Keeper (Conservation), Fitzwilliam Museum, Cambridge; Dinah Eastop, consultant, Conservation and Heritage Studies, formerly Senior Lecturer, Textile Conservation Centre, University of Southampton; Alison Richmond, Chief Executive, Institute of Conservation, UK, formerly Senior Tutor, RCA/V&A Conservation Postgraduate Programme; Anna Zagorski, Senior Project Coordinator, Field Projects, Getty Conservation Centre.

Notes

1 J. Ashley-Smith has discussed the implications for conservation of the terms 'guidelines' versus 'codes', ownership, decision-making and the dangers of 'fashion in conservation'. J. Ashley-Smith, 'The ethics of conservation', *Conservator* 6, 1982, pp. 1–5. For a review of the development of ethical codes as part of growing professionalisation, see M. Corfield, 'Towards a conservation profession', in *Jubilee Conference, Preprints for UKIC 30th Anniversary Conference*, London: UKIC, 1988, p. 6.

2 For a discussion of the 'goods' of professional ethical codes and their moral legitimacy, see D. Koehn, *The Ground of Professional Ethics*, London: Routledge, 1994, pp. 7–9.

3 See M. Brooks, 'International codes of ethics and practice and their implications for teaching and learning ethics in textile conservation education', in Á. Tímár-Balászy and D. Eastop (eds.) *International Perspectives: Textile Conservation, 1990–1996*, London: Archetype, 1998, pp. 74–78.

4 These include intangibility, risk and sustainability; see A. Richmond, 'The ethics checklist – ten years on', *V&A Conservation Journal* 50, 2005, pp. 11–14.

5 See, for example, [A. M. Vaccaro], 'The emergence of modern conservation theory', in N. S. Price, K. M. Talley and A. M. Vaccaro (eds.) *Historical and Philosophical Issues in the Conservation of Cultural Heritage*, Los Angeles: Getty Conservation Institute, 1996, p. 270.

6 See B. Murphy, 'ICOM's evolving perspectives on ethics and museums', *ICOM News*, 58: 3, 2005, p. 4.

7 For example, the revised ICOM *Code of Ethics for Museums*, ratified 2004, based on the 1986 ICOM *Code of Professional Ethics*.

8 This reflects a wider division in thinking and practice. The UK Museum, Libraries and Archives Council 2009 National Action Plan for museums does not mention conservation; see Museum, Libraries and Archives Council, *Leading Museums: A Vision and Strategic Action Plan for English Museums*, London: MLA, 2009.

9 ICOM *Code of Ethics for Museums* 2006. Online. Available HTTP: http://icom.museum/ethics.html#intro (accessed 21 August 2009).

10 See A. Oddy, The Forbes Prize Lecture, *IIC Bulletin* 5, 1996, p. 3.

11 P. Ward, *The Nature of Conservation*, Marina del Rey: Getty Conservation Institute, 1986, p. 9.

12 P. Philippot. 'Historic preservation: philosophy, criteria, guidelines, 1', in Price et al., *Historical and Philosophical Issues*, p. 270.

13 Anon., 'Learning to share more of the magic', *Our Cultural Past –Your Future!* [Newsletter of the ICOM-CC fourteenth meeting], The Hague: ICOM-CC, 2005, p. 1.

14 The Task Force organised well-attended meetings at the fourteenth and fifteenth ICOM-CC conferences. Following the 2008 New Delhi ICOM-CC conference, the Board has undertaken to consider the Task Force's future.

15 S. Cane, 'We need to raise our gaze from the objects', *Our Cultural Past – Your Future!* p. 15.

16 'Terminology to Characterise the Conservation of Tangible Cultural Heritage', unpublished document circulated at the ICOM-CC fifteenth triennial conference, New Delhi, 2008.

17 Dean Sully, cited in S. Jones and J. Holden, *It's a Material World: Caring for the Public Realm*, London: Demos, 2008, p. 28.

18 D. Eastop, 'Conservation as a democratising practice: learning from Latin America. A report from ICOM-CC, Rio de Janeiro, Brazil, 22–27 September 2002', *ICOM UK News* 63, 2006 (December), pp. 22–4.

19 'Using the Ethics Checklist', unpublished document, 1994, London: V&A Conservation Department.

20 American Institute for Conservation, 1994, 'Part one: Code of ethics', in *Directory*, Washington, DC: AIC, 1994.

21 The White Queen tells Alice: 'The rule is jam tomorrow and jam yesterday but never jam to-day.' L. Carroll, *Through the Looking Glass*, London: BCA, 1979 [1871], p. 296.

22 Australian Institute for the Conservation of Cultural Material, *Code of Ethics and Guidance for Conservation Practice for those involved in the Conservation of Cultural Material in Australia*, Canberra: AICCM, 1986. See D. Eastop, 'Introduction', in *Compromising Situations: Principles in Everyday Practice*, Papers for UKIC Textile Section Forum, London: UKIC, 1993, pp. 1–5.

23 Anon., 'Restoration in public can be very successful', *Our Cultural Past – Your Future!* 2005, p. 4.

24 There are, of course, fundamental links between these two conservation practices as Catherine Sease noted: ' … conservation has much in common with ecological conservation. The loss of our archaeological and cultural heritage can be likened to the loss of plant and animal species through overpopulation, urban development, and conspicuous consumption. All are nonrenewable resources whose loss will greatly diminish our lives and the lives of those who come after us.' C. Sease, 'Conservation and the antiquities trade', *Journal of the American Institute for Conservation*, 36: 1, 1997, pp. 49–58.

25 M. Clavir, *Preserving What is Valued: Museums, Conservation and First Nations*, Vancouver, BC: UBC Press, 2002.

26 The corollary of this is a considerable literature discussing conservators' failure to communicate their principles and values; see M. M. Brooks, 'Talking to ourselves: why do conservators find it so hard to convince others of the significance of conservation?' *Preprints, ICOM-CC Fifteenth Triennial Conference*, New Delhi: Allied Publishers, 2008, pp. 1135–40.

27 M. M. Brooks, 'Decay, preservation and the making of meaning', in P. Smith (ed.) *Ways of Making and Knowing: The Material Culture of Empirical Knowledge*, Michigan: University of Michigan Press, forthcoming.

28 C. Brandi, *Theory of Restoration*, Florence: Nardini, 2005.

29 I. Kopytoff, 'The cultural biography of things: commoditisation as process', in A. Appadurai (ed.) *The Social Life of Things*, Cambridge: Cambridge University Press, 1986, pp. 64–91.

30 See, *inter alia*, J. H. Falk and L. D. Dierking, *Learning from Museums: Visitor Experiences and the Making of Meaning*, Walnut Creek, CA: AltaMira Press, 2000; T. W. Luke, *Museum Politics: Power Play at the Exhibition*. Minneapolis, MN: University of Minnesota Press, 2002; G. Bagnall, 'Performance and performativity at heritage sites', *Museum and Society* 1: 2, 2003, pp. 87–103. Online. Available HTTP: http://www.le.ac.uk/ms/m&s/issue%202/ msbagnall.pdf (accessed 20 February 2010).

31 J. C. Podany and S. L. Maish, 'Can the complex be made simple? Informing the public about conservation through museum exhibits', *Journal of the American Institute for Conservation*, 31: 2, 1993, p. 2.

32 A. Xavier-Rowe, 'Communicating the conservation story', *Conservation News*, January 2003, pp. 19–21.

33 G. Basile, 'A few words about a maestro, Cesare Brandi', in C. Brandi, *Theory of Restoration*, Florence: Nardini, 2005, pp. 21–2.

34 Ibid., p. 22.

35 J. Johnstone, *Cleaned Pictures*, Liverpool: Liverpool Libraries, Museums and Arts Committee, 1955/56, p. 1.

36 S. Bergeon, G. Brunel and E. Mognetti, 'Conservation and the public', *Conservation Restauration in France*, Lyon: ICOM, 1999, n.p.

37 J. Johnstone, 'Chairman's preface', in *Cleaned Pictures*, p. 1.

38 H. Scutton, 'Director's preface', in *Cleaned Pictures*, p. 4.

39 The National Gallery's *Meaning and Making* exhibitions have included Holbein's *Ambassadors* (1997) and the Wilton Diptych (1993) while their series *Art in the Making* has examined artists such as Dégas (2004) and Rembrandt (2006). Their 2010 exhibition *Close Examination: Fakes, Mistakes and Discoveries* integrates 'scientific examination, conservation and art historical research to investigate a painting's physical properties'; usefully, the web site includes a reading list on conservation, restoration, scientific examination and technical analysis of paintings. Online. Available HTTP: http://www.nationalgallery.org.uk/paintings/research/close-examination/ (accessed 29 July 2010).

40 J. Wadum, 'Raising awareness at public, professional and political levels', in *Tutela del patrimonio culturale. Verso profilo eureo del restaurato do beni culturali*, Bergamo: Associazione Giovanni Secco Suardo, 1998, pp. 247–2.

41 Podany and Maish, 'Can the complex be made simple?' p. 5.

42 H. Shenton, 'Public engagement with conservation at the British Library', in D. Saunders, J. Townsend and S. Woodcock (eds.) *Conservation and Access*, Dorchester: International Institute for Conservation, 2008, pp. 130–35; '"Behind the scenes tours" of Conservation studios'. Online. Available HTTP: http://www.bl.uk/onlinegallery/whatson/blcc/behindthescenes. html (accessed 29 July 2009).

43 Since 2003 known as National Museums Liverpool.

44 J. Forrester, 'Opening up: the Conservation Centre National Museums and Galleries on Merseyside', *Museum Practice* 7: 3, 1999, pp. 59–61.

45 The Conservation Centre won the 1997 Gulbenkian Prize and the 1997 Interpret Britain Award and was European Museum of the Year 1998. Jim Forrester, 'Opening up: the Conservation Centre National Museums and Galleries on Merseyside', *Museum Practice* 7: 3, 1999, p. 61.

46 2010 exhibitions include a photographic exhibition of a local department store and Best of Merseyside, an exhibition of competition works. Online. Available HTTP: http://www.visitliverpool.com/site/national-conservation-centre-p765 (accessed 28 July 2010).

47 Liverpool Museums, *Reveal: Hidden Stories of Objects*. Online. Available HTTP: http://www.liverpoolmuseums.org.uk/conservation/reveal/ (accessed 21 August 2009).

48 British Museum *Conservation in Focus*. Online. Available HTTP: http://www.britishmuseum.org/whats_on/all_current_exhibitions/conservation_in_focus.aspx (accessed 21 August 2009).

49 *Conservation in Action*, Museum of London, 11 March and 6 May 2009.

50 K. Frame, 'Communicating Conservation at the Historic Royal Palaces', in *Preprints*, *ICOM-CC Fifteenth Triennial Conference*, pp. 1147–53.

51 California Science Center and Getty Conservation Institute, *Fade: The Dark Side of Light*. Online. Available HTTP: http://www.californiasciencecenter.org/Exhibits/ExhibitsForRent/Fade/Fade.php (accessed 26 July 2009).

52 Anon, 'In safe hands', *ICON News*, March 2007, p. 4.

53 Examples include the Royal College of Art (see A. Richmond, 'RCA/V&A Joint M.A. Course in Conservation', in *Ours for Keeps: A Resource Pack for Raising Awareness of Conservation and Collection Care*, London: Museums and Galleries Commission, 1998, 3.21–22 and A. Richmond, 'Exhibitions: how do they do it?' *V&A Conservation Journal*,

April 1977, pp. 14–15); the University of Lincoln (see *Revival: The Art of Conservation*. Online. Available HTTP: http://www.theartofconservation.co.uk/ (accessed 21 August 2009)); the Textile Conservation Centre (*Twentieth Anniversary Exhibition*, Courtauld Institute of Art, 1995). See also Brooks, 'International conservation codes of ethics and practice', pp. 78–79.

54 The author was co-curator/conservator of this exhibition with Simon Cane. *Stop the Rot* won the International Institute for Conservation Keck Award for the promotion of the public understanding and appreciation of conservation. See M. Brooks and S. Cane, 'Creating an exhibition on museum conservation, "Stop the Rot," York Castle Museum', in J. Sage (ed.) *Exhibitions and Conservation*, Edinburgh: Scottish Society for Conservation and Restoration, 1994, pp. 35–44.

55 Podany and Maish, 'Can the complex be made simple?' p. 102.

56 Ibid.

57 Anon., 'The public is first, the money is second', *Our Cultural Past – Your Future!* p. 7.

58 Ibid., p. 7.

59 These vases were broken when a visitor fell down a staircase and the resulting spectacular damage made headlines around the world. See, for example, L. Barton, 'Oops!' *Guardian*, 31 January 2006. Online. Available HTTP: http://www.guardian.co.uk/artanddesign/2006/jan/31/heritage.museums (accessed 17 May 2010); M. Brown, 'After the Wisdom moment, time to tape over the cracks', *Guardian*, 30 March 2006. Online. Available HTTP: http://www.guardian.co.uk/uk/2006/mar/30/topstories3.art (accessed 16 May 2009).

60 This was generously sponsored by a grant from the Conservation Unit, Museums and Galleries Commission. Both organisations are now defunct.

61 The impact of the exhibition was enhanced by lunchtime talks and short courses which allowed visitors to engage more fully with conservation decision-making in relation to the treatment of mummy portraits, paintings, papyrus and silver.

62 Anon., 'CSI: Sittingbourne', *ICON News*, November 2009, pp. 2–3.

63 S. Cane, 'Challenging the Discourse of Conservation: the Development, Function and Position of the Conservation Process in the Museum System', unpublished M.A. dissertation, University of Southampton, 2002.

64 This elegant swan bends its graceful neck to catch little fish amongst the rippling 'water' created by rotating glass rods. Online. Available HTTP: http://www.thebowesmuseum.org.uk/the-silver-swan/ (accessed 8 December 2009). This was also disseminated to the public via a BBC *Inside Out* film. Online. Available HTTP: http://www.bbc.co.uk/mediaselector/check/england/realmedia/insideout/northeast/090114_io_north_east_swan?size=16x9&bgc=C0C0C0&nbram=1&bbram=1&nbwm=1&bbwm=1 (accessed 8 December 2008).

65 Statens Museum fur Kunst, Copenhagen, *The Ferry-Boat to Antwerp*. Online. Available HTTP: http://www.smk.dk/restaurering (accessed 26 July 2009).

66 Nelson–Atkins Museum, *Tempus Fugit*. Online. Available HTTP: http://www.nelson-atkins.org/art/PastExhibitions/tempusfugit/default.htm (accessed 26 July 2009).

67 Canadian Conservation Institute, *Preserving my Heritage*. Online. Available HTTP: www.preservation.gc.ca (accessed 26 July 2009).

68 C. MacIvor, 'CCI launches a new website', *CCI Newsletter* 29, 2002, p. 12.

69 Ibid.

70 Anon., 'The public is first, the money is second', *Our Cultural Past – Your Future!* p. 7.

71 Podany and Maish, 'Can the complex be made simple?'

72 Ibid.

73 This survey was generously funded by the Conservation Unit of the Museums and Galleries Commission. The exhibition curators/conservators did not have input into the development of the interview questions.

74 M. H. Moore, *Creating Public Value: Strategic Management in Government*, Cambridge, MA: Harvard University Press, 1995, p. 27.

75 See, *inter alia*, K. Clark, *Capturing the Public Value of Heritage: The Proceedings of the London Conference*, 25–26 January 2006, London: English Heritage, 2006; G. Kelly, G. Mulgan and S. Muers, *Creating Public Value: An Analytical Framework for Public Service Reform*, London: Cabinet Office, 2002; National Trust, *Demonstrating the Public Value of Heritage*, [London]: National Trust, 2006.

76 Demos is an English think tank which explores issues relating to politics and public policies. Online. Available HTTP: http://www.demos.co.uk/ (accessed 8 December 2009).

77 S. Jones and J. Holden, *It's a Material World: Caring for the Public Realm*, London: Demos, 2008. Funding for this research was raised by the Textile Conservation Centre, University of Southampton.

78 Ibid., p. 18. These would be similar to the Citizens' Juries set up by the Heritage Lottery fund; see L. Forgan, 'Capturing the opinions of the people', in Clark, *Capturing the Public Value of Heritage*, p. 85.

79 A. Xavier-Rowe, 'Communicating the conservation story', *Conservation News*, January 2003, pp. 19–21.

Part IV

VISUAL CULTURE AND THE PERFORMANCE OF MUSEUM ETHICS

22

The body in the (white) box

Corporeal ethics and museum representation

Mara Gladstone and Janet Catherine Berlo

In the twenty-first century, the museum has become an active space of performance and engagement. No longer necessarily neoclassical boxes promoting a received hierarchy of visuality, museums today critically engage the minds and bodies of their audiences from the outside in. From their design and amenities to their exhibitions and public programs, museums now are much more accommodating to the body – in all its forms and diversity – than their predecessors.[1] These changes reflect the shifting currents in artistic practice and art theory over the past forty years that take into consideration audience engagement by challenging the relationships between the visitor, the artist, the museum and its objects.[2] Today's exhibition installations often feature mixed media artworks and objects from varied eras, which frequently move off walls into three dimensions. Such displays engage the body of the audience and, at times, reference the body of the artist.

Yet, the heavy baggage of past representations of the body in the museum still weighs us down. We have chosen to shape this chapter to bring into one conversation two disparate realms: the worlds of contemporary art practice and ethnology. We do this in rejection of outmoded classificatory practices that separate both these literal bodies and these bodies of knowledge. By juxtaposing issues of concern about all bodies and bodily remains, we hope to move beyond tired twentieth-century binaries of "us" and "them." Increasingly, scholars, museum professionals, performance artists and others claim a multitude of ethnicities, cultural backgrounds and belief systems, all of which inform museum ethics in the twenty-first century.

Gunther von Hagens, impresario of the infamous *Body Worlds* exhibitions, once said "*You have to recognize yourself as a specimen.*"[3] Through this brief survey of historical and ethical issues concerning bodies in museums, we aim to demonstrate that anxiety about "specimenhood" underlies much contemporary attention to the body in the museum. For some indigenous peoples, 500 years of colonialism underlies their steely determination to overthrow an oppressive history of specimenhood. For many museumgoers, uneasiness about the frontiers of scientific practice in genomics, cloning and the preservation or cessation of human life seems to make them particularly responsive to museum exhibits of bodies, whether living or preserved. For some contemporary artists, experimentation with specimenhood is the practice of the moment, where purposely becoming the object turns museum dynamics upside down. As artists become objects, we will show that audiences are not merely spectators but crucial elements of museological action. As we move through our necessarily brief history of the body in the museum, we aim to reveal how one's relationship to the body as a museological object, and thus to the notion of specimenhood – whether met with anxiety or an open embrace – is an essential consideration in conceptualizing an ethics of the body on display.

In the title, we place "(white)" *sous rature*, referencing, of course, the idea of the sterile "white box" of the art museum and its galleries, which, by the 1930s, had emerged as an ideal exhibitory practice.[4] The notion of the museum as a box, whether as a building composed of pristine white walls, or as an institutional body comprised of archival preservation boxes, is itself a problematic trope that firmly insinuates the museum into the hegemonic and unwavering timelines of art history. Until the 1970s and 80s, such timelines left little room for populations whose aesthetic and cultural practices had been ignored in dominant discourse. Crucially, it also refers to our ethical concerns with the contrast between the boxes that have historically been constructed by a white majority to delimit the way that non-white bodies have been given expression. Not all the museums discussed in this chapter are "white box" museums. Some consider science, ethnographic or natural history. Nor are all the bodies or artists under discussion people of color; yet, all work within and against the paradigmatic museum model, built upon dominant Euro-American prescriptions for display, use and preservation of art and artifacts, and the wider institutional and archival arrangements that stemmed from them.

A "body in a box" brings to mind a corpse; our title deliberately references the ways that the reifying practices of traditional museum representation have deadened rather than enlivened the presence of the non-white body. This chapter will resuscitate and resituate the body's relationship to the white box museum format through an evaluation of the roles of bodies in diverse museum contexts. These range from the social politics of the body as a collectable object to the dynamics of bodily performance in the museum. It is not our place to articulate here any singular ethics of bodily representation in the museum; ethical standards will vary by region, by nation and by the nature of the institution and its constituencies. Instead, we seek to identify and give credence to the living relationships between body, culture and museum. The body has a place in the museum, and we should embrace and reframe it, so it is welcomed – and so visitors develop an understanding of the ways in which their own bodies are implicated in the bodies on display.

Aboriginal bodies in the museum

Our understanding of aboriginal bodies in the museum cleaves into two temporal horizons: *Before James Luna* and *After James Luna*. The rupture occurred on that February day in 1987 when the Luiseño performance artist first lay down on a bed of sand in an exhibition case in the San Diego Museum of Man, declaring his own body an artifact, in solidarity with all those aboriginal bodies long appropriated by museums (Figure 22.1). "It was my turn to bite back," he announced. "I thought about all our relatives, lying in some museum, on some shelf, in someone's closet, in a box."[5] This was a non-negotiable signal that aboriginal people themselves would

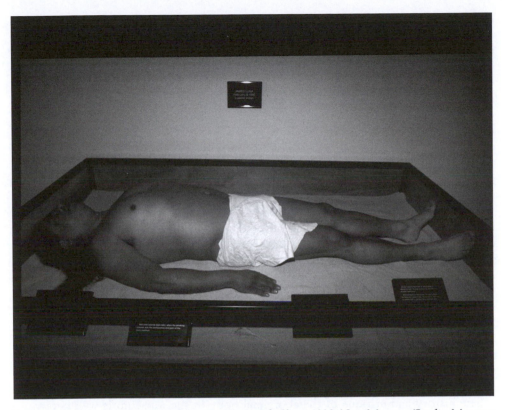

Figure 22.1 James Luna, *Artifact Piece*, in *The Decade Show*, 1990, New Museum/Studio Museum
of Harlem, NYC. Photo credit: Robin Holland. Image courtesy of the artist.

henceforth control the representation of the aboriginal body. It also injected new life
into the unseen museum archives of the past, aligning the objects and artifacts of
Luna's people with living bodies and a living culture.[6]

Displaying the bodies of cultural others for the entertainment and edification of
European and American audiences long predates the institution of the modern
museum, going back to sixteenth-century displays of Aztecs and Brazilian Indians in
Europe. Roslyn Poignant uses the term "the show space" to link the museum with
the fairground, circus, exhibition hall and theatre as "a cultural space that is both a
zone of displacement for the performers and a space of spectacle for the onlookers"
where "historically specific relations of power between colonizers and colonized
were made visible."[7] The Liverpool Museum in Georgian London and P.T. Barnum's
American Museum in mid-nineteenth-century New York, for example, seamlessly
led to the Midway Plaisance at the World Columbian Exposition in Chicago in 1893
and ethnological exhibits at the Field Museum in Chicago and the American
Museum of Natural History in New York.[8]

Three individuals are paradigmatic of the fraught history of the display of aboriginal
bodies in museums: Saartje Baartman for South Africa, Tambo for Aboriginal
Australia and Ishi for Native North America. For our purposes, these named
individuals stand for a more complicated history of the display of mostly anonymous

bodies that is beyond the scope of this chapter. Baartman (1789–1815), a Khoisan woman from South Africa, was taken to Europe in 1810 to be presented as spectacle and scientific curiosity. People in Great Britain and France flocked to see the diminutive "Hottentot Venus" with the large buttocks. Baartman's relative agency in the matter has been much debated. An orphaned indentured servant in South Africa before being taken to England, she testified in a London court that she was willingly on display and paid for her work. Yet she was also subjected to the indignity of close inspection of her genitals by anatomist Georges Cuvier and other men of science. Baartman died at age twenty-six in Paris. She has become an iconic figure of the grotesque excesses resulting from the meeting of colonialism's untrammeled power and the Enlightenment's relentless search for knowledge.[9] Tambo (c. 1864–84) was one of seven Aboriginal people from Northern Queensland, Australia, who were brought to the United States in 1883 to be exhibited. He toured as a "cannibal" in P.T. Barnum's circus, and then was exhibited in "Dime Museums" across the country until he collapsed and died of tuberculosis at twenty, in Cleveland.[10]

Best known in North America is Ishi (c. 1860–1916) – the often described "last of his tribe" of Yahi – who on August 28, 1911 came out of the hills near Oroville, California, malnourished and dressed in rags. Taken into custody and given over to anthropologist Alfred Kroeber at the University of California at Berkeley, Ishi lived the last four and one-half years of his life in the university museum. He worked as a janitor, and museum visitors flocked to see him demonstrate how to knap obsidian arrowheads.[11] James Luna, as a Luiseño Indian man from California, knew Ishi's story well and surely had it in mind as he lay in the San Diego Museum of Man. The stories of these three figures will thread throughout this chapter.

The history and critique of the aboriginal body in the museum is well known. In brief, since the nineteenth-century popularity of living exhibits, and the development of museums, aboriginal peoples have been objectified as living "artifact pieces." Cultural critics might metaphorically use the term "taxidermy" for the whole process of reifying Indians and their objects in an atemporal exhibitionary schema.[12] This has ranged from display of living people (as exemplified by Saartje, Tambo, and Ishi), to dioramas that freeze such a display, to the grasping for some distilled essence of cultural Others by means of their bones and brains.

Dioramas and indigenous bodies

By the end of the nineteenth century, models and dioramas became the way to display native bodies in museums. Franz Boas, for example, designed life-size life groups of Northwest Coast Indian people for the Smithsonian in the 1890s.[13] Elsewhere, dioramas were miniaturized, reducing the display of Native bodies and Native cultures to a doll house-like representation. By the late twentieth century, dioramas came to be seen by most critics as an outdated paradigm. Some Native-run museums continue to use the diorama and life model. The centerpiece of the Mashantucket Pequot Museum in Connecticut (opened in 1998) is a "high tech 22,000 square foot 'immersion environment' diorama"[14] of a sixteenth-century Pequot Village, complete with bare-breasted women at work – a trope long ridiculed by critics of the paradigmatic natural history museum.[15] A far more effective redeployment of the diorama to tell an indigenous story is the Poeh Museum of the Pueblo of Pojoaque, near Santa Fe. Opened in 2005, its 1,600 ft permanent exhibit *Nah Poeh Meng* ("The Continuous Path") tells Pueblo history in small-scale Native-made dioramas. Most notable is the unromanticized view of the violence of the colonizers: surely nowhere in any mainstream museum's historical diorama of the Pueblos would one see a scenario of seventeenth-century life under Spanish rule in which a priest is whipping an Indian – as is displayed at the Poeh.[16]

Performing aboriginality in the twentieth- and twenty-first-century museum

Until recently, when non-European peoples have been brought into the museum, it has generally been to perform their ethnicity. Examples abound from every region. From 1909 to 1912, Maria and Julian Martinez from San Ildefonso Pueblo lived at the Museum of New Mexico, demonstrating their pottery to visitors, as they had in 1904 at the St. Louis World's Fair and other expositions. The often published photo of Navajo sandpainters at the iconic *Indian Art of the United States* exhibit at MoMA in 1941 is a classic image of the Native "artisan" under the surveillance of the non-Native spectator (Figure 22.2). Spectators stand behind a railing, demarcating

Figure 22.2 Navajo Indians executing sand painting, March 26, 1941, during the exhibition *Indian Art of the United States*, The Museum of Modern Art, New York, January 22, 1941 through April 27, 1941. Location: The Museum of Modern Art, New York, U.S.A. Photo credit: Digital image © The Museum of Modern Art/Licensed by SCALA/Art Resource, New York.

the space of display as Navajo men work on their ambitious, ephemeral sandpainting. Dressed for ceremony, the men work in front of a replica of ancient rock art, emphasizing the timelessness of Native practice (despite the fact that this "performance" was coeval with such ceremonies held to protect Navajos going off to fight in World War II).

Since the 1980s, enactments of indigenous identity within museums have more often been volitional performances of agency, sovereignty and knowledge. *Te Maori* (1984–86) is generally acknowledged to be the first national exhibition in which indigenous protocols informed exhibit planning, display and public programming. At the Metropolitan Museum in New York, the St. Louis Art Museum and elsewhere, Maori elders opened the exhibition with both private ceremonies and public performances, educating their audiences that Maori values and protocol drove the exhibits (See Chapter 6).[17] By the 1990s, community-driven enactments of indigenous heritage became far more common.[18]

These acts reflect an emphatic pronouncement of the more empowered relationships indigenous peoples now have with museums. At the grand opening in September 2004 of the National Museum of the American Indian on the mall in Washington, DC, some 25,000 Native Americans and Native Hawaiians marched in procession, signaling a radical restructuring of the relationship between the collective Native body and the apparatus of museums, wherein museums take on a more self-reflexive, open position in their roles as purveyors of knowledge, where input from the community is essential, and considerations of the body must not be assumed.

The afterlives of bodies: cultural taxidermy

Of the moment in *Artifact Piece* when Luna arose from the display case, he wrote:

> Even after the performance I had something to say. The sand around me had been sprayed with water and cornstarch so that my body could be imprinted onto it. After I was carefully lifted off the sand, I would leave a very recent petroglyph, an unmade bed, a recent history, a footprint, a body print of someone who was there, and all of the objects, contemporary and spiritual alike, would point back to that place and that moment when I became the artifact.[19]

So, too, traces of human bodies from across the globe linger in museums with ethnographic holdings: bones, teeth, skulls and other "body print[s] of someone who was there." The metaphorical taxidermy of indigenous peoples in dioramas and ahistorical displays from the late nineteenth to the late twentieth century takes a dangerous turn for the literal when we consider these bodily residues.

In 1897, the seven-year-old Greenlandic Eskimo Minik, his father and four other Greenlandic Eskimos were taken to reside at the American Museum of Natural History (AMNH) to work with Alfred Kroeber and Franz Boas.[20] Four died of pneumonia within eight months; their bodies were autopsied, the flesh stripped from their bones and their skeletons stored at the museum where just weeks earlier these northern visitors had displayed their tools and dined with the anthropologists who later oversaw the removal of their flesh and the treatment of their bones. This brings us back to our three iconic bodies: Saartje Baartman died in December of 1815, and was taken to the anatomical laboratory at Paris's Musée national d'histoire naturelle. Casts were taken of her body, her brain was removed, her genitals were modeled in wax *and* preserved, and Cuvier carefully prepared her skeleton. Her remains were displayed in Cuvier's Cabinet d'anatomie comparée at the Museum until 1977.[21] Upon Tambo's death in Cleveland in 1884, his countrymen tried to conduct the appropriate death rituals, but his body was taken away, embalmed and placed on display in Drew's Dime Museum.[22] Upon Ishi's death in 1916, his body was autopsied and cremated, and his brain sent to the Smithsonian, where it languished for almost a century.[23]

It has been estimated that, before the passage of the Native American Graves Protection and Repatriation Act (NAGPRA) in 1990, the Smithsonian alone held some 18,000 Native skeletons.[24] Hundreds of other museums, research facilities and historical societies contain many more. Since NAGPRA, some have been returned and reburied by their home communities.[25] The publicity generated by these actions has been, in part, responsible for a change in public opinion concerning the exhibition of human body parts. Many more people now agree that the body parts of other people's ancestors do not belong on museum display any more than do their own great-grandmother's bones. Nonetheless, museums of the world are still populated by the brains, bones, heads and other body parts of indigenous peoples.[26]

Appeals made to museums and courts of law for the return of remains highlight the difficulty not only of law and institutional rules on preservation and deaccessioning, but of the deeper implications of the body as art object. In the eyes of the dominant culture, the passing of time only reifies the indigenous body's place in the museum; over time, bodies and bones become distinctly unbodily objects. Only under the advisement of museum staff can body objects undergo an institutionalized deaccessioning, which then confirms that these objects are in fact bodies and not merely objects of study. In essence the indigenous body is transformed from person to body to artifact, and back again. But what to think of indigenous arts that make use of bodily remains as media?

Maori heads and other corporeal remains in art objects

The vividly tattooed heads of Maori men that were steamed, shrunken and dried (called *toi moko*) had an honored place in traditional Maori warrior culture, where heads of ancestors, and of enemies taken as war trophies, were publicly displayed.[27] In the first decades of the nineteenth century, through a robust international trade, many of these heads ended up in European and American museums. H. G. Robley, who had formed a large collection and published a monograph on the topic, sold thirty-five of them to AMNH in 1907, though none is on display.[28] As recently as autumn 2008, two Maori heads were on view in the newly installed Pacific Galleries at the Royal Museums of Art and History in Brussels.[29] The Maori have been urging repatriation of *toi moko* since the late 1990s. More than thirty museums have repatriated *toi moko* to New Zealand, where cultural protocol requires that they be kept in a consecrated vault in Wellington's Te Papa National Museum until their particular cultural origin can be determined.[30]

When city and museum officials in Rouen sought in 2007 to return a Maori head from Musée d'histoire naturelle de Rouen, they were overruled by the Ministry of Culture, which deemed it "a work of art," rather than simple human remains. As such, it was, according to French law, "inalienable." Only in May of 2010 did the French parliament approve their repatriation.[31] Such restitution may seem ethical and sensible, yet further research into the history of the production and sale of these items complicates the issue. By the early nineteenth century, apparently both intertribal warfare and the international market for these "curiosities" caused some entrepreneurial Maori to tattoo captives who were *not* of high rank in order to slaughter them and sell their heads to European traders.[32] The repatriation of such heads to the descendants of their killers does not seem to follow the spirit of the law, yet could anyone in the twenty-first century determine which heads held in museums are actual high-ranking Maori heads and which were those of captive victims?

Mummified and preserved bodies

A formative experience for many urban Europeans and North Americans is a childhood visit to view Egyptian mummies in a museum. This primal exposure to the dead body that "lives on" in the museum normalizes the notion that some bodies – long dead, and from another culture – "belong" in museums. Egyptian mummies and their sarcophagi remain the staples of many museum displays – although even some of them are now in play as objects of repatriation.[33] All are part of cultural and heritage tourism (which sometimes is no more than touristic voyeurism).

In the Andes, mummies from archaeological sites have been displayed in museums for more than a century. Finds of high-altitude Inca offerings of sacrificial victims in the past decades have drawn record-breaking crowds at National Geographic's Explorers' Hall in Washington, DC (1996), at various locations in Japan (1999–2000) and now at local museums in Salta, Argentina, and elsewhere.[34] The thousands of bodies in the Capuchin Monastery crypt in Palermo draw a steady stream of visitors, as do the more than one hundred desiccated bodies in the Mummy Museum of Guanajuato, Mexico.[35] An exhibit drawn from that collection, *The Accidental Mummies of Guanajuato*, opened its North American tour at the Detroit Science Center in October 2009.[36] Several northern European museums prominently feature displays of human remains (so-called "bog people") discovered in a well-preserved state in anaerobic peat bogs. Among the most well known are Yde Girl and the Weerdinge couple on display at the Drents Museum in Assen, Netherlands, and Ötzi the Tyrolean Bog Man at the South Tyrol Museum of Archaeology in Bolzano, Italy.[37]

Mummy exhibits, like Impressionism exhibits, are excellent means of attracting flocks of visitors (and their dollars), so it is no surprise that a profit-making corporation is packaging the three-year North American tour of *Mummies of the World: The Dream of Eternal Life*. Ranging from a tattooed Maori head, to a nineteenth-century Sicilian Capuchin monk, to naturally desiccated mummies from European bogs and the Andes, as well as the obligatory contingent of Egyptian mummies, this self-described "largest mummy exhibit worldwide" promised "record-breaking attendance to science centers and museums."[38] After touring Europe, it opened at the California Science Center in Los Angeles in July 2010 for its three-year North American tour.[39]

Plastinated bodies

The first decade of the twenty-first century witnessed not only the repatriation of human remains but, paradoxically, also an increase in visitors flocking to public venues to see "real" human bodies – principally in the form of preserved cadavers. In July of 2009, Gunther von Hagens announced that the twenty-eight-millionth visitor saw his exhibit *Body Worlds*, which has traveled worldwide since its 1995 premiere in Tokyo.[40] In 1977, this German scientist pioneered the process of preserving bodies through polymer impregnation ("plastination"), which reveals the structure of internal organs.[41] A point of pride for von Hagens is that all bodies in his exhibits were donated by people interested in his project prior to their death, and that he has an extensive waiting list for future plastination and display. Copycat exhibitions such as *Bodies … the Exhibition*, *Bodies Revealed* and *Our Body: The Universe Within* (run by competing companies) do not make such claims, and have been subject to legal investigations as to the origins of the bodies, some thought to be sourced unethically from Chinese prisons.[42]

These exhibitions have been the subject of legal and philosophical debates. Bioethics literature aligns the notion of the ethical display of the body within the parameters of "dignity" in the treatment of the cadaver, this notion assuming a universal understanding of respect for human remains.[43] When government entities conclude that there has been lack of "respect" for the individuals whose bodies are on display, law intervenes. A U.K. exhibition was subject to closure in 2003; one in Paris was shuttered in 2005; *Bodies: the Exhibition* includes a disclaimer, both in the wall text and website, that Premier Events, the organizer, "cannot independently verify that they do not belong to persons executed while incarcerated in Chinese prisons."[44]

These exhibitions provoke the ire of those who boycott them, and cause ethical discomfort among some visitors.[45] In the United States, museums and science centers (among them the Tampa Museum of Science and Industry and the Detroit Science Center) have showcased plastinated bodies. More often, they are mounted in what we might call a mimicked museological context, which lends the bodies an air of institutional seriousness, despite their display in commercial venues. These, such as Manhattan's South Street Seaport and Honolulu's Ala Moana Center, provide a seamless blend of spectatorship, tourism and shopping, putting *Bodies: the Exhibition* on an equal footing with Bath and Body Works and the Body Shop (as the map at South Street Seaport disconcertingly made evident).

Von Hagens has been careful to balance showmanship, humanistic values and scientific education.[46] The exhibition catalogue is filled with respectful essays by philosophers, medical ethicists and biologists.[47] Von Hagens likens himself to Leonardo da Vinci in his interest in depicting the body accurately; others have called him a "latter-day Vesalius."[48] Arguing that anatomists since the Renaissance have used whatever new methods have arisen – from illustration to wax models, photography, CT scans and MRIs – von Hagens believes that it is the anatomist's duty to push the boundaries of technology, and of display of the body. He deliberately places cadavers in poses that recall Classical heroes or Christian saints, including a witty visual reference to St. Bartholomew (typically shown carrying his own flayed skin). Von Hagens compares one of his figures in motion to Umberto Boccioni's

Unique Forms of Continuity in Space (1913) and poses another in front of an anatomical drawing by da Vinci.[49]

Petra Kuppers describes von Hagens's exhibitions as a "self-spectacle" wherein bodies are displayed in a way that strips them of bodily connection to the audience; without individualizing contexts, the universalizing display undermines the human body's complex network. Yet, Kuppers asserts, "the [commercial] success of von Hagens's show ... points to the machine that drives an audience's engagement with their and other bodies" – the museum – where "playing with and bridging the gap between bodies" continues.[50]

Human remains in museums: a coda

The Ethics Code of the International Council of Museums (ICOM), to which all member museums must conform, was adopted in 1986 and revised in 2001 and 2004, and directs that collections of human remains must be cared for "in a manner consistent with professional standards and the interests and beliefs of members of the community, ethnic or religious groups from which the objects originated, where these are known."[51] The passage concerning the *exhibition* of such materials adds that exhibitions "must be presented with great tact and respect for the feelings of human dignity held by all peoples." Of course, as medical ethicists and anthropologists have long pointed out, "human dignity" is a relative concept. For eighteenth-century Maori, the display of tattooed heads added to the prestige of both ancestors and enemies. Some museums take as their guidelines whether the groups from which these bodies came had a tradition of such display.[52] On those terms, Inca and Maori items stay in museums, while most Native North American material does not.

In a lecture at the Musée du quai Branly in 2008, the Director of the British Museum charted a different course, arguing that the encyclopedic British Museum was founded in the eighteenth century in order to "pursue truth without limits," even that "knowledge which is forbidden by the church." It does not bow to the religious preferences of any culture, but serves as a repository of objects documenting social behaviors, from the sacrifice of an enemy and the transformation of his skull into a turquoise mosaic trophy among the Aztec, to the fashioning of a Tibetan musical instrument from human bones "so that even after death the body can go on praising God."[53] While some may dismiss this as mere justification for maintaining control of colonial plunder, others may find it deserves further scrutiny. Should all museums suspend the principles of the Enlightenment in their quest for ethical relations with formerly colonized peoples? Should such encyclopedic museums remain the unquestioned repository for vexed objects, and smaller museums return them? In fifty years will the repatriation efforts of the turn of the twenty-first century be seen in a vastly different light?

The similar ends of Tambo, Ishi and Saartje's time as museological objects suggest that the documentation of their personal histories (however incomplete) and the ability to understand something about them as individuals played a role in the successful repatriation of their remains. In 1993, Tambo's embalmed body was discovered in a Cleveland funeral home. Three Australian Aboriginal elders flew to Cleveland to ceremonially accept the body of their ancestral brother. At the public funeral on the shore of Great Palm Island where Tambo was to be buried, a letter of reconciliation from the Australian Prime Minister was read aloud.[54] In August of 2000, Ishi's brain was reunited with his ashes (held for eighty-four years at Olivet Memorial Park in Los Angeles). A group of Native Californians wrapped his remains in a fox pelt, placed the bundle into a California Indian basket and buried him privately near where he had last lived in the wild.[55] In 2002, Saartje Baartman's remains were flown from Paris to South Africa, to great public celebration, and laid to rest in a grave on a hilltop overlooking the Gamtoos River, near where she had lived. President Nelson Mandela's call in 1994 for her repatriation had been "the first international act of reclaiming cultural property on behalf of the people of a free South Africa."[56] From anonymity, these individuals became underpaid workers, museological spectacles, scholarly specimens and national treasures. While their histories explain the obvious ethical problems of the indigenous body on display, it is only because of their identifiable selves that we are able to connect to them as people with bodies and – despite difference – that we are able to retain the significance of their stories, regardless of where their bodies may now be.

After James Luna: the lives of bodies in contemporary art

Paradoxically, contemporary artists became interested in making art from and with their bodies at the same time that indigenous peoples began insisting upon the return of their biological objects. Display of the living indigenous body in museums of natural history reached its peak of popularity just before fine artists became increasingly interested in non-figurative representation. By the 1960s, anti-colonial movements swept the globe, and subsequent decades saw the questioning of the very presence of human remains in museums. Concurrently, the nineteenth-century ideal of the salon-style exhibition was replaced with the white cube gallery, where "all impediments except 'art' were removed."[57] Abstract paintings seemed perfectly suited to this new museum model. Meanwhile, outside the museum's walls, artists were returning to figurative practice by increasingly using their bodies as performing devices in their artworks.

This revived interest in bodily materials suggests both a broader awareness of and conceptual shift in codes of bodily value and ethics, particularly as the embrace of personal identity and the use of artists' own bodies emerge in contemporary art practice. During its emergence in the 1950s, the body-as-medium largely existed outside the museum in performances derived from modern dance and Bauhaus theater.[58] Mainstream arts institutions rarely offered performance work to their audiences. Such exclusivity was mutual: body-based performance artists were not initially concerned with the museum. For artists of the 1960s, empowered by anti-establishment protests, ignoring the museum as a frame for their works was an indirect form of institutional critique, as well as a way to meld conceptual approaches with sociopolitical issues such as the Vietnam war and feminism. The focus on the body was a means of defying the museum and the rigid sociopolitical structures it represented.

In 1968, Yayoi Kusama orchestrated eight men and women to strip and strike "artistic poses in the fountain of the Museum of Modern Art's sculpture garden" as part of a series of anti-establishment performances around New York City. The event was not museum-sanctioned, and MoMA's security guards tried to remove the nude performers.[59] In the fall of 1970, members of Women Artists in Revolution (WAR) protested the Whitney's abysmal record of exhibiting the work of women artists by leaving tampons and eggs in various public places throughout the museum, to represent women's bodies, if not their art.[60] Though this kind of protest action within the museum was relatively rare, more significant was its inherently provocative nature, encouraging art audiences to engage with art bodies in unaccustomed sites.

Regardless of location, the body had become an art-making tool. Piero Manzoni canned his excrement in *Merda d'artista* (1961), Vito Acconci engaged in his masturbatory performance *Seedbed* (1971) under the floorboards at Sonnebend Gallery and Mary Kelly's *Post-partum Document* (1973–79) detailed her newborn child's daily life with smears of feces and descriptions of bodily activities. By the 1980s, artists such as James Luna began to merge their interests in identity and the body with institutional critiques of the museum.[61] At the Wadsworth Atheneum, Charles LeDray's *Untitled/Tower* (1999–2000) is a virtuoso construction of some twenty-two miniature pieces of vernacular American furniture, each meticulously carved from human bone.[62] The National Portrait Gallery of London's 2009 purchase (for £300,000) of a Marc Quinn self-portrait bust made of his own frozen blood seemed only to engender controversy about the use of British taxpayers' funds.[63]

Producing a self-aware museum audience: James Luna

By the late 1980s, performance was reshaping the way audiences perceived the museum – not simply a temple but a forum, as Duncan Cameron offered in 1971: both a mediated repository and a performative theater for "the second museum age," as Ruth Phillips argued in 2005.[64] While neither Cameron nor Phillips addressed performance art, both were museum directors, and their comments speak broadly to contemporary artistic practice in the museum. With *Artifact Piece* (1987), audiences witnessed a reinvestigation of the shock of 1960s and 70s performance art practices, coupled with a reclamation of the indigenous body in the museum. Luna's performance marked an embodied, postcolonial recovery of aboriginal bodies in museums – a performative refusal of museological taxidermy. The metaphorical unstuffing of the bodily object and replacing it with living flesh suggested that the previous institutional hesitation to remove object status from bodies could only be done by those with an ethical, political and emotional stake. Through didactic labels, Luna offered viewers a historical narrative, pointing out scars on his body, for example, and attributing them to "excessive drinking." These fictional inscriptions played into popular stereotypes about Native American men. Some audience members earnestly believed his performance to be a conventional ethnographic display, expressing shock at discovering the body on display to be alive.

Artifact Piece shifted the power dynamics between museum, artist and audience in two significant ways. First, as Jennifer González explains, Luna used "his body as a flexible sign, pliable enough to accommodate a broad spectrum of projected myths … keenly aware of the limits of corporeal legibility."[65] Lying on a bed of sand in a display case, he reified his own body, thus refusing the institution's authoritative position in identifying objects and naming indigenous bodies.

Secondly, Luna claimed his body as art, not artifact, and reimagined the historical museum encounter between audience and native body. He produced an ethical engagement between audience and object, engendering self-awareness in museum visitors. Luna performed an institutional critique, but it was not his ethical burden to carry alone. Engagement with the audience and the arousal of its emotions became another means of institutional and historical criticism.[66]

While it is easy to classify the museum interventions of artists such as Luna, Coco Fusco and Guillermo Gomez-Peña as representative of a larger "identity art" movement, the work is more complex than simple categorization might suggest. While postcolonial shifts in critical discourse raised awareness about artifact bodies in museums, encouraging their repatriation, this emerged alongside new conceptual approaches to art, the reclamation of the artist's body as a medium and changing, challenging relationships between art audiences and the body. The coupling of performance art with politically engaged concerns shifted the relationship between artwork and audience away from one-way vision focused upon the object, instead encouraging a more reflexive, self-aware audience.

After James Luna: bodily traces

Just as traces of the indigenous body remain imprisoned in museums housing skulls, bones and mummies, in a number of contemporary art projects, the artist's body is only present in the museum through "traces." Luna offered museum visitors his body as an art object, deliberately playing with the notion of "the bodies that were not ours," as Coco Fusco wrote, through a tenuous, embodied museological reclamation.

Other artists use creative practices not dependent on their own bodies as media, producing less direct, if similarly compelling, museum encounters with visitors' bodies. Renée Green has created several installations that include repeated historical references to Saartje Baartman. In *Sa Main Charmante* (1989) Green printed wooden slats with texts describing Baartman's body, but, in order to read the text, visitors had to subject their own bodies to a kind of display: the text was printed on a ladder structure, and was legible only by stepping upon a soapbox while surrounded by large spotlights.[67] Green offered her visitors written words, the only remaining fragments of Baartman's past, and forced them momentarily to take on the performer's role in the spotlight, engaging with these traces through their own bodies.[68]

Fred Wilson is well known for his museological interventions that re-curate art collections. *Mining the Museum* (1993–94) was a response to the omission of the troubled histories of Amerindians and African Americans from many local history museums.[69] Digging into the Maryland Historical Society's archive of household objects, paintings, photographs and documents, Wilson reclaimed hidden artifacts from a turbulent past. He put them on display in unusual juxtapositions, thus visualizing the violent and heretofore unarticulated histories of these absent bodies. Among the most striking juxtapositions were "Metalwork 1793–1880" (ornate nineteenth-century silver drinking vessels surrounding metal slave shackles) and "Cabinetmaking 1820–1960" (armchairs arranged around a whipping post). Audience responses ranged from outright offense and accusations of racism to genuine surprise and tearful, emotional encounters with the objects.[70]

The duality of Wilson's position as both artist and curator allowed him to push the boundaries further than most curators would have. The artist acknowledged the distinct difference between showing work in an alternative space "where you are expecting something unusual" versus a museum, where audience responses are potentially more volatile:

> I'm really interested in surprise and how one reacts on an emotional and intuitive level before the intellectual self kicks in. That synapse seems to happen best when you feel you understand the situation that you're involved in, and the museum setting is one where people feel that they know what to expect and how they're supposed to act. It's a way, once I have people disarmed, to get them to push past their comfort zone.[71]

For Wilson the bodily moment of meeting with an artwork is crucial: the moment before the mind corrects an intuitive response is the space in which the work has its greatest power. Though Wilson selected and arranged the objects on display, his body was not present, nor were the bodies whose histories he highlighted. Yet audience responses seemed to indicate that, though the installations were conventionally arranged, those once absent histories of bodily violence were dramatically understood through a visceral, high-impact museum encounter with objects.

Other contemporary artworks are less formally connected to the body, yet are intimately engaged with body politics, a primary example being the work of Félix González-Torres. Two of his signature displays – the oversize poster and candy piles installed in pristine museum spaces – operate on many levels, referencing the artist's impending absence/death, the absence of others (such as victims of AIDS) and the infinite nature of the museum archive. Though his work is often positioned in the context of death, his broader interest in process is significant as it relates to our concern here with traces.[72] González-Torres avoids figurative representation. Yet his "portraits" are composed of endless piles of the subjects' favorite candies, and reference the bodily passion of both the portrait's subject and the audience, who may select a candy from the "pliant, savory bodies waiting to be plucked and consumed." The artist is less concerned with "ultimate truth" than with "art [that] can be whatever the beholder wants it to be."[73]

In this sense, González-Torres's infinite piles of posters and candy are dependent on the audience body. Their formal qualities alone – colorful, foil-wrapped candies glistening in a perfect pile, or huge reams of paper 4 ft tall in the center of a gallery – seduce the viewer. They are also objects of surprise: the realization that individual objects in the pile can be touched, possessed and consumed in the museum evokes delight, sometimes creating a stream of audience activity to and from his work. In all of these museum encounters, the bodies of the artists are transposed onto the visitors. Interacting with the traces that remain in the museum is akin to engaging with the artist's body.

Extreme bodies, committed audiences

Just as Maria and Julian Martinez lived at the Museum of New Mexico, the performance of living has found its way back into the museum, though not always through bodies of indigenous people. The New Museum of Contemporary Art in New York was one of the first with its 1986 *Choices* exhibition.[74] Museum director Marcia Tucker was aware of the ethical concerns raised by those who move "into dangerous areas of exploration" with their bodies, but saw such risk-taking as both a way to conceptually explore subjects such as temporality, and as a physical means of pushing the psychological limits of art making, as art and life become literally inextricable. Artists such as Tehching Hsieh and Linda Montano – who in *Rope Piece* (1983–84) lived tied together by an 8-ft-long rope for one year, and could not touch each other – were selected because they "drastically alter their lives as a way of making art, and through their work provide living metaphors for states of being, modes of behavior, and other ontological concerns."[75]

Contemporary artists have made living and breathing the museum part of their practice. Bob Flanagan, an artist with cystic fibrosis who battled his disease for more than four decades, worked with his partner Sheree Rose to present *Visiting Hours* at the Santa Monica Museum of Art (1993) and the New Museum (1994). In this signature work, the artist installed a faux hospital room and bed in which he displayed his stricken body to audiences. The installation also included S&M devices alongside videos of his sadomasochistic sexual practices with his partner. Critics decried these videos as torture, but Flanagan's personal view of this violent body work as therapeutic is unmistakable and well documented, a positive foray into palliative "pain-based pleasure."[76]

For museum curators who opt to show this work, the goal is not simply to display personal explorations of the artist-self, but to sanction audience engagement. Consider the decidedly more posh audience experience of Carsten Höller's *Revolving Hotel Room*, which took reservations for a period of ten weeks for the opportunity to sleep in the Guggenheim Museum's legendary foyer in "an operative hotel room outfitted with luxury amenities."[77] For this rare opportunity, reservations booked up immediately. Jerry Saltz, one of the few visitors to document his experience, was open about his museum fantasies: "I have always wanted to have sex in a museum. To me museums are ecstasy machines, places to experience rapture, and the real thing is the real thing." After a night being followed by a museum guard, and then feeling uneasily alone, Saltz woke up refreshed, with a new kind of connection to the building. "The museum had become a cradle of sorts; the environment seemed whole and enveloping. I had the strange feeling of having merged with the structure, like we really had slept together."[78] Saltz's unabashed love for the museum and its cultural representation as a site of history, elegance and power is described in sensual, sexual terms of joy, and his experience leaves him with a feeling that the museum is somehow in him. Art audiences rarely undertake lengthy temporal commitments in their museum experiences with art. Höller's offering presented perhaps one of the only ways a museum audience could realistically undertake such an art project – with sateen bedding, croissants at breakfast and the simplest of challenges: to fall asleep.

In contrast, artists using their bodies as a medium are often willing to undertake physical challenges for art's sake. Marina Abramović's works represent a strenuous commitment to a living performance practice, and in a recent retrospective exhibition at the Museum of Modern Art in New York, she asked the same of her audience. The exhibit included documentation of her earliest performance works, as well as reenactments which were quietly installed among the videos and ephemera as though the bodies were any other sculptural objects. In the opening gallery, tucked into a space between two perpendicular walls, were two unclothed standing performers facing each other, eyes open. Viewers could choose to walk through them, brushing against their skin. Around the corner, framed by gallery walls, two clothed individuals clad in black suits pointed at each other. The liveness of these bodies was genuinely surprising in the context of their conventional installation, whether mounted on a wall, as in *Luminosity* (1997), or lying on a pedestal, as in *Nude with Skeleton* (2002–05). Some visitors were chilled, others excited, but as the exhibit went on, many seemed to become accustomed to the body as object, ignoring the liveness before them, treating the still bodies as any other inanimate art object. While these authors were astonished by the visceral thrill of seeing and touching the living human body in a place like MoMA, we also longed for an acknowledgement or human connection to the bodies we brushed by in "Imponderabilia."

The centerpiece of the retrospective was a new site-specific work, *The Artist is Present* (2010), featured in MoMA's second-floor atrium (Figure 22.3). Abramović performed continuously (seven hours a day, five days a week and nine and a half hours on Friday) for the duration of the exhibit, March 14–May 31, 2010. The prolonged display of Abramović's body was one the museum world has not seen since the times of Saartje Baartman. But was Abramović's body seen with the same curiosity?

Two chairs were positioned in the center of the atrium facing each other; a wooden table was sometimes placed in between the chairs. When visitors arrived,

Figure 22.3 Marina Abramović, *The Artist is Present*, The Museum of Modern Art, New York, 2010. Photo credit: Scott Rudd.

Abramović was already seated, and wall text invited visitors "to sit silently with the artist for a duration of their choosing." Visitors queued up (sometimes for hours), with the majority sitting for under twenty minutes, and with an average of twenty visitors sitting on any given day.

Like her 2005 Guggenheim exhibition *Seven Easy Pieces* that reenacted six significant works by artists from the 1960s and 1970s,[79] this exhibition acknowledged the lack of documentation of twentieth-century performance art with painstaking documentation: every visitor who sat across from her was photographed, with the resulting portrait inserted into an online slideshow. The "portrait" was marked not with a name, but with the date and duration of the sitting, the photographer's name ("photo by Marco Anelli"), as well as the text "© Marina Abramović."[80] In copyrighting these seemingly endless portraits, she renamed the sitters with numbers, like an inventory, and took ownership both of their visage and of that fragment of time in their lives. It is quite a trade: the artist gives the public her body for three months, and in exchange, she keeps your face.

In conceiving of this project, the artist said, "I like the idea [that] ... at the end I'm the same level as the public, very open and vulnerable. That's very important to me."[81] But she also chose to open up her audience to that same vulnerability. The act of audience witnessing was the locus of the artwork, and it was also a site of anxiety, where specimenhood was an ever changing spectacle. Lured in, audiences circled the central space of the gallery, and some gingerly chose to sit with her, while Abramović, ostensibly the art object in question, looked outward, observing them all.

If the act of watching, as a mode of witness, becomes the performative gesture, this can be understood as empowering and activating the visitor.[82] Yet in Abramović's performance work, this activation also projects the anxiety of specimenhood directly upon the visitor. The stress was visible; a surprising number of portraits feature faces with glistening tears streaming down cheeks. Was it hard to be the center of attention? Or was it harder to sit across from a master performance artist who stared vacantly into your eyes, at once existing as an object and treating you as an object, without being able to connect in a fuller, more human(e) way? Was it overwhelming to become the object?

Conclusion: On being a specimen

Two years after James Luna's *Artifact Piece*, in a performance in the form of a docent-led museum tour at the Philadelphia Museum of Art, Andrea Fraser said, "It's nice to feel alive. I'd like to live like an art object."[83] Luna's project signaled a historically critical meeting of institutional critique and conceptual art as performed within the museum. Fraser's work conceived of the museum as a body with which a visitor has an intimate sensory relationship, drawing attention to those sites that every visitor interacts with – toilets, coatroom, water fountain and cafeteria. In *Little Frank and his Carp* (2001), a videotaped performance responding to the Guggenheim Bilbao's audio guide (Figure 22.4), Fraser imagined a personal bodily relationship to the museum by following the audio guide's instructions to feel the limestone walls of the museum as she listened to the narrator's instructions:

Figure 22.4 Video still from Andrea Fraser, *Little Frank and His Carp*, 2001, Six minutes. Image courtesy Friedrich Petzel Gallery, New York.

> Here there is an escape: this space, to which you can return after every gallery, to refresh the spirit before your next encounter ... every surface in this space is curves. These curves are gentle, but in their huge scale powerfully sensual ... Go right up to it. This pillar is clad in ... limestone. Run your hand over them. Squint along the surface. Feel how smooth it is ... [84]

Following the guide, Fraser approached the wall and began to press her body against it. Soon her movement became more active and ecstatic, as she lifted her skirt and moaned, all the time with a digital audio guide held up to her ear. Spurred by an anonymous digital guide, Fraser enacted the sensual relationship that the museum today wants its visitors to have.

As stated at the start of this chapter, cultural vexation about the murky status of "human-being-as-specimen" seems to be at the forefront of our anxieties about and fascination with the body in the museum. On behalf of many, James Luna embraced the hated status of aboriginal specimen to exorcise, reframe and reclaim it. Marina Abramović performed a different kind of institutional critique with her body by using it to lure her audience into contact, and then project specimen status directly upon them.

Each one of us is, in one way or another, the body in the museum, be it as museum patron, artist, aboriginal person, critic, curator or some combination of these. Moreover, we are all implicated in the tangled and vexed history of the body in this cultural box. No set of guidelines will ensure that representations of the body in the museum are presented ethically and responsibly, especially as audiences grow accustomed to for-profit ventures such as *Body Worlds* – exhibitions whose growth is predicated upon the enthusiasm of popular audiences. Many museums are encouraging the presence of the body within their walls in unconventional forms – through installation art, performances and large-scale projects by artists who use their bodies in their creative practice. These very projects, and this institutional openness to new forms of contemporary art as conceptualized via the body, introduce into the museum, with increasing regularity, challenges to the ways in which audience bodies operate and respond to works of art.

Though touch was an extremely important part of seventeenth- and eighteenth-century museum experiences, modern museums abandoned such embodied experiences, in part because of logistics and a sense of preservation, but also because of the emergence of a hierarchy of the senses that paralleled the development of a social hierarchy of the races that came with imperial and colonial ventures.[85] What we are seeing now might be considered an ethical turn back to the initial ways in which museum spaces were used – by people with all of their senses intact and activated – prior to the indigenous body's presence in European museum sites, with their inequitable social systems of power. European consciousness of the existence of the indigenous body and its often tactile aesthetic modes encouraged a primacy of vision over other palpable senses that stripped sensuous moments out of those institutions tasked to offer the public aesthetic experiences. This absence has been theorized as a museological "lost body problem" that can be remedied through a broader conceptualization of embodied aesthetic experiences with art objects, and an embrace of these crucial contact points between visitor and object.[86] The acceptance of the body in the museum today, in all its forms and activities, and with all the ethical concerns of display and reception that come with it, should be heralded as an important moment in the history of museums.

The production of active audiencescapes in response both to challenging, new forms of display for indigenous artifacts, as well as the increasing presence of body and performance art in the museum, ultimately energizes visitors and increases their awareness of their own bodies within the building and among the artworks as much as it situates the audience body in an art-making role. This new way of conceiving the audience's relationship to the contemporary museum is living and embodied; it fully demands our ethical awareness.

Acknowledgments

We are grateful to friends and colleagues Joshua Bell, Marla Berns, Judith Bettelheim, Maia Dauner, Robert Foster, Mary Fox, Leanne Gilbertson, Carol Ivory, Ronald Munson, Karen Kramer Russell, Victoria Pass and Martin Sage, who discussed these issues or read drafts of this chapter. Finally, we are grateful for Janet Marstine's enthusiasm for the project and her deft editorial eye.

Notes

1 For a history of the museum's emergence as a social and political construct, see T. Bennett, *The Birth of the Museum: History, Theory, Politics*, New York: Routledge, 1995.

2 A theory used frequently today in the context of contemporary participatory art practice is relational aesthetics, coined by Nicholas Bourriaud in *Relational Aesthetics*, Dijon: Presses du réel, 2002.

3 *Body Worlds: The Anatomical Exhibition of Real Human Bodies*, DVD, Heidelberg: Institute für Plastination, 2007.

4 See B. O'Doherty, *Inside the White Cube: the Ideology of the Gallery Space*, Berkeley, CA: University of California Press, 1999, first published in 1976.

5 J. Luna, "Sun and Moon Blues," in A. Kiendl (ed.) *Obsession, Compulsion, Collection: On Objects, Display Culture, and Interpretation*, Toronto: Banff Centre Press, 2004, p. 151. Luna repeated his performance of *Artifact Piece* at the New Museum of Contemporary Art in New York in 1990. See N. Peraza, M. Tucker, and K. Conwil (eds.) *The Decade Show: Frameworks of Identity in the 1980s*, New York: New Museum, 1990, pp. 171–2, and plate IL. Of course, the original power of *Artifact Piece* drew from its context in the "Museum of Man," with all that that implies.

6 This influential performance was concurrent with efforts by Canadian and American Native peoples to wrest control of their representations away from non-Native museums, resulting in the convening of the influential Canadian Task Force on Museums and First Peoples in 1988 and the passage of NAGPRA in the U.S. Congress in 1990. See Task Force on Museums and First Peoples, *Turning the Page: Forging New Partnerships between Museums and First Peoples*, Ottawa: Assembly of First Nations and Canadian Museums Association, 1992. For the NAGPRA mandates, see Online. Available HTTP: http://www. nps.gov/history/nagpra/mandates/index.htm (accessed 10 May 2009). Australia's Aboriginal and Torres Strait Islander Protection Act of 1984 and the Council for Aboriginal Reconciliation Act of 1991 similarly sought far-reaching reforms in the relationship between indigenous and settler peoples. Online. Available HTTP: http://www.antar.org.au/ (accessed 15 May 2009).

7 R. Poignant, *Professional Savages: Captive Lives and Western Spectacle*, New Haven, CT: Yale University Press, 2004, p. 7.

8 See, for example, W. Alderson (ed.) *Mermaids, Mummies, and Mastodons: The Emergence of the American Museum*, Washington, DC: American Association of Museums, 1992; R. Altick, *The Shows of London*, Cambridge, MA: Belknap Press, 1978; and R. Rydell, *All the World's a Fair: Visions of Empire at American International Expositions, 1876–1916*, Chicago: University of Chicago Press, 1984.

9 See C. Crais and P. Scully, *Sara Baartman and the Hottentot Venus: A Ghost Story and a Biography*, Princeton, NJ: Princeton University Press, 2008, and R. Holmes, *African Queen: the Real Life of the Hottentot Venus*, New York: Random House, 2007. The effects of Baartman's display trickled back to museum collection practices in her homeland. "European interest in and ethnographic preservation of the Khoisan body has led to the accumulation of thousands of artefacts: today, more than 2,000 skeletons remain in South African museums alone." S. Qureshi, "Displaying Sara Baartman, the 'Hottentot Venus,'" *History of Science* 42, 2004, p. 247.

10 Poignant, *Professional Savages*, passim. On Dime Museums, see A. Stulman Dennett, *Weird and Wonderful: The dime museum in America*, New York: New York University Press, 1997.

11 See O. Starn, *Ishi's Brain: In Search of America's Last "Wild" Indian*, New York: Norton, 2004, p. 147. See also R. Adams, "Ishi's Two Bodies: Anthropology and Popular Culture," in Karl Kroeber and Clifton Kroeber (eds.) *Ishi in Three Centuries*, Lincoln, NE: University of Nebraska Press, 2003, pp. 18–34.

12 On cultural taxidermy, see F. Tobing Rony, *The Third Eye: Race, Cinema, and Ethnographic Spectacle*, Durham, NC: Duke University Press, 1996, p. 99. See also T. Bennett, "The Exhibitionary Complex," *New Formations* 4, 1988 (spring), pp. 73–102.

13 See A. Jonaitis, *From the Land of the Totem Poles*, Seattle, WA: University of Washington Press, 1988, pp. 135–69, and especially figures 50 and 51. On dioramas of Eskimos, see W. Fitzhugh, "Ambassadors in Sealskins: Exhibiting Eskimos at the Smithsonian," in A. Henderson and A. Kaeppler (eds.) *Exhibiting Dilemmas: Issues of Representation at the Smithsonian*, Washington, DC: Smithsonian Institution Press, 1997, pp. 206–45.

14 See the Pequot Museum web site. Online. Available HTTP: http://www.pequotmuseum. org/ (accessed 15 May 2010).

15 At the Seminole Nation's Ah-Tah-Thi-Ki Museum at the Big Cypress Reservation in Florida, the faces in the diorama mannequins are those of living tribal members. J. Holstein, personal communication to authors, 1 May 2009. See also the Museum's web site. Online. Available HTTP: http://www.ahtahthiki.com/ (accessed 15 May 2009).

16 Online. Available HTTP: http://www.poehmuseum.com/exhibits/ (accessed 5 May 2009). This diorama is not pictured on the web site.

17 S. Moko Mead (ed.) *Te Maori: Maori Art from New Zealand Collections*, New York: Abrams, in association with the American Federation of Arts, 1984. For a discussion of Maori exhibit protocols, see C. O'Biso, *First Light: A Magical Journey*, New York: Paragon House, 1989, and D. Newton, "Old Wine in New Bottles and the Reverse," in F. E. S. Kaplan (ed.) *Museums and the Making of "Ourselves": The Role of Objects in National Identity*, London: Leicester University Press, 1994, pp. 269–90.

18 See, for example, *Chiefly Feasts*, which opened at the American Museum of Natural History in 1992, with collaboration from Kwakiutl elders and scholars. A. Jonaitis (ed.) *Chiefly Feasts: The Enduring Kwakiutl Potlatch*, Seattle, WA: University of Washington Press, 1992. The Asian Art Museum of San Francisco regularly features artists demonstrating their creative practice through their AsiaAlive programming. Online. Available HTTP: http://www.asianart.org/ (accessed 15 May 2009).

19 Luna, "Sun and Moon," p. 151.

20 K. Harper, *Give me my Father's Body: The Life of Minik, the New York Eskimo*, South Royalton, VT: Steerforth Press, 2000.

21 Holmes, *African Queen*, pp. 92–101.

22 Poignant, *Professional Savages*, p. 106.

23 See Starn, *Ishi's Brain*, pp. 46–7, 158, and *passim*. Notably, the autopsy was done against Alfred Kroeber's wishes.

24 T. Killion, Smithsonian Director of Repatriation, as cited in Starn, *Ishi's Brain*, p. 316.

25 See K. Fine-Dare, *Grave Injustice: The American Indian Repatriation Movement and NAGPRA*, Lincoln, NE: University of Nebraska Press, 2002; D. Mihesuah (ed.) *Repatriation Reader: Who owns American Indian Remains?* Lincoln, NE: University of Nebraska Press, 2000; V. Cassman, N. Odegaard, and J. Powell (eds.) *Human Remains: Guide for Museums and Academic Institutions*, Lanham, MD: AltaMira Press, 2007.

26 There are, of course, a smaller number of body parts of non-Natives, too. For example, Ishi's brain, while in the Smithsonian, floated in a tank next to that of John Wesley Powell, explorer and ethnologist, who willed his brain to his home institution. See Starn, *Ishi's Brain*, p. 171. Baartman's brain shared storage space with those of many nineteenth-century men of science, including her dissector's. Holmes, *African Queen*, p. 101.

27 The first was "collected" on Captain Cook's 1770 expedition. See B. Hole, "Playthings for the Foe: The Repatriation of Human Remains in New Zealand," *Public Archaeology* 6: 1, 2007, pp. 5–27; and C. Palmer and M. L. Tano, "Mokomokai: Commercialization and Descralization," Denver, CO: International Institute for Indigenous Resource Management, 2004. Online. Available HTTP: http://www.iiirm.org/publications/ (accessed 10 May 2009).

28 Personal e-mail communication from Anthropology Collections Manager Paul Beelitz, 8 May 2009, to authors. They have not been on display since at least the 1970s.

29 Personal e-mail communication from Oceanic art scholar Carol Ivory to authors, 19 May 2009.

30 For a list of more than two dozen institutional repatriations of Maori remains between 2004 and 2008, see Te Herekiekie Herewini, "The Museum of New Zealand Te Papa Tongarewa (Te Papa) and the Repatriation of Kōiwi Tangata (Maori and Moriori Skeletal Remains) and Toi Moko (Mummified Maori Tattooed Heads)," *International Journal of Cultural Property* 15, 2008, pp. 405–46.

31 E. Sciolino, "French Debate: Is Maori Head Body Part or Art?" *New York Times*, 26 October 2007. S. Hardach, "French approve Return of Maori Warrior Heads," Reuters News Service, 4 May 2010.

32 See P. Gathercole, "Contexts of Maori *Moko*," in A. Rubin (ed.) *Marks of Civilization: Artistic Transformations of the Human Body*, Los Angeles: Museum of Cultural History,

UCLA, 1988, p. 172. The Jivaro (or Shuar) of Ecuador and Peru, well known for their tradition of shrunken heads worn as war trophies, also sometimes manufactured such heads solely for commercial trade. See J. Castner, "Shrunken Heads *and Tsantsas*," *Tribal Arts Magazine* 8: 3, 2003 (autumn), pp. 74–79.

33 In 2003, the Carlos Museum at Emory University repatriated the mummy of Nineteenth Dynasty King Rameses I to the Egyptian Museum of Antiquities in Cairo, and it was seen as an important object of cultural patrimony. Egypt's Supreme Council of Antiquities intends many more such repatriations. See "Repatriation: A New Ethos at the Egyptian Museum of Antiquities, Cairo," at the Egyptian Cultural Heritage Organization (ECHO) web site. Online. Available HTTP: http://www.e-c-h-o.org/Repatriation.htm (accessed 10 May 2009). See also H. Mayell, "U.S. Museum to Return Rameses I Mummy to Egypt," *National Geographic News*, 30 April 2003. Online. Available HTTP: http://news.nationalgeographic.com/ (accessed 10 May 2009).

34 The well-endowed National Geographic Society financed and publicized Reinhard's expeditions and retrievals of these ritual offerings, and presumably recoups its costs through its touring exhibitions, television programming, books and home videos on them. See J. Reinhard, *The Ice Maiden*, Washington, DC: National Geographic Society, 2005, pp. 151–9 and 338. Television shows about mummies (mixing education and adventure with a bit of the macabre) have proved that the public's thirst to see and understand the preserved dead is unquenchable. PBS's Nova has produced many such programs; the National Geographic Channel's popular *The Mummy Road Show* aired thirty-seven episodes from 2001 to 2003 and its stars wrote a book about their scientific adventures. R. Beckett and J. Conlogue, *Mummy Dearest*, Guilford, CT: Lyons Press, 2005.

35 On the Capuchin mummies, see A. A. Gill, "Sicily's Crypts," *National Geographic Magazine* 215: 2 (February), pp. 118–29. The Guanajuato Mummy Museum, which expanded and reopened in 2007, has its own multilingual web site, which boasts now "an infrastructure suitable for this exhibition which attracts hundreds of thousands of visitors every year" and contains a "welcome" message from the Mayor of Guanajuato stating that "the mummies are part of Guanajuato's heritage and for this reason we conserve, preserve, and share them with the visitors that come to our city in search of them." Online. Available HTTP: http://www/momiasdeguanajuato.gob.mx/ (accessed 15 May 2009).

36 See L. Aguilar, *Long Live the Dead: The Accidental Mummies of Guanajuato*, Detroit, MI: Detroit Science Center, 2009.

37 See R. C. Turner and R. G. Scaife (eds.) *Bog Bodies: New Discoveries and New Perspectives*, London: British Museum Press, 1995; A. Fleckinger and H. Steiner, *The Fascination of the Neolithic Age: The Ice Man*, Bolzano, Italy: Folio Verlag, 1999. Ötzi has his own web page. Online. Available HTTP: http://www.iceman.it/ (accessed 15 May 2009).

38 See the company's web site. Online. Available HTTP: http://www.americanexhibitions.com (accessed 10 May 2009). See also the dedicated web site of the tour. Online. Available HTTP: http://www.mummiesoftheworld.com/ (accessed 10 May 2009). Perhaps in response to the outcry about the various exhibitions of plastinated cadavers, the web site for the mummy exhibit states: "Mummies are the single direct archive to the human species, the study of which provides great information and data in the context of archaeology, anthropology and science. All mummies in the exhibition originate from established and respected European museum and university collections. The exhibition was prepared in accordance with all recommendations of the International Council of Museums' (ICOM) code of ethics. The exhibition is presented with respect and dignity, acknowledging the interests of the social, ethical and religious groups from which the mummies originate."

39 Personal communication from James Delay, Vice-President for Development, American Exhibitions, Inc., to authors, via telephone, 7 May 2009. After touring Europe, it opened in July 2010 at the California Science Center in Los Angeles. See A. Wieczorek, M. Tellenbach and W. Rosendahl, *Mummies of the World*, New York: Prestel USA, 2010.

40 Online. Available HTTP: http://www.bodyworlds.com/ (accessed 10 May 2009). Its full title is now *Gunther von Hagens' Body Worlds: The Anatomical Exhibition of Real Human Bodies*.

41 In this process, polymers replace the 70 percent of the human body composed of water and lipids, and then harden, allowing bodies to be displayed as life models, as exploded

sections or as other specimens. A medical ethicist associated with von Hagens defines the object on display as "a natural structural model of the human body that makes use of some of the materiality of the original." A. W. Bauer, "Plastinated Specimens and their Presentation in Museums: A Theoretical and Bioethical Retrospective on a Media Event," in G. von Hagens and A. Whalley (eds.) *Gunther von Hagens' Body Worlds: The Anatomical Exhibition of Real Human Bodies*, Heidelberg: Institute für Plastination, 2006, p. 230.

42 *Our Body: The Universe Within* and *Bodies: the Exhibition* are toured by the related companies Premier Exhibitions and American Exhibitions. See the web site of the latter. Online. Available HTTP: http://www.americanexhibitions.com/ (accessed 10 May 2009). They lease plastinated bodies from Dalian Hoffen BioTechnique Company, in Dalian, China. In May 2008, New York Attorney General Andrew Cuomo reached a settlement with Premier Exhibitions that is supposed to end the practice of using bodies of undocumented origin. Online. Available HTTP: http://www.oag.state.ny.us/media_center/ (accessed 10 May 2009).

43 L. Burns, "Gunther von Hagens' BODY WORLDS: Selling Beautiful Education," *American Journal of Bioethics* 7: 4, 2007, pp. 12–23. See also T. C. Jespersen, A. Rodriguez and J. Starr (eds.) *The Anatomy of Body Worlds: Critical Essays on the Plastinated Cadavers of Gunther von Hagens*, Jefferson, NC: McFarland, 2009.

44 For the 2003 London controversy: Online. Available HTTP: http://www.guardian.co.uk/uk/2002/mar/10/arts.highereducation (accessed 10 May 2009). For the 23 April 2009 Blotter story on the Paris closure: Online. Available HTTP: http://www.abcnews.go.com/ (accessed 10 May 2009). For the full text of the exhibition disclaimer: Online. Available HTTP: http://www.prxi.com/nycdisc/index.html (accessed 10 May 2009).

45 In 2007, Elaine Catz, of the Education Department at the Carnegie Science Center in Pittsburgh, resigned in protest over her institution's decision to host *Bodies … The Exhibition*. She now manages "The Anti-Bodies Virtual Protest" web site. Online. Available HTTP: http://mysite.verizon.net/vzexqyla/anti-bodies-virtual-picket-line/ (accessed 15 May 2009).

46 One recent iteration, *Body Worlds and the Story of the Heart*, included huge cloth banners displaying "feel-good" pictures of people, overlaid with philosophical quotations about love and the mysteries of the human heart. Viewed by Berlo at the Buffalo (NY) Science Center, 7 September 2009.

47 In addition to Bauer, already cited, see F. J. Wetz, "The Dignity of the Individual," pp. 240–59, and B. Brock, "The Educating Power of the Sciences," pp. 283–89. For a more hagiographic approach, see C. Moore and C. M. Brown, "Gunther von Hagens and *Body Worlds*," Part 1, "The Anatomist as Priest and Prophet," pp. 214–21. All in von Hagens and Whalley, *Gunther von Hagens' Body Worlds*.

48 Online. Available HTTP: http://www.bodyworlds.com/en/gunther_von_hagens/life_in_science.html (accessed 15 May 2009). See also "A Latter Day Vesalius," *Neurophilosophy*, 19 July 2006. Online. Available HTTP: http://neurophilosophy.wordpress.com/2006/07/19/a-latter-day-vesalius/ (accessed 15 May 2009). In the sixteenth century, Vesalius (known today as "the father of anatomy") not only conducted meticulous dissections of the human body but made precise drawings of its structures, published in 1543 as *De Humani Corporis Fabrica*. In terms of showmanship, von Hagens allowed his exhibit to be used for a scene in the 2006 James Bond movie *Casino Royale*.

49 Von Hagens and Whalley, *Gunther von Hagens' Body Worlds*, illustrations on pp. 284 and 286.

50 P. Kuppers, "Visions of Anatomy: Exhibitions and Dense Bodies," *differences: A Journal of Feminist Studies* 15: 3, 2004, pp. 134–49.

51 Online. Available HTTP: http://icom.museum/code2006_eng.pdf (accessed 15 May 2009).

52 See remarks made by Steven Englesman, Director of the National Museum of Ethnology, Leiden, Netherlands, at the 2008 conference "From Anatomic Collections to Objects of Worship: Conservation and Exhibition of Human Remains in Museums," Musée du quai Branly, 22–23 February 2008. Online. Available HTTP: http://www.quaibranly.fr/en/programmation/scientific-events (accessed 15 May 2009). Englesman's remarks are on p. 20.

53 Ibid. McGregor's remarks are from pp. 44–45.

54 Poignant, *Professional Savages*, p. 251.

55 Starn, *Ishi's Brain*, pp. 264–5.

56 Holmes, *African Queen*, p. 103. In 2002, President Mbeki wrote a letter to the nation on the occasion of her return. Online. Available HTTP: http://www.nathanielturner.com/saartjiebaartman.htm (accessed 10 May 2009).

57 O'Doherty, *Inside the White Cube*, p. 87.

58 See R. Goldberg, *Performance Art from Futurism to the Present*, New York: Abrams, 1988, and T. Warr and A. Jones (eds.), *The Artist's Body*, London: Phaidon Press, 2000.

59 Warr and Jones, *Artist's Body*, p. 82. Forty years later, Kusama's performance has been canonized; an account is now featured on MoMA's online database. Online. Available HTTP: http://www.moma.org/collection (accessed 15 May 2009).

60 See C. Nemser, "The Women Artists' Movement," *Feminist Art Journal* 2: 4, 1973–74 (winter), pp. 8–9.

61 Marcia Tucker offers prime evidence of the institutional resistance that arose as such art began to enter the museum. After her firing from the Whitney, Tucker founded the New Museum in 1977 with a commitment to new artists and art forms (large-scale installations and performance art) not represented in museums and commercial galleries. Marcia Tucker papers, 1957–2004, Research Library, Getty Research Institute, accession No. 2004.M.13.

62 C. Gould, *Charles LeDray, Sculpture, 1989–2002*, Philadelphia: Institute for Contemporary Art, 2002, p. 99. Until it outlawed the export of human bones in 1985, India had been the main source. A brisk trade from West Bengal continues, although increasingly China is the source for human bones, as it is for bodies used in plastination. See S. Carney, "Inside India's Underground Trade in Human Remains," *Wired Magazine* 15: 12, 2007 (December). The purchase and use of human bone for study, display or even art-making is not illegal in the United States; not unexpectedly, it is an international commerce in which ethically dubious practices abound. LeDray does not publicly address his reasons for choosing this medium, and deflects queries about it. See Gould, *Charles LeDray*, pp. 35–38.

63 See V. Acconci and J. R. Kirshner, *Vito Acconci: A Retrospective, 1969 to 1980*, Chicago: Museum of Contemporary Art, 1980; M. Kelly, *Postpartum Document*, Berkeley, CA: University of California Press, 1999; Germano Celant (ed.), *Piero Manzoni*, London: Serpentine Gallery, 1998; and "National Portrait Gallery shows Marc Quinn's frozen blood head," *ArtDaily*. Online, 11 September 2009. Online. Available HTTP: http://www.artdaily.org/index.asp?int_sec=11&int_new=33211. D. Alberge, "National Portrait Gallery criticised over purchase," *London Times Online*, 2 October 2008. Online. Available HTTP: http://www.timesplus.co.uk/tto/news (all accessed 15 May 2009).

64 D. Cameron, "The Museum: A Temple or the Forum?" *Curator* 14: 1, 1971, pp. 11–24; R. B. Phillips, "Re-placing Objects: Historical Practices for the Second Museum Age," *Canadian Historical Review* 86: 1, 2005, pp. 83–110.

65 J. A. González, *Subject to Display: Reframing Race in Contemporary Installation Art*, Cambridge, MA: MIT Press, 2008, p. 37.

66 Space limitations prevent us from considering the important performances by Coco Fusco and Guillermo Gomez-Peña which grew directly out of Luna's work (especially their *Undiscovered Indians* ... , created as a counter-narrative to the Columbus quincentenary). These artists' performative fictions and objectification of their own bodies created a new role for museum audiences by revealing the variety of responses to the art to be part of the art itself. Response to these works attests to a global audience that is – however unknowingly – implicated in the objectification of bodies in museum contexts. See C. Fusco, *English is Broken Here*, New York: New Press, 1995, and Fusco's web site. Online. Available HTTP: http://www.thing.net/~cocofusco/ (accessed 18 May 2009). For a film of *Two Undiscovered Amerindians Visit* ... see Paula Heredia, director, *The Couple in the Cage*, Chicago: Video Data Bank, 1993. See González, *Subject to Display*, pp. 22–63, for descriptions of audience reactions to Luna's works.

67 Online. Available HTTP: http://www.oberlin.edu/amam/Green_Charmante.htm (accessed 21 August 2009). *Charmante* was exhibited at the Allen Memorial Art Museum at Oberlin College, and is now in its collection.

68 Another exhibit that focused on Baartman and Khoisan bodies was the internationally discussed *Miscast: Negotiating the Presence of the Bushmen* (1996) held at the South African National Gallery. *Miscast* considered one fraught history of corporeal fascination and repulsion, ranging from the longstanding objectification of Khoisan bodies (from Baartman to early twentieth-century life casts and dioramas) to aboriginal displacement and genocide. See P. Skotnes (ed.), *Miscast: Negotiating the Presence of the Bushmen*, Cape Town: University of Cape Town Press, 1996, and P. Davison, "Museums and the Reshaping of Memory," in S. Nuttall and C. Coetzee (eds.) *Negotiating the Past: The Making of Memory in South Africa*, Cape Town: Oxford University Press, 1998, pp. 143–60.

69 F. Wilson and L. Corrin (eds.), *Mining the Museum*, New York: New Press, 1994. This was held at the Maryland Historical Society in Baltimore, in association with The Contemporary, where Corrin was curator.

70 Wilson and Corrin included sixteen copies of audience questionnaires as part of the exhibition catalogue, reproduced as though they, too, were artifacts on display. Wilson and Corrin, *Mining the Museum*, pp. 61–76.

71 M. Buskirk and F. Wilson, "Interview with Fred Wilson," in M. Buskirk and M. Nixon (eds.) *The Duchamp Effect*, Cambridge, MA: MIT Press, 1996, pp. 187–90.

72 For further investigations into issues of death, mourning and loss in González-Torres's work, see R. Storr, "Setting Traps for the Mind and Heart: Felix González-Torres," *Art in America* 84, 1996 (January), pp. 70–7. For an essay on his art analyzed as event, see M. Amor, "Felix González-Torres: Towards a Postmodern Sublimity," *Third Text* 9: 30, 1995 (spring), pp. 67–77.

73 N. Spector, *Felix González-Torres*, New York: Guggenheim Museum, 1995, pp. 147.

74 M. Tucker, *Choices: Making an Art of Everyday Life*, New York: New Museum of Contemporary Art, 1986. This was one of the earlier museum exhibitions in the United States to address performance art generally and the ethical questions of body art and endurance in the museum context. M. Gladstone, from an untitled dissertation chapter on performance art and the New Museum, in "Sensing the Museum: Contests of Experience with Contemporary Art," Program in Visual and Cultural Studies, University of Rochester (in progress).

75 Tucker, *Choices*, p. 12. Tehching Hsieh has made six performances in his life thus far; the first five each lasted one full year, and the last thirteen years. His performances are durational explorations of time and space as much as of psychological and physical endurance. In his first, *Cage Piece*, he spent one year in a self-built cage, with access to food and water, but did not speak to anyone (1978–79). See T. Hsieh and A. Heathfield, *Out of Now: The Lifeworks of Tehching Hsieh*, Cambridge, MA: MIT Press, 2009.

76 M. Tucker, "Questing for New Definitions of Contemporary Art," *New York Times*, 29 March 1998, Section 2, 48. For a popular critical perspective, see F. Kaimann, "Victimization as Art: Critics see the growing Body of Work built on Pain and Suffering as perhaps Good Psychology but Questionable Art," *Birmingham News*, 22 January 1995, Lifestyle section, p. 1F. For Flanagan's definitive statement on his creative explorations, see a poem he wrote in 1985, reprinted in B. Flanagan, "Why," *Art Journal* 56, 1997 (winter), pp. 58–9, and D. Cooper, "Flanagan's Wake [reminiscences of Bob Flanagan's career with excerpts from his Pain journal]," *Artforum* 34, 1996 (April), pp. 74–7.

77 Online. Available HTTP: http://www.guggenheim.org/new-york/exhibitions/past/exhibit/1896/3 (accessed 18 May 2009).

78 J. Saltz, "Night at the Museum," *New York Magazine*, 9 November 2008. Online. Available HTTP: http://nymag.com/arts/art/features/51998/ (accessed 18 May 2009).

79 For full documentation of the 2005 Guggenheim reenactments, see M. Abramović, *Seven Easy Pieces*, Milan: Charta, 2007. See also K. Biesenbach (ed.) *Marina Abramović: The Artist is Present*, New York: Museum of Modern Art, 2010.

80 Online. Available HTTP: http://moma.org/interactives/exhibitions/2010/marinaAbramović/slideshow.html (accessed 1 June 2010).

81 Online. Available HTTP: http://www.theartnewspaper.com/articles/Marina-Abramović-takes-over-MoMA/17454 (accessed 1 October 2009).

82 T. N. Cesare and J. Joy, "Performa/(Re)Performa," *The Drama Review* 50: 1, 2006 (spring), p. 173.

83 "Museum Highlights: A Gallery Talk," in A. Fraser, *Museum Highlights: The Writings of Andrea Fraser*, Cambridge, MA: MIT Press, 2004, pp. 95–114.

84 See "Isn't This a Wonderful Place? (A Tour of the Guggenheim Bilbao)," in *Museum Highlights*, pp. 231–260.

85 C. Classen and D. Howes, "The Museum as Sensescape: Western Sensibilities and Indigenous Artifacts," in E. Edwards, C. Gosden and R. B. Phillips, *Sensible Objects: Colonialism, Museums and Material Culture*, New York: Berg, 2006, pp. 199–222.

86 J. D. Feldman, "Contact Points: Museums and the Lost Body Problem," in *Sensible Objects*, pp. 254–67.

23

Towards an ethics of museum architecture

Suzanne MacLeod

Architecture has emerged as one of the defining features of museums and galleries over the last twenty years. In the UK alone, Heritage Lottery Fund has invested some £1.4 billion in museums and galleries since 1995, £977 million of which has funded more than 614 capital build projects.[1] Across Europe and North America museum buildings have been renovated and remodelled, entirely new buildings have been constructed to house existing collections and new museums and new collections have been conceived and built. In the UK, precedents for the scale of the investment and the phenomenal number of capital projects can only be found in the mass building of museums and galleries in the final decades of the nineteenth century and, on a smaller scale, in the expansion projects of the 1930s. At the end of the nineteenth century, it was accepted by ambitious local councils that every town and city of any worth needed a museum and an art gallery. Sometimes these were publicly funded ventures complete with all the compromises that publicly funded projects bring, and at others they were gifts from private benefactors in which the town or city would simply be grateful for whatever it was given. In all cases these projects were driven by a range of interests and relationships but did include, at some level, a vision of society and, in today's language, a vision of community cohesion. There is absolutely no question that later generations have benefited from this foresight and vision.

Since then, the museums profession in its various forms has occupied these spaces and carved out a place and identity for itself based on specialist knowledge, custodianship and varying notions of public education. The recent significant expenditure in cultural infrastructure has, as in other parts of the world, introduced new roles and responsibilities for many museum professionals. Now expected to be project managers, or possibly even the project client, many senior managers have found themselves thrown into major capital projects, sometimes involving high-profile architects and, where the emphasis is necessarily on navigating the complexities and nuances of the architectural process, rather than reflecting on the rights and wrongs of the decision to build or the impact of the project on the wider environment or community.

There are numerous tangible outcomes of the recent investment. The building boom in museums and galleries has provided a much needed upgrading of many existing buildings fit for some of the functions required of the twenty-first-century museum. In Liverpool, for example, the Walker Art Gallery finally managed to create temporary exhibition spaces to sit alongside the permanent galleries, enabling a return to its original function as a space for contemporary art. The building boom has also resulted in the addition of new and architecturally impressive museums in the cultural landscape and high public awareness through media coverage of museums and galleries and the experiences they might potentially offer; Foster and Partners Great Court at the British Museum comes to mind with its monumental glass ceiling. Whatever we feel about some of the buildings constructed and their appropriateness, the opportunity to build has enabled a tangible expression of a resurgence of culture at the heart of society.

Less tangible, but no less significant, the reshaping and upgrading of buildings creaking and crumbling under the weight of decades of use has enabled many museums and galleries to shape a space for themselves and their visitors which better reflects the museum's social values and enables the sorts of user activities now imagined for cultural institutions. New Art Gallery Walsall, for example, is a regional gallery which has won acclaim amongst the architecture *cognoscenti*. The new build has enabled the redisplay of the stunning Garman Ryan Collection formed by Kathleen Garman, wife of sculptor Jacob Epstein, and her friend Sally Ryan and which contains many examples of Epstein's work as well as other significant examples of European art. Housed for years in inadequate space and conditions on the second floor of the central library, the collection now sits at the heart of a dedicated building complete with children's gallery, café, shop, art library with free internet access and temporary exhibition spaces. Such investments in the future are the most significant and important aspects of any museum build. Museum buildings embody the values and experiences of those who built them and enable certain forms of activity and social relationships through their physical form. It makes sense that as time passes and values change, buildings can restrict and work against a museum's aspirations and key messages about their use. Periodic capital development is crucial.

Despite the significance of this phenomenon, there has been little discussion of the ethics of building and the embedded ethics of our new and renewed cultural institutions. In the race to secure funding there has been little detailed critical debate about the ways in which these capital projects might have impacts, big and small, or how they might achieve the kinds of social and organisational transformations that architecture should most certainly set out to create. A great many claims have been made about the success of capital developments but the reality is that we understand very little about the real impact of these building projects on place, community and the individuals who use them. With all this in mind, this chapter aims to stimulate a conversation about ethics and the built cultural environment. It is a difficult subject to access. This is not because it is overly complex or intellectual, but because the ethical dimensions of museum architecture are hidden behind the processes of making buildings and the shiny attention-seeking aesthetics of high-profile examples. The vast and complex nature of these projects inevitably means that an incredible number of decisions need to be taken over a prolonged period of time and attention, understandably, becomes focused on driving the project forward. Similarly, the range of professionals and organisations involved can make building projects difficult to navigate, comprehend and analyse. Invariably, discussion is focused on one major element – what it will look like.

A focus on ethics and a discussion of the ethics of the built environment can provide a way into thinking about the nature of architecture and the ways in which architecture is both an ethical pursuit and embedded – in its physical form – with ethics. These are important ideas with which to engage and the aim throughout has been to attempt to shift the often anecdotal, informal and personal discussion of museum architecture into the field of ethics or, rather (and much more satisfactorily), to draw out the ethical dimensions of museum architecture and begin to identify what might be recognised as elements of ethical consensus on museum architecture within the museums profession. The reasons for doing this are many but do come down to one key driver: if we are able to come to some consensus on the ethical dimensions of museum and gallery architecture, we should be able to move towards a flexible, site specific and usable series of criteria for evaluating new buildings and capital development processes in museums, something which is fundamentally lacking at the moment. Without evaluation, one senses, correctly or incorrectly, that at times the 'wrong' choices are being made on capital projects. A deeper understanding of the ethical dimensions of museum architecture would enable us to identify the real achievements and, ideally, a way forward for future capital development which builds on lessons learned. The chapter asks, what does it mean to think about ethical decision-making in the building of a new museum or art gallery and specifically one that is publicly funded? What complications arise as a result of culture's public utility? As socially responsible organisations – which public museums surely must aim to be – and as sites of free public access to collections, what might we identify as professional ethical consensus on 'good design', 'good process' and 'good building'? Finally, beyond process, can a physical museum building – the end product – have ethical virtue and, if so, how might we begin to define and identify it? These are large and ambitious questions and the following discussions are intended as a starting point, rather than a full-blown, exhaustive account of an ethics of museum and gallery architecture.

An ethics of the built environment

Within the field of architecture there is something called 'an ethics of the built environment', most specifically located in the academic literature rather than in day-to-day architectural practice. Discussion of the ethical dimensions of architecture can be traced back to Plato and Socrates before him and seems obvious when one considers that architecture is about building the physical world in which future generations will live.[2] Approached in this way, it seems to make absolute sense that there would be something called an ethics of the built environment. However, even in the academic field of architecture, this is a seemingly small and contained field of enquiry, reasonably underdeveloped and only now beginning to receive a good amount of attention. As a number of writers have noted, environmental ethics has tended to focus on the natural, rather than the built, environment.[3] However, over the last ten years a body of work has developed which recognises the significance of the ethical dimensions of the built environment, particularly the built *urban* environment. The focus on the urban is directly linked to the size and intensity of cities: some 80 per cent of Europeans and 50 per cent of the global population live in cities. Cities take up only 2 per cent of the Earth's surface and yet account for 75 per cent of the use of natural products, the majority of which come from less developed countries.[4] The built environment is the largest user of energy and at least 50 per cent of all waste produced is building-related.[5] Cities, then, the natural home of museums and galleries, raise a whole range of ethical questions.

Beyond this focus on the urban, the ethics of the built environment is characterised by an ecological logic or systems approach to architecture and building.[6] This logic states that humankind is part of an ecological system where everything exists in relation to everything else and where actions in one realm can and will impact, positively or negatively, in another. Here, the built environment is recognised as having multiple impacts on the natural world. How we build and how we live, then, are entwined and raise questions of utmost importance. As Warwick Fox put it, 'The fate of the "green bits" of the planet is now inextricably bound up with – indeed, effectively at the mercy of – the future of the "brown bits".'[7]

An ethics of the built environment also depends upon a social and cultural understanding of architecture and built environments more broadly. Understandings of architecture do still dominate which see architecture simply as the work and aesthetic outcome of architects – a notion of architecture which explains the rather disconnected and limited nature of architectural ethics. This dominant and powerful understanding sits behind many of the debates surrounding museum buildings and is the cause of many of the problems associated with working with architects on museum projects.[8] However, within the vanguard of the architectural profession (in academia and in practice), a much fuller social and cultural understanding of architecture has emerged whereby designing and building buildings is recognised as a social (and hence ethical) activity. From this perspective, building is recognised as a process of social and cultural production and the built environment is recognised as an embodiment of social values and mores. More than this, the production of a building is only part of the story and it is the peopling of space and the social relationships that are possible and encouraged within the space that will continue to make and remake the built environment.[9] In this sense, architecture or the built environment is also about power and identity; it is about people, their occupation of space and the way they build their identities in and through space. When linked with an ecological approach to the built environment, the social and cultural understanding of architecture enables this system's understanding to be extended to economic and, importantly, social, sustainability and issues of social and economic inequality. As Talbot and Magnoli write:

> The built environment of our cities represents a massive capital investment that, if we make mistakes, commits us irrevocably to long-term patterns of resource use, waste emissions and environmental degradation.
>
> At the same time, the city is the principal locus for change, presenting the greatest opportunity for improving performance and offering the major concentration of essential human resources in terms of vision, information and knowledge. Building more sustainably offers solutions which are simultaneously environmentally responsible, economically viable and socially beneficial – the three touchstones of sustainable development.[10]

The future health of the system then – of the environment, of society and of human experience – depends to a very large extent upon the development of environmentally, economically and socially sustainable approaches to our built urban environment. Indeed, these 'three touchstones' of sustainable development are linked and mutually supportive.

For museums and galleries the third dimension of social sustainability is crucial and is directly linked to the purposes and roles of cultural institutions. If what is required in the sustainable city and for the 'expressive life'[11] are public spaces which create opportunities for participation, identity formation and learning about ourselves, others and the environment, which can create a sense of history, place and belonging and which contribute to the quality of life for all citizens of a locality, then museums have an amazing opportunity to confirm their life-enhancing importance. As Herbert Girardet states, 'We need to revive the vision of the city as a place of culture and creativity, of conviviality and above all else of sedentary living … currently cities are not centres of *civilisation* but *mobilisation* of people and goods. A calmer, serener vision of cities is needed to help them fulfil their potential as places not just of the body but of the spirit.'[12] Museums and galleries have a central role to play in this urgent vision of the future based upon history and place, community and belonging, communication and learning, participation and expression, values already close to the hearts of many publicly funded museums and galleries. Of course programming can and already does go a long way towards enabling the types of civic expression that this view suggests. But it is also fundamentally about the physical stuff of museums – their outside space, their architecture and exhibition hardware and the experiences and possibilities for social interaction and meaning making that those physical environments offer. The difficulty of focusing on the physical stuff of museums should not be underestimated.

In a report which provides an excellent review of the role of museums and galleries in urban regeneration, Simon Tait offers up a whole range of examples of museums actively carving out an important place for themselves as agents of social change and forums for the confirmation and building of cultural identities through specific events and activities. Yet, throughout Tait's report are a number of statements which illustrate the impact of the underlying physicality and reality of museum buildings and building processes. Entwined in case studies of real creativity and social ambition on the part of numerous cultural organisations are comments illustrating the desire within some of those same organisations for a landmark building or an architectural competition: the contemporary hallmarks of civic achievement and success. But, as Tait states, the resulting transformations in physical terms do not always lead to the desired outcomes:

> More problematic now is the physical nature of traditional museums: entrances up broad flights of steps; a front 'information desk' which can be as much a deterrent to the casual visitor as a focus of guidance; subdued lighting required for conservation but creating a sepulchral atmosphere; objects kept behind glass on pedestals; poorly placed and uninformative labels. Although much of that has changed, adapting such building to more contemporary ideas of exhibition and access has been difficult – the British Museum, the V&A, the Walker Art Gallery and even the newly recast

Kelvingrove Museum in Glasgow could still pass as grim tabernacles rather than places of enlightenment.[13]

We might add that adapting museum buildings to contemporary and much needed visions of the environmentally, economically and socially sustainable city has, until very recently, been almost nonexistent.

Towards an ethical consensus on museum building

Why, then, might it be useful to think about a consensus on the ethical dimensions of museum architecture? And why might it be important to do this within the museums profession? At present, there are few mechanisms for evaluating the success of a new museum building or a reconditioned building other than the traditional comparison of form and function; does the building do what those who use it need it to do and is it attractive and usable? This is a good starting point but the obvious difficulty here is that we could be talking about a school or a hospital or a private residence. Also, such questions hardly scratch the surface, let alone enable a deep engagement with the ethics of building and renewal within our sector. Similarly, as the comments above begin to suggest, the criteria for evaluating the success of a new cultural building within the architectural profession are wholly different from, and at times seem diametrically opposed to, the qualities that might be valued within the museums sector.

One useful starting point might be to ask, what is it that is specific to the publicly funded museum and/or art gallery? For example, what does it mean for a socially responsible, mission-led, not-for-profit organisation to engage in a capital development project? What sorts of ethical questions does this meeting of the mission-led organisation with the commercial world of property development raise? What specific challenges, issues and opportunities do these projects bring for those involved and what process of design and decision-making might be best suited to the needs of the museum and its users? Finally, is there such a thing as a virtuous museum building and, if so, what specific characteristics and qualities might define it? In the remaining parts of this chapter these ideas are explored through a discussion of what we might term the ethical dimensions of museum architecture.

Sense of place

Starting from the located nature of all museum buildings and a belief in the desire for architectures which have something to say about that location and which may act in positive ways to build a sense of belonging and identity, sense of place emerges as a crucial ethical dimension of museum architecture. Whether we use the terms 'heritage' or 'history' to describe it, sense of place links to the past life and character of a location, to local building forms and techniques and the stories of occupation and use of the locality. But sense of place is also about the present. It is about the identities of contemporary populations and communities and how these groups and individuals make sense of the built environment and its past uses. As Brook writes:

A place that tells its story, where the layers of past history are evident, and preferably not consciously preserved, is one that expresses a spirit of place ... what is here now makes sense given what was here; it has a coherent narrative that connects its past to its present and could guide its future. Of course, just having a past would not count; everywhere has a past simply by virtue of being in space through time ... there must be significance placed on the coherence of the story and its working connection to the present. Themed street furniture displaying motifs of a town's now defunct cotton industry presumably do not count.[14]

The importance of sense of place is not to be underestimated, linking as it does to identity, a sense of belonging, rootedness and so on. Publicly funded museums and galleries undertaking capital development projects are ethically bound to add to a sense of place in their locale. Such an approach will not only offer something potentially fundamental and life changing into the experiences of local residents and visitors, but will enable the museum to anchor itself as a contemporary addition to the landscape linking past to present and future. Successful examples that we might cite include the National Maritime Museum in Falmouth. This building takes the geography, local building styles and materials as well as the heritage of and future vision for Falmouth into account in its design, an approach which has added great creative depth to the process and resulted in what can only be described as a positively iconic building.[15] The narrative that the building sets up about Falmouth, about that physical place, past, present and future, continues into but also, and importantly, stems from the content and narrative of the new museum; the physical structure of the National Maritime Museum has emerged as an embodiment of its story, speaking to the identities of local communities and adding something of long-term value to the landscape.[16]

The National Maritime Museum provides an example of a unique building which must be deemed a success in terms of the ethical dimension of sense of place. Examples like this in an urban environment are, however, difficult to find and often the characteristics of new museum architecture are more easily described as global rather than local, offering buildings and museum experiences that could be anywhere in the world. Such buildings (and we could list many, many examples) are not created with the museum's or the local community's interests in mind. Rather, and much worse, such buildings speak only to themselves or, occasionally, to an architectural elite.

Process-based design: learning communities

The notion of a sense of place immediately begins to suggest user participation in design. If we are to build museums which enable positive social interactions; which are grounded in place and stem from local perceptions of place and community; and which are economically viable because they offer the right sorts of services and the types of social space the community wants and needs, then users of museums (local residents, regular visitors, staff and other stakeholders) need to be directly involved in design, and not simply in a subsidiary role.[17] Of course, the reality of projects is that they range across a spectrum from no consultation, to some, select consultation, to actually involving stakeholders and users in the design process. Collaboration and even consultation can be a frightening prospect for project teams and difficult to reconcile with the bidding and building process; securing funding for a project can be all-consuming and the forward-lurching processes of building can seem antithetical to the processes of consultation, discussion and negotiation with interested groups and individuals.

This said, there are examples of architects working in a participatory way and genuinely engaging with user groups. At the Sackler Centre for Education at the Victoria and Albert Museum in London, the museum worked with architects SoftRoom to develop an education space which would offer fully accessible and functional spaces for a whole range of arts education activities. The project was directly informed by consistent and detailed consultation with a whole range of stakeholders and users from within and without the organisation, resulting in feedback which directly impacted on design decisions. For example, existing users of the families programme at the V&A provided an incredible resource, feeding their assessment of existing facilities into the design process; research resulted in very tangible outcomes such as the inclusion of cupboards large enough to store pushchairs, bright and welcoming places for users to consume their own food and male and female toilets with baby changing facilities.[18]

Direct involvement of users in design is about more than an ideal of a democratic process and a desire to build what people want; it also offers potential for people (including architects, museum professionals and museum users) to develop new knowledge together. For example, publicly funded capital build projects offer great potential for all those involved to learn more about environmentally sustainable architecture and its social benefits. Indeed, the process of building a sustainable urban future is one that will require communities and individuals to acquire new skills and knowledge. In the museum world we love stories of egotistical designers (and even mild-mannered ones) who come up with design solutions which seem to be at odds with the idea of the public museum. And yet it remains almost impossible to find examples of museum buildings where users of the building have been directly and *equitably* involved in the design process and resultant designed product. Within architectural ethics, there exists a concept of a 'symmetry of ignorance', the idea that all professionals, including architects and museum professionals, have gaps in their knowledge which can be provided by other people.[19] The idea of symmetry is a powerful one, as it suggests parity and equality and helps make the case for fully participatory design processes. Only through a fully participatory design process will the vision of publicly funded urban development as a route to meaningful community learning be realised. Of course such a process would demand a certain kind of architect: one who could use all of their creative and technical skills to realise a new museum building through process-based design.[20]

Organisational learning: journeys of discovery

Where capital projects in museums and galleries have been deemed a success by senior museum managers and their peers, the project has been characterised by an expectation that a major capital build will take the museum and its employees – at all levels of the organisation – on a journey of discovery about their organisation, about their visitors and about their collections. A full engagement with the process of building – of making space within which people will perform in certain ways and which can, through its design, actively enable or disable social relationships – offers up opportunities for a thoughtful and reflective process. For example, at the Victoria and Albert Museum, the making of the British Galleries enabled the organisation to move towards a deeper understanding of mission and philosophy and to learn new knowledge about their users and their collections, a process which has increased capacity and understanding within the organisation.

The idea that the capital project is in itself an investment in the organisation and not simply in the hardware of the institution, a process through which the skills base of the organisation is expanded for the future good of the organisation and the broader profession, is an appealing one. The reality, of course, is that the desire to build and the myriad of decisions and effects that result can often have unpredictable or unanticipated effects. In the UK, for example, one outcome of the availability of funding for capital development has been the weakening in some museum services of in-house design capability, resulting in the loss of a huge amount of creative and technical 'know-how' which may never be recovered (it goes without saying that the outsourcing of design has brought a new creativity to museum design). Clearly, equipping in-house teams to learn new skills and knowledge through capital build projects is crucial to the future of museums if the upgrading of facilities is to be maintained. However, all of this presumes an organisation fully engaged with the process and where the organisational structure allows such meaningful organisational learning to take place; in many large museums, council-run museums and university museums, the sheer size of the organisation often means that the museum is not necessarily the client, a situation which may well be productive on some levels but does interrupt the potential for a smooth and incremental learning journey. Examples abound of architects choosing to bypass the actual client in order to engage more fully with the museum and the people who will occupy the building, but this is often done unofficially and can be a difficult and unpredictable process. The ethical path of organisational learning through capital development is not necessarily an easy one to navigate and, as is often the case with capital projects, ethical issues and dilemmas will emerge later, rather than being particularly obvious at the time.

Value for money

The museum sector has been criticised for jumping on the architecture bandwagon without careful reflection on the long-term impacts of the decision to build.[21] This is absolutely fair and accurate criticism. Many involved in capital projects know that the only way to ensure the future of their museum is to improve increasingly shabby and deteriorating facilities. But the challenge of thinking deeply about whether this is right for the long-term future of museums and galleries and the future good of society is a sobering one. In his book *Museums in a Troubled World*, Robert R. Janes bemoans the relentless desire to build in the cultural sector. He writes:

> Although often likened to a renaissance, this architectural boom doesn't merit this praise, lacking as it commonly does any vigorous intellectual or creative resurgence within the museum itself. In fact, the opposite prevails,

as the 'If you build it, he will come' syndrome readily diverts attention away from a consideration of purpose, values and the requirements for long-term sustainability.[22]

In a similar vein, James Bradburne has described the 'overbuilt' nature of museums as a 'poison pill' condemning museums to increased staffing bills and increasingly stretched revenue budgets, the challenges of which will potentially distract from the mission of the organisation.[23] Like others, Bradburne cites the inherent unprofitability of any mission-led organisation as a salutary reminder to museum directors who see capital development as a route to growth and sustainability, that the economics of this are far from straightforward. Rather, the confusingly titled S curve of visitation whereby visitor numbers rise as a result of a new building but then begin to drop away, is shown time and again to be the reality of living with a capital development project. Janes summarises the argument: 'There is no doubt that bold and creative buildings attract visitors and can provide meaningful visitor experiences, but these inducements are increasingly irrelevant, perhaps malevolent, in a world beset by ... social and environmental pressures.'[24]

Janes's direct criticism of the building boom and its co-conspirators is both refreshing and worrying and immediately brings to mind high-profile examples of shortsighted planning such as The Public in West Bromwich and the first incarnation of the Turner Contemporary in Margate.[25] The Public provides an extreme example of 'overbuilding', leading to bankruptcy, and the first phase of Turner Contemporary was a classic case of faith in an iconic new building to solve the social and economic problems of the ailing seaside town, although the project is now back on track. Both projects have drained millions of pounds of taxpayers' money.

Of course, it is overly simplistic to think that the answer to value for money lies only in strong leadership and a tightly controlled budget. A short-term and reasonable overspend could result in significant long-term savings (making a new building anything but a 'poison pill'), although these types of consideration are rarely evaluated during the building process. Examples of shortsighted cuts such as the selection of cheaper materials which need more upkeep and hence impact regularly on revenue budgets are not difficult to find. In a more fundamental way, however, the desire on public sector projects to minimise costs and avoid an initial overspend, based on a simple financial model of value for money, has undoubtedly contributed to the lack of engagement with sustainable design. The very process of public sector funding and commissioning means that museums and galleries are not always working with contractors who are at the cutting edge of environmental design. This can have a major impact on the technical specifications of buildings and their longer-term carbon footprint. Indeed, the sector as a whole has failed to engage with environmental sustainability in its full sense and green issues are proving stubbornly slow to become established. Examples like the California Academy of Sciences in San Francisco provide a refreshing alternative vision of how sustainability can be built into and become the defining feature of a museum project.[26] Once again, locating such examples in a built-up urban context is close to impossible.

One such example, although very much in its infancy, is the Whitworth Art Gallery in Manchester, a university art gallery on the edge of a major city centre. It sits in a heavily built up environment and has a reputation for cool, thoughtful exhibitions, aided by the stunning 1960s conversion of the original Edwardian galleries. Under the leadership of director Maria Balshaw, the Gallery is in the process of an architectural competition to build a new entrance. The entrance will back onto a public park rather than the university and will act as a direct link to the local urban communities. The new extension will offer a modern and user friendly entrance, separate to the grand and potentially off-putting entrance at the front of the Gallery, and will be driven in its design by a sustainable agenda.

The Whitworth Art Gallery project could potentially provide a model of the synergy between environmental, economic and social sustainability for future developments but, if it is to do this, it will require a longer-term approach to the issue of value for money. Current conceptions of value for money could easily be adapted to the economic argument which states that a carbon neutral building and one with minimal running costs can, in the long term, offer value for money. However, some of the more qualitative elements of environmentally sustainable architecture demand an open-minded approach. The idea of a building made from natural, locally sourced materials which reduces its carbon footprint through the use of natural ventilation sits in contrast to the sealed and tightly controlled environment of the museum and would demand a review of the tight controls placed on environmental conditions in galleries – an issue currently being considered by the National Museum Directors' Conference in the UK and by the international Bizot Group.[27] Of course, the issues here reach far beyond the economic and environmental argument into questions of social sustainability and the role of museums and galleries in cultural life. A building which, through its selection of materials, provides a healthier and more uplifting environment for staff and visitors alike clearly sits very comfortably in a broader vision of the museum as a part of a fulfilling cultural life; no noise from air conditioning, varying levels of light and access to windows, air flows and changes which connect the insides of buildings to life and 'fresh air' outside are highly beneficial to the human spirit and lead to spaces where people want to spend time.[28] Indeed, the green agenda is based on a number of ethical and moral principles that chime with the principles and ethics of the mission-led organisation. Capital development always has been and always will be a part of the museum. Perhaps the question isn't whether we should build, but how, with what and towards what ends, questions which might result in a dynamic and effective model of value for money somewhere in the nexus of budget, environmental responsibility, economic viability and social benefit.

Conclusion. The virtuous museum building

In this chapter, discussion of the ethical dimensions of museum architecture has related mainly to process and to the ways in which process can be directed towards a museum building which might contribute in a very direct way to economic, environmental and social sustainability. The process does pertain at some level to what has been happening already in a good number of museums and galleries but suggests the need for a much fuller and far more radical engagement with the fundamental social possibilities of architecture and a vision of the sustainable city; a large gap exists between current best practice and a fully sustainable approach to museum architecture in an urban context.

The identification of the ethical dimensions of museum architecture – of sense of place, of participatory, process-based design and community learning, of organisational learning and change and of an expanded notion of value for money – enables us to begin to differentiate between museum builds and to separate off, for example, some of the large and small architecture-led projects which have been driven by very different desires and visions of society to those described in this chapter. Such buildings project culture rather than establishing themselves as part of culture and enabling a cultural life which involves everyone. Indeed, the need for differentiation is crucial. Many projects clearly do relate to the rather bleak picture of capital development described by some museum commentators, but others provide examples of thoughtful, capacity-building development that can only be described as a creative resurgence, and still more have enabled the kind of physical reshaping that museums must necessarily go through every fifty years or so to remain relevant and useful to society. The notion of ethical dimensions may, therefore, offer a route to a more detailed and critical assessment of museum architecture, beyond the often celebratory voice of the architectural critic.

But can a building, the physical stuff inside and out and including the displays, be identified as ethical? Can a physical building be embedded with ethics? This is an intriguing question and this chapter certainly begins to suggest some examples of what might be considered the antithesis to the virtuous museum building. What is clear is that built forms are the direct embodiment of the beliefs and values of those involved in their production and their physical form, materials and potential for use will emerge as a result of the choices that are made about the design process. Perhaps, unsurprisingly, in light of all of the above, the question is a little easier to answer if we look to the commercial sector. The Manchester offices of architects Building Design Partnership (BDP) offer office space for 200 staff and also act as a flagship building encapsulating the BDP ethic of sustainable, healthy and usable architecture. Utilising a range of recycled materials, the six-storey building is carbon-neutral, taking advantage of passive ventilation systems which are both environmentally responsible and economically viable. Its south-facing side is clad in a reflective material to reduce solar heat gain, drawing its light instead from the full glazing of its northern canal side wall. Other characteristics include a living roof (specifically designed to attract the Black Redstart, a rare bird species native to British urban areas) and the collection and use of rainwater for flushing toilets; it has been awarded a BREEAM rating of 'excellent'.[29] The new environment has transformed working practices for staff at BDP and the space is used by other businesses and groups in the area, ensuring that the offices and meeting rooms are used out of working hours. The BDP building responds to the context and limitations of its canalside site in the city's Northern Quarter; it is a beautiful building, iconic in its own quiet and sophisticated way. On many levels, one can see that this is a virtuous building and one which provides a glimpse of a usable and sustainable built urban environment.

Acknowledgements

This chapter grew out of a series of interviews undertaken in May, June, July and August 2009. I am extremely grateful to: Moira Stevenson, Manchester Art Gallery;

Sara Hilton, Heritage Lottery Fund North West; David Anderson, Victoria and Albert Museum; Stephen Snoddy, New Art Gallery Walsall; Ken Moth, Building Design Partnership; Jo Beggs, Whitworth Art Gallery; and Nick Gordon, Leicester Museums and Galleries. Thanks also to Jo Digger at New Art Gallery Walsall and Maurice Davies at the Museums Association for helpful and informative email communications and to Bob Janes and Richard Sandell, who provided invaluable feedback on the final draft.

Notes

1 HLF Policy and Strategic Development Department Data Briefing, August 2009, unpublished.

2 For a useful and wide-ranging discussion of architectural ethics see B. Wasserman, P. Sullivan and G. Palermo (eds.) *Ethics and the Practice of Architecture*, New York: Wiley, 2000.

3 W. Fox, 'Introduction', in W. Fox (ed.) *Ethics and the Built Environment*, Abingdon: Routledge, 2000, p. 4.

4 R. Talbot and G. C. Magnoli, 'Social inclusion and the sustainable city', in W. Fox (ed.) *Ethics and the Built Environment*, p. 92.

5 C. Day, 'Ethical building in the everyday environment: a multilayer approach to building and place design', in W. Fox (ed.) *Ethics and the Built Environment*, p. 127.

6 Fox, 'Introduction', p. 1.

7 Ibid., p. 3.

8 S. MacLeod, 'Rethinking museum architecture', in S. MacLeod (ed.) *Reshaping Museum Space: architecture, design, exhibitions*, London: Routledge, 2005, p. 10.

9 See, for example, J. Hill (ed.) *Occupying Architecture: between the architect and the user*, London: Routledge, 1998.

10 Talbot and Magnoli, 'Social inclusion', p. 93.

11 S. Jones (ed.) *Expressive Lives*, London: Demos, 2009.

12 H. Girardet, 'Greening urban society', in W. Fox (ed.) *Ethics and the Built Environment*, p. 28.

13 S. Tait, 'Can museums be a potent force in social and urban regeneration?' September 2008. Online. Available HTTP: www.jrf.org.uk/publications/can-museums-be-potent-force-social-and-urban-regeneration (accessed 13 August 2009).

14 I. Brook, 'Can "spirit of place" be a guide to ethical building?' in W. Fox (ed.) *Ethics and the Built Environment*, pp. 142–3.

15 M. J. Long, *National Maritime Museum Cornwall: the architects' story*, London: Long and Kentish Architects, 2003.

16 P. Higgins, 'From cathedral of culture to anchor attractor', in S. MacLeod (ed.) *Reshaping Museum Space: architecture, design, exhibitions*, pp. 222–3.

17 B. Fowles, 'Transformative architecture: a synthesis of ecological and participatory design', in W. Fox (ed.) *Ethics and the Built Environment*, p. 105.

18 Online. Available HTTP: www.vam.ac.uk/school_stdnts/education_centre/project_diary/index.html (accessed 13 August 2009).

19 Fowles, 'Transformative architecture', p. 107.

20 See, for example, the work of Edward Cullinen. Online. Available HTTP: http://www.edwardcullinanarchitects.com (accessed 24 August 2009).

21 R. R. Janes, *Museums in a Troubled World: Renewal, Irrelevance or Collapse?* London and New York: Routledge, 2009, p. 108.

22 Ibid.

23 James M. Bradburne, 'The museum time bomb: overbuilt, overtraded, overdrawn'. Online. Available HTTP: http://www.bradburne.org/downloads/museums/InstitutioninCrisisWEB.pdf (accessed 24 August 2009).

24 Janes, *Museums in a Troubled World*, p. 111.

25 C. Scott, 'Painting the town pink', *Sunday Times Magazine*, 14 June 2009, p. 11. Anon., 'Margate's Turner contemporary undergoes a sea change', *Building Design*, 2 May 2008.

Online. Available HTTP: www.bdonline.co.uk/story.asp?storycode=3112458 (accessed 24 August 2009).

26 Weald and Downland Open Air Museum, 'Downland gridshell'. Online. Available HTTP: http://www.wealddown.co.uk/Buildings%20and%20Exhibits/gridshell/downland-gridshell.htm (accessed 24 August 2009).

27 National Museum Directors' Conference, 'Reviewing environmental conditions'. Online. Available HTTP: http://www.nationalmuseums.org.uk/what-we-do/contributing-sector/environmental-conditions/ (accessed 24 August 2009).

28 C. Day, 'Ethical building in the everyday environment: a multilayer approach to building and place design', in W. Fox (ed.) *Ethics and the Built Environment*, p. 137.

29 BREEAM is the BRE Environmental Assessment Method for buildings. See their method. Online. Available HTTP: www.breeam.org (accessed 1 March 2010).

24

Museum censorship[1]

Christopher B. Steiner

... they've got to solve this censorship thing.
Thomas Hoving, Director, Metropolitan Museum of Art, 1967–77[2]

In what was eventually uncovered to be an elaborate hoax, performance/installation artist Yazmany Arboleda attempted to set up in June 2008 two impromptu, "guerilla-style" exhibitions in a vacant boutique on New York City's lower West Side.[3] The planned exhibitions, *The Assassination of Hillary Clinton* and *The Assassination of Barack Obama*, were described as "re-installations" to be undertaken independently by the artist in response to what was said to be his prior censorship and forced eviction from two "reputable" Manhattan art galleries.[4] The provocatively titled exhibitions were intended to explore what the artist described as the "character assassinations" by the media of the two leading Democratic contenders in the 2008 U.S. presidential campaign.[5]

Included in the planned Obama exhibition was to be an enlargement of the cover of then Senator Obama's book *The Audacity of Hope* but retitled *The Audacity of Black People*; a photomural showing an image of the Obama daughters captioned "NAPPY HEADED HOS"[6] and the depiction of an enormous black penis wrapped around the white walls of the gallery accompanied by a text panel that read "ONCE YOU GO BARACK..." In the Clinton exhibition, the artist enlarged a magnified close-up photograph of Senator Clinton, appearing ravaged with wrinkles, accompanied by the words "The Face of Experience;" a reproduction of a high-school yearbook page with the phrase "Most likely to compromise" printed next to a teenage photo of Hillary Clinton; and a series of fake campaign posters and bumper stickers, including one that described the candidate as "The Antidote to Niggeritis."[7] This was indeed the explosive stuff of outrage, indignation and potential censorship – racist, misogynist, sexist, ageist and unapologetically offensive art.

But, before the exhibitions were ever installed, their inflammatory titles, which had been stenciled to the storefront's marquis, had attracted not only the attention of curious passers-by but also the United States Secret Service and New York Police Department. Arboleda was detained for questioning and ordered by law enforcement officials to remove the words "assassination" which appeared in association with the names of the presidential candidates. Eventually it was uncovered that the two Chelsea galleries claimed by Arboleda to be the venues of his previous encounters with expurgation and the law, the so-called Leah Keller Gallery and Naomi Gates Gallery, did not actually exist; and, in fact, there were no exhibitions being temporarily shuttered due to pending legal action. "The whole thing was fabricated," the artist admitted to a reporter from *The New York Times*.[8] Arboleda had apparently taken photos of the interior of real art galleries; then, using Adobe Photoshop, he manipulated the digital images to depict his own artworks on the walls. The images were uploaded to web sites on domain names which he had purchased for the project; he included in these web sites phony press releases and fabricated installation shots of the non-existent exhibits.[9] When the story broke, the claims by the artist of having been previously censored in these two art galleries only heightened the interest in what promised to materialize in the storefront installations.

The "censorship" of his shows was reported by nearly a hundred different news organizations around the world, most of which unquestioningly accepted Arboleda's story regarding his previous expulsion from the two Manhattan art galleries. The incident also provoked literally hundreds of comments on *The New York Times*'s web site, as well as on other online forums, that were both in favor of and against the censorship of Arboleda's art. What had been unleashed by these exhibitions-that-never-were was an almost perfectly scripted' re-enactment of the typical litany of reactions provoked by controversial museum exhibitions during the past several decades in the United States. "While the first amendment allows Arboleda to express himself in any way he wants to," wrote one internet pundit, "it also allows citizenry to refuse to attend any gallery that will host this type of offensive material. Galleries considering displaying this particular exhibit should be aware of the backlash they could receive for doing so."[10] Or, "To all those who say it's okay to say whatever they want, do whatever they want, whenever, to anyone, anytime, and to not be able to do so is censorship, are missing the point," opined another outraged commentator. "It's about decency and civility and about a so-called artist with no talent putting up provocative words that do absolutely nothing to bring enrichment into our lives (like art should)."[11] Arguing from the other side of the debate, one reader commented: "I don't find this art show as being offensive at all. Art holds a mirror to society. You either like what you see or you don't."[12]

Apparently, this is exactly the kind of response Yazmany Arboleda was shooting for. "The engagement and the conversation – that's the dialogue ... that's my art" said the artist in an interview.[13] "If it was attention I wanted I would have climbed the side of the *New York Times* building. Instead I chose to take on some of those veneers by inspiring a dialogue, which when it stems from art, is the most effective means of questioning the truths we have come to take for granted."[14] The point of Arboleda's project (which came to be known as *The Keller Gates Project*) became even more clear several months later when he opened, in September 2008, what was described as the last stage of the "performance" – an exhibition, held this time at the Art Directors Club Gallery, which displayed enlarged photocopies of all the comments, opinions, rants and raves from the blog posts and news items generated three months earlier by the *Assassination* "exhibits." In the end, we now know that the exhibitions had indeed not been subject to museum censorship; it was instead museum censorship which *was the subject* of the exhibitions.

The case of Yazmany Arboleda raises many challenging questions about the relationship between art, the media and the law within the context of both museums and commercial art galleries. Was this merely the case of a crackpot attention-seeker looking for quick fame? Or was this a serious artistic intervention into the ethics of art and museum censorship, and an insightful exploration of the boundaries of the freedom of expression? I begin this chapter with a detailed synopsis of the *Assassination* exhibitions because it serves both as a backward- and forward-looking case study. The responses that Arboleda's exhibitions activated encompass the full spectrum of public reactions to incidents of museum censorship and controversial exhibitions in the United States since the height of the so-called Culture Wars in the 1980s and 1990s. In this sense it recapitulates a well-rehearsed dialogue between, on the one hand, staunch proponents of absolute freedom of expression and, on the other hand, the more conservative advocates for civic responsibility and the upholding of shared community values. At the same time, however, the Arboleda case also anticipates an emerging trend in museum approaches to issues of censorship which purposely engage with controversy as a way to provoke a public dialogue and to stimulate an educational forum for better understanding the very nature of both the museum and censorship itself.

I will suggest in this chapter that public demand for the censorship of museums is often generated in reaction to a hierarchical model of museum authority in which an external group (whether it be government, religious, civic or community-based) attempts to critique or control the dissemination of images or knowledge from an institution which the group perceives to be unilaterally powerful, and from which the group feels excluded. The growing trend among museums today to shift from a hierarchical model of authority to a more inclusive model of shared authority, with a greater openness for dialogue and debate, has the potential to transform the nature of museum censorship. Recent incidents suggest that censorship can be "worked out" if the museum and community engage in constructive dialogue about the nature of the offensive material and its provocation to incite controversy. At the same time, however, this shift in the museum's role from being defensive to engaged opens up new questions and ethical considerations regarding the museum's responsibility to its mission and to the public.

Censorship as propaganda in Nazi Germany

While the roots of modern censorship can be traced to earlier origins going as far back as the Renaissance, in the twentieth century one of the most commonly cited examples of museum censorship is the case of National Socialist (Nazi) Germany and Adolf Hitler's attack on modern German art and the work of Impressionists, Expressionists and the avant-garde from across Europe. Working under the direct orders of Nazi propaganda minister Josef Goebbels in the mid-1930s, members of the Reich Chamber of Visual Arts confiscated from German museums and private collections thousands of paintings, prints, drawings and sculptures deemed by the Nazi regime as subversive, immoral or what they simply called "degenerate." Among the artists included in the purge were some of the major figures of early twentieth-century art, including Max Beckmann, Marc Chagall, Otto Dix, Wassily Kandisky, Ernst Ludwig Kirchner, Paul Klee and Emile Nolde. The so-called degenerate works of art were singled out for being either an "insolent mockery" of religion, anti-war,

Jewish, Bolshevist, an insult to the German race or to German womanhood, "Negro" art or even as "total insanity."[15]

In 1937, Adolf Ziegler, National Socialist president of the Reich Chamber for the Visual Arts, organized an exhibition entitled *Degenerate Art* (*Entartete Kunst*) which opened in Munich and then traveled to museums in thirteen cities throughout Germany, attracting more than three million visitors during its tour. Featuring 650 of the Nazi regime's confiscated paintings, prints, drawings and sculptures, the art was installed in Munich in an abandoned warehouse where it was mocked in the gallery space by painted slogans on the walls deriding the artworks as depraved and insane.[16] Part of the public attraction, of course, was a desire to see what had been censored by the state – to witness what was "officially" taboo and forbidden.

While this exhibition is often referred to as the first major example of state-sponsored censorship within the context of an art museum, the case of the *Degenerate Art* show actually stands out as one of the most curious forms of museum censorship in modern history. For unlike most forms of museum censorship, the primary goal of the Nazi regime was not to hide these works from public view (or, as it were, to protect the masses from seeing potentially corrupting and dangerous visual images) but rather it was to make the art known and visible to the largest possible public. "German *Volk*," said Adolf Ziegler at the opening ceremony in Munich, "come and judge for yourselves!"[17]

This notion of censoring-by-showcasing turns on its head the normative model of the "good museum" which needs to be protected from the occasional aberrant idea or image that tries to worm its way into the civic standards of morality and decency for which the institution normally stands. In Nazi Germany, the sites which originally housed the "degenerate" art, and those which were chosen to exhibit the confiscated works in the national tour of the *Degenerate Art* exhibit were not cherished as museums that upheld proper national ideals and moral values, but rather these institutions were portrayed themselves as forces of "evil" that could be enlisted as fodder in a broader campaign of Nazi political propaganda.[18]

When the *Degenerate Art* exhibit traveled to the Dresden City Museum (Stadtmuseum), one entire gallery (the "Dresden Chamber of Horrors") was devoted to an arrangement of paintings that had earlier been confiscated from that museum. The Nazis singled out the long-since-fired museum director, Paul Ferdinand Schmidt, and accused him in the gallery's wall text of misspending the wages of the hard-working German people to purchase such "horror" and "trash." In this sense, the *Degenerate Art* exhibit might better be understood not only as a public censoring of individual works of art but more largely as "an assault on the museum and its power to consecrate works of art."[19] This better explains, perhaps, how the censorship of art in Nazi Germany could occur not by hiding the offensive images but rather by exhibiting them for all to see. The censored works are made impotent (and therefore safe for the museumgoer to look at) because they are exhibited in a *deconsecrated* "temple" of art, where the museum has been stripped of its cultural and moral authority – to be replaced by the power and authority of the National Socialist state. In the case of Nazi Germany it was the museum, even more than any single artist or work of art, which was being censored and portrayed as the enemy of the people.

Museum censorship during the Culture Wars

In the decades following the *Degenerate Art* exhibit, those seeking to censor museum exhibitions have generally aimed not to expose the banned art but instead to conceal or make invisible to the public images or ideas that were deemed subversive, illegal, pornographic, blasphemous, unpatriotic or corrupting. The unintended consequence of these censorship campaigns, however, has been to showcase what might otherwise have gone largely unnoticed. As Judith Butler explains:

> Certain kinds of efforts to restrict practices of representation in the hopes of reining in the imaginary, controlling the phantasmatic, end up reproducing and proliferating the phantasmatic in inadvertent ways, indeed, in ways that contradict the intended purposes of the restriction itself.[20]

Censorship, in this sense, almost inevitably brings greater exposure to the targeted artist, exhibition topic or museum. And, at least for the museum, with that "critical" fame come new questions about responsibility to core mission and how to handle the increased public attention which accompanies controversy.

Beginning in the late 1980s in the United States, Congress became actively involved in censoring selected artists and some of their exhibited works which were perceived to be attacks on the faith or the firmly held convictions of large numbers of individuals or whole communities. One of the earliest works to catch the attention of lawmakers was Andres Serrano's 1987 *Piss Christ*, a large-format photograph of a plastic crucifix submerged in a luminous bath containing the artist's urine. The image, which was punitively singled out and brought up for public inspection on the floor of the United States Congress, was denounced as blasphemous "garbage" and "trash." At stake was a debate on the appropriateness of using public government funding to subsidize a work of art (and then later to exhibit it in a museum gallery) that went against a majority viewpoint on morality and values of decency. Although not funded directly by federal appropriations, Andres Serrano had been awarded $15,000 for *Piss Christ* which was selected as a winner of the Southeastern Center for Contemporary Art's "Awards in the Visual Arts," a competition that was supported by a grant from the National Endowment for the Arts. Eventually, a host of conservative lawmakers, including the Republican Senator from North Carolina, Jesse Helms, rallied around the contentious photograph as a launching pad for a broader attack on the perceived liberalism of the National Endowment for the Arts and the complicity of American museums in exhibiting inappropriate or obscene art.

The censorship campaign that began in 1987 with *Piss Christ* reached a fever pitch just a few years later with an attack on photographer Robert Mapplethorpe's retrospective exhibition *The Perfect Moment*. After an enthusiastic reception at Philadelphia's Institute of Contemporary Art (which organized the exhibition) and the Museum of Contemporary Art in Chicago, the exhibit was scheduled to travel to Washington's Corcoran Gallery of Art on 1 July 1989. The targeting of Andres Serrano's photograph in 1987 had generated a much more systematic attack by a coalition of Christian groups and conservative elected officials waging war on government sponsorship of "obscene" art. Fearing negative publicity and the potential loss of federal appropriations, the Corcoran Gallery of Art cancelled the

Mapplethorpe exhibition three weeks before it was scheduled to open. The Corcoran's abrupt decision sparked a national debate (both within the museum community and in the broader art world) on censorship, public funding of the arts and the role of the museum in upholding First Amendment principles and the doctrine of free speech.

On 8 April 1990, *The Perfect Moment* opened at Cincinnati's Contemporary Arts Center. Those who sought to challenge the museum's decision to host an exhibit that included sexually explicit and homoerotic images chose Cincinnati (known for its conservative values and politics) as the city in which to take "a final stand." Seven of the photographs in the exhibition were deemed to be obscene by Cincinnati law enforcement officials. Five of the seven photographs depicted men in sadomasochistic poses; two of the photographs showed children with their genitals exposed. Both the Contemporary Arts Center and its director, Dennis Barrie, were tried on two counts – pandering obscenity and illegally displaying the images of nude children.[21] If convicted, the museum faced up to $10,000 in fines, and Dennis Barrie faced up to a year in jail and $2,000 in fines. At the trial, a number of expert witnesses, including the exhibit curator, Judith Kardon, were brought in by the defense to "explain" to the jury why the seven Mapplethorpe photographs which were on trial should not be classified as either child pornography or sadomasochistic pornography but rather that they should be understood purely as art. The notorious image of one man urinating into another's mouth was characterized by one defense witness "as a classical composition."[22] At the end of the trial, the jury determined that the works in question were "obscene"; however, they could not establish that the works had no artistic merit.[23] Dennis Barrie and the Contemporary Arts Center were thus acquitted on all charges.

Although the Mapplethorpe trial in Cincinnati was an important mandate for museums to uphold free expression – even under the most extreme pressure from organized interest groups and community outrage – it was a bittersweet victory for the image of museums in America. One of the unpredicted outcomes of the trial was that it served to further entrench the public's perception of museums as being out of touch with the general public and operating according to their own mandate as infallible arbiters of taste and adjudicators of cultural values. As Arthur Danto has suggested in his thoughtful reflections on the trial of Robert Mapplethorpe's photographs, the jurors were demoralized by the art-historical rhetoric and what they perceived to be the erudition of the defense expert witnesses. Under the spell of persuasive arguments made by a parade of credentialed art historians and museum curators, the jurors were bewildered and compelled to agree with these authorities that the images of "men with objects stuck in their anuses" were merely "figure studies." They were convinced by the experts not to trust their own (untrained) eyes – an insinuation that they would really never understand art. Danto concludes by saying, "It was testimony of a kind that created a gap between the populace and works of art – a gap that the NEA had been established to close."[24] So, in the end, victory for the Contemporary Arts Center in a Cincinnati courtroom reinforced a negative popular conception of the hierarchical authority of the museum – an institution perceived to possess unquestioned moral power and the unilateral right to determine what is "right" for the consumption of the museumgoing public.

From censorship to self-censorship

By the time both the Mapplethorpe controversy had unwound, and the exhibit had completed its national tour, the pundits had already predicted that one of the long-term impacts of the trial would be the start of a far more cautious environment within which curatorial decisions would be made. Controversy, in the future, would be avoided rather than embraced. In the film *Dirty Pictures*, a made-for-television docudrama chronicling the events surrounding the trial of *The Perfect Moment*, the character of Monty Lobb, Jr. (president of Citizens for Community Values and one of the leaders of the protest against the Contemporary Arts Center) explains, in the final moments of the film, the prosecution's "hidden" victory in the case against the museum:

> Our victory was won long before that trial; our verdict is in our power to bring prosecution. All across the country these days, people are much more careful about the kind of artworks they show in their museums and galleries. Nobody wants to come up against what Dennis Barrie went through. We sent that message out there.[25]

Artists and curators alike have indeed taken the pre-emptive measures of self-censorship in an attempt to avoid the legal and financial complications of litigious actions against museums and their staff. Many of these internal decisions – exhibition cancellations, the removal of specific objects or the editing of exhibition narratives to downplay or excise particular points of view – have often been controversial in their own right.

In the fall of 1999, for example, the newly appointed director of the Detroit Institute of Arts, British art historian Graham W.J. Beal, abruptly closed its exhibition *van Gogh's Ear* two days after it had opened to the public. The show, curated by Michigan artist Jef Bourgeau, was the first installment of a series of twelve one-week exhibits that were to highlight contemporary art of the past century. The exhibit was full of cliché shock art, including a pile of human excrement, a toy Jesus wearing a condom, a film of a woman taking a shower while menstruating, a jar of urine identified as that used by Andres Serrano to create *Piss Christ* and a Brazil nut held by industrial clamps under a magnifying glass accompanied by the label "Nigger Toe."[26] Having been previously unaware of the exhibit's content, museum director Beal (only two months into his new leadership position) justified his choice to shut down the exhibit "as an act of cultural stewardship, not censorship."[27]

Framing his decision as an issue of curatorial judgment, Beal noted in an interview that "the museum is always selecting works of art, and selection is not censorship." Artist/curator Bourgeau, however, interpreted the cancellation of his show as an act of museum self-censorship – since there were no cries for censorship coming from outside the museum, and two days into the show not a single public complaint had even been voiced against the content of the exhibition. "The show was closed and censored from the inside," said Bourgeau, "which is a new and disturbing twist for the art world."[28] And, along a similar vein, David Walsh, reporting for the World Socialist Web Site (www.wsws.org), accused Graham Beal of carrying out "a preemptive strike against the exhibit, as a means of demonstrating to potential right-wing critics and wealthy donors that the museum plans to do nothing to rock the cultural or intellectual boat. It was a shameful act."[29]

The case of the Detroit Institute of Arts' decision to retroactively cancel the show raises important questions about power and hierarchy in the museum's new role as community voice. Where does the power of self-censorship belong? Where are the boundaries of inclusiveness and free expression? Should the public always be allowed to makes its own decisions about the suitability or appropriateness of an exhibit's content? And how does the museum navigate as both arbiter of quality and taste, on the one hand, and neutral disseminator of knowledge and visual culture, on the other?

No sooner had the buzz died down about the censorship of *van Gogh's Ear*, the Detroit Institute of Arts opened its doors to the traveling international exhibition *van Gogh: Face to Face*, described in the press release as the "first comprehensive exhibition of portraits by one of the best-known painters in the history of art."[30] The news coverage had suddenly shifted from an intense moment of hand-wringing about the disenfranchisement of contemporary art and artists in Bourgeau's shuttered exhibit, to a frenzy of media hype surrounding the greatest art franchise of our day – the Post-Impressionist blockbuster show. The museum drew public attention from both exhibits. While *van Gogh's Ear* was seen by virtually nobody (but widely commented on in the press for its sudden disappearance), *van Gogh: Face to Face* attracted 315,000 visitors – the largest attendance in the museum's history.[31]

The two "van Gogh" exhibits which appeared (and, as it were, disappeared) back-to-back at the Detroit Institute of Arts offer interesting insight into the complexities and nuances of museum self-censorship. The controversial "van Gogh" exhibit was quickly roped off from public view because the newly appointed director feared public outrage from an exhibit that showcased intentionally challenging contemporary art meant to provoke its viewers. But one could argue that hidden within director Beal's decision to close *van Gogh's Ear* was also an awareness of the power of corporate sponsorship and the potential public revenue from *van Gogh: Face to Face* which was scheduled to open on the heels of Bourgeau's "offensive" show. In this sense, the museum was protecting its future income-generating populist blockbuster from any potential backlash or contamination caused by what it perceived as a low-revenue, marginal, intellectualist distraction.

The outrage with which the censorship of *van Gogh's Ear* was met by Bourgeau and others in both Detroit and the broader art world[32] was perhaps exacerbated by the fact that the censored "van Gogh" was followed immediately by a blockbuster "van Gogh." It was as though the museum was now in the business of administering to the public a carefully monitored regime of visual images that it deemed appropriate for public consumption. While the more challenging, push-button contemporary art was judged by the museum's "curatorial" standards to be too dangerous for the public to encounter, saccharine Post-Impressionist masterworks were considered palatable and safe. The public perception of the museum's hierarchical authority was underscored by the van Gogh blockbuster, in which risk-taking had been filtered out of the museum's mission in an effort to better control public reaction and community satisfaction.

From *Sensation* to *Lords of the Samurai*: censorship and the blockbuster

If we've learned one thing from the Culture Wars it is that controversy attracts attention, attention begets crowds and crowds bring euphoria, money and new audiences to museums. In the decade following the media frenzy surrounding *The Perfect Moment*, some museums sought to capitalize on the threat of censorship by purposely provoking their constituents through the exhibition of controversial images or divisive topics. Going against the prediction that the Mapplethorpe trial would inhibit museums from taking on risky topics and would temper their appetite for potentially offending one of their constituent groups, some museums chose to test community standards as a way of promoting their institution and attracting more visitors. In its newly discovered role as community irritant (rather than operating under the authority of its older image as community standard bearer), these museums hoped to generate new streams of revenue by transforming lackluster exhibitions into blockbuster shows. Perhaps the best-known example of this is the notoriously contentious exhibition *Sensation: Young British Artists from the Saatchi Collection*, held at the Brooklyn Museum of Art in late 1999.[33]

Drawn from advertising magnate Charles Saatchi's expansive collection of contemporary British art, the exhibition highlighted the work of some of the most provocative artists of this new generation. Included in the show were Damien Hirst's dead shark and a pig suspended in formaldehyde-filled glass cases; Jake and Dinos Chapman's fiberglass sculpture of naked little girls, some with penises instead of noses and anuses instead of mouths; Mark Quinn's self-portrait bust made from his own frozen blood; and Chris Ofili's painting *The Holy Virgin Mary* (1996) in which the central figure of a black Madonna is surrounded by floating "angels" made from porn magazine cutouts of women's genitalia, and to which the artist affixed a clump of shellacked elephant dung to her right breast. The Brooklyn Museum, Michael Kammen notes, marketed the exhibit as a kind of "freak" show, with a tongue-in-cheek warning label at the entrance that cautioned "the public that the exhibit might cause nausea, vomiting, and other forms of personal discomfort – hype virtually certain to attract people eager to test their own tolerance for terrible and disgusting sights."[34]

The museum's role as *agent provocateur* was a huge success. *Sensation* thrived on its own sensationalism, provoking a loudly trumpeted (but unsuccessful) legal battle spearheaded by New York City Mayor Rudolph Giuliani to censor and close the exhibition, to freeze museum funding and even to evict the museum from city-owned property. These issues have been dealt with extensively elsewhere,[35] but what is of interest here is how *Sensation* can be framed as an alternative model to the more conventional museum practice of generating increased turnstile revenue from the most middle-of-the-road exhibition – the blockbuster show. Normally, the blockbuster eschews controversial or provocative topics in favor of the most familiar, intellectually vacuous and crowd-pleasing subjects and genres – anything from Vermeer to Versace and from King Tut to Harley Davidson.[36] But *Sensation* turned this practice on its head by deliberately courting censorship and controversy with a kind of "bring 'em on" bravado. While there may be room to debate the professional ethics of the practice, the strategy was largely successful in drawing attention to a museum with dwindling attendance and attracting a new, socially engaged audience. *Sensation* helped the museum build exactly the kind of visitorship they wanted. Today, according to the *Washington Post*, the Brooklyn Museum has "the single youngest audience for a general fine arts museum in the country, and the most diverse."[37]

If the typical blockbuster exhibition lies at the opposite end of the spectrum from the exhibition of the radical and unorthodox, it can also be noted that, on occasion, the controversial and the conventional bump into each other, and, in the process, generate a new kind of dialogue that transcends the museum's voice and creates an alternative space for debate and learning. In order to examine this process, let us turn our attention for a moment to the Asian Art Museum in downtown San Francisco which, in June 2009, opened its doors to a heavily publicized blockbuster exhibit entitled *Lords of the Samurai*.[38] Described by the *San Francisco Sentinel* as "one of the most spectacular exhibits ever assembled by its distinguished curators," the exhibition featured over 160 objects of Samurai-related costume and material culture from the Hosokawa family collection and the Eisei-Bunko Museum in Tokyo.[39]

Although praised in the mainstream press, and widely touted as a must-see popular public attraction, the exhibition was not without critics. The museum was faulted for its overt appeal to crass commercialism – the Samurai helmet, for example, that was featured in the exhibition poster and billboards bore an uncanny resemblance to Darth Vader (of *Star Wars*), and the exhibition title itself was a not so thinly veiled allusion to both Michael Flatley's wildly successful stage show *Lord of the Dance* and J.R.R. Tolkien's equally popular *The Lord of the Rings*.[40] The museum also dispatched throughout the Bay Area a character dressed in full Samurai armor and regalia, handing out brochures and posing for photographs.

In addition to the general critiques of commercialism and accusations of surface-depth scholarship, the *Lords of the Samurai* was also targeted by an anonymous Bay Area "guerilla art collective" that engages in "cultural interventions" as a means of challenging the misrepresentation of Japanese culture. In response to this exhibition, the artist group created a parody web site (hosted on the domain www.asiansartmuseum.org) which was designed to look exactly like the official web site of the Asian Art Museum. On the parody site, the artists criticize the Asian Art Museum for perpetuating a stereotype of Samurai culture which glorifies violence, obscures the history of Japan's military imperialism and exoticizes Asian culture and identity by presenting the Samurai as cartoonish fantasy warriors and romanticized cultural Others.

In their intervention, the collective changed the original exhibition title to *Lord It's the Samurai: Myth, Militarism and Man–Boy Love*, and redesigned the iconic poster by transforming the central image of the Samurai's helmet into a Disney-like creature with Mickey Mouse ears. The parody also added a human nose to the warrior's helmet, alluding (as the hypertext link on the web site explains) to a sixteenth-century practice by Japanese invaders of Korea to cut off enemy noses and ship them back to Japan packed in salt. Behind the helmet, in the parody graphic, rises an atomic mushroom cloud, "insinuating a grim linkage between the samurai ethos, modern Japan's imperial hubris and America's ongoing effort to steer world affairs by military means."[41] A version of the modified poster was also printed as a rack card and distributed throughout the Bay Area.

In response to this provocation, the Asian Art Museum created a new section on its web site with the header "Invitation to a Discussion."[42] The museum's statement on the blog summarizes the key points of the artist group's intervention:

> The Asian Art Museum has recently been at the receiving end of some biting humor. An anonymous person (or persons), concealing identity through a privacy service, has created an imitation of the Asian Art Museum website ... While the fake website is humorous in tone, it has a serious intent. It amounts to a critique of the museum's *Lords of the Samurai* exhibition, which it suggests romanticizes the samurai and glamorizes militarism ... It also makes the more general accusation that the museum panders to orientalist fantasies and stereotypes in order to profit from them monetarily (we are a nonprofit organization).

The blog concludes by saying, "Unfortunately, because of their anonymity, we can't directly engage the authors of the fake website. So let's use this blog post to discuss issues of stereotyping and orientalizing." Although the discussion prompted by the blog was quite thoughtful and interesting, it generated only a scant twenty-two responses which were posted between 27 August and 27 September 2009. The intervention itself, however, went "viral" and received wide-ranging media and internet attention, including an article by the art critic of the *San Francisco Chronicle*, an interview on Pacifica Radio, discussion on two Japanese Studies listservs and an extensive exchange of ideas on at least six different blogs.

Several months after the exhibition closed at the Asian Art Museum, the artists who had constructed the web site parody submitted their work to a juried "College Night" art competition held at the de Young Museum in Golden Gate Park.[43] The piece they entered consisted of the documentation of their *Lord It's the Samurai* intervention, with a reproduction of their modified exhibit poster, samples of the rack cards that had been distributed, photocopies of the internet and press coverage and an audio track playing a recorded loop of their radio interview. Their work was accepted in the juried show, but, as the artists installed the piece on the evening of the opening, senior museum staff reportedly interrupted their installation and asked them to remove a large portion of the work. The museum's official position was that the artists were installing more than the jury had seen or accepted, and that it was inappropriate for the de Young Museum to be associated with a critique of a local "sister" institution, the Asian Art Museum.[44] Although the de Young never made a public statement on the incident, the case begs us to ask: what are the ethical responsibilities of one museum to another? Some observers interpreted the whole incident as a calculated provocation by the artists who, they thought, were actually hoping to be censored by the museum. As one writer noted in her comments on the response section of the parody web site, "I think congratulations are in order! The museums' responses were perfectly scripted – how did you manage that? It was like a Borat or Bruno moment where you set them up to act badly. You are a genius."[45]

Whether the artists were purposely courting censorship from the de Young Museum to enhance their point, or whether they simply wanted to present their critique of the Samurai blockbuster as a legitimate artistic intervention, the case illustrates (albeit rather imperfectly) how institutional critique can generate a new level of dialogue on serious issues of representation. The Asian Art Museum did indeed take the critique seriously enough to engage with the anonymous voice of their critics through a web site blog, and the discussion that was generated on the parody site (which was both in favor of the intervention and against it) offered an opportunity for an alternative voice and a more nuanced and complicated reading of *Lords of the Samurai*. Rather than picketing the steps of the museum and demanding that the exhibit be closed, the intervention was a productive contribution that enhanced the exhibition narrative. Like Yazmany Arboleda's *The Keller Gates Project* (2008), this work, too, was about opening up discussion. As one member of the Bay Area artist collective concluded, "We see the success of this action in the debates that have already taken place among folks who might not ordinarily question these kinds of things." In the end, of course, just like the fuss created around so many other museum controversies, the intervention stimulated public interest in the exhibition itself. "This makes me want to go to the Asian Art Museum," declared one respondent on the *San Francisco Chronicle*'s reader response page.[46]

Censorship as dialogue

In the past few decades, museums have sometimes mounted exhibitions of works of art that were considered by previous generations of museum-goers to be offensive or obscene. These exhibitions provide an opportunity for the visitor to understand judgments of taste and evaluations of community standards as historically contextualized phenomena that change or evolve through time. Among the most ambitious of such projects was the Brooklyn Museum of Art's 1990 exhibition *The Play of the Unmentionable*, an installation in the museum's Grand Lobby by conceptual artist Joseph Kosuth (see also Chapter 19).[47] The idea for the exhibition (which was itself funded by the National Endowment for the Arts) came as a direct response to the Culture Wars of the late 1980s and the government attacks on freedom of expression and artistic liberty.

Drawing on over a hundred objects from nearly every department of the Brooklyn Museum's permanent collection, the exhibition sought to showcase the triumph of art to survive (in the protective sanctuary of the museum) the vicissitudes of iconoclasm, racism, imperialism, and state censorship.[48] "Works that eventually come to be seen as masterpieces," Kosuth noted in an interview with Brooklyn Museum curator Charlotta Kotik, "do so precisely because they represented serious problems for their original audiences."[49] Using large-type quotations stenciled on the walls (a subtle reference, perhaps, to the defamatory slogans scrawled on the walls of the *Degenerate Art* show), the exhibit's narrative recounts a history of verbal and textual attacks upon the visual arts. In each case, the survival of the art, and its triumphant acceptance into the canon of great art, is attributed to the power of the museum to preserve works of art in spite of community outcry and demands for its removal or destruction. *The Play of the Unmentionable* sought to engage the museum visitor as an active agent in constructing an interpretation for the objects on view.[50] "Some people appear shocked that such things could ever appear in a museum," says Kosuth, "but my art has always tried to resist a position in which we're supposed to be passive consumers of culture ... The viewers complete the work. They're the other half of the making of meaning."[51]

Building on the kind of project Joseph Kosuth undertook in 1990, museums more recently have continued, in different ways, to use art censorship as a "teaching moment" to engage audiences with critical thinking about community values, the question of obscenity versus art and the role of museum in upholding ethical practices. In 2004, for example, the Newport Art Museum, in collaboration with the Blink Gallery in downtown Newport, mounted a joint exhibition of Rhode Island artist Umberto ("Bert") Crenca's oil paintings and charcoal drawings of monster-like hermaphroditic creatures with grotesquely deformed penises and ovaries. The exhibition, *Frenetic Engineering: Censored/Uncensored*, included works by Crenca that the artist calls "post-apocalyptic, genetically reengineered figurative images."[52] Both sexually explicit and graphically disturbing, these pieces, as Crenca describes them, are "ruminations on the de-evolution of the human species," inspired because he "started to see people as inside-out, with psychology of the human becoming distorted. The figure inside is a little different from the figure outside."[53] Or, put slightly differently, the figures are intended to capture Crenca's idea that "We're kind of fucked up."[54]

Having agreed to show Crenca's work at the Newport Art Museum, curator Nancy Whipple Grinnell became uneasy when she laid eyes on some of the more outrageous images of monstrous erections and misshapen genitals that were to be included in the show. "We're a family-oriented, community-oriented museum," said Grinnell, "and we have a number of audiences to please and don't want to do something that some would find offensive."[55] Although she deemed some of the images "inappropriate for a museum setting," Grinnell wanted to find a workable compromise with the artist. The agreement reached between Grinnell and Crenca was that the museum would show full-sized giclée digital reproductions of the paintings and drawings with the "blush-inducing appendages pixilated out" while the Blink Gallery would show the unaltered originals.[56] Grants from two Rhode Island foundations footed the bill of $14,000 to pay for the cost of reproductions and mounting. In addition, the exhibition featured a video documenting the process of arranging this exhibition of "controversial" material, and the museum hosted a panel discussion entitled "What is Offensive? Freedom of Expression in Museums and Galleries," in which Grinnell and Crenca, among others, participated. Thus the initial impulse toward censorship was transformed collaboratively by both artist and curator into a "teaching moment," and an opportunity for community reflection and discussion on the ethical complexities of exhibiting contemporary art. "We want to carry the dialogue about censorship forward," said Grinnell in the museum's press release, "by providing a forum for interaction between members of the public, artists and intellectuals who write and speak about the issue."[57]

As part of this trend toward engaging museum censorship as a topic of discussion, other exhibitions have been organized specifically to encourage audience reflection on issues of freedom of expression. A traveling installation entitled *Exposing the Censor Within* invites people into a "confessional" booth where they are asked to write their story about self-censorship on an index card. Inside the booth, visitors are posed a series of questions: "Were there times you were afraid to speak up?" "Have you changed what you've written for fear it would get you into trouble?" or "Have you ever stopped yourself from saying something because you thought it might be rude or insulting?" and "Are you glad you stopped yourself?" The completed cards, without author attribution, are then "processed into site-specific poster portraits of self-censorship." The exhibition was first installed at the San Mateo County History Museum in April 2007, and then traveled to the Redwood City Library in March 2007, and eventually to the College Art Association annual conference in Dallas in February 2008. The self-censorship stories that were gathered on the index cards and exhibited in the poster installations are published on line at the web site of the National Coalition Against Censorship.[58] The web site also continues to accept new self-censorship stories which can be posted anonymously to the site, and a version of the exhibit can also be found in the 3D virtual world of Second Life.[59]

Finally, some museums and galleries have tried to engage with censorship by opening up a dialogue that mocks prudishness and openly questions the very nature of moral indignation. A recent exhibition of "fine art nudes and erotica," entitled *Censored*, at the artDC gallery in Hyattsville, Maryland, sought to challenge the taboo nature of human nudity and sexuality through irony and humor. "Our intention," says exhibition organizer Renee Azcra Woodward, "is to poke fun at the long-running practice of moral and social censorship of art by covering any visible genitalia in each work with 'post-it' notes." Visitors, she goes on to say, "will of course be encouraged to take a sneak peak at what's going on underneath the notes."[60] The exhibition, which was intended to draw attention to the "lack of erotic art shows" in the DC area, also offered a "witty approach to a very serious subject."[61] In the end, of course, it is hard to assess the didactic impact of such a project, but the organizers did conclude that "there were more lower 'post-its' peeled back than tops."[62]

What all these exhibits/projects point to (*The Play of the Unmentionable*; *Frenetic Engineering: Censored/Uncensored*; *The Censor Within*; and artDC's *Censored*) is that censorship itself can shift from a dangerous and taboo topic that should be avoided at all cost to a subject of inquiry that, when broached directly, poses instructive challenges and compelling questions for all participants in the museum world – museum administrators, curators, artists and the general public. Museums involved in these sorts of dialogues acknowledge that censorship (and self-censorship) exists all around us in contexts or instances we might not always be aware of. By focusing on censorship as a form of negotiation in which different interests are weighed and measured, the museum or gallery moves beyond a monolithic view of censorship as something imposed from "above" to a multi-dimensional view of censorship as a mediated process which can be explored objectively and even sometimes woven into an exhibition and its narrative framework.

Censorship in an age of shared authority

A recent article by Philip Kennicott, culture critic for *The Washington Post*, points out that since 2001 American museums have been the subject of far fewer controversies and censorship debacles than during the Culture Wars of the 1980s and 1990s. "Over the past decade, small controversies occasionally unsettled the museum world, but they went away quickly, and few gained enough traction to become national issues."[63] The author goes on to ask how one explains the decline in public outrage against museums in the first decade of the new century:

What happened? Was it a cultural or historic change? Self-censorship or a more subtle shift in what museums were exhibiting? Did audiences grow up, or were they just inured to radical art and provocative historical revision?[64]

The answer, according to Kennicott's article, can be found in a blend of several elements. In part, the audience has been desensitized to inflammatory issues by the internet, the media and, in particular, cable television which lowered the bar for what was considered obscene or outrageous. In part, the events of 9/11 deflected attention away from a symbolic Culture War against an internal enemy to the "War on Terror," a real military operation against a new common (and external) enemy. In part, the museum controversies of the 1980s and 1990s have now shifted to other venues – debates over monuments and memorials such as the contentious rebuilding of the World Trade Center site. But the final reason offered by Philip Kennicott for the decline in public outrage against museums is perhaps the most compelling. He suggests that museums have responded to a younger and more diverse generation of museum audiences by breaking down the hierarchical authority of the traditional museum and opening up a space for dialogue and exchange that takes place both within the museum itself and on the internet. "Museums have become more open forums ... New museums specialize in groups and topics that were not always well served by established institutions, and the grand old museums that once dictated much of the cultural dialogue have become more attentive and diverse in what they present."[65] This new opportunity for exchange, one could argue, deflects public dissatisfaction with any given museum decision about what to exhibit or not to exhibit – and thereby short-circuits cries for censorship before they can even take root.

In her 2010 book *The Participatory Museum*, Nina Simon lays out a new paradigm for both individual and community engagement within the framework of a shared authority in contemporary museum culture.[66] Drawing on the concept of a museum as audience-centered institution (i.e., John Cotton Dana, Elaine Heumann Gurian and Stephen Weil) and the notion that visitors construct their own meaning (i.e., George Hein, John Falk and Lynn Dierking), Simon presents a new, dynamic model of participation in which museums enable visitor dialogue (both amongst themselves and with the museum staff) and create the necessary framework for communities of meaning to come together and generate their own agenda. Much of the participation that Simon highlights (and anticipates) occurs as a result of specific steps taken by the museum with interactive design techniques and new strategies of engagement that promote visitor learning, recreation and exploration. The participatory museum is a "place where people are invited on an ongoing basis to contribute, to collaborate, to co-create, and to co-opt the experiences and content in a designed, intentional environment."[67]

The principle of participation is not only an effective way to promote knowledge formation and visitor engagement, it also presents new possibilities for thinking about censorship and self-censorship in the museum. How might the model of the participatory museum – with its emphasis on shared authority and institutional transparency – deal with the threat or potential of censorship more effectively than an older, hierarchal model of the museum – with its emphasis on academic and intellectual authority and its aversion toward transparency and the unencumbered sharing of information about management and operational details? Museum censorship in the United States escalated into a national frenzy at the height of the Culture Wars in the 1980s and 1990s when institutional authority was still an important mandate in the construction of knowledge and values in museums. Many of the most vitriolic censorship battles in that period were caused by the perception held by outsiders (whether they be politicians, religious or civic leaders or community activists) that the museum was an arrogant institution profoundly out of touch with its constituents and its community of visitors. In an op-ed piece published by the *Cincinnati Enquirer* following the trial of *The Perfect Moment*, Monty Lobb, Jr., president of Cincinnati Citizens for Community Values, captures the spirit of the public's attitude toward the hierarchical authority of the museum:

> The Contemporary Arts Center (CAC) sanctimoniously acts as if I and everyone else must silently accept their every artistic fling without public or private comment or criticism. What's more, they expect me to pay for it, or at least part of it. With all the demagoguery about free speech, rights and "censorship," somewhere on the way to the art show CAC forgot my rights.[68]

By opening up a dialogue and engaging its dissenters (as did the Asian Art Museum in San Francisco against its charges of racism and cultural misrepresentation), museums can weave a chorus of disapproval into the very fabric of an exhibition's narrative and its didactic goals.[69] The complexities and contradictions that are often glossed over in the blockbuster exhibition can become a platform for discussion in other exhibits to which public interest would be drawn not because these issues are easily palatable but, on the contrary, because they offer food for critical thought.

Museum censorship and time

Museum censorship can take many forms – from overt, restrictive government actions to block the exhibition of certain images or ideas, to the most subtle and covert forms of manipulation, alteration or self-editing. In almost all cases, however, what has been banned or subjected to censorship generally survives the incident and reappears years (or even generations) later to tell a different story – a story about values and morality in a different time; a story about the capacity of museums to protect what is controversial so that it can be reassessed with the wisdom of hindsight. Consider the fact that in 1938 the Reich Chamber of Visual Arts confiscated from the New State Gallery (Neue Staatsgalerie) in Munich Vincent van Gogh's *Self-portrait* of 1888; the canvas was then sold at auction in 1939, along with hundreds of other works, in order to cleanse Germany of its "degenerate" art and to finance the Nazi war machine. In 2000, the very same picture was showcased at the Detroit Institute of Arts in its blockbuster exhibition *van Gogh: Face to Face*, where it now stood as a symbol not of deviance but of normative splendor. In the sixty years that had elapsed since its confiscation in Munich the very same painting had been transformed from a target of state censorship to a celebrated icon of the art-historical canon. The popularity of van Gogh's self-portrait today stands in sharp contrast to the controversial contemporary works of art from *van Gogh's Ear* – an exhibition that had been censored just months before by the same institution in which the infamous self-portrait now hung.[70]

Seeing the van Gogh painting, few visitors to the Detroit Institute of Arts would have likely connected the image to its history of censorship under the regime of the Third Reich. But what about images from the more recent past whose legacies of censorship are better known? Would it not be difficult today to look at the photographs of Robert Mapplethorpe without associating them with their censorship in the early 1990s? Does censorship become part of an image's permanent identity? And, if so, what is the responsibility of the museum to either preserve this aspect of an object's past or to rehabilitate it to its original context and its "untainted" meaning? Writing about his first "innocent" experience in seeing the Mapplethorpe photographs at the Whitney Museum of American Art before the censorship controversy erupted, Arthur Danto laments, "It is a matter of some sadness to me that no one, ever again, will be able to see Mapplethorpe's work in that way."[71]

In the heat of the moment many censorship debates generate more sparks than light. These sporadic episodes of collective outrage often fail to enlighten us immediately about the broader nature of taste and values in society or about the role (and limits) of a museum to represent its constituents and their different points of view. The challenge for museums today, then, is to find a balance between their institutional mission to educate broadly a diverse and engaged museum audience and to better deal with the occasional and unexpected outbursts of community outrage that sometimes provoke cries for censorship. Rather than trying to avoid controversy altogether, or engage in the kind of self-censorship that dampens the palette of intellectual discourse, museums need to find creative ways to connect with audiences about issues of censorship and to better explore the range of judgments of taste and value that coexist in diverse communities. Taking a page from Yazmany Arboleda's *The Keller Gates Project*, museums might sometimes need to engage directly with censorship itself by preparing their audience to better understand it by making it the subject of their discourse, rather than being engaged by censorship when they least expect it as unprepared subjects of public outrage.

Notes

1 Museum censorship is a vast and complicated topic, the scope of which far exceeds the limitations of space for this chapter. This chapter highlights representative case studies as a way to suggest some of the intellectual and ethical issues involved in museum censorship, both in the past and present. For further research on this topic, and to keep up with the most current cases of museum censorship, I would suggest the following web sites: National Coalition Against Censorship and The File Room, which maintains a virtual archive of censorship cases from around the world. Online. Available HTTP: http://www.ncac.org (accessed 12 May 2010); http://www.thefileroom.org (accessed 12 May 2010). One of the most comprehensive books on the history of censorship in general is D. Jones (ed.), *Censorship: A World Encyclopedia*, Chicago: Fitzroy Dearborn, 2001. For an excellent discussion of the history of museum controversies (including cases of censorship) see S. C. Dubin, *Displays of Power: Controversy in the American Museum from the* Enola Gay *to Sensation*, New York: New York University Press, 1999. And for a history of censorship in the arts,

see E. C. Childs (ed.) *Suspended License: Censorship and the Visual Arts*, Seattle, WA: University of Washington Press, 1997.

2 T. Hoving, interview with Terry Gross, *Fresh Air*, National Public Radio, 1993. Reprint of original transcript on 11 December 2009. Online. Available HTTP: http://www.npr.mobi/templates/transcript/transcript.php?storyId=121335708 (accessed 10 February 2010).

3 Arboleda credits his inspiration for the storefront venue to Richard Prince's 1983 installation of *Spiritual America* (a semi-pornographic nude image of ten-year-old child star Brooke Shields, which Prince had rephotographed) in a rented storefront at 5 Rivington Street in lower Manhattan. See A. M. Gingera, *Richard Prince's Second House*, Parkett 72, 2005, p. 116. Online. Available HTTP: http://www.parkettart.com/library/72/pdf/prince.pdf (accessed 16 May 2010).

4 S. Chan, "'Assassination' Artist is Questioned and Released," *New York Times*, 4 June 2008. Online. Available HTTP: http://cityroom.blogs.nytimes.com/2008/06/04/police-shut-down-assassination-art-exhibition/ (accessed 15 May 2010).

5 It is unclear whether the artist also intended the exhibitions as a kind of word-play on George Bernard Shaw's famous quip, "Assassination is the extreme form of censorship."

6 This is a reference to shock-jock Don Imus's controversial comment in which he described (during his radio broadcast on 4 April 2007) some of the players on the Rutgers University women's basketball team as "rough girls" and "nappy headed hos." After receiving sharp criticism from the NCAA and activist Reverend Al Sharpton, CBS Radio canceled *Imus in the Morning* and heeded the requests of protesters to fire its host, Don Imus. See D. Carr, "Networks Condemn Remarks by Imus," *New York Times*, 7 April 2007. Online. Available HTTP: http://query.nytimes.com/gst/fullpage.html?res=9A07E4D8173FF934A35757C0A9619C8B63&scp=4&sq=imus+nappy&st=nyt (accessed 15 May 2010).

7 D. Segal, "A Young Artist who Mostly Draws Attention," *Washington Post*, Style section, 6 June 2008, p. 1. Online. Available HTTP: http://www.washingtonpost.com/wp-dyn/content/article/2008/06/05/AR2008060504056.html (accessed 16 May 2010).

8 J. Lee "'Assassination' Artist's Trail of Deception," *New York Times*. 5 June 2008. Online. Available HTTP: http://cityroom.blogs.nytimes.com/2008/06/05/assassination-artists-trail-of-deception/ (accessed 16 May 2010).

9 The "piece" consisted of domain names purchased for the fictitious galleries http://www.naomigatesgallery.com and http://www.leahkellergallery.com, as well as websites for the two fictitious exhibitions in which Arboleda inserted digital images of his own art into photographs he had taken of real gallery spaces http://www.theassassinationofbarack-obama.com and http://www.theassassinationofhillaryclinton.com. The so-called exhibitions neither existed in the fictitious galleries, nor were they ever installed in the rented store-front venue. All that ever existed of the exhibits were the fake installation shots on the web sites and the provocative titles that were stenciled on the storefront window. Had the authorities not intervened to demand the removal of the word "assassination" from the exhibit titles, it is unclear from the reporting on the case whether Arboleda actually had any "real" objects to install in the show, or whether everything existed simply as digital imagery that were inserted into the photographs posted on the project web sites.

10 S. Duclos, "Op-ed: Artwork calling Barack Obama's Children 'Nappy Headed Hos' is Offensive," *Digital Journal*, 13 June 2008. Online. Available HTTP: www.digitaljournal.com/article/256083 (accessed 15 April 2010).

11 Reader response to S. Chan, "'Assassination' Artist is Questioned and Released," *New York Times*, 4 June 2008. Posted 4 June 2008 by "chutney28." Online. Available HTTP: http://cityroom.blogs.nytimes.com/2008/06/04/police-shut-down-assassination-art-exhibition/#comment-66871 (accessed 15 May 2010).

12 Reader response to Duclos, "Op-ed: Artwork calling Barack Obama's Children 'Nappy Headed Hos' is Offensive." Posted 14 June 2008 by "666divine." Online. Available HTTP: http://www.digitaljournal.com/article/256083 (accessed 15 May 2010).

13 Lee, "'Assassination' Artist's Trail of Deception."

14 Y. Arboleda, "The Art Offends," *Huffington Post Online*, 29 June 2008. Online. Available HTTP: http://www.huffingtonpost.com/yazmany-arboleda/the-art-offends_b_108281.html (accessed 15 April 2010).

15 S. Barron, *"Degenerate Art": The Fate of the Avant-garde in Nazi Germany*, New York: Abrams, 1991.

16 For an excellent discussion of the *Degenerate Art* exhibition, see C. Zuschlag, "'Chambers of Horror' and 'Degenerate Art': On Censorship in the Visual Arts in Nazi Germany," in Childs *Suspended License*, pp. 210–234.

17 N. Levi, "'Judge for yourselves!' The *Degenerate Art* exhibition as political spectacle," *October* 85, 1998, p. 41.

18 This idea of the "good" museum and the "evil" museum is based in part on a discussion of related issues by Elaine Heumann Gurian. See E. H. Gurian, *Civilizing the Museum: The Collected Writings of Elaine Heumann Gurian*, New York: Routledge, 2006, p. 7.

19 Levi, "'Judge for yourselves!'" p. 57.

20 J. Butler, "The Force of Fantasy: Feminism, Mapplethorpe, and Discursive Excess," *Differences* 2: 2, 1990, p. 108. Quoted in R. Meyer, "The Jesse Helms Theory of Art," *October* 104, 2003, p. 134.

21 I. Wilkerson, "Cincinnati Jury Acquits Museum in Mapplethorpe Obscenity Case," *New York Times*, 6 October 1990. Online. Available HTTP: http://www.nytimes.com/1990/10/06/us/cincinnati-jury-acquits-museum-in-mapplethorpe-obscenity-case.html (accessed 15 May 2010).

22 A. Danto, "Censorship and Subsidy in the Arts," *Bulletin of the American Academy of Arts and Sciences* 47: 1, 1993, p. 38.

23 Institute of Contemporary Art, Philadelphia, "Imperfect Moments: Mapplethorpe and Censorship Twenty Years Later," news release, February 2009. Online. Available HTTP: http://www.icaphila.org/news/pdf/mapplethorpe_pr.pdf (accessed 5 May 2010).

24 Danto, "Censorship and Subsidy in the Arts," p. 38.

25 *Dirty Pictures*, Frank Pierson (dir.), MGM Television, 2000.

26 C. Abe, "Creating a Sensation in American Museum: Art until Now, van Gogh's Ear." Online. Available HTTP: http://jefbourgeau.com/Jane_Speaks%20/creating_a_sensation.htm (accessed 5 May 2010); R. Meredith, "Another Art Battle, as Detroit Museum Closes an Exhibit Early," *New York Times*, 23 November 1999. Online. Available HTTP: http://www.nytimes.com/1999/11/23/us/another-art-battle-as-detroit-museum-closes-an-exhibit-early.html (accessed 5 May 2010).

27 K. Kersten, "An Act not of Censorship but of Stewardship," *Star Tribune*, 8 December 1999. Online. Available HTTP: http://www.americanexperiment.org/publications/1999/19991208kersten.php (accessed 15 May 2010).

28 Quoted in R. Meredith, "Another Art Battle."

29 D. Walsh "Detroit Museum Controversy: Censored Artist defends his Exhibit," 10 December 1999. Online. Available HTTP: http://www.wsws.org/articles/1999/dec1999/dia-d10.shtml (accessed 15 May 2010).

30 Press release, *van Gogh: Face to Face*, 2000–01. Online. Available HTTP: http://philadelphia.about.com/library/weekly/blvangoghpressrelease.htm (accessed 16 May 2010).

31 Detroit Institute of Arts web site, "Museum, Attendance." Online. Available HTTP: http://www.dia.org/about/facts.aspx (accessed 10 May 2010).

32 J. Bourgeau, transcript of interview with K. Paulson, *Speaking Freely*, PBS television, 12 September 2000. Online. Available HTTP: http://www.firstamendmentcenter.org/about.aspx?id=13503 (accessed 10 May 2010).

33 *Sensation: Young British Artists from the Saatchi Collection*, Brooklyn Museum of Art, 2 October 1999–9 January 2000.

34 M. Kammen, *Visual Shock: A History of Art Controversies in American Culture*, New York: Knopf, 2006, p. 294.

35 The exhibition produced a barrage of publications analyzing almost every aspect of the controversy. Some of this literature has been pulled together in L. Rothfield (ed.), *Unsettling "Sensation": Arts Policy Lessons from the Brooklyn Museum of Art Controversy*, New Brunswick, NJ: Rutgers University Press, 2001. Also, see C. Becker, *Surpassing the Spectacle: Global Transformations and the Changing Politics of Art*, Lanham, MD: Rowman & Littlefield, 2002, pp. 43–58; Dubin, *Displays of Power*, pp. 246–76; A. Fraser, "A 'Sensation' Chronicle," *Social Text*, No. 67, 2001, pp. 127–56.

36 R. E. Spear, "Editorial. Art History and the 'Blockbuster' Exhibition," *Art Bulletin* 68: 3, 1986, pp. 358–59.
37 P. Kennicott "After an Age of Rage, Museums have Mastered the Display of Commotional Restraint," *Washington Post*, 31 May 2009. Online. Available HTTP: http://www.washingtonpost.com/wp-dyn/content/article/2009/05/28/AR2009052804119.html (accessed 14 May 2010).
38 Asian Art Museum web site, "Lords of the Samuraí." Online. Available HTTP: http://www.asianart.org/Samurai.htm (accessed 14 May 2010).
39 S. Martinfield, "Exhibition Explores the Many Sides of Famed Japanese Warrior Elite," *San Francisco Sentinel*, 12 June 2009. Online. Available HTTP: http://www.sanfranciscosentinel.com/?p=30916 (accessed 17 May 2010).
40 Asians Art Museum web site. Online. Available HTTP: http://asiansart.wordpress.com/2009/09/03/a-museum-curators-response/ (accessed 14 May 2010).
41 K. Baker, "Samurai Parody takes Jab at Asian Art Museum," *San Francisco Chronicle*, 22 September 2009. Online. Available HTTP: http://www.sfgate.com/cgi-bin/article.cgi?f=/c/a/2009/09/21/DDID19O60Q.DTL (accessed 10 May 2010).
42 Asian Art Museum blog, "Invitation to a Discussion," 27 August 2009. Online. Available HTTP: http://www.asianart.org/blog/index.php/2009/08/27/invitation-to-a-discussion/ (accessed 14 May 2010).
43 Asians Art Museum web site, Online. Available HTTP: http://asiansart.wordpress.com/2009/11/23/censored-by-de-young-museum/#comment-79 (accessed 14 May 2010).
44 This account of the events surrounding the de Young's alleged censoring of the asiansartmuseum.org collective is based on reporting provided by the artists themselves on their web site. There is no publicly available account of the incident from the de Young Museum staff. See "Censored by de Young Museum." Online. Available HTTP: http://asiansart.wordpress.com/2009/11/23/censored-by-de-young-museum/ (accessed 14 May 2010).
45 Asians Art Museum, "Censored by de Young," 23 November 2009. Online. Available HTTP: http://asiansart.wordpress.com/2009/11/23/censored-by-de-young-museum/ (accessed 17 May 2010).
46 Reader comment by "jonvn" on K. Baker, "Samurai Parody takes Jab at Asian Art Museum," 22 September 2009. Online. Available HTTP: http://www.sfgate.com/cgi-bin/article/comments/view?f=/c/a/2009/09/21/DDID19O60Q.DTL&plckFindCommentKey=CommentKey:584df82a-f45a-46bb-b872-baa162357e2e (accessed 17 May 2010).
47 *The Brooklyn Museum Collection: The Play of the Unmentionable*, curated by Joseph Kosuth. Brooklyn Museum of Art, 27 September–31 December 1990.
48 R. Smith, "Art View: 'Unmentionable' Art through the Ages," *New York Times*, 11 November 1990. Online. Available HTTP: http://www.nytimes.com/1990/11/11/arts/art-view-unmentionable-art-through-the-ages.html (accessed 15 May 2010).
49 D. Freedberg, *The Play of the Unmentionable: An Installation by Joseph Kosuth at the Brooklyn Museum*, New York: New Press in association with Brooklyn Museum, 1992, p. 26.
50 G. Glueck, "At Brooklyn Museum, an Artist surveys the Objectionable," *New York Times*, 17 December 1990. Online. Available HTTP: http://www.nytimes.com/1990/12/17/arts/at-brooklyn-museum-an-artist-surveys-the-objectionable.html?pagewanted=all (accessed 15 May 2010).
51 Freedberg, *The Play of the Unmentionable*, p. 28.
52 Newport Art Museum, "New Show at Newport Art Museum enters Discourse on Censorship in the Arts," April 2004. My thanks to Nancy Whipple Grinnell for providing me with a copy of the exhibition's press release.
53 Quoted in J. Margolis, "The Education of Umberto Crenca," *Democratic Vistas Profiles*, No. 1, Chicago: Center for Art Policy, Columbia College Chicago, n.d., p. 2. Online. Available HTTP: http://www.colum.edu/administrative_offices/Academic_Research/PDF_folder/umberto_crenca.pdf (accessed 15 April 2010).
54 Quoted in ibid., p. 2.
55 Quoted in ibid., pp. 1–2.
56 B. Rodriguez, "Bridging the Gap: Umberto Crenca's Frenetic Engineering: Censored/Uncensored," *Providence Phoenix*, 14–20 May 2004. Online. Available HTTP: http://www.

providencephoenix.com/art/other_stories/documents/03861260.asp (accessed 24 March 2010).

57 Newport Art Museum, "New Show at Newport Art Museum Enters Discourse on Censorship in the Arts," April 2004.

58 National Coalition Against Censorship, "Exposing the Censor Within." Online. Available HTTP: http://www.ncac.org/censorwithin (accessed 16 May 2010).

59 Second Life web site. Online. Available HTTP: http://slurl.com/secondlife/Commonwealth%20Island/104/81/30 (accessed 15 May 2010).

60 *Censored*, blog posted 9 March 2010. Online. Available HTTP: http://artdc.com/ (accessed 15 May 2010).

61 J. Cohen, "*Censored*," discussion forum, artdc.org, 13 March 2010. Online. Available HTTP: http://artdc.org/forum/index.php?topic=13381.0 (accessed 15 May 2010).

62 Ibid.

63 P. Kennicott, "After an Age of Rage."

64 Ibid.

65 Ibid.

66 N. Simon, *The Participatory Museum*, Santa Cruz, CA: Museum 2.0, 2010. Online. Available HTTP: http://www.participatorymuseum.org/read/ (accessed 24 May 2010).

67 Ibid, p. 350.

68 M. Lobb, Jr., "The Side of Virtue and Dignity," *Cincinnati Enquirer*, 30 March 1990. Reprinted in R. Bolton (ed.), *Culture Wars: Documents from the Recent Controversies in the Arts*, New York: New Press, 1992, pp. 161–62.

69 Cf. L. Bunch, "Embracing Controversy: Museum Exhibitions and the Politics of Change," *Public Historian* 14: 3, 1992, pp. 63–65.

70 It is also perhaps worth noting here that the Detroit Institute of Arts was the first U.S. museum to purchase a van Gogh canvas – his *Self-portrait* of 1887, which was acquired by the museum in January 1922. Detroit Institute of Arts web site, "The Cultural Gem of Detroit." Online. Available HTTP: http://www.dia.org/about/history.aspx (accessed 4 August 2010).

71 Danto, "Censorship and Subsidy in the Arts," p. 37. Both Kennicott's article and this chapter were written before the Smithsonian's National Portrait Gallery removed (in November 2010) David Wojnarowicz's video *A Fire in My Belly* (1986–87) from the exhibition *Hide/Seek: Difference and Desire in American Portraiture*. The video, which contains a brief scene depicting ants crawling on a crucifix, was taken off display after demands for its censorship from both the Catholic League and Republican leadership in the United States Congress. That decision, made by Smithsonian Secretary G. Wayne Clough, set off demonstrations, panel discussions and Internet debates about censorship in the arts and the relationship between exhibition content and federal funding at the Smithsonian. Protesters set up on the street outside the south entrance of The National Portrait Gallery "The Museum of Censored Art" – a mobile office trailer bearing the sign "Showing the art the Smithsonian won't." A web site for the museum was also created. Online. Available HTTP: http://dontcensor.us/ (accessed 4 March 2011).

25

Ethics of confrontational drama in museums

Bjarne Sode Funch

The individual with an interest in interactivity and challenging experiences has come into focus in contemporary Western culture. In order to address those interests new educational strategies have been developed for museum education. Confrontational drama is one of those strategies that provides the individual with an extraordinary learning experience. "It was a horrifying experience but it was great," a visitor explained after participating in a program of confrontational drama.

The Danish philosopher Søren Kierkegaard once wrote, "If one is truly to succeed in leading a person to a specific place, one must first and foremost take care to find him where *he* is and begin there."[1] This might seem obvious to anyone concerned with education, but what did Kierkegaard actually mean? Finding a person where he or she is, is not as simple as it sounds. Being existentially present is not only a question of being totally attentive to the moment, but also to be present as an individual with one's personal history. Therefore, effective teaching is a question of directing the learner's full attention to the subject matter, and, at the same time, providing a challenge that makes existential growth possible – in other words, engaging the learner in concordance with his or her life experiences. Both requirements are difficult to accommodate within museum education because, even with reliable audience research, it is uncertain who the audience will be and why they are visiting the museum. People who are best served by museums are those who know exactly why they are visiting the museum in question; they are motivated and have a clear purpose for their visit. Most people visit a museum as a leisure activity, or they are tourists, or their visit is part of education. These people usually have no specific aims, and it is up to the museum to engage them. But it is still uncertain if their engagement contributes to existential growth.

Classical museum education

Presentation of original objects is the fundamental strategy of classical museum education. This strategy springs from the museum's obligation to collect and exhibit objects that represent a specific period of history, within a specific domain of human life. Museum professionals are appointed to select those objects that illuminate the area in focus, and the objects are points of departure for telling stories about people in former times, in other cultures and/or in one's own society: how they made a living, how they organized their society, what their conflicts were, as well as what were their values, inventions, rituals, aesthetics, and so forth, and, finally, revealing the nature that makes contemporary life possible. Museums not only preserve those original objects that illuminate human culture, they also exhibit and present these objects to audiences in order to make cultural heritage an asset for life in the here and now.

The educational importance of original objects is based on human reception in which sensation is crucial for conception and understanding of the object and its function in the culture where it belonged. In other words, sensory perception of the original object provides unique conditions for new interpretations because the viewer brings to the experience details that have emotional resonance. Presenting original objects in the museum provides audiences with an option to become familiar with those objects and to carry out their own interpretations. Their reception is not limited to interpretations carried out by communicators and educators.[2]

Original objects are not only fundamental to classical museum education they also make museum education exceptional in comparison to most education in general. However, objects cannot be exhibited without a context. They are exhibited together with other objects, they are classified and organized, and, more often than not, they are accompanied by labels with facts about origin, wall texts with interpretive information and contextual materials such as drawings, videos and photographs.

The defining characteristic of classical museum education is *presentation*. Objects and their interpretive materials are presented to the audience. Exhibitions are traditionally fixed and the audience perceives and receives without being able to interact. Exhibitions are typically characterized by being so called one-way communication.

Classical museum exhibitions may be well documented, thoughtful and beautifully laid out, and may include exceptional objects and scholarship, but they are only engaging to people who already are focused on the topic in question and those who make an effort to become interested. Going back to Kierkegaard's statement, it is only on rare occasions that a classically conceived exhibition offers visitor-centered points of entry and even more seldom provides a personal and existential challenge. On such rare occasions when a visitor becomes existentially engaged, museum presentations are often more profound than any other kind of education because of access to original objects.[3]

Contemporary museum education

Contemporary museum education is characterized by *interactivity*. Objects are no longer just presented within contextual frames, but the audience is invited to interact when they visit a museum exhibition. New technology has made it possible to involve the museum audience in activities and to provide options for learners to choose topics of interest, to produce content and to take part in virtual realities, among other pursuits.[4] Professional museum educators have become prominent members of the museum staff, and, unlike museum curators, who typically work behind the scenes and are invisible to visitors, museum educators are in plain sight and take pride in involving visitors in educational activities.

The strength of contemporary museum education is interactivity, which is not only a result of new technology and the professionalization of museum educators, but also a shift in educational philosophy. Today, it is well known that passive one-way communication is an inefficient educational strategy. The more a person is mentally and physically involved and participates in interactions with other people during an educational process, the more profound the learning experience is. In light of Kierkegaard's statement, museum education today is characterized by offering a diverse range of visitor-centered free-choice learning opportunities that may ignite interest. In other words, ideally, contemporary museum education creates a state of involvement that meets the principle of full attention during the teaching process. However, it is still questionable if the new museum education meets the principle of existential engagement and growth, because the aim of museum education is, as it has always been, to teach topics of cultural heritage without specific consideration of the topic's existential importance to the visitor.

Confrontational drama

Confrontational drama is an example of a contemporary interactive educational strategy. As the term *confrontational drama* indicates, it is an educational strategy that incorporates the principles of drama as they are known from theatre. The drama is fictitious and it involves actors. Drama used as an educational strategy is not a traditional performance with the museum visitors as audience; rather it involves the visitors as fellow actors, and the drama is confrontational in the sense that visitors are not only involved and playing their parts of the drama, they are confronted by professional actors asking questions and making requests, insinuations and sometimes even threats. Before the drama, visitors are generally informed about the subject of the performance and the character of the confrontational drama, and then they give their consent before entering the exhibition. Typically each visitor is given a fictitious name, an identity to perform and a few instructions, but, apart from this, it is largely up to the visitor to improvise when encountered and challenged by professional actors.

Confrontational drama is an educational strategy inspired by *psychodrama*, which is a psychotherapeutic technique introduced by Jacob L. Moreno in the mid-twentieth century.[5] Confrontational drama as an educational strategy is new within museum education and not yet fully developed or researched.[6] Examples of confrontational drama are *Dialogue in the Dark*, an international travelling exhibition in which visitors navigate multi-sensory environments in total darkness guided by blind people, and *Follow the North Star* at the Conner Prairie Interactive History Park in Fishers, Indiana, which is a role-playing experience that takes place at Connor Prairie, a living history site in Indiana, and in which visitors portray a group of Kentucky slaves who try to escape in 1836.[7] *Operation Spy*, at the International Spy Museum in Washington, DC, is a guided group experience in which visitors portray intelligence officers on assignment in a foreign country on a time-sensitive mission. *A Journey Unlike Any Other* which is used as an example in the following pages engages visitors in the role of refugees arriving in Denmark and applying for asylum.

Confrontational drama is a very effective educational strategy. Visitors get physically and mentally involved to such a degree that they are exceptionally present during the play. They have to use all their mental capacities in order to master their part of the drama. This mode requires empathy, consideration, anticipation, intentions and power of speech to be engaged at the right moment. Confrontational drama is fictitious and a certain distance between reality and performance is maintained during the play. But, apart from this distance, confrontational drama involves the visitor in a way that can be compared to an important and intense real life situation. When visitors encounter the professional actors, genuine emotions arise, and since emotions cannot be fictitious, visitors actually experience such feelings as, for example, distress, confusion and humiliation, as well as joy and relief. Visitors become intensively present with all their psychological capacities, and, therefore, the impressions during the drama make a significant educational impact on their personality.

The theme of a confrontational drama as museum exhibition and educational strategy is extremely important to the educational outcome because taking part in confrontational drama is an exceptional experience by itself, and, therefore, can easily become an exciting leisure activity without much impact on learning. On the other hand, when the theme is well researched and staged according to educational principles, confrontational drama may be one of the most efficient strategies within education.

The following example of confrontational drama demonstrates how a current political and humanitarian topic can be the focus of museum education. Only fantasy sets the limits for what topic confrontational drama engages, but topics that involve life experiences and attitudes of others are evidently the most beneficial subjects from an educational point of view because they encourage empathy and the personalization of abstract ideas.[8]

Confrontational drama: an example

An interactive exhibition, titled *A Journey Unlike Any Other*, which took place at the National Museum in Copenhagen in 2000, is a paradigmatic example of confrontational drama.[9] The topic was refugees in Denmark and the exhibition re-enacted the ordeal of refugees, specifically their flight to and arrival in Denmark, with a focus on the application process for residency. The educational aim was to help visitors understand the experience of being a refugee, escaping from their home country, arriving in Denmark to meet the immigration authorities and undergoing a long nerve-racking application procedure to learn if they are rejected and deported, or accepted and awarded residency. The question of accepting refugees in Denmark is continuously debated in the press and most visitors to the exhibition were familiar with some political and humanitarian viewpoints, but, in most cases, audiences lacked proper knowledge of the situation from the refugee's point of view.

After being informed about the nature of the exhibition, each visitor chose an identity among fourteen descriptions of typical refugees coming to Denmark. Each identity was described on a large wallboard, stating place and year of birth, family circumstances and the political situation that made the flight necessary. Before entering the exhibition the visitor was provided with a passport, a colored spot on the forehead for the actors to identify the identity of the refugee in question and some further information about the person they pretended to be during the tour through the exhibition.

The exhibition took up several rooms including a cellar and an outdoor space. Visitors were in each space confronted with actors in roles of soldiers, suspicious people offering their help, immigration police, case officers, etc. The exhibition was designed in such a way that it led visitors sequentially from one space to the other. They first entered a dark cellar with horrifying lighting, noise and sounds. The room simulated a place in the home country, and here soldiers confronted them in the most hostile way. Participants were interrogated, threatened and humiliated by the soldiers and even ran the risk of being jailed in a small pitch-dark closet. After some time, they were able to escape the cellar and get out into a courtyard in fresh air where suspect people approached them with offers to help them escape. They could choose a mock airplane or truck for transportation to Denmark. At the Danish border participants were first met by border police who checked their passports. The border police regarded them with suspicion and asked questions about their identity and flight from home. Afterward, they were held in custody or sent directly to a refugee camp where the application process began. The design of the camp was inspired by actual Danish camps, with barrack-style housing, offices and waiting rooms. Step by step, the visitors were led from one office of authority to another in a process of getting a permit for temporary or permanent residency. They finally received their asylum or were rejected residency.

The actors who played the different parts as case officers, lawyers, psychologists, soldiers and so forth came from the theatre group Terra Nova, under the direction of Toni Cots.[10] They received instruction for the procedures from officials at the Danish Immigration Service and during their preparations they visited a Danish refugee camp, making their own observations in order to give visitors a realistic impression of how it is to be a refugee in Denmark.

Former director of education Jette Sandahl and her staff at the National Museum in Copenhagen curated *A Journey Unlike Any Other*.[11] The exhibition was produced in cooperation with – among others – the Danish refugee authorities. The refugee identities and the scripts for the narrative were based on original accounts, board rulings and court cases executed by the Danish immigration service and the Danish court.

The educational outcome of visiting *A Journey Unlike Any Other* was remarkably promising. The exhibition was extended two weeks because of an overwhelming interest, and, during the eleven weeks it was open, more than 6,500 people participated in this confrontational drama which was maximum capacity. An evaluation[12] based on qualitative interviews with twelve visitors immediately after their visit, and a second time three to four months later, showed that people were deeply moved by the experience and remembered it in vivid detail even months later. People were shocked to discover how refugees are treated by Danish authorities and, even among those who already had a sympathy toward refugees, attitudes were remarkably substantialized. The evaluation, along with comments in the guest book, showed that, in general, people recognized the exhibition as one of the most rewarding museum experiences they had ever had.

Ethics of confrontational drama

Confrontational drama as educational strategy in museums is associated with a number of ethical issues. Hardly any other educational strategy involves the museum visitor in such a personal and challenging way as confrontational drama, and, therefore, ethical principles have to be taken into consideration whenever museums and heritage sites employ it. In this connection, it is important to keep in mind that absolute and indispensable principles of applied ethics do not exist. Applied ethics in medicine, business, museums and other fields is intended to encourage good relationships among people and is influenced by religion, politics and other cultural circumstances; therefore, principles of applied ethics vary from time to time and place to place. The following ethical guidelines suggested for carrying out confrontational drama are shaped by contemporary Western cultural values. Based on my experience evaluating *A Journey Unlike Any Other*, I suggest five general principles from the American Psychological Association's *Ethical Principles of Psychologists and Code of Conduct* (2002).[13] This code of conduct for psychologists working in close relationship with their clients provides appropriate guidelines for ethical issues in confrontational drama.

- *Principle of beneficence and non-maleficence.* Education at museums is carried out to benefit audiences and must not do harm. Museums select and pursue exhibition topics and educational strategies to contribute to visitors' lives and society in general. Museums have a responsibility to reach out to all groups of society, including future generations. Museums must guard against personal, financial, social, organizational or political factors that might lead to misuse of their influence in contemporary and future education. Thus, museums need to refrain from educational approaches that may risk endangering visitors' physical and mental health.
- *Principle of fidelity and responsibility.* Museums establish relationships of trust with the communities they serve educationally. Museum staff members know and accept their professional, ethical and scientific responsibilities to society. Curators and museum educators uphold professional standards of conduct, clarify their professional roles and obligations and assume appropriate responsibilities for their educational service. Museums consult with or cooperate with other professionals and institutions to serve the best interests of their audience.
- *Principle of integrity.* Curators and museum educators seek to promote accuracy, honesty and truthfulness in their educational service. They do not engage in deception and misrepresentation of facts.
- *Principle of justice.* Museums are public institutions founded to serve every member of the society. On the basis of fairness and justice, curators and museum educators ensure that all persons have access to and will benefit from the programs of their museum. They are committed to the theory and practice of social inclusion.
- *Principle of respect for people's rights and dignity.* In their educational programs curators and museum educators respect the dignity and worth of all people, and their rights to privacy, confidentiality and self-determination. Curators and museum educators are aware that special safeguards may be necessary to protect

the rights and welfare of persons or communities whose vulnerabilities impair autonomous decision-making. Curators and museum educators are aware of and respect cultural, individual and role differences, including those based on age, gender, gender identity, race, ethnicity, culture, national origin, religion, sexual orientation, disability, language and socioeconomic status, and they consider these factors in their educational programs and service.

Responsibilities of the exhibition team and actors in confrontational drama

The choice of confrontational drama in museum exhibition and education entails a number of ethical challenges and some are sensitive to such a degree that one may ask why museums should embark on confrontation drama when it is associated with risks for doing harm to the mental health of the visitors. The educational benefits are, as already indicated, the answer to this question. Confrontational drama is an exceptional educational strategy to involve the visitor in an intensive and personally rewarding experience. Confrontational drama is one of the most efficient educational strategies for substantializing insight and a personal stance to a specific subject. It is an experience associated with existential meaning and it will often be preserved in memory for years, if not the rest of life.

Choice of subject is crucial to the educational benefits, and therefore it is up to the curator and exhibition team to evaluate whether the learning potential merits the challenging ethical demands of confrontational drama. Confrontational drama ensures, in most cases, an exciting experience, but if the program prioritizes spectacle over learning outcomes, such an initiative is not in accordance with museums' responsibility to serve their visitors and society in general. Jette Sandahl and the exhibition team at the National Museum in Copenhagen chose to accept the risks of confrontational drama because they believed the topic of immigration to be an important touchstone defining contemporary Danish life and they wanted to promote understanding and acceptance of new citizens.

The exhibition team also chose to accept the risks involved with *A Journey Unlike Any Other* because they understood that, although the project did not incorporate objects from the permanent collection, its interactivity would offer a profound visitor-centered learning experience appropriate to diverse audiences. This perspective reflects the trend in contemporary museum education that prioritizes people over things.

The exhibition team must not only ensure optimal educational benefits based on academic knowledge, they are also responsible to establish that visitors are not harmed, physically or mentally, by participating in confrontation drama. It is obvious that an installation has to be designed to pose minimal risks for the physical health of the visitor; safeguarding the visitor's mental health is equally important, though far more complicated to carry out. While it is difficult enough to define and identify psychological disturbances such as distress, anxiety and loss of concentration, it is even more challenging to prevent such unfortunate consequences. Museum professionals involved in confrontational drama should emphasize to participants its fictitious nature and never make claim or cross boundaries to visitors' private life.

Museums are required to respect visitors' privacy and self-determination; it is up to the individual to decide to what degree they will become involved and museum staff should not exert pressure.

To prevent psychological strain during confrontational drama, museums should take precautions. Visitors under the age of fourteen were excluded from *A Journey Unlike Any Other* because educators considered them too young to process the experience. Furthermore, it is up the exhibition team to design a physical and psychological space for orientation and to create a means by which those who appear hesitant or anxious are encouraged to opt out. In *A Journey Unlike Any Other* the exhibition team reserved a separate room where an educator introduced visitors to the drama. Designers also staggered visitors' entrance so that the educator was able to have direct contact with each person. As the educator explained the subject and dramatic character of the experience to potential participants, s/he also suggested that if anyone was apprehensive about their response to the confrontational character of the drama, they should seriously consider not participating. In addition, the museum educator evaluated each visitor's state of being and those who showed signs of hesitation or anxiety were advised to withdraw. This is not a matter of giving a battery of psychological tests, but rather an assessment of how the visitor responds to instructions and answers questions. Visitors were told that if they are tormented by nightmares, plagued by anxiety attacks or have other signs of psychic distress, they should reconsider their participation. The final decision was generally up to the visitor and they were free as well to withdraw from the drama at any time. The museum educator made sure that no one was pressured by classmates or friends to take part.

In terms of staffing, the exhibition team recruits those individuals from the education department most suited to serve in the all-important orientation role through a record of establishing trusting and transparent relationships with visitors. The exhibition team also ensures that actors participating in the confrontational drama have the skill to perform the characters according to the museum's educational intentions, and that they are experienced with human interactions to such a degree that they are able to evaluate spontaneously if a visitor is shaken up to such a degree that they are not able to continue in a mode of play.

One of the most important roles that educators fulfill in the orientation is conveying the confrontational character of the program in question clearly and with integrity. Any kind of manipulation or deception is unethical even in cases where this might make the drama more provocative. Confrontational drama should be exciting because of the challenging interactions, not because of encounters for which the visitor is unprepared. This does not mean that a person can be informed about every detail of the event since confrontational drama is based on improvisation within a planned structure, but it is important that the visitor is made aware of the demanding character of the drama.

The integrity and skill of the professional actors are crucial for a successful learning experience in confrontational drama. Most visitors are not trained actors, and, consequently, they may feel reluctant to involve themselves. Therefore, it is up to the professional actors to engage participants in such a way that they feel free to join the interaction. The structure of the narrative also facilitates visitors' immersion. For example, the script of *A Journey Unlike Any Other* called for a difficult confrontation as soon as the drama began. Just after entering the exhibition, visitors were accosted by soldiers shouting into their faces, "What a traitor and coward you are!" and commanding them to face the wall and keep their hands up. This stressful entry forced visitors into a mode of play. It was very demanding of the actors because they had both to assume a hostile attitude and, at the same time, be extremely attentive to the visitor's response. Balancing on a knife edge, actors in confrontational drama have to upset the visitor without threatening his or her personal integrity. This delicate balance demands a well-founded sense of empathy. As the interaction takes place, the actor must keep track of the visitor's hold on reality. If a visitor loses contact with the fictitious drama and becomes personally threatened or in other ways intimidated, it is time for the actor to step back and make obvious the fictitious aspect of the interaction. The special quality of emotions is that they are actualized in the present moment and do not differ in quality and intensity if they are caused by circumstances in reality or fiction. In confrontational drama it is a question of getting the visitor emotionally involved on a fictitious level while, at the same time, never threatening personal integrity.

Finally, the exhibition team creates an appropriate debriefing for participants. Because of the intense nature of confrontational drama, visitors need to regain their equilibrium before they return to daily life. When visitors stepped out of *A Journey Unlike Any Other* they were not in the general museum area, but a large room exclusively for debriefing. They were met by a museum educator who helped visitors to process the experience through group and individual conversations and offered them chairs to relax and transition from the experience. In the same room, participants could browse through books and brochures for further reflection on the theme of refugees.

From an ethical point of view, confrontational drama may look like a risky affair, but, actually, if the program is well planned and carried out by people who are aware of their responsibilities, the risk for doing harm to visitors' mental health is minimal, and any possibility of risk is offset by the educational outcomes. Confrontational drama is one of the educational strategies that comes closest to the ideal of Kierkegaard's educational philosophy. The visitor becomes completely alert and, because the emotions during the drama are genuine, consciousness is present to an unusual degree. Moreover, if the subject of the drama is well considered, there is a good chance that the visitor will have an experience of existential value.

Beyond ethical limits

A few examples taken from experimental psychology illustrate how unfortunate a fabricated interaction can turn out if participants' autonomy and personal values are not respected. Museum staff involved in confrontational drama should be familiar with this larger context and understand the potential impact of ethical breaches.

In the early 1960s Yale University psychologist Stanley Milgram carried out a series of experiments on obedience.[14] In response to atrocities committed during the Holocaust he wanted to measure the willingness of experimental participants to obey a person of authority who instructed them to perform acts that conflicted with their personal conscience. Three people participated in the experiment: the first person, an experimenter who conducted the experiment by giving instructions; the second person who was going to learn a list of words; and the third person, the actual subject, who was going to teach the person learning the words. The second person pretended to be a fellow participant who volunteered for the experiment just as did the subject. The experimenter told them that they were participating in an experiment on the study of memory and learning in different situations. The two participants drew lots to "determine" who was going to be the teacher and the student. Unknown to the subject, both slips of paper said "teacher" and, consequently, the subject always got the instructional role. The student was led to a separate room, but could still communicate with the teacher.

Before the teaching began, the experimenter demonstrated an electric shock to the teacher as a sample of what the teacher was supposed to administer to the student in case he made a mistake. The teacher was given a list of word pairs to teach the student. First he read the list of word pairs to the student, and, then, he read the first word of each pair, along with four possible answers. The learner pressed a button to indicate his response. If the answer was incorrect, the teacher would administer a shock to the student, with the voltage increasing in 15 V increments up to a 450 V shock for each wrong answer. The teacher believed that the student received actual shocks, since he could hear the student scream and bang on the door. In reality, the student received no shock. If the teacher wanted to stop the experiment, the experimenter persuaded or even ordered him to continue.

The question was how far the teacher would go in increasing the voltage, and the result showed that about 65 percent of the subjects administered the final 450 V shock, although they often were very uncomfortable by doing so. The experiment was later repeated and varied in a number of ways at Yale University and other institutions around the globe, and the results of these experiments prove Milgram's original findings, that the percentage of subjects who are prepared to inflict fatal voltages is around 65 percent.

Was Milgram's approach acceptable from an ethical point of view? Was it right to deceive the subject in the name of research so that they did not know what really took place? Was it warranted to make the subjects perform acts that conflicted with personal values and conscience? Still, today, it is debated if Milgram and the many who repeated his experiment went too far in an attempt to obtain evidence for their research of the nature of obedience. But, in part, due to such exploitation, most academic research now includes checks and balances including review boards to approve research of human subjects and maintain ethical behavior.

The *Stanford prison experiment* carried out by psychology professor Philip Zimbardo[15] at Stanford University in 1971 also illuminates the dangers of exploitation when using human subjects and applies to issues of control and transparency in confrontational drama. The study focused on the psychological effects of being in a prison in an attempt to investigate if inherent personality traits of prisoners and guards are key factors for understanding abusive behavior in prisons.

Twenty-four undergraduates were selected to live in a simulated prison in the basement of the Stanford psychology building. Those selected were screened to ensure that they were mentally healthy. The experiment was planned for a two-week duration, and began with the local Palo Alto police arresting those who were chosen to play the part of prisoners at their homes and charged with armed robbery. The students went through the procedures of arrest before they were brought to the simulated prison at Stanford where the guards met them. The guards had been instructed to impose a sense of control over the students:

> You can create in the prisoners feelings of boredom, a sense of fear to some degree, you can create a notion of arbitrariness that their life is totally controlled by us, by the system, you, me, and they'll have no privacy … We're going to take away their individuality in various ways. In general what all this leads to is a sense of powerlessness. That is, in this situation we'll have all the power and they'll have none.[16]

The instructions were reinforced by props intended to promote disorientation, depersonalization and deindividualization. Guards sported military clothing, wooden batons and mirrored sunglasses. Prisoners wore ill-fitting smocks, stocking caps and chains around their ankles. Guards referred to the prisoners by numbers instead of names.

Within a few days the experiment grew out of hand. Several guards became increasingly cruel and exhibited genuine sadistic tendencies. Prisoners suffered from humiliating treatment. The second day a riot broke out and was brutally stopped by the guards. After the rebellion was crushed, the prisoners grew increasingly apathetic and, by the end of the experiment, many showed signs of severe emotional distress.

After only six days, Zimbardo had to end the experiment because the participants had internalized their roles to such a degree that their behavior grew out of hand. Even though the experiment was never completed, it reveals quite clearly that ordinary people who are regarded as psychologically well functioning can be convinced, in exceptional situations, to act in unethical ways. The Stanford prison experiment shows, just like the Milgram experiment, how most people are ready to do brutal and evil-minded things to their fellow human beings when they are persuaded by exceptional circumstances. Moreover, in the context of confrontational drama, these ill-fated experiments demonstrate how easily ordinary people can be tempted to turn role-playing into a realistic encounter that may impinge on personal integrity. They underline the necessity of employing transparent orientation procedures as well as professional actors to maintain the distinction in confrontational drama between fiction and reality.

Epilogue

Confrontational drama is a proper answer to Kierkegaard's idea for successful teaching. When people are emotional engaged in topics of existential importance they are not only acquiring new knowledge, their personality has changed. This is reason enough for museums to embark on programs of confrontational drama although such programs demand painstaking preparations and pose ethical challenges. Standards of conduct may be helpful for museums to prepare programs of confrontational drama, but they should never replace empathy and common sense.

Ethical principles can easily turn into moralizing commands such as "You should stop drinking," "You should respect speed limits," and so forth. Morality is not necessarily wrong or harmful, but it is used to control other people. Ethics, as applied to museum studies or other disciplines, is based on philosophical arguments, and such arguments are never absolute; they get their validity within a context. This is true when ethics is applied to the case of confrontational drama. This chapter presents general guidelines but the ruling ethical principles of confrontational drama have to be determined in each individual case.

Notes

1 S. Kierkegaard, *The Point of View for my Work as an Author*, trans. H. V. Hong and E. H. Hong, Princeton, NJ: Princeton University Press, 1998, p. 45; originally published in Danish, 1859.

2 For more about visitor-centered learning, see J. H. Falk and L. D. Dierking, *The Museum Experience*, Washington, DC: Whalesback Books, 1992, and J. H. Falk, *Identity and the Museum Visitor Experience*, Walnut Creek, CA: Left Coast Press, 2009.

3 For more about experiential learning, see D. A. Kolb, *Experiential Learning: Experiences as the Source of Learning and Development*, Englewood Cliffs, NJ: Prentice Hall, 1984.

4 On media-based interactivity, see L. Manovich, *The Language of New Media*, Cambridge, MA: MIT Press, 2001.

5 J. L. Moreno, *Psychodrama*, Vols. 1–3, Beacon, NY: Beacon House, 1946, 1959, 1969.

6 For more about participatory learning at museums in general, including provocative programming, see N. Simon, *The Participatory Museum*. Online. Available HTTP: http://www.participatorymuseum.org/ (accessed 31 May 2010).

7 C. Weinberg, 'The Discomfort Zone: Reenacting Slavery at Conner Prairie', *OAH Magazine of History* 23: 2, 2009. Online. Available HTTP: http://www.oah.org/pubs/magazine/antebellumslavery/connerprairie.html (accessed 4 August 2010).

8 Kolb, *Experiential Learning*.

9 B. S. Funch, 'A Journey Unlike Any Other: An Interactive Exhibition at the National Museum in Copenhagen, Denmark', *Curator* 49: 2006, pp. 205–216. J. Sandahl, 'Creating A Journey Unlike Any Other', *Curator* 49: 2006, pp. 212–214.

10 For more about the theater group Terra Nova see its web site. Online. Available HTTP: http://www.t-nova.org/dansk.html/ (accessed 31 May 2010).

11 Sandahl, 'Creating A Journey Unlike Any Other', pp. 212–214.

12 Funch, 'A Journey Unlike Any Other', pp. 205–216.

13 American Psychological Association's *Ethical Principles of Psychologists and Code of Conduct* (2002). Online. Available HTTP: http://www.apa.org/ethics/code2002.html/ (accessed 31 May 2010).

14 S. Milgram, 'Behavioral Study of Obedience', *Journal of Abnormal and Social Psychology* 67, 1963, pp. 371–378; S. Milgram, *Obedience to Authority: An Experimental View*, New York: HarperCollins, 1974.

15 C. Haney, W. C. Banks and P. G. Zimbardo, 'Study of Prisoners and Guards in a Simulated Prison', *Naval Research Reviews* 9, 1973, pp. 1–17; C. Haney, W. C. Banks, and P. G. Zimbardo, 'Interpersonal Dynamics in a Simulated Prison', *International Journal of Criminology and Penology* 1: 1973, pp. 69–97.

16 A. S. Haslam and S. Reicher, 'Beyond Stanford: Questioning a Role-based Explanation of Tyranny', *Dialogue: Bulletin of the Society for Personality and Social Psychology* 18, 2003, pp. 22–25.

26

Conservation practice as enacted ethics

Dinah Eastop

Conservation interventions can change objects in their material form, in their institutional role and in the meanings attributed to them. This chapter examines how the ethical principles of conservation are invoked and enacted. The focus here is on the relationship between ethical principles and changes in the material and social aspects of objects being treated. Conservation ethics, part of the corpus of ethics within museum practice, can structure conservation practice, and thus has a lasting effect, sometimes for many years.[1]

The ethos or dominant character of current conservation is preventive conservation, which seeks to reduce the effect of material and environmental changes on museum collections by responding to their causes, rather than to their effects. Contemporary practice suggests that it is better to improve the condition of a collection as a whole, rather than to "conserve" only a few artefacts. The idea that "prevention is better than cure" is usually taken for granted, as is the "shared care" model, in which collection care is recognised as a responsibility shared by all museum staff,[2] rather than the sole responsibility of the conservator.

The following study focuses on interventive treatments, "the physical interaction with heritage objects that distinguishes conservation from other heritage activities"[3] while recognising the importance of preventive conservation. Such interventions remain an important aspect of conservation practice, although the dominance of preventive conservation, increased concern about inappropriate interventions and budgetary constraints have made interventive treatments less frequent in the last two decades.[4] When conservation interventions are considered decisions have to be made about what is important and, thus, what features should be prioritised in the intervention. Analysis of this process provides vivid examples of how ethics relates to practice.

What follows is an exploration of the practice of ethics rather than an analysis of ethics as a written code or ethical practice per se. The focus is on the way ethical principles are invoked and what effect they have. An underlying premise of this chapter is that examining what is done with ethics – how it is applied – provides a richer, more nuanced understanding of conservation than merely studying the principles themselves; thus my focus is on both the changes made to objects and the changes in the social meanings attributed to them. This leads to two propositions. The first is that ethics acts as a justification for practice and sustains or reinforces some practices as ethical, which can mean that practitioners get locked into an increasingly rigid ideological position (such as the links made between some art histories and concepts of authenticity). The second is that ethics is viewed as morally neutral; however, the following case studies demonstrate that ethics is culturally and socially contingent.

A conservation intervention arises from a desire to conserve an object, with conservation understood as investigation, preservation and presentation.[5] The decision to conserve will lead to a social process, discussion about what is to be conserved and how. As the conservation intervention proceeds, it may change in response to the results of materials investigation and differences in opinion. At these times ethics may need to be questioned, tested out and elaborated in a social process of consultation. This results in a cumulative, interactive process of material and social change over time. The challenge attempted here is to unravel the evolving relationship between ethics and practice, with the aim of developing a theory of practice[6] which can be articulated and elaborated for each conservation intervention.

Method

The method adopted for this study is to analyse four published accounts of conservation. They serve as case studies, selected because they reflect a variety of conservation interventions, object types and institutions, the interventions are well documented and they have been undertaken by conservators collaborating in respected teams with other museum staff. Each of the four accounts is written by the conservator who undertook the work described and who acknowledges the work of custodians, curators and others who contributed to the decision-making. This analysis focuses on the ethical principles that are invoked by the conservators in their published accounts and how these principles are applied in practice. These principles include thorough documentation (of an object's materials, construction, condition and conservation interventions), fostering preventive conservation, minimal intervention and safely reversible interventions; they also entail a commitment to maintain professional standards, to recognise the rights and interests of originating communities and other user groups and to meet legal requirements.[7]

At each intervention, the interaction of ethical and technical challenges is worked out in practice, demonstrating that conservation interventions are a form of enacted ethics, which explains the importance given in this chapter to examining case studies. Recognising that the implications of ethics are learned in practical action reinforces the significance of considering the institutional and technical specificities of the case studies. The importance of understanding how ethics is applied supports the central proposition of this chapter that conservation interventions are a form of enacted ethics.

The four case studies concern the conservation of: an eighteenth-century upholstered armchair; garments of seventeenth-century silk embroidered with gold and silver; a late nineteenth-century monumental sculpture of the first king of Hawai'i; and *Transparent Tubes*, a plastic sculpture by William Turnbull, 1968. These case studies have been selected to show four contrasting approaches to conservation: retention of the object's original form and materials and removal of later repairs; reconstruction of presumed original form and undoing of later alterations; retention of some later additions followed by repainting; and, refabrication of an artwork. Although different in many ways, the conservation interventions share significant features. Each demonstrates the transformative effects of some conservation practice, and the material and social effects of these changes. In the first example, the conservator transformed an eighteenth-century chair by removing later repairs to reveal the original materials and structure preserved underneath later additions. In the second, transformation was achieved when the conservator reconstructed seventeenth-century garments in order that they could be presented in a form close to their presumed original form. In the third example, structural consolidation and repainting transformed the condition and appearance of the regal sculpture. In the final case, conservators transformed a 1968 sculpture by William Turnbull by viewing it as a prototype that could be refabricated.

The rationale for each intervention and the process of decision-making, which are introduced in the published accounts, are summarised below. In each case the intervention aimed to meet current needs while acknowledging future needs by thorough documentation and use of reversible methods. Each of the interventions (whether the conservative *in situ* upholstery treatment, the radical reconstruction of the seventeenth-century garments, the stabilisation and repainting of the sculpture or the refabrication of the plastic sculpture) sought to achieve similar goals of preserving and presenting what was considered significant. Each case study is summarised with care given to introduce the specific details of the main interventions before ethical issues are highlighted. The technical details are necessary in order to demonstrate that each intervention provides an opportunity to examine the relationship between ethics and practice.

An eighteenth-century upholstered armchair

The first case study concerns a magnificent suite of eighteenth-century upholstered furniture (Figure 26.1) introduced by Kate Gill in "The conservation of four 1760s chairs with original upholstery and top covers of red damask."[8] The carved mahogany suite, which now comprises thirty armchairs, two pairs of settees, window seats and a winged armchair, was commissioned by Paul Methuen for the picture gallery of his Corsham Court residence in Wiltshire, where it remains. The suite is preserved not only in its original setting but also with its original upholstery and silk damask covers. The damask was supplied in 1765 for both the walls and the furniture. The preservation of historic chair frames with their original upholstery, top covers and trimmings is very rare, making the suite of great historical significance, as recognised when part of the suite (sixteen armchairs, the winged armchair and the window seats) was accepted by HM government under the "in lieu [of Inheritance Tax] in situ" arrangement and allocated to Bristol's Museums, Galleries and Archives. The "Acceptance in Lieu" (AIL) scheme enables UK taxpayers to transfer works of art and important heritage objects into public ownership in place of paying inheritance tax;[9] arrangements are sometimes made to leave the objects *in situ*, as was the case at Corsham Court.

Figure 26.1 Armchair from a suite of furniture commissioned in 1765 for the Picture Gallery, Corsham Court, Wiltshire, UK. Composite image showing the chair before and after conservation intervention of 2009. Courtesy of Corsham Court Collection/ Textile Conservation Centre. TCC Ref 2929.

The condition of the suite was assessed in 2005. The red damask top covers had been repaired over the years with patches of various fabrics (some secured with adhesive, some by stitching) and a protective covering of coarse orange-red net. Some repair work was disfiguring and some was beginning to damage the silk damask it was intended to protect. Sixteen of the most fragile upholstered chairs were prioritised for conservation treatment, including an armchair with a sagging seat. The aim of the conservation intervention undertaken at the UK's Textile Conservation Centre in 2009 "was to make the chairs safe for continued open display in their original historic house setting."[10] For the first phase of intervention it was agreed by the custodians (Bristol Museums and Corsham Court) that the orange-red net coverings could be removed. Removal revealed several well-preserved features of the original construction, including welted seams and evidence of shallow tufting. The now visible areas of unfaded damask are orange-red in colour; in exposed areas the damask has a more blue-red hue. After further consultation, Gill removed repair stitching that was distorting or concealing the sharp lines of the welted edge. The second phase involved the removal of the orange-red damask patches. The red damask patches were left in place because they were considered to be later additions of historic significance, as they had been cut from the matching silk damask wall covering behind the pictures in the Picture Gallery.

The third phase combined stabilisation of the fragile damask top covers with camouflage of loss. Gill achieved this by securing custom-dyed patches of a thin but opaque silk fabric overlaid with a semi-transparent silk cloth, dyed various tones to accommodate the unevenly coloured damask. A layer of custom-dyed net, secured by stitching, was then applied to provide both support and protection. Following consultation with the suite's custodians, the net was custom-dyed to match the colour of the aged damask. The fourth phase included the design, manufacture and fitting of a support to the chair with the sagging seat. The support was made so that it could be added without disrupting the original upholstery, be readily removable and appear invisible when the chair is on display. Gill concludes her report by highlighting that *in situ* upholstery conservation treatments are rarely published; she suggests that this may be because such stabilisation treatments are regarded as relatively straightforward and therefore not noteworthy.

Ethics in practice: retaining original form and materials

In Gill's account of the conservation of the 1760s chairs, ethics is embedded in decisions to retain as much of their original form and materials as possible. The intervention is characterized by respect for original materials and construction, observing the principles of reversibility and minimal intervention, documenting all materials and processes, and taking a phased approach. Gill undertook the interventions without removing any element of the original top covers because it was

> a priority to keep original materials with the frames wherever possible so that these important primary sources of material evidence were subject to minimal disruption. Consequently, it was decided that treatment would be carried out in situ ... This approach was extended to the sagging seat of one chair, where a "non-interventive" seat support was proposed.[11]

The significance accorded to the preservation of the chair in the room for which it was commissioned in the 1760s led to respect for certain later additions, namely the red damask patches taken from behind the pictures in the Picture Gallery. Prioritizing original materials and those later additions considered significant is a fundamental feature of textile and upholstery conservation.[12] Respect for original materials is combined with a clear acknowledgment that changes have occurred, e.g. the colour change of the damask. Maintaining the harmonious appearance of the room, for example, between the red damask on the walls, on the recently conserved chair and the others, explains why the conservator dyed the newly applied net to match the changed hue of the damask.

The conservator manifested the principle of reversibility and of "re-treatability" in the choice of stitching (rather than adhesives) to secure patches and in supporting the sagging chair seat with a removable seat support, made of inert materials. The latter intervention also reflects the ethos of preventive conservation where the introduction of catalysts of degradation is avoided; this explains why stable (or relatively more stable) materials (e.g. acrylic sheeting) are preferred for use in museum storage, display and conservation.[13]

Meticulous recording of repairs, original materials and construction highlights the importance attributed to documentation. This is particularly significant for complex, multimedia artefacts because the conservator's close and extended contact with the object allows privileged access to artefacts, and sometimes to components that are concealed by the conservation interventions. The "revelatory" aspect of upholstery conservation is widely acknowledged[14] and links to another important aspect of conservation practice: the phased approach. The phased-treatment approach allowed for discussion between the conservator and the custodians of the suite as new material evidence was revealed during the interventions. Newly revealed evidence can lead to changes in approach or interpretation, resulting in interventions which respond to the specific needs of individual objects and contexts, as will be seen also in the conservation of seventeenth-century silk garments.

Garments of seventeenth-century silk embroidered with gold and silver

Extremely rare garments made of blue silk satin embroidered with gold and silver are introduced by Teresa Knutson in her article "Investigation, engineering and conservation combined: the reconstruction of a seventeenth century dress."[15] The Los Angeles County Museum of Art (LACMA) acquired two garments, a dress and a matching panel/mantle (museum ref. M.88.39), in 1988 because, although the dress had a silhouette fashionable in the 1840s, Edward Maeder, then curator of the Department of Costume and Textiles, recognised that the garments probably dated to the seventeenth century. Knutson describes the work undertaken in 1990–91 to determine the original form of the garments and to reconstruct them in seventeenth-century form.

Conservators examined and documented the materials and construction of the dress in great detail; fold lines, weave faults, thread and stitch types were recorded. Unpicking the newer stitching, while leaving the earlier sewing untouched, revealed that it had been assembled from sixty-two pieces of cloth. Painted and printed representations of late seventeenth-century dress were consulted, as were published patterns of extant garments and accounts of the reconstruction of seventeenth- and eighteenth-century garments. This research supported the curator's view that the garments acquired in 1988 had once formed part of a seventeenth-century ensemble, consisting of three garments: a stomacher, a petticoat (skirt) and a mantua (in the form of a fitted bodice with integral train).

The decision was made to change the garments from their form as acquired by LACMA (dress and panel/mantle) and to assemble them in a seventeenth-century form of stomacher, petticoat and mantua (museum ref: M.88.39a–c). This transformation is described and illustrated in Knutson'a article, which opens with photographs showing the dress front and back "before reconstruction" and later shows the ensemble "after reconstruction," with the mantua, stomacher and petticoat presented in a form characteristic of the period 1680–1710 (Figure 26.2).

Although much of the embroidery was extant, some areas were missing. At the curator's request, the conservator employed painted infills to camouflage areas of loss. The infills enabled the appearance of the embroidered ensemble to be restored while making the additions clearly distinct from the original materials.

LACMA's Department of Costumes and Textiles has actively encouraged debate about the reconstruction. For example, the Department organized a week-long consultation at Hampton Court Palace, UK, in 1997. Interested colleagues (including the author of this chapter) were invited to view the garments and to complete a one-page

Figure 26.2 Woman's Mantua, Stomacher, and Petticoat, circa 1700. (Left) as acquired in 1988
(with a silhouette fashionable in the 1840s), (centre) after the reconstruction of
1990, and (right) in a recent re-display (2005). Gold and silver metallic thread
embroidery on silk satin. a) Dress: Center back length: 56 in. (142.2 cm); b) Petticoat:
Center front length: 35 in. (88.9 cm). Costume Council Fund (M.88.39a-c). Location:
Los Angeles County Museum of Art, Los Angeles, California, U.S.A. Photo Credit:
Digital Image © 2009 Museum Associates/LACMA/Art Resource, New York.

questionnaire which sought information on primary reference material and views
about the reversibility of the treatment. Respondents were asked if, given the same
circumstances, they would have chosen to reconstruct the dress.

A report by curatorial and conservation staff at LACMA[16] stresses the challenges
of the 1990–91 reconstruction and explains that this intervention did not end the
research, which continued into the late 1990s. This on-going research and consultation led to a re-evaluation of the reconstruction of 1990–91. For instance, dress historian Janet Arnold suggested that the sleeves and cuffs were narrower and the train
shorter than she would have expected. It was agreed that LACMA would present
any new findings in the form of an exhibition, rather than in further interventions
with the garments, as "the Mantua was not to be reconstructed again because of its
fragile condition."[17]

In 1998 LACMA displayed the results of research undertaken since 1991. The
display (and another in 2005) included the reconstructed garments but presented
them slightly differently in order to accentuate the verticality of the ensemble; the

more recent research had suggested that such a silhouette was closer to its presumed original appearance. Folds in the train were arranged differently and the mannequin wore a tall headdress; neither modification involved any physical change to the original seventeenth-century materials. McLean and her collaborators note that "However imperfect the current version is, it is a comfortably conservative compromise."[18]

Ethics in practice: reconstruction of original form

In Knutson's account of the conservation of these garments, ethics is embedded in decisions to reconstruct their original form, to ensure that new additions were clearly distinguishable from original materials, to conform to the principle of reversibility and to document all materials and processes. The rarity of surviving examples of seventeenth-century dress provides the underlying rationale for the interventions described; as so few exist, there is a need to preserve them in their presumed seventeenth-century form. (Re)construction was required in order to make the dress recognizable for exhibition as seventeenth-century dress. The intervention of 1990–91 was to "find the original form of the dress."[19] Knutson ends her article by noting that the curator was correct in believing that "there was an authentic seventeenth-century dress hidden inside the altered mish-mash of the fabric pieces" of the garments as purchased in 1988.[20] The form of the LACMA dress as acquired made it anomalous within the history of dress. It did not fit neatly into existing historical narratives: "it had been so severely altered that it did not match the fashions of the seventeenth century – or for that matter the fashions of any historical period."[21]

The practical challenges of matching tarnished metal threads and "ethical concerns about duplicating original processes and making fill-ins too similar to the original" explain the use of painted infills for missing embroidery.[22] This fulfils the need for inconspicuous yet identifiable additions,[23] summarized as the "6 ft × 6 in. rule." This states that conservation interventions should be obvious on close inspection (at a distance of 6 in./150 mm), adhering to the principle of transparency in conservation practice, but not obvious at a viewing distance of 6 ft/2 m, where it might distract from the viewing experience.

The interventions described by Knutson[24] and by McLean and colleagues[25] conform to the principle of retreatability, often seen as an alternative or as complementary to minimal intervention. Conservators handled the treatment in such a way that "the dress could come apart and be reconfigured if it was deemed that the shape is incorrect."[26] Although there is now wide recognition that textiles "are shaped by the complexities of their time of creation, their history of use and period of collection,"[27] there has been little systematic study of the way garments have been altered to meet new needs and conditions, and so the deliberate conservation of such alterations and additions remains the exception.[28] Information about the provenance of the dress[29] provides an insight into the material, functional and social changes that the garments may have undergone since they were made in c. 1700. It is possible that these later additions may be attributed significance in the future. The multi-phase and self-reflexive approach adopted by the curators and conservators at

LACMA, together with the extensive and detailed documentation of the garments, provides the opportunity for such review.

Openness to alternative views and to fostering debate is a welcome feature of textile conservation practice;[30] it recognizes that the values attributed to objects will change as society changes.[31] By referring to the circumstances of the intervention, such accounts of conservation also acknowledge the institutional specificity of some conservation interventions. Knutson points out that the garments were acquired for a museum of art. Understanding conservation (investigation, preservation and presentation) as work in progress, part of a multi-phased project, a process rather than a finished product, is also demonstrated in the third case study.

A sculpture of the first king of Hawai'i

A monumental, painted cast brass sculpture of the first king of a united Hawai'i, standing in the pose of a Roman emperor and dressed in feather regalia (Figure 26.3), is discussed by Glenn Wharton in "Dynamics of participatory conservation: the Kamehameha I sculpture project."[32] The sculpture was commissioned by the Hawaiian legislature in 1878 to commemorate Captain Cook's "discovery" of the islands, thereby linking both Hawaiian state formation and its imperial past. It was designed by

Figure 26.3 Monumental sculpture of King *Kamehameha I*, designed by Thomas Ridgeway Gould between 1878–1880, cast in 1880 and installed in 1882 at Kapa'au, North Kohala, Hawai'i. Composite image showing the sculpture before and after the conservation interventions of 1999–2002. Photograph Courtesy of Glenn Wharton.

the Boston sculptor Thomas Ridgeway Gould, cast in brass in Paris in 1880, shipped to Hawai'i and set up in 1882 on a plinth in front of the courthouse of Kapa'au, a small town in the rural district of North Kohala. A century later the sculpture had become the site of many community celebrations in this culturally diverse district, where nearly everyone respected Kamehameha I as the first king of a united Hawai'i and some local residents held the sculpture in particular reverence.

When Wharton was consulted in 1996 about the sculpture's conservation, he was asked by the cultural heritage authorities in the state capital to make a condition assessment and to develop a conservation plan based on respect for artist's intent. He confirmed the structural weakness of the statue, detected evidence of bronze disease and noted the many layers of overpainting. His examination of the sculpture attracted local interest, and even suspicion from some in North Kohala who resented interference by the state authorities in the capital, Honolulu. During his inspection of the statue several local people told him they liked the painted surface of the sculpture because they valued the lifelike appearance it gave to the king. Local interest in the conservation of the sculpture led Wharton to recommend that its conservation be developed as a participatory project. This proposal was rejected by the cultural authorities in the state capital. However, despite this opposition, a locally based, participatory conservation project was planned and funded as a multiagency partnership, with the state-run Kamehameha Day Celebration Commission overseeing the work, and Wharton as the project conservator.

The conservation interventions (undertaken 1999–2002) required the removal of the many layers of overpainting; one outcome was the detachment of two metal spheres which had been adhered with a modern adhesive (epoxy resin) into the king's eye sockets. Once it was fully documented and structurally safe, and treated with a corrosion inhibitor, decisions had to be made about the finish of the sculpture. Wharton's materials investigation of the sculpture confirmed that the piece was originally gilded and so he assumed repainting the sculpture was inappropriate. This was in line with the views of the cultural authorities in Honolulu who wished to see the sculpture in its original form. However, consultation with local residents showed that the regular repainting of the sculpture was linked to important local celebrations, such as holidays and weddings.[33] After a proactive community engagement programme involving school children, a community vote (ballot) was held to decide whether or not to repaint the sculpture. This resulted in the decision to repaint the sculpture and extensive discussion about the colour of the king's skin and his feathered dress ensued. After much debate, the paint colour for the king's skin was matched to the medium brown of a local assistant on the conservation team.[34] Further consultation led to the reapplication of the bronze spheres into the king's eye sockets. Although they were recognized as additions of the 1970s, they were now considered by the residents of North Kohala to be part of the sculpture, which many residents accorded the respect due to the king himself.

Ethics in practice: retention of later additions and repainting

In Wharton's account of the conservation of the sculpture of *Kamehameha I*, ethics is embedded in the documentation of the statue and its conservation, the stabilizing of its condition and the commitment to the participatory conservation of public monuments. The dominant theme is the questioning of conventional applications of conservation ethics and who should have the power to make conservation decisions. His initial presumption, based on the ethics of respect for artist's intent and the authenticity of original form and materials, was that repainting was inappropriate. Some members of the local community held different views about what aspects of the sculpture should be respected and conserved. As Wharton explains, "Deciding on its conservation could not simply be based on knowledge of Native Hawaiian traditions, nor, given the contemporary social circumstance, could it easily be decided applying conventional conservation principles of authenticity."[35]

With such a culturally diverse community, the question was: who decides and how? Local residents valued the lifelike appearance of "their" sculpture and so Wharton decided that his "initial presumption of straightforward conservation based on artist's intent was inappropriate."[36] Such sensitivity to local concerns explains the adoption of non-standard interventions, such as the reapplication of recent additions (bronze spheres in the eye sockets), resulting in "a negotiated conservation treatment, combined with new ethnographic understandings about how the sculpture fits into local history and contemporary life."[37] This is named in a locally produced DVD, *King Kamehameha: A Legacy Renewed*, suggesting that the recent conservation intervention resulted in the representation of a contemporary view of the king.[38]

Wharton stresses the importance of the local debate engendered by the conservation project. "Some of the most helpful information [about the sculpture] came from reactions to conservation treatment procedures, as the sculpture's surface visually changed through progressive stages."[39] A key feature was that local cultural knowledge was *"elicited through the conservation process itself*, becoming part of an ongoing dynamic process."[40] In terms of social inclusion, the project encouraged "finding value in an active process of exploring versions of the past and deciding how to communicate the past to future generations."[41] The conservation intervention not only changed the material form of the object but also the significance attributed to it; community discussion "made the sculpture more salient on the landscape."[42] Wharton's account also demonstrates the interdependence of conserving tangible and intangible heritage, where the social act of repainting the sculpture of the king was an important aspect of preserving some of its tangible attributes.[43]

Wharton's paper is exceptional in presenting the social dynamics of participatory conservation while recording conventional aspects, such as materials analysis and interventions. Miriam Clavir has highlighted the importance of recognizing and responding to the ever-changing social and physical environments of objects;[44] recent codes of conservation ethics stress the crucial nature of community consultation and participation.[45] Wharton's paper is unusual in portraying the translation of this theory into practice,[46] making explicit the political and economic forces that control decision-making. At the time of writing his account, five years after the conservation interventions, Wharton notes that state administrators in Honolulu continued to withhold funds for maintaining a painted surface rather than the gilded one they had wanted to see restored.[47] Generating heated debate is a feature shared with the following case study.

Transparent Tubes, a plastic sculpture by William Turnbull, 1968

In the final case study, "*Transparent Tubes* by William Turnbull: the degradation of a polymethyl methacrylate sculpture," Stella Willcocks, then a conservator at the Tate Gallery, London, documents the degradation of a modern plastic sculpture.[48] She explains the rationale for replicating its component tubes in order to exhibit the installation. The sculpture, which Turnbull (b. 1922) designed in 1968, consists of eighteen identical tubes made of clear acrylic, each 1.77 m high and fitted with a small circular cap and a larger circular base (Figure 26.4). Turnbull presented the artwork to the Tate Gallery in 1990, when it was noted that the once clear tubes were slightly yellowed; minor crazing on two tubes and tiny droplets of a viscous-looking liquid inside one tube were also reported. These changes had increased considerably by 1996 which led to an investigation of the materials, manufacture and significance of the sculpture.

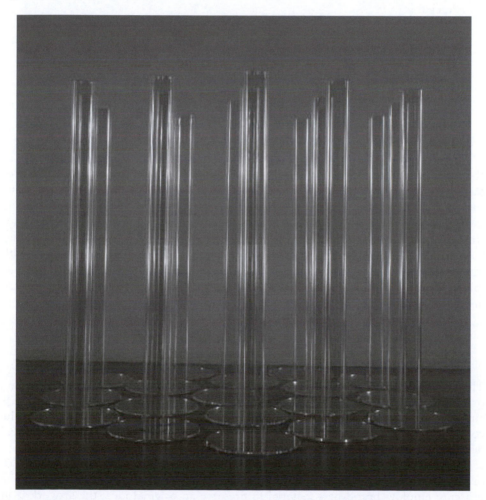

Figure 26.4 Transparent Tubes, designed in 1968 by William Turnbull (b. 1922). © Tate, London

Willcocks explains the processes of manufacturing acrylic (polymethyl methacrylate, pMMA) and the analysis undertaken to understand the materials, construction and deterioration of the tubes. Her conclusion was that the degradation of the tubes was probably due to the method and additives used in making them. As the process of such degradation cannot be reversed, discussions were held among the artist and Tate conservators and curators. Turnbull recognized that the yellowing of the acrylic was irreversible and explained that he intended the work to be transparent. He had no objection to the sculpture being remade. He explained that he had not produced it himself but had supplied a drawing to the manufacturers. This led to the decision, agreed upon jointly by the artist, conservators and curators, to remake the work for exhibition purposes. Willcocks noted, "Refabrication was deemed to be an acceptable means of returning the sculpture to a displayable condition."[49]

At the time Willcocks wrote her report, the refabrication had not taken place, but she introduces the preparatory work and the commissioning process, and concludes that

> Refabrication is a strategy that conservators instinctively dislike, since it runs counter to their training and professional practice. However, one way of viewing the dilemma is to see sculpture like *Transparent Tubes* as a kind of prototype, with the associated problems of any new product. By documenting and attempting to resolve these production problems in collaboration with the artist, conservators can both conserve the history of the idea and assist artists in preserving their original intention.[50]

Willcocks emphasizes the importance of transparency in the process: "details of the refabrication will be acknowledged on the display label and in the catalogue entry for the sculpture."[51] She also notes that conservation of the replica is being considered. Derek Pullen, Head of Sculpture Conservation, Tate Gallery, has since confirmed that the installation has been refabricated and the "restored sculpture has been displayed a few times since it was refabricated and the artist was content with the result."[52] One of the tubes of the 1968 installation has been retained in storage for reference. Pullen ends his update by saying that this project sparked intense debate about replication.

Ethics in practice: refabrication

The difficult issue in this conservation report is the tension between preserving original materials and construction, and preserving evidence of the artist's intent. Is authenticity invested in the original materials, construction and form, or in the conception of the artist? This is an issue of intense ethical, legal and technical debate.[53] The conservation strategy adopted for this artwork sought to preserve a representation (in the form of the refabricated installation) of the artist's original idea or intent of 1968 and not the material presented to the Tate in 1990. In this way the museum employs brand new material to preserve an original idea; the artwork is in the artist's mind, the material form, in this case, is its representation.

Another significant theme is the importance of understanding the properties of materials and their products, which explains the emphasis given to the investigation and documentation of materials and techniques in conservation ethics. Materials characterization is important for predicting the behaviour of both historic material and any new materials that might be used in preventive and interventive measures. Willcocks's investigation of the techniques and additives employed to manufacture acrylic tubes from acrylic sheeting helps to explain the changes seen in Turnbull's *Transparent Tubes* of 1968. In contrast, the stable properties of new acrylic sheeting enabled its use as a seat support in the case of the eighteenth-century seat furniture.

The treatment approach adopted for *Transparent Tubes* at the Tate draws attention to the contingent nature of conservation practice. There is no single view on the discolouration of once transparent plastic sculpture. Turnbull was consulted and explained his preference for transparency, which could only be achieved by replication, as the yellowing was irreversible. The trustees of the Gabo Trust adopted a different approach when presented with the problem of yellowing in Naum Gabo's sculpture at the Tate; their choice was to retain and present the original material even though it was no longer transparent, and to explain the colour change to the public.[54]

Conclusion

Ethics is learnt in practical action so it is instructive to study its applications, which explains the importance given here to re-examining case studies. As these have shown, there is consistency in general principles (e.g. a commitment to documentation, preventive conservation and the reversibility of interventions) and wide variety in applications. Conservation principles and practice are mutually constitutive in the course of the conservation process: practice informs ethics and principles, and vice versa.[55] The case studies demonstrate the primacy usually given to preserving the [presumed] original form of an object over subsequent physical states, including alterations or additions. The privileging of original form often means that its re-establishment is taken for granted as natural and self-evident.[56] Nearly twenty years ago the removal of later additions from the LAMCA dress did not present ethical problems worth noting.[57] Such assumptions are questioned when decisions are made not to preserve or present the original form, as in the case of the recent conservation of the sculpture in Hawai'i.

Greenberg has described conservation as "profoundly contingent,"[58] dependent on the interaction between material and social change, and the processes of decision-making. It is sometimes assumed that the ethics of conservation interventions is fully determined before conservation, but evidence suggests that ethics evolves, is tested and is elaborated during interventions. Cummins argues that it is helpful to consider ethics as an evolving concept.[59] The case studies demonstrate two dynamics. The first are the ethical challenges of interfering with the "real thing," the material, tangible evidence of "museum artefacts." The second is the influence of curators and conservators, and sometimes others, to present (literally re-present) objects in certain ways. This resonates with Pearce's seminal analysis of a coatee [uniform] which has tangible and factual links with the battle of Waterloo (1815) but which can be understood very differently depending on one's point of view and how it is represented.[60] Conservation decision-making highlights different views of the "real thing."

What was considered the "real thing" in the case of the Corsham Court armchair in 2009 was the chair as designed and constructed in the 1760s, together with later additions considered significant. In 1990–91, the seventeenth-century embroidered fabric reassembled in its presumed original form was considered the "real thing." In the case of the conservation of sculpture of King Kamehameha I undertaken between 1999 and 2002 there were conflicting views of what was the "real thing" so that Wharton was faced with the challenge of "honoring artist's intent versus honoring community tradition."[61] What was considered the "real thing" when deciding how to conserve Turnbull's plastic sculpture for the Tate Gallery in 1996 was not its materials and construction of 1968 but the artist's concept of 1968 where the transparency of the tubes was fundamental.

The case studies illustrate the importance of recognizing the material and institutional specificities in applying conservation ethics[62] and the decision-making or decision-influencing powers invested in the maker, the user, the conservator and the curator/custodian/owner, and sometimes the funders. In each case the interventions were instrumental in reinforcing and promoting the museum or site and in demonstrating the expertise of "heritage" professionals. Recent research has highlighted and questioned the power relations and the control of resources within the heritage sector.[63] In the case studies, privileging of the earlier form and materials was important for both the historic house and the museum.

The conservation of the sculpture of the Hawai'ian king demonstrates the benefits of integrating expertise from outside the domain of "heritage" professionals, as well as the resulting ethical and practical challenges. It provides an excellent example of community participation which involved shared decision-making between communities and conservation professionals. It also demonstrates the interconnectivities between conserving tangible and intangible heritage[64] where the act of repainting the sculpture of the king is important in preserving its locally valued material attributes.[65] There is growing recognition that conservation is not only a technical practice but also a social process, requiring new skills, if conservators and other heritage professionals are to become effective facilitators of participatory conservation projects.[66]

Analysis of the case studies demonstrates that social context influences how ethics are invoked and how they are deployed. Ethics, seen as ideology, can be openly debated or quietly taken for granted, depending on particular contexts and their political realities. Conservation interventions require answers to a series of critical and interconnected questions: what features are considered important and should be conserved? To whom are they important and why? Who decides on which intervention is appropriate? Thus, conservation interventions provide sites for contestation and debate. A recent development in conservation ethics and practice is recognizing the importance of such debate. Examining the decision-making process itself and identifying the power relationships inherent in decision-making mechanisms should be acknowledged. This chapter demonstrates "the critical role that the conservator plays in transforming the museum from a temple to a forum."[67]

Conservation itself can become a means of social engagement.[68] The ethics and the practice of conservation are interactive or dialectical. This relationship changes over time, and thus who is involved and whose views should be considered is constrained historically and socially. Analysis of conservation as a process reveals a complex dynamic between the material properties and social meanings of objects. The case studies demonstrate the active role of conservation in prioritizing certain material, social and conceptual elements for conservation over others. Such changes reflect not only the significance attributed to an artefact at any one time, but also the power relations of those making decisions about what is significant. When interventions are viewed as the physical manifestations of museum ethics, conservation practice enacts those ethics.

Acknowledgements

I would like to thank: Richard Sandell for encouraging this contribution; Janet Marstine for editorial advice; Kate Gill for allowing me to read her chapter prior to its publication and the custodians of the Corsham Court suite for permission to publish; LACMA for permission to reproduce images of the mantua, and Catherine McLean, Senior Textile Conservator, LACMA, for allowing me to read, prior to its publication, a paper she, Sandra Rosenbaum and Susan Schmalz prepared; Glenn Wharton for supplying his images of the *Kamehameha I* sculpture; the Tate Gallery for permission to reproduce an image of *Transparent Tubes* by William Turnbull, and Derek Pullen, Head of Sculpture Conservation, for further information; the Institute of Museum Ethics at Seton Hall University and the trustees of the Textile Conservation Centre Foundation for contributing to the costs of the illustrations; and David Goldberg for encouraging critique.

Notes

1 R. E. Child, "Ethics in Conservation," in G. Edson (ed.) *Museum Ethics*, London: Routledge, 1997, pp. 209–15; International Council of Museums, *Code of Professional Ethics*, Paris: International Council of Museums, 1990; J. Weisz (compiler), *Codes of Ethics and Practice of Interest to Museums*, Washington, DC: American Association of Museums, 2000.

2 Museums Association (UK) *Code of Ethics for Museums*, London: Museums Association, 2002, p. 15.

3 J. Ashley-Smith, "The basis of conservation ethics," in A. Richmond and A. Bracker (eds.) *Conservation: Principles, Dilemmas and Uncomfortable Truths*, Oxford: Elsevier, 2009, p. 8.

4 F. Lennard and P. Ewer, "Textile conservation in the heritage sector," in F. Lennard and P. Ewer (eds.) *Textile Conservation: Advances in Practice*, Oxford: Elsevier, 2010, pp. 3–12.

5 D. Eastop and K. Gill, "Upholstery conservation as a practice of preservation, investigation and interpretation," in K. Gill and D. Eastop (eds.) *Upholstery Conservation: Principles and Practice*, Oxford: Butterworth-Heinemann, 2001, pp. 1–9.

6 P. Bourdieu, *Outline of a Theory of Practice*, Cambridge Studies in Anthropology 16, Cambridge: Cambridge University Press, 1977.

7 M. M. Brooks, "International conservation codes of ethics and practice and their implications for teaching and learning ethics in textile conservation education," in Á. Tímár-Balázsy and D. Eastop (eds.) *International Perspectives on Textile Conservation*, London: Archetype Press, 1998, pp. 74–80.

8 K. Gill, "The conservation of four 1760s chairs with original upholstery and top covers of red damask," in Lennard and Ewer, *Textile Conservation*, pp. 171–80.

9 Items accepted under the "Acceptance in Lieu" scheme must be "pre-eminent," i.e. of particular historical, artistic, scientific or local significance, either individually or collectively, and must be in acceptable condition. Online. Available HTTP: www.mla.gov.uk/ ./tax/./AIL_Guidance_Notes_10647_at_12_10_09 (accessed 16 October 2009).

10 Gill, "The conservation of four 1760s chairs," p. 173.

11 Ibid.

12 D. Eastop, "Decision-making in conservation: determining the role of artefacts," in Tímár-Balázsy and Eastop, *International Perspectives*, pp. 43–6.

13 Á. Tímár-Balázsy and D. Eastop, *Chemical Principles of Textile Conservation*, Oxford: Butterworth-Heinemann, 1998, pp. 332–49.

14 K. Gill and D. Eastop (eds.) *Upholstery Conservation*.

15 T. Knutson, "Investigation, engineering, and conservation combined: the reconstruction of a seventeenth century dress," in C. Varnell, C. McLean and S. A. Mathisen (eds.) *Postprints of the Nineteenth Annual Meeting of the Textile Speciality Group of AIC, Albuquerque, NM* [June 1991], Albuquerque, NM: AIC, 1991, pp. 27–45.

16 C. McLean, S. Rosenbaum and S. Schmalz, "A seventeenth century gown rediscovered: work in progress," in *Fashion in the Age of Louis XIV* (forthcoming).

17 Ibid.

18 Ibid.

19 Knutson, "Investigation, engineering, and conservation combined," p. 27.

20 Ibid., p. 43.

21 Ibid., p. 27.

22 Ibid., p. 41.

23 Ashley-Smith, "The basis of conservation ethics," p. 14.

24 Knutson, "Investigation, engineering, and conservation combined."

25 McLean, Rosenbaum and Schmalz, "A seventeenth century gown rediscovered."

26 Los Angeles County Museum of Art, Department of Costumes and Textiles, *Questionnaire: Court Dress*, M. 88.39, n.d.

27 B. Lemire, "Draping the body and dressing the home: the material culture of textiles and clothes in the Atlantic world, c. 1500–1800," in K. Harvey (ed.) *History and Material Culture: A Student's Guide to Approaching Alternative Sources*, London: Routledge, 2009, pp. 85–102.

28 K. Dózsa, "An eighteenth-century Hungarian court dress with nineteenth-century alterations: an example of historicism in the collections of the Hungarian National Museum," in I. Eri (ed.) *Conserving Textiles: Studies in Honour of Ágnes Tímár-Balázsy*, ICCROM Conservation Studies 7, Rome: ICCROM in conjunction with the Hungarian National Museum, 2009, pp. 52–59. Online. Available HTTP: http://www.iccrom.org/pdf/ICCROM_ ICS07_ConservingTextiles01_en.pdf (accessed 17 May 2010).

29 C. McLean et al., "A seventeenth century gown rediscovered."

30 F. Lennard and P. Ewer, "Treatment options: what are we conserving?" in Lennard and Ewer, *Textile Conservation*, pp. 53–62.

31 E. Avrami, R. Mason and M. de la Torre (eds.) *Values and Heritage Conservation*, Los Angeles: Getty Conservation Institute, 2000.

32 G. Wharton, "Dynamics of participatory conservation: the Kamehameha I sculpture project," *Journal of the American Institute for Conservation* (AIC) 47, 2008, pp. 159–73.

33 Ibid., p. 170.

34 Ibid., p. 168.

35 Ibid., p. 164.

36 Ibid., p. 161.

37 Ibid., p. 160.

38 Ibid., p. 172

39 Ibid., p. 162.

40 Ibid., p. 170, italics in the original.

41 Ibid.

42 Ibid.

43 See also L. Smith and N. Akagawa (eds.) *Intangible Heritage*, Abingdon: Routledge, 2009.

44 M. Clavir, "Preserving conceptual integrity: ethics and theory in preventive conservation," in A. Roy and P. Smith (eds.) *Preventive Conservation Practice, Theory and Research*, London: IIC, 1994, pp. 53–7.

45 C. Smith and M. Scott, "Ethics and practice: Australian and New Zealand conservation contexts," in Richmond and Bracker, *Conservation*, pp. 184–96.

46 Wharton, "Dynamics of participatory conservation," p. 162.

47 Ibid., p. 170.

48 S. Willcocks, "*Transparent Tubes* by William Turnbull: the degradation of a polymethyl methacrylate sculpture," in R. Vontobel (ed.) *Preprints of the Thirteenth Triennial Meeting of the ICOM Conservation Committee, September 2002, Rio de Janeiro, Brazil*, London: James & James, 2002, pp. 935–9.

49 Ibid., p. 938.

50 Ibid., p. 939.

51 Ibid., p. 938.

52 Pullen, e-mail to author, 4 October 2009.

53 T. Fiske, "White walls: installations, absence, iteration and difference," in Richmond and Bracker, *Conservation*, pp. 229–40; F. Lennard, "The impact of artists' moral rights legislation on conservation practice in the UK and beyond," in I. Verger (ed.) *Preprints of the Fourteenth Triennial Meeting of the ICOM Conservation Committee, The Hague*, Paris: ICOM, 2005, pp. 285–90; N. Stanley Price, M. K. Talley, Jr. and A. M. Vaccaro (eds.) *Historical and Philosophical Issues in the Conservation of Cultural Heritage*, Los Angeles: Getty Conservation Institute, 1996.

54 R. Barker and P. Smithen, "New art, new challenges: the changing face of conservation in the twenty-first century," in J. Marstine (ed.) *New Museum Theory and Practice: An Introduction*, Oxford: Blackwell, 2006, p. 95.

55 D. Eastop, "The cultural dynamics of conservation principles in reported practice," in Richmond and Bracker, *Conservation*, pp. 150–62.

56 S. M. Viñas, *Contemporary Theory of Conservation*, Oxford: Butterworth Heinemann/Elsevier, 2005, p. 92.

57 Knutson, "Investigation, engineering, and conservation combined," p. 29.

58 D. Greenberg, "Conservation and meaning," in L.E. Sullivan and A. Edwards (eds.) *Stewards of the Sacred*, Washington, DC: American Association of Museums, 2004, p. 45.

59 A. Cummins, "Ethics and heritage," *ICOM News*, 2005, 58: 3, p. 2.

60 S. M. Pearce, "Objects as meaning; or, Narrating the past," in S. Pearce (ed.) *Objects of Knowledge: New Research in Museum Studies*, Vol. I, London: Athlone Press, 1980, pp. 125–40.

61 G. Wharton, "Dynamics of participatory conservation," p. 162.

62 Ashley-Smith, "The basis of conservation ethics," p. 14.

63 Examples include H. Silverman and D. Fairchild Ruggles (eds.) *Cultural Heritage and Human Rights*, New York: Springer, 2007; L. Smith, *Uses of Heritage*, London: Routledge, 2006; L. Smith, "Empty gestures? Heritage and the politics of recognition," in Silverman and Ruggles (eds.) *Cultural Heritage and Human Rights*, pp. 159–71; see also N. Fraser, "Rethinking recognition," *New Left Review* 3, 2000 (May–June), pp. 107–20.

64 For example, Smith and Akagawa, *Intangible Heritage*.

65 M. Clavir, *Preserving What is Valued: Museums, Conservation and First Nations*, Vancouver: University of British Columbia Press, 2002; A-M. Deisser and D. Eastop, "Traditions and conventions in the care of tangible and intangible heritage in Ankober, Ethiopia: a partnership model in practice," in J. Bridgland (ed.) *Preprints ICOM Committee for Conservation, Fifteenth Triennial Conference, New Delhi, 22–26 September 2008*, New Delhi: Allied Publishers, 2008, pp. 1029–34; J. S. Johnson, S. Heald, K. McHugh, E. Brown and M. Kaminitz, "Practical aspects of consultation with communities," *Journal of the American Institute for Conservation* 44, 2005, pp. 203–15; V. Magar, "Conserving religious heritage within communities in Mexico," in H. Stovel, N. Stanley-Price and R. Killick (eds.) *Conservation of Living Religious Heritage*, Rome: ICCROM, pp. 86–93; D. Sully and I.P. Cardoso, "Conserving Hinemihi at Clandon Park, UK," in D. Sully (ed.) *Decolonising Conservation: Caring for Maori Meeting Houses outside New Zealand*, Walnut Creek, CA: Left Coast Press, 2007, pp. 199–219.

66 E. Pye and D. Sully, "Evolving challenges, developing skills," *Conservator* 30, 2007, pp. 19–38.
67 Barker and Smithen, "New art, new challenges," p. 86.
68 See, for example, C. Smith and H. Winkelbauer, "Conservation of a Maori eel trap: practical and ethical issues," in D. Saunders, J. H. Townsend and S. Woodcock (eds.) *The Object in Context: Crossing Conservation Boundaries*, London: IIC, 2006, pp. 128–32; Sully, *Decolonising Conservation*.

27

Bioart and nanoart in a museum context

Terms of engagement

Ellen K. Levy

Artworks informed by nanotechnology and biotechnology are as much ways to study culture as they are themselves objects of study.[1] They avoid a decontextualizing view of aesthetics, instead dealing with possibilities brought about by rapid technological changes. The artists involved utilize an expanding body of knowledge about these technologies to interrogate concepts of the body and its potential transformation. They ask whether and how the technology improves lives and at whose expense, providing viewers with unfamiliar, often invisible entities and highlighting processes that may involve the reconfiguration of matter and the replication of organisms. The body of evidence – the artwork – that accompanies this new information now presents some unprecedented ethical challenges to the museums that host it.

In this chapter I argue that the emergent art forms of bioart and nanoart are introducing critical new variables, which demand that museums consider how to exhibit living matter. However, the humane treatment of animals on display, their housing and protection are only the most obvious concerns. To support a sustainable ethics, museums will increasingly be required to consider other factors, both theoretical and practical. They may need to create new procedures for the shipping of biological artworks and the management and containment of hazardous or contagious materials to safeguard the public. In order to be true to the artists' visions museums may need to provide legal counseling, since many artists now debate the ownership of genetic material. Museums will have to ensure that they impart accurate information in signage and publications since the public may rely on these means for knowledge about nanotechnology and biotechnology. Museums must also be accurate about supporting artistic claims of genetic engineering or nanotechnology, the results of which are likely to be invisible. And they must ensure that scientists have been adequately credited for their contributions. A further concern is that the perennial problem museums face of preserving human dignity can recur in new technological forms. In addition, some works of bioart and nanoart are highly critical of corporations associated with biotechnology and nanotechnology development, and freedom from censorship must be safeguarded. To ensure they are free from the pressures of corporate sponsorship, vulnerable university museums may wish to establish separate endowment funds. As a final point, the acquisition of knowledge has arguably always been the most valuable product of museums as traditionally orchestrated through collections, architectural spaces and displays.[2] Museums must find ways to make bioart and nanoart accessible to a diverse public.

The ethical dimensions of museum display of art dealing with these technologies – nanoart and bioart – overlap but are not identical with those explored by artists. The artists often examine social problems caused by the new technologies whereas the museums must sometimes consider how the art is grappling with these topics since it may implicate them in questionable tactics. Ironically, sometimes the art fuels the very objections that it was intended to probe, prompting the question, "when does the museum's role of being faithful to artists' expressions of social critique interfere with its ethical obligations to protect the public?" This chapter will show that the artists under consideration have never in reality threatened public safety.

Art: the ethics of dual-use technologies

Issues of control loom large in discussions of biotechnology and nanotechnology. Like nuclear applications, these art forms employ dual-use technologies that can bring about both good and harm. As historian Richard Rhodes once noted, "The bomb was latent in nature as a genome is latent in flesh,"[3] implying that, given human nature, nuclear developments were inevitable, as are those of genetics today.

The strategies of artists dealing with biotechnology and nanotechnology sometimes parallel those of artists exploring the nuclear industry. For example, artist Gregory Green claims to have built quasi-functional nuclear devices with materials bought at the typical hardware store, using information publicly available.[4] Green demonstrates that nuclear technology is accessible to anyone today and questions whether the public should be denied access to potentially lethal equipment. Green, himself, conceives of his work as a kind of simulation that lures officials to overextend authority through inappropriate responses, such as arrest.[5] As a result, he has created a public forum for "debate about restrictions of individual liberties and the place of dangerous weapons within a free society."[6] It is important to observe that Green's quasi-functional "bombs" have sometimes needed to be reclassified as models rather than as empty weapons in order for Green to avoid arrest, thus demonstrating their ambiguous status as objects. Although their potential for harm is immense, it is apparent that nuclear weapons have not been used since World War II. Unlike atomic bombs, however, genetically engineered viruses or "nanobots"[7] are invisible, replicable and sustainable, and, therefore, the question of regulations is more critical.

Art dealing with biotechnology can question fundamental classifications of nature and culture. Significant ethical issues concern the production of new species of plants or animals that would no longer be able to propagate because of genomic alterations and, at the other extreme, the possibility that genetically modified organisms would be released into the environment and replace other life forms. Artists consider such issues as genetically modified food, reproductive rights, stem-cell research, ownership of genetic material, the possible resurgence of eugenics and the role that government should assume in establishing regulatory controls.[8]

Nanotechnology, which involves the construction and utilization of tiny molecular devices, similarly stimulates a wide range of expectations. Some believe the minute scale will fulfill its potential in applications that range from nanosurgery and prosthetic devices to molecular computers. Opponents fear the possibility of self-replicating "nanobots" that may damage the body.[9] Artists often address issues of surveillance since nano-scale implants can already direct the behavior of animals.[10]

Nanotechnology derives from materials science and offers the possibility of placing artificial components and assemblies within cells. A related development, nanobiotechnology, involves the interaction of nanotechnology with the body and the environment. Nanotechnology promises to fulfill the goals of complex-systems scientists of making new materials by using nature's own methods of self-organization, as seen in the dispersion modeling of inorganic matter. In addition to scientists and manufacturers, artists and designers have already availed themselves of some of these methods.

From metaphors to realities

The type of museum that displays biotechnology and nanotechnology has become somewhat determinative of the range of problems it encounters, and it is instructive to see how distinct museum genres have responded. Art and science exhibitions that take place at traditional and well-established fine art museums are likely to engage metaphors of science, rather than its processes. Typically, an exhibition such as *The Museum as Muse*, held in 1999 at the Museum of Modern Art (MoMA) in New York, has functioned somewhat like a cabinet of wonder in the sparkle and catholicity of items on display. Such shows might bring to mind exhibitions of earlier centuries when science museums and art museums were not conceived as separate institutions but as conjoined art and science collections such as the Medici collection in Florence.[11] As in the early *Wunderkammern*, viewers are invited to compare diverse collections from natural history and ethnographic museums with varieties of art objects created primarily for esthetic delectation. In nearly all these kinds of exhibitions, science has served as a springboard for the artist to explore subjective realms of poetry and metaphor.

Concurrent with this traditional approach, the Department of Architecture and Design at MoMA has taken a lead in experimental transdisciplinary collaborations between designers and engineers, featuring works dealing with recent technologies. *Design and the Elastic Mind* (February–May, 2008) included an exploration of nanotechnology, showing how designers work with scientists to use principles of self-assembly inherent in cells and molecules. For example, IBM Fellow Don Eigler used a scanning tunneling microscope to spell out "I–B–M." He is known for having positioned thirty-five xenon atoms to create the world's smallest logo in 1989. By including the IBM nano logo, MoMA indirectly pointed out the necessity for artists to develop their own strategies, metaphors and images of burgeoning technologies, apart from those provided by corporations. However, unlike some explicitly provocative displays in other, more experimental museum venues, MoMA's exhibits within this show, even including a project about organ transplantation, were not confrontational.[12]

Museum responsibilities to the living

Design and the Elastic Mind raised the possibility that the fine art museum will increasingly need to contend with living forms of art and their attendant ethics. On rare occasions MoMA has exhibited biological matter. For example, Edward Steichen's display of delphiniums altered by colchicine in 1936 established an early precedent for MoMA to consider maintenance concerns in displaying a living art form. In *Design and the Elastic Mind*, Curator Paola Antonelli stated that she needed to consider an entirely new category of art – semi-living tissue. Making an analogy with the ethical decisions sometimes faced by doctors, she relayed her hesitancy in switching off the "life support system" for bioartists Oron Catts and Ionat Zurr's 2004 art work, *Victimless Leather: A Prototype of Stitch-less Jacket Grown in a Tech-noscientific "Body,"* which required a sterile environment maintained at an appropriate temperature (Figure 27.1).[13] The artwork consisted of a small jacket grown in a test tube using cells made of biodegradable polymer connective and bone. The cultured cell lines formed a living layer of tissue supported by a polymer matrix.

Through a somewhat clinical-looking display, Catts and Zurr intended to "confront people with the moral implications of wearing parts of dead animals for protective and aesthetic reasons … "[14] As theorist Adele Senior has pointed out, visitors allowed to touch such exhibits are ethically implicated, as touching can destroy the tissue through the bacteria and fungi on hands and in the air.[15] In actuality, this experiential aspect was not available to visitors at MoMA since the artwork was sealed off to preserve sterile conditions. In addition to his own provocative practice, Oron Catts initiated the Tissue Culture and Art Project in 1996 to teach tissue culture techniques to other artists.[16] This resulted in SymbioticA, an artistic laboratory within the School of Anatomy and Human Biology at the University of Western Australia. Zurr and Catts's exposure at MoMA offers great incentive to other artists to incorporate wet-lab methods and implies a potential commitment on MoMA's part to exhibiting further work in this vein. MoMA has set a high standard with respect to maintaining living matter in accordance with artistic aims. It does not have an explicit policy about plants, animals or tissue cultures but judges the potential hazards of the work in each instance.[17]

What are museums' ethical responsibilities towards animals? Should animals be used for artistic ends, and should museums display the results? MASS MoCA exhibited works in *Becoming Animal* (May 2005–February 2006) that focused on genetic engineering. The presence of animals in the exhibition led People for the Ethical Treatment of Animals (PETA) to initially protest artist Kathy High's installation, *Embracing Animal*, which involved rats used in medical experiments that had been genetically engineered with oncogenes, making them readily susceptible to cancer.[18] High's work suggests that we reconsider animal rights in relation to their use in medical research. She stated that she wished to show that their housing would impact on their behavior in ways that might negate scientific assumptions concerning their natural behavior.[19] As High recounts, once PETA saw her installation at Mass

Figure 27.1 The Tissue Culture & Art Project (Oron Catts & Ionat Zurr) *Victimless Leather – A Prototype of Stitch-less Jacket* grown in a Technoscientific 'Body,' 2004; Medium: Biodegradable polymer connective and bone cells.

MoCA, PETA endorsed her project, believing that the rats' lives were actually enriched, compared to their typical laboratory environment. At present, all animal research, including clinical studies that involve the general public, must meet current regulatory requirements and oversight. According to U.S. federal law, institutions that use laboratory animals for research or instructional purposes must establish an

Institutional Animal Care and Use Committee.[20] The Animal Welfare Act requires that scientists using live animals in experiments register their activities.[21]

High's installation necessitated docents, gallery sitters, curators and other staff to discuss her work with the visiting public on a daily basis. She described that a vet would come to check on the rats, and staff would clean their habitat regularly. Her experience at MASS MoCA was very positive, since the curatorial, technical and construction staff enabled her to create and maintain the work properly for ten months. High declared her work to be primarily a critique of "pharma" and science institutions. In fact, as she explains, her work also critiqued art institutions as she exposed

> ... the process of using animals as products for medical/pharmaceutical research. The irony is that there are still huge problems with exhibiting animals in a gallery/museum space ... the animals become commodities again – art objects as opposed to laboratory products ... perhaps this is an inherent critique of the gallery system too. By that I mean that this work might really extend and question the actual meaning of the practice of curating = to care.[22]

Museums could justly interpret her statement as a challenge to them to ensure an ethical infrastructure and context for displays that include animals.

It is not yet fully clear how museums should deal with living matter and animals, and this has become a significant issue as we witness recorded acts of violence and cruelty to animals in exhibitions.[23] As only one of many possible examples, Adel Abdessemed's video, *Usine*, made in Mexico (2009), captures different animal and insect species deliberately thrown together into a pen to create a "spectacle of death."[24] On April 20, 2010, the court struck down the 1999 animal cruelty law for infringing on free-speech protections guaranteed by the First Amendment of the U.S. Constitution.[25] Although similar issues have arisen in the past, more guidelines to insure humane treatment of animals may become necessary as the tendency to exhibit living art increases. The College Art Association has, in fact, established a task force in 2010, including artists, art historians and bioethicists to deliberate on the use of human and animal subjects in art.

Encountering new dilemmas

"Teaching art museums" are often expected to play a significant role in campus education through addressing disciplines in addition to art, such as the natural and social sciences. They may encourage staff, faculty and undergraduates to make use of research facilities on campus. As a result, a faculty member or student of the university wishing to conduct artistic research in biotechnology and/or nanotechnology, may gain access to the requisite technological training or develop prospects of collaborating with scientists at their institutions who have those skills. A university museum displaying "artistic research" can become a nexus for educating its students and the visiting public about the science and ramifications of particular technologies.

In 1999, the Henry Art Gallery of the University of Washington (UW) in Seattle launched "Future Forward: Projects in New Media", a special initiative to mount a series of exhibitions of new technologies. Within a few years, it faced several novel challenges regarding the handling of living materials, meeting legal requirements and realizing artistic intentions while safeguarding the public. The first of these appeared when Associate Curator Rhonda Lane Howard developed the exhibition *Banks in Pink and Blue* (January–April, 2000), an installation by artist Iñigo Manglano-Ovalle. The installation called for a cryogenic sperm bank that contained spermatozoa grouped by the presence of the X or Y sex-determinant chromosome, a liquid nitrogen tank and a monitor and video player. The artwork explored ethical issues of assisted reproduction technology, DNA ownership and medical consumer choice. As a prime example, to carry out his self-assigned task within the museum space, the artist needed to legally become a "bank" in order to buy and sell sperm![26] This illustrates how museums may increasingly be compelled to comply with unusual legal requirements.

Two years later, at the same institution, the exhibition *Gene(sis): Contemporary* Art *Explores Human Genomics* (April – August, 2002) explored the potential social, emotional and ethical implications of the completion of a draft of the human genome.[27] The Henry Art Gallery included DNA portraits, abstract "gene-mapping" paintings and digital constructions of transgenic beings. Paul Vanouse's artwork, *Relative Velocity Inscription Device* (*RVID*) (Figure 27.2), necessitated special arrangements.

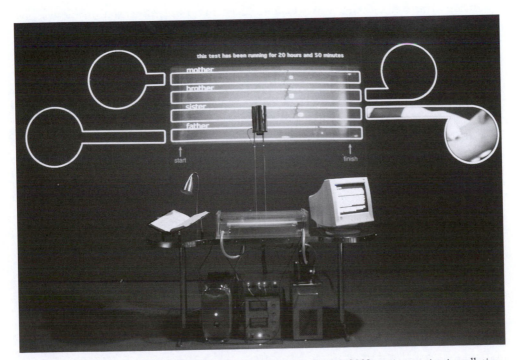

Figure 27.2 Paul Vanouse, *The Relative Velocity Inscription Device*, 2002, an interactive installation, including a computer mediated simulation.

RVID, a meditation about identity, provided a vehicle for the artist to speculate about the likelihood of genetics leading to new abuses of power. Vanouse incorporated the DNA of a multiracial family of Jamaican descent in order to conflate contemporary DNA separation technologies with earlier twentieth-century research methods used by eugenicists. In *RVID*, Vanouse made a subtle point that concerns the notion that DNA evidence can be viewed as a "coded cultural representation," as opposed to irrefutable scientific proof. In this way, he assumed the position of philosopher Bruno Latour and others who argue that science, like art, is rooted in the social sphere, reflecting subjective rather than absolute values.[28]

To fulfill its commitment to an artist's work, a museum must have an appropriate infrastructure for exhibiting it. Vanouse's experiences were similar to those of interactive installation artists, whose displays need constant monitoring and upkeep. However, in addition to using "dry" media, Vanouse and other bioartists often employ "wet" media. Vanouse praised the Henry Art Gallery's diligence in consulting health and safety officers and preparing gels twice a week during the four-month show.[29] Beyond the use of a dedicated microwave and freezer, Vanouse needed to be able to prepare chemicals a few hours before his performative demonstrations since wet biological items are often time-sensitive. Maintaining *RVID* (which the artist states continually runs live DNA experiments) required the museum to change gels periodically. By committing to Vanouse's vision through meeting *RVID*'s novel requirements, the Henry served as a model for other museums showing bioart.

During *Gene(sis)*, the Henry Art Gallery faced two other potential problems: one involved the transport of life forms intended for exhibition. The packaging and transportation of biological materials are subject to strict state, federal and international regulations. Museums must provide assurances that no contaminants or hazardous materials are involved and must conform to rules about containers and labeling.[30] In addition, artists included in *Gene(sis)* were not permitted to include any form of human blood.[31] The curator followed the guidelines of the Environmental Health and Safety Department at UW. In accordance with National Institutes of Health (NIH) rules, artists' works were registered as "laboratory activity."[32] It was left up to the pilots or drivers to decide if they were willing to transport the living art. If not, the museum requested that artists provide an alternate work. The request is problematic since it is tantamount to asking an artist to agree to self-censorship.

The other problem raised more serious concerns. The *Gene(sis)* opening featured the installation piece *Gen Terra* (Figure 27.3), a participatory project by the Critical Art Ensemble (CAE). CAE is an artists' collective whose work has focused on genetics and biotechnology. Many of CAE's projects involve the tools and processes used to engineer genetic materials. *Gen Terra* was additionally intended to engage public action as opposition to corporate control of the practice of genetic engineering. *Gen Terra* included a lab tent, four computer stations and a bacteria release machine. An installation within the makeshift lab presented information about transgenics that enabled viewers to create their own safe, engineered bacteria through the use of a machine.[33] After their "lab work," visitors were asked to make the decision of whether or not to release into the air a benign strain of bacteria from one of twelve Petri dishes of a bacteria-release machine. As described by CAE, eleven of the twelve dishes had wild (non-transgenic) bacteria samples taken locally.

Figure 27.3 Critical Art Ensemble and Beatriz da Costa, *GenTerra*, 2001–2003, Participants manipulated transgenic bacteria in an effort to develop a more nuanced understanding of risk assessment regarding the uses of recombinant DNA.

If the dish with the "benign" transgenic bacteria was selected, a robotic arm picked up the lid of the dish, briefly exposed it and then replaced the lid on the dish.[34]

Were the artist and museum ethically justified in staging such a simulation? Some members of the public might mistakenly have viewed it as real.[35] The art was intended to provoke a discussion on dangerous military tactics and was similar to the approach Gregory Green had used while exploring nuclear capabilities. But the products of biotechnology are harder to detect, thus potentially posing more of a threat. CAE received an unexpected defense of its staged stimulations from medical ethicist George Annas in 2006. His article in the *New England Journal of Medicine* compared the CAE's bacterial "simulations," as led by CAE artist Steve Kurtz, to the U.S. government's own 1950 biowarfare simulations. The government had used the harmless bacteria, *Serratia marcescens*, to determine what dose could be delivered effectively to the population.[36] Annas determined that there was no adequate justification to challenge Kurtz for similar simulations which posed no real harm and were produced on a reduced scale.[37]

The political contexts in which exhibitions take place can certainly influence what kinds of infrastructures museums need. Since CAE performed *Gen Terra* in Seattle just after the anthrax attacks had taken place in the United States, the Henry Art Gallery had to go through lengthy negotiations with environmental agencies and register with the NIH in the interest of public safety. The performance of *Gen Terra* required approval by the UW Institutional Biosafety and Recombinant DNA Committees.

As they negotiated all of these challenges, the Henry Art Gallery was in the unusual position as a university museum of having to access necessary legal advice, recommendations and guidance from appropriate regulatory committees. Robin Held, who was Associate Curator of the Henry Art Gallery at the time, stated that the kinds of state precautions these exhibitions necessitated were highly unusual in art circles but believes that they may become more frequent as biotech art pro-liferates.[38] In the meantime the Henry established important precedents, which have already paved the way for other exhibitions of bioart and nanoart.

As a coda to these issues, Kurtz subsequently became the focus of an FBI bioterrorism investigation. During the spring of 2004, several years following CAE's simulations at *Gen Terra*, Kurtz was assembling work for an upcoming exhibition at MASS MoCA. Kurtz woke to find that his wife had died of a heart attack.[39] He called 911 and, after the police saw laboratory equipment in his home, they notified the FBI. The FBI charged Kurtz under a provision of the Biological Weapons Act that had recently been expanded by the U.S. Patriot Act of 2001. Although the charges were eventually changed to mail and wire fraud before being dismissed as "insufficient on its face," he and geneticist Robert Ferrell were brought before a federal grand jury. His art was confiscated by the Federal authorities, including work scheduled to have been exhibited at MASS MoCA. It is instructive to consider MASS MoCA's decision to open Steve Kurtz's political situation to public discussion. In response to the trumped-up charges leveled at Kurtz and Ferrell, MASS MoCA placed news clip-pings of the legal proceedings on their exhibition walls and invited the public to observe and comment on the ongoing events. Visitors to the museum left numerous messages in support of Kurtz, and the museum, in fact, succeeded in becoming an active forum for airing public policies about genetics. In part, due to MASS MoCA's activism, the assault on Kurtz succeeded in unifying the art world and its publics to his defense. Importantly, MASS MoCA established a laudable precedent in dealing with a potentially fraught political situation.

Contending with the invisible

The results of nanotechnology and genetic engineering are often invisible and may create a problem for traditional Western museums that were established primarily to display aesthetic objects. In actuality, of course, "invisible" art has always existed, including anamorphosis and imagery placed where it could not be seen well or at all. As one notable example, caves with Paleolithic period paintings such as Chauvet that are now closed to the public were apparently also closed to most visitors when they were made. Evidently these caves were found by experts who were able to document footprints in the dust and concluded that the caves were only entered on limited occasions.[40] Museums have featured the ways artists make the invisible visible since the origins of abstract art, although the approach to this subject has tended to shift from spiritual and metaphorical (e.g., "ineffable" art) to the literal (e.g., genetic material and nanoparticles, which are unseen by the human eye).

As theoretician N. Katherine Hayles makes clear, artists restore a crucial dimension of perception by intimating a complex understanding of biotechnology and nano-technology through "embodiment" – tangible physical presentations that have the ability to instantiate what is otherwise invisible.[41] Invisibility also raises the possibility of fraud, since viewers may need to take it on faith that the artists have actually created a molecule or genetically modified organism when they are unseen by the naked eye. Do museums have a responsibility to expose artists who make false claims? How relevant is this critique to artistic aims? Documentation of collaborations and processes has substantiated at least some of the claims made by many of the bioartists active in this field.

According to Professor of Communications Adriana de Souza e Siva, " ... *nano* challenges the traditional concept of what a museum is through three interconnected actions: enlarging what is supposed to be invisible; mixing virtual and physical spaces; and exploring the borderland between the real and the imaginary."[42] The Exploratorium in San Francisco achieved all three objectives in 2006 when it surveyed artistic investigations of nanoscale science, such as Scott Snibbe's *Three Drops* and Victoria Vesna's *Nanomandala*.[43] As Vesna explained, "The ethical questions are less about the work itself, and more in relation to how one develops the work in collaboration with scientists. This is because the science world is very much linked to corporations, pharmaceutical and defense industries."[44] Vesna involves citizens with science policymaking through an open debate and analysis of benefits and risks (both real and perceived) of nanotech. She does this not only through her art, but through an educational program linked with an exhibition site, the Art|Sci Center gallery at UCLA, which she directs along with nanoscientist James Gimzewski. The center's affiliation with the California NanoSystems Institute offers access to scientists and their laboratories and a dedicated gallery for exhibitions. It sets a good precedent by fully crediting scientists along with artists for their contributions. The UCLA School of the Arts and the Department of Design | Media Arts lends its support to the Art|Sci Center, which hosts visiting research scholars and artists in residency from around the world. Vesna's artwork, *Zero@Wavefunction: nano Dreams & Nightmares* (Figure 27.4), includes snippets of information from a variety of sources, including magazines, newspapers, academic papers, science fiction novels, corporate sales and conversations that constitute a continuously growing online database. The purpose is to see how our culture views nanotechnology.[45]

Artists involved with nanotechnology and biotechnology have fostered important collaborations. For example, Paul Thomas, creator of the nano artwork, *Midas*, collaborated with artists Catts and Zurr to realize the scientific portion of his project that necessitated the culturing of skin cells. After their production, Thomas imaginatively visualized the action of self-organized nanobots by applying digital algorithms. He also audified the sounds associated with the cell cultures, bringing a multi-modal dimension to his work.[46] According to Thomas:

> The ethical concern for me is defining boundaries – what the science fiction writer creates is an immunity rather than a community to protect itself from nanobots. An ethical question of what constitutes life at a nano level is my current work. If nano can rebuild nature atom by atom, then where does life as consciousness exist?[47]

The salient point for museums is to develop a context suitable to the philosophical concerns of the artist, particularly when the artist is addressing what it means to make invisibility tangible on a spiritual level. The ethical questions therefore involve the museums in validating that a process invisible to sight has actually been carried

Figure 27.4 Victoria Vesna, *Zero@Wavefunction: nano Dreams & Nightmares*, 2002, Interactive Installation in collaboration with nanoscientist James Gimzewski. Software art by Josh Nimoy.

out and in making certain that the installation of a work is fully in keeping with the artist's content.

Preserving the dignity of the body

Körperwelten, or *Human Body World* (1998), was a controversial exhibition created by Günther von Hagens who developed a process called plastination to preserve real human corpses and body parts. It raised questions about preserving the dignity of the human being. The ethical issues involved both the museum's presentation of the body and the source of these bodies (see Chapter 22).[48] Raising similar problems, in December 2000 at El Gallo Arte Contemporáneo in Salamanca, Spain, artist Santiago Sierra's video documentary *160 cm Line Tattooed on Four People* highlighted the economics of human exploitation. As a result, not only did the artist receive criticism about his means of doing this, but the museum's ethical stance was also indirectly implicated.[49] The Tate collection owns the photodocumentation, raising the issue of the museum's tacit approval of the artist's tactics. As the precedent of Mapplethorpe has demonstrated, museums have a right and perhaps even a moral obligation to show harsh realities.

Media artist Jill Scott's *e-skin* and *Electric Retina* which have been exhibited within the scientific and technical exhibition contexts of the International Society for the Electronic Arts (ISEA) and at the Museum für Gestaltung Zürich offer good counter examples of projects that foster respect for the body. Both works concern technology's ability to extend the body's sensory capacities. *E-skin* addresses ergonomic human–computer interfaces that assist the visually impaired by augmenting navigation and orientation through cross-modal cueing.[50] Her approach continues her fascination with developing ways in which technology can promote agency by supplementing the body with flexible interfaces and emphasizing inter-modal senses like touch and sound. In *Electric Retina* viewers activate videos through sensors that show what an underwater environment would look like, as seen through various defects of vision of zebrafish. Since the zebrafish is a model often used to study the human eye, Scott's neurosculpture promotes empathy for the non-human "others" while modeling eye defects for uses of medical pedagogy. Most of Scott's work solicits the active participation of the viewer. In *Electric Retina*, the sculptural surface references oculars based on human photoreceptors, incorporating dynamic scenes of animated medical imaging that reveal what the eye alone cannot see. Hers is an interpretive vision. The scientific and technical museums that display her work reap the benefits of exhibiting cutting-edge artistic work while avoiding ethical dilemmas stemming from abject content.

Artists such as Scott are enthusiastic about exhibiting their art in science museums and also in the design departments of fine art museums, many of which, like MoMA, have been addressing new interfaces and technologies. Scott believes that these venues mesh well with her artistic aims, but not all artists and viewers concur. Some argue that science venues marginalize the art exhibited, whether through failure of maintenance, architectural restrictions or lack of context. Some science museums (e.g., the old exhibition spaces of the New York Academy of Sciences and Association for the Advancement of Science spaces) have introduced art into structures without

adequate or favorable exhibition display spaces and in which the existent architecture only allowed for makeshift solutions. In most cases, such deficiencies are
offset by contextualizing the art being exhibited and by the prestige of the institution.

Funding conflicts

Institutional contexts and sponsorship can be inconsistent with critical attitudes.
Jacqueline Stevens, an associate professor of the law and society program at the
University of California, Santa Barbara, judged this to be the case in *The Genomic
Revolution: Secrets of Life, Secrets of Death* (May–January, 2001), held at the American
Museum of Natural History (AMNH). The project explored the results obtained by
the Human Genome Project, the application of sequence information in medicine
and agriculture and some of the social issues surrounding its use. Stevens criticized
the AMNH for hanging misleading signage in deference to the exhibition's corporate
sponsors.[51] As examples, Stevens cited signage claiming that "gene therapy will make
most common surgery of today obsolete" and other statements that implied that
biotechnology would significantly enhance life expectancy and conquer disease
within unrealistically short time frames.

Funding, not surprisingly, often comes from corporations which may have financial
interests in how the public views biotechnology. In *The Genomic Revolution* and other
exhibitions such as the Field Museum's traveling exhibition *Gregor Mendel: Planting
the Seeds of Genetics* (2006–08), sponsored by Monsanto, visitors might surmise friction
between some of the critical artistic aims and the corporate goals, which mainly
emphasized the positive aspects of biotechnology. In contrast, museums, like the
Exploratorium, which receive substantial grants from the National Science Foundation
(NSF) in support of their educational roles in scientific understanding, can presumably
have more latitude in the art they show, as compared with museums primarily
dependent upon corporate sponsorship. It would probably be inaccurate to make
sweeping generalizations, however, since many foundations whose wealth may have
derived from corporate investments are focused on improving human and animal
health. Such foundations as the Wellcome Trust and Gulbenkian Foundation that
foster the public understanding of science through art have successfully sponsored
art/science exhibitions within museums of science and have critically examined the
social and political issues raised by new technologies.

Hans Haacke has observed that one sees relatively few exhibitions that would
offend governing boards or corporate donors, and he argues that corporations can
strategically co-opt oppositional forces by burying "negative" sentiments within an
overall positive message, thus neutralizing a critique.[52] Actual censorship is not generally necessary since an effective method of control is to enlist artists in the process of
self-censorship through carrot/stick controls of finance and media opportunities.

Elitism versus populism

Accessibility to content has been a long-standing problem for many kinds of museums,
particularly art museums.[53] Activist artists involved with science have responded by

rethinking the traditional hierarchal positions of audiences and content providers. For instance, a group of artists declaring themselves "amateur scientists" is very concerned with informing the public about scientific issues. These artists challenge the limitations placed on the non-specialist's access to information such as existed during the 1990s, when the "culture wars" involved the resistance of conservative scientists to having the general public intrude on their turf. The resulting art works reflect strategies first developed in the early 1980s by AIDS Coalition to Unleash Power (ACT UP) and feminists protesting the possible loss of agency to the individual as a result of emerging biomedical imaging technologies.[54] During the next decade, leaders of activist organizations, including ACT UP and Women's Health Mobilization (WHAM!), analyzed and critiqued the implications of medical imaging technologies and assisted reproductive technologies.[55] At present, "amateur scientists," inspired by this critique, are producing artwork that utilizes some of the methodologies of science but outside laboratory settings in order to challenge scientific hegemony.[56] These artists believe that the adverse potential of science is so great that it should not be left to scientists and government to make critical policy decisions.

Educational priorities issuing from both museums and artists have conceivably enabled the art-going public to better identify pertinent social concerns regarding new technologies. This has been reinforced by the growing movement called "citizen science," characterized by increasing public engagement of scientists in activities from neuroscience boot camps to the development of open-source primary scientific research, as seen in the *Public Library of Science*.[57]

Conclusion

Museums that exhibit living forms, new molecules or transgenic art may require new infrastructures to ensure the humane handling of animals, implement the proper installation and maintenance of fragile displays and cope with legal problems that, until now, have rarely existed. It is timely that museums undertaking contemporary exhibitions of bioart and nanoart consider whether their current infrastructures can adequately protect and maintain living matter and what they need to do to plan for the future. Living art has raised moral obligations for the institutions that incorporate it, in addition to the other ethical dilemmas explored in this chapter. Because the ramifications of biotechnology and nanotechnology are increasingly part of our daily lives, these media are finding increasing expression in our museums. In the *New York Review of Books*, scientist Freeman Dyson predicted that public perception of biotechnology will most likely become increasingly positive as it is domesticated in everyday life. Dyson stated that "designing genomes will be a personal thing, a new art form as creative as painting or sculpture."[58] Actually, this development is now underway and museums exhibiting such work are hastening the process. However, adaptation is not always regarded favorably by those who view it as inevitably supporting corporate interests, by those artists who resist the process of normalization, itself, or by critics who may view the artists as exploitative of novelty.[59]

Curator Robin Held has claimed that cutting-edge shows about biotechnology may already be a thing of the past since a post-9/11 chill has permeated many museum ventures. But, to the contrary, exhibitions featuring nanoart and bio-technology are taking place on an international scale and are seen at institutions such as the ZKM (Karlsruhe, Germany) and Ars Electronica Center (Linz, Austria). Museums wishing to show nanoart and bioart might give more thought about how to incorporate successful approaches from these and other alternative venues. In contrast to larger art museums, spaces like Wave Hill (Bronx, New York) frequently endorse trans-disciplinary projects and activist concerns since the curators' aims are often identical with those of the artists.

The artworks and museums analyzed here have succeeded to varying degrees in opening up ethical issues of nanotechnology and biotechnology to greater public awareness. Some of the tactics are aggressive and others more meditative; all are informational and some experiential. The danger zones lie in the nature of the artis-tic critiques and in their presentation by museums – whether they consist of inac-curacies or overgeneralizations or whether they offer more nuanced insights into how new technologies can enlarge our choices and quality of life.

In the end, in addition to the humane treatment of animals, one of the most important ethical decisions may involve how well the museum delivers on its man-date to produce knowledge through presenting artworks that can affect public dis-course and influence the understanding of science. Museums may need to consider new terms of engagement for work that reflects some artists' innate mistrust of technologies with roots in the military and of corporations profiting from their spin-offs. Ideally, by providing accurate and transparent public access to pertinent infor-mation, museums will foster public learning about the complex, social ramifications of technologies defining our time and serve as a point of resistance to distortions stemming from government and corporate priorities. Obtaining these desired goals will, in large measure, depend upon how the museum goes about the production of knowledge in relatively unfamiliar areas and with few precedents from which to draw. In addition to the problems discussed, the ephemeral nature of some con-temporary art, coupled with an emphasis on process, will create greater necessity for documentation and project support. Museums may also need to determine whether they have an obligation to collect and maintain work that incorporates living matter. The museum is a key component in identifying a work of art as significant through collecting it and thus insuring its longevity. This decision is decidedly an ethical one since it will determine what is likely to survive into the future.

Creating the conditions conducive to exhibiting nanoart and bioart may help to foster a new type of artist, viewer and museum. Our concepts of artistic media change radically when the artwork consists of living matter or involves invisible molecular devices that have dimensions of between 1 nm and 100 nm (roughly one hundred thousandth the thickness of a human hair).[60] Our ideas of artists are simi-larly affected since, to create such art and to become adept in making it accessible, the political artists among them – some paradoxically functioning as "radical didacts" – must be well versed in the sciences and in media outside the artistic sphere. The viewer will be expected to attend to new information and consider ethical dimensions normally nonexistent within museum settings. Finally, our expectations of fine art museums that show such work are also transformed since their traditional purpose of aesthetic scrutiny must give way to considerations about the production and presentation of knowledge in the fields of concern and to the attendant moral dilemmas. Like photography's famous concept of the "external referent,"[61] the present artistic use of wet-lab, simulation and data visualization techniques are creating new bodies of "evidence." As museums exhibit living matter and new life forms, a network of obligations necessarily follows.

Acknowledgments

Thanks to Paula Antonelli, Paul Cabarga, Beatrice da Costa, Robin Held, Kathy High, Natalie Jeremijenko, Barbara London, Paul Vanouse and Victoria Vesna for providing valuable information for this text.

Notes

1 "Bioart" and "nanoart" are terms used here to include artworks that may respectively reference or incorporate scientific processes of biotechnology and nanotechnology.
2 B. Robertson, "Curiosity Cabinets, Museums, and Universities," in C. J. Sheehy (ed.) *Cabinet of Curiosities: Mark Dion and the University as Installation*, exhibition catalog, Frederick R. Weisman Art Museum, University of Minnesota, 2006, p. 43.
3 R. Rhodes, *The Making of the Atomic Bomb*, New York: Simon & Schuster, 1986, p. 379.
4 Gregory Green web site. Online. Available HTTP: http://www.aeroplastics.net/green_1999/greengr1.html (accessed 17 May 2010).
5 Green made these comments at a panel on 30 September 2005 accompanying the exhibition "A Knock at the Door" at the Cooper Union. Online. Available HTTP: http://www.cooper.edu/art/exhibitions.html (accessed 17 May 2010).
6 Ibid.
7 Nanobots are nanomachines that scientists use to construct objects on an atom-by-atom basis, as described in C. Milburn, "Nanotechnology in the Age of Posthuman Engineering: Science Fiction as Science," in N. K. Hayles (ed.) *Nanoculture: Implications of the New Technoscience*, Chicago: University of Chicago Press, 2004, p. 109.
8 E. K. Levy, "Art Enters the Biotechnology Debate: Questions of Ethics," in G. Levin and E. King (eds.) *Ethics and the Visual Arts*, New York: Allworth Press, 2006, pp. 199–216.
9 G. P. Zachary, "Ethics for a Very Small World," *Foreign Policy*, 14: 3, 2003 (July–August), pp. 108–109.
10 K. Smith, "Monkeys Move Paralyzed Muscles with their Minds," *Nature*, 15 October 2008. Online. Available HTTP: http://www.nature.com/news/2008/081015/full/news.2008.1170.html (accessed 17 May 2010).
11 S. A. Bedini, "The Evolution of Science Museum, Technology and Culture," *Museums of Technology* 6: 1, 1965, p. 9.
12 The project was that of Elio Caccavale. Online. Available HTTP: http://press.moma.org/images/press/press_release_archive/DEMRelease.pdf (accessed 17 May 2010).
13 See business.view in *Economist.com*, 1 April 2008. Online. Available HTTP: http://www.economist.com/business/PrinterFriendly.cfm?story_id=10946762 (accessed 17 May 2010).
14 L. Sandhana, "Jacket Grows from Living Tissue," *Wired*, 12 October 2004. Online. Available: HTTP: http://www.wired.com/science/discoveries/news/2004/10/65248 (accessed 17 May 2010).
15 A. Senior, "In the Face of the Victim: Confronting the Other in the Tissue Culture and Art Project," in Jens Houser (ed.) *sk-interfaces*, Liverpool: Liverpool University Press, 2008, p. 79.
16 With Dr. Stuart Bunt, Catts co-founded SymbioticA, the Art and Science Collaborative Research Laboratory, School of Anatomy and Human Biology, at the University of Western Australia in Perth, to enable artists to engage in wet biology practices in a science department.

17 Paola Antonelli, e-mail correspondence with author, 17 May 2010. MoMA required participants to sign release waivers because of internet access and the Flickr site during the Marina
Abramovic exhibition (2010).

18 *Embracing Animal*, 2005–06, a mixed media installation with video sculptures and lab rats,
was exhibited at MASS MoCA as part of the group exhibition *Becoming Animal*, curated
by Nato Thompson. Online. Available HTTP: http://www.massmoca.org/event_details.
php?id=310 (accessed 17 May 2010).

19 R. Thomas, R. Insel and D. Fernald, "How the Brain Processes Social Information:
Searching for the Social Brain," *Annual Review of Neuroscience* 27, 2004 (July), p. 699.

20 The Institutional Animal Care and Use Committee. Online. Available HTTP: http://www.
iacuc.org/aboutus.htm (accessed 17 May 2010).

21 Animal protocols. Online. Available HTTP: http://grants.nih.gov/grants/olaw/references/
38_6_0609.pdf (accessed 17 May 2010).

22 Kathy High, e-mail correspondence with author, 30 May 2009.

23 The International Council of Museums (ICOM) *Code of Ethics for Museums*, 2006, 2.25
Welfare of Live Animals, states, "A museum that maintains living animals should assume
full responsibility for their health and well being. It should prepare and implement a safety
code for the protection of its personnel and visitors, as well as of the animals, that has
been approved by an expert in the veterinary field. Genetic modification should be clearly
identifiable." Online. Available HTTP: htttp://icom.museum/ethics.html (accessed 17 May
2010).

24 Saatchi. Online. Available HTTP: http//www.saatchi-gallery.co.uk/blogon/art_news/jerry_
saltz_on_adel_abdessemeds_fighting_animal_video/5609 (accessed 27 January 2011).

25 J. Vicini, "U.S. Supreme Court Strikes down Animal Cruelty Law," *Reuters*, 20 April 2010.
Online. Available HTTP: http://www.reuters.com/article/idUSN209833420100420 (accessed
17 May 2010).

26 Robin Held, personal communication with author, 26 January 2009.

27 L. E. Stern, *The Gene(sis) Project: A Laboratory for Arts-based Civic Dialog*. Online. Available
HTTP: http://www.americansforthearts.org/animatingdemocracy/pdf/labs/henry_art_gallery_
case_study.pdf (accessed 17 May 2010).

28 B. Latour, *Science in Action*, Cambridge, MA: Harvard University Press, 1987.

29 Paul Vanouse, e-mail correspondence to author, 30 May 2009; Vanouse stated that many
other museums were unwilling to take on these extended tasks, causing *RVID* to sit out
the rest of the tour.

30 Transportation of Biological Materials. Online. Available HTTP: http://www.lbl.gov/ehs/
biosafety/Biosafety_Manual/html/transportation.shtml (accessed 17 May 2010).

31 L. Lamberg, "Artistic Response to Genomic Research Shown," *Journal of the American
Medical Association* 288, 2002, pp. 1458–1461.

32 Paul Cabarga, Exhibition Manager, Henry Museum of Art, interview by author, 5 January
2009.

33 Creative Capital. Online. Available HTTP: http://creative-capital.org/projects/view/270
(accessed 17 May 2010).

34 Ibid.

35 Critical Art Ensemble. Online. Available HTTP: http://www.critical-art.net/Biotech.html
(accessed 17 May 2010). While studying the history of germ warfare, artist Steven Kurtz
was planning to simulate anthrax and plague attacks, but using harmless agents like *Serratia
marcescens* and *E. coli*.

36 G. J. Annas, "Bioterror and 'BioArt': a Plague o' Both your Houses," *New England Journal
of Medicine* 354: 25, 2006, pp. 2715–2720.

37 Ibid., p. 2718. Annas concluded that " … although the advances of biotechnology that
have potential applications to bioterrorism and biowarfare are scary, even scarier are the
responses – in the name of preventing bioterrorism – of law-enforcement agencies to
legitimate scientists and artists whose actions pose no threat to the public."

38 Robin Held, interview by author, 26 January 2009.

39 L. Lynch, "Culturing the Pleebland: The Idea of the 'Public' in Genetic Art," *Literature and
Medicine* 26: 1, 2007, pp. 180–206.

40 S. P. M. Harrington, "Human Footprints at Chauvet Cave," *Archaeology* 52: 5, 1999 (September–October). Online. Available HTTP: http://www.archaeology.org/9909/newsbriefs/chauvet.html (accessed 17 May 2010). I thank Eve Sinaiko for this example of invisible art.

41 This is a point frequently made by Katherine K. Hayles in *Nanoculture*.

42 A. De Souza e Silva, "The Invisible Imaginary: Museum Spaces, Hybrid Reality and Nanotechnology," in Hayles, *Nanoculture*, p. 31.

43 Art Nano. Online. Available HTTP: http://www.nisenet.org/artnano/perspectives/tom-rockwell/ (accessed 17 May 2010).

44 Victoria Vesna's Interactive Experience. Online. Available HTTP: http://www.digicult.it/digimag/article.asp?id=705 (accessed 17 May 2010).

45 Dreams and Nightmares. Online. Available HTTP: http://www.notime.arts.ucla.edu/zerowave/dreamsnightmares.htm (accessed 17 May 2010).

46 P. Thomas, "midas: a nanotechnological exploration of touch," *Leonardo* 42: 3, 2009, pp. 186–192.

47 Paul Thomas, e-mail correspondence with author, 30 May 2009.

48 N. Ulaby, "Origins of Exhibited Cadavers Questionned," August 11, 2006. Online. Available HTTP: http://www.npr.org/templates/story/story.php?storyID=5637687 (accessed 27 January 2011).

49 M. Spiegler, "When Human Beings are the Canvas," *Art News*. Online. Available HTTP: http://www.artnews.com/issues/article.asp?art_id=1335 (accessed 17 May 2010).

50 J. Scott, "e-skin: Research into Wearable Interfaces, Cross-modal Perception and Communication for the Visually Impaired on the Mediated Stage," in J. Hauser (ed.) *sk-interfaces: Exploding Borders: Creating Membranes in Art, Technology and Society*, Liverpool: FACT and Liverpool University Press, 2008, pp. 63–67.

51 J. Stevens, "Biotech Patronage and the Making of JHomo DNA," in B. da Costa and K. Philip (eds.) *Tactical Biopolitics: Art, Activism, and Technoscience*, Cambridge, MA, and London: MIT Press, 2008, pp. 47–50.

52 H. Haacke, "Working Conditions," *Artforum* 19: 10, 1981, pp. 56–61.

53 V. Zolberg, "American Art Museums: Sanctuary or Free-for-all?" *Social Forces* 63: 2, 1984, p. 381.

54 L. Cartwright, "Gender Artifacts: Technologies of Bodily Display in Medical Culture," in L. Cooke and P. Wollen (eds.) *Visual Display: Culture beyond Appearances*, New York: New Press, 1998, pp. 219–236.

55 P. A. Treichler, L. Cartwright and C. Penley, "Introduction. Paradoxes of Visibility," in P. A. Treichler, L. Cartwright and C. Penley (eds.) *The Visible Woman: Imaging Technologies, Gender, and Science*, New York and London: New York University Press, 1998, p. 9.

56 Da Costa and Philip, *Tactical Biopolitics*.

57 Neuroscience bootcamp. Online. Available HTTP: http://www.neuroethics.upenn.edu/index.php/events/neuroscience-bootcamp (accessed 17 May 2010). Harold Varmus was instrumental in creating a *Public Library of Science*.

58 F. Dyson, "Our Biotech Future," *New York Review of Books* 54: 12, 19 July 2007, p. 1. Online. Available HTTP: http://w7.ens-lsh.fr/amrieu/IMG/pdf/Our_Biotech_Future_7-07.pdf (accessed 17 May 2010).

59 R. Kennedy, "The Artists in the Hazmat Suits," *New York Times*, 3 July 2005, Section 2, pp. 1, 21.

60 P. Galison, "Nanofacture," in C. Jones (ed.) *Sensorium: Embodied Experience, Technology, and Contemporary Art*, Cambridge, MA, and London: MIT Press, 2006, pp. 171–173.

61 R. Barthes, *La Chambre claire : notes sur la photographie*, Paris, 1980; translated as *Camera Lucida: Notes on Photography* by R. Howard, New York: Hill & Wang, 1981.

Index

Page numbers in *italics* denotes an illustration

11-M Memorial (Madrid) 230
400 Men 310–11, *311*
Abdessemed, Adel 450
Aboriginal bodies: in the museum 354–58, *355*
Abramović, Marina 367–69, *368*, 370
Acceptance in Lieu (AIL) scheme 428
access to museums 129, 130–35, 143, 203–6 *see also* admission prices
Accidental Mummies of Guanajuato, The exhibition 360
Acconci, Vito 364
accountability 135, 240–44, 251–52
Acropolis Museum 251
active citizenship 155–57, 159
activism 5, 13–14, 129–43; and Rethinking Disability Representation 136–38
Adams, Donald 212
Addams, Jane 174, 177, 179, 180, 181, 182, 183, 184–85, *185*, 186
admission prices 203, 213–17; arguments against charging 216–17; arguments for charging 214–15; and visitor numbers 216
advertising 213
Aegis Trust 222
Ahmed, Sara 149
AIDS Coalition to Unleash Power (ACT UP) 459
Alcaráz, José 230
alignment: as major factor facilitating good work 42–43, 44–45, 50
alternate reality gaming 323
'amateur scientists' 458–59
American Association of Museums (AAM) 7, 130–31, 189, 288, 293; *Code of Ethics for Museums* 37, 41, 42, 46–47, 80, 302; *Excellence and Equity* report (1992) 45, 46; *Museum Education Principles and Standards* 47
American Association for State and Local History (AASLH) 285, 288
American Institute for Conservation: *Code of Ethics* 334
American Museum of Natural History (AMNH) 358, 458

American Psychological Association: *Ethical Principles and Code of Conduct* 419
Ames, Michael 104
Amsterdam 73
Anderson, Lindsay 197
Anderson, Max 282–83
Angas, G.F. 246
Animal Welfare Act 449
animals: museum's ethical responsibilities towards 449–50
Annas, George 452
anthropology *see* museum anthropology
Antonelli, Paolo 448
Apartheid Museum (South Africa) 175, 185
Apel, Karl-Otto 34
Appia, Kwame Anthony 244, 314
Appleton, Josie 132, 133
applied ethics 6, 8, 27–28, 275, 419
Arboleda, Yazmany 393–95, 404, 409
Archibald, Robert 11, 276
architecture, museum 379–91; and ethics of built environment 381–84; green agenda 389; and organisational learning 386–87; participation with user groups 385–86; sense of place 384–85; and 'symmetry of ignorance' 386; value for money 387–89; virtuous museum building 389–90
Arendt, Hannah 35
Aristotle 29, 31, 38; *Nicomachean Ethics* 26–27
Arnold, Janet 432
Art and Creative Expression (ACE) program 192–93
Art from Africa 311–13
art museum texts 298–314; *Art from Africa* 311–13; *A Bead Quiz* 313; curatorial writing challenge 299–302; ethic of public service 310–11, *311*; ethics of cooperation 309; ethics of disclosure 306–9; ethics of public versus private 313; ethics of shared expertise 311–13; *Gela Mask* 299–301, *300*; *see also* labels and wall texts; *Maasai collects Maasai* 309; experimentations 306–7; *Passion for Possession* 310–11, *311*; *Untold Story* 306–9 Art|Sci center gallery (UCLA) 455

Artifact Piece 354, *355*, 358, 364–65, 369
Artist is Present, The 368–69, *368*
Arts Council England 212
Arvanitis, K. 322
Asian Art Museum (San Francisco) 402–4, 408
Assassination exhibitions 393–95
Association of Art Museum Curators (AAMC) 42, 47
Association of Partners of Palazzo Strozzi (APPS) 281
associational public spaces 35, 36
Attenborough, David 250
attendance, museum: factors encouraging 207; participation rates 203, 204, *205*
Auckland Museum 85, 95, 98, 99, 100, 102, 103, 104, 214
audience development 188–99 *see also* visitors
Auschwitz-Birkenau 227–29
Australia: repatriation in 258–66, 270
Australian Aboriginals 249
Australian Anthropological Society (AAS) 262
Australian Archaeological Association (AAA) 261, 262
Australian Institute for the Conservation of Cultural Material: *Code of Ethics and Guidance* 334
Australian Institute of Aboriginal and Torres Strait Islander Studies (AIATSIS) 262

Baartman, Saartje 121, 355, 356, 359, 362, 363, 365
bacterial 'simulations' 452
Baer, Ulrich 225
Bailey, Stephen 214
Balshaw, Maria 389
Baltimore City Community College (BCCC) 196, 197
Bandelli, Andrea 281, 282
Banks in Pink and Blue exhibition 450
Banksy 246
Barrett, Jennifer 11
Barrie, Dennis 398
Bauman, Zygmunt 146, 150, 154, 159, 160
Bead Quiz, A 313
Beal, Graham W.J. 399–400
Beard, Mary 343
beauty 184
Becoming Animal exhibition 449
Behind the Shadow of Merrick (film) 142
Benhabib, Seyla 35
Benin City: British invasion of (1897) 243

Bennett, Tony: 'The Exhibitionary Complex' 73
Bergen-Belsen Memorial 226
Berry, Wendell 63, 64
Besterman, Tristram 70, 135
Beuys, Joseph 304
'Bilbao Effect' 59
bioart/biotechnology 445–60; and animals 449–50; artist collaborations 455; contending with the invisible 454–56; dilemmas encountered 450–54; elitism versus populism 458–59; funding conflicts 458; museum responsibilities to the living 449–50; packaging and transportation of life forms 452; preserving dignity of the body 457
Birmingham Museums and Art Gallery 137–38, 140
Bishop, Russell 159
Bizos, George 175
Bizot Group 389
Black Box program 193
blockbuster exhibitions 291; and censorship 401–4
Boal, Augusto 155–56, 157
Boas, Franz 356, 358
Bob Jones University Art Museum 118
bodies (in museums) 353–71; Aboriginal 354–58, *355*; afterlives of 358–63; displaying of Maori heads 359–60, 362; lives of in contemporary art 363–69; mummified and preserved 360; plastinated 291, 361–62, 457; preserving dignity of 457; *see also* human remains
Bodies: the Exhibition 361
bodily awareness: and memorial museums 226–27
Body Worlds exhibition 353, 361, 371, 457
'bog people' 360
Bourgeau, Jef 399, 400
Bradburne, James 388
Brighton 240–41
Bristol Museum and Art Gallery 246
Britain: and repatriation 265–66, 268
British Library: Centre for Conservation 338
British Museum 250, 362; conservation exhibitions 338; Great Court 380; and repatriation 265; and spoliated art works 242, 251 'Talking Objects' 156–57, *158*; 'world under one roof' 245
Brook, I. 384–85
Brooklyn Museum of Art 19–20, 172, 292–93, 404; *The Play of the Unmentionable* installation 302–4, *303*; *Sensation* exhibition 401–2
Brown, Alison 248

Brown, Pete 15–16
Brown, Timothy P. 220
budgets, museum 289
Building Design Partnership (BDP) building (Manchester) 390
built environment, ethics of 381–84
business practices (in museums) 285–94; 'blockbuster' exhibits developed by commercial operation 291; budgeting and resource allocation 289; capitalization of collections 288–89; earned income and fund raising 290–91; financial management 288–89; fund raising 292–94; governance 287–88; marketing 292; 'renting' collections 290–91
business tribalism 59–60
Butler, Judith 120, 397

California Academy of Sciences (San Francisco) 388
California Science Center 339
Cameron, Duncan 364
Cameron, Fiona 19
Canadian Conservation Institute (CCI) 343
Cane, Simon 333–34, 342
capitalization of collections 288–89
Capri Batterie 304–6, *305*
Catts, Oron 448, 449, 455
cave paintings 454
Censored exhibition 406
censorship, museum 393–409; and Arboleda 393–95; and blockbuster exhibitions 401–4; and Culture Wars 397–98, 406, 408; as dialogue 404–6; and Mapplethorpe exhibition and trial 397–98, 399, 409; and participatory museum 407–8; as propaganda in Nazi Germany 395–96; reasons for decline in public outrage against museums 407; self-399–400; and time 408–9
Cézanne in Florence exhibition (2007) 279
Chambers, Robert 152–53
charging *see* admission prices
children's museums (US) 194
China: at the Court of the Emperors exhibition (2008) 279–80
Choeung Ek Genocidal Center (Cambodia) 228
Cincinnati Contemporary Arts Center (CAC) 302, 398, 408
citizen science 459
Civil Rights movements 74
civil society 55
Clark Art Institute 191–92, 193
Clavir, Miriam 335, 436
Cleaned Pictures exhibition 336, 337

Clifford, J. 150, 160
Clinton, Hilary 393
Clinton, President Bill 231
codes of ethics *see* ethical codes
Colchester Castle Museum 137
collaborative work 34
collections: access to 204–6; and budgets 289; capitalization of 288–89; 'renting' out 290–91; used for marketing purposes 292
Collections Trust (UK) 327
Collective Conversations (Manchester Museum) 153–54
College Art Association 450
Colonial Museum (renamed Tropical Museum) *see* Tropenmuseum (Amsterdam)
Commission for Looted Art in Europe 242
communities 63, relationship with museums 10 *see also* museum/community partnerships
companies: characteristics of long-lived 60
confrontational drama 414–25; educational benefits 417, 420; ethics of 419–20; examples 416–17; impact of ethical breaches 422–24; *A Journey Unlike Any Other* 416–18, 419, 420, 421–22; and psychodrama 416; responsibilities of the exhibition team and actors 420–22
consensus 6–7, 34–35
consequentialism 28
conservation 332–45, 426–41; communicating of in museums 335–36; democratization of by guardianship 19; eighteenth-century armchair 428–31, *429*, 440; engagement with the public over 333–34; and ethical codes 333, 334; ethics and practice 332–33; on the internet 342–43; participatory 436, 440; phased approach 431; privileging of original form 439; public perceptions of 334–35; and public value concept 344; reconstruction of original form 433–34; refabrication 438–39; retaining original form and materials 430–31; retention of later additions and repainting 435–36; sculpture of King Kamehameha I of Hawai'i 434–36, *434*, 439, 440; seventeenth-century silk embroidered garments 431–34, *432*, 439, 440; as social process 440; *Transparent Tubes* 437–39, *437*, 440
conservation exhibitions 336–42; explanatory/'behind the scenes' model 338–39; impact assessment 343; principles and practice model 339–42; science model 339; single object model 337;

technological model 337;
transformational/revelatory model 337;
virtual 342–43
Conservation In Safe Hands exhibition
(2007) 339
Conservation Science Investigations (CSI)
exhibition (Sittingbourne) 342
consumption, culture as 59
'contact zone', museum as 81, 86,
159–63, 160
contingency, definition 8
ControModa exhibition (2007) 279
Cook, Captain 34
Corcoran Gallery of Art (Washington) 302,
397–98
Cornwall, Andrea 147, 150, 159, 160
corporatism 57, 58
Corsham Court picture gallery 428, 429
cosmic ethics 314
counterpublic sphere 176–77, 185
cowrie shells 117
Crenca, Umberto ('Bert') 405
Crimes of the German Wehrmacht
exhibition 225
Critical Art Ensemble (CAE) 452
Csikszentmihalyi, Mihaly 42
cultural equity 239–52; and accountability
240–44, 251–52; and cultural legacy in
source communities 248–50; issues of
cultural falsification 246–47; and looted
art 242–43, 251; in the public domain
244–45; and repatriation 240–41, 244–45;
and spoilated art works 242; and
transparency 245–46; voice of source
community 247–48
cultural falsification 246–47
cultural patrimony 240
Cultural Resource Center, National
Museum of the American Indian,
Smithsonian Institution (Suitland,
Maryland) 76
culturally sensitive objects: treatment of in
codes of ethics 79–80
culture: as consumption 59
Culture Wars 397–98, 406, 408, 459
Cummins, A. 439
Cuno, James 45–46, 132
curators 257–58, 333; Code of Ethics for 47;
relationship between educators and
46–49; role and duties 47
Curators Committee (CurCom-AAM) 16
Cuvier, Georges 120–21, 356, 359

Damon, William 42
Dana, John Cotton 188–89, 276
Danto, Arthur 398, 409

Darke, Paul 140
de Montebello, Philippe 46
de Young Museum (San Francisco) 403–4
'Decide – Deliberative Citizens' Debates'
project 167–71
decolonization of museums 70, 72–74, 79
Deech, Baroness 242
Degenerate Art exhibition (1937) 396
DeGeus, Arie 58, 60
Delingpole, James 133
democratic pluralism 11
'Democs' game 168
Demos 344; *It's a Material World* report
(2008) 344
deontological theory 28–29
Department for Culture, Media and Sport
(DCMS): *Understanding the Future* 63, 203
Department of Health and Human Services
(DHHS) 194
descriptive ethics 27
Design and the Elastic Mind 447, 448
Detroit Institute of Arts 399–400
Dialogue in the Dark exhibition 416
Dickenson, V. 215
Diggle, Keith 215
digital environment 316–28; codes and
ethics in 316–18; ethics of semantic media
325–27; ethics of sensory media 324–25;
ethics of situated media 321–23; ethics of
social media 319–20
Dingus, Marita 310, 311, *311*
dioramas: and indigenous bodies 356–57
Dirty Pictures (film) 399
disability: representation of 129, 136–40;
social model of 138–39
disability rights movement 138
discourse ethics 26, 34–36, 38
District Six Museum (Cape Town) 232
DNA 451
donors 293
Dordrecht Museum (Netherlands) 334
drama, confrontational *see* confrontational
drama
Drucker, Peter 55, 66
dual-use technologies, ethics of 446–47
Dudley, Sandra 18
dumbing down 132, 134
Dynasty and Divinity exhibition (2009) 250
Dyson, Freeman 459

E-skin 457
Echo-Hawk, W. 77
ecological metaphor 56
economy: impact of on museums 285
Ecsite 165, 170, 171
Edson, Gary 136, 240; *Museum Ethics* 4–5

education *see* museum education
educators: relationship between curators and 46–49; roles of 47
Ego-trap 323, 324
Egyptian mummies 360
eighteenth-century armchair, conservation of 428–31, *429*, 440
Eigler, Don 447
Eind, Gerrit Jan van't 215
El-Bahari, Mohammed 247–48
Electric Retina 457
Elgin, Lord 243
Elkins, James 301; *Our Beautiful, Dry and Distant Texts* 299
Embracing Animal installation 449
encyclopaedic museum 246, 250–52, 362
Entropy Law 65–66
environmental studies 8
Epstein, Jacob 380
ethical codes 7, 16, 26, 36–38, 42, 130, 258; AAM 37, 41, 42, 46–47, 80, 302; and conservation 333, 334; effective use of 38; format 37; ICOM (2006) 37, 79–80, 302, 333, 362; nature and functions 37; and repatriation 261–63; and treatment of human remains and culturally sensitive objects 79–80, 362
ethics 26–39, 275; applied 6, 8, 27–28, 275, 419; descriptive 27; and jurisprudence 7; and law 7; metaethics 27; normative 27; theories of 28–31
European Commission 167
European Union 195
Eurordis 170
Excellence and Equity 45–46, 189
exhibitions, conservation *see* conservation exhibitions
Experimentarium (Copenhagen) 323
experts 26, 33–34
explanatory/'behind the scenes' model: and conservation exhibitions 338–39
Exploratorium (San Francisco) 118, 455, 458
Exposing the Censor Within installation 405–6

Fade: The Dark Side of Light (2008) 339
Fairbrother, Trevor 304, 306
Farhi, Moris 229
feminist theory 6; and contingency in new museum ethics 8–21; focus on collaboration and inclusion 9; and guardianship 18; and representation 112–34
Ferrell, Robert 454
Financial Accounting Standards Board (FASB) 288
financial management 288–89

Fitzwilliam Museum (Cambridge) 340–42
Flanagan, Bob 367
Flynn, Tom 251
Foley, Robert 265–66
Follow the North Star 416
Fondazione Palazzo Strozzi (Florence) 278–82, 283–84
Fortey, Richard 62
Foucault, Michel 4
Fox, Warwick 382
Frank, Anne 222
Fraser, Andrea 369–70
Fraser, Nancy 147
Freire, Paulo 155
Frenetic Engineering: Censored/Uncensored exhibition 405
Freud, Sigmund 146
Freudenheim, Tom 58
Friends of Palazzo Strozzi 281, 282
fund raising 292–94
Fusco, Coco 365
Future Forward: Projects in New Media 450

Gago, Jose Mariano 165
Galla, A. 81
Gallery of Modern Art (GoMA) (Glasgow) 3, 4, 21
Gardner, Howard 12, 42
garments, silk embroidered 431–34, *432*, *439*, 440
GASB 288
Gaskell, Ivan 120
Gaventa, J. 147, 160
Gehry, Frank 59
Geismar, Haidy 18
Gela Mask 299–301, *300*
Gen Terra 451, *452*
gender equality 30
Gene(sis) exhibition 450–51, *452*
genetic engineering 445, 446, 449, 452, 454
genetic material 445, 447
genetically modified organisms 116, 446
Geneva Conventions 275
Genomic Revolution 458
Getty Conservation Institute 337, 339; *The Nature of Conservation* 333
Getty Museum 291
Giamo, Benedict 231
Gill, Kate 429, 430
Girardet, Herbert 383
Giuliani, Rudolph 401
globalization 63
Goebbels, Joseph 118, 395
Gomez-Peña, Guillermo 365
Gonzáles-Torres, Félix 366
González, Jennifer 364

good work (in museums) 41–50;
  components of 42; concept of alignment
  as major factor facilitating 42–43, 44–45,
  50; elements impacting 43, 43; factors
  facilitating the emergence of 44; and
  relationship between curators and
  educators 48–49
Goodman, Nelson 283
GoodWork Project 41–50
Goudriaan, René 215
Gould, Hanna 198
Gould, Thomas Ridgeway 434
Governance 280, 287–88; and Fondazione
  Palazzo Strozzi 280–82; transparency at
  heart of ethical 282–83
Green, Gregory 446, 452
Green, Renée 365
Greenberg, D. 439
Greenfield Village (GV) 212
Gregor Mendel exhibition 458
Grijzenhout, Frans 334
Grinnell, Nancy Whipple 405
Ground Zero (New York) 228
growth model: and museums 65
Grudin, Robert 60
guardianship, ethics of 17–20
Guggenheim Museum Bilbao (GMB) 59
Gulbenkian Foundation 458
Gulug Museum (Russia) 176
Gurian, Elaine Heumann 189, 190, 195

Haacke, Hans 458
Habermas, Jürgen 34–35
Hackney Museum (London) 150, 152
Hague Convention 275
Hamilton, Christopher 252
Hamisi, Kakuta Maimai 309
Hancock Shaker Village (Massachusetts) 288
Hayles, N. Katherine 454
Hein, Hilde 5, 6, 7–10, 12, 13, 15, 41, 46;
  The Museum in Transition 46
Held, Robin 454, 459
Helms, Jesse 397
Henry Art Gallery (University of
  Washington) 450, 451, 452, 454
Henry Ford Museum (FM) 212
heritage: digital 18; and guardianship 6, 17,
  18–19; tangible and intangible 14, 18
Hevey, David 142
Heye, George Gustav 75
Hickey, Sam 147–48
High, Kathy 449–50
Hikurangi 92
Hill, Richard 78
Hillary, Sir Edmund 103
Hindmarsh Island affair 2467

Hiroshima Peace Memorial Museum
  231–32
Historic Royal Palaces 339
Hitler, Adolf 395
Holden, John 344
Holladay, Wilhelmina Cole 118
Höller, Carsten 367
Holocaust 221, 232
Holocaust Memorial Museum (US) 11–12,
  139–40, 222
Homer-Dixon, T. 65
Hood, Marilyn 206
Hoopa Indians 120
Hooper, Chloe 249
Hooper-Greenhill, Eilean 202, 323
Hottentot Venus 120–21
Hoving, Thomas 393
Howarth, Alan 250, 251
Hsieh, Tehching 367
Hull House Settlement/Museum see Jane
  Addams Hull House Museum
Human Genome Project 458
human remains 362–63; exhibiting of
  222–23, 358–59; repatriation of 70, 75,
  77, 258–66, 267–68; treatment of 19, 70,
  77–78, 79–80, 362
human rights 131, 138
Human Tissue Act (2004) 265
humanities: and science 63–64
Hunt, William Holman: The Finding of the
  Saviour in the Temple 140–41
Huyssen, Andreas 233

identity 114–17
Imperial War Museum (London) 138
imperialism 71
importance-performance analysis (IPA)
  207–11, 208, 209, 210
inclusion: criticism of 131–34
Indian Art of the United States exhibition
  (1941) 357, 3578
Indianapolis Museum of Art (IMA) 283;
  Dashboard 283
indigenous peoples 36, 102–3, 104, 353;
  treatment and repatriation of remains 70,
  75, 77, 258–66, 267–68; see also Maori
individualism 6
Ingers 224, 224
innocuous label domination syndrome
  (ILDS) 302, 306, 312, 399
Institute for Conservation and Restoration
  (Vienna) 339
Institute for Learning Innovation 198
interactivity 415–16
International Coalition of Sites of
  Conscience 176

International Council of Museums (ICOM) 131, 189, 260; *Code for Ethics for Museums* 37, 79–80, 302, 333, 362; Conservation Committee 333–34; and repatriation 260, 264–65

Internet: conservation on the 342–43; *see also* Web

interpretation 47–48

intersubjectivity 34

invisible art 454–57

Ishi 355, 356, 359, 362

Istituto Centrale del Restauro (Rome) 336

James, John 207

Jamtili Museum (Sweden) 195

Jane Addams Hull House Museum (JAHHM) (Chicago) 174–86; alternative labelling of Mary Rozet-Smith's portrait project 177–81, *177, 182, 183*; creation of counterpublic space 177, 185; new exhibition and opening up of Addams' bedroom 183–84; 'personal is political' 182–85; public programming 175

Janes, Robert 276; *Museums in a Troubled World* 387–88

Jewish Museum (Berlin) 221

Johnson, Harriet McBryde 139–40

Journey Unlike Any Other, A 416–18, 419, 420, 421–22

jurisprudence: and ethics 7

juvenile offenders: collaboration with museum case study 191–92

Kainai First Nation 248

Kamehameha I, King of Hawai'i, statue of 434–36, *434*

Kammen, Michael 401

Kant, Immanuel 28–29

Karengera, Ildephonse 222

Keller Gates Project, The 393–94, 404, 409

Kellogg, Alice 177

Kelly, Mary 364

Kennicott, Philip 292, 406–7

Kierkegaard, Søren 414, 424

Kigali Memorial (Rwanda) 222

Knutson, Teresa 431, 433, 434

Ko Tawa Exhibition Project 98–102, *100*, 103

Konijn, Elly 281

Kosuth, Joseph 302–4, 404–5

Kothari, Uma 146

Kreps, Christina 10

Kroeber, Alfred 356, 358

Kunst van het Bewaren, De exhibition 339, 340

Kuppers, Petra 362

Kurtz, Steve 452, 454

Kusama, Yayoi 363–64

Label Show: Contemporary Art and the Museum exhibition (1994) 304–6

labels 181–82; alternative labelling project at JAHHM 177–81, *177, 182, 183*; *see also* labels and wall texts, art museum

Laclau, Ernesto 146, 154–55, 159

Langer, Monika 226

Latour, Bruno 451

law: and ethics 7

LeDray, Charles 364

Levinas, Emmanuel 151, 154

Life Beyond the Label exhibition 137

Lipardi, Enzo 166

litigation: and repatriation 268–69

Little Frank and his Carp 369–70, *370*

living art 445–60 *see also* bioart/ biotechnology

living ethics codes 16, 20

Lobb, Jr., Monty 408

locality: museums as keepers of 63

location-based services 321

Lonetree, A. 80

Long Island Children's Museum (LICM) 194, 195, 198

looted art 242–43, 251

Lords of the Samurai exhibition (2009) 402–4

Los Angeles County Museum of Art (LACMA) 431–32, 434, 439

Louvre 118

Lowenthal, D. 241

Lower East Side Tenement Museum (New York City) 196

Lowrance, William 54

Lowry, Glenn 45

Lukes, Sven: *Power: A Radical View* 148

Luna, James 354–55, *355*, 356, 358, 364–65, 369, 370

Lynch, Bernadette 12

Maasai collects Maasai 309

Maathai, Wangari 247, 249

McDonald, Catherine 214

McDonald, Robert 288

MacDonald, Sharon 166

McLuhan, Marshall 276

McRae, Alfie 101

McVeigh, Timothy 231

Mair, Captain Gilbert (Tawa) 92, 98–99, 101

Maish, Susan 336

Malaguzzi, Loris 282

Malaro, Marie 286, 288, 290; *Museum Governance* 287, 291, 292

Manchester Museum 15, 146, 148–49, 151–52, 159, 247; Collective Conversations 153–54, 248; Community Advisory Panel (CAP) 151–52, 153

Manglano-Ovalle, Iñigo 450

Manovich, Lev 18

Manzoni, Piero 364

Maori 18, 85–106, 153–54, 159; and Auckland Museum 103; engagement with museums 95, 96; establishment of Waitangi Tribunal 96; events changing engagement with museums 96; inter-Maori fiction in museums 97–98; kinship philosophy (*whakapapa*) 87–93, *90*, *91*; *Ko Tawa* Exhibition Project 98–102, *100*, 103; operational partnerships with museums 86–87; and *taonga* 92, 93–96, 98, 99–101; and *Te Maori* exhibition 95, 96, 97, 358

Maori heads 359–60, 362

Mapplethorpe, Robert 302, 397–98, 399, 409

marae atea 92–93

market ideology 58

Market and Opinion Research International (MORI) 207

marketing, museum 202–17, 292; and access to museums 203–6; budget for 212; ethical challenges facing 203; pricing policy 213–17; products and services offerings 206–11; promotional tools 203, 212–13; and public relations 213; and visitor satisfaction 206–7; word of mouth 212–13

marketplace ideology: and museums 56–60, 61, 62

Marrin, Minette 132, 133

Martilla, John 207

Martinez, Maria and Julian 357, 366

Mashantucket Pequot Museum (Connecticut) 356

MASS MoCA 449, *454*

materialism: museums and the end of 54–67

Mayer, John 16

Memorial Center Srebrenica 232

Memorial Holocaust Museum *see* Holocaust Memorial Museum (US)

memorial museums 220–33; and bodily awareness 226–27; commemorating political prisoners 226–27; display of human remains issue 222–23; display of images/photographs 223–25, *224*; display of objects and association of objects with events 220–23; politics of remembrance 229–33; tension between tourism and commemoration 227–28; visitor emotions 228–29; visitor presence and physical place 226–27

Memorial to the Murdered Jews of Europe (Berlin) 227

Memorial of the Victims of Communism and Anti-Communist Resistance (Sighet, Romania) 221, 226

Merrick, Joseph 142

metaethics 27

methods: and values 60–61

Methuen, Paul 428

Metropolitan Museum of Art 19

Midgley, Mary 28, 31

Milgram, Stanley 422–23

Mills, Charles 121

Mine Games exhibition 277–78

Minh-ha, Trinh T. 149

Minik, Eskimo 358

Mining the Museum 365–66

Mission Impossible? exhibition (2006) 340–42, *341*

mission statements 44, 45

Missouri Historical Society 276

mobile media 321, 322–23

Mohan, Giles 147–48

money as the measure of worth 58–59

Monitoring Activities of Science in Society in Europe (MASIS) 165

Montano, Linda 367

Moore, Mark 343

moral agency of museums 5, 10, 21

moral pluralism 31

moral virtues 29

moralities: and museums 135–36

Moreno, Jacob L. 416

Mostra dei dipinti di Antonella da Messina exhibition 336

Mouffe, Chantal 154, 155

multidisciplinary approach 33–34, 36

Mummies of the World exhibition 360

mummified bodies 360

Mummy Museum of Guanajuato (Mexico) 360

Munley, Mary Ellen 45

Musée du quai Branly 268

Museo Carmen Funes 244–45

museum anthropology: decolonization of museums 72–74; humanistic turn in 71; impact of National Museum of the American Indian Act (NMAIA) and Native American Graves Protection and Repatriation Act (NAGPRA) on 74–79; and post-colonial critique of museums 70–81

museum boards 60

museum education: classical 414–15; and confrontational drama *see* confrontational drama; contemporary 415–16

museum ethics: contingent nature of the new 6, 8–21; as a discourse of social practice 4; what it is not 6–8
'museum in the everyday' model 322–23
Museum of Fine Arts Boston 304
Museum of London 339
museum marketing see marketing, museum
Museum of Modern Art (MoMA) 45, 48, 447, 448, 449
Museum as Muse, The exhibition 447
Museum of Northern Arizona 289
Museum of Occupations (Tallinn) 224
Museum of Tolerance (Los Angeles) 115
museum workers 41, 55–56 see also curators
museum/community partnerships 146–60; and antagonism 154–55; Collective Conversations programme (Manchester Museum) 153–54; and 'contact zone' ideal 150; developing a practice for active citizens in the museum 155–57; ethical values informing museum as 'contact zone '151–53; and loss of control issue 149–51, 152, 159; power issues 147–48; and privilege 148–49, 159; problems with 154–55
museums: addressing of social inequality potential 205; as bearing witness 64; bridging of divide between humanities and science 63–64; and change 5; closure of 285–86; complex portfolios of 57; decline in funding 57, 203; decline in privilege 56; decolonization of 70, 72–74, 79; distinguishing from other institutions 116; as diversity personified 63; as educational institutions 202; and the end of materialism 54–67; focus on money 58–59; as forum for diverse competing voices 276, 277–78; and marketplace ideology 56–60, 62; and moralities 135–36; numbers worldwide 63; priorities of 114; and renewal 61; as seed banks 62; and short-term thinking 58; as social service providers 188–99
Museums Association (MA) (UK) 58–59, 131
Museums Australia (MA) 259, 260, 263
Museums Computer Group (MCG) 317
Museums and Galleries Lifelong Learning Initiative (MGLI) 198
Museums, Libraries and Archives Council (MLA) 212
Museums for a New Century 189
'museums of victims' 276, 278

Nah Poeh Meng exhibition 357
Nakamura, Jeanne 13

Nanjing Massacre Memorial Museum 223
nanoart/nanotechnology 445–60 see also bioart/biotechnology
Nanoscale Informal Science Education network 172
National Academy Museum and School of Fine Arts 289
National Archives 324–25
National Civil Rights Museum (US) 176
National Conservation Centre 338
National Endowment for the Humanities 183
National Gallery (London) 337
national identity: museums as repositories of in New Zealand 96–98
National Maritime Museum (Falmouth) 385
National Memorial Center Against Expulsions (Poland) 229–30
National Museum of American History 285
National Museum of the American Indian (NMAI) 70, 75–76, 80–81, 85, 358
National Museum of the American Indian Act (NMAIA) (1989) 70, 74–77
National Museum of the American Indian, Smithsonian Institution (New York City) 75National Museum of Australia (NMA) 85, 258–59, 260, 263
National Museum (Copenhagen) 417–18, 420
National Museum Directors' Conference 389
National Museum of History (Taiwan) 213
National Museum of Women's Art 118
National Museums and Galleries (NMGs) 215
National Museums and Galleries on Merseyside (NMGM) 243, 338
National Museums Liverpool 197
National Museums of World Culture (Sweden) 251
National Portrait Gallery (London) 364
National September 11 Memorial and Museum 221
National World War II Museum 115
Native American Graves Protection and Repatriation Act (NAGPRA) (1990) 70, 74–75, 77–79, 266, 359
Native Americans: and passing of National Museum of the American Indian (NMAIA) and Native American Graves Protection and Repatriation (NAGPRA) Acts 70, 74–79; perception of objects as live 76; repatriation of remains 75, 77–78, 266
Natural History Museum (London) 62, 164, 268

Nazi Germany 118, 242; censorship as propaganda 395–96
Nelson-Atkins Museum 343
Nesbitt, Prexy 174
Netherlands: decolonization of Tropical Museum 74–75
New Art Gallery Walsall 380
New Economics Foundation 168
New Jersey Historical Society (NJHS) 193–94, 195, 197, 198
New Museum of Contemporary Art (New York) 367
New-York Historical Society 288
New Zealand 85; museums as repositories of national identity 96–98
New Zealand Museums: Code of Ethics 86
Newark Museum 188, 188–89
Newport Art Museum 405
Ngahue 87
Ngarrindjeri people 240–41, 246, 249
Ngati Whakaue 87, 88, 89, 92, 98, 101, 102
Ngati Whatua 95, 100, 101–2
Nicks, T. 72, 102
Nkondi 312
normative ethics 27
nuclear technology 446

Obama, Barack 393
objectivity 5
objects 7–8, 17, 116; as amenable to symbolism 156; and classical museum education 415; displaying of in memorial museums 220–23; freeing from relegation to fixed objecthood 120; perception of as live by Native Americans 76; and purpose of representation 117; social engagement of 17
Oklahoma City National Memorial 231
One in Four exhibition 137
O'Neill, Mark 134
O'Neill, Onora 146
open-ended exhibitions 118–19
openness, culture of 15
Operation Spy 416
Opoku, Kwame 250, 251
Oppenheimer, Frank 118
Organization for Economic Cooperation and Development (OECD) 195
Orientalism 71
Ostheimer, Rona Tulgan 192
other/otherness 121
Ötzi 360

pa-complexes 92–93
Painting Light exhibition (2008) 280
Pakeha 96, 97

Parry, Ross 18, 19
Parthenon 243
participation rates 203, 204, 205
participatory museum 407–8
"Partners in Learning" Program 193, 194, 195, 197, 198
Passion for Possession 310–11, 311
patronymics 121
Paul Hamlyn Foundation: 'Engagement at the heart of museums and galleries' 157–58
Pearce, S.M. 439–40
Peers, Laura 248
People for the Ethical Treatment of Animals (PETA) 449
Perfect Moment, The exhibition 397–98, 408
'personal is political' 182–85
personal story: as dominant narrative construct 222
Philippot, Paul 333
Phillips, Ruth 364
photographs: display of in memorial museums 223–25, 224
phronesis 38–39
Pieschel, Janet 191
Pinter, Harold 245
Piss Christ (Serrano) 397
Pitt Rivers Museum (Oxford University) 248
plastinated bodies 291, 361–62, 457
Plato 7, 29, 381; Seventh Letter 38
Play of the Unmentionable, The installation 302–4, 303, 404–5
Plaza, Beatriz 59
pluralism 122
Podany, Jerry 336
Poeh Museum of the Pueblo of Pojoaque 356–57
Poignant, Roslyn 355
Portland Museum of Art (Oregon) 248
post-colonialism 8, 9, 17–18, 70–81; and decolonization of museums 72–74; and international museum ethics 79–80; literary context 71; meaning of 71; and Native American Graves Protection and Repatriation Act (NAGPRA) 70, 74–75, 77–79; and National Museum of the American Indian Act (NMAIA) 70, 74–77
post-structuralist theory 17
power: dimensions of 148; and museum/community partnerships 146–47; working of in museum 147–48
Powerhouse Museum (Sydney) 171–72, 202
Pratt, Mary Louise 150
Preserving the Past exhibition (1991) 339, 343
press coverage 213

pricing *see* admission prices
Prince, David 27, 202
principles and practice model: and conservation exhibitions 339–42
privilege 148–49
Proceedings of the American Association of Museums (1917) 41
products and services: and importance-performance analysis (IPA) 207–9, *208*
products and services offerings 206–11
professionalization 4–5
promotional tools 203, 212–13
Providence Children's Museum (Rhode Island) 194
psychodrama 416
psychology 8
public relations 213
public service 42, 45–46, 61
public sphere 55, 176
Public, The (West Bromwich) 388
public value: ethical practice and concept of 343–44
Pukaki 96
Pullen, Derek 438

queer theory 9
Quinn, Marc 364

racism 122–23
radical transparency 14–17
Ralston Saul, John 57
Rancière, Jacques 159
Randolph College 289
reception theory 17
reciprocity 12, 13, 151, 154
refugee communities: museums working with 196–97
Refugee Youth Project (RYP) 196
Reggio Emilia 279, 282
Registrars Committee (RC-AAM) 42
Rehg, William 34–35
Reich Chamber of Visual Arts 408
Reisman, Judith 398
Relative Velocity Inscription Device, The 448, 451
relativism 29–30
repatriation 70, 77, 240–41, 244–45, 256–70, 262–63; and Britain 265–66, 268; criticism of 266; and cultural equity 240–41, 244–45; and ethical codes of professional organisations 260–63; and ethics 257; future debate on 269–70; and government 258–59; and guardianship 19; of human remains 70, 75, 77, 258–66, 267–68; and ICOM 260, 264–65; institutional support 260; jurists and ethics of 268–69; and

litigation 268–69; of Maori heads (*toi moko*) 359–60; and museum industry 259, 265; and United States 266
representation 112–24, 276; conditioning of consciousness 119; as denotative 117; of more diverse communities 131; resisting 119–22; restriction of reality 118
Research Centre for Museums and Galleries (RCMG) 136, 137, 215
Responding to Art Involves Self Expression (RAISE) program 192
restitution 75, 242, 245, 250, 251, 267 *see also* repatriation
restorative justice: and Jane Addams Hull House Museum 174–86
Rethinking Disability Representation 129, 136–42
Revolving Hotel Room 367
Rhode Island Historical Society 289
Rhodes, Richard 446
Richmond, Alison 333
Rifkin, Jeremy 60, 61, 65–66
Robben Island Museum 226
Roberts, Lisa 47
Roberts, Randy 45
Robinson, Helena 19
Robley, H.G. 359
Rope Piece 367
Rose Art Museum (Brandeis University) 289
Rose, Sheree 367
Rosenthal, Norman 243
Rotorua Museum (New Zealand) 95
Rowe, L. Earle 41
Royal London Hospital Museum and Archives 142
Rozet-Smith, Mary 177–80, *177*, 181, 184–85, *185*, *186*
Ruskin, John 215
Rwanda 222–23
Ryan, Kathleen 380

Saatchi, Charles 293, 401
sacred objects: treatment and repatriation of 77–78
Said, Edward: *Orientalism* 71
Salt Lake Art Center (Utah) 192–93
Saltz, Jerry 367
Sandahl, Jette 418, 420
Sandell, Richard 5, 10, 13
Saul, John Ralston 64
Schmidt, Paul Ferdinand 396
Schrag, Anthony 3, 4, *4*, 20–21
Schütz, Chana C. 221
Schwarzer, Marjorie 64
Science: and humanities 63–64

science centers 164–72; ambiguity over social and political role 166–67; challenges faced 167; 'Decide' project 167–71; invisibility of 165–66; open source approach 171–72; participation and engagement with science 164–65; seen as neutral places 166
science model: and conservation exhibitions 339
Science Museum (London) 164
Science Museum of Minnesota (SMM) 166
Science World (Vancouver) 277
Scott, Jill 457
screen memories 222
Seattle Art Museum 306
seed banks: museums as 62
self-appraisal: and museums 114
self-censorship 399–400
self-reflexivity 11, 14
semantic media, ethics of 325–27, 328
Semantic Web 326–27
Senior, Adele 449
Sensation: Young British Art from the Saatchi Collection exhibition (1999) 292–93, 401–2
sense of place 384–85
sensory media, ethics of 324–25, 327–28
Serrano, Andres 397
Serrell, Beverly 180
sexism 119, 122–23
Shannon, J. 76
shared authority 11–12
Sierra, Santiago 457
Silver Swan Conservation Project 342
Silverman, Lois 13, 189, 191, 196, 197; The Social Work of Museums 188
Simons, M. 247
Simon, Nina: The Participatory Museum 407
simulations 324–25
single object model: and conservation exhibitions 337
situated media, ethics of 321–23, 327
Skramstad, Harold 189–90, 198–99
Slave Trade Act: bicentenary of abolition of (2007) 155
Small, Lawrence 287
Smith, James 222
Smithsonian Institution 207, 286, 287, 290, 292, 359, see also NMAI
Snibbe, Scott 455
Snow, C.P.: The Two Cultures 63–64
social inclusion 10–11, 13, 205–6
social justice, and museums 13
social media 11–12, 319–21, 327
social responsibility 6, 9, 10–14, 14, 62, 67, 129, 276
social service providers: museums as 188–99

Socrates 6, 29, 381
Söderman, Eva 221
SoftRoom 386
Sontag, Susan 223
Sopheara, Chea 222
source communities 103–4; cultural legacy in 248–50; relationship with museums 72, 79, 81, 103–4; relationship with their associated values 86–87
South Africa 175
South East Museums, Libraries and Archives Council (SEMLAC) (UK) 193
Souza e Siva, Adriana de 455
specimenhood 353, 354
Spivak, Gayatri 157
spoliated art works 242
Stanford prison experiment 423–24
Stanley, Nick 19
Starr, Ellen Gates 182
State Regional Archives (Sweden) 195
Statens Museum for Kunst (Copenhagen) 342–43
Stayton, Kevin 20
Steichen, Edward 448
Sterling and Francine Clark Art Institute (Williamstown, Massachusetts) 191–92
Stevens, Jacqueline 458
stewardship 276
Stolen Generation 249
Stop the Rot exhibition 339, 340, 342, 343
Stories in Stone exhibition (2006) 337
Sturken, Marita 222
subject/object dualism 113
subjectivism 29–30
suffering: memorial museums and the objectification of 220–33
Sully, Dean 334
sustainability 66, 67, 188, 383
sustainable museum: cultural equity in 239–52
Sweden: and repatriation 265
SymbioticA 449

Taipei Fine Arts Museum (TFAM) (Taiwan) 217
Tait, Simon 383–84
Taiwanese museums 212; participation rates 204, 205; pricing 214–15, 216, 217
Talbot, R. and Magnoli, G.C. 382
'Talking Objects' 156–57
Tambo 355, 356, 359, 362, 362–63
taonga 92, 93–96, 98, 99–101
Taputapuatea 90, 92
Tasmanian Aboriginal Centre (TAC) 268
Tate Gallery (London) 437
Taylor, John 228

Te Kaoreore 87, 88, 90, 92, 93, 96, 98, 101
Te Maori exhibition 95, 96, 97, 98, 358
Te Papa (New Zealand) 83
Te Papa-i-Ouru 87, 88
technological model: and conservation
    exhibitions 337
Trevorrow, Tom 249
Theatre of the Oppressed 155–56, 157
Thomas, Paul 455
tissue culture 448–49
Tissue Culture and Art Project 449
training 20; and ethics education 33
transformational model: and conservation
    exhibitions 337
transparency 245–46; and ethical governance
    282; radical 6, 14–17, 20
Transparent Tubes 437–39, *437*
Trope, J. 77
Tropenmuseum (Tropical Museum)
    (Amsterdam) 73–74, 79, 81
trusteeship 12, 13
truth 184; categories of 175
Truth and Reconciliation Commission
    (TRC) 175
Tucker, Marcia 367
Tuhiwai Smith, Linda 153–54
Tuol Sleng Museum of Genocidal Crimes
    (Cambodia) 222
Turnbull, William 437, 438, 440
Turner Contemporary (Margate) 388
Tyne and Wear Museums 137
Tyne and Wear Museums Service (TYMS)
    205–6

'UK Museums on the Web' conferences 317
UNESCO *Convention* 242
Union of Physically Impaired against
    Segregation (UPIAS) 139
United Nations: Declaration on the Rights
    of Indigenous Peoples 267
United States: decolonization of museum
    74, 75; and repatriation 266
universalizability, principle of 34, 35
Untitled/Tower 364
Untold Story 306–9, *307*
utilitarianism 28, 275

V&A (Victoria & Albert) 203; British
    Galleries 387; *Ethics Checklist* 333, 334;
    Sackler Centre for Education 386
values: and methods 60–61
Van Gogh: Face to Face exhibition 400, 408
van Gogh, Vincent: *Self-Portrait* 408
van Gogh's Ear exhibition 399–400, *409*
Vanouse, Paul 451
Verschachtelt und Behütet exhibition 339, *340*

Vesna, Victoria 455
Victimless Leather 448–49, *456*
Victoria and Albert Museum *see* V&A
virtual exhibitions: and conservation 342–43
virtue ethics 29, 38–39
virtuous museum building 389–90
visible listening approach 279–84
Visiting Hours 367
visitors 276; didactic/dialogic relationship
    with museums 139; factors encouraging
    attendance 207; numbers of and
    admission fees 216; participation rates
    203, *204*, *205*; perceptions of museum
    performance through importance-
    performance analysis 207–11; profile of
    203, 216; satisfaction surveys 206–7
von Hagens, Gunther 353, 361–62, 457

Wadsworth Atheneum 364
Waitangi, Treaty of (1840) 96, 98
Waitangi Tribunal 96
Wake, Drew Ann 277
Wakefield Museum (Yorkshire) 339
Walker Art Gallery (Liverpool) 336, 337,
    380
Wallinger, Mark 132, 133
Walsh, Graham 399–400
Walsh, John 291
Walters Art Museum (Baltimore) 196–97
Warner, Michael 176
Watson, Sheila 17
Web 319–20, 325; ethical challenges of the
    319; Semantic 326–27
web-based exhibitions 342–43
Webber, Anne 242
Weil, Stephen 45, 191, 197, 199
Welch, Peter 14
Wellcome Trust 458
Wellmer, Albrecht 34
Werner Collection 336
West, Aunty Ida 249–50
West, Richard 70, 75, 76
whakapapa 87–93, *90*, *91*
Wharton, Glenn 434, 435, 436, 440
Whitney Museum of American Art 290
Whitworth Art Gallery (Manchester)
    388–89
Whose Muse? 45
Willcocks, Stella 437–38
Wilsdon, James 167
Wilson, Fred 365–66
Winnicott, D.W. 156
Women Artists in Revolution (WAR) 364
Women in Power exhibition (2008) 280
Women's Health Mobilization (WHAM!)
    459

Wong, Amanda 11–12
Woodward, Renee Azcra 406
word of mouth promoting 212–13
Work House (Britain) 176
Working Group on Human Remains
  (UK) 268
World Archaeological Congress (WAC)
  261–62
World Bank 63
World Trade Center: 'Reflecting Absence'
  memorial 230
Wunderkammern 447

Xavier-Rowe, A. 344
"Xpress on Track" program 195–96

Yad Vashem Holocaust memorial (Israel)
  228–29
Yingge Ceramics Museum (YCM)
  (Taiwan) 209–11, *209, 210,* 212,
  215
Yoneyama, Lisa 231
York Castle Museum 339
Young, Iris Marion 11
Young, James O. 244

Zero@Wavefunction installation
  453, 455
Ziegler, Adolf 396
Zimbardo, Philip 423, 424
Zurr, Ionat 448, 455